WebRAD: Building Database Applications on the Web with Visual FoxPro© and Web Connection

Harold Chattaway
Randy Pearson
Whil Hentzen

Hentzenwerke Publishing

Published by:
Hentzenwerke Publishing
980 East Circle Drive
Whitefish Bay WI 53217 USA

Hentzenwerke Publishing books are available through booksellers and directly from the
publisher. Contact Hentzenwerke Publishing at:
414.332.9876
414.332.9463 (fax)
www.hentzenwerke.com
books@hentzenwerke.com

WebRAD: Building Database Applications on the Web with Visual FoxPro and
Web Connection
    By Harold Chattaway, Randy Pearson, and Whil Hentzen
    Technical Editor: Barbara Peisch
    Copy Editor: Farion Grove

ISBN: 1-930919-07-7

Manufactured in the United States of America.

I would like to dedicate this book to my dad.
Besides getting me hooked on computer science,
he also taught me how much fun work can be.

—Harold Chattaway

This book is for those developers
who welcome and enjoy the exploration of new challenges,
and are open to new approaches to solving problems.

—Randy Pearson

Our Contract with You, The Reader

In which we, the folks who make up Hentzenwerke Publishing, describe what you, the reader, can expect from this book and from us.

Hi there!

I've been writing professionally (in other words, eventually getting a paycheck for my scribbles) since 1974, and writing about software development since 1992. As an author, I've worked with a half-dozen different publishers and corresponded with thousands of readers over the years. As a software developer and all-around geek, I've also acquired a library of more than 100 computer and software-related books.

Thus, when I donned the publisher's cap almost five years ago to produce the *1997 Developer's Guide,* I had some pretty good ideas of what I liked (and didn't like) from publishers, what readers liked and didn't like, and what I, as a reader, liked and didn't like.

Now, with our new titles for 2002, we're entering our fifth season. (For those who are keeping track, the '97 DevGuide was our first, albeit abbreviated, season, the batch of six "Essentials" for Visual FoxPro 6.0 in 1999 was our second, and, in keeping with the sports analogy, the books we published in 2000 and 2001 comprised our third and fourth.)

John Wooden, the famed UCLA basketball coach, posited that teams aren't consistent; they're always getting better—or worse. We'd like to get better…

One of my goals for this season is to build a closer relationship with you, the reader. In order for us to do this, you've got to know what you should expect from us.

- You have the right to expect that your order will be processed quickly and correctly, and that your book will be delivered to you in new condition.

- You have the right to expect that the content of your book is technically accurate and up-to-date, that the explanations are clear, and that the layout is easy to read and follow without a lot of fluff or nonsense.

- You have the right to expect access to source code, errata, FAQs, and other information that's relevant to the book via our Web site.

- You have the right to expect an electronic version of your printed book to be available via our Web site.

- You have the right to expect that, if you report errors to us, your report will be responded to promptly, and that the appropriate notice will be included in the errata and/or FAQs for the book.

Naturally, there are some limits that we bump up against. There are humans involved, and they make mistakes. A book of 500 pages contains, on average, 150,000 words and several megabytes of source code. It's not possible to edit and re-edit multiple times to catch every last misspelling and typo, nor is it possible to test the source code on every permutation of development environment and operating system—and still price the book affordably.

Once printed, bindings break, ink gets smeared, signatures get missed during binding. On the delivery side, Web sites go down, packages get lost in the mail.

Nonetheless, we'll make our best effort to correct these problems—once you let us know about them.

In return, when you have a question or run into a problem, we ask that you first consult the errata and/or FAQs for your book on our Web site. If you don't find the answer there, please e-mail us at **books@hentzenwerke.com** with as much information and detail as possible, including 1) the steps to reproduce the problem, 2) what happened, and 3) what you expected to happen, together with 4) any other relevant information.

I'd like to stress that we need you to communicate questions and problems clearly. For example…

- "Your downloads don't work" isn't enough information for us to help you. "I get a 404 error when I click on the **Download Source Code** link on **www.hentzenwerke.com/book/downloads.html**" is something we can help you with.

- "The code in Chapter 10 caused an error" again isn't enough information. "I performed the following steps to run the source code program DisplayTest.PRG in Chapter 10, and I received an error that said 'Variable m.liCounter not found'" is something we can help you with.

We'll do our best to get back to you within a couple of days, either with an answer or at least an acknowledgement that we've received your inquiry and that we're working on it.

On behalf of the authors, technical editors, copy editors, layout artists, graphical artists, indexers, and all the other folks who have worked to put this book in your hands, I'd like to thank you for purchasing this book, and I hope that it will prove to be a valuable addition to your technical library. Please let us know what you think about this book—we're looking forward to hearing from you.

As Groucho Marx once observed, "Outside of a dog, a book is a man's best friend. Inside of a dog, it's too dark to read."

Whil Hentzen
Hentzenwerke Publishing
May 2002

List of Chapters

Table of Contents

Chapter 15: Data Entry on the Web   347

Chapter 16: Extending the Framework   373

Chapter 17: The Mistakes We All Make   403

Chapter 18: Advanced Troubleshooting and Maintenance   415

Appendices (electronic download only)

Acknowledgements

I would like to thank all the people on the FoxPro team at Microsoft for making such a powerful development environment, Visual FoxPro. Also Rick Strahl for developing Web Connection and making Web development so easy. The community support that is so strong on the West Wind support forums has been a tremendous benefit. Responses, usually received in about an hour, from other users like Randy Pearson, Lauren Clarke, and Darrell Gardner have made many big problems disappear quickly. Together, these people have made it possible to have an incredibly fun career!

—*Harold*

It's hard to believe that it has been more than five years since I met Rick Strahl at a VFP DevCon. At that time I was actively weighing potential strategies for migrating my development strategy from a homegrown FoxPro 2.6 framework that had served me well. In the back of my mind, I knew the Web had to be part of my next strategy. But it was hearing Rick's presentation, which featured his Web Connection product, that caused all the right lights to go on for me. Ever since that time, I have been working with Web Connection, and I have enjoyed the numerous opportunities to converse and collaborate with Rick, sometimes in person, but mostly via the West Wind message board.

One of the great pleasures of writing this book was all of the suggestions and help I received from Web Connection developers who gave their time freely in the interest of a better end product. I thank Tom Gehrke, Alan Anderson, Paul Mrozowski, Randy Clark, Steven Black, Terry Voss, and Peter Diotte for their valuable input. Jim Underwood read an early draft of several chapters, and his thoughtful suggestions led to the creation of Chapter 15 on data entry. Three frequent contributors to the Web Connection community, Lauren Clarke, Keith Hackett, and Darrell Gardner, gave their time to perform peer reviews of several of my draft chapters. They each provided thoughtful and valuable input, and greatly improved the quality of what you will read here.

My co-authors, Whil Hentzen and Harold Chattaway, were a pleasure to work with. I thank each of them, both for talking me into joining the authoring team in the first place, and for the comments and suggestions they provided to my chapters. I extend special thanks to Barbara Peisch, our Technical Editor. The challenge of delivering a highly technical book from several authors with vastly different styles is indeed a difficult one. Without Barbara's meticulous technical reviews, extending over many rewrites of some of the chapters, and without her good sense of humor, this book could not have reached the quality it did attain.

Most importantly, I would like to thank Penny Mateer, my life's partner, for encouraging me to undertake this project, and for her patience when that decision led to the consumption of too much of the free time we could have been spending together.

—*Randy*

About the Authors

Harold Chattaway

Harold Chattaway is the principal at WebConnectionTraining.com, which specializes in training seminars and development using Web Connection. He has written for *FoxTalk* and contributed to the book *FoxPro OOP* by Wrox Press. He also speaks regularly at the Boston FoxPro User group, and has spoken three times for Microsoft at DevDays and Client/Server World in Boston and two times at the Great Lakes Great Database Workshop (GLGDW) in Milwaukee. He also runs the www.Bugcentral.com site. Bugcentral is a 100% VFP/Web Connection site designed to allow development teams to track their defects and enhancement requests.

Harold wrote Chapters 1, 2, 5, 6, 7, 8, 9, 12, and 21 and Appendices B and D. Harold can be reached at hchattaway@webconnectiontraining.com.

Randy Pearson

Randy Pearson is a partner with Cycla Corporation in Pittsburgh, PA. He has been developing Visual FoxPro and predecessor solutions for more than 16 years. Randy has spent the past 5+ years developing Web-based applications using West Wind Web Connection with Visual FoxPro. He has spoken at the Great Lakes Great Database Workshop (GLGDW) and at Visual FoxPro user groups, and has written articles for both *FoxTalk* and *FoxPro Advisor*. Randy is also the creator of the well-known public domain "CodeBlock" program (*FoxTalk*, December 1994), which allowed runtime interpretation of uncompiled FoxPro code.

In addition to developing applications for clients, Randy is now spending part of his time mentoring Web Connection developers, and is also developing a commercial framework to be used in conjunction with Web Connection.

Randy wrote Chapters 10, 11, 13, 14, 15, 16, 17, 18, 19, and 20 and Appendix C. Randy can be reached at randyp@cycla.com.

Whil Hentzen

Whil Hentzen is president of Hentzenwerke Corporation, an 18-year-old software development firm that specializes in strategic FoxPro-based applications. He's the author of *Rapid Application Development with FoxPro 2.6* (Pinnacle Publishing) and *Programming Visual FoxPro 3.0* (Ziff-Davis Press). He is the editor of *FoxTalk* and was the series editor for Pinnacle's "The Pros Talk Visual FoxPro" collection. He has also contributed articles to *FoxPro Advisor, Cobb's FoxPro Developer Journal,* and *DBMS*. He has spoken at numerous conferences throughout the United States, Canada, and Europe, including Microsoft's DevCon. Whil is a Microsoft MVP for his contributions to online forums and newsgroups.

Whil wrote Chapters 3 and 4 and Appendices A, E, F, G, and H. Whil can be reached at whil@hentzenwerke.com.

Barbara Peisch

Barbara Peisch is president of Peisch Custom Software, Inc., specializing in custom database application development with Visual FoxPro. She has authored and co-authored various columns, including "The KitBox" for *FoxTalk* and "Customers vs Code: Keeping Your Cool with the Essential Component" for *CoDe Magazine*. Barbara is a Microsoft MVP, and has been a judge for the "Visual FoxPro Excellence Awards." She is also a founding member and treasurer for The FoxPro Developers Network of San Diego.

Barbara can be reached at barbara@peisch.com.

How to Download the Files

Hentzenwerke Publishing generally provides two sets of files to accompany its books. The first is the source code referenced throughout the text. Note that some books do not have source code; in those cases, a placeholder file is provided in lieu of the source code in order to alert you of the fact. The second is the e-book version (or versions) of the book. Depending on the book, we provide e-books in either the compiled HTML Help (.CHM) format, Adobe Acrobat (.PDF) format, or both. Here's how to get them.

Both the source code and e-book file(s) are available for download from the Hentzenwerke Web site. In order to obtain them, follow these instructions:

1. Point your Web browser to **www.hentzenwerke.com**.

2. Look for the link that says "Download"

3. A page describing the download process will appear. This page has two sections:

*   **Section 1:** If you were issued a username/password directly from Hentzenwerke Publishing, you can enter them into this page.

*   **Section 2:** If you did not receive a username/password from Hentzenwerke Publishing, don't worry! Just enter your e-mail alias and look for the question about your book. Note that you'll need your physical book when you answer the question.

4. A page that lists the hyperlinks for the appropriate downloads will appear.

Note that the e-book file(s) are covered by the same copyright laws as the printed book. Reproduction and/or distribution of these files is against the law.

If you have questions or problems, the fastest way to get a response is to e-mail us at **books@hentzenwerke.com**.

Icons used in this book

 Indicates that the referenced material is available for download at **www.hentzenwerke.com**.

 Indicates information of special interest, related topics, important notes, or version issues.

 Indicates a warning or "gotcha."

Chapter 1
Introduction

Presumably you've picked up this book because you want to use Visual FoxPro to do Web development. Well, prepare yourself for some radical changes. My own experience reminds me of what my wife said when my daughter was born. She kept telling me, "Your life will never be the same from this moment on…" At first I did not believe her—after all, how much could a little seven-pound human change my life? Boy was I wrong! It is pretty much the same transition moving from doing traditional desktop development to doing Web applications. All the simple things suddenly become more involved and complicated.

In Visual FoxPro, we have been spoiled. VFP has a mature fully OOP Forms Designer. We can create a library of base classes from which objects on our forms are built. We can simply drag and drop them onto a form and have them bound to a datasource. We can drag and drop a whole table, either local or remote, onto a form and have it become a grid. We have an integrated report writer, not state-of-the-art but very powerful none the less. In short, the entire VFP IDE is wrapped around data. There are no boundaries among the various components, from the language to the forms designer, class designer, and report designer. The entire environment has been designed around building database applications. In building desktop apps, the developer did not have to know about MS Internet Information Server, FTP, SSL, how to secure a Web server from hackers, the complexities of HTML, XML, session management, stateless programming, Web site testing and promotion, browser compatibility, and Cascading Style Sheets. Doing Web development will be like going back to using FoxBASE in some regards. The tools are still very immature compared to desktop tools, but they are getting better rapidly.

VFP has evolved from a simple DOS application, starting with the original FoxBASE program in the early '80s. I'll always remember using Fox for the first time. Without making any changes to my Dbase application, I simply compiled it under FoxBASE and got a tremendous performance boost. Fox has always been about speed in handling data. It proves how even an interpreted language can compete with "native code" environments. With the advent of VFP, the string processing abilities of the language have also been dramatically improved. A great deal of the work in displaying Web pages is in the form of string manipulation. We will see how Web pages can be built using templates that VFP can parse and populate with data, or how an entire table can be converted into HTML in sub-second fashion. The amount of code that is run when evaluating a template is truly amazing. With the data and string manipulation engines in VFP, the response times are so fast that millions of hits a day can be processed by a VFP Web site without too much difficulty.

Things have changed. No longer is it possible to get away with just knowing the VFP language and its design surfaces. The new technologies are not nearly as integrated. The Web page is not a native component of the VFP IDE. Not only is it not integrated, it does not even use the same language to display information. HTML is the language of the Web for formatting information. This is a bit daunting at first, but soon you will be using VFP to write HTML!

This book is intended to serve as a comprehensive introduction for the VFP developer to move into the world of Web development. At the end of many chapters is a "Chapter resources" section that will reference other works that will help in understanding the material. I believe you will find it very exciting to learn about how these technologies work together and how they can leverage the incredibly powerful language that VFP developers have at their disposal. We will be using the Web Connection framework from West Wind Technologies (**www.west-wind.com**) as the basis for all examples in this book. Web Connection is an incredibly robust set of VFP classes that form the foundation for VFP Internet applications. WC is well supported by the author and has a strong development community.

Who should be reading this book?

This book is meant for Visual FoxPro developers who have a good grasp of object-oriented programming (OOP). The Web Connection framework is built on classes, so knowing how to perform subclassing and understanding inheritance is very important. A discussion of OOP principles is beyond the scope of this book. You do not need to know anything about Web development. This book will cover what is needed in HTML, layout tools, and the other related technologies. None of the other tools in VFP are covered other than using the Program Editor. The Forms Designer and Report Writer are not relevant for doing Web development. As different as Web development is from desktop development, Web Connection does allow you to preserve your investment in the VFP language. All of the middle-tier type programming is still done using the VFP language.

So put your thinking caps on and prepare for a new way of doing development!

Chapter 2
What is Web Connection?

Out of the box, Visual FoxPro has no knowledge of how to process a Web request. What Web Connection provides are the foundation classes that are needed to connect Visual FoxPro to the Web. Except for two small DLL files (WC.DLL and WWIPSTUFF.DLL), Web Connection is all native VFP code.

There are classes that handle server functions like waiting for a request, determining what the request is, parsing the incoming data from a Web form, and then sending the result back out to the browser. When a "request" is made of the server, there is the class WWREQUEST. It is responsible for pulling apart a Web form, for example, so its information can be saved and manipulated. On the outgoing side, there is the WWRESPONSE class that contains methods for returning information back to the user, which is the "response" to a "request." This class also contains methods that allow developers to create HTML templates with ASP style tags that can contain VFP expressions. The methods in WWRESPONSE can then parse the template and fill in the template expressions. This is probably one of the most powerful features of Web Connection. This template technology allows the entire VFP language to be exposed to the Web via simple ASP tags. The expression can be as simple as <%=date()%>, which would return the current date, or as complex as a call to a VFP method that makes full use of the VFP data and OOP language.

There are also classes to handle cookie management and session management. One of the biggest changes in Web development is the stateless nature of Web applications. There are no persistent connections from the GUI to the data as there is in desktop apps. This change in development is handled quite nicely in the Web Connection framework. The WWSESSION class allows a user to have a continuous conversation with the server. In short, the WC framework provides all the foundational code that allows a new developer to get a simple Web site up in about 30 minutes.

Apart from the core foundation classes, WC also provides a number of utility classes. One function that is part of the WWIPSTUFF class allows your applications to perform emailing functions. It is possible to programmatically send email whenever an event occurs. For example, when a new customer signs up, you could send an email to your account to notify you. Another very practical use of emailing is when an error occurs in your app, the error trapping code can send you an email notification. WC also provides a WWXML class for XML parsing and generation. You can easily take a Visual FoxPro cursor and convert it to XML with a one-line call. You can also use the WC libraries to parse an XML string and store it into a table. WC also provides the class libraries to implement the MS SOAP protocols. SOAP, or Simple Object Access Protocol, is basically the API for the Web. You can use the SOAP interface to expose methods of your Web site to the outside world. Instead of only providing the traditional Web interface, you could expose links that take SOAP messages. This could allow your users to request and post information from other applications, even desktop applications, without going through the conventional Web form. For example, if your interface requirements are too extensive for a Web page, you could design an application that runs as a normal desktop app but accesses the Web underneath.

You really do not have to know the complete inner workings of the WC framework in order to use it. It is sufficient to know the available functions and methods and build your application using them.

What Web Connection is not

Web Connection does not allow you to take an existing desktop application and simply run it on the Web. Taking a VFP form and duplicating it on the Web is not a trivial task. There are many more events and more form objects available on the desktop. Doing things like page frames in native HTML is virtually impossible. Dynamic HTML is required for something like this, and the browsers (Internet Explorer, Netscape) do not treat dynamic HTML in the same way. The major downside to a Web-based application is accounting for the different run-time environments that can be encountered. In VFP, the same run time is evaluating the form no matter where the app is run. With a Web application, you cannot count on a particular browser always being used and programming to it. Major functional differences exist between browser versions as well.

Also, Web Connection is not a pre-packaged template for building an online store. There is a separate product available called the WebStore for that. WC is meant to be a more general-purpose framework.

Updates

Thanks to the magic of inheritance, updates to the Web Connection framework are very easy. Most of the time, you can simply copy the new class libraries over the old ones. The updates to the WC libraries happen fairly frequently. There are some updates that affect the WCONNECT.H file that contains a large number of #DEFINEs that configure the framework. Also, there might be updates to the WC.INI file. Updates to these files are best done with a tool like Beyond Compare. This is a "vdiff" or "visual difference" tool that will be discussed in detail later on. It allows you to compare two files side by side and move changed lines from one file to the other. It is an extremely helpful tool.

Conclusion

Do not be afraid of all the new terminology! This book is targeted to new Web developers and will cover all these new concepts in detail.

Chapter 3
Installing, Configuring, and Testing Web Connection

Early in school, the difference between an engineer and a technician was explained to us. A technician is someone who can follow instructions and make something work. An engineer is someone who understands not only the "how" but the "why"—the understanding beneath the surface functionality. I've never wanted to be a technician, and as a result, I've never been one to blindly trust the install program—I want to know what's going on underneath as well, so I can change things if I want to. In this chapter, I'll get you started the right way—showing you the hows and whys of setting up a basic development machine. I'll tweak Windows, install Web server software, configure Visual FoxPro, and, finally, install and test Web Connection.

Using Web Connection to build live applications consists of development work on a development machine, and then deployment of the final product on a live server that's running a real live Web server software package. You install the Web Connection framework on your development machine (the same machine that has Visual FoxPro installed), run Web Connection inside of Visual FoxPro, and develop your application using the Web Connection framework and classes as well as your own Visual FoxPro code.

Finally, you build a distributable executable, often referred to as the "Web Connection Server," that will be deployed on your live server. And, of course, there are all of the Web site files, like static HTML files, images, and other things that don't really have anything to do with Visual FoxPro or Web Connection.

Just as you can test a Visual FoxPro application that will run on a local area network by running the app in the Visual FoxPro IDE (or with the Visual FoxPro runtime), you can test your Web Connection app on your development machine by installing a Web server software package on your development machine.

In this chapter, I'll cover the development machine—how to set up a Web server on your development box, how to install Web Connection—the development framework—on your development box, and how to test it all.

Note that I'm not covering the live server at all in this chapter, and just barely touching upon it in the next. You can do everything in this chapter and most of the next on your development machine. Harold will cover the setup of your live server in Chapter 8, "Configuring Server Software," and Chapter 12, "A Web Connection Application from Start to Finish."

Installation
Unlike most PC-based software, Web Connection relies on a bunch of other components. So, before you can install Web Connection, you have to make sure the rest of your system is set up properly.

How it all works

Before giving you step-by-step instructions, though, it's a good idea to have an idea of how the development process works and what the pieces involved are so you know where you're heading.

You're going to have the usual "shrink-wrap" software on your local machine: Windows, some Web server software, and the development version of Visual FoxPro.

You'll also have five pieces to your development environment that are specific to Web Connection projects.

The first is the directory for the project you're working on. This project directory will contain all of your own custom source code, similar to when you create LAN or client/server applications.

The second is the Web Connection framework and classes. You won't copy the Web Connection framework and classes into your project directory. Rather, your project will point to the framework classes in their own directory, just as your other VFP applications point to a common directory for base classes and procedure libraries.

Third is a directory that mirrors the directory on your Web server where your Web site will be located. Most Web sites—even those with a Web Connection component—have oodles of HTML pages, graphics, and other files—and your WC app will need to be able to refer to those in the proper context on your development machine. Thus, you'll have a mirror of your live Web site on your development machine. If you don't, any reference in your application to those files will fail.

Fourth, you'll need directories to house your Web application's EXE and your data. It's always been good practice to separate your data from your application—so that your application doesn't *require* the data files to be in the same directory. With Web applications, this is even more important because if you make a mistake by placing your data files in the wrong place, the entire world could potentially have access to your data.

Finally, you'll need a directory for temporary Web Connection files. This directory stores temporary "messaging" files that are used for communication between the Web Connection ISAPI DLL (WC.DLL) and your own Visual FoxPro application.

Notes about your Web server's root directory

Item number three previously mentioned the directory on your Web server where your Web site will be located. This requires a bit more explanation.

The term "Web server" is one of those terms like "cleave" that means two completely contradictory things. It can mean a physical box that has an IP address where your Web site is located ("our Web server is located in the basement closet"), but it can also refer to a piece of software that runs on a machine. Examples of Web server software are Apache and Internet Information Server. In this chapter, the term "Web server" refers to a software application that receives requests for Web pages, processes those requests, and returns an HTML page to the requestor.

When you configure your Web server software (this process is covered in detail shortly), you'll need to specify a root (or "home") directory.

The default name for IIS's root directory is C:\INETPUB\WWWROOT, and, at least when getting started, many people create directories for each Web site or project under the

WWWROOT subdirectory. This directory will be visible to the outside world (or, at least, in your testing on your development machine, to your Web browser).

The first time you go through this, this may not make a lot of sense, so let's be very specific. When you configure your Web server software, you'll set up a "home directory." This home directory is where a Web server browser will head to look for files when a hit to the root of your domain is received.

In other words, when you enter "www.YourDomain.com" in a browser, the Web server at www.YourDomain.com will try to open the default HTML file in the directory where www.YourDomain.com is mapped on the Web server machine. This might be the C:\INETPUB\WWWROOT directory on that machine, or it might be a subdirectory below WWWROOT. You can also substitute "http://localhost" or "http://127.0.0.1" for www.YourDomain.com when you're working on your development machine. When requests specify a directory below the root, such as www.YourDomain.com/MyApp/home.html, the Web server will check whether you have defined the directory MyApp as virtual, and, if so, follow that virtual mapping to whatever physical folder on the Web server machine you have specified. If you haven't specified the directory name MyApp as virtual, but there is a physical folder named MyApp underneath the Web root, then the Web server will look in that physical folder. (I'll talk about virtual directories shortly.) Once the Web server has located the MyApp directory, it will then look for a file called home.html. If found, that file is returned to the browser. If home.html is not found, an error such as "Page Not Found" is returned.

Notes about your Web server's data directory

Item number four earlier brought up the need for directories to house your Web application's EXE and your data. It's always been good practice to separate your data from your application—so that your application doesn't *require* the data files to be in the same directory.

When you're putting your data on a Web site that's potentially exposed to the world, you'll want to keep it separate from the Web site files so that you can protect it. This technique will also come in handy if you should need to move or change data stores, say, to SQL Server or another back end that may not be located on the Web server itself.

The same thinking goes for the EXE itself—you want it outside of the directory structure that's visible to the outside world so that others can't access the EXE themselves—only through the mechanisms you've set up.

In Web applications, many developers place the EXE itself in the same directory structure, perhaps in a specific subdirectory, as their data. In the examples in the next couple of chapters, the EXE and the data will all be placed in the same directory for ease of use and following along. However, and this is an important point, the EXE doesn't—and shouldn't—require that the data reside in the same directory!

Setting up Windows

I'm going to assume that you're running Windows NT Workstation 4.0 (SP 5 or later) or Windows 2000 Professional. You can develop using Windows 9X, but it's just harder. It crashes more often, and the tools available—such as the Web server—aren't as robust as with NT/2000.

Security

I'm also going to assume you've got both an Administrator account and a user account set up on your development machine. You'll need the Administrator in order to install software like a Web server, but good programming practice dictates that you use a different account during day-to-day work. Remember, the Administrator account has "god" powers (as the Unix weenies like to say), and so you can get lulled into a false sense of functionality if you develop and test as Administrator.

If you regularly switch between Administrator and other user accounts, consider changing the color scheme, background, and other user interface elements for the Administrator account to remind you that you're not logged on as a regular user.

Furthermore, if you're in an office where others have access to your machine, you don't want to be logged on as Administrator and thus expose that type of power to other users. And, finally, if you're logged on as a regular user, you don't have as great a risk in screwing something up as if you are goofing around as "god."

Machine configuration

For purposes of this chapter, I'm also going to assume that you've got access to at least two drives, say, drives C and D. What I've found works best is using drive C solely for Windows and Windows shrink-wrap applications, like Visual Studio. Then I use a completely different drive, such as drive D, for my applications, test data, and so on. I also put my common code, framework code (including Web Connection), and so on, on the second drive as well.

I'm recommending this approach to you so that when you have to reformat your C drive (that's *when*, not *if*), your own programs and data are safe. Furthermore, should you decide to reconfigure your network, say, moving your development materials to another drive—for example, on the network server—you can do so with a minimum of fuss.

However, this isn't an absolute requirement, just my personal preference. The machine I am using to write this chapter (and Chapter 4) uses drive D for the CD-ROM drive, so my development drive is actually drive E. You can put all the stuff I have on drive E on your C drive as well. Just change the references from "E" to "C" in the examples when appropriate.

Drive C: Shrink-wrap software

Specifically, here's what is going to be on drive C: Windows, your Web server software (Personal Web Server or Internet Information Server), and Visual FoxPro.

Drive D: Development materials

The basic idea is to make the directory structure of your development machine look like the structure on your live server. There will be some differences, of course—you won't have the WC framework on your live machine. But the relative locations of your application, the Web site files, and the data files should all be the same whether you're in development or in production, at least when starting out. As you get more sophisticated, you can experiment with alternative approaches.

You don't have to do this, of course. You could have one structure for development and a completely different one for production—and use a "switch" that indicates whether the app is running on the development box or live. But the for the time being, I think it's easiest to make them the same. As you get more experienced, you can go your own way.

So, here's how I'm going to suggest you set up your development drive (from now on, I'll assume that your development drive is drive E):

- A directory for the Web Connection framework and related files. (You may have separate directories for each version of Web Connection if you maintain applications built under different versions. See Chapter 20, "Updating to New Web Connection Versions," for more details.)

- Separate directories for each customer, and subdirectories within those customer directories for each specific project (if you don't have multiple customers—say, if you're a corporate developer, or you do vertical market products—you could axe this layer).

- A separate directory for your own common code.

- Separate directories for the data for each project.

- Separate directories for each project's Web site.

- A directory for Web Connection temporary messaging files, and separate subdirectories within that temp file directory for each specific project.

Thus, your directory structure should eventually look like this:

```
E:
  \WCONNECT
    (Web Connection framework and classes)
  \CUST_ONE
          \PROJ_ONE
                  PROJ_1.PJX
                  PROJ_1.PJT
                  PROJ_1.EXE
                  \SOURCE
          \PROJ_TWO
                  PROJ_2.PJX
                  PROJ_2.PJT
                  PROJ_2.EXE
                  \SOURCE
  \CUST_TWO
          (etc.)
  \INETPUB\WWWROOT
                  \SITE_ONE
                          DEFAULT.HTM
                          (other static pages and files)
                          \SCRIPTS
                                  WC.DLL
                                  WC.INI
                          \IMAGES
                          \ADMIN
                                  ADMIN.ASP
                  \SITE_TWO
  \WSDATA
        \PROJ_1
                PROJ_1.EXE
                PROJ_1.INI
                PROJ1_TABLE1.DBF
```

```
            PROJ1_TABLE2.DBF (etc.)
      \PROJ_2
\WC_MSG
      \PROJ_1
      \PROJ_2
```

You'll install Web Connection into the \WCONNECT directory.

Each of your projects will have its own directory under the appropriate customer directory.

Each project will have a corresponding directory under \INETPUB\WWWROOT. Note that you don't have to place your Web site files under \INETPUB\WWWROOT—you could place them under \WEBSITES, like so:

```
\WEBSITES
      \SITE_ONE
              DEFAULT.HTM
              (other pages and files)
              \SCRIPTS
              \IMAGES
              \ADMIN
      \SITE_TWO
```

Just be sure to point your Web Server software to \WEBSITES instead of \INETPUB\WWWROOT.

You'll have a separate directory for your data. In this example, there's one main directory for data—WSDATA—and the data for each project goes into its own subdirectory, such as WSDATA\PROJ_1.

There are two key points here that bear repeating. First, you'll want to place the working copy of your PROJ_1.EXE in a subdirectory that isn't visible to the Web. The EXE will exist with your project and source code on your development machine, and in its own location on the production server (without the source code, of course). But there's never a need for the EXE itself to be accessible via HTTP.

Second, you'll want to put your data "out of harm's way"—and that means in a directory that isn't accessible from the Web site directory structure. Remember that all the files under INETPUB\WWWROOT are visible to the outside world (assuming there's no additional security set on the subdirectory structure)—after all, that's the whole idea. So if you just enter "www.somesite.com" in a browser, the browser will have access to the files in the directory (and subdirectories) that www.somesite.com points to.

If you put your data under that directory structure, anyone could navigate to that file and open it up, just by entering the following in their browser:

`www.somesite.com\data\very_secret_data.dbf`

Obviously, that would be bad, so you put your data somewhere where it isn't visible. For the time being, we'll just use a directory on the same drive that isn't in the path of the Web site directory structure, but for more security, you could put it on another drive, or even on another machine.

Finally, you'll have a directory for your temporary messaging files, and a subdirectory within that directory for each project or application. More on these temp files, and how important they are, later in this chapter.

Installing a Web server

You can install several different Web Server applications on an NT or 2000 development box; I recommend that you try to mimic your production environment as closely as possible. If you're just goofing around, sure, you can use a "toy" Web server, but that's just going to cause you more work later on.

If you're running NT Workstation, you can install PWS (Personal Web Server) on your NT workstation. If you're running Windows 2000 Professional, you can install either PWS or Internet Information Server (IIS). I suggest you use IIS if you're running 2000 Pro.

Installing PWS on NT4

First off, you find PWS on the Option Pack for NT. Toss the Option Pack CD into your CD drive, and follow the wizard as shown in **Figure 1**.

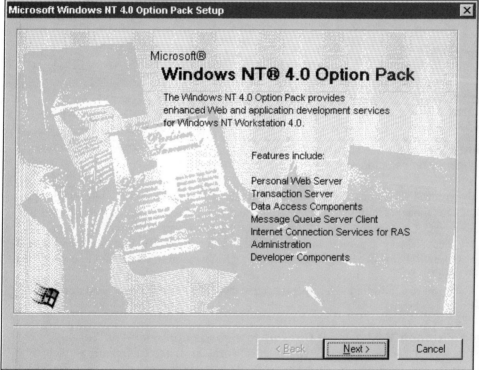

Figure 1. *You'll find Personal Web Server on the NT 4.0 Option Pack.*

If you select the "Custom" option, you'll get to choose which components you want to install from the Option Pack, as shown in **Figure 2**.

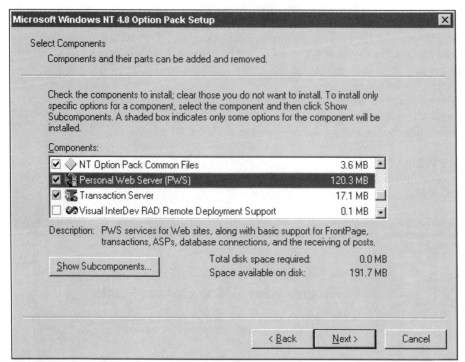

Figure 2*. Select the Personal Web Server option in the Option Pack Setup. Other options may be selected automatically.*

I won't lead you through every single dialog here—they're fairly straightforward. One helpful note, though: During the install, be sure to create a directory called InetPub on drive D, not drive C, if you're following our advice about putting your development files on drive D. Then, when you point to InetPub for PWS, you point to that directory! Make sure you also install Microsoft Management Console (MMC), because it's the tool to use for configuring PWS.

Once you're done with the install, you can manage the Personal Web Server one of two ways.

Using Microsoft Management Console to manage Personal Web Server

The first way to manage Personal Web Server is to drill down into the Internet Service Manager through the Programs | Windows NT 4.0 Option Pack menu chain, as shown in **Figure 3**.

Upon running the Internet Service Manager, you'll get the Microsoft Management Console dialog shown in **Figure 4**. This is a good tool to get used to, since it's also the interface for the Microsoft IIS Web server you'll be running on your live server.

Figure 3. *Use the Programs | Windows NT 4.0 Option Pack | Microsoft Personal Web Server menu to get to PWS.*

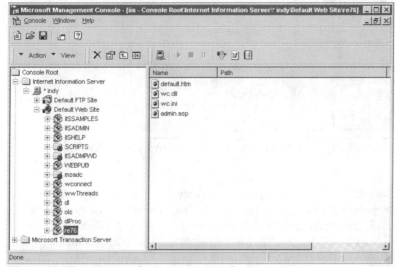

Figure 4. *The Microsoft Management Console is one way to get to the Web server running your development machine.*

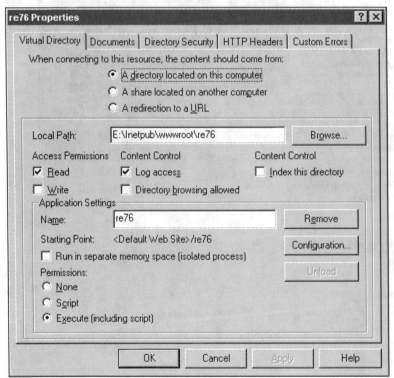 You can run more than one Web server on a single physical machine that's running NT Server or Windows 2000 Server. As you can see in Figure 4, nodes for a Default FTP Site and a Default Web Site are both automatically set up during installation of PWS/IIS. (Setting up multiple Web sites is covered in Appendix E, which is available electronically at **www.hentzenwerke.com**.)

You can run more than one Web Connection application on a single Web site as well. In Figure 4, you can see nodes for the custom DL, OLS, DLPROC, and RE76 Web Connection applications as well as the WCONNECT and WWTHREADS applications that come with Web Connection.

You can view and set the properties for a specific application by right-clicking on the application's node to bring up the Properties dialog, as shown in **Figure 5**.

Figure 5. The Properties dialog for a Web site directory allows you to configure various attributes.

The Virtual Directory tab of the Properties dialog allows you to point to a specific physical directory on the machine, and give that path a shorthand name that you can then use in your URLs. In Figure 5, the virtual name "re76" points to the physical subdirectory "re76" that's found in E:\INETPUB\WWWROOT. The virtual name could have been something else, like HERMAN, ALICE, or MOTORHEAD, if you liked.

Another key property to know about is the default document. When you navigate to a Web site and specify a specific file, such as www.YourSite.com/SomeFile.HTML, the Web server will look for the SomeFile.HTML file and return it to the calling browser if found. But what about when you navigate to a Web site without specifying an HTML file, such as www.YourSite.com? Obviously, the Web server software for that site has to know what file to return when a file isn't named. The Default Document allows the Webmaster for that site to define a file that is returned automatically.

Figure 6 shows how you set the default document in Personal Web Server. (It's the same in IIS.)

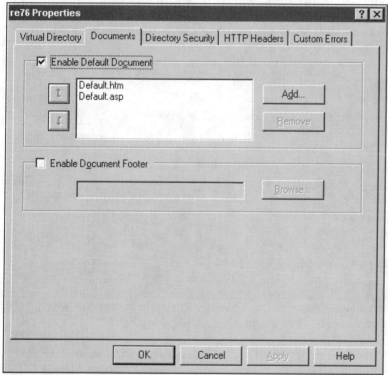

Figure 6. *Use the Documents tab of the Properties dialog to set the default document for a specific Web site.*

As an aside, you'll want to know that this tool is where you go to set the authentication method if you intend to use Windows Authentication when users log into your app. We'll discuss Windows Authentication in further detail in Chapter 13, "Identifying Users and Managing Session Data."

Using Personal Web Manager to manage Personal Web Server
As with most anything in Windows, there are several dozen different ways to do the same thing. As mentioned previously, there are two ways to get to Personal Web Manager. You can also select the Personal Web Manger menu option instead of Internet Service Manager in Figure 3 earlier, or you can click on the second icon from the right in the task bar, also shown

in Figure 3. (The icon looks like, well, I don't really know what it looks like. Maybe like something exploding out of a box?)

Either action will open the dialog shown in **Figure 7**.

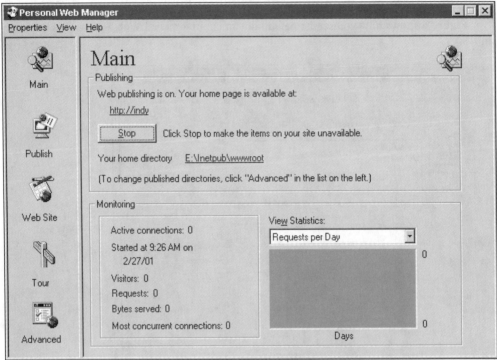

Figure 7. *The Personal Web Manager main dialog allows you to manage your personal Web site and view statistics about it.*

The next three functions on the left menu bar run end-user-style wizards, so I'll ignore them. Clicking the Advanced button at the bottom, though, opens the Advanced Options dialog as shown in **Figure 8**.

You can see that you can drill through the same application directories here as you could in IIS in Figure 4. In addition, you can determine the Default Document on this page, instead of having to go to an additional dialog or tab.

You still have to go to a separate dialog, however, in order to set the home directory of the application and the name of the virtual directory that maps to that physical directory. Clicking on the Edit Properties button in the Advanced dialog will display the Edit Directory dialog as shown in **Figure 9**.

Personally, I use the IIS interface instead of PWS when I'm running NT 4.0. I've found it convenient to create a shortcut to the MMC by dragging it to the Quick Launch toolbar at the bottom of the screen.

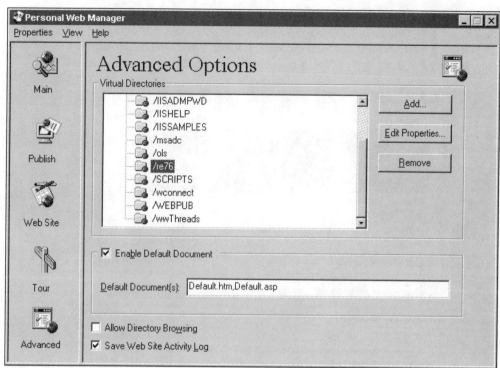

Figure 8*. The Advanced Options page of Personal Web Manager is used to configure virtual directories.*

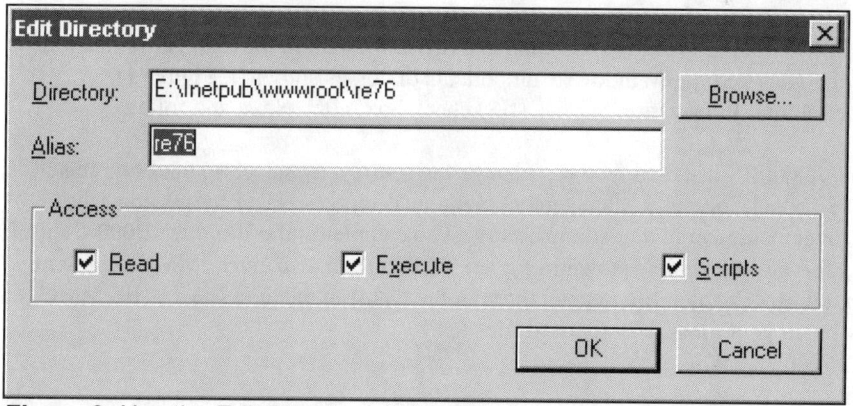

Figure 9*. Use the Edit Directory dialog to set the home directory and virtual name for a specific application in Personal Web Manager.*

Installing IIS on Windows 2000

Installing IIS on Windows 2000 is about as easy as it gets—and that's the way it should be.

Open up the Control Panel from the Start | Settings menu, and double-click on the Add/Remove Programs applet. You'll be greeted by the dialog shown in **Figure 10**.

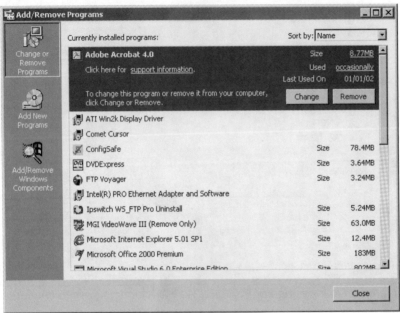

Figure 10. The Add/Remove Programs applet in Control Panel is used to install IIS in Windows 2000.

Click on Add/Remove Windows Components (the third icon in the icon bar on the left side) to open the Add/Remove Windows Components dialog as shown in **Figure 11**.

Check the Internet Information Service (IIS) check box, click Next, and follow the prompts.

Once you've got IIS installed, you can change the settings by selecting the Programs | Administrative Tools | Computer Management menu in Windows NT or by selecting the Computer Management icon in the Administrative Tools applet in the Windows 2000 Control Panel to bring forward the dialog shown in **Figure 12**. You can also enter "MMC" via Start | Run and then tell MMC which file to open through the Console menu in MMC. (IIS.MMC will probably be on your most recently used files list.)

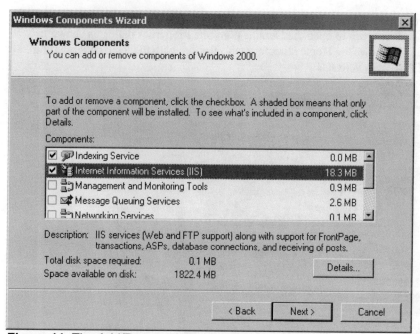

Figure 11. *The Add/Remove Windows Components is used to install programs like IIS in Windows 2000.*

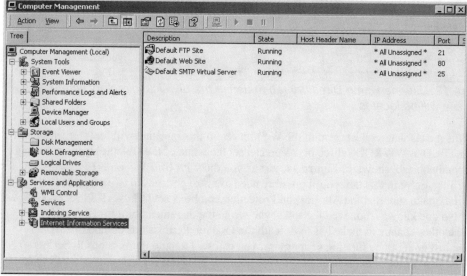

Figure 12. *The Computer Management dialog in Windows 2000 serves the same purpose as the Microsoft Management Console in Windows NT 4.*

In order to point IIS to your Web server directory, right-click on the Default Web Site node, and click on Properties to open the Default Web Site Properties dialog as shown in **Figure 13**. Figure 13 shows the Home Directory tab selected, with the local path pointing toward E:\INETPUB\WWWROOT.

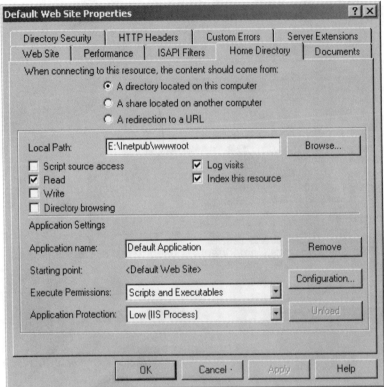

Figure 13. Use the Home Directory tab to define the physical directory where your Web site will be located.

This means that requests sent to the Web server on this machine will look for files in the E:\INETPUB\WWWROOT directory. You can set the name of the Default Document using the Documents tab, shown in **Figure 14**, just as you did with IIS/PWS on NT4.

While you're in this tab, you'll possibly need to make changes to two other controls.

First, make sure that the Application Protection combo is set to Low (IIS Process). Why? No one knows—not even the folks who wrote the documentation for IIS itself.

The other change to make has to do with the Execute Permissions combo box. If you are just going to be running script maps, you can set Execute Permissions to Scripts Only. (I'll cover script maps later.) If you are going to be using Web Connection calls (like wc.dll?YourAppProcess), then you need to set this to Scripts and Executables. For the time being, keep this at Scripts and Executables. If you decide to solely use script maps, you can change this later.

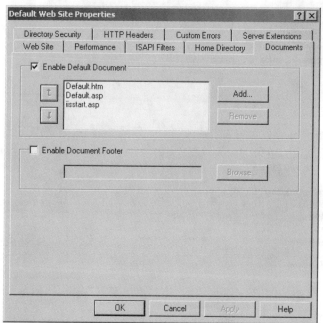

Figure 14. *Use the Documents tab of the Properties dialog to set the Default Document.*

Installing Visual FoxPro

You've most likely already installed VFP. I suggest that, if you haven't already done so, you create a directory on your development drive where you can stuff all of those little developer utilities that you have accumulated over time. Then, create an add-on to the VFP system menu that calls those utilities.

However, don't stop there. In your system menu add-on, create a second menu pad that displays all of the VFP projects that you're working on, and from that menu pad, call a program that switches to those projects and sets your paths and any other settings as you need. You could even data-drive this so that when you add new apps, you just add a row to a table instead of recompiling.

Here's the nuts and bolts of one way to do this.

First, set up VFP to start in the root of drive D (use the Start In text box of the Properties dialog of your shortcut on the Windows desktop). Once you do so, you can load VFP and make sure that the default directory is D:\ with the CD command in the Command Window.

Next, create a CONFIG.FPW file that contains the following lines:

```
path = d:\devutil
command = do d:\devutil\gofoxgo.prg
```

Place this CONFIG.FPW file in the root of drive D, so that VFP finds it during startup.

Third, create a directory called DEVUTIL on drive D. You'll create your add-on menu and program in this directory so that it's available from everywhere.

Create a VFP project, named GOFOXGO, in \DEVUTIL. The main program in this project, called GOFOXGO.PRG, looks like this:

```
* set the system menu back from whence it came
set sysmenu to default
* install class browser
do (_browser) with 0
* run the menu add-on
do GOFOXGO.MPR
* make sure we're in the root
set default to \
* modify the VFP title bar to reflect
* the current version of VFP as well as
* the current directory
modi wind screen title "We're rocking in " + vers() ;
    + "  (" + sys(5) + sys(2003) + ")"
* open the Debug Output window
activate window "Debug Output"
* open up the data session window
set
* set focus to the Command Window
keyboard "{CTRL+F2}"
* get rid of any echoes
clear
return .t.
```

There's actually a lot of stuff in this short little program, but the key is running the GOFOXGO menu about six lines down from the top. Here's how to create this menu.

1. Use the Menu Designer to create the GOFOXGO menu with two pads. Once you do so, you'll have two menu bars defined, similar to the Menu Designer shown in **Figure 15**.

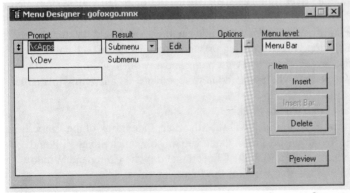

Figure 15. The GOFOXGO menu has two pads, one for custom apps and one for developer utilities.

2. Click the Edit button next to the Dev submenu and create the menu bars, as shown in **Figure 16**.

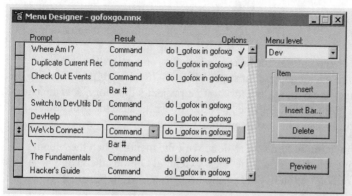

***Figure 16**. The Dev menu contains bars for a variety of developer utilities as well as an option to run Web Connection.*

3. You'll see that each menu calls a routine in GOFOXGO.PRG named L_GOFOX. Now, back to the menu call for each menu bar. The complete menu call is:

```
do l_gofox in gofoxgo.prg with prompt()
```

As you can see, the L_GOFOX routine is passed the prompt of the menu bar as a parameter.

4. The L_GOFOX routine in GOFOXGO.PRG looks like this, in part:

```
***************************************************************************
func l_gofox
***************************************************************************
parameter m.tcNaCust
do case
case upper(m.tcNaCust) = "WEB CONNECT"
  set defa to d:\wconnect
  set path to \devuti65;\wconnect;\wconnect\classes\;\wconnect\tools\
  do ("wcstart")
case upper(m.tcNaCust) = "WFBHS 76 REUNION"
  set defa to d:\hwapps\rw76
  set path to \devuti65;source;\wconnect;\wconnect\classes\;
  set path to \wconnect\tools\
  modi proj RW76 nowait
  keyboard "{CTRL+F2}"
<more cases for other menu options>
endcase
modi wind screen title "We're developing in " + vers() ;
    + "  (" + sys(5) + sys(2003) + ")"
clear prog
return .t.
```

The previous listing shows two examples of how this subroutine works. The first sets up Web Connection if you click on the Web Connect menu option under the Dev menu pad. It changes the default directory to \WCONNECT, and then sets up the path. Finally, it runs WCSTART, which adds the Web Connection menu to the VFP system menu.

The other case statement illustrates a sample call to an application. Under the Apps menu pad, there's a menu bar that says "WFBHS 76 REUNION." Clicking on that menu bar changes the default directory to that project's directory, sets the path properly, opens the project manager (the "nowait" doesn't pause the program at that point), and then returns focus to the Command Window.

5. One more thing to mention before you're done with the menu. When the Menu Designer is the active window, select the View | General Options menu and be sure to check the Append option button in the Location box as shown in **Figure 17**.

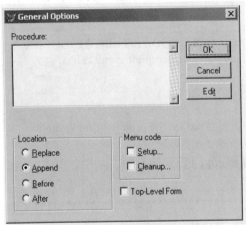

Figure 17. Be sure to select the Append option button in the Location option group so that the menu is added onto to the Fox system menu.

If you don't, you could inadvertently find yourself with the VFP system menu gone, and just your Apps | Dev menu in its place.

When the GOFOXGO menu runs, the Apps and Dev menu pads are added on to the end of the VFP system menu, as shown in **Figure 18**.

We're developing in Visual FoxPro 07.00.0000.9262 for Windows {E:\DEVUTIL7}

File   Edit   View   Format   Tools   Program   Window   Help   Apps   Dev

Figure 18. The Apps and Dev menu pads are added on to the end of the Visual FoxPro system menu.

Setting this mechanism up once will save you a ton of typing as well as a fair amount of head-scratching when an errant path or default directory causes "unexpected results to occur."

Installing Web Connection

It should be obvious, but just in case it isn't, you need VFP on the machine on which you're installing Web Connection. There are two reasons for this. First, at the conclusion of the Web Connection install process, it will attempt to run some VFP programs, and it won't be able to if you don't have Fox installed. Second, Web Connection is an application framework—in other words, just a bunch of VFP programs and class libraries, which by themselves don't do much. You'll need VFP to develop Web Connection apps.

The first step, then, is to run the install. As of this writing (and we see no reason that it's going to change any time soon), Web Connection comes as a self-extracting EXE. Just double click on that EXE from within Windows Explorer.

The first thing that will happen is that the install program will tell you that "the install program creates a full installation directory structure for Web Connection. This is not a temp install, so choose carefully," as shown in **Figure 19**. This means that you're actually creating the directory structure that the framework will be placed into, so don't point to a directory like "C:\TEMP" or "C:\SOMEDUMBNAME" because you'll have to live with it unless you want to reinstall. I suggest you choose D:\WCONNECT (or whichever drive your development stuff goes on).

Figure 19. *The first step in the installation process warns you to pick your installation directory carefully.*

After you click OK in the warning message dialog, the installation routine's self-extractor will ask you for the directory to unzip into, as shown in **Figure 20**. Click the Unzip button next. The Run WinZip button is really only there if you've already done an install but for some reason need to unzip and re-install some, but not all files. I've never even found a need to use this button.

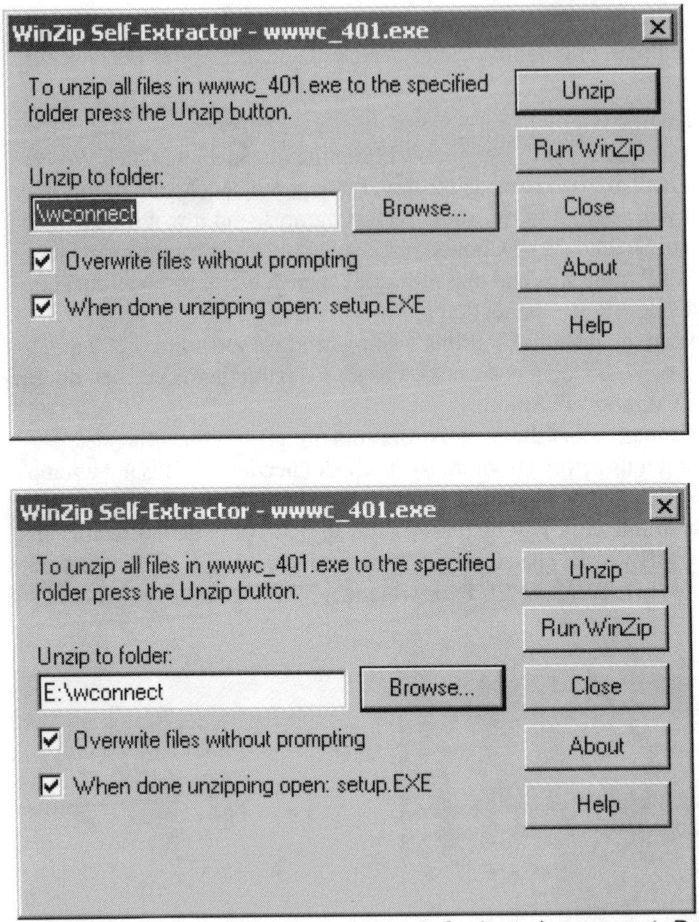

Figure 20. The installation routine defaults to \wconnect. Be sure to include the drive letter if necessary when you pick the directory and enter the directory name in manually.

Eventually, after all the unzipping and extracting is finished, the install program will run a Visual FoxPro program that starts the Setup Wizard. (That's why you need Visual FoxPro installed on the machine!) The Visual FoxPro program will also open the Web Connection CHM file to the Setup Wizard Help topic to guide you along. The instructions are pretty good, but a couple of steps could use additional elaboration.

The first screen you see will be the Select a Web Server dialog as shown in **Figure 21**.

Note that when you choose a Web server, the names in the Web Connection Web Servers combo box don't match the names of the Microsoft products. ("You call it Peer Web Services, I call it Personal Web Server—let's call the whole thing off!")

Next, you'll be asked to specify the temporary file path, as shown in **Figure 22**. This is really, really important and requires a bit of preliminary explanation.

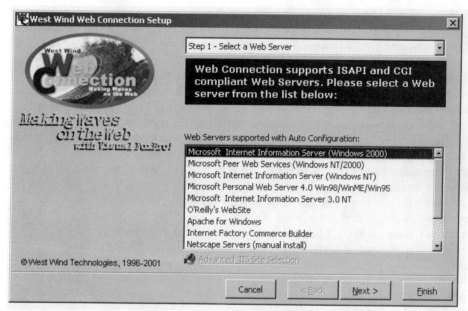

Figure 21. Select a Web Server is the first step of the Setup Wizard.

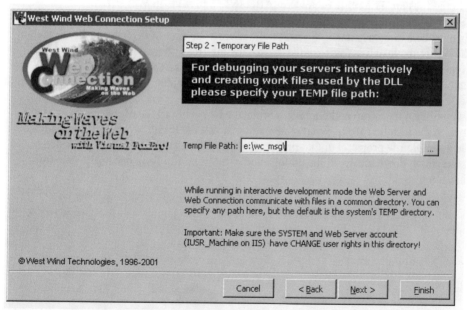

Figure 22. Specify the directory where Web Connection will create temporary files for communication between the Internet connector DLL and your Visual FoxPro application.

A call to a Web Connection application involves a URL something like so:

```
http://www.somesite.com/wconnect/wc.dll?wwdemo~TestPage
```

The WC.DLL file is a small C++ application that connects the Internet to your Visual FoxPro application. The DLL creates a temporary file using the rest of the string (in this case, "wwdemo~TestPage") on the Web server's hard disk. The values in this string are the names of classes, methods, and parameters passed to those classes and methods.

The Visual FoxPro application that you wrote using the Web Connection framework then picks up this temporary file, parses out the names of the classes, methods, and parameters, executes those methods, and returns an HTML page to WC.DLL that is then returned by the Web server to the user.

Now, just where do you think that temporary file is going to be created? Yes, in the directory specified in this step of the Setup Wizard.

As a result, since the WC.DLL is going to be writing (and then deleting) temp files all willy-nilly, the Web server account has to have Read, Write, and Delete rights in this directory.

The wizard defaults to the TEMP directory that's usually hanging around on drive C, but you'll want to change this to wherever you want to keep your temp files, as described in the file structure description earlier in this chapter.

The temp directory is specified in the application's INI file (if you name your Web application ABC.EXE, the INI file will be called ABC.INI) and the WC.INI file. The specific values in the files are TEMPFILEPATH in ABC.INI and PATH in WC.INI.

Next, you'll be asked to specify what the Script and HTML Path is, as shown in **Figure 23**. This must be a directory under the path defined for your default Web site in IIS or PWS.

The rest of the install is fairly painless—follow the Help file and prompts.

At the end of the wizard's processing, you'll be greeted with a summary screen and installation notes, as shown in **Figure 24**. This is good information—read it and remember that it's been copied to the Windows clipboard.

WC will then try to run and compile a project, and it will fail. Don't worry about it—it's just a bug in the install process. What's happening is that the install process is trying to compile a sample file project, but that project file is open, and thus it can't be compiled. Close everything down (close all the dialogs and exit Visual FoxPro), and we'll start from scratch again.

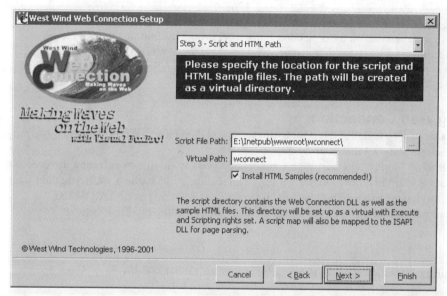

Figure 23. Specify the Script and HTML Path in Step 3 of the Setup Wizard.

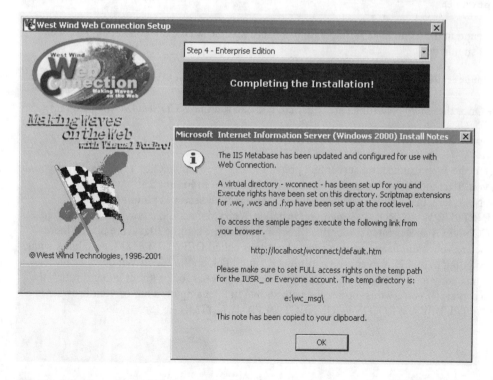

Figure 24. The wizard finishes with a summary of installation notes that you'll want to read carefully.

Testing your Web Connection installation

Once you've installed the Web Connection framework, you may find that you've closed Web Connection (and VFP, for that matter). The first few times you do this, it's easy to get confused and forget how to "get back in" and get things running. So instead of just running from the install program, let's start from scratch.

Running Web Connection

Assuming that you've installed everything properly, and then closed Web Connection and VFP, here's how you start things up again.

First, load up FoxPro and start Web Connection. You can do this by selecting the cool link you put on your developer toolbar within VFP (see Figure 16 earlier), or, if you didn't get to that yet, by changing to the \WCONNECT directory and running WCSTART.PRG.

Once you do so, you can do two things to verify what's going on. First, enter

```
cd
```

in the Command Window to make sure you're in the \WCONNECT directory. Second, issue the

```
? set("path")
```

command in the Command Window to make sure that the Web Connection path has been set. It should be

```
\wconnect;\wconnect\classes\;\wconnect\tools\;\wconnect\console\
```

Once these two conditions are satisfied, you can run the WCDEMOMAIN program:

```
do wcdemomain
```

to start the Web Connection server and prepare to run Web Connection requests. Once you do so, you'll get the Web Connection server window shown in **Figure 25**.

Next, let's make a request. Remember that your Web server is pointing to E:\INETPUB\WWWROOT. When you installed Web Connection, a new directory called \WCONNECT was created under this directory, and some sample files were placed there. These are your sample application files. One file is called DEFAULT.HTM, and that's what we're going to run. However, you can't just double-click on the file in Windows Explorer— by doing so, you'd simply be opening the file in the browser, but without going through the Web server. (If you try this, notice the path shown in the navigation bar of your browser is E:\INETPUB\WWWROOT\WCONNECT\DEFAULT.HTM.)

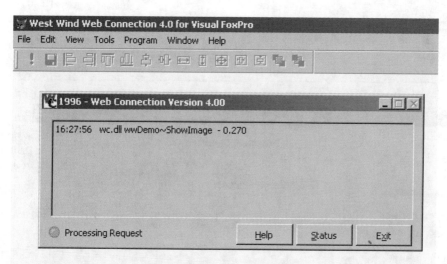

Figure 25. *Every time Web Connection processes a request, a line will display in the edit box in this window. See Figure 28 for an example.*

Thus, you need to enter the following in your browser's address window:

```
http://localhost/wconnect/default.htm
```

This says several things: First, the **http:** says to use HTTP as the protocol (instead of, say, FTP or the local file system). This ensures that you're not going to use the operating system's regular file opening mechanism, like when you double-click in Explorer, or select File | Open in Word or Excel.

Second, the **localhost** part means that you're running the Web server software on this machine. (You could also specify the IP address of 127.0.0.1 instead of "localhost".) If you wanted to run the Web server on another box, you'd call the Web server on that box (assuming that Web Connection is installed on that box):

```
http://www.thatbox.com/wconnect/default.htm
```

So the http://localhost is now pointing to the root of INETPUB\WWWROOT. Since the Web Connection samples are not in the root, but in the WCONNECT directory, you need to navigate there. Thus you'll include the WCONNECT string to specify which directory—and the DEFAULT.HTM string to indicate which file you want to open. (Note that if you defined DEFAULT.HTM as the default document in IIS or PWS, you don't have to add DEFAULT.HTM in your browser.)

You'll get a display like the one shown in **Figure 26**.

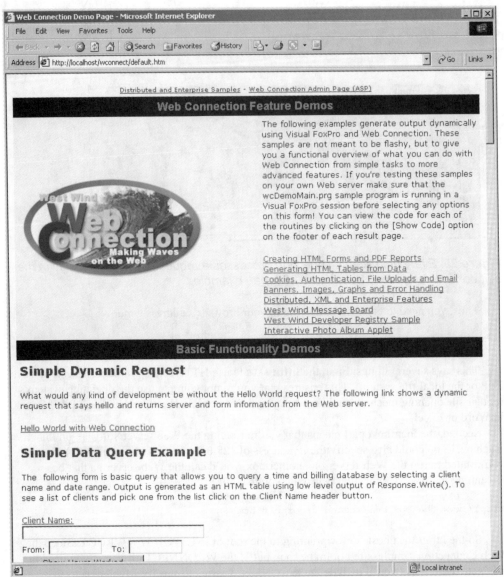

Figure 26. *The default HTML page of the Web Connection sample application.*

Clicking on the "Hello World with Web Connection" hyperlink in the bottom left of Figure 26 will make your first Web Connection request. If everything is set up properly, you'll get the page in **Figure 27**.

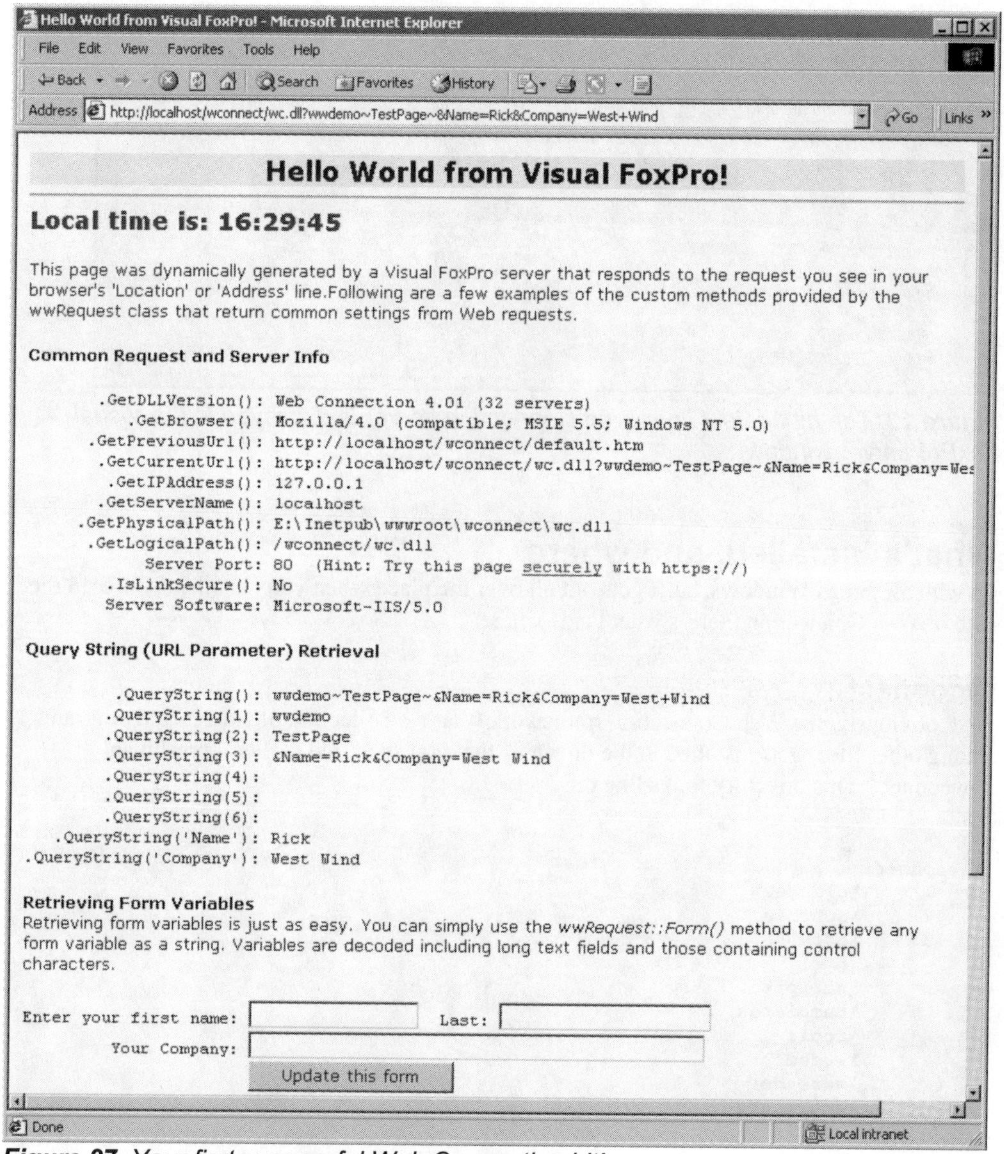

Figure 27. Your first successful Web Connection hit!

If you look back in your Visual FoxPro application, you will also see a line displayed in the Web Connection server window, shown in **Figure 28**. Congratulations! You've just served your first live Web hit from Visual FoxPro.

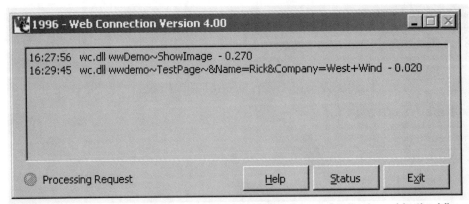

Figure 28. The hit against your Web Connection server is displayed in the Visual FoxPro server window.

What's installed, and where

As with all things Windows, stuff gets put all over the place when you install software. In the case of Web Connection, here's what lands where.

\wconnect

First, obviously, the Web Connection framework (that's a collection of classes and programs, among other files) gets installed in the directory that you specified earlier—presumably d:\wconnect. This directory looks like this:

```
D:
  \wconnect
              \classes
              \console
              \docs
              \html
              \scripts
              \templates
              \tools
              \wwdemo
              \wwreader
              \wwthreads
```

We don't have to go into huge detail on each of these. Suffice it to say that the classes you'll be using are in the \classes directory, and we'll get to the other stuff as need be.

\inetpub\wwwroot\wconnect

The demo HTML files get installed in a directory called "\WCONNECT" underneath the Web server directory—called, for example, \INETPUB\WWWROOT\WCONNECT. Just as you'll install your own Web site's HTML files under INETPUB\WWWROOT, Web Connection places its demo HTML files in the \INETPUB\WWWROOT\WCONNECT folder. The default page for the Web Connection demo app, DEFAULT.HTM, is located here, as are a bunch of other related files and images.

This directory also houses WC.DLL, which is the actual application that services the requests from the server.

Drive C
The Web Connection install program installs several things on drive C even if you place the Web Connection framework on drive D.

First, a copy of WWIPSTUFF.DLL is placed in the WINNT\SYSTEM32 directory and registered automatically. The West Wind Help icon's BMP is placed in the WINNT directory as well, but you shouldn't have to worry about that.

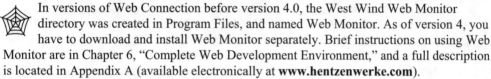 In versions of Web Connection before version 4.0, the West Wind Web Monitor directory was created in Program Files, and named Web Monitor. As of version 4, you have to download and install Web Monitor separately. Brief instructions on using Web Monitor are in Chapter 6, "Complete Web Development Environment," and a full description is located in Appendix A (available electronically at **www.hentzenwerke.com**).

How Web Connection works inside
Let's walk through a request, step by step.

To begin with, your Web server (IIS or PWS) is running, waiting to receive requests from browsers. Your VFP/WC application is also running—you've executed your EXE and there's a VFP Web Connection Server window open on your Web server's screen, like in Figure 25.

You enter a URL that includes "WC.DLL" as part of its string into your browser, like so:

```
http://localhost/wconnect/wc.dll?wwdemo~TestPage~&Name=Rick&Company=West+Wind
```

and that URL is sent to and received by your Web server. The Web server software sees that it has "WC.DLL" and looks for that file in the \WCONNECT directory. WC.DLL writes out a file in the messaging directory described earlier—like D:\WC_MSG\WC. This temp file includes everything about this request, including (but not limited to) the entire URL string.

Your Visual FoxPro EXE is running, waiting for a file to arrive in the messaging directory. Your EXE has a timer in it (courtesy of the Web Connection classes that are built into your project), so the EXE checks the messaging directory every once in a while. (See Chapter 11, "Managing Your Configuration," to see how to change the timer interval.)

When the file arrives in the messaging directory, your Visual FoxPro application parses the information in the file and uses that info to decide which method of which class to call in order to process the request. The following listing shows you the type of information in the file that lands in the messaging directory.

```
********  Form Variables  ********

********  Server Variables  ********

Output File=e:\wc_msg\WWC1A8.tmp
DLLVersion=Web Connection 4.01 (32 servers)
wcConfig=e:\inetpub\wwwroot\wconnect\wc.INI
REQUEST_METHOD=GET
```

```
QUERY_STRING=wwdemo~TestPage~&Name=Rick&Company=West+Wind
Executable Path=/wconnect/wc.dll
PATH_TRANSLATED=e:\inetpub\wwwroot
SCRIPT_NAME=/wconnect/wc.dll
PHYSICAL_PATH=e:\inetpub\wwwroot\wconnect\wc.dll
SERVER_PROTOCOL=HTTP/1.1
SERVER_SOFTWARE=Microsoft-IIS/5.0
SERVER_NAME=localhost
SERVER_PORT=80
REMOTE_HOST=127.0.0.1
REMOTE_ADDR=127.0.0.1
HTTP_REFERER=http://localhost/wconnect/default.htm
HTTP_USER_AGENT=Mozilla/4.0 (compatible; MSIE 5.01; Windows NT 5.0)
HTTP_COOKIE=WWTHREADID=A513CP4E
GMT_OFFSET=-21600
ALL_HTTP=HTTP_ACCEPT:image/gif, image/x-xbitmap, image/jpeg, image/pjpeg,
application/vnd.ms-powerpoint, application/vnd.ms-excel, application/msword,
*/*
HTTP_ACCEPT_LANGUAGE:en-us
HTTP_CONNECTION:Keep-Alive
HTTP_HOST:localhost
HTTP_REFERER:http://localhost/wconnect/default.htm
HTTP_USER_AGENT:Mozilla/4.0 (compatible; MSIE 5.01; Windows NT 5.0)
HTTP_COOKIE:WWTHREADID=A513CP4E
HTTP_ACCEPT_ENCODING:gzip, deflate
```

In this specific example, the class is named "wwdemo" and the method is named "TestPage." Additionally, the TestPage method accepts some parameters—namely Rick&Company and West+Wind—and returns some data, as shown in Figure 27, via the Web server.

In your own application, you'll be creating a class and writing methods that will be called instead of wwdemo and TestPage. Those methods will do things like present HTML pages that ask for user input, accept and validate data entered into those HTML pages, use that data to dig stuff out of databases (or stuff that data into databases), and build HTML strings that are returned to the users in their browsers.

And you know how to do all that stuff—writing Visual FoxPro code and manhandling databases, right?

By the way, note that you don't have to write the code that parses the URL string into the class name, method name, and list of parameters—that's all part of the Web Connection framework, as is a whole bunch of other good stuff.

For the time being, we're going to ignore everything that happens inside the Web Connection framework. That will be explained in detail in Chapters 12 and 16 (as well as in pieces of virtually every other chapter of the book). Chapter 4 will explain how to build your own process class and add methods to it that perform some basic but common tasks.

When something goes wrong

In a perfect world, everything would have worked perfectly to this point. You'd have executed every command and function properly, gotten the right responses in return, shot all the bad guys, kissed the girl, and ridden off into the sunset.

But it ain't a perfect world. There is a topic, "Setup troubleshooting," in the Web Connection Help file that describes some typical problems. Sometimes it helps to hear an explanation more than once, though, so let's discuss those items as well as a few other things that might have happened to you by now.

Authentication dialog appears

First, you might run into the dialog in **Figure 29**, most often when clicking on a link that contains a reference to WC.DLL.

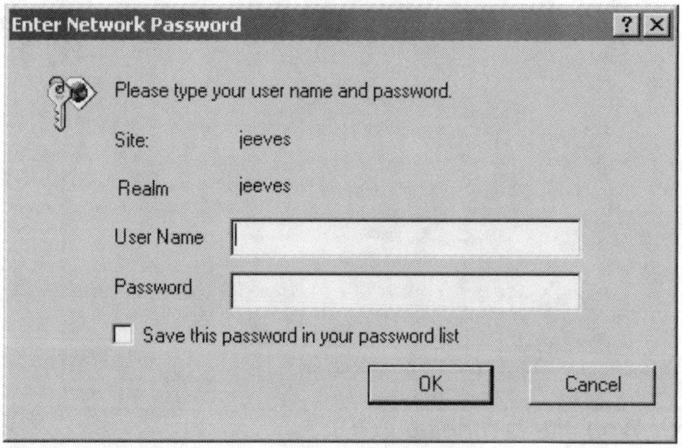

Figure 29. The Authentication dialog.

The cause for this is incorrect permissions being set for directories. In other words, you're not allowed access to a directory that you need access to. Remember how Web Connection writes a temporary file to WC_MSG\YourApp? If you don't have permission to access that directory (so you can write a temp file to that directory), then Windows is going to ask you to login, just like if you tried to get to any other directory that you didn't have permission to access. See the next topic for details about setting permissions properly.

Nothing happens when clicking on a WC.DLL link

Next, suppose you click on a WC.DLL link, but nothing happens. Well, technically, it's not that "nothing" happens—rather, it's that you don't get the page you wanted. Often you'll get a "Page not found" response in your browser. Here are some things to check.

First, is your Web server software (IIS or PWS) running? You can check whether your Web site server is running in IIS by clicking on Start | Programs | Administrative Tools | Computer Management, and then drilling down into the Services and Applications node, to the Internet Information Services node, and seeing what the status of your Web site node is (in the "State" column in the right pane), as shown in **Figure 30**.

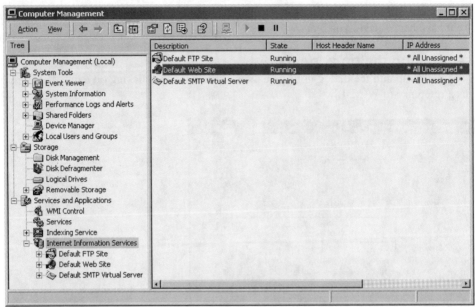

Figure 30. *Checking whether your Web site is running in IIS.*

Second, make sure your Web server software is operating correctly—try putting a simple HTML file in the directory that contains your WC.DLL, and then call that through your browser. Don't just double-click on the file in Windows Explorer—use the full syntax of

```
http://localhost/YourDir/YourSimpleHTMLFile.htm
```

and see whether the file is displayed properly in the browser. If the file doesn't display properly (or at all), it probably means that your Web server software is messed up. Fixing that problem is beyond the scope of this book. I've had luck just uninstalling IIS and reinstalling it, but you may be faced with a complete reinstall of Windows at some point. Do not pass Go, do not collect $200.

Third, make sure that your temp directory (for example, D:\WC_MSG\YourApp) has *full* access for the IUSR_<machine name> Web Account, where <machine name> is the name of the computer. Remember, WC.DLL is writing (and then erasing) files to this directory for each hit processed. If the WC.DLL "user" only has Read permissions, then the hits will fail because the files can't be created.

To check this, go into Windows Explorer (not Internet Explorer), right-click on the directory D:\WC_MSG, and select Properties. In Windows NT, you'll see the dialog shown in **Figure 31**.

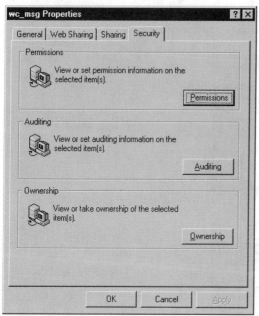

Figure 31. Select the Security tab of the directory's Properties dialog.

Then click on the Permissions button in order to determine which users have which rights to this directory, as shown in **Figure 32**. You should remove Everyone and add ISR_MACHINENAME with Full Control. Note that IUSR_ isn't a member of Everyone by default, so unless you've added IUSER_ to the Everyone group yourself, you need to add IUSR_ here. Harold discusses this in detail in Chapter 12 too. You can refer to that chapter for advice on privileges.

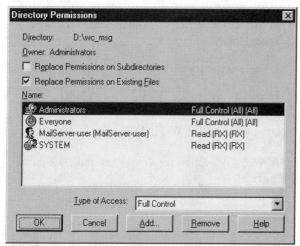

Figure 32. The Directory Permissions dialog in Windows NT shows you which users have which rights for a given directory.

In Windows 2000, you'll immediately get the dialog shown in **Figure 33** after clicking on the Security tab. Set up the appropriate users with the appropriate rights.

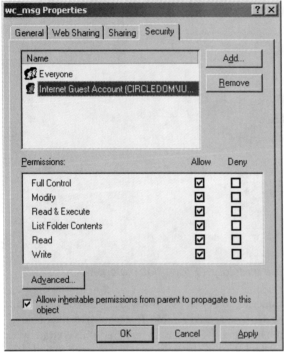

Figure 33. *Setting user access and rights only requires one dialog in Windows 2000.*

Fourth, make sure your Visual FoxPro Web Connection server is running, as shown in Figure 25 earlier in this chapter.

If it is, but hits aren't showing up in the edit area of the server window, there could be several things wrong. Try entering the following into your browser:

```
http://localhost/wconnect/wc.dll?_maintain~ShowStatus
```

(If you're typing this URL manually, that's an underscore after the question mark, not a space.) The page shown in **Figure 34** will display.

Compare the values in this screen with the values in the WC.INI file in the \INETPUB\WWWROOT\WCONNECT directory.

You can also go into the Visual FoxPro Web Connection server window and click on the Status button to get the dialog shown in **Figure 35**.

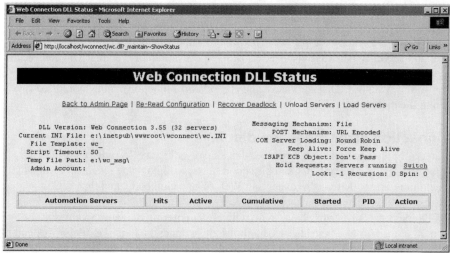

Figure 34. The Status page for Web Connection.

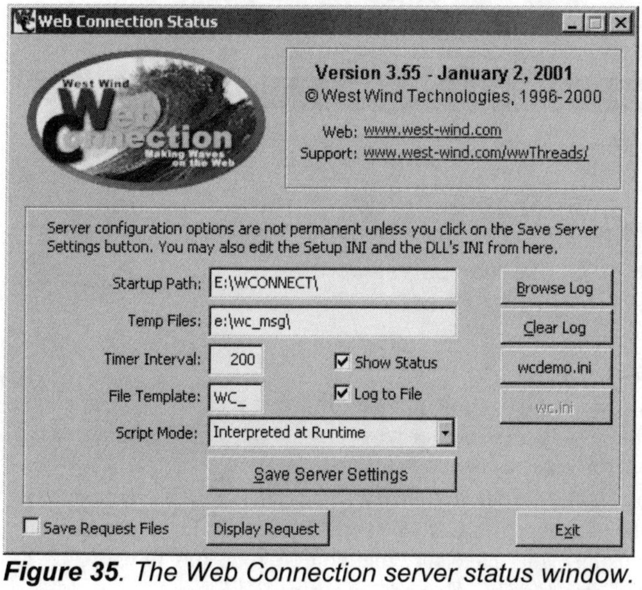

Figure 35. The Web Connection server status window.

Make sure that the values in Figure 35 match the values in Figure 34. A common mistake is for the Temp Files paths in WC.INI and YOURAPP.INI to be different. They need to be identical, or else WC.DLL will be putting the Web Connection messaging files in one directory but your application will be looking for them in another. (Note that the WC.INI button will be disabled until the first hit is processed by Web Connection. This is because, using file-based messaging, your Visual FoxPro application does not know the physical location of the WC.DLL and WC.INI files.)

See Chapter 11 for more information about these settings, what they mean, and how they work.

Fifth, see if you are getting temp files written in your messaging directory. Resize your Web Connection server window, your browser, and Windows Explorer so that you can see all three windows at the same time. Select the messaging directory (for example, e:\wc_msg\wc) in Explorer, and hit your WC.DLL link (say, the Hello World function). You should see two files written to the messaging folder.

Web Connection error message displays

If you get an error message in a Web page like that shown in **Figure 36** (with a colored bar across the top and text in reverse), it's actually good news, well, to some extent. It means that Web Connection is firing, that you're executing Web Connection code, and that WC is returning a result.

Typically, these types of errors have to do with either entering the wrong values in the URL (misspelling the names of the classes, methods, or parameters, like "TextPage" instead of "TestPage") or errors in the Visual FoxPro code itself.

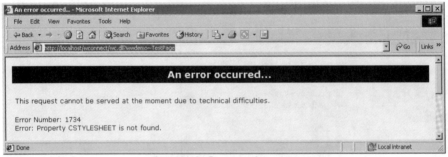

Figure 36. An error page that Web Connection serves up.

Save As/Download dialog

If you get a Save As or Download… dialog like shown in **Figure 37**, it means that your server isn't configured correctly, or that the wrong Web server was selected during installation and setup, or that something else went wrong.

The first thing you want to do is make sure that your \WCONNECT virtual directory was created properly in IIS. Bring up the Management Console (see Figure 4 or 12, depending on which version of Windows you're using), and make sure that you've got a \WCONNECT virtual directory. Also check that the directory has Execute or Script and Execute rights selected, as shown in Figures 5 and 13, depending on which OS you're using. Finally, make sure that you stop and restart IIS after you make any changes. Windows and IIS cache so much information that the only sure way to make sure that your changes take effect is to reboot your machine.

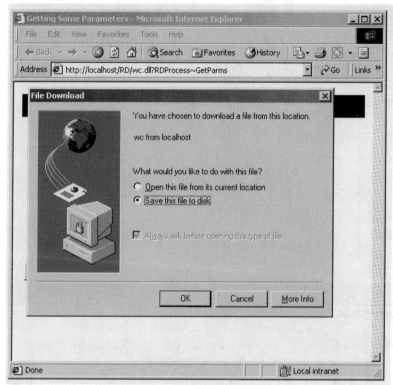

Figure 37. *The Save As/Download dialog.*

Cannot update the server

If you are moving from one version of Visual FoxPro to another, or upgrading Web Connection, you may need to update WC.DLL. It is possible to receive a message like that shown in **Figure 38**.

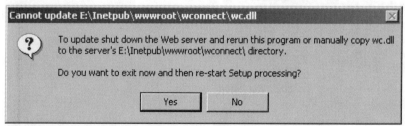

Figure 38. *The Cannot update WC.DLL error message.*

You'll need to stop your Web server software. Here's how to do so. First, open up your Web server software control panel—the Computer Management for Windows 2000 with the IIS node highlighted is shown in **Figure 39**.

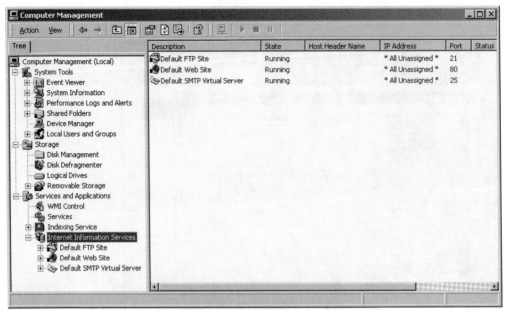

Figure 39. *The Computer Management dialog for Windows 2000.*

Then select the Web site of interest—for most purposes, it will be "Default Web Site"—and right-click to bring up the context menu, as shown in **Figure 40**.

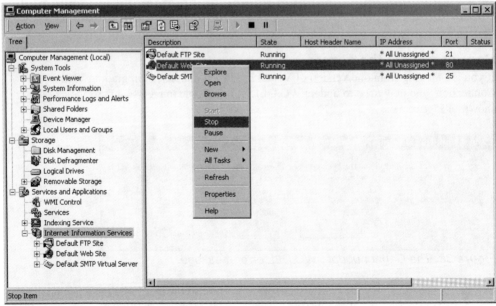

Figure 40. *The context menu for a service under IIS allows you to start and stop that service.*

Select the Stop menu option, and wait a few moments. Eventually, the State column entry will change to "Stopped." Copy over your WC.DLL (or perform whatever other tasks you need to), and then perform the same steps, but selecting "Start" in the context menu.

Conclusion

Getting Web Connection installed and running is a straightforward process but one that involves a lot of steps and many chances for things to go wrong. If the steps in this chapter don't work for you, consult the Web Connection message board at **www.west-wind.com/wwthreads** for additional help.

Now it's time to build our first real application!

Chapter 4
Your First Web Connection
Application

Once you've got the Web Connection demo running, you're probably all anxious to do your own thing. In this chapter, I'll show you how to create your first Web Connection application, how to run and test it, how to start modifying code, and, gasp, even how to access data!

I'm going to start you out on the right foot from the very beginning. When you create a project using the Web Connection wizard, Web Connection will place the project in the WCONNECT directory—along with all of the Web Connection framework code—and your project very definitely doesn't belong there.

As noted in the introduction to this book, there are many possible development environment architectures, and I'm not purporting to claim that the approach I describe in this chapter is the only one, nor the best one. But it's straightforward and, for lack of a common standard, one that you can use as you get started. As you progress through this book, you may find techniques and styles described later on by Harold and Randy to be more to your liking. Feel free to mix and match as you desire.

This chapter's sample application

In this chapter, I'm going to show you how to create your first Web Connection application. I'll start with a variation of "Hello World," just so you can follow the process involved in creating, running, and testing all of the pieces. Then I'll show you how to reference static files in your application, such as simple HTML pages and image files.

Next, I'll create some methods that allow the application to talk to data. In order to keep things simple, I'll use a single table of companies and products that are categorized by industry category and type of product. Using a search screen that allows the user to query this table by industry category and product type, I'll show you how to get input from the user, query the database, and return the results of that query. Once that's working, I'll discuss how to provide simple maintenance functions—add, edit and delete—to the query functionality just built.

Finally, I'll move the application to a live server, just to show you the pieces involved. Setting up the live server (both hardware and software) will be discussed in complete detail in Chapter 12, "A Web Connection Application from Start to Finish," but this will give you a running start.

A review of your directory structure

I'm going to assume that you've already gone through the drill in Chapter 3, "Installing, Configuring, and Testing Web Connection," so VFP and Web Connection are installed and running. However, just to make sure, I'll review what your directory structure should look like. For the sake of this discussion, I'll assume that all of your development is being done on drive E, and that the Web Connection framework files are in E:\WCONNECT. (That's because the machine I'm using while writing this chapter has a CD-ROM drive D.) If you have a one-drive machine, just replace "E" with "C" in the following discussion.

First, you'll need a directory in which to place your new Web Connection project. If this is being done for a customer, you could create a customer directory on drive E, and then a subdirectory underneath that customer's directory for this project. If you're just goofing around, why don't you create a directory called, say, "WCAPPS," and underneath it, create a directory for your first project, say, WR04. That stands for WebRAD, Chapter 4.

Next, you'll need a directory where you'll put the Web site files for this project. To make your life easier, how about E:\INETPUB\WWWROOT\WR04?

You'll also need a directory for those all-important temp files. I suggest E:\WC_MSG\WR04.

Finally, you'll need a directory where you'll put your data files for this project. Again, for sake of argument, I'll use E:\WSDB\WR04 (the "WSDB" stands for "Web Site Databases"). Whatever you do, *don't* put your data underneath the INETPUB\WWWROOT directory, because on your live server, that directory will be accessible by anyone who can get to your Web site.

Creating your project

The first step in creating your new Web Connection project is to start VFP and load Web Connection. I know, you thought I was going to say, "Take out a piece of paper and do your analysis and design." Well, for the time being, I'll assume that you've already done that. I mean, this is a simple one-table system.

So, once you've loaded VFP, changed to the \WCONNECT directory, and run WCSTART, you should have the Web Connection menu pad added to the end of your VFP system menu, as shown in **Figure 1**.

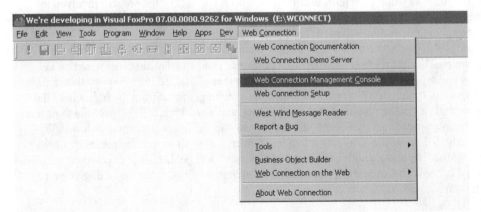

Figure 1. *Running WCSTART adds a Web Connection pad to the Visual FoxPro system menu.*

You may want to double check that you're set up properly. Make sure that the current VFP directory is \WCONNECT and that the path (using SET('path')) is:

```
\wconnect
\wconnect\classes
\wconnect\tools
\wconnect\wwipstuff_samples
.\classes
..\
.\console
```

Some of our sharp-eyed readers have noted that they put this in a WAIT WINDOW NOWAIT box as part of the setup code—making it easier to notice a mistake due to a setup routine that went astray.

Select the Web Connection Management Console menu option, and you'll be greeted with the main Web Connection Management Console dialog, as shown in **Figure 2**.

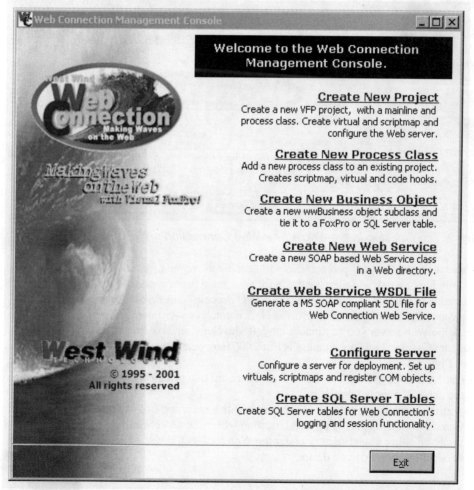

Figure 2. Launch the Web Connection Management Console to create new projects.

Select the Create New Project hyperlink in the Web Connection Management Console dialog, and you'll get the first step in the New Project Wizard, as shown in **Figure 3**. Note that the Web Connection Help file also loads at this point—depending on the position of the moons as well as the karma of your development machine, the Help file may overlap the wizard dialog. Just Alt-Tab to get back to the wizard if needed.

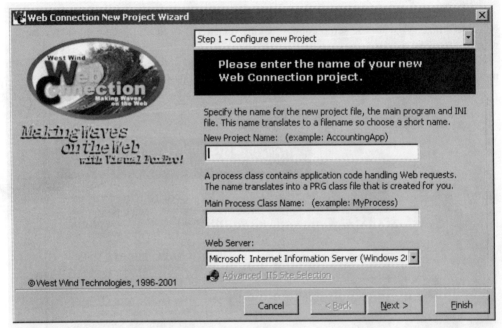

Figure 3. *The first step in creating a new Web Connection project is to name it.*

Enter the name for your project (this will become the name of your VFP project, so don't use a really long name), and then the name for your main process class (for the time being, just add the name of your project in front of the word "Process"). In future projects, you can change your mind about your main process class naming conventions.

Pick the Web server you're running on your development box (hopefully you took my advice from Chapter 3 and are running NT or 2000, so you can just grab IIS and be done with it)—see **Figure 4**.

Click Next to go to Step 2 in the wizard. There are two pieces to this step. The first is to select the name of a virtual directory.

A virtual directory provides the Web server with a mapping from a realm name like www.yoursite.com to a specific physical location where the server can find files. This physical location can be either a subdirectory under the Web root with the same name, or it can be any other physical location that you desire.

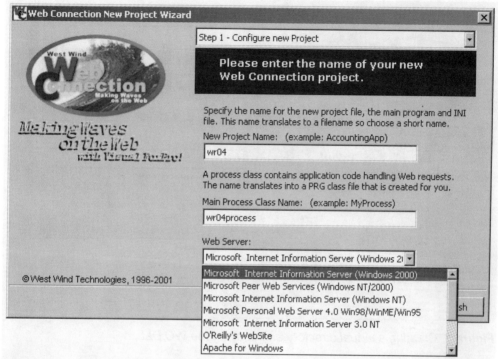

Figure 4. The Configure New Project dialog after a new project has been named.

As a result, then, the user will be entering a domain name and a virtual name into their browser, and the Web server will be translating that information to a physical location on a hard disk.

It looks like creating a virtual directory is optional, but I suggest that you choose to do so. You'll want Web Connection to act as if there is a virtual directory whether you use a different name for the physical location or not. You'll be setting properties for that virtual that are different from the properties of the default Web site.

Check the Create Virtual Directory check box, and then enter the name for your virtual directory, and point to the actual path that it will represent. Note that Web Connection will try to guess what the path will be, by appending the name of your project to the location of the Web server home directory, as shown in **Figure 5**. It's perfectly fine for the virtual name and the subdirectory name to be the same, and, in fact, doing so can be less confusing.

Note that by checking the Create Virtual Directory option, the Web Connection wizard will actually have IIS create a virtual directory. You could do this yourself, of course, by going into IIS and creating a virtual directory, but by letting Web Connection do it, Web Connection also sets other things properly—things like script maps and setting up access permissions properly. We'll cover this stuff later in Chapter 12, but it's good to know that for now, it's being taken care of for you.

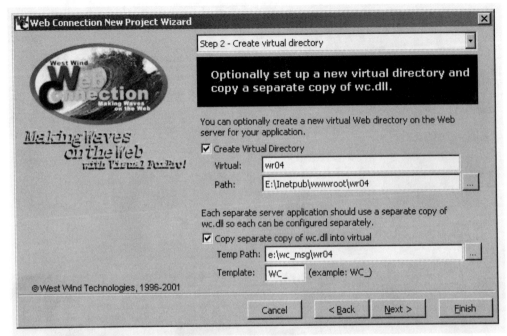

Figure 5. *Creating a virtual directory and copying the WC.DLL.*

The dialog makes the second part of Step 2 in the Web Connection Setup Wizard confusing. The dialog appears to be asking whether you want to copy a separate copy of the WC.DLL (and create a Web Connection INI file to go with it) into the virtual or not. However, what's not clear is that this task must be performed—if you don't have the wizard do it for you, you'll have to do it yourself manually. The dialog is asking whether you want Web Connection to do it for you, or if you want to do it yourself later. (Blech!) There is not an alternative of not making a separate copy one way or another. Let Web Connection do it!

Thus, you'll want to check the "Copy separate copy" check box.

Next, change the Temp Path value to match the folder you create for temporary files for this project. In this example, that temp path would be E:\WC_MSG\WR04.

The template is the extension used for files placed in the temp file directory. If you place temp files for each Web Connection application into their own temp directory, then you can leave this as "WC_"—if, for some reason, you need to have multiple applications put their temp files all in the same directory, then you'll want unique template names for each application, so that each application creates files with different extensions.

Click Next to go to Step 3 in the wizard, where you can define a script map. Like the temp files, scripts maps are powerful and important, but require a bit of explanation. Please take the time to read through this!

Remember that a Web server can process three types of files:

- Those that are simply sent back to the user's browser, such as straight HTML

- Those that are executed (such as EXEs and DLLs)

- Those that are pre-processed, such as ASP files

To understand what a script map is, let's look at how a URL is processed at the server. When you enter a URL with a file name that has an extension of, say, HTML or GIF, the server knows that it's to find the file and deliver a copy back over HTTP to the user.

Some files, however, well, you don't want to send them to the user. Instead, you want them to be processed on the server. EXEs and DLLs, for example, right? Servers can be configured to automatically run certain types of files instead of delivering the file back to the user. That's what the "Execute" setting for a virtual directory means—that EXEs and DLLs, for example, are to be executed on the server instead of delivering the EXE or DLL file back to the user like an HTML file would be.

For reference, go back to Chapter 3, and look at Figures 5 (for NT) and 13 (for Windows 2000). You'll see where you set the Scripts/Execute permissions for a directory on the Web server.

Now, let's go one step further. Some files aren't just delivered back to the user, nor are they "executed" on the server. ASP files, for example, fall into this third category. When a Web server gets a URL that includes a file with an ASP extension, like this:

```
http://www.somewebsite.com/SomeFile.ASP
```

the Web server knows that this file should be handled in a special way. How does it know this? There's a lookup table in IIS, associated with the Web server that has the "ASP" extension in it. (See the "Setting up script mapping" section of Chapter 12 for details about how to set up script maps directly in IIS.)

The Web server sees the "ASP" extension and automatically looks for a DLL called ASP.DLL. (The server knows this because the entry in that lookup table I just mentioned matches the ASP.DLL next to the extension "ASP.") The ASP file is processed by the ASP.DLL, and the results are returned by the Web server to the user.

So far, so good, eh?

Now, what if you could define your own extension, similar to "ASP," and then attach it to some DLL? Groovy, eh? In fact, it'd be even groovier if you could use that lookup table I just mentioned to do so, right?

A Web Connection script map is just this—a definition of an extension for a file that is processed by the WC.DLL. (So, when you think about it, a script map should actually be called a "script extension," doncha think?) This definition is placed in the lookup table automatically from Web Connection by this New Project Wizard (see, I told you we were just taking a short detour). And, of course, the Web Connection framework knows how to interpret a URL that has a predefined script map.

So, instead of entering a string into your browser like this:

```
http://www.somesite.com/wc.dll?SomeClass~SomeMethod
```

you could enter a script map, XXX (remember, you could think of "XXX" as a "script extension" if that makes it easier), that would be mapped to the WC.DLL in the IIS lookup table. Then, you could enter this string instead:

`http://www.somesite.com/SomeMethod.XXX`

This provides you with a couple of benefits that I'll talk about in depth later. The bottom line, for now, is that Step 3 in the New Project Wizard is where you determine whether or not you want to define a script map, and, if so, what it is. See **Figure 6**, where I define a script map of "WR," and link it to the WC.DLL in the WR04 directory.

There's actually a lot to using script maps the first time around. I discuss the topic in more depth in the section "Using script maps instead of calls to WC.DLL" later in this chapter, and Harold covers it in more detail in "Setting up script mapping" in Chapter 12.

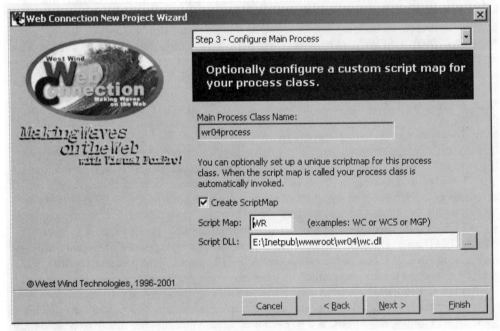

Figure 6. Naming the script map and identifying the script map DLL.

Okay, back to the wizard. Click the Next button, and then, finally, create the project by clicking the Finish button in the Step 4 dialog, as shown in **Figure 7**. Ever wonder what the difference is between clicking the Finish button in the Step 3 dialog in Figure 6, and clicking the Finish button in the Step 4 dialog in Figure 7?

You could shortcut Step 4 by clicking on Finish in Step 3—it's just that the final page in Step 4 shows you what all of the selections you've made are in a summarized screen. If you realized that you made a mistake, you could go back via the Back button and change something. You could certainly click Finish earlier if it is offered.

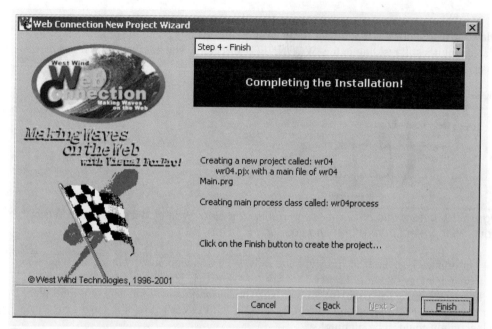

Figure 7*. The Finish dialog displays the settings you've chosen.*

As of Version 4.0, Web Connection will then offer to stop and restart IIS for you, as shown in **Figure 8**. If you select Yes, a DOS box will display stopping and starting command lines. It may take a minute or two for the operation to complete on your machine.

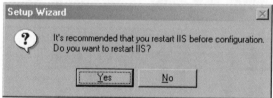

Figure 8*. Web Connection offers you the opportunity to automatically stop and restart IIS after clicking Finish in the wizard.*

The Web Connection wizard will now do its thing, creating a project file, adding files to it, and copying files as you directed with the wizard. Eventually, the wizard will attempt to build an EXE from the project, as the WAIT WINDOW in **Figure 9** shows, but will fail because some files are in use.

Figure 9*. The WAIT WINDOW indicates that the New Project Wizard is attempting to create a new EXE file.*

You'll get the error message in **Figure 10**. Click OK and move on. However, do *not* follow the instructions in the Project Build error dialog! At this point, the project has been created, but it's still residing in the \WCONNECT directory. The next step is to move the project where it belongs *before* creating your first EXE.

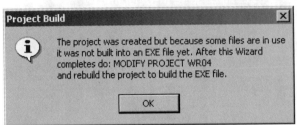

Figure 10. Ignore this error message during the New Project Wizard startup. You'll move your project before creating your first EXE anyway.

Unfortunately, even if the project build fails, Web Connection will launch a test page for the new project, as shown in **Figure 11**. I say "unfortunately" because if you click on any of the hyperlinks in the test page, the hit will fail. The reason they will fail is because the Web Connection server isn't running—after all, the EXE didn't even get built in the previous step, so it certainly couldn't be running!

You might want to keep the browser open to this page, and after you move your project and build the EXE, you'll be ready to test, instead of having to open up your browser again and enter the test URL.

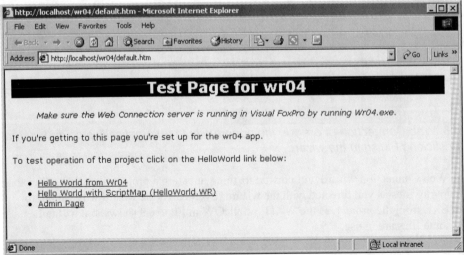

Figure 11. The test page for your new project allows you to test the server and the script map.

Before I get to moving the project, though, take a look at the contents of the address bar in the browser. You'll see that the link to this test page doesn't include the great big long URL to

E:\INETPUB\WWWROOT\WR04—just simply the call to the Web server (localhost or 127.0.0.1), the virtual directory (wr04), and the name of the test page (default.htm). If you wanted to, you could have set up your virtual directory to extend way deep into the bowels of the file system directory, pointing to a subdirectory buried in layers of subdirectories, but still reference a test page simply via the virtual directory name.

Now, after you've clicked OK in the error dialog in Figure 10, you'll be returned to the Visual FoxPro IDE, and your Project Manager window and the Web Connection Management Console window will both still be open. I've found it easiest to close the WCMC window, and then get out of Fox completely, in order to make sure there aren't any loose files open.

Moving your project

If you open up Windows Explorer, you'll see a bunch of new files in the E:\WCONNECT directory (or whatever you named the directory where you installed the Web Connection framework), most of which start with the name of your project, as shown in **Listing 1**.

Listing 1. The contents of the Web Connect directory after creating project WR04.

```
Volume in drive E is DEV
Volume Serial Number is 9D58-C911

Directory of E:\wconnect

01/11/25   04:44p       <DIR>          .
01/11/25   04:44p       <DIR>          ..
01/11/25   04:40p                2,909 bld_Wr04.prg
01/11/25   03:29p       <DIR>          classes
01/10/17   11:41p                  210 config.fpw
01/11/22   04:21p       <DIR>          console
01/11/03   11:41a              670,203 console.EXE
01/11/25   04:44p                    0 dir1.txt
01/11/22   04:21p       <DIR>          FoxCentral
01/11/22   04:36p       <DIR>          html
01/11/22   04:21p       <DIR>          scripts
01/10/18   09:14p               19,892 setup.EXE
01/10/18   09:14p               20,404 setup70.EXE
01/11/22   04:21p       <DIR>          SoapSamples
01/11/22   04:21p       <DIR>          templates
01/11/22   04:21p       <DIR>          tools
01/11/22   05:23p                1,348 wcdemo.ini
01/11/22   04:43p                6,585 wcdemomain.FXP
01/11/22   04:36p               14,914 wcDemoMain.prg
01/11/03   11:50a            3,672,992 wconnect.chm
01/10/17   10:18p                8,804 wconnect.h
98/07/27   02:19a                1,078 wconnect.ico
00/04/14   12:20p               44,404 wconnect.wav
01/10/20   03:46p                  559 wconnect_override.h
01/11/22   04:43p                3,070 wcstart.FXP
01/10/10   03:40a                3,967 wcstart.PRG
01/11/25   04:40p                  217 Wr04.ini
01/11/25   04:42p              143,088 Wr04.PJT
01/11/25   04:42p                3,143 Wr04.PJX
01/11/25   04:40p               11,842 Wr04Main.prg
01/11/25   04:40p                2,111 wr04process.prg
01/04/16   01:07a                3,329 wwbanners.DBF
```

```
01/11/22  04:44p        <DIR>              wwdemo
01/11/22  04:22p        <DIR>              wwDevRegistry
01/10/17  10:07p               75,776 wwipstuff.dll
01/11/22  04:22p        <DIR>              wwIPStuff_samples
01/11/22  04:22p        <DIR>              wwreader
01/11/22  05:23p                  661 wwRequestLog.DBF
01/11/22  05:23p                1,280 wwRequestLog.FPT
01/11/22  04:27p        <DIR>              wwthreads
01/10/18  09:24p                9,379 _readme.htm
              26 File(s)      4,722,165 bytes
              15 Dir(s)   1,201,762,304 bytes free
```

The one file that has your project name in it, but doesn't begin with the name of your project is at the beginning of this listing: BLD_WR04.PRG.

If you still haven't created the project directory that you're going to keep your project files in, now is the time to create it, as well as the SOURCE directory underneath.

Next, move (don't copy) all of your project's files from the \WCONNECT directory to your project directory. (Don't forget to close those files in VFP first! That's why I just exit VFP completely.) Then move the XXProcess.PRG (where XX is the name of your project) files to the source directory. Do not move XXMain.PRG to your source directory! If you do, and try to run the PRG, Web Connection will look for your application's INI file in the source directory. When it doesn't find it, you'll end up with unexpected results that are very hard to track down. (The error message "WWC_SERVER is not found" is one symptom.) You should end up with something like this (using "WR04" as the name of the project):

```
E:
  \WCAPPS
        \WR04
        bld_wr04.prg
        wr04.ini
        wr04.pjx
        wr04.pjt
        wr04main.prg
           \SOURCE
           wr04process.prg
```

Get back into Fox, change to that project's directory by selecting the project's menu option (set up via the GOFOXGO tool described in Chapter 3), open the project, click on the Rebuild project option button, check the Recompile All Files check box, and all of the files should be brought into the project if they weren't already. Remember that the GOFOXGO routine I described in the previous chapter includes "SOURCE" as part of the path when changing to the project's directory, so you may have to fiddle around a bit if you don't do it that way.

If you don't use the GOFOXGO mechanism, you'll find that the project will complain about not being able to find the Web Connection framework files, so you'll need a different way to make sure your paths are set up properly. One way is to manually set the default directory and path. After loading Visual FoxPro, you could type the following into your Command Window:

```
    set defa to <name of your application directory>
    set path to source; \wconnect; \wconnect\classes\; \wconnect\tools\;
\wconnect\wwipstuff_samples\
```

Another way, espoused by our technical editor, is to create a CONFIG.FPW file in the project's directory that specifies the path, and then create a desktop shortcut that opens VFP in that directory.

Testing your project

It's white-knuckle time now. Time to build your EXE and test it.

First, rebuild your project again, and be sure to select the Win32 executable/COM server option group in the Build Options dialog, as shown in **Figure 12**.

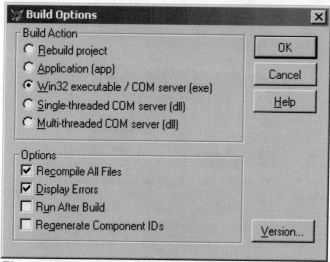

Figure 12. Be sure to check the Recompile All Files check box when rebuilding your EXE.

Next, run the EXE by double-clicking on it in Explorer. (Technically, you could also DO WR04.EXE in the Command Window in VFP.) You'll get the server window as shown in **Figure 13**. Running the executable—what we know as "running a program" in LAN and client/server apps—is referred to as "running the server." At some point, you may be asked, "Is the Web Connection server running?"—this question means, "Have you run the EXE so that the server window is displayed?" like in Figure 13. (There are cases where you won't have a visible instance of the server, but we'll cover that in Chapters 12 and 14.)

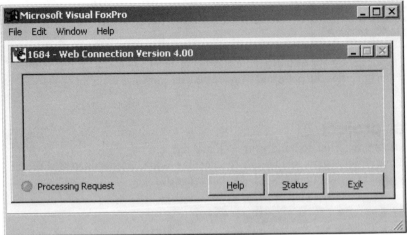

Figure 13. *The Visual FoxPro Web Connection server window.*

So far, so good. Now it's time to test whether it's really working. Open up your browser, and enter:

```
http://localhost/wr04/default.htm
```

or whatever the name of your virtual directory is. (What you are doing here is displaying the default.htm file that's located in E:\INETPUB\WWWROOT\WR04.) You'll get the same browser window as shown in Figure 11. Click on the first hyperlink, and you should get a new page in your browser, as shown in **Figure 14**.

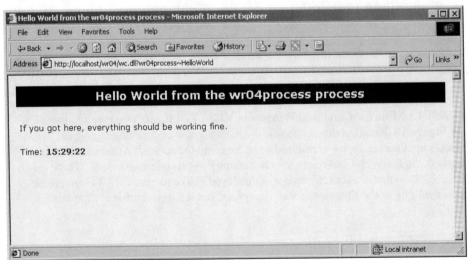

Figure 14. *Your first successful Web Connection request from your own project.*

Look over to your server window, as shown in **Figure 15**, and you should see a line of text describing what the server just did—process a request and make a call to the Hello World method of the WR04Process class. Where did this Hello World method come from? It's always generated as part of the Process class that is created when you create a new project from the Web Connection Management Console.

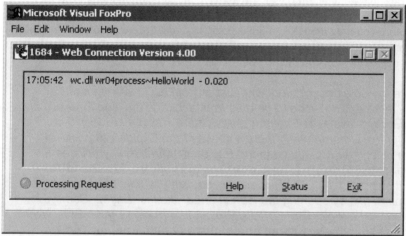

Figure 15. *The Visual FoxPro Web Connection server window displays the results of hits to the server.*

After you've made your first successful hit, you can click the Status button in the Web Connection server window and see that the WC.INI button is finally enabled.

Now it's time to start making some modifications. Go ahead and click the Exit button in the server window.

Optimizing your development environment—just a bit

Before we start cranking out oodles of Fox code, though, it's worth spending a few moments to make your life easier. You're going to find that you will be doing a few things over and over again—running the server, and making page requests in your browser.

You'll notice that for this first test, I had you build an EXE and run it from outside of Visual FoxPro. Do you have to do that each time you test? Yeah, it's not a big deal to build an EXE, switch over to Explorer, find the EXE, and double-click on it, or to open the drop-down in the browser, find the link you want, and execute it. But it's still more work than you really want… What if we could make both of those functions single clicks? Or what if we didn't even have to build an EXE at all?

As the saying goes, the idea is to keep the iteration time shorter than your attention span. Personally, I need all the help I can get. I'll show you how to speed up time if you want to build an EXE each time, and then how to avoid building the EXE at all, until you're ready to deploy to your live Web server.

EXE shortcut

The first thing to do is create a shortcut to the EXE on your taskbar.

Open Explorer, click on your EXE file, and drag it to the Quick Launch toolbar in the taskbar (the area immediately to the right of the Start button), and you'll be all set. Well, almost all set. Once you have created a half-dozen apps, you'll end up with a bunch of EXE shortcuts files that all look alike—they'll all have the same orange Fox head for the icon.

As a result, before you drag the EXE to the taskbar, assign a different icon to the project. If you're short of artistic skills, you can find a bazillion ICO files on drive C using Find in Explorer. Place a copy of an icon you like in your project directory.

NOTE *Note that this doesn't work with just any old ICO file—the icon has to be a 32x32 icon to be able to attach, and the icon for the EXE won't display in Explorer unless there's also a 16x16, 16-color icon in the ICO file. Unfortunately, there's no way from Explorer to positively tell what type of icon an ICO file is. In the Explorer Search tool, you'll see the size of the various ICO files—1K files don't contain both the 32x32 and 16x16 icons, while it seems that the 2K files usually do. But I've only been able to positively confirm this by opening the icon in a tool like IconEdit32. See the online Help under the topic "Project Tab, Project Information Dialog Box." You can get IconEdit32 from **www.zdnet.com/pcmag/pctech/content/16/12/ ut1612.001.html**, and you can find a shareware version called IconEdit Pro at **www.iconedit.com**.*

Then, open the Project Manager (don't have it docked), and select the Project | Project Info menu option from the VFP system menu. Select the Project tab, click on the Attach Icon check box in the lower right, as shown in **Figure 16**, and navigate to the ICO file you want. I grab a copy of the ICO file I want and put it in the project's directory so that I have it for the life of the project.

Next time you build your EXE, this icon file will be attached to the EXE. However, it will still not be attached to the shortcut in the Quick Launch toolbar. Right-click on the shortcut in the Quick Launch toolbar, select Properties, click on Change Icon, and, using the Browse command button, navigate to the ICO file (*not* the EXE file that's provided as the default file for the Current Icon). Click on OK in the Change Icon dialog, then on Apply and OK in the Shortcut Properties dialog, and your new icon will display instead of the orange Fox head on the Quick Launch toolbar.

From now on, you can just click on the EXE shortcut in the Quick Launch toolbar after building the EXE inside VFP. But that's still a lot of work. How about running your Web Connection server from within your Visual FoxPro development environment?

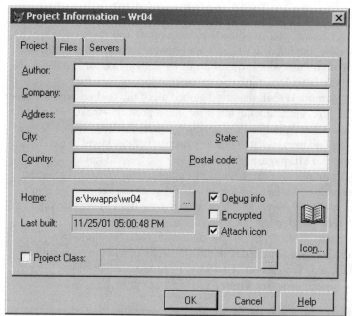

Figure 16. Use the Project Information dialog to attach an icon to the EXE for easier identification in the taskbar.

Running your Web Connection server inside VFP

When you're building regular Visual FoxPro applications, you're probably used to testing your programs by issuing a

```
do someprogram
```

command in the VFP Command Window. Wouldn't it be nice if you could do this with your Web Connection applications as well? Well, you can, usually.

Either issue the

```
do wr04main
```

command in the VFP Command Window, or, if you're the type to keep your Project Manager open, click on the wr04main item in the Code tab, and then click the Run button. (I keep the Project Manager open all the time with the wr04main item highlighted, so I just have to keep hitting Run—about as few steps as is possible.)

Note that occasionally Web Connection and Visual FoxPro get confused. You may need to rebuild your project completely, or even get of Visual FoxPro and start it up again in those cases.

HTML page shortcut

In just about every project you work on, you're going to have multiple calls to Web Connection methods. After a while, the list of URLs in your browser address drop-down can be pretty lengthy—particularly if you use your browser for other things, like surfing the Web. Thus, it can be difficult to find the exact hyperlink you're looking for.

What I've done is create a dummy HTML page and embed all of the URLs I regularly use in it. (These URLs have the full link, including the http://localhost prefix, to make sure that the request is routed through the Web server, not just the operating system's file system.) Then I put a shortcut to that HTML page on my taskbar. Thus, it's just two clicks to get to any URL I need—one to call up the dummy HTML page, and a second one for the real link.

Note that the shortcut to the dummy HTML page is just opening the HTML page in the browser via the file system—not through the Web server—but that's OK, because we don't need that page processed through the Web server. The key is that the links in the dummy HTML page make the correct requests through the Web server.

In fact, I take this idea one step further. I divide the dummy HTML page into two columns—the left column contains links for the development machine, and the right column has matching links that go to the live Web server. That way, I can test the live server from my development box with just a couple clicks. See **Figure 17** for an example.

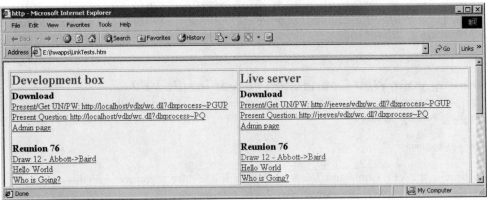

Figure 17. Create a dummy HTML page with links to your development box and your live server for easy access to your Web Connection application's functions.

Want life to be even better? Make this dummy HTML page your home page in your browser, so you can get to this page with the Home button any time your browser is open.

Another option is to create a new folder under your "Favorites." Call it something like "Development projects." Then you can add the main page for each of your virtual directories to this folder. You can also create another folder for the "Live server" links. The disadvantage to this technique is that you don't see the development and live links side-by-side, as you do on the dummy HTML page.

Help file shortcuts

Hopefully you'll find this book so spellbinding that you'll be referring to it day and night. But it can be inconvenient to keep flipping through it—why not refer to the CHM file that comes along with the source code downloads?

I've found it very useful to put shortcuts to several CHM files on the taskbar. The shortcuts I have on my taskbar open the Hacker's Guide, the Web Connection Help file, and this book.

As our technical editor mentioned, you may find that you can sure get a lot of shortcuts building up that way. Barbara puts her shortcuts into groups, and has the groups on the taskbar.

Opening up and adding code to the project

The previous discussion is all well and good, but you're itching to get your hands dirty, aren't you? Okay, let's open up the project and start writing our own code.

Get back into Fox, switch to your project's directory, and click on the Code tab in the Project Manager, as shown in **Figure 18**. I personally keep the Project Manager docked, and just open the Code tab itself.

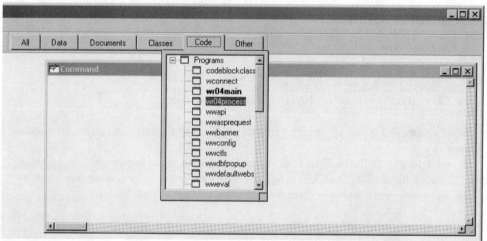

Figure 18. *Open up the process class program via the Code tab in the Project Manager.*

The action happens in the WR04Process program, so open it up and look for a method called Hello World, as shown in the following listing.

```
****************************************************************
FUNCTION HelloWorld()
***********************

THIS.StandardPage("Hello World from the WR04Process process",;
            "If you got here, everything should be working fine.<p>" + ;
            "Time: <b>" + TIME()+ "</b>")
```

```
ENDFUNC
* EOF WR04Process::HelloWorld
```

Now, there are two types of programmers: the cautious ones, and the ones who are now selling insurance. Thus, I won't blame you if you want to take it slowly and make a slight tweak to the existing Hello World method, just to prove to yourself that you can do it. How about the following?

```
THIS.StandardPage("Well, go-oo-oolly, Andy, looky here! ",;
                  "Wait till I go tell Aunt Bea!<p>" + ;
                  "Time: <b>" + TIME()+ "</b>")
```

To make it easy on yourself, just copy the existing THIS.StandardPage call and modify the copy. Then comment out the original call. If you rebuild the project, creating a new EXE, you very well might end up with an error message like in **Figure 19**. (In fact, if you don't run into this at one point or another in your Web Connection programming career, you're just not trying very hard.)

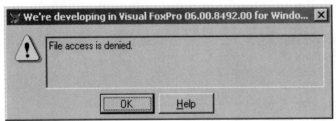

Figure 19. You can't rebuild an EXE if it's already running.

What's happened is that you haven't shut down the Web Connection server (the window in Figure 14).

Click on the icon in the taskbar, click on the Exit button in the server window, and then rebuild the EXE again. Run the EXE (using that nifty shortcut on your taskbar that's part of the GoFoxGo program!), and then enter the following request in your browser:

```
http://localhost/wr04/default.htm
```

If you click the "Hello World" link this time, you should end up with a new page in your browser, like in **Figure 20**.

Okay, so we're genuine programmers now. But we're just running an EXE and returning the results of a simple function. Let's move on.

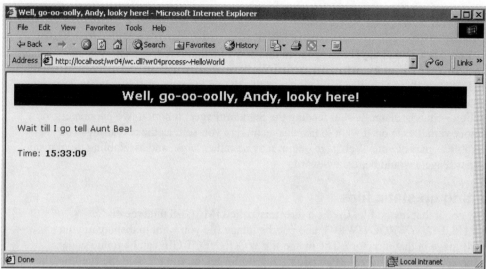

Figure 20. *The results of your revised Hello World program.*

Accessing static (non-Web Connection) files

It's time to expand the scope of this application to include static files. One example might be an image file that you want to embed in your generated Web page.

You'll want to do one thing first. That "thing" is to put code in your Web Connection app that will reference (and display) other files.

Referencing static files

The next step is to make some modifications to the process program that contains the Hello World function we just modified. I'm going to show you how to create a new function that references a static image file, and call that function instead of Hello World in the URL.

First, shut down the server (click on the Exit button in the server window).

Next, fire up VFP (if it's not already running), open your project, and open the WR04Process program file. Add the following code, say, in front of the Hello World function. (You could put it after, instead, if you wanted to—just make sure that your new function is located after the DEFINE CLASS command near the beginning of the code, and before the ENDDEFINE statement at the end of the Process program file.)

```
*************************************************************************
FUNC ShowStatic()
*************************************************************************
m.lcTitle = "This is a WC request with a static file"
m.lcPage ;
  = [This is the West Wind Logo:] ;
  + [<br>] ;
  + [<p><img border="0" src="images\wconnect.gif" ] ;
  + [ width="180" height="105"></p>] ;
  + [That was the West Wind Logo.]
```

```
this.StandardPage(m.lcTitle, m.lcPage)
ENDFUNC
```

You'll notice that the HTML code in this new function refers to a GIF file that's located in the "images" directory, wherever that is. We'll set that up in a second.

The other thing to notice is that in the Hello World function, the actual data was sent to StandardPage(). In this new function, I'm using the same standard Web Connection function—StandardPage()—but feeding the StandardPage() function two parameters via memory variables. You'll want to use this technique yourself, as the text strings you assemble as part of your Web page output may be rather large, and assembling them inside StandardPage() would be, er, awkward.

Setting up static files

Now, about that image file. Create a directory called IMAGES underneath \INETPUB\WWWROOT\WR04, and put the image file you want to display in your HTML page in that directory. The image file WCONNECT.GIF can be found under \wconnect\html\formimages. If you don't, or you forget, or you mess up the spelling, the image won't display in the page—and you'll get a big red X where the image should be.

Running your app

Time to test. Run WR04MAIN or rebuild your EXE, and run the EXE (using that nifty taskbar shortcut described earlier). Then open up your browser. Enter the following URL:

```
http://localhost/wr04/wc.dll?wr04Process~ShowStatic
```

You should get a page returned in your browser that looks like **Figure 21**.

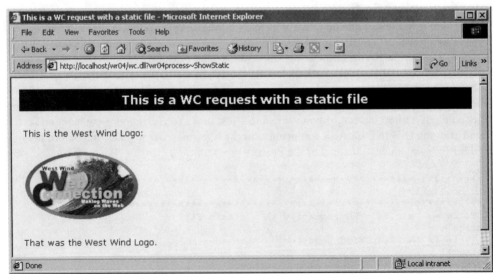

Figure 21. The results of a Web Connection hit that references a static file.

Accessing data

It's a pretty silly database application that doesn't actually have data in it, eh? Well, the same type of techniques I used to reference static files can be used, after a fashion, to reference data. Neat-o!

The sample application I'm going to demonstrate in this section is a simplified version of the Resource Database from Hentzenwerke's Web site. If you're not acquainted with it, the Resource Database contains listings on a variety of developer resources—consultants, training videos, events, third-party tools, vertical market applications, and so on. Users can select the type of resource they're looking for—utilities, for example—as well as keywords, and then display all listings that match that query.

In this example, I'm simply going to allow the user to select records that match a particular type of resource. In other words, I'm going to pull out all records where the value matches the contents of the Type field.

Setting up your database

The first thing to do is set up the resource table. The table, RES.DBF, is going to go into the WSDB\WR04 directory. The structure looks like this.

```
iidres I
ccategory c(10)
ctype c(20)
cnares c(100)
cnaf c(15)
cnal c(15)
cnao c(50)
ca1 c(30)
ca2 c(30)
ca3 c(30)
ccity c(20)
cstate c(10)
czip c(15)
ccountry c(25)
cgeoloc c(10)
cvoice c(15)
cfax (c15)
ctollfree1 c(15)
ctollfree2 c(15)
curl c(100)
cemail1 c(50)
cemail2 c(50)
mdesc m
cadded c(10)
tadded t
cchanged c(10)
tchanged t
```

The domain for the cType field contains the following values: Books, Consultants, Events, Magazines, Training, Courseware, Tools, Vertical Market Apps, and Videos. Thus, the user will be able to query the table for all records in any one of these types.

Opening your database

The next thing to do is enable your application to see the data. Remember, unlike the static image file we used in the previous example, your data will not be in the Web server directory structure, and, thus, will not be directly visible to the app.

What we need is a "file opening" mechanism, much like you probably use in your day-to-day desktop applications. Open up the WR04Main program, and look for the SetServerProperties method. In this method, you'll see the following line:

```
*** Add any data paths - SET DEFAULT has already occurred so this is safe!
```

This is where you'll want to add your file opening code. The following code *would* work:

```
*** Add any data paths - SET DEFAULT has already occurred so this is safe!
select 0
use \WSDB\WR04\RES shared
```

but it would be a bad idea. Hard-coding the entire path name in the USE command, that is. If you just have one or two tables, maybe you could get away with it—at least for introductory testing. But it's a bad habit to get into.

Why? First of all, if your app grows (and apps never get smaller, do they?), and you add more tables, you potentially enter into a maintenance nightmare. Imagine if you had 10 or 15 or 20 tables—and then you decided to change the location of where your data is stored.

Second, while I've been recommending to you that you keep your development and live machine structures similar, that's not always practical, or possible. And if that's the case— either now, or becomes the case in the future—then you'll need to create a file opening mechanism that can do double duty: open tables in one location on your development box and in another location on the live server.

So, what's a better way? There are actually two issues here: 1) setting the path to the location of the tables in one place, so you don't have to make multiple changes if the path changes; and, 2) providing a mechanism so that you can point your app at tables in one location during development and a second location during production.

You can handle the first issue by setting your path under the "Add any data paths" line, and then creating a separate function that opens tables. For example:

```
*** Add any data paths - SET DEFAULT has already occurred so this is safe!
set path to (set('path')+'; YourPath')
this.OpenTable("RES")
```

And then, right after the ENDFUNC statement of the process method in the server, you'd have a function called OpenTable that would look like the code in **Listing 2** that our technical editor uses.

Listing 2. The OpenTable function to generally open tables.

```
function OpenTable
parameter tcTableName, tcAlias
* Opens table named in tcTableName parameter.
* If tcAlias is specified, table will be
```

```
* opened with that alias.
* Leaves table/alias selected
* Returns .T. if successful, .F. if not

local llSuccess, lcOldOnError

lcOldOnError = on('Error')
on error llSuccess = .F.

llSuccess = .T.
if empty(tcAlias)
 if not used(tcTableName)
  select 0
  use (tcTableName) again shared
 else
  select (tcTableName)
 endif
else
 if not used(tcAlias)
  select 0
  use (tcTableName) again alias (tcAlias) shared
 else
  select (tcAlias)
 endif
endif

on error &lcOldOnError

return llSuccess
```

A better way is to read the data path from the application's INI file (WR04.INI) instead of hard-coding it with a SET PATH command. First, you need to include your data path in your application's INI file. In the bottom section of WR04.INI, I've modified the Datapath line to reference the \wsdb\wr04\ path that heretofore had been referenced in the SET PATH command.

```
[Wr04process]
Datapath=\wsdb\wr04\
Htmlpagepath=e:\inetpub\wwwroot\wr04\
```

Next, here's the code you'd use in the SetServerProperties method of WR04MAIN instead of the SET PATH (or DO PATH) business. And while you're at it, you might add a belt and suspenders to the SET PATH statement, and throw a couple of debugging statements in as well:

```
*** Add any data paths - SET DEFAULT has already occurred so this is safe!
lcDataPath = THIS.oConfig.oWR04process.cDataPath
debugout "lcDataPath is " + m.lcDataPath
this.cPathOriginal = set("path")
set path to this.cPathOriginal + "; " + (m.lcDataPath)
m.lcX = set("path")
debugout "Path is now " + m.lcX
this.OpenTable("RES")
```

The first line, with the reference to THIS.oConfig.oWR04Process.cDataPath, is explained more fully in Chapter 11, "Managing Your Configuration"; for the time being, you can replace the "WR04Process" string with the name of your own project.

Note that if you forget this step—adding code to open your tables—the code you write in your process method will eventually try to do something with a table, and since that code knows nothing about, nor can it find that table, it'll pop open a File Open dialog on your server box. Since the user of this application—running a browser in Texas or Germany or New Zealand—isn't sitting in front of your server, they can't deal with the dialog.

You'll also want to know that you don't have to explicitly close the table at any point. Since your application (and, presumably, your data) will be available all the time, you won't need to close the table. Whenever you shut down your Visual FoxPro Web Connection server, the table will automatically be closed, just like any Visual FoxPro executable does. You may be wondering if one instance of an open table is shared by all the hits serviced by the WC server—and, yes, it is.

Now that the table is available for access, it's time to get stuff out of it.

Presenting parameter selections to the user

We're going to present an HTML page to the users that allows them to choose which records they want to retrieve from the database. Technically, this could be done with a static page that you put together in FrontPage or another HTML editing tool. However, we're going to build it from a function that we're going to put in our WR04Process class, and then call via Web Connection.

Doing so provides two benefits. First, we'll call a second WR04Process function from this page, so you'll start to get an idea of how to daisy-chain one page to the next. And, second, it's just a short jump to make this static HTML page data-driven. For example, the categories are currently hard-coded in the HTML code, but it would be pretty easy to create the categories on the fly by querying the resource database and building the list of query options from those values.

Just so you know where we're heading, **Figure 22** shows you a picture of the parameter page that we're going to build in a moment.

Note that the URL in the address bar has a typical Web Connection call, with the final function named "GetParms." In your own live application, you'd typically have a hyperlink that says, "Click here," and would have the following link in it:

```
Click <a href="/wr04/wc.dll?wr04process~GetParms">here</a>
```

You can probably guess that we're going to need a new function in WR04Process.PRG. It's going to look like **Listing 3**.

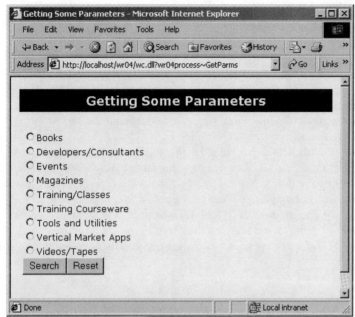

Figure 22. *The query screen requests parameters from the user.*

Listing 3. *The GetParms function that is called by a Web Connection call.*

```
************************************************************************
FUNC GetParms()
************************************************************************
m.lcTitle = "Getting Some Parameters"
m.lcPage ;
  = [<form action="/wr04/wc.dll?wr04process~GetAndShowResults" method="post">]

m.lcPage ;
  = m.lcPage ;
  + [<input type="radio" value="Books" name="RadioType">Books<br>] ;
  + [<input type="radio" value="Consultants" name="RadioType">] ;
    + [Developers/Consultants<br>] ;
  + [<input type="radio" value="Events" name="RadioType">Events<br>] ;
  + [<input type="radio" value="Magazines" name="RadioType">Magazines<br>] ;
  + [<input type="radio" value="Training" name="RadioType">] ;
    + [Training/Classes<br>] ;
  + [<input type="radio" value="Courseware" name="RadioType">] ;
    + [Training Courseware<br>] ;
  + [<input type="radio" value="Tools" name="RadioType">] ;
    + [Tools and Utilities<br>] ;
  + [<input type="radio" value="Vertical Market Apps" name="RadioType">] ;
    + [Vertical Market Apps<br>] ;
  + [<input type="radio" value="Videos" name="RadioType">Videos/Tapes<br>]

m.lcPage ;
  = m.lcPage ;
  + [<input type="submit" value="Search" name="B1" tabindex="98">] ;
```

```
    + [<input type="reset" value="Reset" name="B2" tabindex="99"><br>] ;
    + [</form>]

this.StandardPage(m.lcTitle, m.lcPage)
ENDFUNC
```

There are four important pieces to this little bit of Visual FoxPro and HTML code.

The first thing to realize is that this is building HTML strings in Visual FoxPro. I used the square bracket delimiters because more often than not, single and double quotes will be needed in the strings presented to the user.

The second is the option button (those old-fashioned HTML folk still call it a radio button) syntax code. You can learn more about this syntax in Chapter 9, "How a Web Page Works," but it's important now to point out that the "type" describes what kind of input control is going to be displayed—an option group, a text box, a check box, or whatever.

The "value" is the value of the control that you'll look for when determining which option button the user selected, while the "name" is the name of the control that you'll use to determine which control on the HTML page the user was working with. This is the same as how it works in Visual FoxPro.

If you had two option groups, one for the Type of Resource and the other for the Geographic location, you'd could name one of them "RadioType" and the other "GeographicLocation." The values for the RadioType option group would be "Books," "Videos," "Events," and so on, while the values for the GeographicLocation option group would be "Alabama," "Alaska," "Arkansas," and so on. The text string after the close of the angle bracket is the text that will display on the HTML page after the option button image.

And, finally, the <br> is an HTML code for a line break—much like a carriage return/line feed combination.

The third piece is the definition of the command buttons on the form. The types of command buttons are predefined—"submit" will execute whatever is defined as the form action, while "reset" will set the values in all controls on the page back to the values they held when the form was first displayed. So, if you seed a control with a value and then display the page like that, but the user then edits that value and then clicks Reset, the value of the control goes back to the original value.

The fourth and final piece is the definition of the form action—what will happen when the Submit button is clicked. In our case, we're going to make a call to a second WR04Process function, called GetShowResults, and it's this function that will determine which option group button was selected, do the query of the table, and then display the results.

Digging data out of your database

Next, we need to run a query using the parameters that the user selected, and then present the result set to the user in another page as shown in **Figure 23**. As Garth said in "Wayne's World" when they were setting up the satellite relay to intercept Mr. Big's cell phone calls, "This is almost too easy!"

Listing 4 shows the code for the GetAndShowResults function.

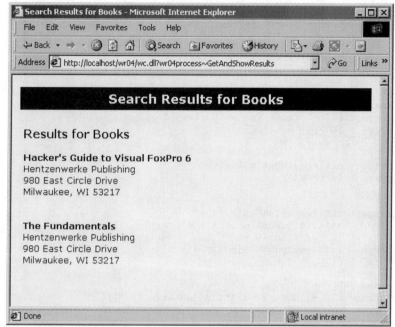

Figure 23. *The results of the query screen.*

Listing 4. *The GetAndShowResults function that is called by a Web Connection call.*

```
**********************************************************************
FUNC GetAndShowResults()
**********************************************************************
local m.lcSearchForWhat, m.lcUSearchForWhat, m.li, m.lcPage

* get the value of the control from the GetParms page
m.lcSearchForWhat = alltrim(request.form('RadioType'))
m.lcUSearchForWhat = upper(m.lcSearchForWhat)

* dig the data out of the table
sele cNaRes, cNaF, cNaL, cNaO, cA1, ;
     cA2, cA3, cCity, cState, cZip, ;
     cVoice, cFax, cTollFree1, cTollFree2, cEmail1, ;
     cEmail2, cURL, left(mDesc,200) ;
     from RES ;
  where upper(cType) = m.lcUSearchForWhat ;
  order by cNaRes ;
  into arra aWhat

if _tally = 0
  * no resources for this Type
  m.lcTitle = "Search Results for " + m.lcSearchForWhat
  m.lcPage = [Type = ] + upper(cType) + [!<br>]
  m.lcPage = m.lcPage + [UpperSrchForWhat = ] + m.lcUSearchForWhat  + [!<br>]
  m.lcPage = m.lcPage + [No Records for ] + m.lcSearchForWhat
```

```
else
  * label the page with the name of the resource
  m.lcTitle = "Search Results for " + m.lcSearchForWhat
  m.lcPage = [<font face="Verdana" size="3">]
  m.lcPage = m.lcPage + [<b>Results for ] + m.lcSearchForWhat + [</b></font>]
  m.lcPage = m.lcPage + [<br><br>]

  * loop through all resources found
  for m.li = 1 to alen(aWhat,1)
    m.lcPage = m.lcPage + [<font face="Verdana" size="2">]
    m.lcPage = m.lcPage + [<b>]

    * resource name
    m.lcPage = m.lcPage + alltrim(aWhat[m.li,1])
    m.lcPage = m.lcPage + [</b><br>]

    * company name
    m.lcPage = m.lcPage + iif(!empty(aWhat[m.li,4]), ;
                          alltrim (aWhat[m.li,4]) + [<br>] , "")
    * Address 1
    m.lcPage = m.lcPage + iif(!empty(aWhat[m.li,5]), ;
      alltrim (aWhat[m.li,5]) , "")
    * Address 2
    m.lcPage = m.lcPage ;
      + iif(!empty(aWhat[m.li,6]), [, ]+ alltrim (aWhat[m.li,6]), "" )
    * Address 3
    m.lcPage = m.lcPage ;
      + iif(!empty(aWhat[m.li,7]), [, ]+ alltrim (aWhat[m.li,7]), "" ) + [<br>]
    * City/State/Zip
    m.lcPage = m.lcPage + alltrim (aWhat[m.li,8]) + [, ]
    m.lcPage = m.lcPage + alltrim (aWhat[m.li,9]) + [  ]
    m.lcPage = m.lcPage + alltrim (aWhat[m.li,10]) + [<br>]

    * space between this resource and the next
    m.lcPage = m.lcPage + [<br><br></font>]
  next
endif

* output the results
this.StandardPage(m.lcTitle, m.lcPage)
ENDFUNC
```

There are, again, several specific pieces of code that are important. The first is the Request.Form function. It grabs the value of the control passed as the parameter—in this case, the RadioType option group. (Remember that "RadioType" is the name we specifically gave to the control in the GetParms function—we could have called that option group "Herman" or "Hilda," and then would have issued a Request.Form("Herman") call.)

The second thing is to convert the value to all uppercase. The reason I don't do this when assigning the value to the variable m.lcSearchForWhat is that I'll want the proper case version around when I display the results to the user.

You'll probably find that, in the beginning, interpreting the value of the controls on HTML pages is one of the trickier things to get right. It seems that the value is always the wrong case, or its type is not what you thought it would be—numeric when you thought it would be character, or vice versa. As a result, having the original value from the control around is useful when you have to debug.

Once I've found what type of Resource the user is interested in, I grab the appropriate records from the RES table, and then put together the results string that are going to be displayed to the user by moving through the resulting array row by row.

Once the whole string has been assembled, I use Web Connection's StandardPage() function to output the results.

You'll notice that in this piece of code, I don't use one huge statement to put together the value for m.lcPage. This is because it can be tough to hunt down a syntax error in a 25-line string concatenation. If you build a series of smaller strings, Fox will tell you exactly which line to look at if you mismatch parentheses or forget a comma—and it happens to all of us. And Fox is plenty fast at building strings—there generally isn't a performance penalty.

Even so, some of the strings can be hard to decipher at first—a well-structured convention for formatting your code will help readability and debugging considerably.

As you can see, using StandardPage can be flexible, to a point. But what if you wanted a different look for your title? Building the entire page into a single string can also become a pain. Fortunately, the Response object has two functions—Write and WriteLn—that allow you to write out a single line at a time. The difference between them is that with Write, you must specify where the carriage returns go. WriteLn includes a carriage return at the end of each line. There are also HTMLHeader and HTMLFooter functions to make creating a more customized header and footer easier, and ShowCursor for a quick way to display a table. An example of how to use these functions is shown in **Listing 5**, using the same output we generated earlier.

Listing 5. _The GetAndShowResults function using an alternate set of functions for HTML presentation._

```
**********************************************************************
FUNC GetAndShowResults()
**********************************************************************
local m.lcSearchForWhat, m.lcUSearchForWhat, m.li, m.lcPage, aHeaders[8],
lcTitle

* get the value of the control from the GetParms page
m.lcSearchForWhat = alltrim (request.form('RadioType'))
m.lcUSearchForWhat = upper(m.lcSearchForWhat)

* dig the data out of the table
sele cNaRes, cNaO, cA1, ;
    cA2, cA3, cCity, cState, cZip, ;
    cVoice, cFax, cTollFree1, cTollFree2, cEmail1, ;
    cEmail2, cURL, left(mDesc,200) ;
    from RES ;
  where upper(cType) = m.lcUSearchForWhat ;
  order by cNaRes ;
  into cursor What

with Response
  if _tally = 0
    * no resources for this Type
       .HTMLHeader([Search Results for ] + m.lcSearchForWhat)
    .WriteLn([UpperSrchForWhat = ] + m.lcUSearchForWhat  + [!])
    .WriteLn([No Records for ] + m.lcSearchForWhat)
  else
```

```
    * Write a grid that shows the result
       * Format an array to hold the column headings
       * (ShowCursor will use the field names as column
       * headings if you don't)
       aHeaders[1] = "Resource"
       aHeaders[2] = "Company"
       aHeaders[3] = "Address"
       aHeaders[4] = ""
       aHeaders[5] = ""
       aHeaders[6] = "City"
       aHeaders[7] = "State"
       aHeaders[8] = "Zip"
       * Define a string to use as the page title
       lcTitle = "Results for " + m.lcSearchForWhat
    .ShowCursor(aHeaders, lcTitle,,,)

    * Button for bottom
    .WriteLn([<form method="POST" name="form1" id="form1" ;
       action="/wr04/wc.dll?wr04process~GetParms">])
    .WriteLn([<p><center><input type="submit" name="btnSubmit" value="Done">])
  endif
  .HTMLFooter()
endwith

ENDFUNC
```

The ShowCursor function uses the currently selected alias, so we must send the results of the query to a cursor instead of an array. There are several parameters available for ShowCursor that increases its flexibility. I recommend you read the "wwResponse:: ShowCursor" topic in the documentation that comes with Web Connection for some additional ideas.

Updating your database

While getting data out of your database is all well and good, it's pretty likely that you'll want to put data into it as well—rather, let your users put data into it. I won't go into any detail here in this part, because it's all just Visual FoxPro database stuff that you already know how to do.

For example, in order to add a record, just take the data the user has entered into the controls on a form, using the request.form functions to get the values. Then add a record to a table with the APPEND BLANK or INSERT INTO commands, and use those values from the Web page as values to put into the new record.

Editing is nearly as easy. Find an existing record by asking the user for a value that you can use to locate the matching record in the table. Use the request.form function to find out what value they entered. Then SEEK that value in a table, and either return values from a successfully found record or present a message to the user that the record was not found. Deleting works similarly—let the user find the record they want to delete, and then just get rid of it from the table like you normally would.

Of course, you can run into a number of tricky situations—that's why we'll cover advanced topics and a whole host of tricks and traps later in the book. But you've already got the fundamental plumbing for your Web Connection apps covered here.

Using script maps instead of calls to WC.DLL

Step 3 of creating your project earlier in this chapter was to identify the script map (or, as I suggested a better name would be, the script extension). I even made a quick reference to how a Web Connection script map would be used in place of the long URL containing "wc.dll" but then skipped on ahead. Now it's time to show you how to use script maps in the previous examples. I'll walk through each example and show you the comparable syntax for the script map.

Script map syntax

The first example was a simple call to the "Hello World" method in wr04process that looked like this:

```
http://localhost/wr04/wc.dll?wr04process~HelloWorld
```

The script map version of this would be:

```
http://localhost/wr04/HelloWorld.wr
```

The next example was to reference a static file, such as an image file. The call that did this was:

```
http://localhost/wr04/wc.dll?wr04Process~ShowStatic
```

The script map version would be:

```
http://localhost/wr04/ShowStatic.wr
```

Finally, the calls to present the user with a series of choices were:

```
http://localhost/wr04/wc.dll?wr04Process~GetParms
```

and then inside the GetParms method to present the results:

```
m.lcPage ;
  = [<form action="/wr04/wc.dll?wr04process~GetAndShowResults" ;
    method="post">]
```

The corresponding script map versions would be:

```
http://localhost/wr04/GetParms.wr
```

and

```
m.lcPage ;
  = [<form action="GetAndShowResults.wr" ;
    method="post">]
```

Benefits to script maps

As you can see, there's not a lot of mystery to using simple script maps like those in the previous few examples. They can get more complex, as you'll see in Chapter 12. Still, you may be asking, why bother? There's a lot to learn—what's in it for you to learn yet something else?

First of all, they're shorter to type, and that means that you're less likely to make a mistake. And the fewer mistakes you make, well, that's got to be good, right? Second, using a script map means that the reference to WC.DLL, as well as the internals of your application, are hidden from the user. This means that the user may not be aware that you're running a Web Connection application, or how your application is structured, and the more information about the internals of your Web site that you can keep hidden from the outside world, the better.

Deploying your application to a live Web server

Tell me your eyes aren't lighting up right now. This is, of course, the ultimate goal—to deploy your application to a live Web server.

Chapter 12 will cover the development of a full application from start to finish, including deploying to your live server. You may want to get a taste of how this works before then, so I'll briefly walk you through the steps required to configure and deploy this simple WR04 Web Connection application to a live server.

The steps involved are:

1.   Setting up the directory structure on your live Web server.

2.   Getting the files of your application to the server.

3.   Testing.

Setting up your live Web server directory structure

For the most part, you'll need directories on your live server that match the ones on your development box. You won't have your development project, Visual FoxPro, or a copy of Web Connection on your live server, but everything else on your development box will have a match.

The first directory you'll need to have set up is where your Web site will be located—when you're starting out, that would be \inetpub\wwwroot, just like on your development box. Since your live server may have a different number of drives than your development environment, the drive designation may be different.

In any case, you'll set up your Web server software (IIS) just like you did on your development box, together with identifying the Web server's home directory and default document as shown in Figures 13 and 14 in Chapter 3.

You'll then need to create application-specific directories underneath your Web server's home directory, like so:

```
\inetpub\wwwroot\wr04
```

This directory is where the "WR04" Web site will reside. Your home page, all other static HTML files, graphics, and any other files will all reside in this directory (or in a subdirectory below it, such as \images). You'll also need to create an ADMIN directory under this directory.

Note that I'm skipping the drive designation in these examples. The second directory you'll need to create is for Web Connection's temporary messaging files. Again, it's a good idea to make these the same as your development box, like so:

```
\wc_msg\wr04
```

The third directory you'll need to create is where the good stuff will be—your data and application files. As noted earlier, you don't have to keep your data and application files in the same directory—indeed, your application should never assume that your data is in the same directory. For sake of simplicity in this example, they're both going in the same place.

This directory would again be called

```
\wsdb\wr04
```

like it was in your development environment.

Getting your application's files to the server

You'll notice that I used the highly technical term "getting," instead of "copying" or "moving" or some other such highfalutin terminology. That's because we're going to employ different means to "get" different files to the server. In some cases, we'll simply copy files (you could also FTP or PCAnywhere them); in other cases, we'll use more sophisticated and complicated methods.

First, you'll copy WC.DLL and WC.INI into \inetpub\wwwroot\wr04. You'll also copy your Web site files—your default home page, your static HTML files, and all that stuff. This directory should be an identical version of \inetpub\wwwroot\wr04 on your development box.

You'll also copy ADMIN.ASP and WESTWIND.CSS to the ADMIN subdirectory. (If you don't include the WestWind cascading style sheet, ADMIN.ASP will show up in Times New Roman instead of a sans serif font.)

Next, you'll copy your data (databases, tables, indexes, memo files, and anything else needed) to \wsdb\wr04.

Finally, you'll install your application's EXE and INI file into \wsdb\wr04 as well. However, this is not simply a matter of copying those two files over to the live server. There's really no need to install the Visual FoxPro development environment on your Web server (although many developers do). And if you do, you'll need to make sure you satisfy all of the licensing issues involved.

Thus, you'll need to install the Visual FoxPro runtimes on your live Web server as well. If you're using Visual FoxPro 6.0, it's a matter of copying the runtime files along with your EXE file. If you're using Visual FoxPro 7.0, however, it's more complicated.

Essentially, you'll use InstallShield Express, a custom version of InstallShield that comes bundled with Visual FoxPro 7.0, to create a complete installation package that includes your EXE and INI file as well as the appropriate Visual FoxPro runtimes. When you're asked for the target directory during the InstallShield process, you won't use the default of "Program

Files\Your Company\Your Application"; rather, you'll specify "\wsdb\wr04" (or whatever your directory is called on your live Web server).

 I've included a lengthy paper on how to use InstallShield to distribute Visual FoxPro 7.0 applications along with the other downloads for this chapter, available from the Hentzenwerke Web site.

Administering your live Web server

Okay, just as your eyes lit up in anticipation of the goodies in the previous section, your shoulders are probably drooping right now. "Administration"? That sounds suspiciously like "maintenance," and we all know how much developers like "maintenance." But you have to do it, and it's even more important here, because if you don't set up administration properly, outsiders can take control of your Web Connection application.

The ADMIN.ASP file in your \inetpub\wwwroot\wr04\admin directory allows you to perform a variety of maintenance tasks on your Web Connection application without having to be sitting at the server box itself.

In order to bring up the maintenance page, execute the ADMIN.ASP page in your browser, like so:

```
http://LiveServerIPOrName/wr04/admin/admin.asp
```

You'll get a page like the one shown in **Figure 24**.

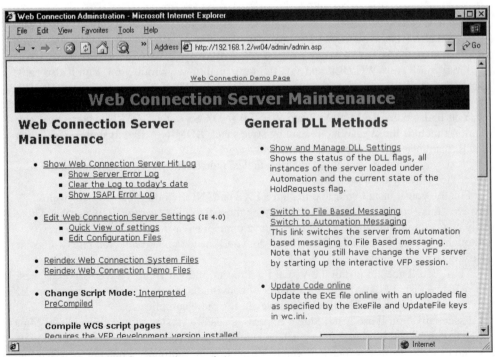

Figure 24. The Web Connection maintenance page.

Now, remember that the world has rights to see \inetpub\wwwroot\wr04—after all, it's your Web site, right? That also means that they have access to the ADMIN subdirectory, and thus, ADMIN.ASP... unless you stop them. You can do this through a two-step process.

First, rename ADMIN.ASP to something else, like MYADMIN.ASP or something else that you'll remember but that's not easily guessed. If you have directory browsing turned off, users won't be able to peruse through the ADMIN subdirectory to see what the file name might be.

The second step is to restrict access to running this page by making a couple of entries in WC.INI that's located in \inetpub\wwwroot\wr04. The first thing to change is the name of the admin page that Web Connect looks for. Look for the entry like this:

```
;Admin Page that is used for Backlinks from various internal pages
;Use a full server relative Web path!
AdminPage=/wconnect/Admin.asp
```

And change the value of the AdminPage entry to something like so:

```
AdminPage=/inetpub/wwwroot/wr04/admin/MyFirstAdmin.asp
```

The second entry to change is just above this one, in the section that looks like so:

```
;*** Account for Admin tasks      REQUIRED FOR ADMIN TASKS
;***          NT User Account   -  The specified user must log in
;***          Any               -  Any logged in user
;***                            -  Blank - no Authentication
AdminAccount=
```

Change the value of the AdminAccount entry to something like so:

```
AdminAccount=Administrator
```

where Administrator is a Windows NT account on the server box. Once you do this, when a user opens the admin page, they'll be greeted with a Windows NT login screen and will be required to log in before getting access to the admin page.

When something goes wrong

Yes, it happens. You push the "go" button, but nothing goes. Here are some of the common mistakes developers new to Web Connection typically make, introduced by the phenomena that the user is experiencing.

The first, and possibly the most frustrating, problem is when the dialog shown in **Figure 25** appears after you make a request. I caused this error to happen by using the name of the physical directory instead of the virtual directory that WC.DLL is located in. As a result, instead of processing the WC.DLL call, the browser thinks you're trying to download the file, just as if you had typed in the name of a ZIP file contained in a hyperlink. You can also get this dialog when you don't have execute rights in the proper directories.

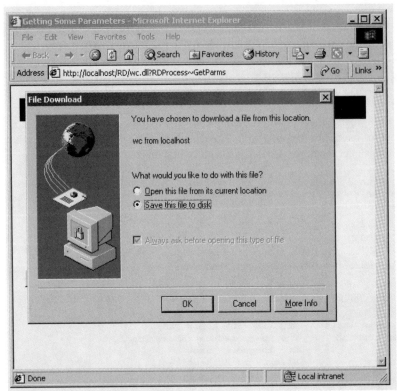

Figure 25. *The dialog that appears when you confuse the names of your virtual and physical directories.*

Next, you may run into the dialogs shown in **Figure 26** and **Figure 27**. These are preceded by the thermometer bar in the bottom of the browser taking its own sweet time, and then hanging up perhaps a third of way across. These errors occur when the server is not running—in other words, you forgot to click on the EXE before making the call in the browser.

Figure 26. *One dialog that appears when the Visual FoxPro Web Connection server is not running.*

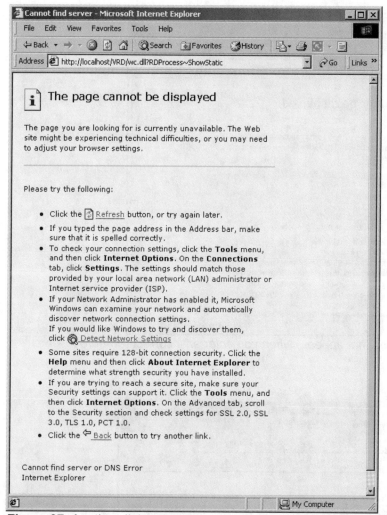

Figure 27*. Another dialog that appears when the Visual FoxPro Web Connection server is not running.*

The same error can appear if you enter incorrect information into the browser's address bar. In **Figure 28**, I've entered a nonexistent IP address for the server (999 is never a valid number in an IP address).

Okay, now let's assume that the server is running, but you're still banging your head against problems. The error page shown in **Figure 29** (the text in the band at the top of the page is yellow in color and says "Unhandled Request") indicates that you entered the name of a process that doesn't exist. In this case, I entered "RDPocess" (no "r") instead of "RDProcess" in the URL.

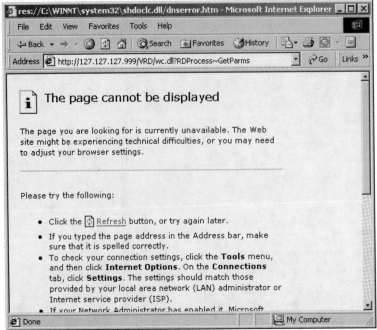

Figure 28*. The dialog that appears when you enter an incorrect IP address for the server.*

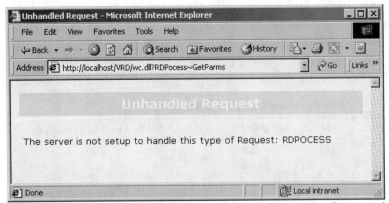

Figure 29*. The error message that appears when you refer to a class that doesn't exist.*

Similar to the previous problem, **Figure 30** shows what happens if you make a request to a function that doesn't exist in the process method. In this case, I entered "GetParm" instead of "GetParms" (with an "s").

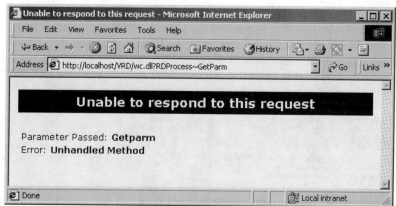

Figure 30*. The error message that appears when you refer to a method that doesn't exist.*

The next few errors have to do with a problem in front of the keyboard—you and your coding! **Figure 31** shows what happens when you forget to include a command in your program that returns results in an HTML page, like the StandardPage() function.

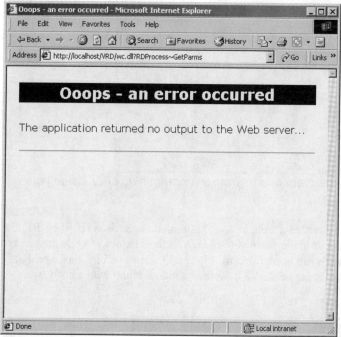

Figure 31*. The error message that appears when you forget to send output back from your application.*

Figure 32 shows what happens when you make an error in your code that isn't detected when you compiled. For example, I included a reference to a nonexistent variable, m.clX, in the code that is used to assemble the string to be returned at the HTML page. This display will only appear if you are not running your app directly from the PRG, and Debugmode in the H file is set to .F. Otherwise, instead of this display, you'll get a VFP-style error message on the server, and eventually the browser will display the same display as shown in Figure 28.

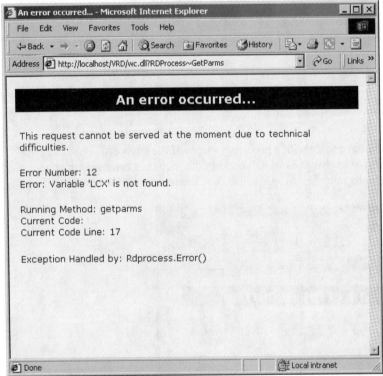

Figure 32. The error message that appears from a programming error inside your Visual FoxPro application.

What happens when you reference a table in your Main method, such as HERM.DBF, but HERM.DBF doesn't exist, or isn't in the place you told the method to look? While the server starts up, it'll warn you that it has run into problems. **Figure 33** shows you the message that will show up in the upper right corner of the VFP runtime window along with a not-yet-completed server window.

```
Startup wwServer Error: 1-File 'e:\wsdb\rd\herm.dbf' does not exist.
setserverproperties
```

Figure 33. One error message that appears when you reference a table that doesn't exist in the startup (MAIN) program.

Now, suppose that you don't reference a nonexistent table in your startup code, but later, while you're trying to do some data crunching—for example, doing a SQL SELECT from a table—but that table doesn't exist (because you forgot to put it there, or because you misspelled it in your SELECT statement). What then, huh?

You'll get the mysterious File Open dialog as shown in **Figure 34**—however, it's worse than that. On your development box, where the Web server software and your application are running on the same screen as the user's browser, you'll see the File Open dialog. If you attempted to deploy this live, though, the screen on your live Web server will be where the File Open dialog displays—not on the screen where your user has their browser open. All they'll see is a Web page that eventually tells them that the request timed out, and they'll never know why.

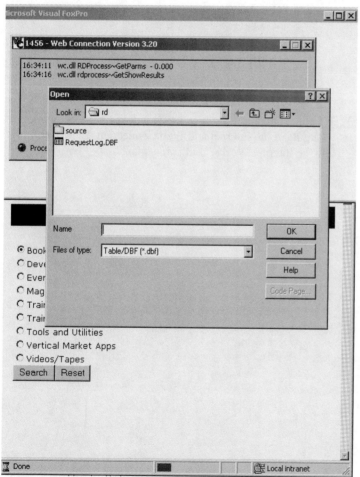

Figure 34. The error message that appears when you reference a table that doesn't exist in your code.

There are, of course, more errors than these—given the mixture of operating system, Web server software, Visual FoxPro, Web Connection, and your own programming, it's impossible to foresee every possible error. But these are the common ones. If you run into another, your best bet is to head on over to the Web Connection message board at **www.west-wind.com/wwthreads**.

Finally, I've even had a situation where the Web Connection framework "disappeared," and I started getting error messages indicating that the framework classes or files referenced by WCONNECT.H couldn't be found. In those cases, I've found that making a trivial change to WCONNECT.H (like adding a space to the end of a line), saving the file again, exiting everything, rebooting my machine, and rebuilding all files did the trick.

Another trick that sometimes helps is simply rebuilding all classes and programs in the Web Connection framework, like so:

```
cd \wconnect\classes
compile *.prg
compile classlib *.vcx
```

Conclusion

You've now built your first Web Connection application and seen it do a couple of simple things. Now it's time to get into the guts of the Internet and Web Connection. Harold will get you started in Chapter 5, "How the Internet Works," with an explanation of how the Internet works.

Chapter 5
How the Internet Works

Before you can deploy a Web Connection application, you need to have a Web site. If you've been fuzzy on the plumbing behind Web sites, you need to read on. In this chapter, I will cover the basics of how IP addressing works, how domains are registered, how routing works, and what happens when things do not work as they should.

IP addressing, registering Web sites, domain names, routers—why do you have to worry about these things? Well, these are the elements that make the Internet what it is: a vast INTERconnected NETwork. When you build your first Web Connection application that will live on a Web server, it helps a great deal to know what happens over this network. When doing more traditional LAN-based Visual FoxPro applications, the network drive was basically like a local drive with a longer wire attached to it. There was no fundamental difference in development techniques, outside of multi-user considerations, than if it lived on your local C drive.

Today, the Web developer needs to know how the various pieces fit together. This chapter will cover the necessary technologies so you can talk intelligently with the various people (registration companies, data centers) necessary to get a Web site up and running.

IP addressing—how Internet servers find each other

IP (or Internet Protocol) addresses are the phone numbers for the Web. Just as with the phone system where every phone has a unique number, each site on the Web has a unique address. The IP address is a 32-bit number that uniquely identifies a Web address. While a 32-bit address can accommodate 2^{32} (4,294,967,296) addresses, this is turning out to be a small number of addresses by today's demands. The originators of this system did not anticipate the explosive growth the Internet has gone through. There are new devices such as PDAs, Web phones, and even appliances that will each need their own IP address. There is a new system being worked on now that will greatly increase the number of addresses, but it will be quite a number of years before it can be implemented. Another reason for the shortage is that not long ago, just by asking, huge blocks of IP address were given out when no need was actually shown. Today, when a company asks for a block of addresses, it must produce network diagrams and detailed plans as to when the addresses will be used. If they are not used within a certain amount of time, they can be taken back.

The 32-bit IP number is made slightly more friendly by being commonly written in dotted decimal notation. This notation divides the 32-bit number into four 8-bit fields. The 8-bit blocks are each separated by a decimal point (see **Figure 1**).

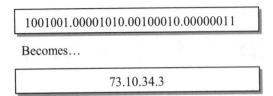

Figure 1. Translation of binary IP address into "dotted decimal" notation.

Each number has to range from 0 to 255 and is called an octet because there can be 2^8 (256) possibilities for each number. When you connect to the Internet using a dial-up account with an Internet Service Provider (ISP), you are most often given what is called a dynamic IP address. You can see this IP address in Windows 2000 by bringing up a DOS command window after you have established a connection and typing in IPCONFIG. This utility will print out the current IP address for your machine. In the listing IPCONFIG produces, there will be a line for "Subnet Mask:" and "Default Gateway:". These will be described later in this chapter. The next time you dial up, you will most likely be given a new IP address. The ISP routers, however, have assigned the port to which you are connected for this dynamic IP, so during the time you are logged in, the outside world knows how to find your machine.

As I will discuss later, these octets are not used just because they make it easier for humans to record and IP address (who could get 001110001010111, right?). The Internet is designed with 255 CLASS A accounts that correspond to each of the numbers in the first octet. (Well, not really—some of the numbers are reserved for special purposes, but we'll ignore those for the moment.) All of the routers on the Internet know how to talk to a router who knows a router and so on that can talk to each of these 255 top-level accounts. Each one of them knows the routes to the 255 addresses that are in the second octet. Hence Class A Account 3 knows how to talk to a router at 3.1, one at 3.2, one at 3.3, and so forth. Each of these knows how to talk to the 255 that are below it, so 3.2 knows how to talk to 3.2.1 and 3.2.2 and 3.2.3, for instance. If your router doesn't know how to contact an address, it asks the top level and then asks the router supplied by this top level and so on.

When you connect to the Internet from your corporate desktop, you are typically sitting behind a "firewall." This device prevents the outside world from seeing the computers on the inside network. Firewalls act as the gatekeeper between a trusted (corporate) network and an untrusted network such as the Internet. Your corporate IP address—the one for your specific machine—is also dynamically assigned, but is typically what is called an "unroutable" IP. This address is not recognized out on the open Internet. The firewall does the routing from the outside to individual computers. The Internet is only seeing the one IP associated with the company—the IP of the firewall. The internal network does not have a presence beyond the firewall.

This use of sub-networks, or "Sub-nets," decreases the demand for IP addresses and gives more freedom to network administrators. Each time they need to add on a machine or reconfigure the network in any way, the outside world does not have to know about it. The outside world is still only seeing the address associated with the firewall. The firewall does its routing of data to and from computers inside the firewall through the use of "ports." Ports are analogous to a house with multiple doors. The house has one address, but if you want to see Joe, you go though door #1; if you want to see Mary, you go through door #2. The router is simply keeping the associations between the doors (ports) and the people (desktop computers). A "static" IP address is the kind you will get when you host your machine in a data center. You are assigned a permanent IP address that identifies your Web site.

What makes up a domain name? (How humans talk to the Internet)

One of the first steps you need to consider in creating a Web site is determining what are you going to call it. Then you need to get approval for it and get it into the Internet system. This process is called registering your domain. Obtaining a Web address, or domain, is a simple process. Coming up with a domain name that is not yet taken may take some time, however.

There are four components to a Web address. They are the protocol, host name, second-level domain, and top-level domain. The parts that someone can register are the top-level and second-level domain (see **Figure 2**).

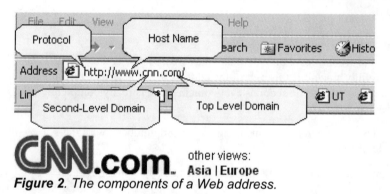

Figure 2. The components of a Web address.

Protocol

Let's take a look at each of these components. The first component, the protocol, basically dictates what type of client software you will use to connect to the site. If the protocol is "http," or hypertext transfer protocol, you will most likely be using a browser such as MS Internet Explorer. HTTP is a protocol that allows applications to communicate over the Internet. HTTP can be used by non-browser applications as well. A later section discusses how to use the West Wind library WWIPSTUFF to have a Visual FoxPro desktop application act as a front end to the Web. If the protocol is "FTP," or file transfer protocol, you will most likely be using an FTP client such as WS-FTP for the purpose of transferring files from your development machine to the production server. WWIPSTUFF also has FTP methods built into it that allow FTP operations from a desktop Visual FoxPro application. The setting up of an FTP site for your domain is covered in the next chapter.

Host name

The next component is the "host" name. This host name tells visitors once they have found your main site (detailed in the next section) where to go next. If they are to visit your main homepage, the host name would usually read "WWW." If you have different servers for different corporate functions, that function can replace the more typical "WWW" host name.

A familiar example is the set of multiple addresses that Microsoft maintains. Microsoft's main homepage is at **www.microsoft.com**. But different Microsoft divisions can have variations on the Microsoft domain. The Microsoft software developers network (MSDN) has an address of msdn.Microsoft.com. This allows the authoritative domain name server for Microsoft to route all MSDN traffic to another physical Web server, thereby distributing the load and segmenting content by department.

Any word can appear in the "host" section of the address. All of these variations are handled by this entry in the authoritative DNS server (described later). If you want to use "account.yourdomain.com," you are not required to register this with any of the registrars. You are registering the top-level and second-level domain components. The host component is handled at the local level. As seen in the Microsoft example earlier, this technique can be used to route traffic to department-level Web servers such as sales.yourdomain.com or support.yourdomain.com.

Second-level domain

It is the next component, the second-level domain, that takes creativity to come up with. This has to be chosen very carefully since it is this part of the address that will associate your visitors with your product or service. The second-level domain name is really completely unrestricted. The only rules are:

- All characters must be alphanumeric, meaning letters and numbers, with the exception of a hyphen (-).

- The hyphen cannot be used at the beginning or the end of the domain name.

- The second-level domain name has a maximum character length of 63.

Top-level domain

When choosing a top-level domain, you have a choice of three unrestricted domains. These are:

- .com—Commercial sites. This is by far the most used extension for commercial use.

- .net—Usually used by Internet Service Providers.

- .org—Used mainly for non-profit organizations.

The "restricted" top-level domains are:

- .int—A restricted domain name for international databases and organizations established by international treaties.

- .gov—A restricted domain name intended for any kind of government agency or office but which is now only for U.S. federal government agencies. State and local agencies are being registered under the country domain of .us.

- .mil—A restricted domain name for use only by the U.S. military.

- .edu—A restricted domain name originally intended for all educational institutions but now limited to four-year colleges and universities.

In addition, there are also a host of top-level domains coming into vogue now such as .cc and .tv. These are rather worthless domains. These two-letter codes are actually country abbreviations and are being sold as a means to raise cash for the respective country. Some may seem to have some relevance, but only out of pure luck like the .tv domain. They are similar to the bogus "Presidential Coin" collections that are minted in the country of Liberia or some other Third World country. They are made to look official and of some value, but they actually have no value beyond what the holder of them gives them. So for any commercial site, stick with .com. In 2000, there were several new top-level domains approved for use by the Internet Corporation for Assigned Names and Numbers (ICANN) (see **Table 1**). ICANN was created by the government to commercialize the domain name registration system, to maintain the root name servers, and to allocate IP addresses.

Table 1. The new Internet top-level domain names.

TLD	Purpose
.aero	Air-transport industry
.biz	Businesses
.coop	Cooperatives
.info	Unrestricted use
.museum	Museums
.name	For registration by individuals
.pro	Accountants, lawyers, and physicians

ICANN has not authorized any registrar to accept any domains using these new top-level domains. The process is still being formalized.

How to register your domain name

There are many registration services. For a complete up-to-date listing, visit **www.icann.org/registrars/accredited-list.html**. This list is maintained by ICANN. All registrars must be accredited by ICANN. For our examples, we will use Network Solutions (**www.networksolutions.com**). When you first navigate to the Network Solutions Web site, there is a search text box where you can type in the domain name you are trying to register. The process of just making sure the domain is available can take a long time. You need to type in the middle part of the domain name, as it would be entered into a browser.

For example, if you want to check www.yourdomain.com, you would enter yourdomain in the text box. There is a drop-down for the extension you would like. For yourdomain, do not bother trying to register any brand names or trademarked names. The case law is becoming clearer on this issue. Any domains that are registered trademarks or people's names will be retained by those parties. It is best to come up with a completely original domain. There can be variations on existing names, such as using hyphens. There are also variations of names using common prefixes and suffixes. For example, you could have e-yourdomain.com, eYourdomain.com, yourdomainCentral.com, or yourdomainOnline.com. You could also come up with other combinations that look reasonable. If your domain choice is available, you will get a confirmation page letting you know that you can have it.

This first page, which is from the Network Solutions homepage, allows you to start the search for your domain name (see **Figure 3**). You provide the name of the domain and the top-level domain you wish to have associated with it. .com is the default. Click on the GO! button and a search is done for that domain. If it is already taken, you will get a page saying it is unavailable but with variations on the name that you may want to try.

Figure 3. *Searching for an available domain name at Network Solutions.*

If it is available, you get a notification page with other possible variations of interest. For example, if you chose "yourdomain.com," it might be a good idea to register the .net version also.

After confirming that your domain name is not taken, you will be asked for some contact information. You will need a billing contact, administrative contact, and technical contact. The technical contact would usually be the person at the Web hosting facility where your site is hosted. This is the person who makes the Domain Name Server (DNS) entries. After the contact information, you will need to provide DNS information (see **Figure 4**). This will be explained in more detail shortly. The DNS server information is available from your hosting company. Some hosting companies provide this as a service. If not, it is quite easy to do. The hosting company's Webmaster can provide the addresses and names of the DNS servers. If they have a support page, it is most likely supplied there as well.

As the screen in Figure 4 shows, there are entries for the primary and secondary DNS servers. The secondary DNS is used if the first one is offline. DNS servers are explained in detail in the next section. After this, you will have to supply payment information. Once the registration process is complete, the Webmaster at your hosting company will receive an email with the domain information you provided. He will then make an entry in the primary domain server that was listed in the screen shown in Figure 4. This entry will map that domain name to a specific IP address that sits on either your co-located server or one of their shared or dedicated servers.

Figure 4. Supply authoritative domain server names and addresses.

If you use REGISTER.COM to register your domain names, they can provide DNS servers for you. This can be much more convenient if you are comfortable with it. Register.com has a "Domain Manager" that allows you to choose a specific domain under your account and then manage all aspects of it. You can use their DNS servers or you can have another DNS server be authoritative. It is simply a matter of entering in an IP address for the domain you are managing. Register.com also allows you to add your own email accounts. Again if you are comfortable doing this, it cuts out the middle man.

Figure 5 shows the new "directory" entry in the authoritative DNS server. The domain that was registered, "yourdomain.com," serves as the corporate directory for all other sites that have the same top-level and second-level domain.

For this example, there is a DNS server called OAK. The "host" part of the address can be mapped to any IP address. So when this entry is found through the process described next, this can then tell the incoming request what machine can service the request. The authoritative DNS server can be though of as the "information desk" in a corporate office building. You would walk up to the desk (DNS server) and ask, "Where is your sales department?" The reply "Sales is on the 5th floor, suite 210" is equivalent to the DNS server telling the incoming Web request that "sales.yourdomain.com" is located on a particular machine (floor) at a particular IP address (suite). As mysterious as the Internet may seem to be, its inner workings have everyday analogies back in the "real world"!

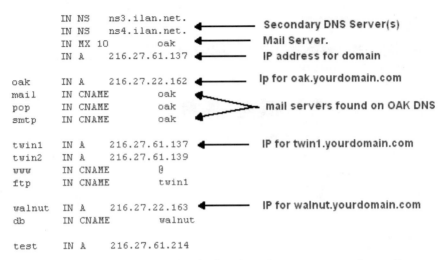

Figure 5. The entries in the authoritative domain name server for a site.

How does the world know where my site is located?

Routers

I'm going to talk mostly about human-level addresses (domain names) and Internet addresses (IP addresses), but way at the bottom, at a level that most of us never have to see, there are boxes that actually send electronic pulses or light pulses to each other. These are the routers. They know which wire or fiber optic cable to send a pulse down to talk to another router, which talks to another and so on until the pulses are turned into messages that Web servers can understand. You can think of these as the telephone operators back in the switchboard days—they get a call and plug in the right wire to make a connection between the person calling and the person being called. Routers do this for us on the Internet. The role of routers will be covered in greater detail in the "bonus" chapter "Setting up a Network for Web Connection Development," which is available electronically at **www.hentzenwerke.com**.

After your site is registered, the new site information is placed in what are called "root name servers." These are the master "white pages" for the Internet. There are 13 geographically separate root servers that tell the world where your site is located. The 13 root domain servers are listed in **Table 2**.

Network Solutions updates the root name servers every night. Even if you use another registration company like **www.register.com**, they still forward your domain registration information through to Network Solutions. They are the ones that maintain the master database of Web domains.

Table 2. *Listing of the root name servers.*

Name	Organization	City, State	Country	URL
A	Network Solutions, Inc	Herndon, VA	USA	http://www.netsol.com
B	Information Sciences Institute, University of Southern California	Marina Del Rey, CA	USA	http://www.isi.edu
C	PSINet	Herndon, VA	USA	http://www.psi.net
D	University of Maryland	College Park, MD	USA	http://www.umd.edu
E	National Aeronautics and Space Administration	Mountain View, CA	USA	http://www.nasa.gov
F	Internet Software Consortium	Palo Alto, CA	USA	http://www.isc.org
G	Defense Information Systems Agency	Vienna, VA	USA	http://nic.mil
H	Army Research Laboratory	Aberdeen, MD	USA	http://www.arl.mil
I	NORDUNet	Stockholm	Sweden	http://www.nordu.net
J	(TBD)	Herndon, VA	USA	N/A
K	RIPE-NCC	London	UK	http://www.ripe.net
L	(TBD)	Marina Del Rey, CA	USA	N/A
M	WIDE	Tokyo	Japan	http://www.wide.ad.jp

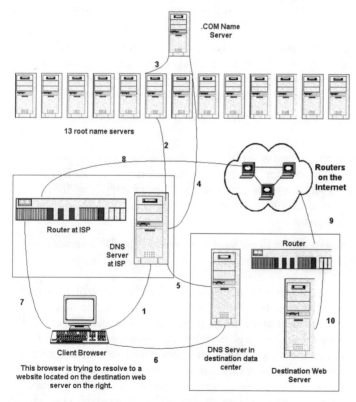

Figure 6. *Getting from a browser to a Web server.*

Let's say the first person to hit your site is located in Boston, and the server that holds your Web site is located in California. These are the steps he goes through to get to your server (see **Figure 6**):

1. The person who queries your site first has to have a machine connected to the Internet. This can be done through a variety of mechanisms, from a corporate LAN connection that's connected through a high speed T1 (or faster) line to a dial-up connection over conventional phone lines. In any case, the machine will be set up to talk to a Domain Name Server. This is a server that performs the translation between domain names such as www.yourdomain.com and the IP address that represents that domain. The address of this DNS machine is usually automatically provided by the ISP or is configured through the Windows Network applet. So when the user first types www.yourdomain.com into the browser, the browser talks to the local DNS server and asks it, "Hey, do you have an entry for www.yourdomain.com?"

2. In this case, the DNS Server does not have an entry for this site yet, so it forwards the request to one of the root name servers (RNS). When the RNS server is queried, it looks at the top-level domain designation of .com and determines the address of the name server that handles all .com domains. It passes this address back to the local DNS server.

3. The name server for .com domains is then asked if it knows about www.yourdomain.com. It does have an entry for this domain. What it has, though, is simply the primary DNS server information that was entered in when the site was registered. It has the IP address of the "authoritative domain name server."

4. The information about the authoritative DNS is passed back down to the local DNS server.

5. A request is then sent to the authoritative DNS machine asking, "Hey, do you have any information on this domain?" It does have the information since it is listed as the authoritative DNS. It has a record that has the matching IP address. The authoritative server is usually located in the same data center where www.yourdomain.com is located.

6. This IP address is then passed back to the local DNS server. This DNS server now keeps a record of the IP address for future queries.

7. The IP address is then sent back to the original browser. The "name resolution" part of the query is now over. The process of finding a Web site's IP address from a domain name is exactly equivalent to the process a person uses to make a phone call to a person for whom they do not have a phone number. If you need to look up a phone number, you use a phone book to resolve the person's name with his phone number. The phone system does not work by names; it routes calls based on the phone number. The Internet is very similar. The use of domain names is for human convenience only. The name resolution phase relates the human-readable domain name to the IP address that is equivalent to the site's "phone number." Once the IP address is found, the final routing phase begins. The browser then sends this IP

address to the "Default Gateway." This is a router that is configured in the machine's network dialog in the Control Panel (see **Figure 7**).

8. This "gateway" is a router that contains a table of IP addresses. If the destination server starts off with "216," for instance, it looks to see whether it has an entry for IP's that start with this number. If it does, it sends this request on to the router that knows how to handle IP address that start with this number. If it does not have an entry for this IP address, it sends the request further up the chain to the other routers that are connected to the "Default Gateway" router. These routers have physical ports with connectors similar to phone jacks. Each of these ports is mapped to an entry in the router table. The router table knows what IP addresses are handled by each port. So when a request comes in, the router can switch the request down to the matching port.

9. This may point directly to the final server, or it may send the request on to yet another router that has more specific information.

10. Eventually this process reaches the router to which the machine is directly connected. This final router has attached to one of its ports the server that holds www.yourdomain.com. When this server was last booted up, the router became aware of its presence and an entry was made in its router table that mapped that specific port to that machine's IP address that was assigned by the Webmaster in that particular hosting company. So whenever a request comes into that router looking for the IP address for www.yourdomain.com, it knows what port to switch the request to. This is the Internet version of the old manual telephone switchboards. The operator would take an incoming request and route it to a specific port for that phone number using jumper cables. Now the same thing is done using electronic switching.

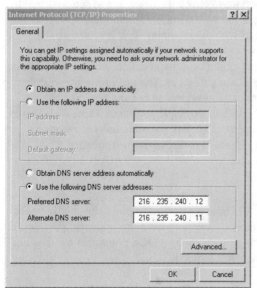

Figure 7. Windows 2000 Professional property sheet for DNS server.

After this first request, steps 2, 3, 4, and 5 are eliminated. The final IP address is now stored in the local DNS server. If you were to type in the IP address of the site into your browser instead of the domain name, the name resolution steps just outlined would not have to take place.

What makes this process more efficient the next time around is how the DNS servers cache their information. The Internet would be choked with traffic if these steps had to be done for each request. Any of the DNS servers along the way can cache the information they have acquired during the initial search. But they do not cache the information forever. There is another entry made in the authoritative DNS server for each domain called the TTL, or Time To Live. The value of this item tells other DNS servers how long to keep the information around. Some routes are never visited again, and to keep all the routing information in the machine permanently would be stretching resources a little too far. This TTL value will cause the cached information to be timed out and deleted.

There is one very important drawback to this, however. If the authoritative DNS server for "yourdomain.com" changes for whatever reason—say, because you change hosting companies—the new location for the Web site may not be accessible directly for days or even weeks. Since the TTL value could be a week, all the DNS servers that have cached information about this domain will not be updated with new information for that period of time! The best workaround for this problem is to retain access to the old server for the time it takes to get the cached information updated. On the old site, the homepage can contain what is called a "redirect meta tag." This tag tells the incoming request to go to your new site. You have to specify that new site using an IP address and not the domain, of course! A listing of these important "meta tags" will be covered later in the chapter on HTML.

When something goes wrong

There will be times after your site is up when people will call up and complain that your site is not accessible. First, it is important to check the obvious and see whether the site is indeed up and running. If you have a site with dynamic content like a Web Connection application, it is important to check to see that a dynamic link is returning the expected data. (Don't worry if you don't know what this means. There will be more on this later.) Many monitoring tools that are used in data centers simply check to see that the Internet Information Server (IIS) is up and running. This is not sufficient. The machine may be able to serve up a static page, but maybe your Web Connection executable is hung for some reason. You need to be using tools like PING and TRACERT to troubleshoot Internet and Web Server problems and a tool like West Wind Web Monitor to make sure dynamic links are working. The first two tools are discussed next, and Web Monitor 1 is discussed in Appendix A (available electronically at **www.hentzenwerke.com**).

PING

If you run into problems, the first action you should take is to try and "ping" the site. PING is an acronym for Packet Internet Groper. It also takes its meaning from the submarine term used to see whether anything is lurking about. To do a ping, bring up a DOS command window and type in "ping www.yourdomain.com." A sample result looks like this:

```
Pinging bugcentral.com [216.235.240.51] with 32 bytes of data:

Reply from 216.235.240.51: bytes=32 time=220ms TTL=112
Reply from 216.235.240.51: bytes=32 time=220ms TTL=112
Reply from 216.235.240.51: bytes=32 time=411ms TTL=112
Reply from 216.235.240.51: bytes=32 time=210ms TTL=112

Ping statistics for 216.235.240.51:
Packets: Sent = 4, Received = 4, Lost = 0 (0% loss),
Approximate round trip times in milli-seconds:
Minimum = 210ms, Maximum =  411ms, Average =  265ms
```

It simply sends out four packets to the site and measures round trip time. If the site cannot be reached, there will be a message that the packet has timed out. This simply checks to see whether the server is responding. For more detailed information, a trace route may be necessary.

Trace routes

Assuming that the site is up and running, it may be necessary to ask the user to get a trace route from their location to the server. A trace route can be derived from a Windows tool called TraceRT.EXE. This tool takes as a parameter the address of the destination Web site. It then produces a table showing all the hops it took to go from the client to the server. As the prior routing example suggests, it may take upwards of 30 hops to go the complete route. Over the course of traversing all this distance, there can be a lot of problems encountered that are out of your hands. The analogy drawn between the Internet and a "super highway" is pretty accurate.

If you were to give directions to your house to a friend and he was traveling across the country, you would not be responsible for construction delays, accidents, or detours. Well, the same applies to the Web as well. Many people are not aware of this yet, so it may take some time to educate your users on this fact. The trace route exposes all of these construction delays and detours. Many times delays are caused by cut fiber optic cable, excessive traffic, a downed router, or a corrupted router table. The latter problem struck Microsoft in January 2001. A bad router table was uploaded to a router, and all of its sites were inaccessible for a day!

To perform a trace route, simply call up a DOS command window by typing CMD.EXE into the Open box when you use the Start | Run command. At the DOS prompt, type in "tracert www.yourdomain.com > badroute.txt". This will pipe the results to a text file called badroute.txt. When done, open this up in Notepad. What you will see is something like the following.

```
TraceRoute to host

Timeout 3
Start from hop 1
Maximum Hops 30

#    Address         Host Name                    Msg Type Time
1    24.128.28.1     ndrtr01-ndswt02-vlan8.ne.mediaone.netTTL Exceeded 17 ms
2    24.128.190.61   lwgsr01-ndgsr02.ne.mediaone.netTTL Exceeded 16 ms
3    24.128.190.58   lrgsr01-lwgsr01.ne.mediaone.netTTL Exceeded 13 ms
4    24.128.190.53   wbgsr01-lrgsr01.ne.mediaone.netTTL Exceeded 14 ms
5    12.125.39.9     Unavailable                  TTL Exceeded 19 ms
```

```
6    12.123.40.98    gbr1-p70.cb1ma.ip.att.net        TTL Exceeded 15 ms
7    12.122.5.53     gbr3-p70.cb1ma.ip.att.net        TTL Exceeded 17 ms
8    12.122.2.13     gbr4-p10.n54ny.ip.att.net        TTL Exceeded 21 ms
9    12.122.5.241    gbr1-p60.n54ny.ip.att.net        TTL Exceeded 22 ms
10   12.123.1.41     gr1-p350.n54ny.ip.att.net        TTL Exceeded 27 ms
11   157.130.0.13    Serial1-1-0.GW2.NYC2.ALTER.NETTTL Exceeded 372 ms
12   146.188.178.158 144.ATM2-0.XR2.EWR1.ALTER.NET TTL Exceeded 392 ms
13   146.188.176.158 292.ATM7-0.XR2.BOS1.ALTER.NET TTL Exceeded 436 ms
14   146.188.177.213 190.ATM8-0-0.GW3.BOS1.ALTER.NETTTL Exceeded 426 ms
15   137.39.135.214  rcn-gw.customer.ALTER.NET        TTL Exceeded 370 ms
16   199.232.56.60   fe11-0-0.gw1.mbo.ma.rcn.net      TTL Exceeded 345 ms
17   146.115.12.252  gw-sw1.mbo.ma.rcn.net            TTL Exceeded 327 ms
18   209.6.3.42      Unavailable                      TTL Exceeded 293 ms
```

The query packets that are sent out by the trace route program are the basis for this report. The first packet is given a TTL value of 1. Each router along the way decrements this TTL value by 1. So the first packet that hits the first router gets its TTL value decremented to 0, which sends the results back to the initiating machine. To get to the second router in the path, the trace route program sends out a packet with a TTL value of 2. This repeats until it has tried 30 hops. Most trace routes take fewer than 30 hops. The second column in this report shows the IP address of the router. The third column shows the name of the router, and the fourth column shows the time it took to get through this router in milliseconds. On routes that are slowing down, you will see high values for the bad hops. What is interesting here is that if you rerun this trace route, you will probably get a different set of hops. In the Internet world, there is no permanent dedicated connection between the client and the server as there is in a telephone connection. The data sent between the browser and server can take different routes from second to second. The decision about where these packets of data will go is made by the routers, the brains behind the Internet.

Conclusion

In this chapter, we explored the process by which Web sites are registered and made known to the world, and how the world actually finds a Web site. Humans know Web sites by their human-readable names such as **www.cnn.com** or **www.hentzenwerke.com**. These are meant for humans only, however. Computers do it by the numbers. The process by which names are converted to numeric addresses form the first step in finding a Web site. This process is just like looking up a name in a phone book and finding the phone number associated with that name. Domain Name Servers (DNS) perform this very same function for users of the Internet. All of these interconnected DNS servers are part of a huge distributed database that "learns" about new Web sites on a need-to-know basis.

Of course, things do not always work the way they should. Tools like PING and TRACERT help troubleshoot where the path is cut or slow.

Chapter resources

- Network Solutions: **www.networksolutions.com**

- Register.com: Another domain registration company. Easier to use than Network Solutions. Allows customers to manage email addresses and DNS entries through a Web interface.

- Understanding IP Addressing: **www.3com.com/nsc/501302.html**. Very detailed and technical discussion of IP addressing.

- Hyper Text Transfer Protocol Specification: **www.ietf.org/rfc/rfc2068.txt**

- List of country top-level domains: **www.iana.org/cctld/cctld-whois.htm**

- Listing of authorized registration companies: **www.icann.org/registrars/accredited-list.html**

- Author-run site with code updates and training videos: **www.webconnectiontraining.com**

Chapter 6
Complete Web Development Environment

In this chapter I will cover the complete Web environment for the development machine. I will cover all the software needed and how to configure it.

The development environment needed for doing Web development requires a number of new software tools for the Visual FoxPro developer. It used to be that all you needed was Visual FoxPro, but no more! It is now necessary to have HTML authoring tools, remote control software, file transfer utilities, and a local Web server. All of these tools work in concert to build, test, and deploy your Web site. This chapter will discuss the best way to utilize them.

Development machine

Table 1 describes the required and optional tools for the development machine.

Table 1. Software tools for Web development.

Software	Description
MS Windows 2000 Professional	Desktop version of Windows 2000. Has integrated IIS. (Alternative: Windows NT Workstation.)
Visual FoxPro, version 6 (with Service Pack 3) or higher	Full development version of Visual FoxPro needed. Need IDE.
West Wind Web Connection	Need all class libraries of framework including WC.DLL.
WS-FTP (or equivalent FTP client software)	FTP client software. Needed to transfer files from local machine to remote production server.
WinZip (Optional)	Must have utility for compressing files. Greatly speeds file transfer times.
HTML Authoring tool (for example, GoLive or FrontPage)	Needed to create and manage HTML Web content.
PCAnywhere (Optional) or equivalent remote control software	Needed for remote control of production server. Have full access to host machine. Must be installed on development machine and production server.
Windows 2000 Terminal Services	Better alternative than PCAnywhere. Much lighter weight and seems to be faster. Lacks file-transfer option of PCAnywhere, thus making FTP client software a must.
West Wind Web Monitor (practical necessity!)	West Wind site monitoring tool. Can be used to check dynamic content for specific return values. Sends email alerts when a site is down. A must. (Comes with Web Connection.)
Beyond Compare (Optional)	Great tool for checking visual differences between program files. Double-pane view into two files.
West Wind Help Builder (Optional)	Excellent tool for building HTML- or CHM-based help. Template driven. Can import VFP class libraries for documentation.

I'll assume that Visual FoxPro is already installed on the development system. Installation of Web Connection was covered in Chapter 3, "Installing, Configuring, and Testing Web Connection." I will cover the use of the other tools on this list. Detailed instructions on use can be found with the respective product. This is more a discussion on the functions the different tools provide and why they are needed.

IIS on Windows 2000 Professional

Internet Information Server (IIS) comes with the Windows 2000 Professional CD. However, it is not installed by default. To install it, simply go to Start | Settings | Control Panel | Add/Remove Programs | Add/Remove Windows Components. In the list of Windows Components, IIS is listed second. Check it off and proceed with the installation. There are two main differences between IIS on Windows 2000 Pro and Windows 2000 Server:

1. On the Professional version, you can only have one IP address bound to the machine. There is either one Web site in the WWWROOT directory or all sites are virtual sites off of the root.

2. There can only be around 10 simultaneous Internet connections to the machine at any one time. This makes it impractical for hosting a public website. Only being able to use 1 IP address is manageable, but only allowing 10 connections is not.

Start the Microsoft Management Console for IIS by going to Start | Settings | Control Panel | Administrative Tools | Internet Services Manager. This brings up the screen shown in **Figure 1**.

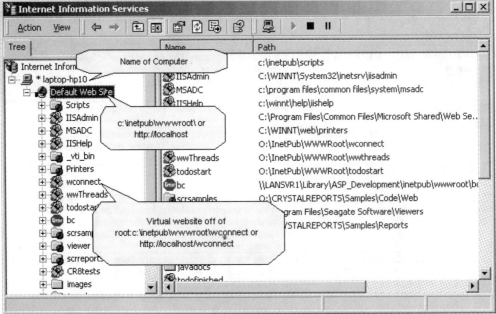

Figure 1. Internet Information Services Management Console.

This console is what maps physical directories on your machine to Web site addresses. It also allows you to set site permissions and define script maps and default pages. The IIS sites shown in Figure 1 translate into the physical directories shown in **Figure 2**.

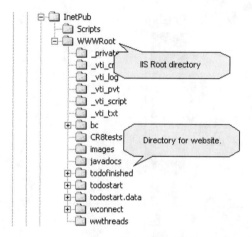

Figure 2. Typical directory structure for Web sites.

In this book, a simple task management system called "TODO" will be used as a basis for how to build a Web Connection application. To create a new virtual Web site for the TODO application, simply select "Default Web Site" in the IIS console. Right-click and choose New | Virtual Directory. This starts a wizard that walks you through the process of creating a site. The first step in the wizard asks for the name of the site (see **Figure 3**).

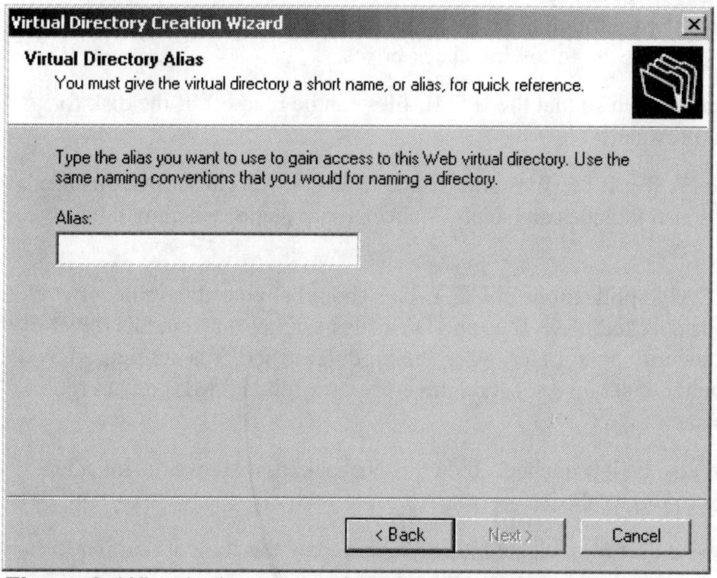

Figure 3. What is the name of the new virtual directory?

To create a site for the sample application being used in this book, type in "todo" as the alias name. The second step asks for the name of the physical directory on your machine that holds the HTML content (see **Figure 4**). This directory must already exist.

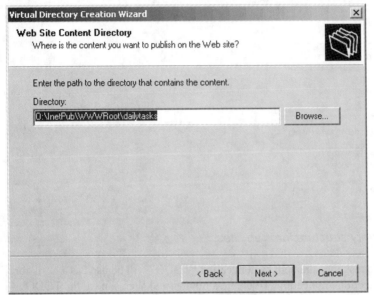

Figure 4. Where is the site content located?

The next step sets the access permissions for the site (see **Figure 5**). This is a very important step in the process. I'll cover each in detail. Remember that anything you do during these wizard steps can be modified through the IIS MMC console.

The screen in Figure 5 presents the following check boxes:

- Read: This has to be chosen so that the HTML files can be read off of the disk for display back to the browser.

- Run scripts (such as ASP): If the Web site will have any ASP style scripts, this needs to be checked. This also includes any Web Connect script pages, which will be covered later.

- Execute (such as ISAPI applications or CGI): This should almost always be left *unchecked*! If this is checked, EXE files and DLL files can be run from this directory. This could pose a security hole. Later, when the production server is configured, you will see that it is better to set up a separate directory off of the HTML content root for holding DLL files such as WC.DLL.

- Write: This should also be left unchecked. If this is checked, it allows the outside world to write files to this Web site.

- Browse: This allows a user to navigate to the site and view the contents similar to Windows Explorer. This should also be left unchecked.

Click Next and then Finish to complete the creation of the Web site's virtual directory. Setting up this Web site will be covered again in Chapter 12, "A Web Connection Application from Start to Finish."

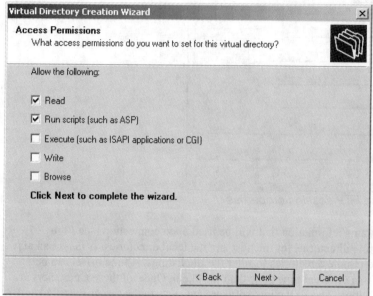

Figure 5. What permissions will the site have?

WS-FTP

WS-FTP is file transfer protocol (FTP) client software. This is the software that resides on the development machine and transfers files to the production server. The production server must have an FTP server installed. Installation of the FTP server will be covered in the next chapter on server configuration. When WS-FTP is first started, you will see the dialog shown in **Figure 6**.

When creating a new connection to the server:

1. Click on the New button.

2. Provide a name for the new connection in the Profile Name field.

3. Provide the IP address of the FTP site you need to connect to.

4. Host Type specifies the OS that you are connecting to. It is best to leave it as "Automatic Detect."

5. You do not want to connect to your production server as an "anonymous" user. This will be discussed later on, but anonymous access allows anyone to connect to your server without a password! There should be a Windows username set up on the server that can be used here. Provide the username and password.

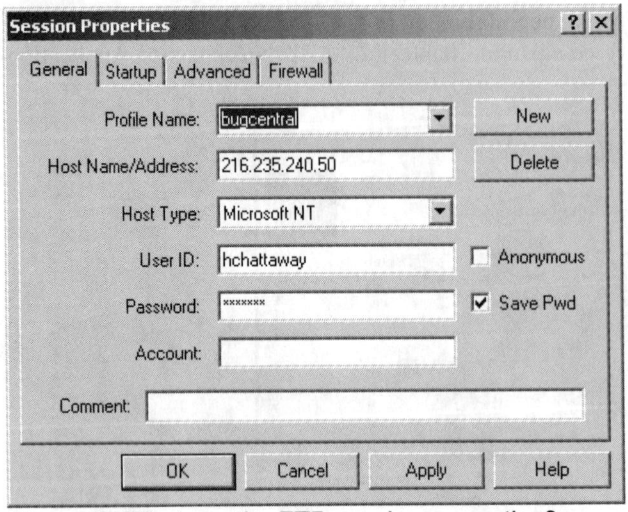

Figure 6. What are the FTP session properties?

The Startup tab contains information that will be used upon connection (see **Figure 7**). You can supply the starting directories for the host and the local directories. A mask can also be supplied for local and remote directories to filter the file listings. A time offset can be supplied if the server is in a different time zone than the client. Once all these parameters are specified, click the OK button. The FTP client software connects to the server specified and the screen shown in **Figure 8** appears.

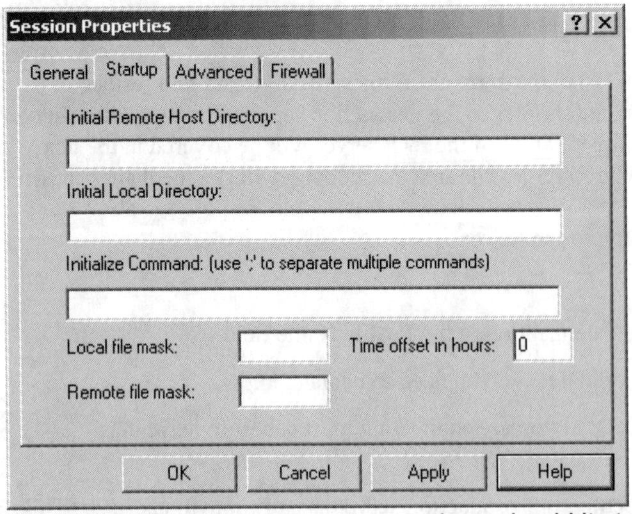

Figure 7. FTP startup parameters—where should it start?

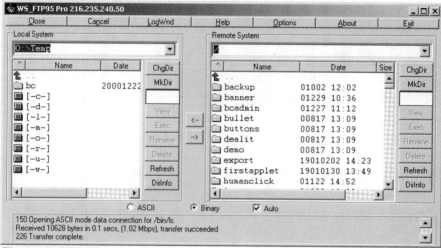

***Figure 8**. FTP "Explorer" window.*

The "Remote System" side represents the server that you are connected to. You can navigate down the FTP site from the root of the FTP site and to any "Virtual" directories that were created on the server for this FTP site. Virtual directories will be covered in detail later. You can perform standard directory and file operations such as file deletions and directory maintenance. If you wish to upload a file from the local system to the remote, simply click on the file name and either drag it to the remote system or click on the right arrow button in the middle of the screen. Multiple files can be selected by using either Shift-Click or Ctrl-Click. A convenient way to use this tool is to sort your local files in descending date order. This groups the most recently changed files at the top of the local listing. This tool will be revisited later when we start transferring files to the production server.

Most Web site authoring tools such as the ones covered in this chapter have their own integrated FTP clients. So in GoLive, for example, after creating new Web pages, you can upload them to the production server right through GoLive. However, Visual FoxPro does not have an integrated FTP client, so using a client like WSFTP for transferring tables and other application files is still necessary.

WinZip

WinZip has become one of the mandatory tools of any software developer. It's a very elegant utility that magically reduces the size of files for faster uploading and downloading over the Internet. When you are working over a dial-up connection, this is particularly important. It performs its magic rather simply. It scans the file that is being compressed for repeating patterns. These repeating patterns are remembered in a dictionary that shows the original string and the shorter tokenized version of the string. The original file is expanded back to its original size by replacing the tokens with the original string. Visual FoxPro database files tend to compact very tightly. Encrypted Visual FoxPro executables do not compact much at all. The latest version of WinZip (see the link in the "Chapter resources" section) installs itself on the right-click menu of Windows Explorer. This way it is easy to select a file, right-click, and send it to a ZIP file. The interface to the WinZip program is shown in **Figure 9**.

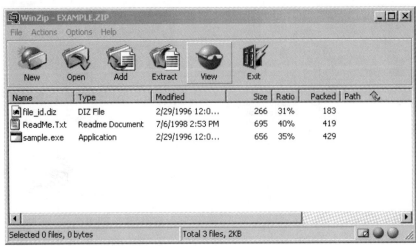

Figure 9. *The WinZip interface.*

Files can be viewed from the WinZip interface without having to save the file to disk. Simply select the file and click on "View." The proper host application will be launched for the file type. Files can be added to a ZIP file through the interface shown in Figure 9, or files can be selected from the Windows Explorer interface and added via the right-click menu. When moving data from the development machine to the production server, it can be a good idea to zip the tables first. Since it is still very common to be connected to the Internet via a dial-up connection, zipping files can be crucial. However, doing file transfer over a T1 line from a corporate office can be faster than going through the process of zipping and then sending.

HTML authoring tools

There are a number of very good Web authoring tools available. The major choices are Microsoft FrontPage, Adobe's GoLive, Dreamweaver, and HotDog, among others. GoLive actually handles ASP style code better than FrontPage and is geared toward a more technical crowd than FrontPage is.

FrontPage

FrontPage allows the masses to create and publish Web sites. FrontPage (see **Figure 10**) comes with Microsoft Office, so it is readily available.

FrontPage 2000 has a tabbed interface for layout (normal), HTML, and previewing. One advantage of GoLive is that it allows you to be in layout view and have a source view window open at the same time. The two windows are kept in sync so you can edit in either view. The Preview tab in FrontPage, as well as any other tool, only renders the HTML content and does not run any script code that might be in the page.

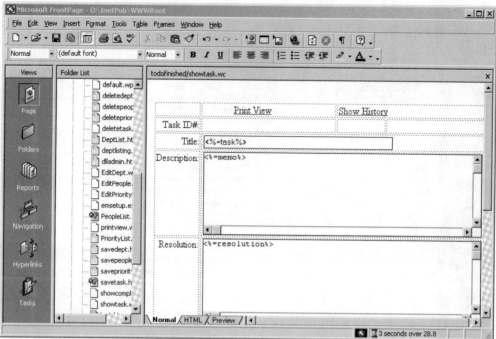

Figure 10*. FrontPage 2000 interface.*

FrontPage can be used to edit single pages or an entire Web site. Typically it is used to manage an entire site. When a "Web" is created in FrontPage, it creates a site project similar to the Project Manager in Visual FoxPro. With this, you can edit the pages and easily update the live site through the "Publish" feature. This feature is built in and does not require an FTP client like WS-FTP. It can be a little slow, however, since it needs to compare the files on the live site with the local files and checks to see what has changed. It keeps these files in sync by using its own database of sorts. When a Web is created, it creates a series of directories that start with _vti. These directories hold FrontPage's databases that manage site content. If another tool is used to transfer site content, FrontPage's databases get out of sync and can no longer be used until they are rebuilt.

A very handy feature of FrontPage is the canned reports. If you click on "Reports" in the left-hand Views column, the screen shown in **Figure 11** appears.

You can drill down into any one of these reports simply by double-clicking on the report name in the first column. To view all the pages with broken hyperlinks, double-click on the "Broken hyperlinks" row. This will show all pages with broken links. To fix one of the pages, just double-click on it also. This is a powerful way to manage site content very easily.

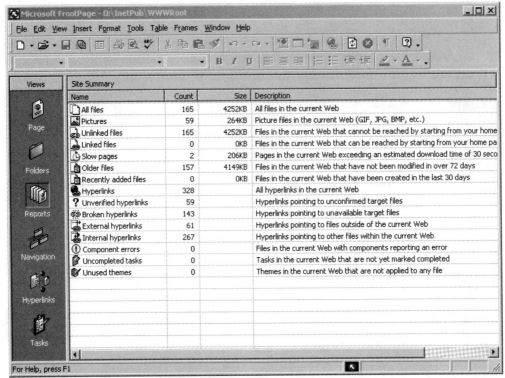

Figure 11. *Canned FrontPage reports.*

GoLive

GoLive 5.0 from Adobe is an excellent tool for developers. **Figure 12** shows the GoLive Site Manager. On the left is the local view of your Web site, and on the right is the FTP view of the production server. Files can be simply dragged and dropped between local and remote. There is no need for third-party FTP software for transferring HTML files.

The design surface in GoLive is excellent for seeing layout and code views at the same time. In **Figure 13**, the Layout tab is selected and the source window is layered on top of that. The source window is an "always on top" window, so switching between the two is not frustrating. Also, any changes you make in the source view will be updated right away in the layout view.

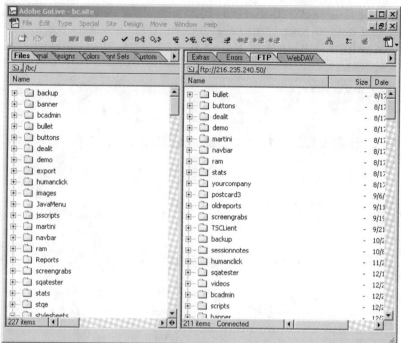

Figure 12. GoLive's Site Manager.

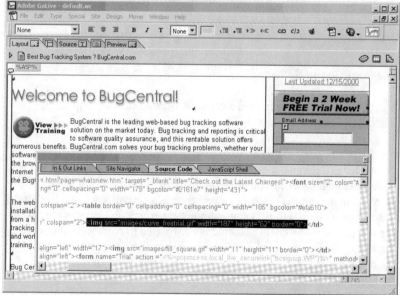

Figure 13. The GoLive design surface.

For this book, we will be using HTML-Kit from Chami Software to view HTML source code. It is a free authoring tool with some very nice features for HTML beginners. It is downloadable from **www.chami.com/html-kit/**. It is a sophisticated text editor that allows for easy insertion of HTML tags and for HTML validation using the utility TIDY (see **Figure 14**).

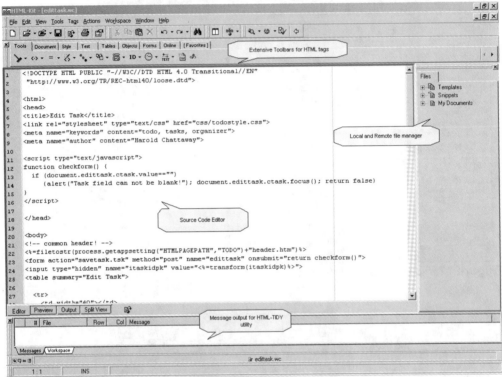

Figure 14. HTML-Kit from Chami Software.

The interface is great for beginning users and advanced users alike. The chapter on HTML will cover this tool in detail.

PCAnywhere

PCAnywhere from Symantec is a remote control software utility (see **Figure 15**). A remote control program becomes mandatory when you are administering the production server in a data center. If there is a problem with the machine, travel time is an eternity when a live site is down. PCAnywhere is an excellent tool to remotely administer servers. PCAnywhere must be installed on the server as a service. The client machine is configured to connect to the server using the server's IP address. Once connected, PCAnywhere shows the server's desktop in its window. From here you have total control of the server just as if you were sitting in front of the machine. Of course, in order for this to work, the server has to be in a healthy state. If the machine is hung for any reason, PCAnywhere will not be able to connect. For this reason, it is always important to have a human available in the data center who can reboot the server if needed.

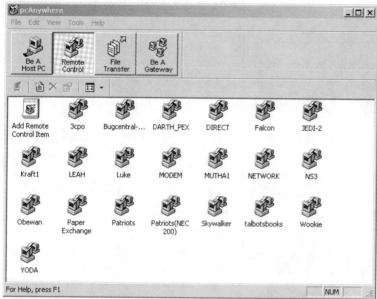

Figure 15. *PCAnywhere's listing of remote connections.*

PCAnywhere also has file transfer ability built in. An Explorer-like interface is used to show local and remote files. Files can be easily moved in either direction. On-the-fly file compression is also used to greatly reduce transfer times. Starting with version 8 of PCAnywhere, remote control of the server happens over the Internet. This means you can dial up to your local ISP's phone number and control a machine across the country. In the old days, you had to connect to the host machine via a modem on both ends.

Windows 2000 Terminal Services

PCAnywhere is an excellent tool, but if Windows 2000 Server is being used on the Web server, Terminal Services might be a better alternative. Terminal Services can be installed during the installation of Windows 2000 Server as an integrated component of the operating system. This will be covered in more detail in Chapter 8, "Configuring Server Software." The Terminal Services client is a very lightweight client. From the server, disk images of the client install can be created. It only takes two 3½" floppies to store the client. On the Windows 2000 Server machine, click on Start | Programs | Administrative Tools | Terminal Services Client Creator. This will copy the disk images to two floppies. The Terminal Services client application created from this server is not tied to this server. It can be used to connect to any Windows 2000 Server. Since the install is so small, another option is to place a zipped version of the client on the server in a Web-accessible directory. This way, it is possible to simply point to the ZIP file using a browser, download it, and install it on whatever machine you are currently on. This is very handy if you are away from your primary machine and need quick access to the server. It is much easier and quicker to install the Terminal Services client on a machine instead of having to have the PCAnywhere CD. Since Terminal Services client installation is so small, it is very easy to erase when you are done. The Terminal Services client screen could not be simpler, as you can see in **Figure 16**.

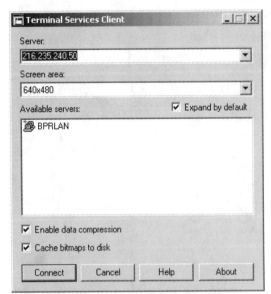

Figure 16. *The Terminal Services client.*

In the "Server" drop-down, the IP address of the host machine is supplied. The "Screen area" drop-down specifies the size of the window that displays the host machine. The "Available servers" drop-down allows navigation to a server that is on an accessible LAN. "Enable data compression" and "Cache bitmaps to disk" help speed data transfer and screen painting. When these settings are complete, simply click on the Connect button and it will attempt to communicate with the host machine. If a connection is made, a private desktop instance is shown in the Terminal Services client window. Unlike in PCAnywhere, this session is private to the connection. A person sitting at the console of the host machine is not able see what is being done in any particular session. When PCAnywhere connects, a host operator can see all of the mouse movements and keystrokes. In Terminal Services, all sessions are kept isolated from each other and the console. This is an important feature that PCAnywhere does not have. PCAnywhere only allows one connection at a time. Terminal Services' ability to allow multiple connections is the mechanism by which Microsoft will allow Office and other applications to be rented as a service. A central server can house these applications, and client machines can utilize them without any additional software installed on the client machine. The setup and configuration of Terminal Services is covered in the next chapter. Unlike PCAnywhere, there is no file transfer function available in Terminal Services, thus making access to FTP client software more important.

VNC (Virtual Network Computing)
VNC or "Virtual Network Computing" is a free utility from AT&T labs. This is a remote control utility like PCAnywhere and Terminal Services but with a few important differences.

- It has both a server component and viewer. The server component can run as a service under Windows 98, ME, and Windows 2000 Professional. It does not require Windows 2000 Server like the server component of Terminal Services.

- It is very small. The program fits on a floppy and can be run from a floppy. No installation of the viewer is necessary.

- It sees the same desktop that you would see if you where in front of the machine you are attached to. Terminal Services "sees" a virtual desktop, it is not what you would see if you sat in front of the Windows 2000 Server console you are attached to. Seeing the actual desktop has advantages. Some software that is run under Terminal Services interacts only with the actual desktop and not the virtual one that Terminal Services creates. This creates a problem wherein certain dialog boxes are not visible and the application appears to hang. You then need to go to the server in question and answer the dialog there. With VNC you are always seeing the actual desktop.

VNC is a important utility to have available. If you are using it on a local LAN, you can connect to the machine acting as the server via computer name. If you are on the public Internet, you can connect via IP address. When the VNC server component is installed as a service, it will prompt for a password. Then when ever the client viewer connects, you will be prompted for a password before being connected to the desktop.

It does not have any file transfer ability built in. Like Terminal Services, you need to have an FTP client available to do any file transfers.

West Wind Web Monitor

The West Wind Web Monitor tool is a very important site-monitoring utility. Basic monitoring services in a data center simply check to see whether the Web server is responding to HTTP requests. But being able to serve up a static Web page does not mean that an application serving up dynamic content is healthy and responding. It is possible that the Web Connection application is hung and not responding to dynamic requests. Web Monitor allows you to specify a dynamic link and what is expected to be returned if the link is responding. Web Monitor will then automatically check the site at predefined intervals. If the link fails, an email notification can be sent out and a link can be executed that, for example, restarts the Web Connection application. This tool allows you to employ an around-the-clock technician to watch over your site! A great many times, this tool will take care of any problems without any human intervention. It is comforting to know that the site is being checked and kept healthy 24x7.

In **Figure 17**, the link, the return value expected, and the polling interval are defined.

The "Search result for" value is a substring that is searched for in the HTML code that is returned by the "URL to monitor" link. This utility needs to run on a machine other than the server. If it is run on the server and the server crashes, Web Monitor will not be able to send out a notification that the site is down! It is best to place it on a machine that can be left on all the time and has a constant connection to the Internet.

On the Contact Info page (see **Figure 18**), email information is provided. The email addresses entered will receive notification from Web Monitor when a link test fails.

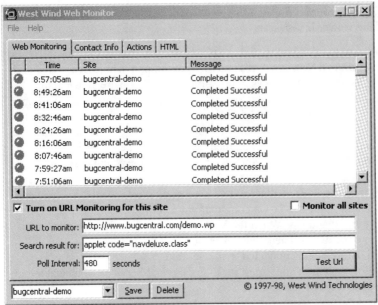

Figure 17. *West Wind Web Monitor setup, where you define the link and the expected return value.*

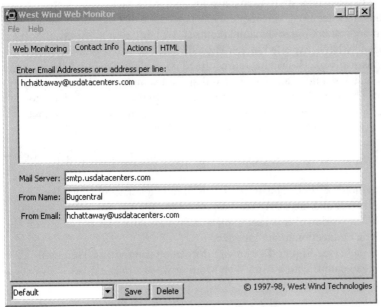

Figure 18. *Email information for when a link fails.*

An email server needs to be accessible in order for this to work. Usually the data center where your site is hosted will make a mail server available.

The Actions page (see **Figure 19**) specifies what actions to take when a link fails.

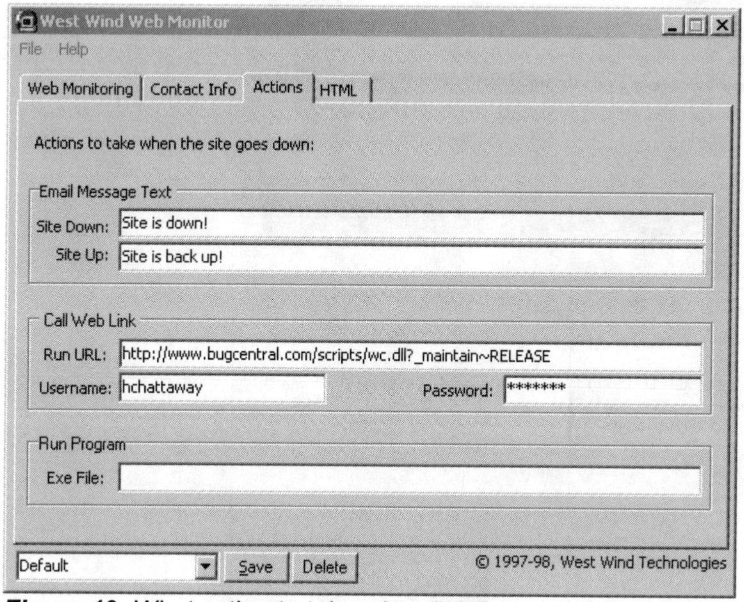

Figure 19. *What action to take when link fails.*

The "Email Message Text" area is where the message of the text is supplied for when the site goes down and when it comes back up again. If the link fails, "Run URL" specifies what http link to run. Typically it is the "release" link for the Web Connection DLL file. This will release the COM servers, and the next hit to the site will restart them. There can be many reasons why the test link may fail. It may be that:

- The COM server has crashed and is hanging the Web server.

- IIS is grabbing 100 percent of the processor and preventing any requests from being processed. This happens every so often.

- There is a problem with the Internet path. The server may be functioning normally but there may be a problem with a router or cut fiber along the way.

- The hardware has failed (hard disk crash or loss of power).

Web Monitor has no way of knowing the reason the link failed, just that it did.

Beyond Compare
Beyond Compare by Scooter Software (**www.scootersoftware.com**) is one of those "must have" utilities. It is a very powerful program that allows two separate files to be compared side

by side. Beyond Compare highlights the differences between to two files and allows them to be synchronized by merging the differences line by line (see **Figure 20**).

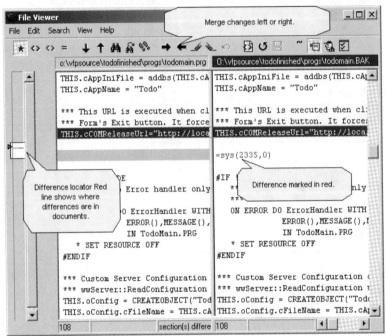

Figure 20. Beyond Compare.

Beyond Compare can be most helpful when a new version of Web Connection is released. If there were changes to WCONNECT.H or any of the INI files, Beyond Compare can visually merge in the new changes. Also, if there is a difference in behavior between the development and production versions of an HTML page, Beyond Compare can highlight the differences. Besides comparing file content, it can also compare directory contents. It will highlight any differences in directory contents and structure. Sessions can be named and recalled for later comparison. It was originally written to support multiple developers working on the same code base. It can merge changes into a final build version. This is similar to what Microsoft's SourceSafe does. Beyond Compare, however, is not integrated into the Visual FoxPro Project Manager and does not support checking source files in and out from a repository. For further details on SourceSafe, check out Ted Roche's book *Essential SourceSafe*, from Hentzenwerke Publishing.

West Wind Help Builder
Help Builder, from West Wind Technologies, greatly helps in producing professional-grade Help systems. It is a tool written in Visual FoxPro to cater to the special needs of the Visual FoxPro community. It is capable of producing HTML Help files as well as Windows CHM

files.[1] The HTML file format produces a framed window with the Help index in the left frame with hyperlinks that navigate to the matching content in the right frame. When writing Help, it uses a plain text editor for entering in both text and HTML tags. There is a preview feature that displays a "Web view," which switches the display of plain text to a rendered display of the HTML. There is also a "browser preview lock" button that will additionally display the rendered HTML in an instance of your default browser. **Figure 21** shows the West Wind Help Builder editor.

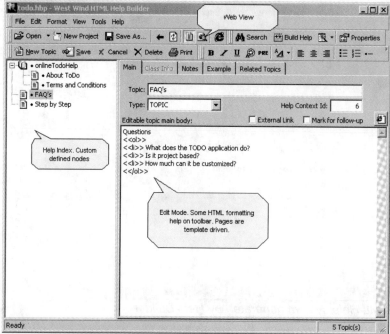

Figure 21. *West Wind Help Builder editor.*

The editor interface has two major sections. On the left is the Help index tree. This tree can be custom designed with any number of top-level nodes and subnodes. When HTML is built from this content, this tree is converted into a list of hyperlinks to each respective page (see **Figure 22**). The main edit window on the right contains the content of each Help topic. The pages that are created from this are based on ASP style templates. There is a set of templates provided in Help Builder. The information provided in the sections in Figure 21 is simply inserted into the page template. Help Builder does not have a WYSIWYG layout for editing like FrontPage or GoLive. The content is typed in its raw format. There are some basic formatting toolbar options, like bold, italics, and help in creating ordered and unordered lists. To view how the content will actually look, you must switch to "Web View" using the icon marked in Figure 21. Entries into the Notes, Example, and Related Topics tabs may be used

---

[1] Help Builder relies on the compiler in Microsoft HTML Help Workshop to create CHM files. Therefore, it is required that you also have HTML Help Workshop installed if you want to create CHM files. This product is free, and it can be downloaded from Microsoft's Web site.

flesh out the specific Help topic, appearing as "Remarks," "Example," and "See Also" sections. Under the hood, all this Help information is being stored in a Visual FoxPro table.

To generate an HTML help file, simply click on "Build Help" and the dialog shown in **Figure 23** will appear.

You can create either a compiled Help file (CHM) or an HTML version of the Help content. Also specify where the Help files are to be generated. The final output of this wizard is a frame-based HTML Help system, as shown in Figure 22.

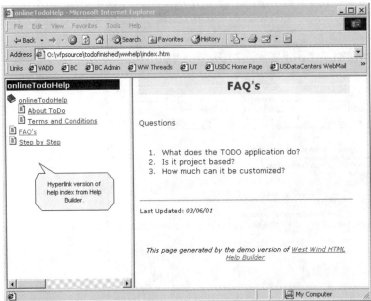

Figure 22. Final HTML Help system generated by Help Builder.

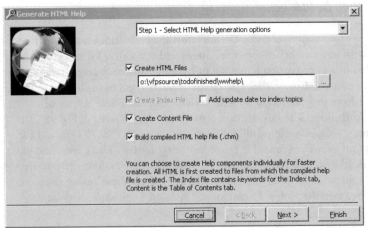

Figure 23. Generating HTML Help.

Help Builder can be used to create generic Help files or Help files specifically for Visual FoxPro programs and class libraries. It has the extra intelligence built in to parse a Visual FoxPro program file and place the functions, class methods, and class properties into a Help file. Special comment blocks can also be inserted into the source code that Help Builder knows how to parse and format into its help system. This way, you can have one source for your program and Help content (the PRG file) instead of maintaining two separate files.

Web browsers

Last but not least on the list of development software are Web browsers. This has become in large part a religious war between Microsoft Internet Explorer (IE) and Netscape (NS). There are significant differences between IE 5x and NS 4.x. They utilize Cascading Style Sheets differently and have a different implementation of Dynamic HTML (DHTML). Programming for cross-browser compatibility is very difficult. There often has to be code bracketing to support the different implementations.

When Netscape 6 was released in late 2000, it parted ways with Netscape 4.x. It was totally rewritten and conforms more closely with the W3C standards committee on HTML4 and CSS. It was a very frustrating change, because code that worked in NS4.7 suddenly did not work in NS6. It wasn't so much that NS6 was broken, just that now it is adhering to the standards. This has made cross-browser programming much easier. It is now possible to program DHTML forms for both browsers without using code bracketing. All the screen shots of HTML forms in this book will be from IE.

Even though code is not written using a browser, it is the browser that renders the HTML content, and it is the browser that interprets the scripting language embedded in the Web page. Since it is the browser that has the final say as to how the HTML looks and how the page behaves, it is an integral part of the development process. In order to test the appearance of your application as your users will see it, you should have a representative collection of browsers at your disposal. Your selection depends on your user community. At minimum, you should test under NS 4.x, NS 6.x, and IE 5.x.

Conclusion

As you can see from all the tools covered in this chapter, the self-contained development environment of Visual FoxPro is simply not enough anymore. There are so many different technologies involved in producing a Web site that the days of a one-tool development environment are over. Visual FoxPro allows the developer to retain an enormous advantage going forward: The entire language can be used, all database access stays the same, and, thanks to Web Connection, all of these features are available from within a Web page, not just a program file.

While learning all of these other tools and technologies is very time consuming, it is this very process that is so exciting. With the aid of these other tools, Visual FoxPro is transformed into one of the most powerful Web tools on the market. As with desktop development, the use of Visual FoxPro continues its tradition of making difficult projects seem easy. Projects can still be completed in less time and with fewer people than with most other development languages.

Chapter resources

- **FTP client software:**

    - **WS-FTP**: FTP client software. **www.ipswitch.com/**

    - **CuteFTP**: **www.globalscape.com/**

- **WinZip**: Windows file compression utility. **www.winzip.com**

- **Web Connection**: Framework for Visual FoxPro Web applications. **www.west-wind.com**

- **HTML authoring tools:**

    - **GoLive**: Adobe's Web authoring tool. **www.adobe.com**

    - **FrontPage 2000**: Microsoft's Web authoring tool. **www.microsoft.com/windows/IE/**

    - **HTML-Kit**: Free authoring tool. **www.chami.com html-kit**

    - **HotDog** authoring tool: **www.sausagetools.com/index.php**

- **Remote control software:**

    - **PCAnywhere**: **www.symantec.com**

    - **VNC** (Virtual Network Computing): **www.uk.research.att.com/vnc/index.html**

    - **ControlIt** (formerly "Remotely Possible"): **www.ca.com/products/controlit.htm**

    - **Carbon Copy** (one of the originals!): **www.compaq.com/services/carboncopy/**

    - **Win 2000 Magazine Buyers Guide** to remote control software: **www.win2000mag.com/Files/7220/7220_01.pdf**

- **Beyond Compare**: Visual Difference tool. **www.scootersoftware.com**

- **HTML Help Builder**: Help authoring tool. **www.west-wind.com**

- **HTML Help Workshop**: Microsoft's Help authoring tool, needed for the creation of CHM files. **http://msdn.microsoft.com/library/tools/htmlhelp/wkshp/download_main.htm**

- **www.webconnectiontraining.com**: Author-run Web site with Web Connection training material.

Chapter 7
Server Hardware and Hosting

We saw in Chapter 6 only one side of the equation—getting the development machine set up with all of its software. When it comes to deploying the newly developed Web site, a Web server must be built that will be connected to the Internet. This chapter will focus on building this machine and getting it connected to the Web.

In Chapter 6, "Complete Web Development Environment," familiar territory was covered. The development machine was covered along with some new software tools. Some are handy to have even if you're not doing Web development. This chapter, however, will probably be all new material. It covers the notion of taking your locally developed application and transferring it to a machine that will reside on one of the millions of connections on the Internet. Conventional desktop Visual FoxPro applications have to be distributed via disks. An application update requires burning new disks or CDs. With Web applications, however, it is simply a matter of updating the server, and instantly the whole world has the new application. This one aspect of Internet development is the most compelling: one point distribution. This chapter will cover those areas that are necessary to make this process successful.

The machine that will serve as the production Web server needs some special consideration. The Internet makes your product or service available to the entire world. There are no set hours of operation; the Web site needs to be up and responding 24x7. If there is frequent downtime, users will not be back a second time. This worldwide audience can keep the site active around the clock. When users in the United States are asleep, European and Asian users are pounding on the site. With this in mind, the server needs to be ultra-reliable. The mindset with the server is to keep it very lean on software and unnecessary hardware. There is no need for fancy video or sound cards or a full installation of MS Office or Visual Studio. Let's take a look at the various hardware considerations when building a Web server. The following discussion assumes the Web Connection application, the data, and the HTML content are on the same box. SQL Server is not used for this example.

Memory

For optimum speed, do not use less then 256MB of memory in a Windows 2000 Server. The extra memory eliminates a great deal of disk access by caching more of the data in memory.

Processors

The average processor speed is currently around 800 MHz. The newest Intel chips are now over 1 GHz. If the site that is being built will be generating a lot of traffic, it would be a good idea to plan on a server with two processors. If multiple copies of the Web Connection application need to be loaded, it is best to be able to have multiple processors available to spread the load. If multiple EXEs are loaded on one processor, they will always be waiting for the other EXE to finish with its current task. A multi-processor box is the only way to take advantage of multiple application threads.

Hard drives

Hard drives are the single biggest factor in determining Web server performance. Very fast ultra-wide SCSI drives will increase performance far more than a faster CPU or additional memory. It is wise to make sure the server has multiple ultra-wide SCSI hard drives. The fastest drives now spin at 15,000 rpms. Even 7200 rpm drives are very adequate. One of the key differences between an IDE and SCSI configuration is that SCSI drives multi-task. IDE drives are accessed sequentially. The multi-tasking ability of SCSI greatly increases throughput. Also, it is best to use multiple hard drives to spread disk access. **Table 1** shows a typical configuration for three hard drives.

Table 1. Hard drive layout for a system with three physical drives.

Drive	Size	Content
Physical drive-0 Operating system partition	3GB NTFS partition Drive C:	Operating system only. Allow at least 3GB when using Windows 2000 Server.
Physical drive-0 Swap file partition	200-500MB NTFS partition. Drive D:	Have only one file in this partition, which is pagefile.sys. This will permanently eliminate the pagefile fragmentation problem.
Physical drive-1 NT CD partition	500MB NTFS partition. Drive E:	In a server down emergency, it is best to have the CD installed on the server.
Physical drive-1 Application and database partition	Remaining 2-4GB of drive with NTFS partition. Drive O:	Web Connection COM servers and tables get installed here. Directory structure is discussed in Chapter 8, "Configuring Server Software."
Physical drive-2 Web htm/GIF/content partition	All of drive NTFS and used only for Web content. Drive P:	All HTML content is stored in this partition. Directory structure is discussed later.

RAID drives

RAID is an acronym for Redundant Array of Inexpensive Disks. The reason for having a RAID configuration is to write data to multiple places at the same time to help guard against single points of failure. If the server being used only has one drive, when that drive fails, the site is down for a long time. Even if there is a recent backup, it will still take considerable time to install the new drive and reconfigure the box. In a RAID system, a drive can crash and the site still keeps running. There are several types of RAID configurations (see **Table 2**).

The most common choices are RAID 1 and RAID 5. In RAID 1, there is a complete backup of all data at any time. The disk controller is writing information to both disks simultaneously. With this, the drives should also be "hot swappable." If one of the drives fails, it can be replaced, and the disk controller will rebuild the new drive. With RAID 1, there is one drive dedicated to be the backup. Hard drive prices have become so reasonable, however, that dedicating a hard drive just for backup is not an issue. The up-to-date, full backup that is always being done far outweighs the minimal one-time cost of the hard drive. Also, RAID 1 is very fast since data is being written to both disks through different I/O paths.

RAID 5 came about due to the smaller hard drive sizes that were available only a short time ago. If a server needed 35GB of space, it was necessary to have an array of seven 5GB hard drives. Today, however, it is not a problem to get an IBM 40GB hard drive for well under $200. Also, if one of the disks in a RAID 5 array fails, it can greatly slow down the whole box. There is significant overhead required to work around the failed drive. When a new drive is swapped in for the failed one, it can also take quite a while to get it back in sync. So, with the larger hard drives that are now available at a very low cost, RAID 1 can be an excellent solution for ensuring server uptime.

Table 2*. RAID configurations.*

RAID level	Description	Fault tolerance	Performance	Relative cost
0—Striping	Data is striped across the RAID set of disks; no configuration. parity is maintained.	None. If one disk fails, the data is lost.	Excellent. The fastest RAID level.	Equivalent to the cost of disks in a non-RAID system.
1—Mirroring (Duplexing, if two RAID controllers are used)	Identical date is written simultaneously to two disks.	Excellent. Depending on the implementation, failover can occur immediately.	Very good. Reads a bit faster than it writes.	Very expensive. For every drive, a second drive is needed for backing it up.
2	All data is striped across both data and parity disks. All disks must be accessed in parallel.	Good.	Superseded by RAID 3.	Slightly less than RAID 1.
3—Striping + parity drive	Similar to RAID 2, but parity data is stored on a dedicated drive.	Very good, but all fault tolerance is lost if the parity drive fails.	Moderate.	Least expensive. Only part of drive is used for parity information needed to rebuild contents.
4	Similar to RAID 3, but with multiple independent disk reads instead of synchronized read and writes to the array.	Very good.	Moderate.	Same as RAID 3.
5—Distributed data guarding	Instead of a dedicated parity drive, data and parity information is interleaved over all drives in the array.	Excellent. Two drives in a RAID 5 array must fail to cause the array to fail.	Read: excellent. Write:	Same as RAID 3.
6	RAID 5 + extra parity information.	Most excellent. Three drives in a RAID 5 array must fail to cause the array to fail.	Similar to RAID 5, but writes are a bit slower.	Slightly greater than RAID 5. Extra disk for additional parity information.
10	RAID 1, but with mirrored pairs instead of single drives.	Excellent. Two drives must fail for the array to die.	As fast as they come on reads; almost as fast on writes.	Same as RAID 1.

NIC cards

It is a good idea to have two Network Interface Cards (NICs) installed in the server. One is used for connection to the Internet, and the other NIC card can be used for doing backups to a central tape unit. Most data centers run 100 Base T connections to the machines, so the NIC cards should match this speed.

There is no need for a monitor in a data center environment. There is generally one monitor for each 5-8 computers. A KVM (keyboard, video, mouse) switch connects these machines to one monitor, one keyboard, and one mouse so data center staff can access the machines when needed. Space is at a premium in a data center, so these switches save a lot of space and power.

Hosting options

When choosing to host with a particular hosting company, there are several issues that you need to be aware of. First, you should find out the size of the company. Many "hosting" companies are one-man shops that simply co-locate a server in another company's data center. This can be okay, but bear in mind that such a company has less control over the hosting environment if they themselves are using some other company's facilities. The following sections address the various services and features of a data center and the choices you'll need to make when choosing a company. They are listed in order from least expensive to most expensive.

Do-it-yourself hosting

The very low end of hosting options is to host the server yourself. If you are doing anything other than beta testing your site, this is not a recommended path to take. If the site is for non-commercial purposes, it may be appropriate. Assuming your Web site will be identified with a URL and not just an IP address, you would need a static IP address. This allows the domain name that has been registered for your site to be permanently associated with a specific IP address. Typically, when a dial-up service is used the IP address assigned to your machine changes from connection to connection. While it is possible to obtain a permanent IP address from a dial-up service, dial-up connectivity is by no means reliable enough for a commercial Web site. Not to mention how incredibly slow a dial-up connection is. In some locations, DSL lines are available. These are much faster than dial-up lines, but most providers would not allow commercial use of the line.

If a static IP address is not possible, another alternative is to use a "dynamic DNS" service. Providers of this service act as the authoritative DNS service, and if the IP address of the server changes, they update the DNS record entry automatically. So if as in the previous example, the IP address changes because the connection was broken, when the new IP address is allocated upon reconnection, the DNS record for the Web site will be updated to repoint to the new address. There are third-party utilities that can be placed on the server to continuously monitor the IP address.

In a corporate location, it is possible to obtain a T1 line for connectivity. T1s are much faster and more reliable. A single T1 line can carry about 51 30kbps dial-up connections at the same time. This means 51 fully loaded dial-up connections simultaneously. Since this is rarely the case, the number of users that can be browsing your site can be far higher. The cost of a T1 line is around $800 - $1000/month, however.

Besides the drawbacks of these options, there are other important factors. Web users expect the site to be up 24x7. What is most lacking in a "do-it-yourself" environment is redundancy. In a home and even an office location, it is unlikely there will be dual network and power feeds. These become necessary in real e-commerce sites. Also, it is unlikely that there is generator backup power in this environment. When the power goes out, as it certainly will, generator backup is mandatory to take over after the 15 minutes of power that a UPS unit provides. So while the do-it-yourself approach is initially cheaper, it will most certainly cause many headaches and will most likely cause the site to be less than inadequate to serve any commercial purpose.

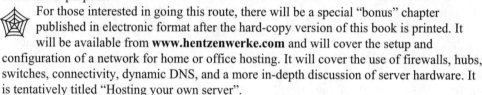

For those interested in going this route, there will be a special "bonus" chapter published in electronic format after the hard-copy version of this book is printed. It will be available from **www.hentzenwerke.com** and will cover the setup and configuration of a network for home or office hosting. It will cover the use of firewalls, hubs, switches, connectivity, dynamic DNS, and a more in-depth discussion of server hardware. It is tentatively titled "Hosting your own server".

Shared, co-location, managed co-location, or dedicated?

There are usually several alternatives available when it comes to the server arrangements. Let's go over each of them from least expensive to most expensive.

Shared

For Visual FoxPro hosting, shared is really not an option. Due to the nature of how a Web Connection application needs to be configured, it is unlikely a hosting facility would allow such an application to be hosted on a shared box. As you will see later, setting up a Web Connection application involves registering a COM server with the Registry. While trivial to do, this makes data centers nervous. Also, unless security on the box is extremely well managed, it is all too easy for one Visual FoxPro application to poke around on the server and get at any other DBFs that may be on the machine. It is very easy to write a little program that utilizes recursion to completely catalog an entire machine within a couple of seconds.

Also, for many maintenance operations, it is very handy to be able to use PCAnywhere to connect to the machine. However, this gives you console-level control of the machine, another nerve-racking experience for a data center. As you shall see, Windows Terminal Services can also be used to remotely access a machine, but in Administration mode, Terminal Services only allows two connections at a time. With a shared box, this is most likely not enough. Also, it is common on a shared server that if an update is done to any system files, such as a new MDAC installation, the other sites that may not have needed the update will stop working. The rates that shared servers are able to garner along with the hassles of managing them makes these very unattractive for everyone. Data centers can only make money on these if they never have to touch them. These are best left to static FrontPage or plain HTML sites.

The one hosting company that could do shared Web Connection sites is DNGSolutions.Net. They specialize in hosting Web Connection applications and go to the lengths necessary to secure your application from these kinds of problems.

Co-located

A server can be "co-located" at the hosting facility. This arrangement involves the client supplying the machine, and the data center just rents the floor space, the power, and the connectivity to the Internet, also known as "ping, power, and pipeline." There is usually no Service-Level Agreement (SLA) with simple co-location. The data center cannot make any guarantees as to how the server was constructed and configured, so they are not going to stand behind the server. Basic co-location can run anywhere between $350-$450 per month. For many budgets, this is affordable for hosting. If this is the case, it becomes even more important to build a solid server. Any time data center personnel are needed to restart the server or perform some emergency procedure, you will be charged around $75 per hour.

The style of machine that should be used for co-location is the rack mount variety. Most data centers would require rack mount as opposed to tower systems, to maximize space. Dell and Hewlett Packard make some of the best Web servers. If co-location is the choice, it is important to go with a name brand system. Co-located servers get the minimum of monitoring services, if any. At most it will receive a basic "ping" monitoring. This only tests to see that the machine is responding to basic ICMP messages. ICMP (Internet Control Message Protocol) is a low-level diagnostic protocol used to troubleshoot network problems and is used in the PING and TRACERT utilities. It will not test to see whether an application is responding correctly. For this function, the West Wind Web Monitor tool fills an important niche. It is necessary to check to make sure the application is returning the correct HTML for a specific request.

If you are supplying your own machine, make sure that all components are on the hardware compatibility list. The link to this list can be found in the "Chapter resources" section. Problems with incompatible hardware can be extremely difficult to track down and fix in a production server. There are some video cards, for example, that are not compatible with Visual FoxPro. In certain cases when Visual FoxPro tries to write to the screen, the video card conflict can cause the machine to "blue screen," resulting in a corrupted system. Making sure all hardware is on the compatibility list will go a long way in building a stable server. Another excellent site in the "Chapter resources" section is "Troubleshooting strategies." This Microsoft site gives detailed explanations about troubleshooting hardware. This is a site worth bookmarking!

Managed co-location

If a data center offers managed co-location, it usually starts with the co-location services and adds on additional monitoring. These take the form of monitoring for CPU utilization, disk space, and other load analysis. Also, with managed co-location the customer usually gets a higher level of support if the site goes down. There is an "escalation" policy. The customer provides a series of phone numbers, email addresses, and pager and cell phone numbers that can be used in an emergency.

Dedicated hosting

In this configuration, the level of service is generally the same as in the preceding case, but the data center supplies the machine and all hardware. It is built and configured to their specifications. Here the customer is basically renting the machine. An example of what might be included as an entry-level dedicated configuration follows:

HP NetServer LPr servers with Pentium III 700 MHz processors
Base configuration includes:

- Single PIII 700 MHz processor

- Dual 9.1GB Ultra2 HS hard drives—RAID 1

- 512MB memory

- Dual 10/100 NIC cards

- HP NetRAID 1Si

Available options include:

- Up to 2x PIII 700 MHz processors

- Up to 1GB memory

- Up to 3x NIC cards

- 2x 18GB HS Ultra2 hard drives—RAID 1

The RAID 1 configuration provides mirroring between the two 9.1GB hard drives. These drives spin at 10,000 rpm. At this speed for most Web Connection applications, the loss of having the OS, swap file, and data spread out over multiple drives is not very significant. These offerings can be re-spec'ed for each use, and additional hard drives can be added. It is important that the hard drives be "hot swappable." This means that if a hard drive fails, it can be switched out while the machine is running. If the drives are mirrored as described here, the server will be able to proceed with no downtime. When the new drive is plugged in, the server will re-sync them. This re-syncing can take a bit of time, but it prevents the server from being offline. If you expect to need more than two instances of your Web Connection application to handle the server load, it would be a good idea to configure this machine with dual processors. It is best to load each processor with 2-3 COM servers. More than this results in diminishing returns.

Loss of control

With managed hosting comes a loss of total control over the box. Many developers are used to having "root" access to the machine. This means control at the desktop level. This is typically given up in order to have a Service-Level Agreement (SLA, discussed later). The hosting company cannot guarantee a level of service if outside parties are able to tamper with the machine. This can be a big hurdle for most site managers and developers to get over. This also requires a great deal of confidence in the abilities of the technicians and engineers at the data center. Depending on how the SLA is written, it may not be possible to simply FTP up a new Web page. It would first have to be given to the data center staff with an implementation plan, and they would then upload it to the site. A test script would need to be run through to ensure the new change did not break anything. If anything does go wrong, there must be a rollback plan.

This same update procedure would be required for the Web Connection COM servers as well. A new EXE would be given to the data center staff, and they run the update procedure, test it, and have a rollback procedure if necessary. Also, before any updates are done, the site would be backed up. Actually, the data center staff is doing no more than what the developer would be doing, and actually the developer would have to show the staff how to update a COM server. But the point is, the data center would have no one else to blame if something went wrong and can therefore make guarantees.

These formalities can be a good thing. These are steps that should happen anyway. However, it still is a leap of faith to turn over this much control to someone else. If the site being built is a major e-commerce site, or any other source of recurring revenue, this is probably the way to go. If this is not a comfortable arrangement, however, a purely co-location solution may be better. As you shall see, a co-located server can be easily managed remotely through the use of Terminal Services.

If a fully managed solution is chosen, make sure the staff has the proper credentials. In an SLA contract, the data center should state any certifications the staff has. Make sure there are fully qualified people doing these maintenance routines. If it is necessary to explain to them how to restart IIS if something fails, or what a HTML page is, be extra careful before handing over the keys to the site!

Physical facilities

There are a number of considerations to take into account with regard to the physical layout of the data center. Some data centers utilize a raised floor. This looks great and brings to mind the images of the old mainframe data centers, but in reality they do not provide any real value to the hosting experience. They add a "wow" factor and contribute to the marketing aspects of the data center, but do not get nervous if the data center you are looking at does not have raised floors. Let's take a look at the types of racks that are available, UPS backups, connectivity, security, and fire suppression.

Racks

There are three basic types of rack systems available.

Open racks are the least expensive but also the least secure. There can be multiple clients in the same rack. All the wiring, connectivity, and power is out in the open (see **Figure 1**).

Locked cabinets provide more security. They are completely enclosed but only house one client at a time. This makes them more expensive (see **Figure 2**).

Condo units are a nice compromise (see **Figure 3**). They allow a customer to rent a section that is around 3' high. All power and connectivity is protected. Someone opening up the top unit cannot get access to the power and connectivity of the second unit. These are a good middle ground between the first two options.

Figure 1. Open rack.

Figure 2. Locked cabinets.

Figure 3. Condo unit.

Cages are the top-of-the-line solution if you have a large amount of equipment that needs tight security. Cages are locked steel units that are bolted to the floor (see **Figure 4**). Data center personnel will have access to the cages if there are any problems. A top-of-the-line solution has a top-of-the-line price. Cages can run as much as $6,000 per month! The site being hosted needs to generate some major revenue to justify this expense!

Figure 4. Cages.

Power

There are two levels of protection needed in a serious data center. The first line of defense is a UPS unit (see **Figure 5**). Many data centers use an Uninterruptible Power Supply (UPS) at the rack level. These units can have approximately six computers plugged into them. However, these units can only supply power for about 10 minutes before they are drained. Another solution for really serious data centers is UPS units that back up the entire data center. USDatacenters Inc. in Massachusetts has the largest UPS system that APC has ever produced. It has 2 megawatts worth of battery backup. However, this is still a short-term solution. What is needed for extended power outages are on-site generators. The UPS units are really only meant to supply power during the time it takes the generators to start up and supply the necessary power. There is also a series of enormous switches that switch the source of power from the street to the generator after they are up to full power.

For the sites that simply must not go down, the servers can also have dual power supplies, each with isolated power feeds. Top-tier data centers will have dual independent power feeds at the server. So if one source of power goes down, the machine can utilize the other separate feed through the other power supply unit.

Figure 5. UPS units.

Connectivity

Depending on the size of the data center, connectivity for the data center itself may range from a CAT5 cable to a fiber bundle, as shown in **Figure 6**. CAT5 cable has connectors similar to telephone wire that gets plugged into the data center router at one end and into the NIC card in a Web server at the other end. A CAT5 cable is rated for 100 Mbits per second. The kind of connectivity fiber provides, however, is in an entirely different league.

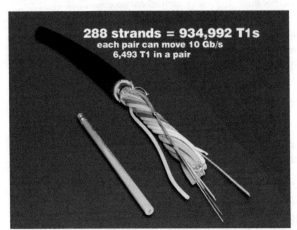

Figure 6. Major fiber for some serious connectivity!

Table 3 summarizes the various levels of connectivity available.

Table 3. Levels of connectivity.

Circuit name:	Capacity	Number of dial-up connections @30kbps
DS0	64kbps	2
T1, DS-1	1.544Mbps	51
E1, DS-1	2.048Mbps	68
T2, DS-2	6.312Mbps	210
E2	8.448Mbps	281
E3	34.368Mbps	1,145
T3 or DS3	44.736Mbps	1,491
OC-1, STS1	51.840Mbps	1,728
Fast Ethernet	100.00 Mbps	3,333
OC-3, STS3	155.520Mbps	5,184
OC-48	2.488Gbps	82,962
OC-96	4.976Gbps	165,925
OC192	10Gbps	333,333
OC-255	13.21Gbps	1,040,333

Redundancy

Another important consideration is redundancy in the data center. If the data center has only one connection to the Internet and that connection fails, the whole data center will go dark. There are bound to be times when an upstream provider to the data center has a connection problem. Data centers with redundant connectivity use routers that can switch between multiple feeds without interruption of service. This is a key feature of a data center. It is virtually guaranteed that at some time a connection will go down upstream. The data center needs to ensure there is not a single point of failure. The top-tier data centers even have redundant connectivity down to the server. Multiple NIC cards can be used in case one of them fails. Some data centers are closer than others to the Internet "backbone" and rely less on other companies for connectivity. It is important to find out about these other possible upstream providers and learn about there reliability also.

Service-Level Agreements (SLAs)

A Service-Level Agreement (SLA) is a contract between the data center and the client guaranteeing a certain level of service and uptime of the data center facilities. The SLA states what the facility has to offer in the way of fire protection, air conditioning, network uptime, and customer response time to problems. If the uptime component is not met, for example, the SLA will typically state how the customer will be compensated. For different ranges of downtime, the customer will get a credit on their monthly recurring bill. For example, if the site is down for five minutes, there might be a credit for a half-day of billing. This is an important document to have when signing up for service. If the facility does not offer one, there are no guarantees of service.

IP addresses

Not all data centers actually own the IP address that will be assigned to your Web site. If your hosting company simply co-locates your box at another data center, it may be that this other data center actually owns the IP address assigned to your Web site. This is an important fact to discover. If the owner of the IP wants it back, all sites using those addresses have to be reconfigured in a Domain Name Server (DNS) so the domain points to the new IP address, wherever that may be. It is usually the company that owns the IP address that runs the authoritative DNS server for the matching Web site. Make sure where this is and who is allowed to make changes! Your site could be offline for a while if the IP address changes without sufficient notice! If the DNS servers are not managed by the hosting company, it should be in the SLA that notice will be given in the event the IP address has to be changed.

Other services

There are some other key services that a data center can offer. Let's take a look at these not-so-optional services.

Site traffic reporting

The proper analysis of the site traffic is vital to the success of the site. There are many Web sites that have no monitoring. A site administrator needs to know:

- Where the traffic is coming from.

- What search engines are being used.

- What keywords are being used.

- What browsers people are using.

- What the most used directories are.

- What errors are occurring.

- What the daily/hourly load is.

- How many megabytes of data are being transferred.

One of the best tools for doing this is WebTrends. This tool will take the raw text files produced by IIS and produce formatted charts and graphs that make sense of all this data. This will be covered in detail later in the book. WebTrends can be set up as a service with the reports scheduled to run at any time interval and emailed automatically to any address. These reports are crucial; make sure the data center provides this service. If a co-located machine is being used, this software can be installed and configured by the client.

Backups and disaster recovery

Backups are also a vital part of running a Web site. Ideally, the data center should administer daily backups with offsite storage. Generally, a backup procedure is not included in basic co-location; it must be purchased separately. Any of the managed packages should include it, however. Tape backup units are not needed in each machine. The data center should have a central robotic tape machine that automatically backs up the servers on a scheduled basis. The backups are performed through a separate NIC card, so Web site performance does not have to contend for the same connection. Here is an example of a comprehensive backup policy:

- Daily incremental backups occur Monday through Sunday.

- Weekly full backups occur at the end of the week.

- Monthly full backups occur at the end of the month.

- Weekly tapes are brought offsite and held for one month and then put back into circulation.

- Monthly full backups are held for one year.

The newer backup software can even back up open Visual FoxPro tables. There is no need to make sure the tables are closed when the backup is in process. Part of the backup strategy that a data center provides is its disaster recovery plan. If the machine crashes, how fast can the machine be restored? If a file is accidentally deleted, how responsive are they to locating the backup tape and restoring it? These kinds of things should be clearly stated in the SLA described earlier.

Conclusion

Proper configuration of the server is vital when there is a single point of distribution for your product or service. The machine has to be built with a different environment in mind from a development workstation. The production server (or servers) needs to be as reliable and autonomous as possible. Ideally, it should be like the space probes NASA sends to the outer planets. Those probes, once gone, can never have another human hand touch them. Shoot for this when building the server!

Chapter resources

- DNG Solutions: This hosting company specializes in Web Connection hosting. They know how to provide support in the data center for Web Connection. They can provide help in getting your site going, setting up script maps, and so forth. **www.dngsolutions.net**

- Web Trends Site Reporting: **www.webtrends.com**

- Backup software by Veritas: **www.veritas.com**

- Hardware compatibility list: **www.microsoft.com/windows2000/upgrade/ compat/default.asp**

- Windows 2000 Resource Kit: **www.microsoft.com/windows2000/library/ resources/reskit/WebResources/default.asp**

- Troubleshooting strategies: **www.microsoft.com/WINDOWS2000/library/ resources/reskit/samplechapters/fnhb/fnhb_trb_efjy.asp**

- ICMP protocol overview: Provides links to PING and TRACERT. **www.freesoft.org/CIE/Topics/81.htm**.

- How the Internet is constructed: A great Resource for learning what hardware makes up the Internet. **http://backofficesystems.com/tips/internet/backbone.htm**

- Excellent description of how RAID works: **www.pcguide.com/ref/hdd/perf/ raid/index.htm**

- RAID Advisory Board: **www.raid-advisory.com/rabguide.html**

Chapter 8
Configuring Server Software

In Chapter 7 I discussed server hardware and considerations in hosting the server in an Internet data center. In this chapter, we will take a look at how to best configure the server with the software required. I will cover IIS, FTP, site security, and the necessary utilities.

The book *Weaving the Web* by Tim Berners-Lee, the inventor of the World Wide Web, states, "The job of computers and networks is to get out of the way, not to be seen. This means that the appearance of the information and the tools one uses to access it should be independent of where the information is stored—the concept of location independence... file names should disappear; they should become merely another form of a URI...". The best way for this ideal notion of the Web to become reality is to build Web servers that run 24x7x365. When a Web server becomes unstable or offline, people are immediately reminded that the files they are looking at are not on their local machines and the illusion of "location independence" is broken (see **Figure 1**).

User should not care.

Desktop File   Web File

Figure 1. *Location independence of content.*

So in order to achieve this goal, Web servers need to be stable, and they must be configured to recover quickly from any problems that might occur. The software that is required on a Web server is different from what is needed on the development machine. **Table 1** lists the software that I will cover for server software.

Table 1. *Server software.*

Software	Description
MS Windows 2000 Server (Could use Windows NT)	Server version of Win2k. This will be used for the remainder of this chapter.
Visual FoxPro Runtime (Required)	Just the Runtime is needed on Server. A small Visual FoxPro app and distribution disks can be created.
Internet Information Server (IIS) (Required)	Provides HTTP services to allow publishing of HTML content.
File Transfer Protocol (FTP) (Required for remote uploads)	Provides FTP service to allow file transfers.
WinZip (Optional)	Helpful for transferring the live files down to the development machine.
WC.DLL (Required)	Licensed copy of Web Connection for the server. Just the DLL component needs to be on the server. The Visual FoxPro class libraries will be compiled into your VFP COM Server.
Windows 2000 Terminal Services or PCAnywhere (Required)	Needed on the server so client machines can attach.
VFP file repair tools (A practical requirement!)	Very important to have for emergency file repair and regular maintenance (www.abri.com).
Reindexing utility	DIRT is a freeware index recovery tool that works quite well.

Installing Windows 2000 Server

The installation of Windows 2000 Server is actually quite an easy process. Assuming the box meets the basic requirements, Windows 2000 Server can be installed without a hitch. To make this as smooth as possible, make sure the basic requirements listed in **Table 2** are met.

Table 2. *Windows 2000 Server hardware requirements.*

Component	Minimum requirements	Comments
Processor	32-bit Pentium 133 MHz.	For the price, on a production server 700 MHz is good.
Free hard disk space	One or more hard disks where %systemroot% (C:\WINNT by default) is located on a partition with at least 671MB of free space (2GB is recommended).	The boot partition should be at least 3GB. Windows 2000 takes up a lot of space, and after the OS and some application software, 2GB will be gone fast!
Memory	64MB for networking with one to five client computers; 128MB minimum is recommended for most network environments.	If you will be running multiple Web Connection executables, 256MB should be the minimum.
Display, keyboard, and mouse	VGA monitor capable of 640x480 (1024x768 recommended).	In the data center, the server will most likely share these through a KVM (keyboard, video, mouse) switch with other servers to save space.
CD-ROM drive	12x or faster recommended; not required for network installations.	
Additional drives	High-density 3.5" disk drive, unless your CD-ROM is bootable and supports starting the Setup program from a CD-ROM.	

Once these basic hardware requirements have been met, follow these steps:

1. Check all hardware (network adapters, video drivers, sound cards, CD-ROM drives, PC cards, and so on) for compatibility by checking the Windows 2000 Hardware Compatibility List (HCL). Check it out online at **www.microsoft.com/windows2000/ server/howtobuy/upgrading/compat/default.asp**.

2. Make sure the BIOS is up-to-date for Windows 2000.

3. Identify how you want to partition the hard disk drive on which you are going to install Windows 2000 Server. In Chapter 7, "Server Hardware and Hosting," there is a table showing a possible hard drive configuration. Lay this out ahead of time.

4. Choose a file system that meets your requirements and provides the services you need. Choose NTFS for a Web server. There is nothing on any drive that anyone in the outside world needs to see! NTFS allows you to set security at the directory and file level to prevent intruders.

5. Select a licensing mode. You can switch to per-seat from per-server mode after installation, but not to per-server from per-seat. On a Web server, the per-server license is what you want. Anonymous Web site access and FTP connections do not require a Client Access License (CAL); only authenticated non-IIS connections do.

6. Windows 2000 is excellent at detecting hardware, but make sure you have all device drivers handy.

7. If your CD-ROM drive is not bootable, have four 3.5" high-density floppies for creating the installation disks.

You can make these bootable installation disks by running the Makeboot.EXE program in the \bootdisk subdirectory of your installation CD. Makebt32.EXE is a 32-bit application that runs on Windows NT and Windows 2000. You can upgrade an existing Windows NT system to Windows 2000 or install Windows 2000 on a machine that has been "Fdisked," or wiped clean.

Let's assume that you will do the installation using the bootable floppies. After inserting the first disk and turning the machine on, one of the first things that the installation program detects is the drive configuration. Here are the steps that the installation program goes through in getting the drive formatted and partitioned.

1. Setup displays the Windows 2000 Server Setup screen, prompting you to select an area of free space or an existing partition on which to install Windows 2000. This stage of setup provides a way for you to create and delete partitions on your hard disk.

2. For this example, I am assuming all drives are unformatted and unpartitioned. The first drive is where Windows 2000 will be placed.

3. Make sure that the unpartitioned space partition is highlighted, and then type *c*.

4. Setup displays the Windows 2000 Setup screen, confirming that you've chosen to create a new partition in the unpartitioned space and informing you of the minimum and maximum sizes of the partition you might create.

5. Specify the size of the partition you want to create (3000MB), and then press Enter to continue.

6. *Note:* Although you can create additional partitions from the remaining unpartitioned space during setup, it is recommended that you perform additional partitioning tasks after you install Windows 2000. To partition hard disks after installation, use the Disk Management snap-in.

7. Setup displays the Windows 2000 Setup screen, showing the new partition as C: New (Unformatted).

8. Make sure the new partition is highlighted, and press Enter.

9. You are prompted to select a file system for the partition.

10. Use the arrow keys to select "Format the Partition Using the NTFS File System," and then press Enter. Remember, all drives should be NTFS. A drive can be converted after the fact from FAT to NTFS by using the CONVERT utility.

11. The Setup program formats the partition with NTFS. After it formats the partition, Setup examines the hard disk for physical errors that might cause Setup to fail and then copies files to the hard disk. This process will take several minutes.

12. Eventually, Setup displays the Windows 2000 Server Setup screen. A red status bar counts down for 15 seconds before Setup restarts the computer.

When the computer restarts, it will be running in a Windows interface—no more DOS! During this phase of the installation, the installation program is gathering information about the system. It will be:

1. Installing device drivers.

2. Setting regional settings.

3. Asking for user name and organization.

4. Asking for licensing mode (for a Web server it should be per-server).

5. Asking for computer name. This is the name the machine will be known by if it is on a network.

6. Asking for an administrator password. Passwords are a very important part of security! No matter what facilities are provided to secure a Web server, if the passwords are chosen poorly, the whole Web server can be compromised. Passwords should not be the same as your username, should not be "ABC" or "123." They should, however:

      a.   be at least seven characters long;

      b.   be mixed case and include letters, numbers, and symbols; and

      c.   have at least one symbol character in the second through sixth position.

7.   Asking for what components are to be installed. The following components need to be installed at a minimum; each one will be shown in detail:

      a.   Terminal Services. Terminal Services can be installed in *one* of two modes: Application or Administrator mode. Choose Administrator mode. More on this later.

      b.   Internet Information Services (IIS).

      c.   File Transfer Protocol (FTP).

      d.   Monitoring Tools.

      e.   Windows Media (if there is going to be any streaming media content).

After this has finished, installation of Windows 2000 itself is complete.

Connecting the development and server machines for testing

Before the server is moved to the data center, the development machine configured in Chapter 7 can be connected to the server configured in this chapter. It is a good idea to network them together in the office so you will understand all facets of communicating with the server before doing it remotely.

Assuming both the development machine and the server have NIC cards in them, the only other thing you need is a cross-over CAT5 cable. A source for cabling is **www.pcconnection.com**. When the two machines are directly connected, the development machine can see a site on the server by simply using the name of the server in the address line in the browser. For example, the application that we will develop later in the book would have an address like this: http://testserver/todo. In this example, TESTSERVER is the name given to the server machine, and TODO is a Web site on that box. The networking is automatically taken care of by simply connecting them with the cross-over CAT5 cable. There will be a separate bonus chapter in electronic format that will cover how to set up a small network for Web Connection development.

Installing the Visual FoxPro Runtime

For the server environment, it is only necessary to install the Visual FoxPro Runtime libraries. If a command line environment is needed, which it often is for performing browsing and maintenance, the best solution is to use Randy Pearson's CODEBLOCK utility. CODEBLOCKCLASS is distributed with Web Connection in the "classes" subdirectory.

This is a pretty amazing piece of code. It allows for the execution of blocks of Visual FoxPro code without the need to compile it first. It basically macro-expands each line of code dynamically. This code is the heart of Web Connection's ability to interpret Web pages with embedded Visual FoxPro code. The Web page is converted into a TEXTMERGE document and run through CODEBLOCK. This process will be shown in detail in Chapter 10, "Getting in Tune: Overcoming Conceptual Hurdles." The interface to CODEBLOCK is shown in **Figure 2**. It provides a run-time command window whereby single lines or blocks of code can be entered and run.

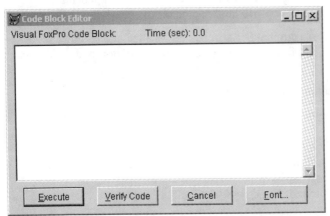

Figure 2. *The CODEBLOCK command window.*

The best way to package this for the server is to create a project with only CODEBLOCK as part of the project. Compile the project as an executable and use the Setup Wizard to create a set of distribution disks. **Figure 3** shows the CMDWINDOW project with the CODEBLOCKCLASS as the only program. This one EXE with the runtimes should fit on two 3.5" floppies. The details on doing this are:

1. Create a new project folder called CMDWINDOW. This folder will be the home directory of the CMDWINDOW project file.

2. Create a new project called CMDWINDOW by typing MODI PROJ CMDWINDOW.

3. Click on Add and navigate to the Web Connection CLASSES folder, and then select CODEBLOCKCLASS to add to the project. This will automatically become the main program in the project.

4. Click on Build and choose Win32 Executable/COM Server.

5. Click OK.

6. Build the EXE to the same directory.

7. When completed, type DO CMDWINDOW in the command window and the form shown in Figure 2 will appear.

8. Then, if you are using Visual FoxPro 6, the Setup Wizard can be used to create the distribution disks. If you are using Visual FoxPro 7, there is a special version of InstallShield that is being distributed in the Visual FoxPro 7 box.

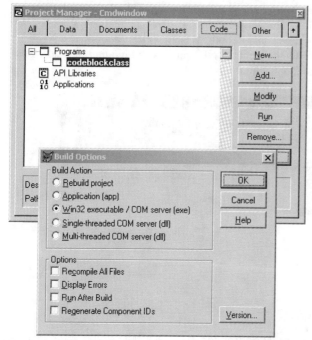

Figure 3*. Project to create a command window for the server.*

Setting up Internet Information Server (IIS)

The installation of IIS on Windows 2000 Server is taken care of when the main OS is installed. It is ready to go right away. Setting up Web sites is also very similar to setting up sites on Windows 2000 Professional. The main difference is that all the sites on Professional are set up as virtual sites off the WWWROOT directory. This is because Professional can only have one IP address bound to the machine. On Server, multiple IPs can be used and can be assigned to their own Web sites. This way there is no sharing of IP's between the sites.

Binding IP addresses to the server

Before a Web site can be set up, IP addresses have to be assigned to the server. The hosting company where the server is located will be able to provide the IP addresses. There is a charge for IP addresses, but it is reasonable. Also, depending on the level of service that you've paid for, the hosting company might configure the server with the necessary IPs. If simple co-location is being done, however, it will be up to the customer to set up the addresses.

If the server is being built and tested in an office first, it can utilize IP addresses from the "private" IP address space. These IP addresses are meant to be used strictly on internal networks. The ranges are 10.0.0.0 to 1.0.255.255.255, 172.16.0.0 to 172.31.255.255, and 192.168.0.0 to 192.168.255.255. These addresses can be bound to the NIC card while the machine is on a private LAN. These numbers can be used for the Web site being built, and when the server is moved into a data center, the public IP addresses can be used and bound to the site. The private IP addresses, though, are very useful for testing. This topic will be covered in detail in the bonus networking chapter mentioned earlier.

When IP addresses are added to a server, the IP addresses are being "bound" to a NIC card in the server. The first step then is to choose what NIC card we are binding the addresses to. Here are the steps to bind the IPs to the machine:

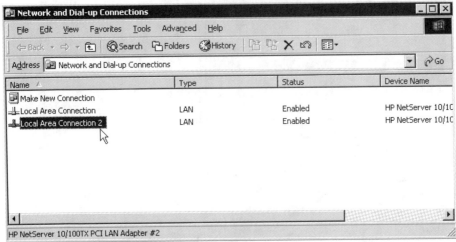

Figure 4. Selection of the NIC card for IP addresses.

1. Click on Start | Settings | Network and Dial Up Connections Settings. As in **Figure 4**, there will be a listing of the NIC cards in the machine as Local Area Connection x. As discussed in Chapter 7, it is a good idea to have more than one NIC card in a server. One will be for Internet access, and the other would typically be for backups to an in-house tape library. In this example, Local Area Connection 2 is the Internet NIC card.

2. Double-click on the NIC card, and a summary dialog box appears for the card. If you have more than one protocol installed, select "Internet Protocol (TCP/IP)." Make sure the check box is checked, and then click on the Properties button to bring up the dialog shown in **Figure 5**. This is where the addresses to the DNS servers and primary routers are kept. These two devices were discussed in Chapter 5, "How the Internet Works." Storing the address of the DNS server and primary router here is how the server knows to connect itself to the outside world. When you are directly connected to the Web, the first radio button set would be "Use the following IP address." The IP address supplied in the next box is the primary address of the server. "Subnet mask" allows for the creation of "subnetworks" within the data center. Servers that are on the same subnet can communicate without going through the main routers. If not on a subnet, the value of this would be 255.255.255.0 for a class C address. "Default gateway" is the address of the main router. This would be the router used to start the process of locating another server on the Web, as discussed in Chapter 5. The next two boxes hold the addresses of the primary and secondary DNS

servers. These servers perform the function of converting an address such as www.yourdomain.com into an IP address. When this is complete, the router with the address specified in "Default gateway" takes over and locates the target server with the newly resolved IP address.

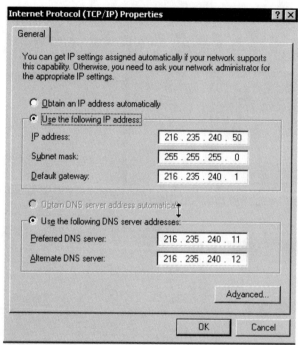

Figure 5*. TCP/IP properties for the NIC card.*

3. To enter more than one IP address, click on the Advanced button. This allows for the entry of multiple addresses for servers that will house multiple sites. This dialog is shown in **Figure 6**. The list box shows all current IP addresses. To add additional addresses, click on the Add button.

4. On the bottom of the dialog in Figure 6 are the default gateways or routers. Multiple gateways can be added here as well.

5. On the DNS tab, multiple DNS servers can be added (see **Figure 7**). It is important that there be more than one DNS server listed here. If the first DNS server becomes unavailable, the second one will be used. Ideally, they should also be in separate facilities and on separate networks. If they are on the same network and the network goes down, having a backup DNS server will be of no use! The hosting company will provide the addresses of the DNS servers.

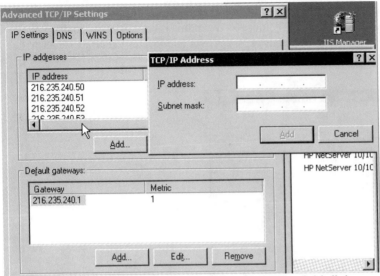

Figure 6. *Listing of the server's IP address and the Add dialog.*

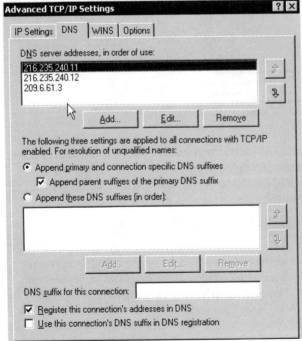

Figure 7. *DNS server addresses.*

Creating a new Web site

When creating a new Web site in Windows 2000 Server, the main difference is the availability of more than one IP address. When creating a new site, the directory must already exist. So before beginning these steps, make sure the directory structure shown in **Figure 8** already exists on disk.

Figure 8. The directory structure for the "TODO" application.

Then follow these steps to create a new site:

1. Launch the IIS Management Console via Start | Programs | Administrative Tools | Internet Services Manager.

2. At the top of the tree control on the left portion of the screen, click on the name of the server.

3. Right-click and choose New | Web Site.

4. A wizard will start, which walks through some basic steps.

5. The first step asks for the name of the site. For this example, we will name it "TODO." The sample application that will be developed in Chapter 11, "Managing Your Configuration," will be the "TODO" task management system.

6. Next, the wizard asks for the IP address for the site (see **Figure 9**). The IPs that appear in the drop-down were the ones entered in the previous steps showing how to bind IP addresses to the server. The SSL port for this Web site will be grayed out unless there is an SSL certificate installed on the server.

7. Next, the physical location on disk needs to be entered. The directory must already exist on disk. There is no way to create the directory from inside the wizard. Keep in mind the issues discussed in Chapter 7. The drive that will hold the HTML content should be on a different drive from the application and data if possible.

8. The final step is to set basic permissions for the site. The default permissions as seen in **Figure 10** are to Read and Run scripts. It is not a good idea to give Execute permissions on the root. This directory on most Web sites allows anonymous access, and keeping this directory as locked down as possible is mandatory. Any executables including the Web Connection DLL file should be in a separate "scripts" directory where the appropriate rights can be set. Write access should never be allowed in the root, and no one should be able to get directory listings, so Browse should also be turned off.

9. Click Next to complete the wizard and create the new site.

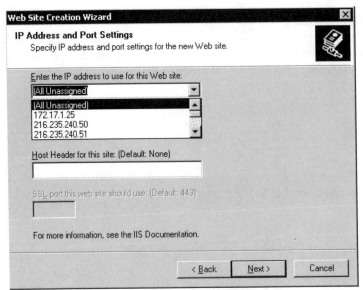

Figure 9. Choosing an IP for the new Web site.

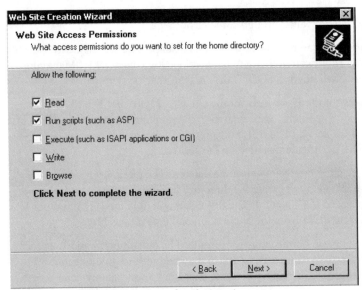

Figure 10. Site permissions for the root.

Setting Web site permissions

While the site's root directory requires anonymous access, the directories "scripts" and "admin" require some special permissions. For the "scripts" subdirectory, Execute rights need to be set so that the Web Connection DLL file can be executed. Doing this is straightforward:

1. Launch the IIS Management Console via Start | Programs | Administrative Tools | Internet Services Manager.

2. Using the tree control on the left side of the Manager, select the "scripts" directory below the "TODO" home. Right-click and choose Properties. Set the "Execute Permissions" to "Scripts and Executables" and click on OK.

3. Securing the "admin" directory requires a couple more steps. The "admin" directory is where the Web Connection administration page (admin.asp) and any application-level administration pages will live. The admin.asp page administers the Web Connection COM servers, while any application-level admin page would provide functions like performing backups, special back-end query forms, debugging links, reports for management, and so forth. This type of functionality should not be exposed by anonymous access! Settings need to be changed on the Web server and in the server's file system. The first thing you need to do is to disallow anonymous access to the "admin" directory. Disallowing anonymous access forces the Web server to send a password dialog to the client browser. The user will need to provide a valid username and password that has been set up to allow access to that particular directory on the server. It only needs to be entered once by that browser instance. All subsequent requests from that browser will append the authentication information to that request so no further dialogs will appear. With Web Connection, there is additional security that should be added. In the WC.INI file, there is an "AdminAccount" setting that checks that every Web Connection administration request is authenticated. This makes sure a malicious user cannot directly type in a Web Connection administration link. In Chapter 11, the configuration of the INI files is covered in detail.

4. In the IIS tree control, select the "admin" directory under "TODO" root.

5. Right-click and choose Properties. Click on the Directory Security tab, and then click on the Edit button for "Anonymous Access and Authentication Control." The dialog shown in **Figure 11** appears.

6. Uncheck the "Anonymous access" check box and check off "Basic authentication." A dialog will appear warning that with basic authentication enabled, the passwords will be transmitted in clear text and could be intercepted. If this is perceived to be a major risk, an SSL certificate for the site would encrypt all traffic from and to the server and client. Integrated Windows authentication only works with IE browsers and does not work through HTTP proxy servers. This is really best left for intranet environments where these factors can be controlled. Leaving this checked is okay here. Examples of the kind of back-end admin pages that can be used will be discussed in Chapter 12, "A Web Connection Application from Start to Finish." Click OK three times to save, and now anonymous access has been removed for the "admin" directory.

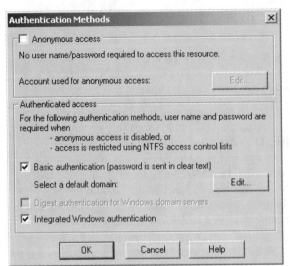

Figure 11. *Turning off anonymous access to the "admin" directory.*

Setting directory-level permissions

Now the Web site permissions have to be coordinated with NTFS permissions in the directory where these admin pages reside. First create a user account that is designed to be the administrator account for that site:

1. On the server select Start | Programs | Administrative Tools | Computer Management, and when the tree control for Computer Management appears, select Users.

2. Right-click and select New User. Supply an admin account name for the site, such as "todoadmin." When supplying a password, make it a strong password as described in the beginning of this chapter. Just check off "Password never expires" for this account. When the user is created by clicking on Create, it now appears on the right side in the list of all users.

3. Select this new user from the complete list, right-click, and select Properties. Click on "Member of" and add the local "Administrators" group to the list.

Now we are going to take this new user and change the directory permissions for the "admin" directory so it only allows this user to log in.

1. Using Windows Explorer, navigate to the "admin" directory under the new "TODO" site. Right-click and select Properties. Then click on the Security tab. The dialog in **Figure 12** appears.

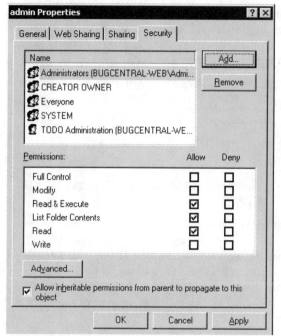

Figure 12*. Setting directory-level access permissions. (Change!)*

2. Initially the "Everyone" group appears in the list. Make sure this group is removed! In order to remove the Everyone group, uncheck "Allow inheritable permissions from parent to propagate to this object." Then select the Everyone group and click on Remove as shown in Figure 12. "Administrators" and "System" should be left in the list. The only other user that really needs to be in here is the new "todoadmin" user. To do this, simply click on the Add button, scroll down the user list, and double-click on the "todoadmin" user. This user can have "Full Control." Then click OK to save.

Now when an admin user navigates to the admin.asp file that will reside in this directory, they will be prompted with a username and password dialog. If the username and password entered match the information supplied earlier, the admin.asp page will be displayed. Any other access to files in that directory will not require re-entering the username and password. The browser remembers this information and sends it to the server on each submission. There are some additional security settings that can be set in the WC.DLL file that resides in the "scripts" subdirectory. These will be covered in Chapter 12.

Setting up FTP access

File Transfer Protocol (FTP) is the means by which HTML content, new EXEs, and Visual FoxPro data will be transferred to the server. When Windows 2000 Server is installed, it is important that FTP services be installed too. There are many FTP clients available on the Web. Microsoft Internet Explorer version 5 and greater even provides reasonable FTP client services. Here I will discuss WS-FTP. Some HTML authoring tools have an FTP client built into the product such as Adobe's GoLive or the HTML-KIT authoring tool used in this book. Before these can be used, however, the server must be configured to accept FTP connections. Configuring FTP is easier than setting up a regular Web site:

1. Launch the IIS Management Console via Start | Programs | Administrative Tools | Internet Services Manager.

2. At the top of the tree control on the left portion of the screen, click on the name of the server.

3. Right-click and choose New | FTP Site.

4. A wizard launches and walks through the process. The first step is to name the FTP site. Supply a name such as "TODO-FTP." Click Next.

5. Next, it prompts for the IP address that will be used for the FTP site. The IP address that was used for the Web site can be used here for the FTP site. The same IP address can be used since the Web site goes through port 80 and the FTP site goes through port 21. This is analogous to there being one address for a house, but multiple doors to enter the house by. You can enter the house at 12 Main St. by going in either the front door (port 80) or the back door (port 21). Each will get you to a different room at the same street address (IP address).

6. Next, it prompts for the physical directory on the server that you want the FTP site to be associated with. This will be the location where files are sent when the FTP client connects. In this example, it would be \inetpub\wwwroot\todo for the HTML content.

7. Next it prompts for basic permissions. Should it have Read and Write? Since the purpose of FTP for the most part is to transfer files back and forth, both of these should be checked.

8. When this is done, the FTP site is created. It will be listed in the IIS tree control in the top portion of the list and is represented by a folder icon.

FTP permissions

The default permissions for the Web site created earlier had anonymous access. However, FTP sites are different! The setting for FTP sites should *not* allow anonymous access. FTP sites are notorious for being hijacked by hackers and used to store pirated software and porn. Unless the FTP site is being monitored closely for traffic levels, this can go unnoticed for a long time. So the next step is to turn off anonymous access:

1. Select the FTP site in the IIS tree control.

2. Right-click and choose Properties. The tabbed property sheet will appear for the site. On the first page, make sure that logging is turned on. This will record all activity to the site.

3.   Click on the Security Accounts tab. De-select "Allow Anonymous Access." This will only allow users with accounts on the server to connect with their FTP client. Save these changes by clicking on OK.

Virtual FTP directories

The site created previously can be used to transfer HTML content to the Web site. However, in order to use the same connection to transfer Visual FoxPro data, a "virtual" site can be created off of the main FTP site. This way, the FTP client can connect using the same connection, but can access the virtual directory by specifying the virtual directory name. This is an important part of getting files transferred, so here are the steps:

1.   Select the FTP site created earlier in the IIS tree control.

2.   Right-click and choose New | Virtual Directory.

3.   In the first wizard step, supply an alias for the virtual site. In this example, "todoapp" will be used.

4.   Next, supply the path to the application's home directory. If the application's root directory is used, the FTP client will be able to navigate to any of the subdirectories as well, including the data and EXE update directory we'll cover later. So for this directory it could be \vfpapps\todo\.

5.   Next, supply the basic permissions. In this case, allow both Read and Write permissions. The site is now completed. Click on Finish, and the virtual site is created. You will see how to use the FTP client to update content in Chapter 12.

Securing your Web server

Security is one of the most important aspects of running a Web site. The only way people will do business with the site is if they believe the site keeps any personal and financial information secure. This is largely about perception. In everyday life, people give away credit card and personal information to total strangers in order to conduct business. When handing over a credit card at a gas station or telling an operator your credit card information over the phone, no one really knows what is happening to it. Traditional businesses have the advantage of many years of existence that has given people a sense of security. The Internet does not yet have that luxury.

Some security questions that need to be answered at a moment's notice are:

• Where are the tape backups stored?

• How quickly can the backups be restored on a different server?

• Who is allowed physical and remote access to the server?

Depending on your level of service, backups may not be a part of the package. Make sure you know exactly what to expect in this regard. If backups are done, where are they stored? Many data centers have their own on-site vault to store backups. Once a month they may be moved off-site to a secure facility like Iron Mountain. If the computer is broken into and all data is destroyed, how quickly can the remote and local copies be retrieved? You need to know the answers to these questions before there is a problem. Some other points to keep in mind are:

- When setting up user accounts, make sure that all users have their own usernames! If everyone shares an account, there is no real auditing taking place. If there is any question as to who had access to a machine, you must be able to have separate accounts to track activity. Whether you are utilizing managed services or are co-locating, make sure the Event Log is being examined for possible hacker attacks. A hacker attack will appear in the logs as repeated attempts by an account every couple of seconds. There are monitoring tools by companies like Internet Security Systems that can monitor for hacker attacks by looking for common tactics hackers use. When these are identified, it is possible to back-track to find out where the hacker is located. It is then possible to deny access to the site based on the IP address of the attacker. It is then a good idea to notify the authorities. These break-ins are treated very seriously.

- If Telnet is not going to be used, disable it. If it will be used, create a special group called "TelNetClients" and assign to it only the people who really need access to this service. When this group exists, Telnet will only allow these people access to the service. To disable Telnet:

    1. Click on Start | Administrative Tools | Services.

    2. Select Telnet from the list of services.

    3. Right-click and select Properties.

    4. From the StartupType drop-down," select Disabled.

    5. Click on OK to save.

- Restrict access to directories. As discussed before, access to a site's "admin" directory should require authentication. If someone gets to the admin.asp file, they can cause problems. See Chapter 11 for information about setting additional security in the WC.INI file.

- Create directories for each file type on your site that needs protection and assign access rights to that directory, letting the file inherit the settings. Setting permissions at the file level can be impossible to maintain and error-prone.

- Make sure FTP sites do not allow anonymous access. There might be a case where customers have FTP privileges, but this is rare. If FTP privileges are needed, it typically would be to allow users to download information. So an account could be created to allow Read access but not Write access. Some reporting functionality might allow customers to download their data. These customers could have an account that allows downloads but prevents them from uploading files.

- Log all FTP activity so there are records.

- Delete all unnecessary script maps from IIS. The only ones that need to be active are the ones that are specific to the Web Connection application. Script maps are covered in detail in Chapter 12.

Some important things to be aware of

In this section I'll cover some important areas of IIS management. These areas will greatly help in keeping your site healthy and provide for a better user experience.

Auto-restart of IIS

One of the harsh realities of IIS is that every so often, it can get corrupted. This can appear in the form of the INETINFO.EXE process grabbing 100 percent of the CPU. When this happens, the site becomes completely unresponsive. Or the process can grab 50 percent of the processor and all CPU usage never drops below this. It becomes the new minimum. At this utilization, the site responds but is very slow. There is a little known utility in Windows 2000 called IISRESET.EXE. This can be used in place of re-booting the server itself. When this utility is used, IIS is restarted with all related services in a few seconds. The users really do not even know it happened. Windows 2000 is configured to use this utility automatically if IIS hangs. To see this, do the following:

1. Click Start | Programs | Administrative Tools | Services.

2. Locate the IIS Admin Services entry and double-click.

3. On the Properties tab, select Recovery.

4. This dialog tells Windows what to do if IIS fails. It should state to "Run a file." When this is chosen, the File text box is activated. It should point to C:\winnt\system32\iisreset.exe.

One thing you can do to gain easy access to this utility is create a desktop shortcut that points to it. From the desktop:

1. Right-click and select New | Shortcut.

2. Point to C:\winnt\system32\iisreset.exe.

3. Supply a name for the shortcut and click Finish.

A new desktop icon is created that will execute this EXE. Even when the CPU is 100 percent utilized, Terminal Services can still connect and will allow for this shortcut to be run. Once it is, utilization should drop down to 0. This also has the effect of reloading the Web Connection COM servers that will be built in Chapter 12.

Task Manager can quickly show what level the processor is running at. Task Manager is started by right-clicking on the task bar and choosing Task Manager. Click on the Performance tab to see a real-time graph of the performance.

Custom error messages

When surfing a site, there is nothing more annoying than seeing one of the standard Windows error messages for a missing page or access denied. The site administrator has complete control over what is displayed back to the user when these errors occur. On the property sheet for the site:

1. Launch the IIS Management Console via Start | Programs | Administrative Tools | Internet Services Manager.

2. Select the Web site (TODO).

3. Right-click and choose Properties.

4. Select the Custom Errors tab.

5. Scroll down the list and select error 404 (File not Found).

6. Click on "Edit Properties."

7. Leave "Message type" as File. You can also navigate to another URL or run a link to your application that can process this error in whatever way you wish, such as sending an advisory email to the administrator.

8. In the File text box, navigate to the HTM file that will serve to replace the default error message. If custom error messages are used, it is a good idea to create a subdirectory off the site root to hold the custom error pages. In this example, the page \inetpub\wwwroot\todo\cust_errors\err404.htm could be pointed to.

9. Click OK twice, and the custom error page is now in place.

10. To test, navigate to the site and point to a file that does not exist—this custom page will appear instead!

Using custom error messages really makes for a much more professional-looking site. These pages can utilize the look and feel of the rest of your site so that every page consistently uses the same logos and fonts.

Performance Monitor

Performance Monitor, or "perfmon," is a utility that allows administrators to spy on what is happening at a very low level in the server. Basically it allows an administrator to specify different "counters" to keep track of. One can track CPU utilization, disk utilization, CPU queue, page faults, and about 100 other server metrics. This is an advanced topic that would probably take an entire book; however, it does bear a discussion here. Depending on the level of service that was contracted for at the data center where your Web site is hosted, it may not be necessary to use perfmon to monitor your own server. Depending on the agreement, it may not be possible to even run perfmon if root-level or desktop access is not permitted. However, if you are co-locating, this utility can be run through Terminal Services.

If your solution is a fully managed service, the data center is most likely using a Simple Network Management Protocol (SNMP) tool like HP OpenView. These types of tools have two components, a manager and a client. The client resides on the server and monitors the server's resources and reports back to the manager component in the Network Operations Center (NOC). It allows the engineers to specify alerts for any process running on the machine. So if one of them passes or drops below some given threshold, the NOC is alerted or maybe even the service can be restarted automatically. For instance, in the case where IIS can use up 100 percent of the processor, OpenView can be set to monitor this and alert the staff when it happens. Another important data point to collect is available disk space. Disk space can be used very quickly if the site is active. Both the IIS logs and even Web Connection's WWSESSION table can consume a large amount of space. If drive space is used up, the site COM servers crash on every hit and make for a very nasty problem. OpenView can be configured to monitor disk space. If this is not available, the Web Connection application could also be set up to monitor disk space and notify admin personnel when space runs low. Some type of monitoring is necessary since on a live server, it is very difficult to free up disk space!

To configure perfmon:

1. Click on Start | Programs | Administrative Tools | Performance.

2. This launches the perfmon interface. The tree control on the left side of the screen shows the different parts of performance monitoring. The node called "System Monitor" is the main screen. It is here where the counters can be added and viewed on the real-time moving graph. The graph color-codes all chosen counters, and as each counter is selected in the listing, the line representing that item is highlighted in the graph.

3. Add counters by clicking on the plus sign (+) in the toolbar. The dialog shown in **Figure 13** appears.

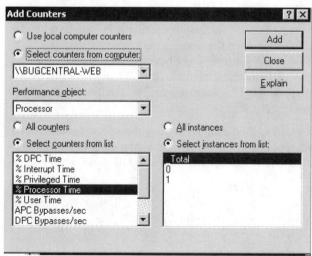

Figure 13. Adding counters into Performance Monitor.

4. Counters on computers other than the local machine can be selected. The "Performance object" drop-down selects what class of counters are to be looked at. Figure 13 shows the counters available under the Processor object. Some of the most important counters are:

   a. Processor: % Processor Time—This is the counter that IIS has been known to max out. If this is very high, but the NIC card and disk I/O is low, then there is a processor bottleneck.

   b. System: Processor Queue Length—This shows the number of threads waiting in line to be processed. If this counter has two or more threads always in the queue, there could be a bottleneck here too.

   c. Memory: Available Bytes—There should always be around 10 percent of memory free for peak usage.

   d. Network Interface: Bytes Total/sec—This counter displays the amount of bandwidth being squeezed through the NIC card. Check to make sure the numbers being reported here are not the maximum amount that the card can handle. There needs to be some headroom for peak times.

   e. Physical Disk: % Disk Time—If this counter is high, but the processor and NIC traffic is low, the drives could be causing a bottleneck. Even if every page is being cached, there is still disk activity to write the IIS logs to disk. To optimize disk usage, turn off logging for those directories that do not need it. For example, the images directory does not really need to be logged. Using the IIS Manager, select the images directory using the tree control, right-click, and bring up its property sheet. Uncheck "Log visits" for this directory and save changes.

   f. Process: Private Bytes—One very interesting counter is Private Bytes under the Process group. This reports on the memory allocated to a specific running process. If a process is suspected of having a memory leak, the Private Bytes value would gradually increase. See "Finding Leaks in COM Objects with Perfmon" in the "Chapter resources" section for an interesting discussion on this topic.

5. After selecting counters, the graph will be updated to show the selected counters. To enable highlighting of the selected counter in the list, click on the lightbulb icon in the toolbar. **Figure 14** shows what a populated perfmon looks like.

6. The current perfmon counters can be saved to a file so they do not have to be selected each time. Simply select Console | Save as. The file will be saved in the WINNT\System32 directory with an MSC extension by default. It is best then to create a desktop shortcut to this file so perfmon can be easily launched with all necessary counters in place.

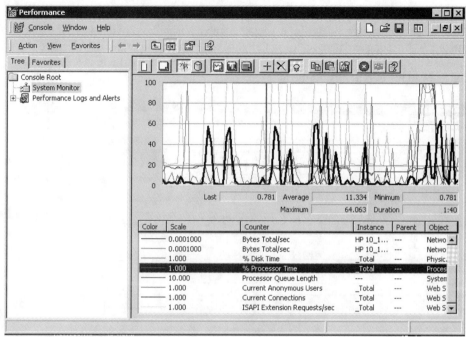

Figure 14*. Performance Monitor.*

7. Alerts can also be set for any counter. When alerts are defined, the "Performance Logs and Alerts" service is turned on in Windows 2000 and the Perfmon GUI does not have to be active. Alerts can write the event to the Event Log, send a network message, start recording performance data, or run a program.

    a.   Expand "Performance Logs and Alerts" node.

    b.   Select and right-click on "Alerts."

    c.   Select "New Alert Settings."

    d.   Enter a name for your settings.

    e.   From the General tab, click on the Add button to select a counter to monitor.

    f.   Decide what level is to be monitored and whether the check is over or under this value (for example, Processor Utilization over 90%).

    g.   Click on the Action tab and decide on a course of action when an alert is reached.

Visual FoxPro utilities

These utilities are essentially mandatory for the proper administration of any Web Connection site. There are a number of tools that provide similar functionality, but the ones discussed here, while not an endorsement, have been shown to do an excellent job.

DIRT, or Database Index Repair Tool (DIRT.EXE)

This utility is used to manage index files associated with a Visual FoxPro database container (see **Figure 15**). It reads the database, logs in all indexes, relationships, and RI rules into a meta database of its own. This way, if the index files become corrupted, there is an external reference that can be used to rebuild the indexes.

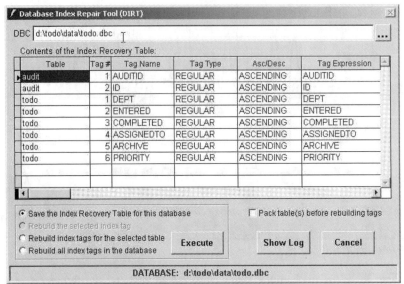

Figure 15. *Database Index Repair Tool (DIRT)*.

This utility or one like it should be used to re-create the index tags, ideally, about once every couple of weeks. This tool will drop the existing indexes and rebuild them from scratch. Simply performing a REINDEX on a table will not fully optimize the index file. Also, if the index is corrupted, REINDEX may not fix the problem.

Recover

Recover, from Abri Technologies (**www.abri.com**), can be an absolute lifesaver. There can be some rather troublesome corruption problems with Visual FoxPro tables that use memo fields. One form of corruption will cause the Visual FoxPro COM server to terminate with no errors when the corrupt portion of the table is traversed. When this happens, not even Dr. Watson is triggered; the Visual FoxPro process simply goes away. This can be an extremely difficult problem to track down. This type of error cannot even be caught by the normal ON ERROR routines, either. If all of a sudden there are a great many COM server restarts happening, this might be the problem. Since it can happen only when a certain area of a table is accessed, the table may look and behave properly most of the time. Also, there is the more common error stating, "Memo file is missing or invalid." When Recover is run, it will analyze the table header for problems and for tables with memo files, scan the link between the table and memo file, and determine whether there are any corrupt pointers between the two. It will report on the errors and correct them. **Figure 16** shows the Recover interface.

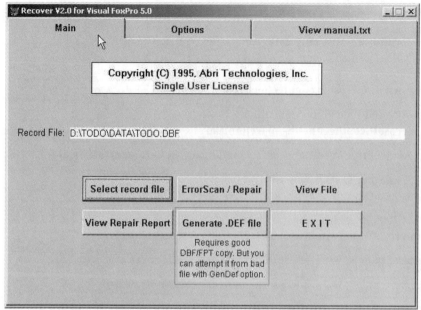

Figure 16. The Recover utility from Abri Technologies.

The Generate .DEF file option should be run before there are problems with the tables. This is a meta file that holds information on the structure of the table. Similar to indexes, if a table gets corrupted, it may be impossible to recover the table with no external information.

The full version of Recover can be used from within an application to check for corruption automatically. For instance, whenever the Web Connection application starts up, it may be a good idea to scan the tables for possible corruption. Recover needs exclusive use of the tables, so during startup is a good time to do it. It can recover memo fields automatically, and it then writes the results to a log file. If any corruption occurred, an email could be sent automatically to an admin person to make them aware of the problem.

Conclusion

In this chapter, I covered many topics that are new to most Visual FoxPro developers. The setup and configuration of a Web server can be another world. Even if you decide to go with complete management in a data center, it is still very important to be aware of all aspects of server configuration if for no other reason than to make sure the hosting company is doing it right! With the cost, however, of a fully managed solution, most developers and site managers would probably go with a co-location solution. In this case, all server management is left up to the customer. In order to fulfill the illusion of "location independence" with regard to content, the server needs to be stable and secure. With the topics covered in this chapter, along with the chapter resources listed next, the job of building a solid server will be significantly easier.

Chapter resources

- **www.webconnectiontraining.com**: Author-run training site. Updates to code and training videos available here.

- Logging: **www.microsoft.com/technet/ecommerce/LogCandA.asp**

- Performance and Reliability Monitoring: **www.microsoft.com/technet/iis/prfrelmn.asp**

- Setting Alerts: **http://msdn.microsoft.com/library/techart/smartalerts.htm**

- Finding Leaks in COM Objects with Perfmon: **http://msdn.microsoft.com/library/techart/perfmon.htm**

- Windows 2000 Resource Kits: **www.microsoft.com/windows2000/techinfo/reskit/default.asp**

- IIS Restart Features: **www.microsoft.com/technet/iis/restart.asp**

- Web Server Tuning: **www.microsoft.com/technet/iis/iis5tune.asp**

- IIS Exception Monitor: **www.microsoft.com/technet/iis/tools/ixcptmon.asp**

- Creating User and Group Accounts: **www.microsoft.com/technet/win2000/win2ksrv/crusegrp.asp**

- Custom IIS Error Messages: **www.microsoft.com/technet/iis/custerr.asp**

- IIS Security Checklist: **www.microsoft.com/technet/security/iis5chk.asp**

- Inside the Registry: **www.microsoft.com/technet/winnt/inreg.asp**

- HP Openview, Server Monitoring Tool: **www.hp.com/ovw/**

- Recover Table/Memo Recovery Utility: **www.abri.com**

- Database Index Repair Tool (DIRT): Available in the Download area of **www.universalthread.com**.

- Internet Security Systems: **www.iss.net/**

- Simple Network Management Protocol (SMTP): **www.rad.com/networks/1995/snmp/snmp.htm**

Chapter 9
How a Web Page Works

The language used on a Web page is HyperText Markup Language, or HTML. Hypertext is the part of the Web that allows for the linking together of Web content through the use of clickable "hyperlinks." The markup language defines the document form. Remember back in grade school getting an essay back, "marked up" with symbols stating that an item should be capitalized, or a new paragraph should begin here? Well, that is pretty much what HTML does for a Web page. In this chapter I will cover what makes up a well formed Web page, what the different sections are, how to use JavaScript for form validations, and how Web Connection can process a page that contains embedded expressions.

HTML is yet another technology that new Web developers need to understand. When developing Visual FoxPro forms using the form designer, developers had the luxury of a fully object-oriented design surface that was seamlessly integrated with the data engine. It was possible to simply drag and drop fields from a table onto the form and have the resulting text box bound to the data field. When designing an HTML form, there is no integration between the form objects and the data engine. Also, there are no object-oriented form objects in HTML. In Visual FoxPro, developers had the easy life. It was possible to create class libraries of the base form objects, give them custom looks and behaviors, and make full use of inheritance to allow for easy maintenance. In HTML, the closest thing to inheritance is Cascading Style Sheets, or CSS. CSS is what brings uniformity and easy site maintenance to Web development. Web pages should not be designed without them!

In this chapter, I will use the HTML-Kit authoring tool from Chamai Software. It is a free tool, easy to use, and very well supported. See the "Chapter resources" section for the download site. The forms that will be used to build the "TODO" application in Chapter 12, "A Web Connection Application from Start to Finish," will be dealt with in detail here. These forms are simple but utilize most of the principals needed to build complex forms using HTML and Web Connection.

A brief history of HTML

Tim Berners Lee developed HTML in the early 1990s. Mr. Lee was the inventor of the World Wide Web as we know it today. HTML was born out of the need at the CERN High Energy Research Labs in Europe to tie together the documents from researchers from all over the world. The scientists and engineers brought their own machines and software, and trying to get them to communicate was a difficult task. HTML was developed as a standard document format that could be used over the existing network protocols.

HTML was based on SGML, or the Standard Generalized Markup Language, which had been in use for some time already. SGML had already been using "tags," or instructions enclosed in "<>" angle brackets, to denote the form of the document. Mr. Lee made every effort to keep the form of HTML very similar since people were already familiar with the syntax of SGML. As it turned out, this syntax choice also made it very easy for humans to read and understand the code that made up a Web page. As you'll see, the various tags that make up a Web page give the document structure. In other words, HTML tags are to a Web page what steel beams are to a building. They provide the structure, but they do not necessarily determine the outward appearance. Cascading Style Sheets determine the appearance of a Web page, like a façade determines a building's appearance. Structure and appearance need to be separated, as we shall see.

The editor interface

The HTML editor that will be used in this chapter is HTML-Kit from Chami Software (see the "Chapter resources" section). There are many HTML authoring tools available, such as Adobe's GoLive and Macromedia's Dreamweaver. Dreamweaver is a very sophisticated authoring tool with some great features. It would be beyond the scope of this book, however, to get into using a tool like Dreamweaver. HTML-Kit is a highly glorified "Notepad" editor that provides preview ability and some great add-on utilities (see **Figure 1**). Its menu system allows for the insertion of all of the HTML elements as well as Cascading Style Sheet attributes. So instead of having to type in all the HTML tags, you can select and insert them from the menu system. There is also an integrated FTP client to make it simple to upload the files to the production server. For easy viewing of the HTML code used in this chapter's examples, HTML-Kit is a great choice. It is easy to use and makes it easy for beginners to learn their way around an HTML document.

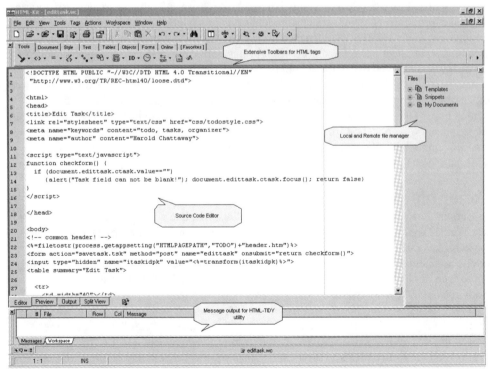

Figure 1. The HTML-Kit authoring tool interface.

However, for more advanced site management and HTML authoring ability, Macromedia's Dreamweaver is an excellent choice. Dreamweaver has an extensible development environment, very much like Visual FoxPro's. It has an integrated JavaScript interpreter that can be used to interact with the Web page under development similar to the way Builders in Visual FoxPro can interact with a Visual FoxPro form in the forms designer. One of its most powerful features is its template technology. Unlike templates in HTML-Kit and virtually every other tool, Dreamweaver's templates provide the ability to create a "baseclass" form. When this base template is updated, all pages that are based on this template are updated too! This makes for greatly simplified site management. Though it is not a base class in the same sense as a real object-oriented base class, it provides basically the same benefit.

The Tools tab in HTML-Kit along the top of the editor is used to gain access to different categories of HTML tags. Under the Forms tab are all the form object tags. You can insert textboxes, dropdowns, and list boxes from here. The Preview tab allows you to see the page rendered in a browser. This is not a WYSIWYG editor, so it is necessary to switch back and forth between the Editor and Preview tabs. Remember that this will not correctly evaluate the embedded ASP tags in the page. Previewing does not cause the page to be evaluated by your Web Connection application!

On the right side of the editor is the File interface. This allows you to specify local directories within the editor for easy access to your files. You can also specify FTP sites to make it easy to drag and drop files from your local machine to a production server.

An important step in validating Web pages is to validate them against the HTML standards. You can easily do this in HTML-Kit by choosing Tools | Check Code Using TIDY from the main menu. This will find any errors in the HTML code that doe not adhere to the standards for the version of HTML used in the Web page. The standard that the TIDY utility will apply to the page is specified by the DOCTYPE definition at the top of the Web page. This is described in detail later.

The example "TODO" application

The example used in this chapter and described in detail in Chapter 12 is a task management system called "TODO." This is a simple but very useful application that will be used to illustrate many of the key features of Web Connection and Web development in general. This chapter will focus on how the Web pages are constructed and how a developer can improve the user experience. The application allows users to enter tasks, assign them to others, and assign status and priority. Reports can be run that list all tasks for ADMIN users or tasks filtered only to the current user. Once the task is completed, "Date Complete" and "Solution" can be filled in. While many sample applications do not have a practical application, this one could be installed either locally or on an intranet and serve a very useful purpose.

Different techniques for generating a page

There are three different techniques a developer can use to generate a Web page using Web Connection:

1. *Templates:* Templates in Web Connection are pages that contain both HTML markup tags and Active Server Pages (<%=%>) style expressions that contain any valid

Visual FoxPro expression. Templates are used in the TODO application. The first page described in this chapter is a template page. The location on disk for templates is referenced by the HTMLPAGEPATH entry in the application's INI file. There could be another custom entry made to point to the location on disk where the templates are stored. For example, the HTMLPAGEPATH setting could be used for static HTML pages that require no processing by Web Connection. Then there could be another custom setting called SCRIPTPAGEPATH that is the path to the directory holding dynamic pages such as scripts and templates. These templates do not have to be stored in the Web site's root directory with the regular HTML pages. Since these pages are first read and parsed by Visual FoxPro and Web Connection, they can be stored in any directory the developer sees fit. The Web site root directory is a valid place to store them, but they do not have to be there. For the examples shown in this book, static and dynamic pages will reside in the same directory. One advantage to using templates is that you can make updates to Web pages by simply FTPing a new page to the site. A new Web Connection EXE does not have to be uploaded. File extensions are usually not .HTM. An extension of either .WC or .WCT can be used to identify it as a Web Connection template page.

2. *Scripts:* Scripts are Web pages that contain HTML tags as well as Visual FoxPro code blocks. TASKLIST.WCS is an example of a script page. An example of a use for scripts is where an HTML table is laid out in a Web page editor. The HTML table will represent rows of a Visual FoxPro cursor. In order to have the HTML table rows repeated for each cursor row, those tags are wrapped in a SCAN/ENDSCAN loop. Any Visual FoxPro language construct can be included on a Web page by enclosing it in <% %> delimiters. This technique is described in greater depth in Chapters 10 and 12. The location of these files follows the same rules as described for templates. Here, like templates, if a change is needed the new page simply has to be FTPed up to the server. For script pages, the extension is usually .WCS.

3. *Generating pages from Visual FoxPro:* In some cases it may be necessary and easier to generate Web pages manually from within a Web Connection application. This works best for simple pages. Using templates or scripts that are laid out using an HTML authoring tool and then modified to contain ASP expressions is generally the easiest way to develop a site. Some developers have laid out pages in FrontPage, for example, and then cut and pasted each of line of code into their Web Connection application using the WRITE() or WRITELN() function to output each line individually. This approach is very cumbersome and breaks the link between the HTML authoring tool and the HTML code. Also, if any changes are needed to the generated page, a new EXE must be uploaded and swapped out with the old EXE.

It is generally best to use the tool most appropriate for the underlying language. Visual FoxPro is not an editor for HTML, and an HTML authoring tool is not the best editor for Visual FoxPro. With this in mind, templates fit this rule the best. Scripts are a great technique to use when necessary as long as a lot of Visual FoxPro code is not embedded in the Web page.

The TODO sample application

In this book, a sample "TODO" application is used to illustrate how to use Web Connection. It is a task management application that can be used to record your daily checklist of activities. It consists of a main task list, which is a simple listing of all tasks you have entered. Each one contains a hyperlink to a page showing the detail of that task. Entries can be added with a description of what the task is, whom it is assigned to, and when it is due. The task list can be filtered to show only your tasks or everyone's. This application is included with this book's source code, available at **www.hentzenwerke.com**, and can be used however you like.

How is this Web page rendered?

The Web page shown in **Figure 2** is displayed when the user clicks on a particular TODO item in the main listing. This is the rendered version of the EDITTASK.WC file that is stored on the Web server. The method EDITTASK is executed in the CLASS_TSK file. It is described in detail in Chapter 12, but briefly this translates to the link http://localhost/todo/edittask.tsk?id =1000. This method then performs a query and pulls out the record in the TODO table with a primary key of 1000. Then the EDITTASK method calls the Web Connection framework method EXPANDTEMPLATE() with the following line:

```
response.expandtemplate(PROCESS.cHTMLPAGEPATH+"edittask.wc",loHeader)
```

Web Connection then opens up the file EDITTASK.WC on disk and begins the parsing process. It is looking for ASP tags like <% %>. ASP is a technology, not a language. Any language can be utilized inside of these delimeters. When using Web Connection to parse a template, the language inside these delimeters will be Visual FoxPro.

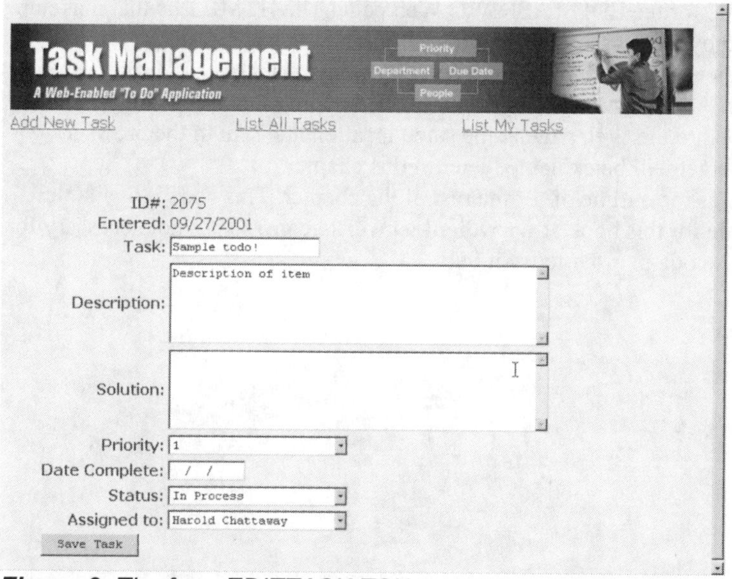

Figure 2. The form EDITTASK.TSK.

Any expression contained within the <% %> delimeters is evaluated and the result is inserted back into that location. The only requirement is that the result of the expression be a character string. The resulting page is what is then sent to the browser to be rendered. All of the ASP-style tags are evaluated on the server! The expression can consist of a simple in-line statement such as <%=date()%> or can be a call to a 1000-line method. There is really no limit to what can be done with these expressions. The ASP tags serve as a window into the entire Visual FoxPro language. The expression has access to any value currently in scope at the time of evaluation. So after the server gets done evaluating all of these expressions on the page, the hard-coded HTML page is then sent back to the browser that requested it. The browser reads in the HTML page and does some parsing of its own. It determines what objects (text boxes, dropdowns, text areas) are going to be used and displays the visual representation of these in the browser. It evaluates any JavaScript that may need to be run as the page is loading. It also determines whether there are any external links to this page like GIF or JPG images. If there are any references to such files, it opens up another channel and sends a request to the server to retrieve it. So after all the parsing, validating, and link resolution is complete, you should be looking at a fully formed Web page. As you can imagine, there is a lot of work that goes on to fully render a page. And still a great deal of the transmitting is done over dial-up modem connections that run no faster than about 56K.

It is a good idea to keep your audience in mind. If your Web page is targeted to users sitting at home, it would be best to keep the pages very "lite"—low on graphics. If your user base is mostly a commercial crowd sitting on fast fiber connections, you may have some more leeway.

What makes up a Web page?

To understand what makes up a Web page, let's take a look at the "TODO" data entry form that is part of the application that will be developed in Chapter 12. The HTML shown in **Figure 3** is the source code for the EDITTASK.WC Web page. The HTML tags that make up a Web page are processed by a browser. It is the browser's job to correctly interpret the HTML tags and display them on a Web page. The ASP-style tags that contain Visual FoxPro expressions are processed on the server. When the embedded expression is evaluated, the resulting string is inserted into the Web page at the same location and sent to the browser. How these two pieces interact will be explained later in this chapter.

 Figure 3 will serve as the outline of for the rest of the chapter. This code is available with the source code for this book at **www.hentzenwerke.com**, so it's not necessary for you to re-create this code in order to try it out.

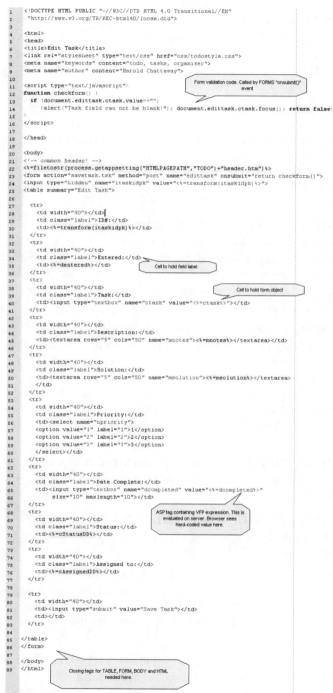

```
1   <!DOCTYPE HTML PUBLIC "-//W3C//DTD HTML 4.0 Transitional//EN"
2     "http://www.w3.org/TR/REC-html140/loose.dtd">
3
4   <html>
5   <head>
6   <title>Edit Task</title>
7   <link rel="stylesheet" type="text/css" href="css/todostyle.css">
8   <meta name="keywords" content="todo, tasks, organizer">
9   <meta name="author" content="Harold Chattaway">
10
11  <script type="text/javascript">
12  function checkform() {
13    if (document.edittask.ctask.value=="")
14      {alert("Task field can not be blank!"); document.edittask.ctask.focus(); return false)
15  }
16  </script>
17
18  </head>
19
20  <body>
21  <!-- common header! -->
22  <%=filetostr(process.getappsetting("HTMLPAGEPATH","TODO")+"header.htm")%>
23  <form action="savetask.tsk" method="post" name="edittask" onsubmit="return checkform()">
24  <input type="hidden" name="itaskidpk" value="<%=transform(itaskidpk)%>">
25  <table summary="Edit Task">
26
27    <tr>
28      <td width="40"></td>
29      <td class="label">ID#:</td>
30      <td><%=transform(itaskidpk)%></td>
31    </tr>
32    <tr>
33      <td width="40"></td>
34      <td class="label">Entered:</td>
35      <td><%=dentered%></td>
36    </tr>
37    <tr>
38      <td width="40"></td>
39      <td class="label">Task:</td>
40      <td><input type="textbox" name="ctask" value="<%=ctask%>"></td>
41    </tr>
42    <tr>
43      <td width="40"></td>
44      <td class="label">Description:</td>
45      <td><textarea rows="5" cols="50" name="mnotes"><%=mnotes%></textarea></td>
46    </tr>
47    <tr>
48      <td width="40"></td>
49      <td class="label">Solution:</td>
50      <td><textarea rows="5" cols="50" name="msolution"><%=msolution%></textarea>
51      </td>
52    </tr>
53    <tr>
54      <td width="40"></td>
55      <td class="label">Priority:</td>
56      <td><select name="npriority">
57      <option value="1" label="1">1</option>
58      <option value="2" label="2">2</option>
59      <option value="3" label="3">3</option>
60      </select></td>
61    </tr>
62    <tr>
63      <td width="40"></td>
64      <td class="label">Date Complete:</td>
65      <td><input type="textbox" name="dcompleted" value="<%=dcompleted%>"
66          size="10" maxlength="10"></td>
67    </tr>
68    <tr>
69      <td width="40"></td>
70      <td class="label">Status:</td>
71      <td><%=cStatusDD%></td>
72    </tr>
73    <tr>
74      <td width="40"></td>
75      <td class="label">Assigned to:</td>
76      <td><%=cAssignedDD%></td>
77    </tr>
78
79    <tr>
80      <td width="40"></td>
81      <td><input type="submit" value="Save Task"></td>
82      <td></td>
83    </tr>
84
85  </table>
86  </form>
87
88  </body>
89  </html>
```

Callout annotations:
- (line 12) Form validation code. Called by FORMS "onsubmit()" event
- (line 35) Cell to hold field label.
- (line 39) Cell to hold form object
- (line 71) ASP tag containing VFP expression. This is evaluated on server. Browser sees hard-coded value here.
- (line 89) Closing tags for TABLE, FORM, BODY and HTML needed here.

Figure 3. Sample HTML page.

The header section of an HTML page

The section of the Web page that comes before the <BODY> tag is not displayed in the browser. This area of the document is meant to hold meta tags and scripting functions that can supply form validation or Dynamic HTML (DHTML) functionality. Let's look at each one in more detail.

- **DOCTYPE:** Line 1 of the listing is for specifying the DOCTYPE. This Document Type Definition (DTD) is for the use of form validators only, for now. In Microsoft Internet Explorer 6, using this tag will turn on strict compliance checking for the document. There are utilities that check the validity of HTML forms to make sure they adhere to certain standards. Since there are a number of versions of HTML out now, the validator has to be told what version to check the document against. The DOCTYPE tag does just that:

  - **<!DOCTYPE HTML PUBLIC "-//W3C//DTD HTML 4.01//EN" "http://www.w3.org/TR/html4/strict.dtd">** This declares the document to be HTML 4.01 Strict. Strict is a trimmed-down version of HTML 4.01 that stresses structure of presentation. Out-of-date elements, frames, and link targets are not allowed in Strict. By adhering to the strict definition, Web authors make their pages accessible and easy to adapt to style sheets.

  - **<!DOCTYPE HTML PUBLIC "-//W3C//DTD HTML 4.01 Transitional//EN" "http://www.w3.org/TR/html4/loose.dtd">** This declares the document to be HTML 4.01 Transitional. HTML 4 Transitional includes all elements and attributes of HTML 4 Strict but adds presentational attributes, out-of-date or "deprecated" elements, and link targets. HTML 4 Transitional recognizes the relatively poor browser support for style sheets, allowing many HTML presentation features to be used as a transition toward HTML 4 Strict.

  - **<!DOCTYPE HTML PUBLIC "-//W3C//DTD HTML 4.01 Frameset//EN" "http://www.w3.org/TR/html4/frameset.dtd">** This is a standard specially for pages using frames.

  - **<!DOCTYPE HTML PUBLIC "-//W3C//DTD HTML 3.2 Final//EN">** This specifies that the page adheres to the 3.2 version of HTML. Most browsers support this version of HTML fully.

The form validator goes out to the DTD file specified in the DOCTYPE URL and retrieves the specification in use by that page. The validator can then compare the current page to the specification to see how it matches the definition. HTML-Kit has one of these validators built in (HTML-TIDY) and will do the validation and present a report showing the errors in the page.

- **<HTML>:** This tag on line 4 tells the browser that what follows is HTML code. As you shall see later, non-HTML instructions can be placed above this line.

- **<HEAD></HEAD>:** The HEAD section, or header, contains page-level information. This is where META tags, the page title, style sheet references, and JavaScript code reside.

  - **TITLE tag:** This tag defines the text that will appear in the title bar of the browser window. In most cases this is just the name of the site.

  - **LINK tag:** This tag defines the CSS file that will be used to define the appearance of the site. There will be a detailed section on style sheets later on. LINK tags can also be used to reference other types of files, such as external JavaScript function libraries. This will be demonstrated later.

  - **META tags:** These tags can provide additional information about the page to search engines and also special instructions to the browser that can tell the browser how to cache the current page. The most common meta tags are "keywords" and "description." The keywords tag is what the indexing engines from the various search engines use to determine your ranking in those engines. How search engines work and how to best promote your site is covered in a later chapter. The description meta tag is used by most search engines to provide a two- or three- sentence description of your site in the listing report. How to use meta tags will be covered in Chapter 21, "Marketing Your Web Site."

  - **SCRIPT tags:** The script tags tell the browser that what is contained within the script tags is a scripting language and not HTML tags. Typically the scripting language is JavaScript, or JScript in Microsoft Internet Explorer. JavaScript is used in all modern browsers. VBScript as a scripting language is only used in Internet Explorer. It is JavaScript that is used to add form validation and Dynamic HTML (DHTML) functionality to the page. Using JavaScript, the Web developer can access the Document Object Model (DOM). The DOM is what exposes the page elements and allows them to be controlled through code. This will be very familiar to Visual FoxPro programmers who have worked in the form designer. There are very close equivalents on a Web page to the syntax Visual FoxPro developers are accustomed to using.

The <BODY> section of an HTML page

The <BODY> section of a Web page contains the tags that are used to display information in the browser. This is the section where all of the form objects live.

Common menu and banner

One of the first things that is done in the <BODY> section is to pull in a common menu system that will be used throughout the application. In line 14, the Visual FoxPro function FILETOSTR() is used to read the file HEADER.HTM from disk and convert it into a string that is then reinserted back into the page. This HEADER.HTM file does not contain any ASP tags that need to be evaluated, so returning it as a string is sufficient at this point. This is a very convenient way to have a consistent menu and banner for the entire site that is easy to maintain. Any changes that are made to the menu system or banner are instantly made available to all pages when this technique is used. If the code in HEADER.HTM lived on every page in the site, maintenance would be a nightmare. The smallest update to the menu system would have to be done to all pages. The three menu commands available in this menu are Add Task, List all Tasks, and List my Tasks. Each of these will be covered in Chapter 12.

Give your page some <FORM>

The <FORM> tag as shown on line 15 will form a wrapper for all the form elements such as text boxes, text areas, and list boxes. When a Web page is submitted back to the server, the values of any objects that reside between the <FORM></FORM> tags will be sent to the browser as a series of name/value pairs. Let's see what the various attributes of this tag are:

- **ACTION=:** The ACTION attribute tells the server what should be done when the page is submitted. In Web Connection applications, this would typically be a call to a custom method in the Web Connection application. In this example, the method SAVETASK will be executed inside the CLASS_TSK file. The mechanics of script mapping will be covered in detail in Chapter 12. Basically the action SAVETASK.TSK is mapped to the method SAVETASK in the CLASS_TSK procedure file through the use of a CASE statement in the main program. Very simple, but very powerful and elegant. This ACTION is initiated when the user click on a SUBMIT button like the one defined in line 81. This is a special type of button that is associated with the FORM tag that contains the button. FORM tags cannot be nested, so there is never any confusion as to what FORM tag a SUBMIT button belongs to.

- **METHOD=Post:** The METHOD attribute specifies whether the browser is to send form values to the server, or retrieve information from the server. The POST value tells the browser to send the form values to the server, as opposed to the GET value, used for retrieving information from the server. When submitting a form, the METHOD will always be POST. Hyperlinks send their request to the server in the form of a GET with any additional information being sent to the server on the URL. For example a GET request might take the form of http://localhost/todo/edittask.tsk?id=1000.

- **NAME="EDITTASK":** This attribute allows any scripting that may be on the page to refer to the form by a name. For example, instead of referring to a page element as "document.form[0].lastname.value="Smith"", it can be referred to as "document.edittask.lastname.value="Smith"".

How values are stored on a page

When designing a conventional Visual FoxPro form, it is sometimes necessary to store information in a form property. This piece of data may or may not be displayed in a form object. In a Web page, you have pretty much the same ability. As can be seen on line 24, a form property can be created by using:

```
<INPUT TYPE="hidden" NAME="itaskidpk" VALUE="<%=transform(itaskidpk)%>">
```

This form object stores the value in an invisible object that can be referenced through scripting and is submitted along with all the visible form elements. Here is an example of how easy it is to reference a Visual FoxPro field value. Simply enclose the expression in the ASP tags and make sure the value returned to the page is a string. The TRANSFORM() function is perfect for this since it will convert any data type to a string with the value trimmed both left and right. Any values associated with visible form elements are submitted with the page and do not need a "hidden" version of the property.

Storing data as hidden form variables is an easy way to carry forward information from one hit to the next. As you shall see in Chapter 12, all Web requests are independent. There is no knowledge whatsoever from one request to the next as to what the last request was and who made it. So if there is any information that needs to be carried forward to the next request, a good place to store that data is in hidden form variables.

Placing form elements on the page

When laying out a Web page, you typically use the <TABLE> element to position elements on a page. This tag allows the creation of as many rows and columns as you need. In our example, there are three columns used. The first column is used to create a left-hand margin, the second column is for labels, and the third is for holding the form element such as a text box. Some attributes for the <TABLE> tag are:

- **Width="x":** This controls the total width of the table in either pixels or a percentage basis. If using percentage, it is not generally a good idea for it to be 100%. The page has a much better appearance with both left-hand and right-hand margins. A percentage of 90% works well. In order for the appearance to be consistent, it is best to design to a fixed width for most pages. For example, the minimum horizontal resolution is 800 for most people. So width="800" will fix the width of the table to be 800 pixels.

- **Border="x":** This defines whether there is a visible border. This is more a personal preference, but many times a border of "0" looks best. This controls the outside border of the table, not the lines that separate the rows and columns.

- **Cellpadding="x":** This sets the distance between the border and the contents of the cell.

- **Cellspacing="x":** This controls the distance between the cells. This in effect makes the lines separating the rows and columns larger or smaller.

There are two sub-elements to the <TABLE> tag:

- **<TR></TR>:** This tag creates a new row within a table. The closing </TR> tag must be used after the last cell in the row.

  - **Align="right|left":** This controls horizontal alignment of cell contents.

  - **Valign="top|middle|bottom":** This controls vertical alignment.

- **<TD></TD>:** This tag creates individual cells within a row. These elements should hold one object only. If two TEXTBOX elements were placed in one cell, for example, the appearance would be very hard to control. There are some attributes to the <TD> tag that can be used to help control appearance.

- **Align="right|left":** This controls horizontal alignment of cell contents.

- **Valign="top|middle|bottom":** This controls vertical alignment.

- **Height="40":** This attribute controls the height of the cell in either pixels or percentage. This attribute is available for the <TR> element as well. It is common to have to force the height of row to a specific value to create the proper spacing.

- **<TH></TH>:** This tag is used to create a header for each column. This makes the header bold and centered. This is an accessibility guideline requirement.

More and more it is becoming important to make sure Web pages can be used by people with various disabilities. For example, the "title" attribute should now be used on all form objects. This makes it possible for agents to actually read the page to a person who is blind. See the reference in the "Chapter resources" section for accessibility guidelines. For any developers who are doing work for government agencies, it will be a requirement very soon to make Web sites accessible to all!

By setting the table width as well as cell widths and heights, correct placement of form elements can be achieved. Most HTML forms designers allow this to be done visually. The simpler HTML-Kit editor used in this chapter does not have a WYSIWYG editor, but Adobe's GoLive and Macromedia's Dreamweaver do. Dreamweaver has the most sophisticated one in the bunch. While the preceding display attributes can be set directly in the page, you will see later that it is best to externalize these attributes in a style sheet. Style sheets can be a Web designer's best friend!

Common form objects

The form elements that are available on a Web page are pretty similar to what is available in the Visual FoxPro form designer. The one huge difference is that HTML objects do not support inheritance. So the designer does not have the luxury of creating a class library with customized versions of all the controls. However, as you shall see shortly, style sheets bring some of this convenience to a Web page.

This section will cover the key form objects and show how they are used within a Web Connection application. For a more complete explanation of HTML objects, see the "Chapter resources" section. Let's take a look at these objects one by one:

- **<input type = "textbox" name = "ctask" value="<%=ctask%>" size="30 " maxlength="50">** This object is the equivalent of the textbox object in Visual FoxPro.

In file "edittask.wc" on server	As browser sees it
<input type = "textbox" name = "ctask" value="<%=ctask%>" size="30 " maxlength="50">	<input type = "textbox" name = "ctask" value="Create edituser form" size="30 " maxlength="50">

- **input type="textbox":** This creates a standard single-line text box field.

- **Name="ctask":** This name is used when the form is submitted to the server to identify the associated value. The listing of name/value pairs simply lists each field and its current value. This can also be used by JavaScript embedded in the page to read and set the value of that object. If using this to display table values, the object name should be the same name as the field in the table. This makes for much more readable code.

- **Value="<%=ctask%>":** The value attribute sets the value that will be displayed in the text box. The value can be derived from an ASP expression as shown here. This is typically a field name in a table or a memory variable. It can also be a call to a custom method. The value should be enclosed in quotes. Remember, all data types on a Web page are character! If there are no quotes and there are spaces in the value string, the value when read will be truncated after the first space.

- **Size="30":** This sets the visible size of the field on screen. This is typically the size of the field in the corresponding table.

- **Maxlength="50":** This can be used if the size attribute needs to be set lower to conserve screen real estate. Maxlength will limit the maximum number of characters entered into that field. So if the field is 50 characters in length, but there is only room to show 20, size could be set to 20 and maxlength to 50, and any characters over 20 will scroll in the text box. Remember, the size attribute has to be set manually. When a field is dropped onto a Visual FoxPro form, this is set automatically. If this is not set properly and the on-screen size is larger than the width in the table, characters will be truncated when stored in the field!

- **<input type="checkbox" value="<%=cadmin%>" name="cadmin" checked>** The checkbox object can be used to set flags. In this example, there could be an admin field in the user table. If checked, that person would have administration rights. The "checked" attribute determines whether the box is initially checked when the form is displayed. The way this would be handled with script is to create an expression that checks the current value and then returns the string "checked" or nothing. For example, <%=iif(cadmin="Y","checked","")%> could be used to dynamically output the correct definition for this object. *Tip:* Since the only data type that a form value can have is character, it makes more sense in many cases to define the matching field in the table to be character also. In this example, an ADMIN field would typically be of type logical. However, if it is made character and either a "Y" or an "N" is used, it eliminates a lot of unnecessary data conversions. Of course, this technique should not always be used! For example, it is always a good idea to store dates as dates so date functions can be used easily!

In file "edittask.wc" on server	As browser sees it
<input type="checkbox" value="<%=cadmin%>" name="cadmin" checked>	<input type="checkbox" value="Y" name="cadmin" checked>

- **\<input type="password" value="" name="password" size="10"\>** The password field is the same as the "textbox" field except the on-screen characters are replaced with "*" as the user types. This is only a screen effect; the data is still sent as clear text to the server when the form is posted! The only way around this is to have an SSL certificate installed on the server and for the link to be secure.

- **\<input type="submit" name="save" value="Save!"\>** The Save button works along with the \<FORM\> it resides in. When the Submit button is clicked, all form values that are inside of the \<FORM\>\</FORM\> tags are sent to the server for processing. These are made available to your Web Connection application as a series of name/value pairs. Web Connection functions such as request.form() are used to parse this list of name/value pairs to return individual posted values. The "value" attribute here is used to set the label text.

- **\<input type="reset"\>** This simply resets all fields within the current \<FORM\>\</FORM\> tags to the values they had when the page was first displayed.

- **\<input type="radio" value="radioValue" name="default"\>** This tag would be repeated for the number of buttons needed. The name attribute ties them all together. So if there were three radio buttons all with the same name, when the form is submitted, the value of the one that is chosen is what gets sent to the server. The same technique shown earlier for the checkbox object can be used here to pre-select a button when editing data. The following expression can be used on each radio button to determine which one is pre-selected.

  ```
  <%=iif(cpaymethod="I","checked","")%>
  ```

  If the radio buttons were used to select the method of payment (Invoice, Credit card, or Purchase order), each radio button could check to see whether the stored value matched its value. For example, the radio button for selecting Invoice could be:

  ```
  <input type="radio" value="I" name="cpaymethod"
  <%=iif(cpaymethod="I","checked","")%>>
  ```

  Each of the other radio buttons would check to see whether its cpaymethod was equal to either "C" for Credit card or "P" for Purchase order.

- **\<input type="file" name="fileGetterName" size="16"\>** This is a powerful form object that allows users to upload local files to the server. This is useful if you want your users to be able to upload attachments such as Word DOC files or pictures such as JPG files. This object creates a Browse button that allows the user to navigate to a file on the local network. When the file is chosen, its full path is shown in the textbox object. Forms that allow this type of upload must use the enctype="multipart/form-data" attribute in the \<FORM\> tag! This embeds the contents of the file along with the other form content during the POSTing process. If this encoding is used, instead of using request.form() to retrieve form values, request.GetMultipartFormVar() must be used. To retrieve the embedded file itself, the Web Connection function request.GetMultiPartFile() is used. The file is returned as a string and can then be saved to disk with strtofile() or stored in a memo field.

- **\<textarea name="mnotes" cols="40" rows="4"\>\<%=mnotes%\>\</textarea\>** The textarea object is equivalent to the editbox in Visual FoxPro. This is used to enter in freeform text for input into a memo field, for example. This is different syntax from the textbox object shown earlier. TEXTAREA requires a closing \</TEXTAREA\> tag. Instead of having a VALUE attribute, the value that is to be displayed appears *between* the \<TEXTAREA\> and \</TEXTAREA\> tags. So in the example shown here, the value of the memo field "mnotes" is displayed using the ASP expression \<%=mnotes%\>.

  - **cols="40" rows="4":** This simply sets the size of the text area.

  - **Name="mnotes":** This serves to name the field when submitted to the server and allows for manipulation through scripting.

In file "edittask.wc" on server	As browser sees it
\<textarea name="mnotes" cols="40" rows="4"\>\<%=mnotes%\>\</textarea\>	\<textarea name="mnotes" cols="40" rows="4"\>Create a form that allows for the maintenance of users.\</textarea\>

- **\<Select\>\</Select\>** This object is used to create a dropdown list box. The example from Figure 3 has hard-coded values in the dropdown.

```
<select name="nPriority" size="1" >
    <option value="1">1</option>
    <option selected value="2">2</option>
    <option value="3">3</option>
</select>
```

  - **name="nPriority":** Names the matching value for submission to the server and for scripting.

  - **Size="1":** Determines the height of the dropdown. A value of 1 makes it a dropdown. A value greater than 1 makes it a scrolling list box.

  - **\<option value="1"\>1\</option\>:** The \<option\> elements create the rows in the dropdown. The value is what is returned to the server. The string appearing between the \<option\>\</option\> tags is what is displayed to the user. This string does not necessarily need to match the value attribute for the option, but instead can consist of more readable text. Adding "selected" after "option" in the opening tag will show the dropdown with this option pre-selected.

The preceding example shows a hard-coded dropdown. Quite often, however, in a Web Connection application you will want to have the values pulled from a table dynamically. There is a class definition in the wwDBFPopup program file called wwDBFPopup. This allows the current open cursor to be used to populate a dropdown. In the TODO application shown in Chapter 12, this function is used to generate a dropdown of users and statuses.

```
SELECT NAME ;
  FROM (THIS.cdatapath+"users") ;
ORDER BY cusername ;
  INTO CURSOR tnames

    lopopup=CREATEOBJECT("wwDBFPopup")

    lopopup.cKeyValueExpression="cusername"
    lopopup.cDisplayExpression="tnames.cusername"
    lopopup.cFormVarName="userfilter"

    lopopup.caddfirstitem = "No Filter"
    lopopup.cselecteddisplayvalue = THIS.cUserFilter
    lopopup.BuildList()

    cPeople = lopopup.GetOutput()
```

- The property cKeyValueExpression determines the value that will be used for the value="x" attribute.

- The property cDisplayExpression" is the expression that will be inserted between the <option></option> tags. This is what the user will see.

- The property cFormVarname is what the name attribute is set to.

- The property CaddFirstitem is optional. This can be used to show a message such as "Select an item…" as the first element in the list.

- The property cSelectedDisplayValue can be used to pre-select an item in the dropdown. This would be used if a value is already stored in a table and an edit screen is being presented to the user. For example, the current value of the dropdown would need to be shown instead of "Select an item…"

- The BuildList() method then creates the HTML code and the GetOutput() method returns the HTML code as a string. This variable can then be referenced using an ASP tag like <%=cPeople%> in a Web Connection template page. The HTML code generated by wwDBFPopup will be inserted into that location!

Scripting the Web page

JavaScript is a huge topic that is beyond the scope of this chapter. The book *The JavaScript Bible*, by Danny Goodman, is one of the best references on JavaScript. It is listed in the "Chapter resources" section.

This chapter should serve as a good introduction to the topic and will make you aware of some of the things that can be done with JavaScript.

In order to perform form validations on the client and to generate and manipulate HTML dynamically, the developer must also know how to write scripts. The most widely used language for writing scripts is JavaScript. The Microsoft browsers support two scripting languages, VBScript and JavaScript (or JScript), while all modern browsers understand JavaScript.

Back in 1995, Netscape needed a new language to allow for easy integration of Web pages with its new support for Java. Brendan Eich was charged with developing a new language to fill this need. The original name given to the new language was "LiveScript." This reflected its ability to interact with the Web page. However, a marketing decision led to the name being changed to JavaScript. It was deemed an easier language to learn than Java and did not need a complicated IDE to use. Until the most recent versions of IE and Netscape, writing cross-browser JavaScript was a nightmare. Lots of code bracketing was needed to test for what browser version was being run. Now with IE 5.5 and Netscape 6.01, much of the language works unchanged across these browsers.

The ASP style expressions we have seen so far are executed on the server. JavaScript is executed in the browser. It is the browser that has the built-in interpreter for the JavaScript language.

Why use client-side scripting?

Many of the functions that can be done with JavaScript on the client can be done on the server as well. Many forms when submitted perform validations on the server, and an error page is sent back if there are any problems. However, doing the validations on the client is a lot more interactive. There are no delays in processing, no blinking screens.

Okay, so how do I do simple form validations?

In order to validate fields on a form, there must be a place where the script code can sit until called. The place for form validation functions is in the <HEAD> section of the Web page. Here is a simple example to illustrate how validations are performed:

```
<!DOCTYPE HTML PUBLIC "-//W3C//DTD HTML 4.0 Transitional//EN"
"http://www.w3.org/TR/REC-html40/loose.dtd">
<html>
<head>
<title>Todo Validation Example</title>
<script type="text/javascript">
function checkform() {
  if (document.edittask.ctask.value=="")
    {alert("Task field can not be blank!"); document.edittask.ctask.focus();
return false}
}
</script>
</head>

<body>
<form action="savetask.tsk" name="edittask" method="post" onsubmit="return
checkform()">
<table>
  <tr>
    <td>Task:</td>
    <td><input type="text" value="" name="ctask"></td>
  </tr>

  <tr>
```

```
    <td><input type="submit" value="Save!"></td>
    <td></td>
  </tr>
</table>

</form>
</body>
</html>
```

The JavaScript function checkform() lives in the <head></head> section of the Web page. The browser must be told that what follows is JavaScript, so the code is enclosed in the <script></script> tags. The checkform() function is invoked when the form's Submit button is clicked. The onsubmit event handler specified in the <Form> tag traps this event. This event handler will execute the checkform() function before the form is actually sent to the server. If the function returns a TRUE, the form is sent on its way. If the validation fails, a message box is displayed warning the user that a field is empty. After the alert message box is displayed, the ctask text box get focus by using its focus() method. The notation used to specify an object is very similar to the way it is done in a Visual FoxPro form. Instead of document.edittask.ctask.value, in a Visual FoxPro form it would be thisform.ctask.value. **Figure 4** will help you visualize how the DOM in a Web page corresponds to the DOM in a Visual FoxPro form

Comparing the DOM's between a web page and Visual FoxPro

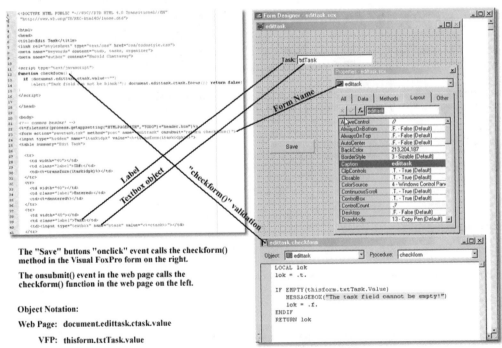

The "Save" buttons "onclick" event calls the checkform() method in the Visual FoxPro form on the right.

The onsubmit() event in the web page calls the checkform() function in the web page on the left.

Object Notation:

Web Page: **document.edittask.ctask.value**

VFP: **thisform.txtTask.value**

Figure 4. Comparison of Web page and Visual FoxPro DOMs.

Here are some key points to keep in mind when coding in JavaScript:

- JavaScript is case-sensitive! Make sure all variable names match case in all locations. In the preceding example, the name of the text box is ctask, so the reference in the function checkform() has to be ctask also. cTask would not work!

- The expression being evaluated after an IF statement must be enclosed in parentheses.

- If multiple lines of code are being executed like in the preceding IF statement, they must be grouped together by braces {}.

- The code that makes up a function must also be grouped together by braces {}.

JavaScript caution

Even if you include client-side validation using JavaScript, you should also validate all important data on the server. This is because: (1) some browsers either don't support JavaScript or allow users to turn JavaScript support off; and (2) client-side validation can be easily hacked. Thus you should always double-check the validity of data at the server. Your client-side efforts are not wasted, however, as they do improve the user experience and reduce the load on the server.

JavaScript libraries

After working with JavaScript for a while, you will most likely develop libraries of functions that will need to be used across multiple pages. A great source for JavaScript examples is **www.brainjar.com**. One of the examples of DHTML that is shown on the site is a dropdown menu system that was written using JavaScript and style sheets. The list of functions that are needed to run the menu system could be put into a JavaScript library file and referenced on each page that uses the menu. This can be done like this:

```
<script src="mainmenu/menufunctions.js"></script>
```

This also goes in the <HEAD> section of the Web page. This has the effect of pulling in all the code from the referenced JavaScript (js) file so that the Web page can make use of the included functions. This is very much like the SET PROCEDURE TO command in Visual FoxPro. This menu system provides the Web page with a Windows-type menu system. One of the goals of Web-based applications is to not make the user learn a different way of using the application. The Web application should have the same type of interface that users are accustomed to using. The Web is a different delivery mechanism for applications, but it does not have to be whole new user interface experience. **Figure 5** shows this JavaScript menu system.

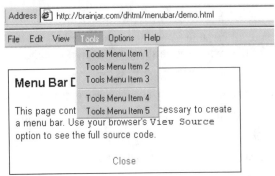

Figure 5. *Dropdown JavaScript menu system.*

When using a menu system like this in Web page, a common complaint from users is, "When I scroll down the page, I have to scroll back up to the top to choose another menu item—that's too much work!" Well, one of the cool things that JavaScript allows you to do is to dynamically change the form in response to user actions. The menu bar is positioned with absolute coordinates. There is a property "top" that specifies the top position of the menu bar. Using the form's onscroll event, anytime the user scrolls the form, the new top position of the menu system is reset and the menu is always positioned at the top of the visible Web page! This is a very cool and very practical use of JavaScript. An example of this is included in the source code for this book, available at **www.hentzenwerke.com**. **Table 1** summarizes some key events that occur on a Web page. For a complete list of available events, consult *The JavaScript Bible*, mentioned in the "Chapter resources" section. These can be trapped, and script can be written to handle the event further.

Table 1. *Some key Web page events and Visual FoxPro equivalents.*

Event	Description	Closest Visual FoxPro analogy
Onblur	Occurs when an object loses focus.	Lostfocus()
Onchange	Occurs when the contents of an object change.	Interactivechange()
Onclick	Occurs when the left mouse button is clicked.	Click()
Onfocus()	Occurs when an object receives focus.	Gotfocus()
Onload	Fires when an object is loaded. Frequently used in the <FORM> tag to call a script after a form has fully loaded in the browser.	Form init()
Onscroll	Occurs when the user scrolls the Web page. Used in preceding example to dynamically move the main menu.	Form's Scrolled event
Onsubmit	Occurs just before a form is submitted to the server. Used primarily for form validation scripting. If the function returns TRUE, the submission proceeds; otherwise, the form is not submitted. Use an alert() message box to notify the user of validation problems.	Click event of a form's Save button.

All scripting for these events must be very thoroughly tested across browsers! Browser compatibility is a tricky area and must be tested. See the listings for *The JavaScript Bible* and the Microsoft DHTML reference in the "Chapter resources" section.

Style sheets: Why you need them

Life without style sheets is not pretty, literally and figuratively. Most beginners making their first Web page will use the toolbar in their page designer to apply formatting to text on the page. Using this technique, the presentation tags are embedded in the page and wrap around the text they affect. Here is a common example: Let's say you are designing a maintenance form for users. As discussed earlier, you would probably have a table with two columns. The first column holds the labels, and the second column holds form objects such as text boxes. You decide that all labels should be red on the form. So, naturally, you swipe the mouse to select it, and choose red from the Text icon on the toolbar and make the selected text red. Great! That was easy! Now you go ahead and create an entire site using this same technique. A total of 20 forms are created, all with red labels created in the same way as the first. The following snippet of HTML shows the code that this technique produces:

```
<font color="#FF0000">Lastname:</font>
```

The <font> tag wraps around the text with a color attribute specifying the color to be used. Now, your first critic (your manager) looks at the pages and thinks the red color is a bit too harsh on the eyes and want you to use blue instead. If you're thinking you can simply change a base class somewhere like you can in Visual FoxPro, you are wrong! You would need to open up each Web page and manually change the color attribute! Or a slightly better solution would be to use a global search and replace. But these techniques are pretty archaic by today's standards. What is needed is a way of separating what's on the page from how it looks. This is where style sheets come into the picture! The best solution is to have definitions of how various pieces of the Web page should look in a separate file and have each Web page reference this library of definitions. There is a very simple way of doing this. In the <HEAD> section of each page, insert a reference like this:

```
<link rel="stylesheet" type="text/css" href="css/todostyle.css">
```

This line instructs the browser, upon loading the page, to retrieve the file todostyle.css in the css directory below the site root, and use the styles defined in it when they are referenced in the page. The HREF could also point to a style sheet that resides at another URL. For example, it could point to www.mycompany.com/stylesheets/todostyle.css. So why use style sheets? Well, in order to change the look of your entire site, all that you need to do is update the style definitions in this one file. The next time a page is loaded that references this style sheet, it will inherit the new definitions. No editing of individual pages is required! This is the closest you will get to the convenience of creating base classes in the Visual FoxPro form designer.

How style sheets are structured

Style sheet files are stored in plain text fields with an extension of .CSS for cascading style sheets (more on this later). You can use something as simple as Notepad. What is highly recommended, though, is a tool called "TopStyle" (see the "Chapter resources" section). This provides an IDE designed just for style sheets. It allows the user to pick style properties from a menu, formats the sheet, and provides some very powerful reports.

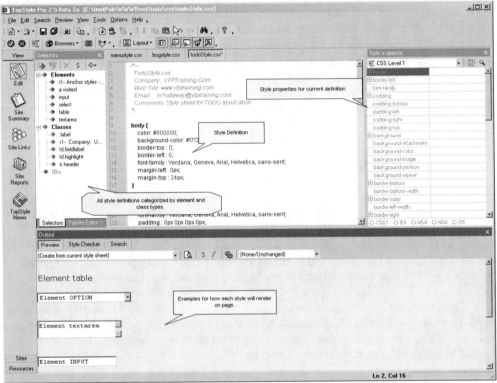

Figure 6. The TopStyle style sheet editor.

Figure 6 shows the IDE for TopStyle. It makes creating correct style sheets a breeze. The Style Inspector in the right panel shows all available properties for each style definition you are creating. The left panel organizes all the definitions into either element or class definitions. And the bottom panel shows a sample Web page with the current style applied to it. Some of the most helpful features of this product are the reports it provides:

- *Orphaned classes:* This report displays style sheets containing classes that are not used in any HTML documents that reference this style sheet. It's a great report for cleaning up the style sheet of dead definitions.

- *Undefined classes:* This report shows all classes that are used in an HTML page that are not defined in the referenced style sheets.

- *Class usage:* This report shows each defined class and where it is used in the entire Web site. It displays a list of files, and you can double-click on a file name to open the file for editing.

It is best to start off in TopStyle by creating a "site." A site is like a project file in Visual FoxPro. You specify the root folder, and TopStyle is then able to create reports linking the pages with all the style sheets that the pages reference.

Element definitions

Element definitions are style definitions that act on the pre-defined HTML form element tags. For example, all pages that reference the todostyle.css style sheet as shown in the Figure 6 would use the style definition for the BODY tag automatically. The designer would not have to reference this style definition explicitly. If you wanted all your TEXTAREAs to have a consistent appearance, you could use a definition like this one:

```
textarea {
  font-size: 10pt;
  font-family: "Courier New"
}
```

The format for a style definition is shown in **Figure 7**.

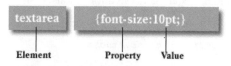

Figure 7. Style definition.

The property and value must be separated by a colon (:), and the property/value pair must be enclosed in brackets {}. A semicolon separates each property/value pair. The list of property/value pairs can all be on one line or on separate lines as shown earlier. TopStyle can automatically format a style sheet file to be on multiple lines. This does make it much easier to read. By having an element definition for all the basic form elements, you can be assured that all of these objects will look the same on all of the pages that reference the common style sheet. A page can have a reference to more than one style sheet, but there should be only one style sheet that defines the standard look and feel for all pages. The style sheet included for the sample "TODO" application in Chapter 12 could be used as a template for other projects as well.

By specifying an element style for all the form elements, all objects throughout the entire site will look exactly the same. It is a good idea, for example, to have all text boxes and labels use the same font, color, and size. For example, there is a definition for the <SELECT> object in the todostyle.css sheet that defines all occurrences to be of the same width.

```
select {
  font-size: 10pt;
  font-family: "Courier New";
```

```
    width: 200px
}
```

This definition states that all <SELECT> objects or dropdowns will be 200 pixels wide, as well set setting the font to 10 point Courier New.

One very interesting use of style sheets is for users to choose their own "themes." With a common set of style definitions, this becomes quite easy. The background color for each page can be controlled by creating a definition for the <BODY> tag. For example, if the following definition is used for the <BODY> tag, it becomes easy to change the background of each page in the entire Web site based on a theme. The background-color property controls the page color for any page that references the todostyle.css sheet.

```
body {
    color: #000000;
    background-color: #f7f2d0;
    border-top : 0;
    border-left : 0;
    font-family : Verdana, Geneva, Arial, Helvetica, sans-serif;
    margin-left : 0px;
    margin-top : 24px;
}
```

On a user profile form, you could provide a dropdown with some pre-defined themes. They could simply be choosing the background color for all of the forms, for example. This could then be saved in the user's profile, and when the pages are generated for that user, an ASP tag with the following expression could be used:

```
<link rel="stylesheet" type="text/css" href="css/<%=process.ctheme%>">
```

Assuming a user needs to log in first, the login routine could look up the chosen theme in the user profile, store it to a session variable, and, when each form is rendered, the current theme name could be built into the prior link dynamically—pretty cool! In this example, what would change between each theme is the value of the background-color property. Remember, the preceding expression is evaluated on the server when the process.ctheme property is in scope. So by the time the browser sees the form, it is hard-coded. The name of the theme that is chosen would correspond to the name of the style sheet. For example, if there was a theme called "Earth Tones," the file on disk could be called earthtones.css. It is this file name that would appear where the <%=process.ctheme%> expression sits in the preceding code line. There would be a separate style sheet for each theme.

Font control

Since Web sites can be run on any platform anywhere in the world, the developer has little control over what fonts will be installed on the client machine. It is important that the site developer use the font-family property correctly so the page content will render properly on the client machine. As in the preceding example, multiple fonts can be listed on the font-family line. If Verdana is not installed on the client machine, the next font, Geneva, will be used. This will continue down the list until a font is found that is installed on the machine. If none of the named fonts are installed the machine, the browser on the client machine will use a

Sans Serif font to render the text. This is the last entry in the comma-delimited list. Serif fonts are proportional and have "serifs," or the tiny decorations that appear at the end of the main strokes in letters (see **Figure 8**).

Figure 8. *Serif on Times New Roman.*

Sans Serif fonts are fonts that do not have these tiny decorations; examples include Helvetica and Geneva. By being able to specify what font families to use, the developer retains some control over how the Web page will be rendered. If the font-family property is not used, the page could come out looking very different from what you intended!

If any object within the BODY needs a different font, the font-family property can be used on specific objects and that will override the definition in the BODY style.

Class definitions

Class definitions can be used for non-element tags. In our first example, we wanted to create a label that has a common site-wide definition. So instead of our HTML looking like this:

```
<td>font color="#FF0000">Lastname:</font></td>
```

it should look like this:

```
<td class="label">Lastname:</td>
```

Then, in the referenced style sheet, we have the following definition:

```
.label {
  font-family : Verdana, Geneva, Arial, Helvetica, sans-serif;
  color : Blue;
  font-weight : bold;
  text-align : left;
}
```

Now, any time you want to create a label with the standard pre-defined look, you simply use the class attribute and specify the label style definition. In almost all cases, the label will be in its own table cell, so the class reference is enclosed inside of the <TD> tag and will then affect anything within that element. Just to be clear, the class names should be pretty generic. By this I mean that the name of this definition should not be "bluelabel," for example. Naming it just "label" makes it very easy to simply change the style definition to make it any color you like. This allows for *very* easy site maintenance. Updates to the interface become trivial if the right class definitions are defined in an external style sheet. **Figure 9** shows an example of the todostyle.css style sheet and how it affects the look of the edittask Web page from the "TODO" application in Chapter 12.

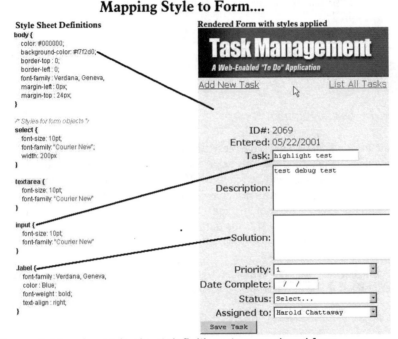

Figure 9. Mapping style sheet definitions to a rendered form.

Pseudo-class selectors

There are other types of style definitions that are implied. For example, the <A> tag or anchor tag is used to define an embedded hyperlink. A common need is that when a user moves the mouse over the link, something about it should change to let the user know it is a link. Very often, it is given an underline or the background color changes. Let's see how we can do the latter. In our todostyle.css style sheet, there is a definition that looks like this:

```
/*-- Anchor styles -*/
a:hover {
  color: Red;
  text-decoration: underline;
  background : Yellow;
}
```

There is a pseudo-class selector available for the anchor tag called "hover." This, if defined, is used when a user hovers over a link. Since this is an element definition, it will be used wherever the <A> tag is used automatically. And since the hover class is pre-defined for the anchor tag, this does not have to be explicitly defined either. It will be used automatically when a user moves the mouse over the link. This definition will make the text red and the background yellow. **Table 2** lists the pseudo-class selectors for the anchor tag.

Table 2. *The pseudo-class selectors for the anchor tag.*

Name	Description
:visited	Any link that has already been clicked on.
:hover	A link that is currently being moused over.
:active	Any link that is about to be clicked.

At times it may be necessary to make special versions of element definitions. For example, let's say there is a frame on the left side of the Web page that will hold the site menu, and the background color is yellow. If the preceding a:hover definition was used on those links, the user would never see the hover effect since the hover background color and the frame background color are the same. So another style sheet definition is needed:

```
/*-- Anchor styles -*/
a.menu {
  color: blue;
}

a.menu:hover {
  color: black;
  text-decoration: underline;
  background : red;
}
```

This definition will make the text black and the background color red when the user mouses over the link. Since this definition has a name to it, it would not be used automatically by the links in the menu frame. In order to reference it, we need to use the class attribute.

```
<a href="edituser.wp" class="menu">Edit Users</a>
```

This technique of specifying the element tag, a period, and then a name can be used on any element tag to create specific versions of styles for each element.

So how do style sheets "cascade"?

The term "cascading style sheets" applies to how various levels of style definitions are applied to the final rendering. The closer a style definition is specified in a Web page, the more weight it has. For example, the definition for the element INPUT could appear in one of three places.

* It could appear in an externally linked style sheet as :

```
input {
  font-size: 10pt;
  font-family: "Courier New"
}
```

* It could appear as an embedded style definition anywhere in the page prior to use as:

```
<style>
input {
  font-size: 10pt;
```

```
     font-family: "Courier New"
}
</style>
```

- Or it can appear as a STYLE definition within the element tag:

```
<input type="textbox" style="font-size: 10pt; font-family: 'Courier New'"
value="">
```

The third variation overrides the second, and the second would override the first. So it is possible to have a site-wide style sheet that is referenced by the LINK tag in the header, but to have the style that is used for rendering cascade down to the definition used either at the page level (as in the second version) or at the element level (as in the third version).

Finally...

So, after all the form elements have been added to the page, it is time to make sure the page has all of the matching closing tags. For example, the body of the Web page started off with the <BODY> tag. There must be a matching closing body tag (</BODY>) to complete this section. Similarly there must be a closing form tag (</FORM>) and a closing HTML tag (</HTML>). This is just like having to match parentheses in Visual FoxPro code with nested functions.

Conclusion

The topic of HTML and style sheets is probably what will cause the new Web developer the most frustration. Even as deep as Web Connection is, it is still all Visual FoxPro and most Fox developers should be able to get through it. HTML, JavaScript, and style sheets, however, are all new and not intuitive at first. If you start off using style sheets from the beginning and are aware of what they and JavaScript can do, you are off to a great start. Going back and retrofitting a Web page with style sheets is a very painful process. Using them correctly from the start, however, will make your work go much faster and make site maintenance much easier as well. If you find yourself working for days on a single page to get it right, it will become incredibly frustrating. Visual FoxPro developers are used to constructing pages rapidly, and using HTML may seem like you are going back to FoxBase days! Study the concepts in this chapter and read the resource material, and it will be much easier.

Chapter resources

- **www.webconnectiontraining.com:** Author-run site with updates to code, videos, and more examples for developing in Web Connection.

- HTML-Kit home page: **www.chami.com/html-kit**

- Dreamweaver home page: **www.macromedia.com/software/dreamweaver/**

- TopStyle Style Sheet Editor: **www.bradsoft.com**

- Online HTML Validator: **http://validator.w3.org/**

- **http://msdn.microsoft.com/library/default.asp?url=/workshop/author/html/ reference/elements.asp**: Microsoft's online guide to all HTML objects.

- **http://msdn.microsoft.com/library/default.asp?url=/workshop/author/dom/ domoverview.asp**: Excellent MSDN online resource for DHTML overview. Lists all properties, events, and methods with explanations of each.

- **www.w3.org/TR/html4/**: World Wide Web Consortium standards document for HTML 4.01.

- **www.w3.org/TR/REC-CSS2**: Cascading Style Sheet level 2 Standard.

- *The JavaScript Bible*, by Danny Goodman: **www.amazon.com/exec/obidos/ ASIN/0764533428/ref=bxgy_sr_text_a/104-4309761-0938307**

- *Cascading Style Sheets: The Definitive Guide*, by Eric Moyer: Published by O'Reilly Press, ISBN 1-56592-622-6.

- HTML Table Specification: **www.ietf.org/rfc/rfc1942.txt**

- Web Accessibilities Policy: **www.w3.org/WAI/Policy/#255**

Chapter 10
Getting in Tune: Overcoming Conceptual Hurdles

Making the transition to Web application development can be a challenge. A few lucky people feel right at home and become immediately productive. Some feel like they are on another planet, and never get there at all. This chapter is for everyone in between.

Over the past several years I have spent countless hours on the West Wind support forums answering questions from new developers. During that time I have gradually recognized several key concepts that people don't always "get" when they are just starting. These are concepts for which, once you understand them, there is no looking back. On the other hand, developers who fail to migrate to Web development are usually those who never grasp some of these concepts.

Each of these topics is also covered in other chapters of this book; however, the basic concepts have been collected here to provide a point of focus for people who are new to Web Connection development or Web development in general.

There are 10 separate concepts, each covered in a separate section of this chapter. The concepts are:

1. a basic explanation of how Web Connection enables you to connect your Visual FoxPro data to the Web;

2. an explanation of why you need a separate C++ DLL file (WC.DLL), and where your Visual FoxPro code fits in;

3. a brief introduction to the "stateless" nature of the Web (Concepts 4, 6, 7, and 8 also are really just issues of state);

4. passing "parameters" between Web pages;

5. understanding the Request and Response objects (plus other primary Web Connection objects);

6. realizing that one Visual FoxPro instance is servicing multiple users at once;

7. improving performance by running more than one instance of your server application;

8. seeing the huge difference between Web forms and Windows forms;

9. validating user input; and

10. a brief introduction to the (optional) Web Connection template and script technology.

Concept 1: How the machine works—just the basics

Okay, you may have installed Web Connection and verified that the samples do actually run on your server. Possibly you have even created a page or two of your own and managed to get them to display in a browser. But you have never quite understood why it works, and you certainly would not feel comfortable trying to diagnose any problems that might occur. Further, although many steps are involved, you might not be sure which ones happen automatically and which ones you must implement.

Table 1 presents a simplified list of the steps that take place in file-based messaging. For each step, if you have specific responsibilities, these are noted.

Table 1. Steps that occur in file-based messaging.

What happens	Your involvement
When a hit arrives at the Web server (IIS), the server makes a call to the Web Connection ISAPI connector program (WC.DLL), which receives all of the information about the request. Web Connection creates a temporary file with this information in a format that can be read by the Web Connection framework code in your Visual FoxPro application. The file is written to a pre-arranged folder as specified in an INI file option.	None.
In the meantime, your Visual FoxPro application (the Web Connection server application) is running continuously and includes a timer that repeatedly looks for these new request files. When a new request file is found, your application reads the information and calls the Process method in your main program, which then parses the URL of the request in order to select the appropriate class and method to be used for processing the request.	Very little. If you use the Web Connection wizards, this main program code is written for you.
Each processing class (derived from the Web Connection framework wwProcess class) has its own PRG file with a name that matches the class. Based on the determination of which class to use, the appropriate PRG file is called.	Very little. If you use the Web Connection wizards, these files are created for you with the basic plumbing in place.
The URL is further processed to see which method of the class is responsible for processing the request. Once determined, that method is called and the request is processed.	This is where 99 percent of your work occurs. You write the individual method code for each "page" in your Web application. The Web Connection framework sets up the Request and Response objects for you. Your job is to read any details you need from the Request object, and use that information to fill the Response object with an HTML result page. In doing so, you may also be performing other actions such as querying data, saving submitted information to a database, sending email, and so forth. Although some of these actions are facilitated by classes in the framework, you are responsible for all of the orchestration.
After you have completed filling the Response object with the HTML result, a file with a pre-designated name is automatically created as a signal that the request processing is complete.	None.

Table 1. Continued.

What happens	Your involvement
Upon seeing this signal, the ISAPI program (WC.DLL) grabs the HTML response you created and returns it to the Web server, which in turn sends it back to the user for display in the browser. The temporary files used during the entire process are then deleted.	None.

Although, strictly speaking, you can install Web Connection and even implement some basic applications without understanding the underlying machine, I cannot imagine advancing far without facing the need to assimilate this knowledge. A true understanding can help you:

- troubleshoot unusual problems;

- optimize application performance; and

- explain how Web Connection operates to others, such as clients or management who might question your choice of this product.

File-based messaging—the complete sequence

Although the preceding explanation provides all you really need to know, some developers will be curious to explore the Web Connection framework source code in more detail. For file-based messaging, the following sequence describes both the steps taken and the classes and components involved:

1. The ISAPI connector application WC.DLL receives a request through the Web server (Microsoft Internet Information Server) and creates a temporary request file (for example, WC_*.TMP) in a specified directory. This file includes the name of the return file that is to be created by your application with the HTML result.

2. In the Server object (class wwServer), a timer member object (class wwFileTimer) regularly calls the CheckForMessageFile method, which looks for new request files. This method performs file locking, resizing, and deleting functions in a safe manner, such that two or more file-based instances can run simultaneously without the possibility of more than one instance processing the same request.

3. In the Server object when a new request file is found, the timer calls the framework ProcessHit method in the Server object.

4. The ProcessHit method then calls the Process method in your application's main program (for example, wcDemoMain.PRG).

5. A DO CASE structure in the Process method of your main program parses the incoming URL and calls the correct application program to process the specific page (for example, wwDemoProcess.PRG).

6. Your application program instantiates a **Process** object (defined in the same PRG) as a subclass of wwProcess, from which you use the Response object to construct the HTML to return.

7. The Process object also instantiates a Response object, passing it the required return file name, as determined from GetOutputFile method of the Request object (class wwRequest).

8. The Init method of the Response (HTML) object creates a file with the file name that was determined from the Request object.

9. When the response preparation process is complete, the ProcessHit method back in the Server object calls SendReturnMessageFile, which causes a 0-byte .RET file to be written to the temp directory.

10. During this time, WC.DLL continually polls for the creation of this file name with a .RET extension, which is a signal that the temporary response file is ready. When it sees the .RET file, WC.DLL grabs the corresponding .TMP file contents to give back to the Web server.

COM messaging—what's the difference?

Web Connection also provides for a higher-performance messaging mechanism using COM. Chapter 14, "COM vs. File-Based Messaging," discusses COM messaging in detail. For now, it is important just to know that this option is available to you in the future, and that you will be able to convert your system to use this mechanism without making any changes in your Visual FoxPro code. Knowing that this option is available in the future, and requires no specific planning at the outset should be very comforting.

There are just a few fundamental differences between file-based messaging and COM messaging:

- Rather than writing temporary files that your application looks for, WC.DLL instantiates your application as a COM server using the equivalent of CREATEOBJECT(), and then passes messages to your application when a new request has been received from the Web server.

- Instead of using a timer and polling for new requests, your application is called directly by WC.DLL when it is time to process a new request. This eliminates the latency inherent in file-based messaging when new hits arrive, but they are not seen until the next timer interval. Performance is improved even further with COM messaging, because message files do not have to be created for each hit.

- Finally, instead of writing output files with your HTML response that WC.DLL needs to continually look for, you simply return the HTML response as a string from your COM server back to WC.DLL. This again both avoids latency and precludes the creation of an additional file on each hit.

In addition to these differences, WC.DLL is multi-threaded and has a pool manager that can instantiate more than one instance of your application to allow for simultaneous processing on machines with sufficient processing power. (Note that even using file-based messaging, it may be possible to run more than one instance of your application to increase total server performance.)

Concept 2: Why is there a C++ DLL and where does my VFP EXE fit in?

A Visual FoxPro desktop application is compiled into an executable (EXE file), and users run that. Because your Web Connection application is also compiled into an executable, developers are often confused about why users cannot just run that. In other words, why do users have to browse to the WC.DLL instead of simply something like http://yourdomain /wconnect/yourVfpApp.exe?

The reason lies in the nature of the Internet Services API (or ISAPI). This is the API that Microsoft Internet Information Server (IIS) uses to provide for multi-threaded, high-performance Web applications. Any application (DLL or EXE) that is referenced in a URL in a virtual directory that has execute rights must be compliant with either ISAPI or the older, less efficient common gateway interface (CGI). Basically a Visual FoxPro application is not capable of interfacing with IIS in this manner, and thus an ISAPI-based C++ "connector" program is needed to provide the ISAPI interface, handle multi-threading and pooling issues, and so forth. It is this small ISAPI application (WC.DLL is less than 100KB) that allows your Visual FoxPro application to be connected to the Web.

Concept 3: The stateless nature of the Web

Before you even start with Web Connection, you will probably hear that "the Web is stateless." Perhaps you will read about the "disconnected" nature of the Web. What do these statements mean and how do they affect you?

This concept is best explained by examining how a desktop application operates and then seeing how a Web application differs.

In a desktop application, the user connects to numerous resources, and often remains connected for long time periods, perhaps until closing the application. These resources include file handles, database connections, COM/DCOM object references, and so forth. The application is fully in control—monitoring user activity, ensuring proper resource disconnection and cleanup, and many similar activities.

A user's "session" on a Web site is nothing like this. First, the user does not open a new application; rather, he or she just navigates the browser to a new location. Second, other than brief connections to the Web (HTTP) service, the user does not connect to any resources at the remote site. The HTTP connection itself tends to be brief—generally just long enough to transfer the request and receive the response from the Web server. (Connections can persist longer for performance reasons under HTTP 1.1, but there is never an expectation that the user is connected between one page and the next during a Web visit.)

In the most general sense, as each brief connection is made, the Web server has no idea whether that connection is from a brand-new user, or one who has already been navigating through your site. This may sound ominous at first. How, after all, could you provide much of a user experience if you respond to each hit without knowing what the user has been doing? Clearly applications such as shopping carts are more intelligent than that.

The secret to managing this "stateless" condition is to convince the browser to identify itself upon successive hits to your site. There are several techniques to accomplish this identification, including use of cookies, license plates, and authentication. You can then employ this identification scheme on the server to store temporary information during the user session. By doing this, you can reconstruct the user's session environment as needed while processing each hit, and can thus provide a consistent end-user experience. Chapter 13, "Identifying Users and Managing Session Data," presents a full discussion of these concepts and the various tools and techniques available to you for managing state within a stateless Web.

Concept 4: Passing "parameters" between Web pages

A complete Web application consists of one or more distinct Web pages that the user sees and interacts with. In a Web Connection application, each of these pages is created from a different method in one or more process classes. In any but the simplest of Web applications, there is a need beyond simple hyperlinks to pass data between one page and another. Or, to look at it in reverse, when you are processing a new request, you will often need to know how the user got there and other information about what else the user has done during this visit to your site. In other words, your method needs to establish the context from which it can construct a response. Some examples of these needs include:

- In a page called DisplayCustomer, which queries a database and displays information about a single customer, you need a way of knowing which customer to display.

- In a page called ReceiveFeedback, which processes a feedback form contained on your site, you need to be able to determine what the user entered into each of the form fields.

- In a page called FinalCheckout, which processes the purchases a user made while browsing your Web store, you need to be able to accumulate all of the items the user has added to his or her shopping cart.

- In a page called SaveUser, you need to know whether the user just came from the AddNewUser page or the EditExistingUser page, so that you take the correct database action.

- If your site allows the user to set display preferences (for example, low-graphics mode, large fonts, or a color scheme choice), you need the ability in each of your pages to determine what the user's choices have been and persistently honor those choices during the entire visit to your site.

There are three specific techniques in which information is made available between one hit and another. These are very different from one another. Often, for any one specific need, only one of the three is appropriate. Learning and understanding these three methods is essential to becoming a successful Web application developer. These techniques are used throughout this book and in the Web Connection demo application. Take whatever time is necessary to become completely comfortable with each. The three basic techniques are:

1. Passing parameters in the URL.

2. Submitting variables via HTML forms.

3. Storing and retrieving session information.

Some Web developers use a fourth technique of attempting to save the settings on the client machine using separate cookies for each parameter. This technique is subject to both hacking and cookie size limitations and should not be used.

The following sections present the basics of employing each of these techniques and describe the types of situations in which each is appropriate for use.

URL parameters

Parameters can be passed between one page and another in the physical URL that is used to hyperlink from one page to the next. Web Connection uses the first two positions in the URL as its own parameters to decide which class and method are to be used to process a request. Beyond that, your application is free to use any additional parameters that it sees fit.

A URL that has no additional parameters might look like this (for brevity, I will display only relative URLs, instead of full URLs like http://yourDomain/yourVirtual/...):

```
wc.dll?CustPages~DisplayCustomer
```

This is a basic Web Connection URL, which indicates to use the DisplayCustomer method in the CustPages program to process the page. Depending on the nature of the method, this will not provide sufficient information to allow your method to process the page. In this example, you would need to know which customer to display. The customer ID, in essence, is a required parameter for the method; however, your Web Connection methods are never called with parameters.

The secret is to embed the required information in the URL itself, so that your method can retrieve it (using the QueryString method of the Request object). URL parameters can have either an ordinal position or a name. Examples of each of these, in a request to display the customer whose ID is 9999, would look like:

```
wc.dll?CustPages~DisplayCustomer~9999
wc.dll?CustPages~DisplayCustomer~&custID=9999
```

Although Web Connection supports using either of these formats, the former (ordinal position) is strictly inferior and should not be used. To see why you should prefer the parameter name technique, first observe the code you would use to read in the requested customer ID:

```
lnId = VAL( Request.QueryString( 3))        && ordinal case
lnId = VAL( Request.QueryString( "custID"))  && name case
```

The advantage of the latter technique should be obvious: In the former case, you have to remember the specific position number that each parameter occupies, while in the latter, you refer to each parameter by its name. This may seem unimportant in this example, which has but one obvious parameter; however, consider what happens when your method requires two, three, or even more parameters. With the former technique, you would be forced to keep track of the order in which the parameters must appear. With the latter, you simply string them together, in any order, using their names.

The proper time to use URL parameters is when you can specify all of the parameters in advance when constructing a page, and the user simply needs to click on the specific hyperlink to proceed to the next page. Consider a page that contains a list of all of your customers, and you want the ability to construct a hyperlink from each name in the list to the corresponding detail page for that customer. In that case, you know how to construct each link before the user sees the list, because you are enumerating all possible choices, rather than asking the user to enter some type of search criteria in a form.

Form variables

Often you will face situations that are not as simple as the examples discussed earlier. In order to provide the thread from one page to the next, you may need to prompt the users to supply information about their needs.

For example, in a product search form, the user may have the option of selecting a product type from a drop-down list and optionally entering search text with a portion of the product name. When the user presses the Search button, he or she navigates to the page that displays a list of matching products. How do you go about constructing this list? You cannot check for URL parameters, because you could not know what the user was going to select from the list or type in the text box. The answer in this case is that the user's browser transmits all of the form selections made by the user and transmits those to your server as form variables. The request that you receive comprises both the URL and the form variables. Web Connection makes it easy to read these variables, using the Form method of the Request object. So in this example, you could read in the user's selections, construct and execute a SQL query based on those selections, and display back a list of matching products.

Using form variables is the appropriate technique when the user is going to make a series of choices on one page, and those choices will be used on the subsequent page to construct a response.

Let's look at the case of the product search form mentioned earlier. This form has a text box, asking the user to enter a product name to search for. Assign the name attribute of the text box in your HTML file with name="txtProduct". Also, define the action to run in the form tag so it calls a method called "FindProducts":

```
wc.dll?MyProcess~FindProducts
```

In the FindProducts method of MyProcess, you have the following line of code:

```
lcProduct = Request.Form("txtProduct")
```

You now have a variable, lcProduct, you can use in your FoxPro code to find the product or products requested by the user.

Session variables

Each of the previous techniques, URL parameters and form variables, handles situations where information from one page is used when processing the very next page. Sometimes your needs extend beyond this immediate temporal relationship. Instead, when processing one page, you may require information that spans several different pages the user has visited and actions the user has taken.

Consider the example of an online store. Users are typically free to wander through your site, examining products and adding some of those products to their "shopping carts." When they finally decide to check out and purchase their items, you need to be able to accumulate all of their previous selections. Additionally, the users may have identified themselves at the start of the session with a login screen, so you'd need to track who they are throughout their shopping experience. Although possible, designing your site to track information like this using URL parameters would be a nightmare. Instead, the recommended technique is to store the user selections in session variables.

Using session variables, you create a method for identifying users from one hit to the next as they navigate through your site. The most common identification technique is through the use of cookies. User identification techniques are discussed in detail in Chapter 13. Once you identify a user, you can store any information about that user's selections on the server using session variable technology. Web Connection stores these values in a special session table (both DBF and SQL Server are supported). Whenever needed, you can read back any session variables and take action as needed. By using session variables, you break the dependence between one page and another and are much more prepared to allow the users to navigate your site in their own preferred sequence.

Concept 5: Request, Response, Session… Oh, my!

As developers explore Web Connection for the first time, they usually start by studying several of the examples in the demo application. The code they encounter is replete with references to several standard objects, including Response, Request, Session, Server, and even Process.

It also appears that these object references can be used almost anywhere, suggesting that they are not local, but must be either private or (gasp!) public in scope. Nevertheless, attempting to use these object references in certain locations, such as in server methods in the main program, can result in "variable not found" errors. Finally, these variables are not named using the familiar Hungarian notation, wherein you might expect names like poResponse (if private) or goResponse (if public). This non-standard naming prevents you from making assumptions as to the variable scope.

So, what is going on here? When can you use these object references and when can you not use them? And finally, why does Web Connection not follow standard naming practices?

These variables are created for convenience purposes only. They are declared to be private in scope in the Process method of the wwProcess class. Because it is this method that calls any of your individual method code, these variables are always available to (1) all of your detailed Process methods; (2) any objects instantiated from those methods (such as business objects); and (3) any templates or scripts that you render.

There are, however, places where you cannot refer to these variables, primarily in any code that is called before the wwProcess::Process method itself. This restriction applies primarily to the server code in the main program. Here, you can refer to the Server object itself simply as THIS and the Request object using THIS.oRequest. (There is no need to refer to the other three objects in server code.)

A second place where you cannot refer to these convenient object references is in your own Process method. If you need to add functionality to the Process method, the standard approach in Web Connection is to override the method, add any custom code, and then call through to the framework via DODEFAULT. Thus, any code you place in your own Process method will not yet have access to these variables. (You can always use THIS.oResponse, THIS.oRequest, THIS.oSession, THIS.oServer, and THIS to refer to the same five objects if needed.) You may think that a way around this limitation is to call DODEFAULT at the beginning of your Process method, followed by any custom code you need. This will not work! The default Process method in Web Connection will call whatever method was passed in the URL before returning, and the remainder of your code will be run too late, or may not be run at all!

Finally, there is a good reason why these variables are named as they are, apparently ignoring standard naming conventions. Active Server Page (ASP) technology uses the names Request, Response, and Session within its scripting environment to refer to the corresponding objects in the ASP environment. By using the same names, and by designing the classes to often use the same method names as used in ASP, it is possible for developers and page designers with ASP experience to become productive more quickly with Web Connection.

Concept 6: One Visual FoxPro instance—multiple users served

In a desktop or network application, your entire application is run by each user in parallel. In other words, your executable and the Visual FoxPro run-time libraries are executed on each workstation. As such, when your application is run by a network user, it is loaded into the memory of the user's workstation, and thus it is serving a specific user, and you can perform all sorts of special setup code that is specific to that user. With each subsequent form action or menu choice that user selects, your code already knows who the user is, and can continue to act accordingly until the user logs off or exits your application. Further, except for "abnormal events" (such as hardware failure or your user turning off the computer with the "big red switch"), you can count on running standard cleanup code for each user when they exit.

A Web application is nothing like this!

First of all, your users do not run Visual FoxPro at all. They are only running a Web browser, such as Microsoft Internet Explorer or Netscape Navigator. Your Visual FoxPro application runs *unattended* on a server, usually the same machine as the Web server. Second, and most important, your Visual FoxPro application is serving multiple users serially. Except in the most lightly loaded situations, successive hits that your application services will be from different users. Thus you cannot create code that simply sets up the environment based on the first user to hit your application and then continue to assume each hit is from that user. Examples of problematic coding techniques include:

- Setting environment variables and expecting them to be unchanged upon the next hit for the same user. (Alternative: Be certain to check that your environment is as needed when processing a request. Also, use standard best practices for restoring the environment as you found it, particularly if you change dangerous variables such as SET EXACT ON, which can be a disaster in a Web Connection application.)

- Assuming record pointers have not moved between successive hits from the same user. (Alternative: Always be certain that you establish that the correct tables are open and that the proper records are utilized. Otherwise, you might change a different record from the one the user was editing, which could be catastrophic.)

- Using pessimistic locking techniques. If, for example, you present someone with an editing form and lock that record, who knows whether that user will ever complete the task you offered? The user may instead use the Back button to visit another part of your site, or might even navigate to Monster.com to look for a different job. (Alternative: Never lock a record between Web hits. Instead, navigate back to the record when and if the user requests to save any edits and verify that the record has not been changed by another user.)

Further, if you attempt to migrate code from a network application that establishes the user's environment, you would have to execute that code on every hit, since the user keeps changing. This will probably incur much too big of a performance hit to be practical for most situations. Chapter 13 presents the entire topic of identifying and tracking users in detail and includes strategies for managing this situation.

Concept 7: Multiple Visual FoxPro instances—one user served

Now that you feel comfortable with the fact that your application is serving multiple users at once, I will complicate matters further: Each successive hit from the same user may not necessarily be handled by the same instance of your application. There are many possible reasons why this could occur, ranging from server reboots to decisions to run more than one simultaneous instance of your application for performance and scalability reasons.

Consider the impact of these possibilities. For example, suppose your application renders an HTML page to a user and that page includes a hyperlink that navigates to another dynamic page that is part of your application. If that user clicks on the link, their hit will not necessarily be processed by the same instance of your application as the one that rendered the first page.

You may have read the last paragraph and asked, "How could that be?" Or perhaps instead, "What does that mean for my application?" The answer to the first question is simple. There are two situations where this occurs. In both file-based and COM messaging modes, Web Connection allows multiple instances of your Visual FoxPro application to be run simultaneously, on one or more servers, taking care of incoming Web hits. Each hit is serviced by the next available (idle) instance without regard to user identity. Thus, if more than one instance is running, it is purely random whether successive hits from the same user are serviced by the same application. In addition, whether or not you run multiple instances, your application can certainly stop and be restarted between one hit and the next for any user. This could occur due to many factors, including anything from a server reboot to the normal loading and unloading of instances due to load when using COM messaging. The important point to understand is the user has no permanent handles or affinity settings that produce any consistent thread between successive hits.

The second question of what this means to your application is more difficult to answer. The general principle is to avoid any code that makes assumptions that an entire user session will be serviced by a single instance of your application while it is running. Here are some guidelines for complying with this principle:

- Do not attempt to track user state in any memory-based structure such as a cursor or an array. This information is not available to other instances, and would also be destroyed if your application were stopped and restarted. For example, you could be used to tracking the current user ID in your applications using a public (or high-level private) variable. This technique fails in a Web application, because the current user changes from one hit to the next.

- Do not create dependencies between successive hits that make an assumption that the next hit will be processed by the same running instance. An example is moving a record pointer to a specific record to render an HTML editing form, and then assuming that the pointer is still correctly positioned when the user eventually submits his or her changes. In fact, your application may have processed hits from tens or even hundreds of other users while the user in question was completing his or her edits.

- Do not perform any special actions when your application terminates, such as user cleanup or forced logouts, that would impact how the next user might be processed by another instance of the application.

- Think of your application as being a multi-user Visual FoxPro application. Because more than one instance can be running at one time and accessing the same data, you need to employ the same techniques you use in network applications. For example, try to RLOCK() a record just before saving changes, and then UNLOCK just after. If the lock fails, you can report back to the user with a nicely formatted HTML page (perhaps saying, "Please try again later"), instead of having the user see a Visual FoxPro error message ("Record is in use by another"). Similarly, the use of transactions concluding with either a commit or a rollback is superior to allowing the user to bump up against raw database error messages.

- To ensure that your application handles these situations properly, be certain to test its operation with multiple instances running. This is easy to accomplish even in file-based mode: Simply build your application into an EXE and start two or more instances of it from Windows. Be sure to have more than one user hit your application from different browsers on different machines when doing this testing.

- If you ever find yourself trying to implement an idea using global (PUBLIC) variables, you are definitely doing something wrong!

Concept 8: Web forms are not Windows forms!

One of the most difficult areas for developers who are new to Web applications is understanding the use of forms. Web forms differ from the forms deployed in a desktop application in many significant ways. I will try to present the main concepts behind Web forms and highlight the differences between using forms on the Web and in a desktop application.

Basic attributes of desktop forms

In most desktop applications, a form is synonymous with a single window that is part of the application. That form can either be modal or modeless. When forms are modal, the user must take an action (such as clicking an OK button) before anything else can be done in the application. When forms are modeless, more than one form can exist at once, and users can generally switch between open forms to suit their needs. When multiple modeless forms are open, the user can generally perform tasks in a random order—actions performed in one form do not affect the other forms, unless the application logic dictates otherwise. Although a modeless form need not be closed immediately, the application has control over all such forms, and can take any necessary action if the user tries to exit the application without closing any open forms.

Modern desktop development languages support a rich set of controls that handle most development needs, and often can also support add-on controls, such as third-party ActiveX controls when the built-in controls are not sufficient. These controls can often be bound to data sources, such that user actions can be saved to the database with little or no code involved. Control sources can be of a specified data type, such that data entry is limited to values of that type (for example, numeric or date) without writing any code. Finally, in desktop applications, the application generally has control over events at a granular level, often down to the individual keystroke.

Basics of a Web form

Almost nothing from the preceding two paragraphs applies to Web forms. A Web form is part of a larger HTML page, all of which appears in a single browser window. In fact, a single page can contain more than one form. The user often cannot distinguish how many forms are on any given page. Modal forms are generally impossible to create, and there is much less application control over what the user does with any form, because of the disconnected nature of Web applications. For instance, your application may send a blank form to the user, but you have no guarantee that the user will ever respond. If you are designing for cross-browser compatibility, Web forms are limited to a very basic set of controls—much fewer than offered with modern desktop languages. Text boxes only support character values, so editing numeric and date values requires special care during validation.[1] These controls cannot be easily bound to data sources without using third-party classes or writing your own control classes. Finally, Web forms are not "live" per se, in that your application is completely out of the picture until the user fills out the entire form and submits the entire form back to the server.

What this means is that you need to learn the concepts of Web forms from scratch. Your users may well see text boxes and command buttons on a Web page and not even realize the difference between those and similar controls in a desktop application; however, your work in rendering and processing these controls is completely different. In the remainder of this section, I will present some of the concepts in more detail.

---

[1] In fact, everything in an HTTP request and an HTML document is a string. You have no protection from strong data types, and generally must convert all non-character data to strings on the response side, and convert from strings back to other data types on the request side.

Structure of a Web form

A single form on a Web page consists of an opening <form> tag, a closing </form> tag, and any form elements (controls) that are found between those tags. The form must exist between the <body> and </body> tags of the HTML page. More than one form can appear on any Web page; however, these forms can neither overlap nor be nested. Improperly structured forms are difficult to troubleshoot, because different browsers respond in different ways to improperly structured forms.

Form elements include text boxes, text areas (similar to Visual FoxPro edit boxes), check boxes, radio buttons, list boxes (both single- and multiple-selection), hidden elements, and command buttons (both textual and graphical).

The most basic Web form usually includes one or more controls for the user to enter information and a command button to "submit" the form. The form tag's Action attribute indicates the server location to which the form variables are to be submitted. Here is an example of the HTML used to render a form with two text boxes and one Submit button:

```
<form method="POST" action="wc.dll?forms~ProcessUserInfo">
   <b>Your Name: </b><input type="TEXT" name="txtName" value="" size=20><br>
   <b>Email: </b><input type="TEXT" name="txtEmail" value="" size=50><br>
   <input type="SUBMIT"name="cmdSubmit" value="Submit Data"><br>
</form>
```

This form prompts the users for their name and email address. If they submit the form, it will be handled by the method indicated by the Action attribute, in this case ProcessUserInfo.

Two or more forms on one Web page

As indicated previously, more than one form can be included on a single Web page. This has both advantages and disadvantages. If the user will clearly want to use either one form or the other, a multiple-form page can be a convenient launching point from which users can navigate in differing directions.

On the other hand, having two or more forms can be confusing to users, particularly if more than one of the forms appears to apply to them at a single time. If your users fill out form elements from each of two forms, what do they do next? Whichever form they submit will result in their input to the other form being lost and ignored. Perhaps worse than this, the users may not even be able to tell whether they are working with one form or two! Observe the Web page shown in **Figure 1**.

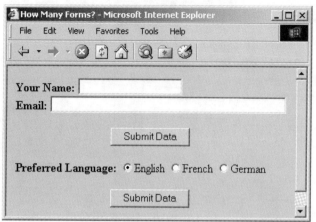

Figure 1. *Can you tell how many forms are really on this page?*

From examining this page you cannot tell whether there are two distinct forms, or a single form with two Submit buttons. Why would a user care? Well, suppose that a user had filled out the entire form (which often have many more than two fields) and was about to submit the form, when he noticed the little language preference option below. If this page consists of a single form, the user could now choose his preferred language and then submit the form by pressing either button. If instead the page consisted of two separate forms and the user clicked the second button, all of the data he typed into the first form would be lost.

Don't put your users through aggravation like this! Most users are not even sophisticated enough to realize there could even be an issue with this page. If your page must have this appearance, handle all elements within one form. Better yet is to eliminate the ambiguous design. In this example, the language preference could have been offered on the home page or some other point in the application.

A classic example of this problem appears on sites that include an "instant poll" or some other type of survey on all of the pages. If these are included on pages where the users also have an important form to fill out, you must make certain that they are not distracted by other options that interrupt the main purpose of the page. The next section covers a closely related problem with forms.

Ensuring forms get submitted

One of the biggest quality problems on Web sites involves the failure of user-provided data being submitted and processed. **Figure 2** presents a page that showcases the problem.

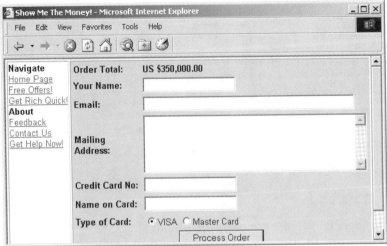

Figure 2. *Menu options can distract users from the task at hand.*

The overriding purpose of this page is to present the user with a form to process the order and specify shipping and credit card information. Nevertheless the page includes a menu with six other options. If the user fills out the form, *but fails to click the Process Order button*, the order is never processed! This could have been the user's intention, which is fine; but a very common problem is that users do not realize they have to press the Submit button, rather than simply filling out the form and clicking on some other menu option. This problem is exacerbated when the form is sufficiently lengthy that the Submit button scrolls off the viewable area on some browsers.

Various techniques can be used to work around this problem. You can repeat the Submit button at the top of the form. You can include fancy notes advising users that their order is not complete until they click the Submit button. None of these completely eliminates the problem, but each one helps with specific users. A better solution is to *eliminate the menu entirely* when important forms are presented. In this case, you can include a second Submit button with a caption of "Cancel Order" and then act accordingly. The user now has only two choices of how to proceed, which gives you much better control and chances of success.

Relating form elements to data—single record case

The preceding examples have involved blank forms for users to fill out. Very often, you will want to create forms to allow users to edit existing data. It is very important to understand how to relate data in your database to elements on your Web forms.

The key to these forms is in the NAME attribute of each form element. When you click a Submit button, the browser traverses the form and sends an encoded string of all form elements for which you have entered values using a syntax of <name>=<value>. WC decodes this string for you and provides the Request.Form(<name>) method, such that if you know the NAME that you gave each element, you can read the entered value back in.

Thus, each element on the form must have a unique name (and one that you can re-establish when you're reading the form) in order for Request.Form() to be able to distinguish one element from another. For a single record form, this is pretty easy. For example, you could name each form element the same as the underlying Visual FoxPro field name. A better convention is to prefix the form name with a three-letter prefix indicating the form element type. For example, a character field named Email might be edited in a form text box with a name of txtEmail. Assuming your code has already located the correct record, you can first render the text box using code such as:

```
Response.Write( [Email: ] + [<INPUT TYPE="TEXT" NAME="txtEmail" VALUE="] + ;
    TRIM( Email) + [" SIZE=20 MAXSIZE=] + TRANS( LEN( Email)) + [">] )
```

Then, when the form has been submitted, you can read the new value using code such as:

```
lcEmail = Request.Form( "txtEmail")
IF NOT ALLTRIM( m.lcEmail) == ALLTRIM( Email)
   REPLACE Email WITH m.lcEmail
ENDIF
```

Relating form elements to data—multiple record case

The previous approach works well when you are editing a single record; however, you may find cases where you want to edit several records in one form. A typical example is editing several child records in a table. There is no equivalent to a Visual FoxPro grid element in HTML. Nevertheless, Web pages are free to vary in length, so you can construct a form that presents child records in a table, and the page can grow with the number of child records.

But with multiple-record forms, you must give each form element a unique name. Because you are trying to edit the same fields from multiple records, you cannot just use the field name, or you end up with several form elements all with the same name, and there would be no way for Request.Form() to distinguish between these. The solution is to combine some primary or candidate key value for the record with the field name, so that you create a deterministic name for the form element corresponding to each field of each record.

Let's look at a basic example where you have a cursor of three fields from a Book table:

```
ID - integer primary key
Title - character (50)
BestSeller - logical
```

Now suppose you want to allow all second and third fields of these records to be edited at once. You cannot just use the name Title or txtTitle, for example, in your text box, since you would have several form elements all with the same name, and the browser would send them in such a way that your application could not tell them apart. So, you use that unique primary key value as your discriminator:

```
WITH Response
  .Write( [<table boder=1>] )
  SCAN
    .Write( [<tr>] )
    .Write( [<td><input type='TEXT' name='txtTitle_' + TRANSFORM(ID) + ;
      [' value='] + TRIM(Title) + [' size=] + TRANSFORM(LEN(Title)) + ;
      [></TD>] )
    .Write( [<td><input type='CHECKBOX' name='chkBestSeller_' + ;
```

```
      TRANSFORM(ID) + ;
      ['] + IIF( BestSeller, [ checked], []) + [ value=ON></TD>] )
   .Write( [</tr>] )
  ENDSCAN
  .Write( [</table>] )
ENDWITH
```

Note that we append the unique ID value (the primary key) onto the NAME of each text box and check box. This is critical to the second step, when you read in the values. In the form processing code, you use the exact same names when you call Request.Form—that is the whole key to how forms work. Remember, the browser is sending you back the name that you provided in the first place.

```
LOCAL lcTitle, llBestSeller
SCAN
   lcTitle = Request.Form('txtTitle_' + TRANSFORM(ID))
   llBestSeller = ( Request.Form('chkBestSeller_' + TRANSFORM(ID)) = "ON" )
   * Now take whatever action you want here, for example:
   REPLACE Title WITH m.lcTitle, BestSeller WITH m.llBestSeller
ENDSCAN
* Note: Assumes same records are in the SCAN as when form was rendered.
* If not a viable assumption, a little more checking is needed.
```

It is vital that you understand this mechanism before you proceed; otherwise, you will keep spinning your wheels. Note that this is not a Web Connection phenomenon—this is just how HTML forms work.

By the way, you may find it helpful when debugging form problems to insert something like this in your code as a debugging step in your second (form processing) method:

```
THIS.StandardPage("Form Variables", STRTRAN( Request.cFormVars, "&", "<br>"))
```

Try inserting this into your code and see what it tells you. You can comment out this line of code when you are not debugging. Once everything is working, you will see nicely delineated form variable names.

Check box and radio button differences

Check boxes and radio buttons on Web forms have some differences over their Windows counterparts. Most striking is that the text that appears adjacent to the square box (for check boxes) or circles (for radio buttons) is not part of the control itself. Because of this, the user cannot click on the text to select an item, but rather must click within the small box or circle. This is a constant annoyance for people used to the more flexible behavior in desktop forms. Fortunately, some browsers now offer relief. Starting with Version 4 of Microsoft Internet Explorer and Version 6 of Netscape Navigator, you can use the LABEL tag to wrap a form control with associated text, which results in the more familiar behavior of being able to click the text to select a value. For example:

```
<input type="CHECKBOX" id="myCheck" name="myCheck">
  <label for="myCheck">Click my box or my text!</label>
```

As a further point of interest, note that the prior example uses the same value for the ID and NAME attributes. Although this works for single check boxes, it would not work for radio buttons, because all individual radio buttons from one group must have the same NAME value. When I create radio buttons, I use a convention for the ID attribute of using the NAME value with an underscore followed by an index value. For example:

```
<input checked type="RADIO" name="fruit" id="fruit_1" value="oranges">
  <label for="fruit_1">Oranges</label>
<input type="RADIO" name="fruit" id="fruit_2" value="apples">
  <label for="fruit_1">Apples</label>
```

Concept 9: Validating user input

Validating user input is problematic in Web applications, because the users are not communicating with your application as they are filling out individual form elements. Instead, the entire form gets submitted at once for your application to process.

It is possible to include client-side JavaScript in your Web forms to perform some validation so that users get immediate feedback about what they entered before submitting the values to the server. Unfortunately, this is yet another technology for you to learn. Further, you can never guarantee that valid values are submitted, because of browser differences and the ability of clients to bypass or turn off the JavaScript. Therefore, even if you attempt to perform some validation at the client end, you must assume that all submitted values are potentially invalid.

Because invalid submittals are possible, and even likely, you must determine how you will handle these situations when they arise. One technique used by many Web sites is to process the submittal using a different URL from the one that rendered the form in the first place. In a Web Connection environment, this equates to one method for form rendering and a second for form processing. Using this technique, when validation errors arise, a message is displayed to the user indicating the problems that were found, and generally suggesting that the user click the Back button to fix the problems and submit the form again.

I find this to be an undesirable approach. One problem is that some users may not understand how to operate the Back button. Second, once they do navigate back to the form, the validation error message is no longer visible. Unless the problem was a simple one, the users may need that message while they are correcting the form. Finally, some techniques for forcing content expiration may result in the form becoming blank in some browsers, thus forcing the users to re-enter all of the previous data, when they might have only needed to fix a single field value.

A much better approach is to use the same Web Connection method for both form rendering and processing. I determine up front whether the request is a result of a form submittal. An easy way to make this determination is to check whether the current HTTP Request method is GET or POST, as follows:

```
llPosted = Request.ServerVariables( "REQUEST_METHOD") = "POST"
```

In my form-processing methods, I also set variables lcCancelCaption and lcSubmitCaption to the actual text captions on the form buttons. I can then refer to these variables *both* in the code that renders the buttons and in the code that determines whether either button was pressed. By using this technique, I ensure that the code continues to function correctly if the button captions are ever changed. (All of my forms have Cancel buttons to support users who don't understand Web site navigation via the Back button, or if I have a specific place I want them to go if they cancel.) All of this results in code such as the following, which would be part of a method in a process class, using a simple form with two fields, where the only validation rule is that neither field be empty:

```
LOCAL lcCancelCaption, lcCancelURL, lcSubmitCaption, ;
  lcValidMsg, llPosted, lcVar1, lcVar2
llPosted = Request.ServerVariables( "REQUEST_METHOD") = "POST"
lcCancelCaption = 'Cancel'
lcSubmitCaption = 'Search'
lcCancelURL = 'wc.dll?myapp~HomePage'
lcValidMsg = ''
IF NOT m.llPosted
  * Not submitted yet, create default form element values:
  lcVar1 = ''
  lcVar2 = ''
ELSE   && form submitted
  IF Request.Form( 'cmdsubmit') = m.lcCancelCaption
    Response.Redirect( m.lcCancelURL)
    RETURN .F.
  ENDIF
  * OK. Read form vars:
  lcVar1 = Request.Form( 'var1')
  lcVar2 = Request.Form( 'var2')
  * Validate:
  IF EMPTY( m.lcVar1)
    lcValidMsg = m.lcValidMsg + 'Var 1 cannot be empty.<BR>'
  ENDIF
  IF EMPTY( m.lcVar2)
    lcValidMsg = m.lcValidMsg + 'Var 2 cannot be empty.<BR>'
  ENDIF
  IF EMPTY( m.lcValidMsg)  && Everything checked out!
    * Do whatever the intention of the form is, then
    * display some result, such as:
    Response.ExpandTemplate( "ResultPage.wc")
    RETURN .F.  && no further processing needed
  ENDIF
ENDIF
* Now render the form:
WITH Response
  IF NOT EMPTY( m.lcValidMsg)  && problems were noted
    .Write( [<P ALIGN=CENTER><FONT COLOR="red"><B>] + ;
      [Validation Problems Encountered!</B><BR>] + ;
      m.lcValidMsg + [</FONT></P>] )
  ENDIF
  * Display the form:
  .Write( [<form method=post>] )
  .Write( [Search Item 1: <input type="TEXT" name="var1" value="] + ;
    m.lcVar1 + [" SIZE=20><BR>] )
  .Write( [Search Item 2: <input type="TEXT" name="var2" value="] + ;
    m.lcVar2 + [" size=20><br>] )
  .Write( [<input type="SUBMIT" name="cmdSubmit" value='] + ;
    m.lcSubmitCaption + ['> ])
  .Write( [<input type="submit" name="cmdSubmit" value='] + ;
```

```
  m.lcCancelCaption + ['> ])
 .Write( [</form>] )
ENDWITH
```

This type of flow control works well in Web Connection applications. Observe that you first determine whether the form is being submitted vs. simply being displayed for the first time. (This means your method is processed at least twice for each user—once when they first see the form and again when they submit the form.) If the form has not been submitted, you create blank values for the form elements and render the form. If instead the form is being submitted, you read each form variable's value, and check all the validation rules. Each rule violation results in a message being concatenated to the lcValidMsg variable. If after checking all rules, this variable is still empty, the entire submittal is valid and you can proceed with the intended result.

The key behavior occurs when validation problems are encountered. In this case, you display the validation error messages, followed by re-rendering the form. The form will display the values the user already submitted, and he or she can use that combined with the error messages to fix the values and resubmit. This is all accomplished in one step without any need for use of the Back and Forward buttons.

Validation tips on certain Visual FoxPro data types

Text boxes on HTML forms are all character-based. If your forms include text boxes representing fields of some other data types, there is no way to convince the client browser to understand this and limit keyboard entry in the ways that Visual FoxPro forms have always worked for you. Even character fields have some nuances. Following are some tips on using text boxes in HTML forms:

- When rendering a text box for entry of numeric values, you will need to use the Visual FoxPro TRANSFORM() function to convert the initial value to a string to be

  embedded in the VALUE attribute of the INPUT tag. For example:

  ```
  .Write( [<input value="] + TRANSFORM(m.lnPrice) + [" name="txtPrice">])
  ```

- When processing the submittal of numeric form elements, you cannot simply use the Visual FoxPro VAL() function to convert the string back to a numeric value. You should also consider stripping any commas, dollar signs, and other unwanted characters that can cause VAL() to return the wrong value. A typical approach for ignoring formatting characters in a string might look like:

  ```
  lnPrice = VAL( CHRTRAN( Request.Form( "txtPrice"), ", $", ""))
  ```

- When rendering fixed-length character fields, you should TRIM() their value first. If you do not do this, the browser will fill the text box with the trailing spaces, and the user cannot easily add characters to the current value. This will be either confusing or annoying, depending on the user's level of understanding; neither of these is a good outcome.

- Date fields are very problematic, because you cannot tell the browser to restrict the text input to valid date fields. There are countless approaches available on the Internet for dealing with this shortfall in HTML. Most of these involve client-side JavaScript. You are welcome to explore such options, but you must still assume that any date entry might be invalid when it is submitted to your application. The approach I use is to read the form variable and use the Visual FoxPro CTOD() function to convert the input to a date value. CTOD() returns an empty date if the string cannot be reconciled by Visual FoxPro to a valid date value. If the date value is empty, you can display an appropriate error message. This approach should be combined with a form that includes a note suggesting the proper date format in the first place.

Concept 10: Templates vs. scripts—huh?

Just after Web Connection developers become comfortable with some of the basics, whereby HTML output is produced entirely in Visual FoxPro code, they may start to encounter the terms "templates" and "scripts." They may wonder what these terms really mean and whether it is really necessary to learn about them. On the other hand, producing all HTML output line-by-line in code may start to seem inefficient. Perhaps their organization has good Web page designers who use WYSIWYG page editing tools, such as FrontPage, who could not be utilized if all pages were created from pure Visual FoxPro code.

The answer to these dilemmas is that the template and script technology should be explored to determine whether it will help create a better development environment. New Web Connection developers often have trouble understanding what this technology is and how they would use it. To understand it, consider that there are in fact three techniques to produce HTML output for a single Web request. These are not mutually exclusive—you can use whichever one best fits your needs and development preferences for each type of request. The three techniques are:

- **Entirely in code:** This is the simplest method to get basic dynamic output to a Web page. Using this approach, process code simply scripts the Response object, usually issuing either a series of Response.Write calls or, in very simple cases, by a single call to StandardPage.

- **Using templates:** A template is a separate file that is just like a normal HTML page, except that Visual FoxPro expressions can be inserted between the special delimiters <%= and %>. Instead of simply returning the file contents to the browser, a special merge operation is performed, wherein any expressions between these delimiters are evaluated at run time and the resulting string is inserted in place of the delimited expression. This merge operation is performed in your process code by calling the ExpandTemplate method of the Response object, passing the file name containing the HTML-like template. For example, if the template file included the string:

```
<h2>Produced by Visual FoxPro, Version <%=VERSION()%>, on <%=DATE()%></h2>
```

the Visual FoxPro version and today's date would be inserted into the output string. A template can also contain self-contained blocks of Visual FoxPro code that are executed as though they were individual subroutines. Each such block of code *must* return a string, which is merged into the HTML output in place of the code block. These code blocks appear between the special delimiters <% and %> (same as expression delimiters, except for the missing = sign). Examples are discussed later.

- **Using scripts:** Just like a template, a script is also a separate file that is like an HTML page, and can also contain Visual FoxPro expressions and code segments. Visual FoxPro expressions are merged in the same manner as with templates. The biggest difference is that code blocks do not have to be self-contained and do not use RETURN values. A script can contain much more flexible structures with pure HTML inserted between structural components, such as between SCAN and ENDSCAN statements. Unlike templates, nothing is merged into the output in place of the code blocks. (You can always use Response.Write if your code needs to insert a string in that place.) The merge operation is performed in your process code by calling the ExpandScript method of the Response object, passing the file name containing the HTML-like script.

So, the *big difference* between templates and scripts relates to the type of code blocks that can be inserted. In templates, only self-contained blocks can be used and each one must return a string. In scripts, you have much more flexibility, such as to wrap literal HTML with repeating structures such as SCAN-ENDSCAN, or conditional structures, such as IF-ELSE-ENDIF blocks. To see the difference between templates and scripts, consider the case where you have issued a query in your Process method and have an open cursor that you want to display in an HTML table with one record per row. In a template this table might look like:

```
<table>
<tr><th>Field #1</th><th>Field #2</th></tr><!--Column Headings-->
<%
PRIVATE lcOut
lcOut = ""
SCAN
  lcOut = m.lcOut + '<tr><td>' + Field_1 + '</td>' + ;
    '<td>' + Field_2 + '</td></tr>'
ENDSCAN
RETURN m.lcOut && must RETURN a string in templates!
%>
</table>
```

While the rest of the template file might look much like plain HTML, the preceding is mostly Visual FoxPro code. It would be difficult to train visual Web page designers with no Visual FoxPro experience how to create pages in this way. With a script, you have much more flexibility and control. To produce the same output, this portion of your script would look like:

```
<table>
<tr><th>Field #1</th><th>Field #2</th></tr><!--Column Headings-->
<% SCAN %>
  <tr>
    <td><%=Field_1%></td>
    <td><%=Field_2%></td>
```

```
    </tr>
<% ENDSCAN %>
</table>
```

   This is much more like true HTML. In fact, you could easily imagine laying out the table with a visual editor, and then just inserting the SCAN loop and the field expressions. Further, training someone without Visual FoxPro experience to make these transformations is much more straightforward. The only difference in processing code is whether you use the ExpandTemplate or ExpandScript method of the Response object.

   You can do anything with a script that you can do with a template, and much more. On the other hand, templates can be processed more efficiently than scripts, which can have a great impact on performance and throughput of your server application. In general, you should never use scripts where templates will suffice. So, once you get comfortable with the difference, you can evaluate which to use on a page-by-page basis. Further, if a page starts out as a template, and you later add requirements that seem to necessitate using a script, it is generally not difficult to transform the page and change your Process method to call ExpandScript instead of ExpandTemplate.

   Debugging both scripts and templates is more challenging than debugging pure Visual FoxPro code. Web Connection does attempt to provide error information back to the browser when errors occur, but this is not always enough. You can set breakpoints and use other familiar debugging techniques, but learning how best to deploy your debugging skills in a script or template processing environment can be an arduous process. One technique that works for some problems is to insert a SET STEP ON statement directly within a code block of the script or template. For problem scripts, a better option is to pre-compile as discussed in Chapter 12, "A Web Connection Application from Start to Finish," after which standard Visual FoxPro debugging techniques can be deployed. For templates, create all variables required by the template as private prior to executing the template, which allows you to check these values in the debugger if necessary.

   Table 2 summarizes the differences between templates and scripts.

Table 2. Templates vs. scripts.

Characteristic	Templates	Scripts
Can be compiled?	No	Yes
Execution speed	Fast	Slow (when not compiled)
Supports Visual FoxPro expressions?	Yes	Yes
Types of Visual FoxPro code blocks supported	Stand-alone blocks only	Can be split (for example, separate SCAN and ENDSCAN wrapped around HTML)
How to insert results from a code block	Code block must RETURN a string	Response.Write() anywhere in the code
Calling syntax	Response.ExpandTemplate()	Response.ExpandScript()
Debugging technique	Check variable values prior to calling ExpandTemplate()	Try pre-compiling problem scripts, which allows standard debugging techniques

Visual FoxPro 7 gives us another option

Before version 7 of Visual FoxPro, your choices were limited to either producing HTML strings in code or using scripts (or templates) to merge expressions within an HTML layout.

With Visual FoxPro 7 come excellent new textmerge features that improve the options for code-based response generation. Review the following example code:

```
LOCAL lcTxt AS STRING
lcTxt = "<table border=1>"
SCAN
   TEXT TO lcTxt ADDITIVE TEXTMERGE NOSHOW
     <tr valign=top>
       <td><%=Field_1%></td>
       <td><%=Field_2%></td>
       <td><%=Field_3%></td>
     </tr>
   ENDTEXT
ENDSCAN
Response.Write( m.lcTxt + [</table>])
```

This is pure Visual FoxPro code, but it actually looks much more like the example of a Web Connection script shown previously, because of the amount of HTML that can be constructed without requiring Visual FoxPro delimiters.

The key to this resides with the TO <memvar> clause that has been added to TEXT/ENDTEXT in Visual FoxPro 7. This allows you to include textmerge construction within your code without resorting to the creation of temporary files, thus making the option much faster and easier to maintain.

This new feature allows for a hybrid approach between pure code and scripts that may prove desirable to many Web Connection developers.

For the curious: How templates and scripts work

You can certainly use templates and scripts without ever needing to know anything beyond what has been presented so far. Nevertheless most Visual FoxPro developers are curious and want to understand how these mechanisms actually function.

Templates are much simpler than scripts to process, which also accounts for the difference in performance between the two mechanisms. A template can be processed in a linear fashion. All text that is not between delimiters is considered to be pure HTML and is dumped straight to the output stream in large chunks, which is very fast. Whenever a Visual FoxPro expression is encountered, a simple EVALUATE() is performed and the result is appended to the output stream (non-character results are first TRANSFORMed). Blocks of code are executed using CodeBlock, and the character return values are again appended to the output stream.

Scripts present a more difficult situation. Blocks of code do not have to be self-contained. In the preceding script example, one code block is simply "SCAN" and the other "ENDSCAN", which obviously cannot be executed by themselves or Visual FoxPro errors would result. Clearly something more clever is happening behind the scenes.

In fact, what happens is the entire script file is first converted completely to Visual FoxPro code, and then that code is run in its entirety using either CodeBlock or by compiling and running it. The converted version of the previous partial script file might look like:

```
TEXT
<table>
<tr><th>Field #1</th><th>Field #2</th></tr><!--Column Headings-->
ENDTEXT
SCAN
   TEXT
   <tr>
     <td><<Field_1>></td>
     <td><<Field_2>></td>
   </tr>
   ENDTEXT
ENDSCAN
TEXT
</table>
ENDTEXT
```

Three things have happened. First, all of the plain blocks of HTML have been wrapped in Visual FoxPro TEXT-ENDTEXT blocks, so that plain text actually becomes executable code, and the entire script can be executed. Second, the delimiters of all expressions have been converted to the Visual FoxPro TEXTMERGE delimiters << and >>. Third, all of the Visual FoxPro code blocks have been extracted from their delimiters. The result of this is that the Web Connection framework can now SET TEXTMERGE ON and execute this code while routing the output to a file whose contents can then be read and sent as the HTML response.

These explanations have been simplified for the purpose of this book. Developers who license the full version of Web Connection receive source code and the very curious can explore the ExpandTemplate and ExpandScript methods of class wwResponse, in addition to worker classes wwEval, wwScriptResponse, and wwVfpScript, all of which play a role in this complex mechanism.

Conclusion

There are several difficult concepts with which a developer must come to terms when shifting from desktop to Web development. In this chapter, I have attempted to introduce some of the most common of these concepts. The time taken to get comfortable with these ideas will pay for itself many times over.

Chapter 11
Managing Your Configuration

A production Web application includes many configurable aspects and several file locations. Configuration files provide the key for managing all of the requisite settings in order that all of the pieces work together.

A complete Web Connection application involves the coordination of several components. Each component has one or more settings, such as specifying file locations. These settings can vary between your development and production environments. This chapter looks at both the individual settings and the mechanisms provided for maintaining them. I first examine the structure and contents of each of the two configuration files. Later in the chapter, I present the mechanics of how these files are created, when they are read, and how to make changes to configuration settings.

Configuration file overview

The configuration settings for a Web Connection application are maintained in two separate INI files. The first configuration file includes the settings used by the ISAPI connector (WC.DLL). This file must be named WC.INI and must be located in the same physical folder as the WC.DLL file.

The second configuration file includes settings used by your Visual FoxPro application. This file should have the same root name as your Visual FoxPro project files. Thus, if your project is named DemoApp.PJX, your configuration file would be named DemoApp.INI and be located in the same folder as your project.

I will now dive deeply into everything you might need to know about these files and their maintenance; but first, I must offer one piece of advice. Your first reaction might be to look at the names and sheer number of configuration settings and become overwhelmed. Don't be! Although there are many settings available to help fine-tune your application, there are very few with which you need to become familiar immediately. Some you may never use at all. If you have set up your directory structures as recommended in the earlier chapters of this book, and you use the Web Connection New Project wizard to create your application, initial copies of INI files will be created for you that require little or no modification for you to get started.

Why not just one configuration file?

A logical question for a first-time Web Connection developer to ask is why there needs to be two separate INI files for a single application. The answer lies in the architecture of how the Web Connection engine operates. Primarily, the ISAPI connector (WC.DLL) and your Visual FoxPro executable do not reside in the same location. These two components are not even required to know the whereabouts of each other. In fact the two could even be on different machines. As such, it makes sense to have separate configuration files for the two, thus allowing maximum flexibility in deployment and scalability options.

This need is particularly evident when you consider how Web Connection implements its file-based messaging mechanism. The WC.DLL component communicates with your Visual FoxPro application via temporary files that are written and read in a pre-arranged location and with pre-established file extensions. This entire mechanism relies on each INI file having identical settings for both the temporary path name and the temporary file extension. Without these exact matches, your Web Connection application will not respond to a single Web hit!

Inside the WC.INI file

The WC.INI file includes all of the configurable parameters that are used by the ISAPI connection code in WC.DLL. The settings in this file tend to remain fixed once your application is running. The only time you make further changes is if you change something about how the application is deployed (for example, if you switch between file-based messaging and COM servers). Further, the settings in this file are generally not used by your Visual FoxPro application, and with one key exception (discussed later), the settings in this file are completely independent of the settings in your application's configuration file.

If you use the Web Connection New Project wizard, a WC.INI file is automatically created for you and placed in the proper Web folder together with the WC.DLL file. You can also create this file manually by copying the WC.INI file from the scripts folder of the Web Connection installation and editing the setting for your application. **Figure 1** shows a typical WC.INI file with most of the comments (identified with a leading semicolon) removed.

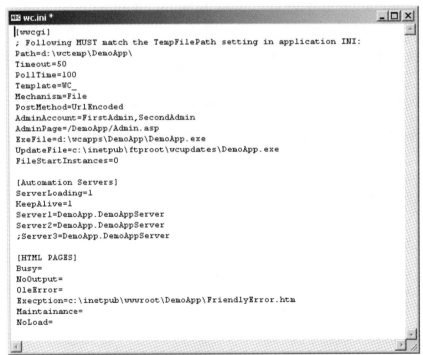

Figure 1. Contents of a typical WC.INI file.

Table 1 presents each of these settings in detail. As you can see, most of these are either optional or can be left at the Web Connection default value without further consideration. Pay particular attention, however, to the Path setting. Erroneous Path settings are among the most common mistake for new Web Connection developers. Also note that each setting must appear under the correct INI file section ([wwcgi], [Automation Servers], or [HTML Pages]), because Web Connection uses standard Windows API functions, for which the section name is a parameter, to read INI file settings.

Table 1. *This table presents each setting from the WC.INI file.*

Setting	Usage notes	Required?
Path	The full path to the directory where temporary files are exchanged during the file-based messaging process. Unless this setting exactly matches the TempFilePath setting in the application INI file, your Web Connection application will fail to respond to even a single Web hit! (Example: d:\wctemp\DemoApp\) (Note that, while the trailing backslash is not specifically required for this setting, it is for other Web Connection path settings, and should always be used.)	Yes. Critical under file-based messaging. Also used with both messaging mechanisms to determine location of wcerrors.TXT error log file.
Timeout	Time in seconds that WC.DLL will wait for your Visual FoxPro application to respond sending a "No Output" error message back to the user. See the NoOutput option below for customizing this message. (Default: 50 seconds.)	Yes.
PollTime	Under file-based messaging, determines how frequently (in milliseconds) WC.DLL checks to see if your Visual FoxPro application has returned a result page. (Default: 100 milliseconds)	Yes, for file-based messaging only.
Template	Determines file extension used for temporary files created under file-based messaging. The default is WC_, which you should never change unless you are trying to run two separate Web Connection applications via the same temporary directory (a practice that is strongly discouraged). Must match exactly the Template setting in your application INI file!	Yes, for file-based messaging only.
Mechanism	Controls whether WC.DLL communicates with your Visual FoxPro application using file-based messaging or via COM. (Possible settings: File or Automation)	Yes.
PostMethod	Always leave this set to URLEncoded. Vestige of a previous design option.	Yes.

Table 1. *Continued.*

Setting	Usage notes	Required?
AdminAccount	Comma-delimited string of Windows user accounts that are allowed to access various administrative functions. Leaving this blank allows anyone accessing the site to perform these functions. Setting this to "Any" allows any authenticated Windows user to perform these functions. (Note: If your virtual directory is set to accept Integrated Windows Authentication (formerly called "Windows NT Challenge Response Authentication"), it must also be set to accept Basic Authentication in order for Web Connection to check whether the user is one of those specified in this setting. Refer to Chapter 8, "Configuring Server Software," for details of configuring Microsoft Internet Information Server.)	No.
AdminPage	URL to the Web page with links to the administrative functions. The default is to use the admin.asp file, which is provided by Web Connection and is installed automatically if you use the wizards. If WC.DLL is located in a separate folder, this URL must include the relative or absolute path required to locate the file.	No.
ExeFile	Full path and file name to your Visual FoxPro executable file. Used for automatic code updates (under COM). Also used in conjunction with the FileStartInstances setting under file-based messaging to automatically start your executable after a server reboot. (Example: d:\wcapps\DemoApp\DemoApp.exe)	No, but noted features become unavailable if not provided.
UpdateFile	Full path and file name to the location where you will upload new versions of your EXE to the production server. For maximum flexibility in off-site management, I recommend that this be a password-protected FTP directory. Used for the automatic code update feature under COM messaging to allow an updated EXE file to be replaced while the Web server is running. (See Chapter 14, "COM vs. File-Based Messaging," for a discussion of performing automatic code updates.) (Example: c:\inetpub\ftproot\wcupdates\ DemoApp.exe)	No, but automatic code update feature becomes unavailable if not provided.
FileStartInstances	Controls how many copies of your executable to start automatically under file-based messaging. Upon receiving the initial hit to your application, WC.DLL will start one or more instances of your executable if this setting is greater than 0. Under certain circumstances, particularly on unattended servers, this can help automatically recover your site after a server reboot. Leave this set to 0 if you do not want to have your application automatically started in this way. (Default: 0)	No, used under file-based messaging only.

Table 1. *Continued.*

Setting	Usage notes	Required?
ServerLoading	Under COM messaging with multiple instances, this affects whether each subsequent hit is cycled between the instances ("round robin" loading) or based on load requirements. (Values: 0 = load-based, 1 = round robin)	Applies to COM messaging only.
KeepAlive	Under COM messaging, affects whether, after 6-8 minutes of inactivity, your Visual FoxPro COM server is allowed to shut down. If it is allowed, the next hit suffers the performance drag of waiting for the instance of Visual FoxPro to start back up. For an application that is used infrequently, setting this to 0 allows your Visual FoxPro application to terminate, so that the server can use the system resources for other services. There are obvious trade-offs here that must be weighed based on specific circumstances. (Values: 0 = Normal, 1 = Keep Alive)	Applies to COM messaging only.
Server1	Class name for the first instance of your Visual FoxPro COM server. (Example: DemoApp.DemoAppServer)	Applies to COM messaging only.

Server2, …	Second and subsequent instances of your COM server. The number of these lines in the WC.INI file controls how many instances (up to 32) of your Visual FoxPro application will be instantiated and managed by WC.DLL. An approximate rule of thumb, for a machine dedicated to your application's use, is to allow two instances per processor.
	In general, each of these settings will have exactly the same value. For example, specifying:
	    Server1=DemoApp.DemoAppServer
	    Server2=DemoApp.DemoAppServer
	    Server3=DemoApp.DemoAppServer
	would tell Web Connection to create three instances of your application.
	You can also install your application on remote servers and create further instances via DCOM. If you do this, you specify the machine name for remote instances:
	    Server4=DemoApp.DemoAppServer,
	    OtherMachine
	See Chapter 14 for a discussion of COM server deployment.
		Yes, when you want more than one server instance. Applies to COM messaging only.

Table 1. *Continued*.

Setting	Usage notes	Required?
Busy	Allows you to specify a custom Web page to be displayed in place of the automatic message that WC.DLL provides, if your Web application is busy, such that the request cannot be handled. This should be a full file system path and file name. Your application is "busy" if a new hit is received by WC.DLL and none of your Visual FoxPro COM servers are available, because they are processing other hits. (Example: c:\inetpub\wwwroot\DemoApp\Errors\ Busy.htm)	No.
NoOutput	Same as above, but covers the automatic response when your application fails to provide a response in the requisite period of time as specified in the Timeout setting above.	No.
OleError	Same as above, but covers the automatic response when an OLE error occurs while WC.DLL is trying to call your application.	No.
Exception	Same as above, but covers the automatic responses when an internal error occurs in WC.DLL itself. If this unexpected condition ever arises, notify West Wind immediately. (Note that some versions of Web Connection had an incorrect spelling of "exception" in wizard-generated copies of WC.INI.)	No.
Maintainance (sic)	Same as above, but covers the automatic responses when you have set the maintenance flag. Note the required non-preferred spelling!	No.
NoLoad	Same as above, but covers the automatic responses when an OLE error occurs while trying to load your COM server.	No.

You now have a good idea of what settings are specified in the WC.INI file. The next section presents the second configuration file, which is your application INI file. Following that, the remaining sections of this chapter discuss how each of these files is created, used by your application, and maintained.

Inside your application INI file

Your Visual FoxPro application INI file has two levels of configuration settings. First are those settings that affect the entire application. Second are those settings particular to each sub-application, or "process." This structure is maintained with the application INI file by placing all of the application-wide settings in the [Main] section, and then by creating a separate section for each process (for example: [Process1], [Process2]). In most applications, there are more settings in the [Main] section, and these settings are more frequently subject to modification than in each Process section. Each of the Process sections tends to have only two or three settings, such as the path or connection string to the underlying database, and these settings seldom change.

Introducing the configuration object

Although the INI file represents the physical manifestation of your application settings, your application does not have to read directly from that file. Instead, the Web Connection framework provides a class, wwServerConfig, that encapsulates the usage of this file. Not only does this absolve you of the need to call Windows API functions in order to read the INI file settings, but it allows for changing the physical implementation in the future (such as storing settings in the Registry or in XML files) without having any impact on your application code.

The configuration object that you instantiate from the wwServerConfig class has one property for each corresponding setting in the [Main] section of your application INI file. Further, in order to encapsulate the hierarchy of individual Process sections, this object has one additional property for each of these sections, which is an object reference to a child object. Each child object then includes one property for each setting for that process.

A picture could be worth 1,000 words here, so in **Figure 2** you can see an example application INI file, while in **Figure 3** you can see the matching Visual FoxPro class definition code.

Figure 2. Contents of a typical application INI file. This application has two sub-applications or "processes."

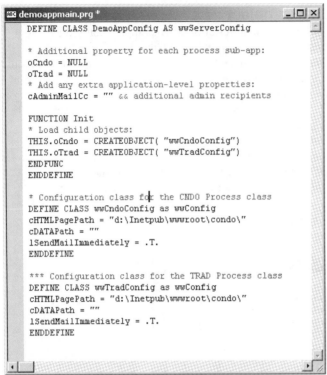

```
demoappmain.prg *                                    _ □ ×
    DEFINE CLASS DemoAppConfig AS wwServerConfig

    * Additional property for each process sub-app:
    oCndo = NULL
    oTrad = NULL
    * Add any extra application-level properties:
    cAdminMailCc = "" && additional admin recipients

    FUNCTION Init
    * Load child objects:
    THIS.oCndo = CREATEOBJECT( "wwCndoConfig")
    THIS.oTrad = CREATEOBJECT( "wwTradConfig")
    ENDFUNC
    ENDDEFINE

    * Configuration class for the CNDO Process class
    DEFINE CLASS wwCndoConfig as wwConfig
    cHTMLPagePath = "d:\Inetpub\wwwroot\condo\"
    cDATAPath = ""
    lSendMailImmediately = .T.
    ENDDEFINE

    *** Configuration class for the TRAD Process class
    DEFINE CLASS wwTradConfig as wwConfig
    cHTMLPagePath = "d:\Inetpub\wwwroot\condo\"
    cDATAPath = ""
    lSendMailImmediately = .T.
    ENDDEFINE
```

***Figure 3**. Visual FoxPro code that creates the object hierarchy that encapsulates the reading and writing to the application INI file shown in Figure 2.*

As I mentioned earlier, the configuration object has an additional child object for each process. In the specific example shown in Figure 3, there are two of these child objects. Notice the two CREATEOBJECT statements in the Init method, which instantiate these Process objects.

If you study and compare these two figures, there are several important aspects of which to make special note, since they all help in the understanding of the relationship between the Visual FoxPro classes and the physical INI file:

1. Although I stated there was a one-to-one relationship between lines in the [Main] section of the INI file and properties in the main configuration class, you'll note several lines in the INI file that don't match up with properties in the code. The explanation is that the DemoAppConfig class is based on the framework wwServerConfig class, and all of the "missing" properties are already defined as properties of that parent class. These parent properties are therefore default configuration object properties *that apply to all Web Connection applications*. As such, you do not need to repeat these properties in the class constructor code, unless you specifically want to override any framework default values. See the next section, "Built-in application INI file settings," for a description of each of these default properties.

2. The property names differ from the INI file setting names, in that the property names are prefixed with a character that appears to indicate its data type. This is not simply a convention to aid in readability, but rather *a requirement for these classes to operate.* The wwServerConfig class actually parses each property name, and uses the first character to perform automatic type conversions, after reading the corresponding value from the INI file. Thus, if you find the need to add additional configuration settings to your application, the property names must correspond to the INI setting names in this manner. For example, to add a numeric setting that limits the number of records displayed in a search result to 100, you would add a property called, say, nMaxSearchRecords to your configuration class, while the corresponding INI file setting would simply read MaxSearchRecords=100. Detailed examples of adding new INI settings are presented later in this chapter.

3. Perhaps most importantly, you will notice that the values do not match between the properties in the Visual FoxPro code and the settings in the INI file. The point is that the Visual FoxPro code simply sets up the right object hierarchy and creates the right property names. The actual run-time values for those properties are maintained in the INI file.

I cannot overemphasize the need to understand these points, particularly the last one. The Web Connection framework provides a great way to encapsulate the mechanics of working with configuration settings. But you need to feel somewhat comfortable that you understand the relationship between the Visual FoxPro code and the INI file structure. Once again, your Visual FoxPro code simply creates the object hierarchy with the requisite properties and data types. The run-time production values, as you would expect, are those in the physical INI file.

Built-in application INI file settings

As I just discussed, there are several properties built into the wwServerConfig object that correspond to configuration settings that will apply to every Web Connection application you create. These appear in the [Main] section of the application INI file. Following is an overview of these settings:

- **AdminEmail** (property cAdminEmail) is the email address of the Web site administrator. Web Connection uses this internally to send out automatic notifications when errors occur in your application, depending on the setting of AdminSendErrorEmail. You can also use this setting for your applications' own email functionality, such as the return address for outgoing messages. *Caution:* Because this is used in the "from" field of outgoing SMTP messages, this must be a single address, rather than a comma-delimited list.

- **AdminMailServer** (property cAdminMailServer) is either the domain name or IP address of the SMTP server machine that is to be used for outgoing messages. If you are using the IIS SMTP service, this can be the name or address of the local machine.

- **AdminSendErrorEmail** (property lAdminSendErrorEmail) is a flag that controls whether Web Connection automatically sends an email message whenever a Visual FoxPro error is encountered in your application. Whether set to send messages or not,

Web Connection responds to the client with a generic HTML error page. This setting only applies when your application is compiled with the DEBUGMODE compiler directive in WCONNECT.H turned off.

- **TempFilePath** (property cTempFilePath) is a vital setting that directly affects Web Connection file-based messaging. This setting specifies the full path to the folder where temporary files are placed. This setting must exactly match the Path setting in the WC.INI file, or your entire application will fail to operate. The trailing backslash is required for proper operation.

- **Template** (property cTemplate) is used in conjunction with the TempFilePath setting to specify the file extension for the temporary files used in file-based messaging. This setting must exactly match the Template setting in the WC.INI file, or your entire application will fail to operate.

- **LogToFile** (property lLogToFile) is a flag that controls whether each hit is recorded to a log file (which can be either a Visual FoxPro database table or a SQL Server table).

- **SaveRequestFiles** (property lSaveRequestFiles) is a flag that controls whether temporary file copies are made for each incoming request and outgoing response. Allowed values are on and off, which are converted to configuration object logical property values of .T. and .F.. *Warning:* Turning this option on greatly impedes your application performance and throughput. You should use this for debugging and troubleshooting only!

- **ShowServerForm** (property lShowServerForm) is a flag that controls whether your application displays a status window that shows hits being processed. Under file-based messaging, it is normal to keep this option on. Allowed values are on and off, which are converted to configuration object logical property values of .T. and .F..

- **ShowStatus** (property lShowStatus) is a flag that controls whether information is displayed in the server window that shows hits in an edit region as they are processed. This setting works in conjunction with the ShowServerForm setting. Allowed values are on and off, which are converted to configuration object logical property values of .T. and .F..

- **UseMTS** (property lUseMTS) is a flag that controls whether Microsoft Transaction Server (COM+) is automatically assumed and invoked. This topic is beyond the scope of this book, and the setting should always be turned off. Allowed values are on and off, which are converted to configuration object logical property values of .T. and .F. Note that this setting does not impact the ability of your application to host middle-tier components that themselves are part of COM+ packages. Your Web Connection application does not need to run under COM+, because the pool management features built into WC.DLL provide an alternative approach to handling simultaneous hits to your site.

- **ScriptMode** (property nScriptMode) determines whether script files (WCS) should be precompiled (2) or executed using CodeBlock (3). When developing and testing your application, the default value of 3 should be used. Later, in the performance tuning stages of your application cycle, you may be able to improve performance of your scripts by switching to precompilation mode. See Chapter 12, "A Web Connection Application from Start to Finish," for a presentation of how to deploy scripts in your applications.

- **TimerInterval** (property nTimerInterval) applies only to file-based messaging and controls the frequency in milliseconds at which the timer fires to look for new files in the temporary file directory. The default of 200 milliseconds can be adjusted lower on a dedicated machine to improve performance, or higher on a machine that hosts other services to reduce the load that your application places on the disk system and other resources.

- **ComReleaseURL** (property cComReleaseURL) is the URL to be used under COM messaging to allow automatic releasing of your Visual FoxPro application from memory. This setting allows you to release your Visual FoxPro application using the Exit button on the server form when your application is deployed under COM messaging. This is necessary because your application, which is a COM server, has been instantiated by WC.DLL and therefore must be released by WC.DLL. By specifying a URL in this property, when you press the Exit button, an HTTP request is made to WC.DLL to release the COM server instances. The value of this property should include a complete URL, such as http://localhost/myapp/wc.dll?_maintain~release.

Adding a main INI setting

Beyond the built-in settings of the [Main] section of your application INI file listed previously, you may occasionally find the need to add a configurable setting of your own. This is a good choice when you encounter something that you want to let your administrator control without having to recompile your application. By studying the built-in settings in the previous section, you should get a feeling for these types of settings.

An example, as shown in Figure 2, is the addition of an administrative "cc" list for email messages. As I discussed earlier, you cannot simply add names to the AdminEmail property, because that is used in the "from" field of outgoing messages, and this is required to be a single email address. But suppose you want to send some messages to more than one administrator. One solution would be to add a configurable setting that is used for these additional addresses. All that is required is to add a line for the new setting in the [Main] section of the INI file, and a single property to the main configuration class definition, as shown in Figure 3, and subsequently the system administrator can revise this setting as the desired recipients change. I discuss how you read and make use of these settings in your application code later in this chapter.

Typical process INI settings

In addition to the built-in application settings that are part of the [Main] section of the INI file, there are two settings that are added by default to each child process:

- **DataPath** (property cDataPath) is added by default for your use in identifying the physical path to the database used by that process. This property is a convenience that is provided for your own use in the application. Your application can use this setting in different ways. You could choose to add the data directory to your Visual FoxPro path, using the Web Connection function Path, after which you could USE and SELECT your data with no path prefixes required; or you can reference the data path property directly in your data access code.

- **HTMLPagePath** (property cHTMLPagePath) is added by default for your use in identifying the physical path where various HTML and related files are stored. This setting can be useful in cases where your Visual FoxPro application needs to read or manipulate these files. This setting is often used when processing Web Connection scripts or templates, or when publishing static HTML files.

Adding a process INI setting

Much like adding a setting to the [Main] section of the INI, you may also need to add settings to a single Process section. This is done in exactly the same manner—simply add a new line for the setting to the INI file, and a property to that class definition. Figures 2 and 3 show an additional line (Sendmailimmediately) and an additional property (lSendMailImmediately) that have been added to allow the application to decide whether email messages are sent in real time, or queued to be sent later by another component. Note again that the Web Connection framework automatically handles the job of converting string settings of on and off in the INI file to logical property values of .T. and .F. I discuss how you read and make use of these settings in your application code later in this chapter.

How the INI files are initially created

You must have a WC.INI file accompanying your WC.DLL file in order for your system to function at all. If you use the New Project wizard from the Web Connection console, this file is created for you with all of the settings established to allow your new application to function. You can also choose to create this file manually by making a copy of the WC.INI file from the scripts folder of your Web Connection installation directory, and editing the settings as needed. If you are new to Web Connection, the wizard approach is probably more straightforward and less error-prone.

The same wizard will also create a new application INI file in the same folder where your new Visual FoxPro project is created, which is the folder where Web Connection is installed. Further, if you modify your application by adding an extra process class, the New Process wizard will modify both your main program and the application INI file to add the new class and section, respectively.

As you can see, Web Connection provides tools so that you do not have to create these files by hand.

How and when the INI files settings are read

It is important to know both how and when each of the INI file settings are read. There is a distinct difference between the two.

The WC.DLL file reads all of the settings in the WC.INI file when it is first loaded into the Web server's memory space. This occurs on the first hit that references your application. The DLL file tends to remain in memory even if your Visual FoxPro application is not active. As such, once it has been loaded, you generally cannot edit WC.INI manually and expect the changes to be recognized without completely stopping and starting the HTTP service. Fortunately, as discussed later in this chapter, there are other live mechanisms that work well for making immediate changes to these settings.

The application INI file is read when your Visual FoxPro application first starts. The file is parsed and the properties in your configuration object hierarchy are loaded with matching values from the INI file. Further, when your Visual FoxPro application terminates, in any case where a property value does not correspond with the INI file, the INI file is updated. This actually means that you can start your application with a partial or missing INI file and a proper one will be created for you, providing your application can function with the default property values in your class constructor code.

How to read and use INI settings in your application

Now that you are aware of all of the settings available to you, and how to add new settings, you need to know how to make reference to these setting values in the process class of your application code. The primary configuration object is always available via a server property oConfig that maintains an object reference. Thus you can refer to:

```
THIS.oServer.oConfig
```

Further, if you use the default Web Connection practice that provides a private variable Server, you can even refer to simply:

```
Server.oConfig
```

Each of the child configuration objects is available as an object reference of the main configuration object. Thus, using the example in Figure 3, which shows a hypothetical application with a process named "Trad", you could refer to the "Trad" process configuration object via:

```
Server.oConfig.oTrad
```

Putting this all together, if you need to refer to the path to the database for that process class, you might use code such as:

```
LOCAL lcDataPath
lcDataPath = Server.oConfig.oTrad.cDataPath
USE ( m.lcDataPath + "Customer" )
```

You probably would not want to repeat this code throughout your application every time you wanted to open a data table. Fortunately, both the database path and the HTML file paths are so frequently needed that the wwProcess class already has two properties that are available for storing these paths. Although these properties aren't initialized automatically, it's easy enough to do. The following code, if placed in the Process method of your process class, will make these two paths readily available throughout all of the methods in that class:

```
THIS.cDataPath = Server.oConfig.oTrad.cDataPath
THIS.cHTMLPagePath = Server.oConfig.oTrad.cHTMLPagePath
```

Now in any of your methods you can just use code like:

```
USE ( THIS.cDataPath + "Customer" )
```

If instead your data is all stored in a Microsoft SQL Server database, you would no longer care about file system paths, but might instead want to store a connection string as a configurable parameter.

Reading settings from WC.INI

In general, the settings in WC.INI are used strictly by WC.DLL and are not needed in any of the Visual FoxPro methods that you will construct. There can, however, be occasional exceptions that you discover as your needs advance. Fortunately, Web Connection now includes a Request object method named GetWcIniValue that handles these needs. The method takes two parameters, for key name and section name; however, the latter defaults to the main [wwCGI] section, which covers most needs.

The most likely setting that you will want to read is the AdminAccount setting. By using this setting you can create your own maintenance functions and then restrict access to the same users who are allowed access to the built-in Web Connection maintenance functions. An example follows:

```
LOCAL lcAdminAccount, lcUserId, llResult
lcAdminAccount = UPPER( THIS.oRequest.GetWcIniValue("AdminAccount"))
IF NOT EMPTY( m.lcAdminAccount ) && user specified
  lcUserId = UPPER( THIS.oRequest.GetAuthenticatedUser())
  DO CASE
  CASE EMPTY( m.lcUserId ) && not logged in
  CASE m.lcAdminAccount == "ANY"  && anyone is OK
    llResult = .T.
  CASE "," + m.lcUserId + "," $ "," + m.lcAdminAccount + ","
    * User ID is found in the comma-delimited list of admin accounts.
    * Note the use of commas to avoid accepting one user whose ID is
    * a subset of another user's ID.
    llResult = .T.
  ENDCASE
ELSE  && no login requirement
  llResult = .T.
ENDIF
IF NOT m.llResult
  THIS.oResponse.Authenticate( THIS.oRequest.GetServerName() )
ENDIF
RETURN m.llResult
```

How to change INI settings on production applications

As I discussed earlier in this chapter, INI file settings are read in and used in such a way that you cannot simply edit these files while your application in running and expect to be able to see those changes take effect. In fact, in the case of the application INI, these changes would be overwritten with the old values as soon as your Visual FoxPro application terminated! In the case of the WC.INI file, the changes would eventually be used, but possibly not until the Web service was stopped and started (or the machine rebooted).

Fortunately, Web Connection offers several better mechanisms to enable you to make changes to each of these file settings. Further, the changes can be made via the HTTP protocol, thus enabling easy remote administration of Web Connection applications.

The easiest way to edit settings in either of the configuration files is via a Web Connection method itself named EditConfig that is included in the wwMaint.PRG file and is built into each new Web Connection project by default if you use the wizards. The server administration Web page admin.asp that is provided with Web Connection includes a link directly to that method. **Figure 4** shows this administration page, and the arrow indicates the link to click to bring up the INI editor window, which is then shown in **Figure 5**. You can also summon the editor directly by entering the URL of http://<path>/wc.dll?wwMaint ~EditConfig. Although it may seem to be a security risk to allow these files to be edited via a Web interface, all of the methods in wwMaint.PRG are protected, so that only those users specified in the AdminAccount setting in WC.INI can access these methods. If you prefer not to make these methods available via the Web, you can always comment out the lines of code in your main program that call wwMaint.PRG.

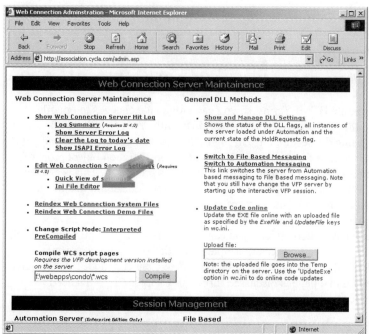

Figure 4. On the standard admin.asp page is a link to the INI File Editor.

Figure 5. The INI File Editor page provides forms for updating either configuration file.

Note that these are separate HTML forms, so you can only make changes to one file at a time. Web Connection handles these two forms slightly differently. After making a change to your application INI file (using the second form in Figure 5), the changes are saved and your Visual FoxPro application re-reads them immediately into the configuration object property values, so that these changes take effect when the very next hit is processed. This is not the case for changes made to WC.INI via the first form. Instead, when you submit this form, the physical changes are saved to disk, but you get a response that provides an option to read these settings immediately. **Figure 6** shows this response. You click the reload link to have your changes take effect immediately. Alternatively, you can reload the settings from your WC.INI file to the configuration object by calling the http://<path>/wc.dll?_maintain~readSetupIni URL. After WC.DLL reloads these settings, it displays the Web Connection DLL Status page. The information presented on that page is discussed further in Chapter 18, "Advanced Troubleshooting and Maintenance."

Figure 6. When you make changes to the WC.INI file, you get the option to reload these settings, making the changes take effect immediately.

In addition to the Web interface for editing the INI files, as shown previously, you can also modify settings from the Web Connection server console while your application is running. The main Visual FoxPro server form includes a Status command button. Pressing that button brings up the dialog shown in **Figure 7** from which you can initiate, among other options, the following actions that relate to configuration settings in the INI files discussed in this chapter:

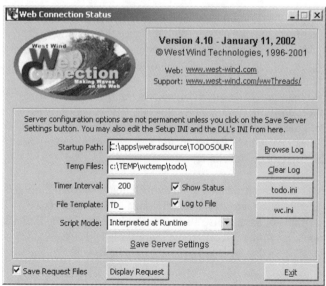

Figure 7. This dialog appears when you click the Status button on your Web Connection server form. Notice that the wc.ini button is disabled until a hit is processed.

- The third button (just beneath the Clear Log button) is labeled with the name of your application INI file. Pressing this button simply opens the INI file using the default editor application for such files on the host machine (typically Notepad). There is no connection between this editor and the running Visual FoxPro application. As such, any changes you make *do not take effect* until you stop and restart the Visual FoxPro application. This is a point of confusion to some developers and administrators.

- There are also five text boxes and two check boxes that show the current settings of seven important server properties. These are live settings in that they are each bound to the related Server object properties. This allows you to test changes to these settings without making any physical change to the application INI file. Once you confirm that the change works, you can press the Save Server Settings button and the changes will be written to the INI file. (Also, be aware that if you are running multiple instances of your application, any effects of editing these form controls will only apply to the instance from which you pressed the status button. Once you conclude that the changes achieve the desired result, save the settings, stop all instances, and start them up again so that they each read the updated server settings.)

- Finally, there is a command button that allows access to edit the WC.INI file. This is the fourth button in the vertical row of command buttons. This behaves in the same manner as the preceding button, in that in simply opens an editor window, wherein you can make changes to the WC.INI file. Again, these changes do not take effect when you save the file. Instead, you must either stop and restart the Web service, or request that WC.DLL re-read its configuration using the http://<path>/wc.dll?_maintain~readSetupIni URL.

- Finally, there is an interesting behavior to the wc.ini button in that it is disabled unless your application has processed at least one Web hit since the Visual FoxPro executable was launched. This is because, using file-based messaging, your Visual FoxPro application does not know the physical location of the WC.DLL and WC.INI files. Nevertheless, your application is capable of discovering this location from information provided in the temporary file that encapsulates the first request to be processed. The Web Connection framework handles this entire discovery process for you, and enables or disables the wc.ini button on the status form accordingly. This behavior, particularly the disabled state of the command button, confuses many new (and some seasoned) Web Connection developers.

In the preceding sections, you have been introduced to many techniques for maintaining your application's configuration. The choices may seem overwhelming at first. I offer two points of potential comfort. First, you do not have to use all of these techniques; instead, think of them as providing you with options. Second, as you become more skilled with Web Connection, you will appreciate the choices that have been made available to you.

When things go wrong

Configuration problems represent one of the most common sources of difficulty for the Web Connection developer. These problems occur most often when you move files, install on a different machine, or add new features to your application. The best tool for diagnosing these problems is a clear understanding of the mechanics I have presented in this chapter. In this section I present some common symptoms and their diagnosis.

Symptom: Your application does not respond when tested from a browser, and after a long delay the browser displays some (often misleading) message, such as "cannot find server."

Diagnosis: One possibility is simply that you failed to start your Visual FoxPro application. The second possibility is that the Path setting in the WC.INI file does not match the TempFilePath setting in your application INI file. In either case, WC.DLL is properly writing temporary files but they are not being serviced by your application. Another possibility is that you've moved the application to another machine, but haven't created the temporary files directory specified in the TempFilePath setting.

Symptom: Clicking on the Exit button on your COM server form fails to cause the application to exit.

Diagnosis: The setting of ComReleaseURL is incorrect in your application INI file. This should be set to a full URL that terminates with wc.dll?_maintain~release. (Example: http://www.myCompany.com/wconnect/wc.dll?_maintain~release)

Symptom: Clicking on a maintenance link repeatedly prompts you for authentication, even though you enter a valid user ID and password.

Diagnosis: There are three different possible explanations: (1) You are logging in using a different user ID from that specified in the AdminAccount setting in WC.INI. (2) You have altered the AdminAccount setting after incoming hits have been made to WC.DLL, such that the configuration settings have already been loaded into memory. The only solution to this is stopping and starting the Web service or rebooting the server machine. (3) You have listed specific users in the AdminAccount setting, but your virtual directory is configured to use only Integrated Windows Authentication. In this case, you need to alter the security setting for the virtual directory so that Basic Authentication is also used. This is required in order for Web Connection to be capable of determining the user ID. Refer to Chapter 8 for details of how to configure Microsoft Internet Information Server.

Chapter 12
A Web Connection Application from Start to Finish

In Chapter 4, the Web Connection Project Wizard was used to automate the process of beginning a new application. In this chapter we will look at how a Web Connection application works under the hood. This is necessary in order to fully understand and debug an application. We will explore INI file setup, directory structures, class definitions, script mapping, and deployment. This process will make the reader comfortable in tackling future Web Connection applications.

The number of new technologies that a Web developer has to be knowledgeable about can be rather overwhelming at first. On the Visual FoxPro side of Web development, expert knowledge of Object-Oriented Programming (OOP) is very important in the Web Connection framework. On the browser or client side, learning HTML, JavaScript, and Cascading Style Sheets (CSS) can add to the already steep learning curve. There are some upfront steps you can take to organize your workspace to make these new technologies easier to deal with. We'll explore directory layouts, code generation utilities, and macros that help create a consistent development environment. We'll then use this environment to create our first complete Web Connection application. This application will demonstrate the major features of Web Connection and lay the foundation for a solid understanding of the underlying Web technologies.

The "TODO" sample application

The task management system that we'll build in this chapter is an application that will be of real use to you when it's completed. It can be used on a corporate intranet, or utilized as part of a commercial site. It is easy to integrate into an existing site or it can live on its own. This application will serve as the example to cover the following new material in Web development.

- Setting up INI files

- Session Management

- Working in File-Based Mode

- Practical uses of templates and scripts

- Emailing

- The importance of a "queryengine" class

- Advanced Debugging class

- Deploying an application as a COM server

- Configuring a COM server for auto-start

- Updating a production server with the new EXE

Let's set up the development environment first to make things easier going forward.

Setting up the Visual FoxPro work space

There are a number of tricks that can be used to make the development of applications much more efficient. One technique is to make use of the Visual FoxPro system toolbar as a place to access frequently used custom tools. The best way to install these custom menus is to create a program that is run when Visual FoxPro is started. This can be set by clicking on Tools | Options | File Locations and scrolling down to the "Startup Program" entry. Click on Modify and enter the path to where the VFPStart.PRG program (see **Listing 1**) is located. The Visual FoxPro dialogs are shown in **Figure 1**.

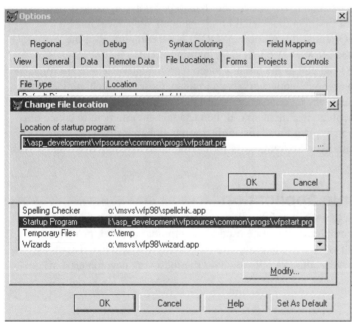

Figure 1. Setting the Visual FoxPro startup program to install custom menus.

Listing 1. Source code for VFPStart.PRG.

```
LOCAL lnBars,lnNewBar
lnBars = BARCOUNT("_MSM_TOOLS")
lnNewBar = lnBars + 1

lnNewBar = lnNewBar + 1

DEFINE BAR lnNewBar OF _MSM_TOOLS ;
```

```
PROMPT "WebRad Project Wizard"
ON SELECTION BAR lnNewBar OF _MSM_TOOLS ;
  DO \webradsource\radwizard\radwizard.exe

lnNewBar = lnNewBar + 1

DEFINE BAR lnNewBar OF _MSM_TOOLS ;
  PROMPT "GenDBCX" KEY CTRL+G, "Ctrl+G" ;
  MESSAGE "Run GenDBCX..."
ON SELECTION BAR lnNewBar OF _MSM_TOOLS ;
  DO ..\gendbcx\gendbcxListing
```

Of course, this sample startup program can be used to configure the development environment any way that is deemed productive. Some developers might want to install a menu item to run the reindex routine, DIRT, or other valuable tools that would be worthwhile to install on the system menu. The paths that are shown in the code listing would of course be updated to reflect the location of these files on your machine. When this program is run, the menus will be installed at the bottom of the system tools menu.

One must-have utility is PJXSEARCH from **www.stevedingle.com**. This utility allows you to search the current project file for a string. Unlike most other search utilities, PJXSEARCH will also search property values for a string. So if it is necessary to find all locations where the string "m.lastname" appears, this will search all files in the project for this string and return the file names in a grid. Simply double-click on the line and the editor pops open ready to edit.

WebRadX

In Visual FoxPro 7, developers have at their disposal one of the coolest features of any development environment. The IntelliSense that is built into VFP 7 is extensible. VFP code can be attached to any abbreviation. When that abbreviation is typed and the space bar is pressed, VFP 7 looks to see whether there is an entry for it in the FOXCODE.DBF table. If there is, code in the DATA memo field will be executed to perform any function you wish. Included as part of this book's source code are additional entries for the FOXCODE table called "WebRadX." They are new IntelliSense entries that run code to generate some commonly used snippets of Fox code. To get a better understanding of how IntelliSense works in Visual FoxPro 7, check out *What's New in Visual FoxPro 7* by Tamar Granor, Doug Hennig, and Kevin McNeish (Hentzenwerke Publishing). The following entries can be imported into your local FOXCODE table easily.

1. Unzip the source code for the book into a directory.

2. In the Command Window, open up the FOXCODE table using the _FOXCODE system variable:

    ```
    use (_foxcode) again shared
    ```

3. Now pull in the new IntelliSense records:

    ```
    append from \webradsource\todosource\common\data\webradX
    ```

4. Close the Foxcode table:

```
use
```

Now the macros detailed in the following sections will be available to you during development!

WebRadInsert (WRI)

This macro will generate a SQL INSERT statement for the table in the current work area. If the table you need the INSERT statement for is fairly wide, it can be tedious to construct the statement. At the point in your code where you need to enter the SQL INSERT statement, make sure the table is open in the current work area and simply type in WRI {SPACE}. This will cause the code in **Listing 2** to execute.

Listing 2. WebRadX SQL Update Extension code for IntelliSense.

```
*****************************************
** WebRad IntelliSense Extensions
** Harold Chattaway
** hchattaway@webconnectiontraining.com
** http://www.webconnectiontraining.com
** Inserts SQL INSERT command into current location in code.
*****************************************
LPARAMETERS oFoxcode

IF oFoxcode.Location #1
    RETURN "WRI"
ENDIF

oFoxcode.valuetype = "V"

local cInsString
cInsString = ""

if used()
    nfields = AFIELDS(lafields)

    cInsString = "INSERT INTO " + ALIAS() + [ (]
    cFieldList = ""
    cMemString  = ""

    FOR fldidx = 1 TO nfields

        *--- build string of field names
        lcvar = "m." + lafields[fldidx,1]
        cFieldList = cFieldList + lafields[fldidx,1] + ;
            iif(fldidx=nfields,") ",", ") + iif(mod(fldidx,5)=0,";" + chr(13),"")

        *--- build string of VALUES's
        cMemString = cMemString + lcvar + + iif(fldidx=nfields,") ",", ") + ;
            iif(mod(fldidx,5)=0,";" + chr(13),"")

    ENDFOR

    cInsString = cInsString + cfieldlist +" ; " + chr(13)+ ;
```

```
       " VALUES (" + cMemString
ELSE
   RETURN "WRI"
endif

RETURN cInsString
```

This code is stored in the FOXCODE table's Data field. An object reference to the FoxCode object is passed as a parameter by FoxPro to the code in the Data field. See the topic "FoxCode Object Reference" in the VFP online Help for information about the properties available for the FoxCode object. The record for this macro has the ABBREV field set to "WRI." The code simply runs through all the fields for the currently open table and concatenates two strings in parallel. One string is the field list and the other string is the "VALUES." It assumes that the values to be inserted are from memory variables designated with "m.fieldname." The newly built SQL INSERT command will be inserted in the same place the "WRI" abbreviation was typed in.

WebRadUpdate (WRU)

This IntelliSense abbreviation works in the same way as the preceding one does. This command inserts into the current location a SQL UPDATE command. Simply type in "WRU {SPACE}" and a SQL UPDATE command is inserted based on the currently open table. Before trying to execute the code inserted by the WRU macro, you must complete or remove the WHERE clause (see **Listing 3**).

Listing 3. *WebRadX SQL Update IntelliSense extension.*

```
*******************************************
** WebRad IntelliSense Extensions
** Harold Chattaway
** hchattaway@webconnectiontraining.com
** http://www.webconnectiontraining.com
** Inserts SQL Update statement into current location in code
*******************************************

LPARAMETERS oFoxcode

IF oFoxcode.Location #1
   RETURN "WRU"
ENDIF

oFoxcode.valuetype = "V"

IF USED()
   LOCAL nfields, cUpdateString

   nfields = AFIELDS(lafields)

   cUpdateString = ""

   FOR fldidx = 1 TO nfields
      lcvar = "m." + lafields[fldidx,1]

      *-- if formvar exists, build SQL Update field list...
```

```
    cUpdateString = cUpdateString + IIF(EMPTY(cUpdateString)," ", ", ") +
lafields[fldidx,1] + " = " + lcvar + IIF(MOD(fldidx,5)=0,";" + CHR(13),"")

    ENDFOR

    RETURN "UPDATE " + ALIAS() + " SET ;" + CHR(13) + cUpdateString + " WHERE "
ELSE
    RETURN "WRU"
ENDIF
```

WebRadRequest (WRR)

When you want to retrieve the values of a table from a Web page, it is necessary to write a series of REQUEST.FORM(fieldname) commands to read those values. For a table with many fields, this is a lot of typing! The easy way, of course, it to let VFP do the work for you using IntelliSense. The entry in **Listing 4** generates all the code needed to retrieve a table's values from a Web page.

Listing 4. WebRadX IntelliSense extension for generating REQUEST.FORM().

```
*******************************************
** WebRad IntelliSense Extensions
** Harold Chattaway
** hchattaway@webconnectiontraining.com
** http://www.webconnectiontraining.com
** Insert a series of REQUEST.FORM() commands based on currently open table
*******************************************
LPARAMETERS oFoxcode

IF oFoxcode.Location #1
    RETURN "WRR"
ENDIF

oFoxcode.valuetype = "V"

IF USED()

    nfields = AFIELDS(lafields)
    cfieldlist = ""
    cvaluelist = ""
    cReqText = ""

    FOR fldidx = 1 TO nfields

        DO CASE

            CASE INLIST(lafields[fldidx,2],"F","I","N","Y")
                cReqText = cReqText + [m.]+lafields[fldidx,1]+[ =
val(request.form(]+lafields[fldidx,1]+[))]   + CHR(13) + CHR(10)

            CASE INLIST(lafields[fldidx,2],"D")
                cReqText = cReqText + [m.]+lafields[fldidx,1]+[ =
CTOD(request.form(]+lafields[fldidx,1]+[))]   + CHR(13) + CHR(10)

            CASE INLIST(lafields[fldidx,2],"T")
```

```
        cReqText = cReqText + [m.]+lafields[fldidx,1]+[ =
CTOT(request.form(")+lafields[fldidx,1]+["))]   + CHR(13) + CHR(10)

        CASE INLIST(lafields[fldidx,2],"L")
          * If a checkbox is used for Logical fields, the VALUE of the form
          * may not be "Y"! It could also be "YES" or "NO" or whatever the
          * VALUE attribute is set to.
          cReqText = cReqText + [m.]+lafields[fldidx,1]+[ =
IIF(request.form(")+lafields[fldidx,1]+[")="Y",.t.,.f.)] + CHR(13) + CHR(10)

        OTHERWISE
            cReqText = cReqText + [m.]+lafields[fldidx,1]+[ =
request.form(")+lafields[fldidx,1]+["))]   + CHR(13) + CHR(10)

      ENDCASE

    ENDFOR

    RETURN cReqText
ELSE
    RETURN "WRR"
ENDIF
```

Of course, you may not need a REQUEST.FORM() for each field in the table, but this gives you a big head start. This code determines what the field type is and uses the correct function to convert the form-based character data to the proper data type that is stored in the table.

GENHTMLFORM

Another powerful WebRadX extension is GENHTMLFORM. A very common and tedious task is creating a form to maintain lookup tables like the STATUS and USERS table in this chapter's TODO application. The GENHTMLFORM greatly simplifies this. Simply open the table that needs a maintenance form. In the Command Window, type in GENHTMLFORM {space}. You will get a prompt for the name of the form and the form action. It will then generate an HTML page with two columns. The first column has the field label and the second column has a form object for the field's data type. For example, memo fields get a <TEXTAREA> and logical fields get a checkbox object. The table is then wrapped in a <FORM> tag with the name and action supplied in the initial prompts. This string of HTML is then placed on the clipboard. Then simply switch to your HTML authoring tool, and paste the code into the <BODY> section of the page. From here you can delete any fields that do not need to be edited, like primary keys. It would also be a good idea to edit the source code for this routine to customize the generated HTML code to use your style sheet classes.

These few examples of how to make use of VFP 7's IntelliSense are simple examples. But they should get you thinking about what can and should be automated. Always take notice of what repetitive tasks are being performed during the course of development. If they are something that can be coded, IntelliSense may be the solution!

HEADER

It's a good idea to have a header at the top of each of your programs with information about the author and copyright, and possibly some contact information. The HEADER entry for

FoxCode does just this. Open a new PRG for editing, type HEADER, and press Space. A complete program header will be filled in. Of course, you'll want to customize the information filled in by this function. Open the Data field for the HEADER record in FoxCode, and customize it how you wish.

Macro to reset environment

Before each build and after each error that might occur, it is a good idea to clean up the development environment. Repeatedly typing "clear program" and "clear all" can amount to a lot of typing throughout the course of a day. A much easier way of handling this is to create a macro to do this for you. The macro in **Listing 5** is a good starting point.

Listing 5. Macro used to reset the environment.

```
1._genscrn=_foxcode
2._foxcode=""
3.Set development on
4.clear all
5.release all
6.clear program
7.set sysmenu to default
8.set procedure to
9.set classlib to
10.close data all
11.clear
12.do ..\common\progs\vfpstart.prg
13.set path to progs, data, ..\common\progs, ..\common\classes, ..\wc,
..\wc\classes
14._foxcode=_genscrn
```

Line 1 is used to store the current location of the FOXCODE.DBF table, which holds the IntelliSense entries. The _genscrn system variable is used because line 4 does a CLEAR ALL and system variables are not affected by a CLEAR ALL. Because _genscrn hasn't been used since the 2.x days, it can be safely used for this purpose.

Then, in line 2, blanking out the _FOXCODE system variable turns off IntelliSense. This prevents IntelliSense from popping up while each of the next macro lines are typed out in the Command Window. Line 3 is necessary because in Web Connection there is a SET DEVELOPMENT OFF statement executed if the server is not being run in debug mode. If the server crashes before the SET DEVELOPMENT ON statement is run, you will be wondering why no new changes are taking effect when a program is run from the Command Window. Line 12 re-runs the VFPStart program, and line 13 sets the paths to the locations that every application can reference. It is important to specify the path to the Web Connection home directory. This is where the WCONNECT.H file, which is referenced at the top of every class library, resides. Then, in line 14, the original value of _FOXCODE is reassigned to re-enable IntelliSense. Macros can be created by simply doing the following:

1.   Click on Tools | Macros.

2.   Click Record.

3. Supply a keystroke that will invoke the menu. Alt-C is appropriate for this macro since it "clears" out the environment.

4. In the Command Window, simply type in each of the lines from Listing 5.

5. Click on Tools | Macros and click on OK to stop recording.

6. Finally, click on Tools | Macros again and click on Set Default to make these the default macros on startup.

TODO application feature set

To get started with the TODO application, **Table 1** lists the feature set that will be in this application.

***Table 1**. Feature set listing for the TODO application.*

Feature	Solution technique
Require that users log in so records can be stamped with user id.	Use the wwsession object to maintain state from hit to hit.
Track title, description, resolution, date entered, assigned to, entered by, status.	Create Visual FoxPro "TODO" table to hold fields. Fields assigned to, entered by, status will be foreign keys (integer) to lookup tables.
Reference a table of users that can be used to assign TODO items to.	Maintain separate table of users with a primary key that will be referenced in the TODO table.
Reference a pre-defined list of possible statuses.	Maintain separate table of status codes with a primary key that will be referenced in the TODO table—COMPLETE, IN PROCESS…
Provide each page with a common header section for menus and filtering.	Each page will use a tag to evaluate and include a common page header. <%=expandtemplate("pagehead.htm")%>
Filter list of tasks to show only items entered by or assigned to the current user.	
Provide listing of tasks with alternating colored rows for readability.	Use a SCAN loop inside of a Web Connection script page to control the appearance of the listing.
Have a page for entering tasks.	
Have maintenance pages for users and status.	Use Web Connection templates with embedded expressions (<%=title%>) to display and edit table content.
Use a separate "Query Engine" for all data access.	Create a class library that encapsulates all data access. Keep queries in a "querydefs" table.
Provide email notification of new tasks to assignee.	Use the SENDMAIL() method to send email from within the application.

The flow of development in this example will be first to develop the application on a development machine running Windows 2000 Professional. The server will be connected to the development machine with a cross-over CAT 5 cable. The configuration of these machines will be as described in Chapters 6, 7, and 8. When the application has been finished on the development machine, it will be migrated to the server using FTP and managed with Terminal Services or VNC (Virtual Network Computing from AT&T Labs).

Class hierarchy

There are five main classes in the Web Connection framework: WWSERVER, WWREQUEST, WWPROCESS, WWRESPONSE, and WWSESSION.

- WWSERVER: This class is responsible for handling the two modes available to Web Connection, file-based and COM-based. It abstracts out the methods so when methods are called, your application does not have to know which mode it is running in. It also creates an instance of WWREQUEST. The INIT method of WWSERVER configures the server by reading the application's INI file. The main program instantiates the server. Unlike the other classes, the instance of the server class is not destroyed after each hit, but remains running as long as your app remains running. Anything that needs to be done on startup and not on every hit can go here. For example, it is okay to open up your application's tables here and they will be left open during the lifetime of the server, assuming they are not explicitly closed in code. Also, the reading of the application's INI file is done here so that INI settings are available application-wide by referencing a property.

- WWREQUEST: The request class is responsible for gathering all the information that will be needed to complete the request being made of the server. It contains methods that allow HTML form data to be retrieved, along with querystring information that might be provided by a hyperlink.

- WWPROCESS: This class contains the application code needed to process the Web request. This class holds the application-specific methods that implement the business logic.

- WWRESPONSE: This class is responsible for sending the result of the Web request back out to the browser. It contains a number of methods for formatting HTML, some of which are:

    - ShowCursor(): This converts the current cursor to an HTML table. It uses the fields' names as column headers by default but can also be custom formatted.

    - ExpandTemplate: Herein lies the real power of Web Connection. This reads in an HTML file that has been designed as a template, parses it, and fills in the Visual FoxPro expressions contained within ASP delimiters (<% %>) with the expression value. Expressions can be simple variable references or calls to custom methods.

    - ExpandScript: This method allows Visual FoxPro code to be embedded in a Web page. The page is read in, converted to a PRG file, and executed.

- WWSESSION: This class is responsible for maintaining state during your application.

It is through the understanding of these five classes that sophisticated applications can be built. From the server's point of view, a client (most likely a Web browser) is making a request of the server. The information needed to fulfill this request is contained within the wwrequest object. The wwprocess object takes this information, processes it, and formulates a response using the wwresponse object. This response page is then sent back to the browser. This request/response cycle is repeated over and over again until the user ends the session.

Ya wanna know a secret?

Before seeing how classes will be managed for this TODO application, you need to understand how a link on a Web page translates into a "DO" command that all Visual FoxPro developers are familiar with. In **Figure 2**, the relationship is pretty straightforward.

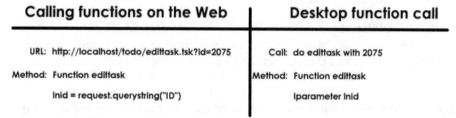

Calling functions on the Web	Desktop function call
URL: http://localhost/todo/edittask.tsk?id=2075	Call: do edittask with 2075
Method: Function edittask	Method: Function edittask
lnid = request.querystring("ID")	lparameter lnid

Figure 2. *Mapping a URL to a Visual FoxPro function call.*

The example on the right is what most developers are used to seeing in a desktop application. However, in a Web application, the parameters would not be passed with the WITH clause. As we shall see shortly, the parameters to the function are parsed out of the data sent to the server by the Web page using the request.querystring() function. The methods that are in the process class and the request class perform this simple transformation. When a Web request is processed, the address as shown in the address bar of Internet Explorer is parsed and assembled into a conventional Visual FoxPro method call. The full address as shown is passed to the server via the WC.DLL file. It is the Process method of the WWPROCESS class that parses this address to determine what method to call. Therefore, it is important that if you place any code in the Process method of your application's subclass of WWPROCESS, you call DODEFAULT() from your application's Process method, or copy the code from the WWPROCESS class to your own Process method.

Once inside the method called in the address ("ShowTask" in this case), the parameters must be retrieved via calls to the QUERYSTRING method in the WWREQUEST class. As an example, the ShowTask method has these commands to retrieve parameters:

```
lnid = VAL(REQUEST.querystring("id"))
```

This particular technique of using QUERYSTRING() shows how we can use named parameters in a Web Connection application. The parameter's "name" is determined by the text to the left of the equal sign (=) and immediately after the ampersand (&) for each parameter in the address bar. We specify the name of the parameter we wish to retrieve by sending that name to the QUERYSTRING function. Remember that all values retrieved from a Web page or URL are of type character. You must convert the data to the appropriate data type before using it in Visual FoxPro! In the preceding line of code, the VAL() function is necessary.

It is also possible to retrieve positional parameters using QUERYSTRING() by passing it the position number. For example, since I know that the ID is the first parameter sent in the address, I could have used VAL(Request.Querystring(1)) to retrieve the ID in the preceding code.

Once read by the QUERYSTRING() method, these values can then be used as if they were passed in using a conventional LPARAMETER statement. This is really all there is to processing requests from the Web. The job of the WC.DLL ISAPI connector is to pass these links as text to the Web Connection application so it can parse and convert them into conventional method calls.

Class management

When using the Web Connection Management Console to create a project, it simply creates a single Process class that will hold the logic for the application. This is fine for many small Web apps; however, it can become rather difficult to maintain one monolithic file. This is of course true in a conventional desktop application as well and does not change when doing Web applications. Let's take a look at a technique to help organize our classes that utilizes IIS script mapping.

Script mapping allows extensions in Web addresses to be mapped to a DLL file like the WC.DLL file that ships with Web Connection. After a script map has been created, the end result is analogous to what is present in a Windows environment. In a Windows environment, from Windows Explorer, if a file with a DOC extension is double-clicked, Windows knows that any file with a DOC extension is associated with Microsoft Word and so Word is launched and the DOC file is displayed. This mapping ability with URL addresses entered into a browser provides similar functionality. A custom extension can be created that maps to the WC.DLL file that is processing hits for the Web site. Then, in the MAIN program for the application, there is a CASE statement that evaluates what the extension is and routes the request to the class file that has been set up to handle those particular requests. (See **Figure 3**.)

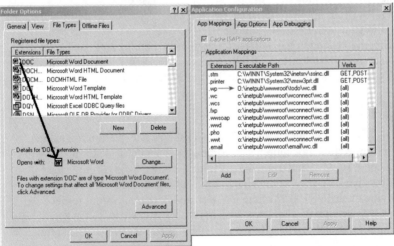

Figure 3. *Registered file types in a local file system perform the same function as script mapping on a Web site.*

For example, in our TODO application the extensions in **Table 2** will be used.

Table 2. The script mapped extensions.

Script mapped extension	Class name
TSK	Class_tsk: Methods handle all task maintenance operations.
USR	Class_usr: Handles all user maintenance operations such as adding and editing.
MNT	Class_mnt: Performs all maintenance operations: backups, system reports, reindexing of files.
WP	Class_wp: Generic requests.
WCT	Web Connection Template: For displaying the DEBUG.WCT form. This form needs to be executed on disk.

A common issue that comes up is where the application-wide methods should go. There will be some methods that all classes need. So how can the classes be designed to handle this?

Easy! It was stated earlier that all of the application-specific methods go in a subclassed version of the WWPROCESS base class. To make a common class that all other process classes can access, a top-level class can be "spliced" into the inheritance tree. This is more easily shown in **Figure 4**.

With this class tree, any reference to "this.method()" in class_tsk will flow up to class_top if the specified method does not exist in class_tsk. This process of subclassing WWPROCESS to have a CLASS_TOP and then CLASS_TSK in our example here may seem confusing at first. However, this is no different from traditional desktop development using the form designer. When designing a Visual FoxPro form, it is considered a good practice not to place any of the base class form objects directly on the form. It is strongly recommended that you first subclass the base classes and create a "class library" of custom controls. It is then possible to have yet another level of subclassing to make more specific versions of the controls. For example, the first level of subclassing might make Times New Roman the font for all textbox objects. The second level of subclassing might make a special textbox that uses a font color of red to show negative values. This is what is being accomplished here with Web Connection classes. Think of WWPROCESS as the TEXTBOX base class. CLASS_TOP and CLASS_TSK are more specific subclasses of WWPROCESS.

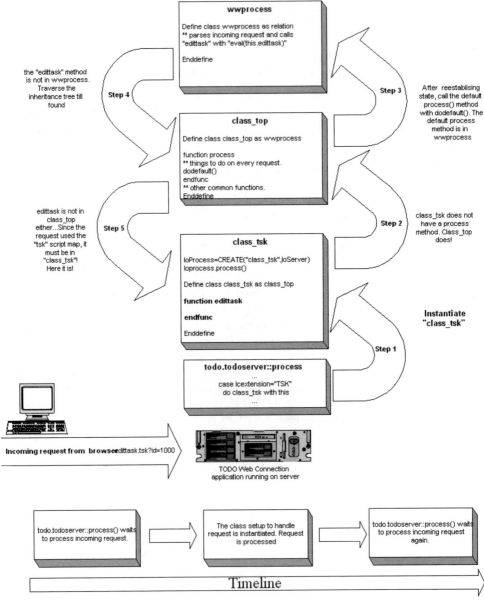

Figure 4. Processing a request.

Configuring the TODO project

In this section we'll establish the directory structure and set up the application's INI files.

Directory structure

 The directories on the development machine for holding the Visual FoxPro source code for this application are as shown in **Figure 5**. This directory structure is contained within the ZIP file for this chapter's source code.

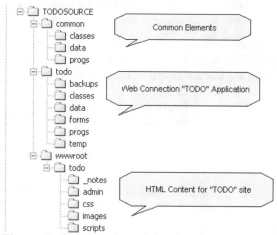

Figure 5. Directory layout for development machine.

The "TODO" directory holds the project file for this application and any application-specific files such as custom classes and data. The "common" directory holds common utility programs that we will see in the next section. The WWWROOT directory holds the HTML source code for the TODO application. Not shown in this directory node are the Web Connection source files. Somewhere on your development machine would be your copy of Web Connection that contains all the Web Connection framework classes. Wherever this might be, a PATH command can make these files available to the TODO project file.

 Please read the TODOInstallation.DOC file included with this book's source code for a detailed explanation of how to install this application. It discusses INI file settings and IIS settings. Also, there is a narrated video (TODOInstall.EXE) included that walks through an actual install session. This will greatly help beginners understand all the steps. The video has a built-in viewer. No installation is necessary; just run the executable and it will play.

Setting up script mapping

In the TODO application, script mapping works with the class hierarchy described earlier to make the application design very easy to work with. For the example here, there will never be any URLs that specify the WC.DLL file in the address. Out of the box, most Web Connection addresses use the form http://localhost/todo/scripts/wc.dll?class_tsk~addtask. This approach requires explicit pathing to the WC.DLL file. The first parameter is the class library that contains the method specified in the second parameter. Using script mapping as described here, this becomes http://localhost/todo/addtask.tsk. This is a shorter, more intuitive calling method. This is also consistent with the notion of executing programs on the Web the same way they would be executed on the desktop. For instance, in a desktop app you would most likely double-click an icon that has an associated EXE in the form "d:\apps\todo\todo.exe." You're basically replacing the drive letter with HTTP in the Web version so the request is processed on the Web instead of locally.

The New Project Wizard that was discussed in Chapter 4, "Your First Web Connection Application," creates some script maps for you automatically. It is important, however, to know how to do this manually as well. Let's go through those steps now.

1. If you are running Windows 2000, click on Start | Settings | Control Panel. From this list, double-click on Administrative Tools and then Internet Services Manager. Since this will be used a lot, it would be best to place a shortcut on the desktop to access it. With Internet Services Manager selected, right-click and choose "Send to Desktop (create shortcut)". If you are running Windows NT 4, find the file called IIS.MSC in your Windows\System32\Inetsrv directory, and create a shortcut from that.

2. Expand the tree control and select the "TODO" Web site.

3. Right-click and select Properties.

4. The first tab shown is Virtual Directory. In Windows 2000, at the bottom of this tab, Application Protection should be set to Low and Execute Permissions should be Scripts only. For Windows NT, make sure "Run in separate memory space" is not checked, and under Permissions, select Execute.

5. Click on the Configuration button. This will bring up the dialog in **Figure 6**.

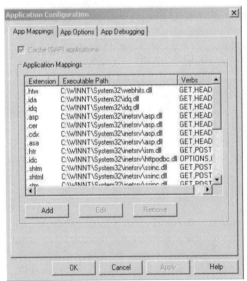

Figure 6. Creating script map entries.

6.   Click on the Add button to view the dialog shown in **Figure 7**.

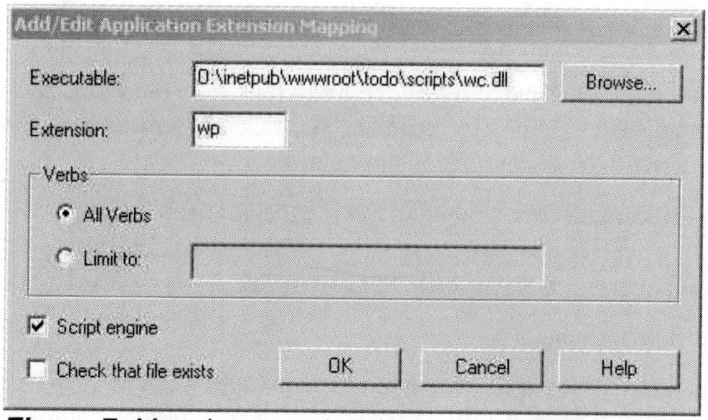

Figure 7. *Mapping an extension to the WC.DLL file.*

7.   To create a script map for wp, type in the full path and name of the WC.DLL, or navigate to the WC.DLL file for this Web site.

8.   For an extension, type in wp.

9.   Leave the "Script engine" check box as is and click OK.

10. This script map will now be added back to the dialog shown in Figure 6.

11. Repeat these steps for the other script maps: USR, TSK, MNT.

The last piece that ties the script maps to the matching Visual FoxPro methods is the CASE statement in the main program (see **Listing 6**). There is a CASE statement for each script map. Each CASE statement then routes the request to the matching CLASS library.

Listing 6. *CASE statement in TODOMAIN for branching.*

```
OTHERWISE
    *** Check for Script Mapped files for: .WC, .WCS, .FXP
    lcPhysicalPath=THIS.oRequest.GetPhysicalPath()
    lcExtension = Upper(JustExt(lcPhysicalPath))

    DO CASE

    CASE lcextension = "WP"
        DO class_wp with THIS

    case lcextension = "USR"
        do class_usr with this

    case lcextension = "TSK"
        do class_tsk with this

    case lcextension = "MNT"
        do class_mnt with this
```

This code snippet looks at the full path of the request sent to the application by using the request.GetPhysicalPath() method. Then, using the built-in Visual FoxPro function JUSTEXT(), the extension is extracted. This is then evaluated in the CASE statement to determine what class is set up to handle a request of this type. To handle a request with a TSK extension, the third CASE statement would be TRUE, so the request would then be routed to CLASS_TSK. Inside of this class are all the methods for handling task-related items. The methodology for creating a well structured Web Connection application is:

1. First analyze how the application will be segmented. Divide the application into logical units. For each feature set, create a different class. In the case of the TODO app, all users, tasks, and maintenance features have their own class.

2. For each feature set, create a script map.

3. For each script map, create a CASE branch in the main program's Process method.

4. Then in each class file, create methods for the functionality needed.

How TODO's first method is created

The first method that will be tested for this app is the obligatory "Hello World" test. The method HelloWorld will be put in the class_wp class library. So let's see how class_wp gets hooked in.

In the method SetServerProperties in TODOMAIN, the CLASS_TOP library needs to be opened. Since this is the template for the other class libraries, it must be made available when the other classes need to be instantiated. So the first section of TODOMAIN looks like **Listing 7**.

Listing 7. TODOMAIN.

```
******************************************************************************
*FUNCTION TodoMain
****************************
***    Created: 11/19/99
***    Function: Web Connection Mainline program. Responsible for setting
***              up the Web Connection Server and get it ready to
***              receive requests in file messaging mode.
******************************************************************************

*** This is the file based start up code that gets
*** the server form up and running
#INCLUDE WCONNECT.H

*** PUBLIC flag allows server to never quit
*** - unless EXIT button code is executed
RELEASE goWCServer
PUBLIC glExitServer, goWCServer

SET TALK OFF
SET NOTIFY OFF
glExitServer=.F.

DO WHILE !glExitServer
```

```
#IF !DEBUGMODE
    SET DEBUG OFF
    SET STATUS BAR OFF
    SET DEVELOP OFF
    SET SYSMENU OFF
#ENDIF

*** Allow shut down by system
ON SHUTDOWN DO ShutIt IN TodoMain.PRG
SET PROCEDURE TO wr-response ADDITIVE

*** Load the Web Connection class libraries
DO WCONNECT

** <Load any custom libraries here> **
SET PROCEDURE TO class_top ADDITIVE
SET PROCEDURE TO debugprocess ADDITIVE
SET PROCEDURE TO security ADDITIVE
SET PROCEDURE TO queryengine ADDITIVE
** </Load any custom libraries here> **

*** Load the server - wc3DemoServer class below
goWCServer = CREATE("TodoServer")

IF TYPE("goWCServer")#"O"
    =MESSAGEBOX("Unable to load Web Connection Server",48,;
        "Web Connection Error")
    RETURN
ENDIF

*** Make the server live - Show puts the server online and in
*** polling mode
READ EVENTS

*** Done
    ON SHUTDOWN
ENDDO

ON ERROR
RELEASE glExitServer
RELEASE goWCServer

SET SYSMENU ON
SET DEBUG ON
SET DEVELOP ON
SET STATUS BAR ON
SET TALK ON

RETURN
```

This section of TODOMAIN is only executed when run in file-based mode. So the section labeled <load any custom libraries here> is needed to make these libraries available when running in file-based mode. When run as a COM server, the TODOSERVER class, which is defined immediately after this section, is instantiated directly by WC.DL. When run as a COM server, all procedure files are available without the need to issue a SET PROCEDURE TO command. When run in file based mode, the line goWCServer = CREATE("TodoServer") instantiates the server, reads the INI file settings described later, and the READ EVENTS command waits for the first request to be processed.

Class_top will contain all common methods that are needed by the other classes, and it also contains the common code that will be run on each request (see **Listing 8**). Since each request is sent through class_top first, this is the perfect place to manage sessions and reestablish state. Also, all application-wide properties are defined here. All the other classes can access them simply by using "this.property." The code on session management, security, and reestablishing state will be covered in detail later. There will also be other application wide methods that reside in this class that will be covered later as well.

Listing 8. CLASS_TOP showing hooks for session, security, and reestablishing state.

```
****************************************************************************
*PROCEDURE class_top
***************************
***   Function: Processes incoming Web Requests for todoproc
***             requests. This function is called from the wwServer
***             process.
***       Pass: loServer -   wwServer object reference
****************************************************************************
#INCLUDE WCONNECT.H
#DEFINE TIMEOUT 14400

*************************************************************
DEFINE CLASS class_top AS WWC_PROCESS
    *************************************************************

    ******************************************************
    ***   <CommonProperties>
    ******************************************************
    cdatapath = ""
    chtmlpagepath = ""
    ctemppath=""

    username = ""
    USERID = 0
    admin=""
    header= .null.

    security = .NULL.

    ******************************************************
    ***   </CommonProperties>
    ******************************************************

    ***********************************************************************
    * Function todoproc :: Process
    ***********************************
    *** If you need to hook up generic functionality that occurs on
    *** every hit, implement this method then call DoDefault() to
    *** get the default Request Processing functionality. See docs
    *** for more info on how to customize wwProcess::Process behavior.
    ***********************************************************************
    FUNCTION PROCESS
        *--- create a Response and Request object reference!
        Response = THIS.oResponse
```

```
REQUEST = THIS.oRequest
PROCESS = THIS
SERVER = THIS.oServer

*** We'll need to create a custom HTTP header so we can
*** potentially add the Cookie to it
Header=CREATE("wwHTTPHeader")
Header.DefaultHeader()

LOCAL ARRAY laPostused[1,2]   && Holds workarea snapshot.

********************************************************
***   <Assign path items from Config object to properties>
********************************************************
THIS.chtmlpagepath = SERVER.oConfig.oTodo.chtmlpagepath
THIS.cdatapath = SERVER.oConfig.oTodo.cdatapath
THIS.ctemppath = SERVER.oConfig.oTodo.ctemppath
********************************************************
***   </Assign path items from Config object to properties>
********************************************************


********************************************************
***   <SessionManagement>
********************************************************
THIS.osession = CREATE("wwsession")
SESSION = THIS.osession
SESSION.nSessionTimeout = TIMEOUT
*** Retrieve the session Cookie...
lcCookie=REQUEST.GetCookie("TODOID")

*** Check if we have a valid Session
IF !SESSION.IsValidSession(lcCookie)
    SESSION.oRequest = REQUEST

    *** Nope - we have to create the session
    lcCookie=SESSION.NewSession()

    *** And add a Cookie to the Request Header
    loHeader.AddCookie('TODOID',lcCookie)
ENDIF
********************************************************
***   </SessionManagement>
********************************************************


********************************************************
***   <SecurityManagement>
********************************************************
security = CREATEOBJECT("security")
IF !security.login()
    RETURN
ENDIF
********************************************************
***   </SecurityManagement>
********************************************************


********************************************************
***   <ReestablishState>
********************************************************
THIS.username = SESSION.getsessionvar("username")
THIS.USERID = VAL(SESSION.getsessionvar("userid"))
```

```
      THIS.admin = SESSION.getsessionvar("admin")
      *******************************************************
      ***   </ReestablishState>
      *******************************************************

      DODEFAULT() && run code for current request.

      *******************************************************
      ***   < Close tables/cursors opened during last request.>
      *** if the table was not opened up originally it will
      *** be closed..
      *******************************************************
  AUSED(laPostUsed)
  LOCAL lni
  FOR lni= 1 TO ALEN(laPostUsed, 1)
     IF ASCAN(server.aOpendbfs, laPostUsed[lni,1])= 0
        USE IN (laPostUsed[lni,1])
     ENDIF
  ENDFOR

      *******************************************************
      ***   <Cleanup Code>
      *******************************************************
      RETURN .T.
  ENDFUNC
ENDDEFINE
```

Class_wp is subclassed from class_top and contains any generic function that does not fit in any other class. For now, it will just contain the HelloWorld test method (see **Listing 9**).

Listing 9. CLASS_WP with HelloWorld method.

```
* Program....: CLASS_WP.PRG
* Author.....: ** Harold Chattaway **
* Date.......: March 8, 2000
* Compiler...: Visual FoxPro 06.00.8492.00 for Windows
* Abstract...: class module for miscellaneous methods...□
* Changes....:
*******************************************************************
LPARAMETER loServer
LOCAL loProcess

#INCLUDE WCONNECT.H
#DEFINE TIMEOUT 14400

loProcess=CREATE("class_wp",loServer)

IF VARTYPE(loProcess)#"O"
   *** All we can do is return...
   WAIT WINDOW NOWAIT "Unable to create Process object..."
   RETURN .F.
ENDIF


*** Call the Process Method that handles the request
loProcess.PROCESS
```

```
RETURN

DEFINE CLASS class_wp AS class_top

*************************
function helloworld
*************************
this.StandardPage("Your First Web Request","Hello World!",loheader)
endfunc
Enddefine
```

What was covered up to here is really the template for all Web Connection applications. A class_x that is based on class_top, which in turn is based on the base class WWPROCESS. Class_x contains the functionality for a particular feature set. Any common methods are kept in class_top so all other process classes can reference them with a simple this.method() reference. That's all there is to it!

After these programs have been added to the project, the project can be compiled into an EXE file. Then:

1. From the Command Window, type in "DO TODO". The Web Connection server window will appear waiting for a request.

2. Launch an instance of Internet Explorer and in the address box, type in http://localhost/todo/helloworld.wp.

3. This request is intercepted by the WC.DLL file because of the script map that was created earlier. WC.DLL then creates a temp file in the TEMP directory specified in the WC.INI file. This temp file contains all the information needed to process the request. The content of a typical request is shown in **Listing 10**.

Listing 10. Contents of a messaging file

```
********  Form Variables  ********

********  Server Variables ********

Output File=c:\temp\wc\WWC71.tmp
DLLVersion=Web Connection 3.35 (32 servers)
wcConfig=O:\inetpub\wwwroot\todo\wc.INI
REQUEST_METHOD=GET
Executable Path=/seminartodo/helloworld.wp
PATH_INFO=/seminartodo/helloworld.wp
PATH_TRANSLATED=\\laptophp10\o$\InetPub\WWWRoot\todofinished\helloworld.wp
SCRIPT_NAME=/seminartodo/helloworld.wp
PHYSICAL_PATH=\\laptophp10\o$\InetPub\WWWRoot\todofinished\helloworld.wp
SERVER_PROTOCOL=HTTP/1.1
SERVER_SOFTWARE=Microsoft-IIS/5.0
SERVER_NAME=localhost
SERVER_PORT=80
REMOTE_HOST=127.0.0.1
REMOTE_ADDR=127.0.0.1
HTTP_USER_AGENT=Mozilla/4.0 (compatible; MSIE 5.5; Windows NT 5.0)
GMT_OFFSET=-18000
```

```
ALL_HTTP=HTTP_ACCEPT:*/*
HTTP_ACCEPT_LANGUAGE:en-us
HTTP_CONNECTION:Keep-Alive
HTTP_HOST:localhost
HTTP_USER_AGENT:Mozilla/4.0 (compatible; MSIE 5.5; Windows NT 5.0)
HTTP_ACCEPT_ENCODING:gzip, deflate
```

This information is available for each request, provided you checked "Save Request Files" on the Status screen of the Web Connection server. Simply click on the Status button in the server window. Then click on Display Request | Last Request Info. Later on you'll see a technique that can append this information onto the bottom of the response page for much easier viewing.

The PHYSICAL_PATH variable is what is parsed by the Process method to determine what associated class to run. So in this example, since the address line contains a WP extension, the Process method in TODOMAIN routes the request to the CLASS_WP class. This class is instantiated, and since it is based on CLASS_TOP (DEFINE CLASS class_wp as class_top), CLASS_TOP's properties and methods are made available. CLASS_WP has the method HelloWorld, which is the JUSTSTEM() portion of the full path. This method is run and the following line is executed:

```
response.StandardPage("Your First Web Request","Hello World!",loheader)
```

Since the response object is responsible for generating all output in response to the request, the line "Hello World" is sent out to another temporary file with the name specified by the "Output File" server variable. This name was generated by WC.DLL and it is waiting for that file to be generated by TODO.app. When the response is finished, the file is closed. WC.DLL now sees the file on disk, so it sends it back up the wire to the originating client where it can be viewed. The result is shown in **Figure 8**.

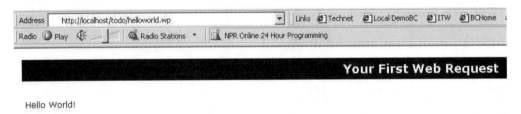

Hello World!

Figure 8. *The first TODO Web request!*

Using the CONFIG object

Near the top of the Process method in CLASS_TOP, the method assigns the value from the INI files for HTMLPAGEPATH, DATAPATH, and TEMPPATH to properties of CLASS_TOP for easy reference. The right hand side of **Figure 9** shows the section of TODOMAIN that sets up the CONFIG object. The SETSERVERENVIRONMENT() method in TODOMAIN instantiates the TODOSERVERCONFIG() class. This class specifies any custom properties and sections that may appear in the application's INI file. For the TODO application, we need a section for custom properties for TODO itself, the Query Engine, and the Debug class. In TODOSERVERCONFIG::INIT(), the properties oTodo, oqeconfig, and odebug are defined. These will serve as object references for TODOCONFIG, QECONFIG, and DEBUGCONFIG, respectively.

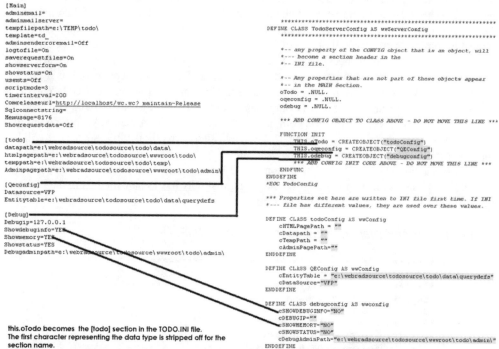

Figure 9. How the Config classes in TODOMAIN map to TODO.INI.

When defining properties in the Config class, the first character is the data type. This first character is not written to the TODO.INI file. If the data type is an object as OTODO is, Web Connection makes it a section in the INI file. The name is derived from the property name starting at the second position. So "oTodo" becomes the "todo" header in the TODO.INI file. The properties of that object then become a set of name/value pairs in that section of the INI file. If any new properties are added to the class definitions for these configuration classes, they are written to the INI file when the application is first started. Using the WWCONFIG class as shown here is a very simple way to drive the behavior of your application via settings in the application's INI file. Since the Query Engine and Debug class are separate from the application it self, they warrant their own section. Finally, any properties defined in TODOSERVERCONFIG that are not objects become name/value pairs in the "[MAIN]" section of the TODO.INI file. Randy Pearson has a more detailed explanation of the configuration object in Chapter 11, "Managing Your Configuration."

Keeping track of the users

Web applications are a series of disconnected conversations with a Web server. Probably the biggest conceptual leap for Visual FoxPro developers is this very fact. In a desktop application, a Visual FoxPro form is bound to the data, whether it is on the local hard drive or on a LAN server. In a Web application there is no such luxury. Each hit to the server is independent. The data that appears in any Web form is not bound to the source. When that form is submitted there must be a way to tell the server its context. Reestablishing state with the server is a novel problem that must be addressed by new Web developers. If the request shown in Figure 8 is repeated over and over again, the Web server has no idea where the request is coming from. (Even though you can usually ascertain the client IP address, this is not a reliable indicator of a specific user.) There are times, however, when it is necessary to know whether the request coming in is part of a session and not just independent hits. For example, on a Web site where no purchasing is being done and no preferences need to be saved, it may not be important for your purposes that the server keep track of who you are from hit to hit. However, on Amazon.com, it is very important. On Amazon, keeping track of the session so your shopping cart can be tracked and filled correctly is vital. So next, it will be important for this application to remember sessions.

There is a base class in Web Connection called WWSESSION. It contains all the methods needed to track users through the site. To plug it in, it simply has to be called from the Process method of the CLASS_TOP class (see **Listing 11**).

Listing 11. *Session management code in CLASS_TOP.*

```
**********************************************************
*** <SessionManagement>
**********************************************************
THIS.osession = CREATE("wwsession")
SESSION = THIS.osession
SESSION.nSessionTimeout = TIMEOUT
*** Retrieve the session Cookie...
lcCookie=REQUEST.GetCookie("TODOID")

*** Check if we have a valid Session
IF !SESSION.IsValidSession(lcCookie)
   SESSION.oRequest = REQUEST

   *** Nope - we have to create the session
   lcCookie=SESSION.NewSession()

   *** And add a Cookie to the Request Header
   header.AddCookie('TODOID',lcCookie)
ENDIF
**********************************************************
*** </SessionManagement>
**********************************************************
```

It is inserted just before the call to DODEFAULT() in the Process method of CLASS_TOP. This is shown in Listing 8. The class is instantiated and a reference is stored to "SESSION". The nSessionTimeout property of the session class controls how long, in seconds, the session can be inactive before timing out. On each hit, an attempt is made to retrieve the cookie "TODOID." The first time a user hits the site, this cookie will not exist. So a new session is created. This has the effect of creating a new record in the WWSESSION table. This table has one record for each session. The Sessionid field stores the unique session id that was generated by the Newsession() method. This same id is then stored as a cookie back on the user's browser by using the AddCookie method. The actual text sent back to the browser as the result of the request in Figure 8 is shown in **Listing 12**.

***Listing 12**. HTML output from the Hello World test.*

```
HTTP/1.1 200 OK
Content-type: text/html
Set-Cookie: TODOID=0DI15WWH8; path=/
<html>
<head>
<title>Your First Web Request</title>
</head>
<body color="#FFFFFF" style="font:normal normal x-small Verdana">
<table border="0" cellpadding="5" width="100%">
  <tr><td align="center" colspan="2" bgcolor="#000000">
  <font color="#FFFFFF" size="4" face="Verdana"><b>
Your First Web Request</b></font>
  </td></tr>
  <tr><td><br><p>
  <font face="Verdana" size=2>
Hello World!</font>
  </td></tr>
</Table>
<p></BODY>
</HTML>
```

The browser intercepts everything above the <HTML> tag as commands and not as display information. The first line tells the browser what protocol is being used. The second line tells it what type of text is being sent. And the third line tells the browser to create a cookie called "TODOID" and assign it a value. The rest is passed on to the rendering engine so that it can be displayed. This cookie persists until the browser session is ended. When a cookie exists, it is automatically sent back to the site that created it so that it can be determined whether this session already exists in the WWSESSION table. If it does, session information can be retrieved and the "conversation" can be picked up right where it left off.

A very close everyday analogy can serve to illustrate this technique. Most everyone has had to call a customer "support" line more than once. The really poor support lines have you tell them the entire problem over and over again for each person you speak with. There is nothing retained between phone calls. This would be similar to a Web site that asked for your name, address, and phone number on every single hit instead of remembering it through session logic. This could get extremely annoying, to say the least. Whereas with a top-notch support line, you simply give them your account number or telephone number, and they immediately know your entire problem. In a Web application, the "account number" is the cookie value. It is simply used to tell the server who you are so the conversation can continue on from request to request. Many people get upset over the use of cookies, but the exact same idea has been used in customer relations for decades!

Refer to Chapter 13, "Identifying Users and Managing Session Data," for more information on managing users and sessions.

Table structures

The table layouts for this sample application have been kept very simple. **Figure 10** shows a snapshot of the DBC file.

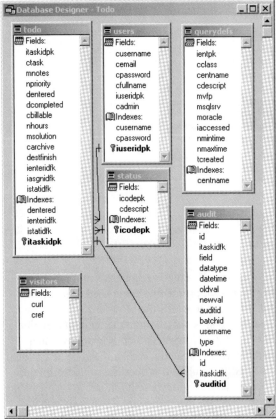

Figure 10. Table design for the TODO application.

There are some fields in the TODO table that will not be displayed on screen in the examples presented in this chapter. But when the samples are shown, it will be easy to add these onto the HTML forms if you wish. The format used to name the fields uses the data type + fieldname. If the field is used a foreign key, like "ienteridfk," the name ends with "fk." A primary key field like "itaskidpk" uses "pk" to denote Primary Key. All field names are kept to 10 characters. One problem with using longer field names is that they get truncated to 10 characters whenever a table is created that uses those fields. Even though the DBC allows for longer field names, it is more convenient to keep them to 10 characters. This problem can come up if you need to create a table from a SQL SELECT. It can also be an issue if you are extracting data into a DBF file that will be shared with another program. In Visual FoxPro 7, if you need to create a writable temporary result set, you can use the new READWRITE clause for the SQL SELECT command. This does away with the need to create a table on disk and the problem caused by having long field names truncated in free tables.

The first data request

The first thing that will be done when navigating to the TODO site will be to show a listing of all the tasks in the TODO table. To make the function that lists these tasks the default home page for this site, a "default" document needs to be set for the site. In most sites, either default.htm or index.htm is set as the default home page. But it is possible to make any page a default home page, even a page that is dynamic in nature. To set a custom default home page:

1. Launch Internet Services Manager using the desktop shortcut as discussed earlier.

2. Select the TODO Web site, right-click, and select Properties.

3. Click on the Documents tab.

4. Click on the Add button.

5. Type in "listtasks.tsk" and click OK.

6. Listtasks.tsk is added to the document list.

7. Click on the up arrow button until it is first in the list (see **Figure 11**).

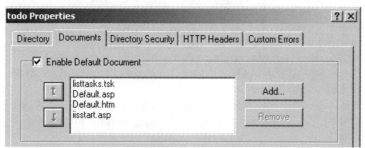

Figure 11. Setting the default document.

By specifying a home page with a TSK extension in conjunction with the script maps that were set up earlier, this page request will be routed to the CLASS_TSK library and the listtasks method will be run. One small "gotcha" when defining a home page document is that even if the document is 100% dynamic in nature, there must be a file on disk with the same name. The file does not have to contain anything, it just needs to exist. So using Notepad, create a file with the name "listtasks.tsk" and place it in the sites home directory. This file is included with this book's source code.

Since the purpose of listtasks is to filter the query to only entries entered by or assigned to the current user, a login routine is needed. If the current user has their CADMIN flag set to "Y" in the user table, then they will see all entries, not just ones assigned to them. Since it is necessary to check on each hit that a user is logged on, the best place for this is in the CLASS_TOP library.

Login routine

Immediately after the Session Management section in CLASS_TOP, the code in **Listing 13** will check to see that the current user is logged in. Since the first time someone navigates to the TODO application they will not be logged in, this code will force the display of a login page that will ask for the username and password. When entered, it will then proceed to the home page, which is listtasks.tsk. Subsequent hits to the site by the same user will pass the login test and the login page will *not* be displayed.

Listing 13. Security hook in CLASS_TOP.

```
********************************************************
***   <SecurityManagement>
********************************************************
security = CREATEOBJECT("security")
IF !security.login()
    RETURN
ENDIF
********************************************************
***   </SecurityManagement>
********************************************************
```

The SECURITY class library, which is part of this book's source code, was adopted from an example in the Web Connection documentation. It simply reads the username and password off of the login page and executes a SQL SELECT statement to find this user in the USER table. The sample code for the book works with DEMO for username and password. If found, a session variable is created that records the username and user id value. Since this session record is tied to the TODOID cookie created earlier, it is retrieved on subsequent hits by the code in the <SESSIONMANAGEMENT> section of the CLASS_TOP library without having to ask the user for it each time.

After a successful login, it is necessary to record session variables so subsequent hits can pick up the conversation. In the SECURITY class, the code in **Listing 14** authenticates the login and writes out session variables.

Listing 14. AUTHENTICATE method in SECURITY.PRG.

```
IF THIS.Authenticate(lcUsername, lcPassword )
    *** Write the user into the session table
    SESSION.SetSessionVar('Username',lcUsername)
    SESSION.SetSessionVar("userid",THIS.USERID)
    SESSION.SetSessionVar("admin",THIS.Admin)

    *** <source of visit>
    cReferral = REQUEST.querystring("referral")
    cPreviousURL = REQUEST.getPreviousURL()

    IF !EMPTY(cReferral)
        header.addcookie("referral",cReferral)
    ENDIF

    *--- where did they come from? HAC 02/26/01
    IF !EMPTY(cPreviousURL)
        header.addcookie("previousURL",cPreviousURL)
    ENDIF

    oquery = CREATEOBJECT("QueryEngine")
```

```
oquery.executesq("LOGVISITS")


*** </SOURCE OF VISIT >

*--- send them on their way!
response.ReDirect(SESSION.GetSessionVar("Destination"))
RETURN .T.

ELSE
    *-- redisplay login page...
    response.expandtemplate(PROCESS.cHtmlpagepath+"login.wct",header)
    RETURN .F.
ENDIF
```

The SETSESSIONVAR() method in the session class creates an entry in the VARS field of the WWSESSION table.

```
<destination>http://localhost/todo/listtasks.tsk?</destination>
<username>hchattaway@webconnectiontraining.com</username>
<userid>1</userid>
<admin>Y</admin>
```

They are written as XML tags for easier reading and parsing.

Reestablishing state

On any future hit after a login, the cookie TODOID exists and the session variable "username" exists in the LOGIN() method of the security object, so the user is not presented with the login screen again. It is necessary, however, to reestablish state with the code in **Listing 15** in the Process method of the Class_Top class.

Listing 15. Code to reestablish state in CLASS_TOP.

```
****************************************************
***   <ReestablishState>
****************************************************
THIS.username = SESSION.getsessionvar("username")
THIS.USERID = VAL(SESSION.getsessionvar("userid"))
THIS.admin = SESSION.getsessionvar("admin")
****************************************************
***   </ReestablishState>
****************************************************
```

The call to GETSESSIONVAR() retrieves the named session variable from the VARS field of WWSESSION and assigns it to whatever variable you choose. This combination of SETSESSIONVAR() and GETSESSIONVAR() can be used throughout the application to persist data across Web hits.

The need for a "Query Engine"

With the first dynamic page ready to be generated, it is necessary to go over the importance of having a separate data access class or "Query Engine." For the first method that will generate our list of tasks, it is common to write such a class with inline SQL code such as in **Listing 16.**

Listing 16. Improper way of using SQL.

```
****************************************
FUNCTION ListTasks
****************************************
select todo.itaskidpk, todo.npriority,padr([<a
href="edittask.tsk?id=]+transform(itaskidpk)+[">]+trim(todo.ctask)+[</a>],80)
as ctask, dentered, status.cdescript,users.cfullname  ;
from todo left join users on todo.iasgnidfk = users.iuseridpk  ;
left join status on todo.istatidfk = status.icodepk  ;
where todo.ienteridfk = process.userid or todo.iasgnidfk = process.userid ;
into cursor tasklist ;
order by npriority, dentered

response.expandscript(THIS.cHTMLPAGEPATH+"tasklist.wcs",3,Header)
USE IN tasklist
```

Now imagine three months down the road, it becomes necessary to upsize to SQL Server and there are dozens of locations throughout the application with inline SQL statements that need to be upgraded. This is an extremely time-consuming process that involves an enormous amount of testing to convert. What would be easier is to create a single class for all data access and centralize all logic in this class. This way, any data store changes that may occur down the road can be handled in one location, and your application-level code will not have to be changed or even be aware there was a change. It would be possible to change from using Visual FoxPro native tables to using SQL Server via ADO or ODBC or returning data as an XML string by using SQL Server 2000 HTTP queries. Any and all data access is encapsulated in one class. So the means by which the data is retrieved becomes irrelevant. Using a Query Engine class, the previous code becomes that shown in **Listing 17.**

Listing 17. Preferred technique for executing SQL commands.

```
****************************************
FUNCTION ListTasks
****************************************

IF PROCESS.admin != "Y"
   server.oQueryEngine.executeSQ("LISTMYTASKS")

ELSE
   server.oQueryEngine.executeSQ("TASKLISTALL")
ENDIF
response.expandscript(PROCESS.cHTMLPAGEPATH+"tasklist.wcs",3,Header)
```

The executeSQ() method takes as a parameter the name of the query to retrieve. The resulting query is now open in the current work area. The SQL statements are stored in a table called QUERYDEFS and has the structure shown in **Listing 18**.

Listing 18. _Structure for QUERYDEFS table._

```
Structure for table: E:\WEBRADSOURCE\TODOSOURCE\TODO\DATA\QUERYDEFS.DBF
Number of data records:        12
Date of last update:           01/12/2002
Memo file block size:          64
 Code Page:                    1252
            Field        Field Name      Type        Width     Dec
               1         IENTPK          Integer      4
               2         CCLASS          Character    20
               3         CENTNAME        Character    60
               4         MDESCRIPT       Memo         4
               5         MVFP            Memo         4
               6         MSQLSRV         Memo         4
               7         MORACLE         Memo         4
               8         IACCESSED       Integer      4
               9         NMINTIME        Numeric      8          5
              10         NMAXTIME        Numeric      8          5
              11         TCREATED        DateTime     8
```

The CENTNAME field is referenced in the executeSQ method call. A description can be supplied in the MDESCRIPT memo field. The mVFP, mSQLSRV, and MORACLE memo fields contain the SQL statements that would otherwise be in line. These fields allow you to easily switch between back ends. Currently this class works with Visual FoxPro only, but by centralizing data access in this class, back ends can be switched easily in the future. The IACCESSED field records how many times the query was run. NMINTIME and NMAXTIME record the minimum and maximum elapsed times of the query. These metrics can be useful when analyzing site performance.

The executeSQ() method retrieves the QUERYDEFS record for the named query, and macro expands the SQL statement stored in the table. A SQL string can be assigned using the Query Engine's SETSQL() assign method, in case the query is ad hoc and is not stored in the table. There are assess and assign methods, GETSQL() and SETSQL() for the cSql property. This can be used to pass in a SQL string instead of looking one up in the entity table. There is also a GETRECORDS() method for returning the number of records in the result set, and a GETELAPSED() method to return the elapsed time of the query. Also, the executeSQ() method will use the enhanced SYS(3054) showplan function if Visual FoxPro 7 is being used. There is a new parameter on SYS(3054) that can save the showplan results to a memory variable. By using a centralized Query Engine, all queries can make use of this functionality, so valuable debugging information on query performance can be accumulated and presented back to the developer. A special debugging class will be shown later to present the showplan information as well as POST data and DISPLAY STATUS and DISPLAY MEMORY information.

Using an HTML page template

The HTML-Kit authoring tool has the means to use page templates. The page template used for this book is shown in **Listing 19**.

Listing 19. *Simple page template.*

```
<!DOCTYPE HTML PUBLIC "-//W3C//DTD HTML 4.0 Transitional//EN"
 "http://www.w3.org/TR/REC-html40/loose.dtd">

<html>
<head>
<title></title>
<link rel="stylesheet" type="text/css" href="css/todostyle.css">
</head>
<body>
<!-- common header! -->
<%=filetostr(process.cHTMLPAGEPATH+"header.htm")%>

</body>
</html>
```

To create and use this template, do the following:

1. Launch HTML-Kit.

2. Click on File | New Document.

3. Type in the preceding HTML code.

4. Click on File | Save as Extra | Save as Template.

5. Supply author, description information in the form and select the section to save it in.

6. Then, to use it, click on File | New… and select the template from the list. Your new page will be primed with the code in this template.

The line containing FILETOSTR() is used to insert a common header into each page. This header is not a valid HTML page by itself. It simply contains the HTML code to insert the site graphic and also contains the three links that form the basic menu for the TODO application. It is important to segment out the header like this. It greatly reduces maintenance when menus change or any other common look-and-feel issue needs to be updated. Since the header is inserted dynamically each time the page is hit, the header file can be updated and all pages will immediately see the update when they are displayed. Also, there is a link to pull in a common site-wide style sheet. Style sheets were discussed in Chapter 9, "How a Web Page Works." Each page's custom content would be inserted below the FILETOSTR() line between the <BODY></BODY> tags. There is a detailed explanation of how a Web page is constructed in Chapter 9.

Displaying the task list using a script page

After a successful login, the next method that is run is listtasks. This is the link specified in the ACTION clause of the LOGIN page. With the use of the QUERYENGINE class and the Web Connection framework class WWRESPONSE, the method to list out the main TODO table is only a few lines long (see **Listing 20**).

Listing 20. The listtasks method in CLASS_TSK.

```
*****************************************
FUNCTION ListTasks
*****************************************
oQuery = CREATEOBJECT("QueryEngine")
IF PROCESS.admin != "Y"
  oQuery.execute("LISTMYTASKS")

ELSE
  oQuery.execute("TASKLISTALL")
ENDIF

response.expandscript(THIS.cHTMLPAGEPATH+"tasklist.wcs",3,loHeader)
USE IN tasklist
```

In order to have something to list out, a couple of TODO items can be added manually first. The form that will add new records to this table is in the next section. LISTMYTASKS and TASKLISTALL are entries in the QUERYDEFS table. The Web Connection framework class, RESPONSE, has a very powerful method called EXPANDSCRIPT(). This method converts an HTML page that contains Visual FoxPro code into a Visual FoxPro program that then creates an HTML document.

The three steps a script page goes through are shown in **Figure 12**. Step 1 is the file before processing occurs. Step 2 is the intermediate PRG file that expandscript() generates and then executes. Step 3 shows the page as the browser sees it. All of the scripting elements are removed by the time it gets to the browser to be rendered. What is left is a plain HTML file.

In the Web Connection Script file tasklist.wcs, there is an HTML table defined that will hold the contents of the cursor TASKLIST from the precding query. Using an HTML authoring tool, the table is laid out and the table cells are filled with the ASP tags to display the appropriate fields. The resulting rendered page is shown in **Figure 13**.

How a scriptpage is executed

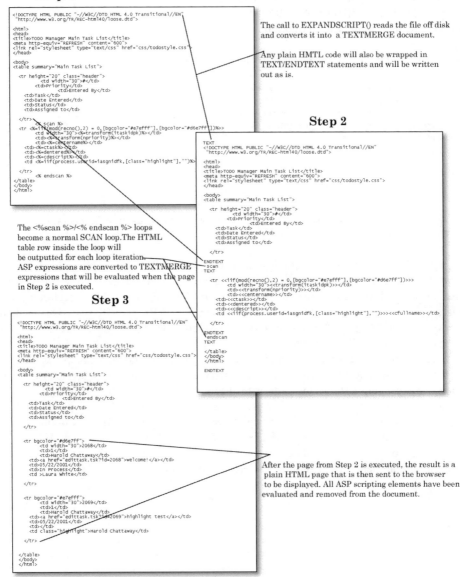

Step 1

```
<!DOCTYPE HTML PUBLIC "-//W3C//DTD HTML 4.0 Transitional//EN"
   "http://www.w3.org/TR/REC-html40/loose.dtd">

<html>
<head>
<title>TODO Manager Main Task List</title>
<meta http-equiv="REFRESH" content="600">
<link rel="stylesheet" type="text/css" href="css/todostyle.css">
</head>

<body>
<table summary="Main Task List">

   <tr height="20" class="header">
       <td width="30">#</td>
       <td>Priority</td>
               <td>Entered By</td>
   <td>Task</td>
   <td>Date Entered</td>
   <td>Status</td>
   <td>Assigned to</td>

   </tr>  <% scan %>
   <tr <%=iif(mod(recno(),2) = 0,[bgcolor="#e7efff"],[bgcolor="#d6e7ff"])%>
       <td width="30"><%=transform(itaskidpk)%></td>
       <td><%=transform(npriority)%></td>
       <td><%=centername%></td>
   <td><%=ctask%></td>
   <td><%=dentered%></td>
   <td><%=cdescript%></td>
   <td <%=iif(process.userid=iasgnidfk,[class="highlight"],"")%>>

   </tr>
   <% endscan %>
</table>
</body>
</html>
```

The call to EXPANDSCRIPT() reads the file off disk and converts it into a TEXTMERGE document.

Any plain HMTL code will also be wrapped in TEXT/ENDTEXT statements and will be written out as is.

Step 2

```
TEXT
<!DOCTYPE HTML PUBLIC "-//W3C//DTD HTML 4.0 Transitional//EN"
   "http://www.w3.org/TR/REC-html40/loose.dtd">

<html>
<head>
<title>TODO Manager Main Task List</title>
<meta http-equiv="REFRESH" content="600">
<link rel="stylesheet" type="text/css" href="css/todostyle.css">
</head>

<body>
<table summary="Main Task List">

   <tr height="20" class="header">
       <td width="30">#</td>
       <td>Priority</td>
               <td>Entered By</td>
   <td>Task</td>
   <td>Date Entered</td>
   <td>Status</td>
   <td>Assigned to</td>

   </tr>

ENDTEXT
scan
TEXT

   <tr <<iif(mod(recno(),2) = 0, [bgcolor="#e7efff"],[bgcolor="#d6e7ff"])>>>
       <td width="30"><<transform(itaskidpk)>></td>
       <td><<transform(npriority)>></td>
       <td><<centername>></td>
   <td><<ctask>></td>
   <td><<dentered>></td>
   <td><<cdescript>></td>
   <td <<iif(process.userid=iasgnidfk,[class="highlight"],"")>>><<cfullname>></td>

   </tr>

ENDTEXT
endscan
TEXT

</table>
</body>
</html>

ENDTEXT
```

The `<%scan %>`/`<% endscan %>` loops become a normal SCAN loop.The HTML table row inside the loop will be outputted for each loop iteration. ASP expressions are converted to TEXTMERGE expressions that will be evaluated when the page in Step 2 is executed.

Step 3

```
<!DOCTYPE HTML PUBLIC "-//W3C//DTD HTML 4.0 Transitional//EN"
   "http://www.w3.org/TR/REC-html40/loose.dtd">

<html>
<head>
<title>TODO Manager Main Task List</title>
<meta http-equiv="REFRESH" content="600">
<link rel="stylesheet" type="text/css" href="css/todostyle.css">
</head>

<body>
<table summary="Main Task List">

   <tr height="20" class="header">
       <td width="30">#</td>
       <td>Priority</td>
               <td>Entered By</td>
   <td>Task</td>
   <td>Date Entered</td>
   <td>Status</td>
   <td>Assigned to</td>

   </tr>


   <tr bgcolor="#d6e7ff">
       <td width="30">2068</td>
       <td>1</td>
       <td>Harold Chattaway</td>
   <td><a href="edittask.tsk?id=2068">welcome!</a></td>
   <td>05/22/2001</td>
   <td>In Process</td>
   <td >Laura White</td>

   </tr>


   <tr bgcolor="#e7efff">
       <td width="30">2069</td>
       <td>1</td>
       <td>Harold Chattaway</td>
   <td><a href="edittask.tsk?id=2069">highlight test</a></td>
   <td>05/22/2001</td>
   <td></td>
   <td class="highlight">Harold Chattaway</td>

   </tr>

</table>
</body>
</html>
```

After the page from Step 2 is executed, the result is a plain HTML page that is then sent to the browser to be displayed. All ASP scripting elements have been evaluated and removed from the document.

Figure 12. How a script page is converted into a TEXTMERGE program.

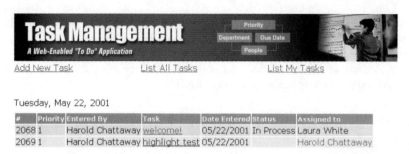

Figure 13. *Fully rendered tasklist.wcs script page of the code in Step 3 of Figure 12.*

The data rows of the HTML table in Figure 13 are the result of the SCAN loop discussed earlier. Laying out a row in HTML and wrapping it in a SCAN loop is almost exactly what is being done in the Visual FoxPro Report Designer. In the Report Designer, a report header section contains the column headers and then a single data row is laid out with the correct spacing and expressions that represent the column data. Then, when the report is run, Visual FoxPro loops through the active cursor and replicates that single data row for each row in the cursor. In our example here, the expandscript() method is providing very similar functionality.

When is an extension just an extension?

In the preceding example, the file extension WCS (Web Connect Script) was used for the tasklist script page. When the expandscript() method is used to run a script page, it is not necessary to create a script map in IIS for the file extension used. The file name is specified explicitly in the expandscript() method call. If the site was designed so that users could point their browsers at tasklist.wcs, there would be a need to have an IIS script map for "wcs." Quite often, however, a script map will be utilized to call a method in the application and that method contains the bulk of the logic. The method then calls the expandscript() method, which references the script page on disk to display the results.

Pros and cons of scripts and templates

Exposing the entire Visual FoxPro language through the use of simple ASP tags in a Web page is extremely powerful to say the least. Anything from a simple expression to a call to a large function can be referenced in one of these ASP tags. It is important to know the correct usage of each to leverage the power where appropriate.

One of the problems with scripts is that they can be slow to run. There are two modes that they can run in: interpretive and compiled. When running in interpretive mode, the page is executed using CodeBlock. This program uses macro expansion to run a program. While it is an extremely powerful utility, there is a lot of overhead in running a program this way. The other mode, compiled, saves the converted page as an FXP file and then executes that compiled program to generate the final page. In this mode, execution speed runs at normal Visual FoxPro speed—fast! However, if a new page is uploaded, the page has to be recompiled. If the page is run in interpretive mode, a newly uploaded page will run right away.

Also, it is not good practice to keep a lot of Visual FoxPro code in an HTML page. That is not its "natural environment" and as such, will not be as easy to maintain. HTML editors are not as good as the Fox editor at editing Fox code. While it is very powerful to put some Visual

FoxPro code in a script as in the prior example, it is mainly for simple display purposes. Any involved business logic really needs to reside in the application's EXE file.

Templates should be used when there is no need for logic or looping constructs in the Web page. Template execution is much faster than evaluating a script page, and it allows full access to the Visual FoxPro language as well, through function calls.

Single instance, single-user. Multiple instances, multi-user!

One of the other fundamental differences in Web applications is multi-user issues. In a typical desktop Visual FoxPro application running on a LAN, each desktop user accessing data on a file server is sharing the tables sitting on the file server. On a Web server, the point of view changes slightly. If there is only one EXE needed to process the requests coming in on the site, then the tables are seeing only one user, the single EXE handling the requests. It is the IIS Web server that is seeing multiple users coming in over the Internet connection. These requests are then queued and processed by your Web Connection application.

It is vitally important to plan for the need for more than one EXE to handle the load. When the site becomes more and more popular, that single EXE may not be able to handle all the requests in a timely manner. If it is decided to launch another EXE to service more requests, suddenly the tables are seeing two users and not just one! So all the data access logic now has to accommodate multiple users. Some items to consider:

- SET EXCLUSIVE must be set off.

- When running SQL queries, INTO CURSOR is still okay because Visual FoxPro manages the file names on disk automatically by generating random file names.

- If doing INTO TABLE queries, the developer must now manage the file names manually so there is no chance of collision between the multiple EXEs! For example, the QUERYENGINE class described earlier creates tables with a random file name. To determine the alias that was used for this table for future reference, use the ALIAS() function right after the call to the query engine. This is the same situation that arises in desktop applications as well. In desktop apps, however, you have the option of directing temporary tables to the user's local hard drive, avoiding any clashing of file names. On a Web server, however, each user is using the same hard drive.

```
server.oQueryEngine.executeSQ("BLANKTASK","TABLE")
cAlias = ALIAS()

*-- prime table
INSERT INTO (cAlias) (ienteridfk, dentered) ;
    VALUES (PROCESS.USERID, DATE())
```

The line cAlias = alias() allows the newly created table to be referenced more easily. Since the table does not have a consistent name, it is easy to reference it by "(cAlias)" during the rest of the request.

Seeing it for yourself!

All of the source code discussed here comes with the book. Once the software is installed:

1. Build an EXE from the project file.

2. DO TODO to start the Web Connection server window.

3. Start a new browser session.

4. Navigate to http://localhost/todo. The default page for the site was set up to be listtasks.tsk. Since no login has occurred yet, the login page will be displayed.

5. Type in DEMO for the username and password.

6. The page shown in Figure 13 will appear in the browser.

7. Click back to the running Web Connection application, and the listtasks.tsk request will be listed in the server window.

After each and every change it is best to build a new app and test the functionality. The shorter the development/test cycle is, the faster the overall development will be. Wrapping too many new features in a test makes it very difficult to isolate the problems when they occur! It is necessary to be able to know as soon as possible what new feature is responsible for any errors that appear.

Adding a TODO item

The first menu item from the common header file is a hyperlink that calls ADDTASK.TSK. This is a link that will also get routed to the CLASS_TSK class library. The ADDTASK method simply creates a blank record from the TODO table and then displays the EDTTASK.template page using EXPANDTEMPLATE() (see **Listing 21**).

Listing 21. The ADDTASK method in CLASS_TSK.

```
********************************
FUNCTION addtask()
********************************

     *--- get blank record.
     server.oQueryEngine.executeSQ("BLANKTASK","TABLE")
     cAlias = ALIAS()

     *-- prime table
     INSERT INTO (cAlias) (ienteridfk, dentered) ;
        VALUES (PROCESS.USERID, DATE())

     cStatusdd=PROCESS.GenDropDowns("status","","istatidfk")
     cAssignedDD=PROCESS.GenUserDropDown(iasgnidfk,"iasgnidfk")

     response.expandtemplate(PROCESS.cHTMLPAGEPATH+"edittask.wct",header)

ENDFUNC
```

The QUERYENGINE class is used to execute a SQL SELECT statement that returns an empty cursor. This is done by using a WHERE clause of itaskid = -1.

This will always fail, resulting in an empty cursor. The SQL INSERT statement is then used to prime the cursor with some default values. The functions GenDropDowns() and GenUserDropDown() reside in CLASS_TOP and are common functions that can be referenced from anywhere using the PROCESS object reference. GenDropDowns() creates an HTML drop-down object and is passed the name of the code table to use, the initial value to set the drop-down to, and the name of the HTML form object that will hold the drop-down. The idea here is that other code tables like STATUS will have the same structure so that this common function can be used to generate a drop-down from them. GenUserDropDown() provides the same functionality for the user table.

With the cursor primed with data and the drop-down code sitting in their respective variables, the EXPANDTEMPLATE() call will use the EDITTASK template page to populate the page with data. A template is utilized here instead of a script page, because the page simply needs to have references to the fields and the drop-down variables evaluated and inserted into the page. No other conditional logic or looping constructs are needed here. A small snippet of code from the EDTTASK page looks like **Listing 22**.

Listing 22. HTML snippet showing ASP tags evaluated by Web Connection.

```
<tr>
    <td width="40"></td>
    <td class="fieldlabel">ID#:</td>
    <td><%=transform(itaskidpk)%></td>
</tr>
<tr>
    <td width="40"></td>
    <td class="fieldlabel">Entered:</td>
    <td><%=dentered%></td>
</tr>
<tr>
    <td width="40"></td>
    <td class="fieldlabel">Task:</td>
    <td><input type="textbox" name="ctask" value="<%=ctask%>"></td>
</tr>
```

The ASP style expressions are evaluated by EXPANDTEMPLATE() and the result is inserted into the same location. The first expression is simply written out as plain text to the form since the ID# field is not editable. The same is true of the Entered field. The TASK field, however, is editable. So the HTML object TEXTBOX is used and the ASP expression <%=ctask%> is used to provide the initial value of the textbox. When adding a task, this value will always be blank. But the same form is being used to display existing populated records so the field name is always referenced whether or not it is filled in. The fully rendered page will look like **Figure 14**.

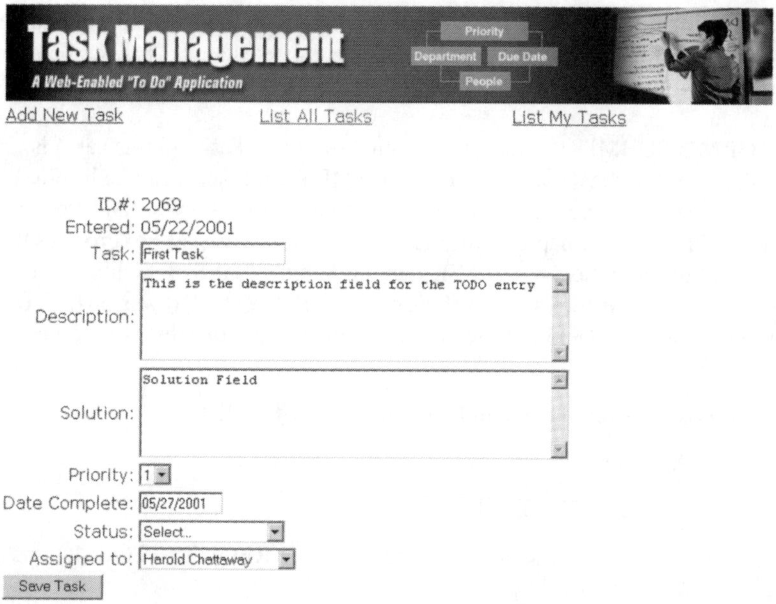

Figure 14. The final Edit Task HTML form.

Saving a TODO item

After the previously described Web page is displayed and filled in, there needs to be a way to execute the save routine back on the server to insert the data into the TODO table. The mechanism that allows this is the ACTION clause on the HTML FORM tag. This is illustrated in **Listing 23**.

Listing 23. The HTML FORM tag.

```
1.<body>
2.<!-- common header! -->
3.<%=filetostr(process.cHTMLPAGEPATH+"header.htm")%>
4.<form action="savetask.tsk" method="post" name="edittask">
5.<input type="hidden" name="itaskidpk" value="<%=transform(itaskidpk)%>">
.
.
.
6.<input type="submit" value="Save Task">
7.</form>
8.</body>
```

In line 4, the ACTION clause states that when the form is submitted using the Submit button defined on line 6, everything between the <FORM></FORM> tags will be sent to the server. In line 5, the HIDDEN form variable is used to carry forward the ID of the TODO item that is being displayed. Displaying the ID# as plain text as shown in the prior listing does not make the ID value available for posting to the server. So to carry this value forward, the HIDDEN form variable must be used. If a new record is being added, this form variable will have an ID of 0. If it is for an existing record, it will be greater than 0. This can be tested for in the save routine, and then either a SQL INSERT or a SQL UPDATE can be used where appropriate.

So when the FORM's SUBMIT (which has a caption of "Save Task" in this case) is clicked, the data will be sent to the server. Any of the HTML form objects can be inserted between the <FORM></FORM> tags. Text boxes, radio buttons, drop-downs, and freeform text fields can be placed here. See Chapter 9 for more details. When Visual FoxPro sees the incoming request, it will execute the SAVETASK method in the CLASS_TSK library. The first thing that needs to be done is to read the values of the FORM data that was posted. Here is where the WebRadRequest (WRR) IntelliSense entry comes in handy (it was described in the beginning of this chapter).

1.   In the Visual FoxPro Command Window, open up the TODO table.

2.   Open up the CLASS_TSK library.

3.   Create a function called SAVETASK.

4.   Simply type WRR and hit the space key. The following REQUEST.FORM() lines will be generated automatically.

5.   The complete function is shown in **Listing 24**.

Listing 24. The SAVETASK method in CLASS_TSK.

```
FUNCTION savetask
    ********************************
    *--- get all fields...
    m.ITASKIDPK =  VAL(REQUEST.FORM("ITASKIDPK"))
    m.CTASK =  REQUEST.FORM("CTASK")
    m.MNOTES =  REQUEST.FORM("MNOTES")
    m.NPRIORITY =  VAL(REQUEST.FORM("NPRIORITY"))
    m.DCOMPLETED =  CTOD(REQUEST.FORM("DCOMPLETED"))
    m.CBILLABLE =  REQUEST.FORM("CBILLABLE")
    m.NHOURS =  VAL(REQUEST.FORM("NHOURS"))
    m.MSOLUTION =  REQUEST.FORM("MSOLUTION")
    m.CARCHIVE =  REQUEST.FORM("CARCHIVE")
    m.DESTFINISH =  CTOD(REQUEST.FORM("DESTFINISH"))
    m.ienteridfk =  VAL(REQUEST.FORM("IENTERIDFK"))
    m.iasgnidfk =  VAL(REQUEST.FORM("IASGNIDFK"))
    m.istatidfk =  VAL(REQUEST.FORM("ISTATIDFK"))


    IF EMPTY(m.ITASKIDPK)
       *-- NEW Insert record
       server.oQueryEngine.executeSQ("ADDTASK")
       PROCESS.ShowMessage("Task was Added!")

    ELSE
       *-- Update
       server.oQueryEngine.executeSQ("UPDATETASK")
```

```
    PROCESS.ShowMessage("Task was Updated!")
ENDIF

ENDFUNC
```

The WRR WebRadX IntelliSense entry correctly wraps the VAL() function around any fields that are numeric and the CTOD() function around date fields. The QUERYENGINE class is used again here to save the data. If the m.itaskidpk variable is empty, a new task is being added. There is a SQL INSERT statement in the QUEYDEFS table with the name ADDTASK. This is executed with the executeSQ() method and the data is saved. If the m.itaskidpk variable is not empty, a SQL UPDATE command is executed to update the existing record. Of course, any DBC table defaults or triggers are respected when adding data this way. For example, on the itaskidpk field in the TODO table, there is a default value of lnextid("TODO"). This UDF generates a unique ID value by keeping a system table of the next ID value for any table. The parameter passed is the name of the table that needs a new ID. The source code is available on the Hentzenwerke Web site.

The same technique used to maintain the TODO table is used to maintain the other tables in this example. For the STATUS and USER tables, there must be ADD, EDIT, SAVE, and DELETE methods. This example is pretty straightforward; however, on more involved tables, there might be a lot of code that needs to be executed to bring up a blank record. For instance, the generation of multiple drop-downs might be necessary. In these cases, it might be best to combine the ADD and EDIT methods into one EDIT method. If a new record is being added, pass in a -1 value for the key. If editing an existing record, the parameter would be the PK for the record in question. This technique eliminates the duplication of code that would occur if there were separate ADD and EDIT methods.

Cleaning up after yourself

With the first request processed, it is important to see how we can clean up the environment after each request has been processed. During the processing of a request, it is possible to open up many cursors and create a number of tables. Some of these tables are not opened up explicitly, so the developer cannot be aware they need to be closed. SQL SELECT statements can open up additional instances of tables in new work areas, for example. The approach with table management taken in the TODO application is to open up all needed tables when the server is started and close down all other tables opened up during the course of processing a request when that request is finished. To open up the tables initially, the TODO application runs a function called OPENTABLES() in the TODOSERVER INIT() method in TODOMAIN.PRG (see **Listing 25**).

Listing 25. Code in TODOMAIN to open up tables and capture open tables.

```
DEFINE CLASS TodoServer AS WWC_SERVER OLEPUBLIC
    *************************************************************
    ***   Function: This is a subclass of the wwServer class
    ***             that is application specific. Each Web Connection
    ***             server you create *MUST* create a subclass of the
    ***             class and at least implement the Process and
    ***             SetServerEnvironment methods to receive requests!
```

```
************************************************************
*** Add any custom properties here
*** These can act as 'global' vars

*--- application specific config items from INI file.
oQueryengine = .NULL.

*--- array to hold open tables.
DIMENSION aOpenDbfs[1,2]

PROTECTED FUNCTION INIT
   DODEFAULT()
   *--- Config object properties have been set...
   *--- set data path using path specified in INI file...
   DO PATH WITH THIS.oConfig.oTodo.cDatapath

   *-- open tables in DBC.
   =opentables("todo")

   *--- instantiate Query Engine.
   THIS.oQueryengine = NEWOBJECT("queryengine","queryengine.prg")

   *-- remember the initial tables that have been opened.
   =AUSED( THIS.aOpenDbfs )
```

The function OPENTABLES() cycles through all the TABLE entries in the TODO database container file. The DBC name is passed as a parameter to OPENTABLES(). *These tables can be found because in the line just before calling OPENTABLES() we used the PATH procedure to set the path to the value for the data path that was specified in the TODO.INI file.* The PATH function is in WWUTILS.PRG. The INIT method also instantiates the Query Engine and its tables are opened up as well. Then the function AUSED() is used to take a snapshot of all open tables and their work areas. The array aOpenDbfs will hold the name of the table and its work area. This is a property of the SERVER class so it is available application-wide. After the current request's methods are run as illustrated in Figure 4, any tables that have been opened need to be closed. The code shown in **Listing 26** is after the DODEFAULT() statement in CLASS_TOP's PROCESS() method.

***Listing 26**. Code in CLASS_TOP to close tables/cursors opened during the last request.*

```
************************************************************
*** <Close tables/cursors opened during last request.>
*** if the table was not opened up originally it will be closed..
************************************************************
AUSED(laPostUsed)
LOCAL lni
FOR lni= 1 TO ALEN(laPostUsed, 1)
   IF ASCAN(server.aOpendbfs, laPostUsed[lni,1])= 0
      USE IN (laPostUsed[lni,1])
   ENDIF
ENDFOR
```

```
***********************************************************
***   <Cleanup Code>
***********************************************************
```

This section of code takes a snapshot of the work areas after all requests have been processed and stores that information to the array laPostUsed. This array and the array aOpenDbfs created in TODOMAIN are compared. Any table from array laPostUsed that does not appear in array aOpenDbfs is closed. The result of this is that the data environment always shrinks down to its original state after each request. This is a very simple way of managing the work areas!

When the Query Engine is asked to create a TABLE, it creates it in the directory specified by TEMPPATH in the TODO.INI file. After a day of activity, this directory could become quite full! An easy way to get rid of these files is to create an old-fashioned BAT file that deletes everything in this directory. Then, in Windows 2000 it can be run as a scheduled event once or twice a day to make sure the directory stays clean. For example, there could be a batch file named CLEAN.BAT and it could reside in the C drive's root directory. All it needs in it is the following:

```
DEL \temp\todo\data\*.*
```

Whatever directory was specified in the INI file for TEMPPATH in the TODO section of the TODO.INI file should be specified in this BAT file! Then, do the following in Windows 2000:

1. Go to Start | Programs | Accessories | System Tools | Scheduled Tasks.

2. Create a new scheduled event by double-clicking on "Add scheduled event."

3. Point to the file that will be scheduled. In this case it is the CLEAN.BAT file.

4. Specify how often it should be run and at what time.

5. Enter the user account it should use when executed. It will impersonate this account. This makes it possible to run programs when the desktop is logged out.

6. Click Finish. The task is now scheduled to run automatically!

This batch file will only be deleting files that have been closed by the cleanup routine discussed earlier. Any open files still in use will not be deleted by this batch file.

Extending the framework with a DEBUG class

One of the more common questions is, "How do I know what is being sent to the server?" An "exclusive" for this book is the following class library, DEBUGPROCESS, which will append all the POSTed form variables, server variables, DISPLAY STATUS, DISPLAY MEMORY, and, in Visual FoxPro 7, SHOWPLAN results to the response page. This means that whenever a page is submitted or a link is clicked, the resulting RESPONSE page can contain the preceding information appended to the bottom of the page. There are several reasons why the technique shown here is so powerful:

- For beginners and even seasoned Web developers, it is important to be able to see easily what data the server is receiving. It can be tedious to go back to the Web Connection server window and then click on Status | Display Request | Display Last Request Info. The DEBUG class simply appends onto the bottom of the RESPONSE page.

- When running COM servers using impersonation (described later), the Web Connection server window is not visible. So there is not even the option of viewing the REQUEST information here. Thus, when the servers are deployed on a production server, the DEBUG class will still allow you to see what is being sent to the server. This is very important since it is not always possible to exactly duplicate a bug on a development machine that appears on a production server.

- There is a separate administration Web page for the DEBUG class. This page allows an admin user to turn debugging on and off. It also controls whether DISPLAY MEMORY, DISPLAY STATUS, and SHOWPLAN information is included.

- If debugging a live site, it is not desirable for viewers to suddenly see this debug information appended to every page. So the DEBUG class will only append this information for the user at the same IP address that initially turned it on! This allows the administrator to gather real-time debugging information on the production server without anyone knowing. Pretty cool!

- The SHOWPLAN output allows you to see how your queries are optimized on the server. You may have created indexes locally but not on the server. This will help you find these kinds of problems. The DEBUGPROCESS class creates a CSHOWPLANRESULTS property, which the QUERYENGINE class updates. After each query is run through the QUERYENGINE, it concatenates the SHOWPLAN results together and the DEBUGCLASS outputs it as shown in **Figure 15**.

- This class contains the ERROR() method that would be used if the DEBUGMODE constant in WCONNECT_OVERRIDE.H is set to .F.. This ERROR routine returns a Web page showing the error message and complete call stack using the new Visual FoxPro 7 ASTACKINFO() function. It also saves a snapshot of the environment at the time of the error to the DEBUGTEMPPATH directory specified in the oDebug Configuration object in TODOMAIN. It saves the following files, which are given random names. The name used is displayed in the returned error page in the browser:

  - A memory file using SAVE TO. Can easily restore the memory variables at the time of the error.

  - A text file with LIST STATUS information.

  - A text file with LIST MEMORY information.

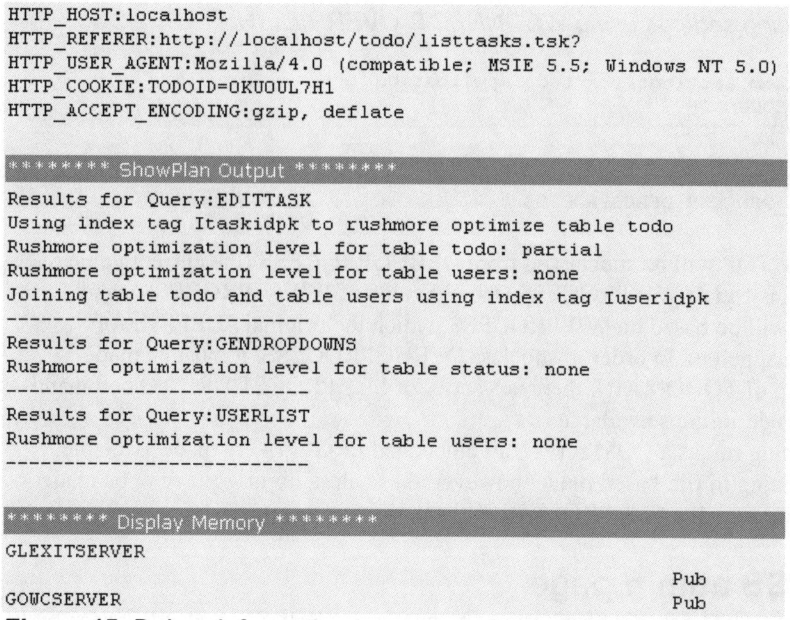

```
HTTP_HOST:localhost
HTTP_REFERER:http://localhost/todo/listtasks.tsk?
HTTP_USER_AGENT:Mozilla/4.0 (compatible; MSIE 5.5; Windows NT 5.0)
HTTP_COOKIE:TODOID=OKUOUL7H1
HTTP_ACCEPT_ENCODING:gzip, deflate
```

```
******** ShowPlan Output ********
Results for Query:EDITTASK
Using index tag Itaskidpk to rushmore optimize table todo
Rushmore optimization level for table todo: partial
Rushmore optimization level for table users: none
Joining table todo and table users using index tag Iuseridpk
-------------------------
Results for Query:GENDROPDOWNS
Rushmore optimization level for table status: none
-------------------------
Results for Query:USERLIST
Rushmore optimization level for table users: none
-------------------------
```

```
******** Display Memory ********
GLEXITSERVER
                                                                  Pub
GOWCSERVER                                                        Pub
```

Figure 15. *Debug Information is appended onto RESPONSE page.*

So now what we need to do is "splice" this new class into the inheritance tree so that it is accessed on every hit. The place where this happens, as has been shown, is in CLASS_TOP. The class definition for CLASS_TOP states that it is based on WWC_PROCESS. This is a #DEFINE constant in the WCONNECT.H file. As described earlier in this chapter, the WCONNECT_OVERRIDE.H file can be used to override settings in WCONNECT.H, and this is precisely what needs to be done to "splice" the new DEBUGCLASS into the inheritance tree. The WCONNECT_OVERRIDE.H file that ships with the source code already points to the DEBUGPROCESS. This process is reviewed in greater detail in the chapter "Extending the Framework," but some of this process bears repeating here.

The reason for using #DEFINES to specify various parent classes is to make it easy to extend the framework. In order to use a custom version of any of the base Web Connection classes, it is only necessary to override the #DEFINE in the WCONNECT_OVERRIDE.H file and recompile the project. The new class will then be used in place of the original base class. To complete the object hierarchy, the new custom class must be based on the original Web Connection base class. This is what "splicing" means. The inheritance tree flows from the application-specific process class to the subclassed base class and then to the base class. Remember, this is just like the subclassed text box that shows red for negative values, which in turn is based on a Times New Roman subclassed text box, which is subclassed from the text box base class form object. So, to splice in the DEBUGCLASS, the WCONNECT_OVERRIDE.H file contains that shown in **Listing 27**.

Listing 27. Overriding settings using WCONNECT_OVERRIDE.H.

```
*--- HAC Note:Custom settings for todo application
     #UNDEFINE DEBUGMODE
     #UNDEFINE WWC_PROCESS

     #DEFINE DEBUGMODE .f.
     #DEFINE WWC_PROCESS DEBUGPROCESS
```

So now CLASS_TOP will be subclassed from DEBUGPROCESS (the current value of WWC_PROCESS) instead of WWPROCESS (the old value of WWC_PROCESS), and DEBUGPROCESS will be based on WWPROCESS, which the original #DEFINE for WWC_PROCESS mapped to. In order to subclass DEBUGPROCESS, it must be made accessible. At the top of TODOMAIN, there is a series of SET PROCEDURE TO commands that make these class definitions available.

If the EXE is being run as a COM server, all embedded PRG files are made available automatically. If running in file-based mode, however, these class libraries have to be made available manually through the SET PROCEDURE statement.

DEBUGCLASS admin page

DEBUG.WCT is a template page that is executed by navigating to the page itself. The Debug.WCT file is located in the admin directory under the virtual directory for the site. It is best to call up this page in a separate browser on your machine. This way, the browser dedicated to Debug.WCT can be used to toggle on and off the RESPONSE information for the form in the main browser window. The extension WCT is handled in the TODOMAIN program and is evaluated by the Web Connection WWSCRIPTMAP class. The page needs to be run so the current IP address can be inserted in the text box. Clicking on "Toggle Debug Information" writes a setting to the application's INI file that sets SHOWDEBUGINFO=ON. A new section is created in the INI file called "DEBUG" (see **Figure 16** and **Listing 28**).

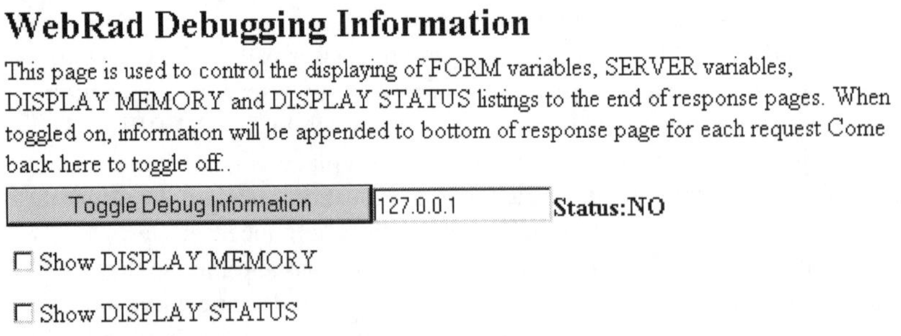

WebRad Debugging Information

This page is used to control the displaying of FORM variables, SERVER variables, DISPLAY MEMORY and DISPLAY STATUS listings to the end of response pages. When toggled on, information will be appended to bottom of response page for each request Come back here to toggle off.

| Toggle Debug Information | 127.0.0.1 | Status:NO |

☐ Show DISPLAY MEMORY

☐ Show DISPLAY STATUS

Figure 16. The DebugClass admin page.

Listing 28. *Settings in TODO.INI that control the DEBUGPROCESS class.*

```
[Debug]
Debugip=127.0.0.1
Showdebuginfo=YES
Showmemory=YES
Showstatus=YES
Debugadminpath=\webradsource\todosource\wwwroot\todo\admin\
debugtemppath=\webradsource\todosource\todo\temp\
```

The DEBUGIP entry is set to the IP shown on the DEBUG.WCT form. Checking the "Show DISPLAY MEMORY" or "Show DISPLAY STATUS" check boxes sets the corresponding entries in the INI file also. These settings are kept in the INI file because they need to be remembered from hit to hit and are not associated with any particular user, so the WWSESSION table is not the place for them. So the first time the Toggle Debug Information button is clicked, it will write the entries to the TODO.INI file. Then, the response page that is generated for any request will have the debug information appended to the bottom of the page as shown in Figure 15.

For new Web Connection developers, this information can offer some real insight into what is being sent to the server and how a request is processed. All the name/value pairs that are listed can be accessed with the REQUEST object. For example, to retrieve the MNOTES value, a call to REQUEST.FORM("MNOTES") would do the trick. A call to REQUEST.GETLOGICALPATH() would return the value of SCRIPT_NAME. Basically all the methods in WWREQUEST are written to parse the FORM VARIABLES and SERVER VARIABLES sections of Figure 15. These two sections contain all the information needed to fulfill a Web request.

By using the other two check boxes on the DEBUG form, the current memory variables and STATUS can also be displayed. Seeing a snapshot of this information on the production server can be very helpful in analyzing problems.

The links on the DEBUG form use a scriptmap of MNT for maintenance. The class library CLASS_MNT is based on WWC_PROCESS and not CLASS_TOP like the other class libraries. This is so that links on the DEBUG page do not force the user to log in to the application. If CLASS_MNT were based on CLASS_TOP, the user would be forced to log in to the application to perform maintenance functions, which really is not necessary. More maintenance functions will be shown shortly that will use this trick. Not having to log in to the application is different from not being authenticated on the server! The ADMIN directory where the DEBUG page resides still needs to have NT security associated with it to keep out anonymous users. The two most important sections can be FORM VARIABLES and the SHOWPLAN output. Very powerful!

It is highly recommended to always leave this DEBUGPROCESS class spliced into the class hierarchy. This way, all the debugging information discussed earlier is available simply by setting the SHOWDEBUGINFO = ON in the TODO.INI file using the Debug.WCT page. This is much easier than changing the #DEFINE constant, recompiling the project, and updating the live site with a new EXE!

Administration Web page

Another important aspect of running a Web site is having an administration page that allows various maintenance tasks and reports to be run through a browser interface. It can be important to run these tasks remotely using terminal services, or locally, right at the console. One of the most basic tasks is to perform a backup of the data. Depending on the level of service available at the data center, a tape backup should be done. But having a backup of the Visual FoxPro tables in another directory on the same server can be a huge convenience. If there is a need to get the data restored quickly, having it in DBF format can save a lot of time!

Another HTML page that comes with this book's source code is called TODOADMIN.HTM. This page would be in the ADMIN directory for the site. This page needs to be protected with an authenticated password too! The first function on this page will be a hyperlink to BACKUPTABLES.MNT. This function looks like **Listing 29**.

Listing 29. Backing up tables.

```
*******************************
Function BackupTables
*******************************
SET PROCEDURE TO class_backup additive
oBackup = CREATEOBJECT("class_backup")

oBackup.cBackupPath = "backups\"
oBackup.cEmailList = ""
oBackup.cFTPBackupSite = ""

oBackup.backup()

*-- response page will be the accumulated messages generated during
*-- backup...
cMessage = "<PRE>"+oBackup.cMessage+"</pre>"
response.write(cMessage)

RELEASE oBackup
Endfunc
```

It instantiates a class called class_backup in the class_backup class file. This utility class takes a list of tables from the application and backs them up to a directory defined by the property cBackupPath. The list of tables is stored in the file called BackupFileList.TXT in the application directory. The backup utility uses a SQL SELECT statement to perform the copy. The backup class concatenates a string to the cMessage property that will inform the user of the success of each file as it is being backed up. Any error messages encountered during the backup are also recorded to this property. Upon completion, the backup class can send an email to an account notifying that person of the backup. It can also FTP the backed up files to another physical machine if an FTP address is set to the cFTPBackupSite property. A call to the backup method actually performs the procedure. When completed, the calling program can query the cMessage property and report that back in the response page.

One common reason for doing a backup of this sort is to provide a copy of the data that can then be FTPed down to a development machine. This technique does not require the site to be turned off. This backup utility can also be packaged as a stand-alone EXE that can be scheduled using the Windows 2000 scheduler utility. This is a very important routine that can be scheduled to run every night or even several times a day. Often having only one backup each day is not sufficient. Some users cannot stand to lose a whole day's worth of work. The complete source code for this utility is included with this book.

Some other common maintenance routines that can be included on the maintenance page are:

- Re-indexing of tables
- Packing of tables
- Customer listings
- Sales reports
- Marketing reports
- Accounting reports

The Web Connection administration page

The administration page that comes with Web Connection is called admin.asp (see **Figure 17**). Admin.asp and any application-specific admin page you create should reside in the admin directory under the site's home directory. This way, they are all in one place and can take advantage of the same directory-level security. The links on the admin.asp page control the WC.DLL file. Some of the more important links on this page are:

- Show and Manage DLL Settings: This shows the current status of the WC.DLL that is processing the requests for the site. You can:

  - Load and unload the running servers

  - Switch into maintenance mode. This turns off the servers and prevents the next hit from starting them up again.

  - View each running server and see the load each one is processing.

- Update Code Online: This allows a running COM server to be updated without taking the site down. The UPDATEFILE entry in the WC.INI file points to the location of the new EXE. Clicking this link shuts down the running servers and copies over the new EXE to the location specified by the EXEFILE entry in the WC.INI file. It happens fast enough whereby no users will even notice. Even though there is a button on this page to navigate to the new EXE on your computer, there is no way here to upload it! You will need to use an FTP client to actually get the new EXE to the server!

- Show Web Connection Server Hit Log: This displays a bar chart of the past 24 hours of activity. It queries the WWREQUESTLOG table and groups by the hour to obtain data. These are hits processed by the WC.DLL.

- Show ISAPI Error Log: This is a report showing any errors generated by the WC.DLL file. If a request times out, there will be an entry here. This data comes from the WCERRORS.TXT file.

- Edit Configuration Files: This allows the INI files to be edited online. If site traffic increased and another COM server instance was needed, the WC.INI file could be edited to launch another instance of the server.

- Unload all Servers but one and Hold Requests: This shuts down all COM servers but one and prevents the others from loading so tasks requiring exclusive use can be run.

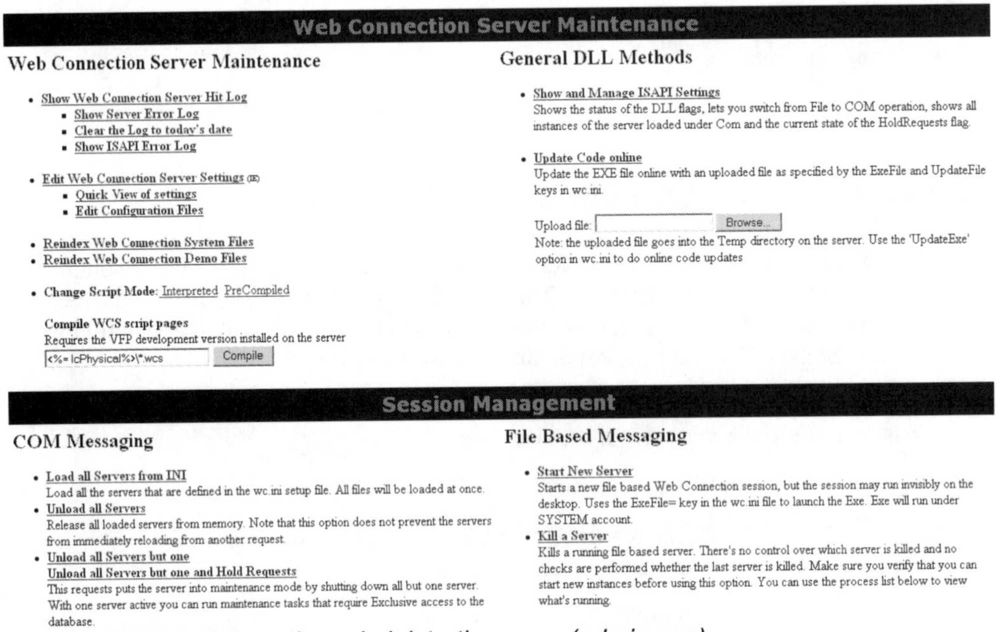

Figure 17. Web Connection administration page (admin.asp).

As shipped by West Wind, the admin.asp page has /WCONNECT/WC.DLL for all of its links. This is assuming the directory structure that the Web Connection Project Wizard uses. The convention here has been to place the WC.DLL file in a directory called "scripts" under each Web site. So to make admin.asp work, you need to do a search and replace on "/wconnect/" and replace it with "../scripts/".

Running as a COM server

Up until now, the TODO application has been running in file-based mode. This meant that the WC.DLL file and the TODO.EXE file were talking to each other via files on disk. All the form variables and server variables that where shown earlier are passed in physical files. This mode is fine during testing and development, but when it comes time to deploy the application on a live server, file-based mode has some drawbacks. The most severe of these is easy updating of the EXE and auto-starting of the server before Windows login.

Fortunately, Web Connection is designed in such a way that switching between these two modes is as simple as clicking on a hyperlink. To run TODO.EXE as a COM server on the development machine, do the following:

1. Build the TODO project as an EXE. From the project build menu, select "Win 32 executable/COM Server" and click OK. Check "Run after build" on.

2. The first time an EXE is built, the Project Manager built it as a MULTI use EXE. It needs to be set to SINGLE. From the system menu, go to Project | Project Info... Click on the Servers tab and change "Instancing" to "Single," and then rebuild the project.

3. Visual FoxPro automatically registers the EXE in the local Registry as a COM server because in TODOMAIN the DEFINE CLASS statement for defining the server uses the OLEPUBLIC keyword. This tells Visual FoxPro to make this EXE visible to the outside world. It is important to also check the "launch" and "access" permissions on the COM server at this point using the "state-of-the-art"<g> utility DCOMCNFG. To do this:

   a. Click on Start | Run.

   b. Type in "dcomcnfg" and hit Enter.

   c. The DCOMCNFG interface appears. It shows a list of all the COM objects that are registered on the local machine. Scroll down to the "todo.todoserver" entry.

   d. Click on the Properties button.

   e. Click on the Security tab.

   f. Select "Use Custom Access Permissions" and click on the Edit button within that group.

   g. Make sure the "iuser_ machinename" and "iwam_ machinename" accounts are listed. If they are not, click on Add and select them from the list of available users on the local machine.

   h. Click OK.

   i. Perform the same check on the "Use Custom Launch Permissions" section, making sure the "iuser_ machinename" and "iwam_ machinename" accounts are listed.

   j. Click OK to save and update rights.

4. Using a browser, navigate to http://localhost/todo/admin/admin.asp. This displays the admin page shown in Figure 17. Although you didn't need the Web Connection Web server running to run the admin.asp file, you do need it running for any of the links on this page. Click on the "Show and Manage ISAPI Settings" link. You can then click on the "COM Mode" link in the upper right to switch from file-based to COM-based. This tells the WC.DLL file to do the equivalent of a

CREATEOBJECT("todo.todoserver") to instantiate the TODO.EXE as a COM server on the next site hit. The response page to this link states the WC.INI files has been updated and the "mechanism" entry has been set to Automation.

5. In the same browser session, navigate to the TODO home page at http://localhost/todo.

6. You should see the TODO server window pop open, and the first request should appear in the list. Since you have not logged in, the login form should be the first form to appear.

7. As the site is navigated, all hits will appear in the server window.

That's really it! For further insight into COM-based vs. file-based mode, please see Chapter 14, "COM vs. File-Based Messaging."

Transferring the TODO application to the server

Now it is time to start transferring the TODO application to a server box. Chapter 8, "Configuring Server Software," discussed how to configure IIS and FTP access to a site on the server box. This will not be repeated here but will be covered in this section's video. The main difference when moving the application to the server is configuring the application to run as a COM server. While the application can be run in file-based mode on the server, it is not recommended for a production site. Maintenance is far easier in COM mode. Please see Chapter 14 for more details. During development, the application is run in the Visual FoxPro development environment as either an APP or EXE file. On the server, however, only the Visual FoxPro runtime needs to be installed to run the TODO.EXE file. You do not need the full development environment. All the other files that need to be on the server are listed later. Okay, so how does the TODO.EXE file get instantiated? When a request comes into the Web site that involves a dynamic link such as http://localhost/listtasks.tsk, the TSK is a script mapped extension that is associated with the site's WC.DLL file. IIS executes the WC.DLL file and passes the link information to it. The WC.DLL in turn reads the WC.INI file, and in the [Automation Servers] section there is an entry Server1=Todo.TodoServer. This is used by WC.DLL to do the equivalent of a CREATEOBJECT("todo.todoserver"). Windows looks up TODO.TODOSERVER in the Registry, finds the location on disk where the EXE lives, and then instantiates it.

The scenario here is that the server is temporarily connected to the development machine via a cross-over CAT 5 cable. It simply goes from one NIC card to the other to form the network. A hub can be used also, but in that case a cross-over cable would not be needed. The IP addresses that can be used on the server at this point to create the Web site can be from the private IP address space as specified by RFC-1918 specification listed in the "Chapter resources" section at the end of this chapter. During initial testing, these IPs allow for realistic testing. A full Web site can be created instead of just a virtual site. After you are satisfied the server is running properly, you can disconnect it from the development machine and move it into a data center. At that point, the permanent IP address can be added and the IP address changed on the site.

Let's review the steps needed to configure the server software (more details are in Chapter 8):

1. Install IIS and FTP services during OS installation.

2. Bind the allocated IP addresses to the server.

3. Create a directory for the HTML content: c:\inetpub\wwwroot\todo\.

    a. Create a scripts, admin, images, and css subdirectories off of the site's root.

File	Destination
WC.DLL	\inetpub\wwwroot\todo\scripts\
WC.INI	\inetpub\wwwroot\todo\scripts\
Admin.asp	\inetpub\wwwroot\todo\admin\
JPGs and GIFs	\inetpub\wwwroot\todo\images\
Todostyle.css	\inetpub\wwwroot\todo\css\
All HTML content and script pages	\inetpub\wwwroot\todo\

    b. Using Windows Explorer, change directory permissions on the admin directory and remove "Everyone" access. Specify the accounts that have access to this directory!

4. Create a directory for the TODO.EXE and associated data. For this example, the path will be \comapps\todo\. Also create a data subdirectory. If possible, put this on a different drive from the virtual directory.

File	Destination
TODO.EXE	\comapps\todo\
TODO.INI	\comapps\todo\
Wwipstuff.DLL	\comapps\todo\
All tables and DBC	\comapps\todo\data\

5. Start the IIS Management Console and create a new Web site.

    a. Set the isolation level to "low."

    b. For the site's root directory, set Execute Permissions to "Scripts only."

    c. For the scripts directory, set Execute Permissions to "Executables."

    d. Click on the Configuration button and create script maps for tsk, usr, mnt, and wp. Point to the \inetpub\wwwroot\todo\scripts\wc.dll file.

    e. On the Documents tab, make "listtasks.tsk" the default home page.

    f. Make any changes necessary to the INI files. For example, in COM mode you may want to load more than one server. You most likely will need to change the paths specified in the app's INI file. You'll also need to set the EXEfile path and UpdateFile path in the WC.INI.

6. Create a new FTP site to allow uploading of HTML content.

    a. The FTP site can use the same IP address that the Web site uses. Remember, since they use different ports (doors), the IP can be the same.

     b.   Create a virtual FTP directory off of the main FTP site that points to the TODO.EXE home directory. A name such as EXEHOME can be used for the virtual name.

7.   Bring up a DOS Command Window. (Some things never change! Working in Windows 2000 Server and still needing to use a DOS window!)

     a.   Switch to the drive the TODO.EXE is located on.

     b.   Type in cd \comapps\todo.

     c.   To register the TODO.EXE COM server in the Registry, type in todo.exe /regserver.

     d.   Or you can bring up the Start | Run window and supply the full path on the command line:

```
regsvr32 X:\comapps\todo\todo.exe
```

8.   Now set permissions on the TODO.EXE file so it can be launched.

     a.   Click on Start | Run | DCOMCNFG | OK.

     b.   Select TODO.TODOSERVER from the list of applications.

     c.   Click on the Properties button.

     d.   Click on the Identity tab.

     e.   Select the "Interactive user" radio button.

9.   Check access and launch permissions.

     a.   Click on the Security tab.

     b.   Select "Use custom access permissions" and click on Edit.

     c.   Make sure Administrators, Interactive, IUSR_machinename, and IWAM_machinename are listed. If not, add them. These permissions allow the WC.DLL file to access the COM server.

     d.   Click OK to save.

     e.   Perform the same check on the launch permissions.

     f.   Save the results and exit DCOMCNFG.

10.   From a browser on the development machine, execute the helloworld.wp link: http://192.168.1.1/helloworld.wp. (This IP address is one from the private address space. You could use any of the addresses allocated for private Internet usage. See the "Chapter resources" section at the end of this chapter for information on private addresses.) This is a script mapped extension that will execute the HelloWorld method in the class_wp library.

11. In the TODO server window, there should be an entry for helloworld.wp, and in the browser window should be the output "Hello World!"

12. To get the TODO home page to render, the listtasks.tsk link needs to be made the default document.

    a.   Start the IIS Manager.

    b.   Highlight the TODO site, right-click, and choose Properties.

    c.   On the Documents tab, add listtasks.tsk and move it to the top of the list. Save your changes.

    d.   In the browser, navigate to the TODO home directory: http://192.168.1.1/.

    e.   This should list out the current contents of the TODO table.

Okay, these steps got the TODO application up and running on the server. However, with the way it is currently configured, the machine has to be logged in in order for the server window to appear. This is not the proper solution. Even though Windows can be configured to log in in automatically upon startup, this creates a huge security problem. The ideal way of doing this is to have the COM server start automatically without the server being logged in and without any human intervention. This becomes extremely important in a data center environment where there is no one readily available.

Configuring the server for "autostart"

Autostart is what allows developers to get a better night's sleep. If in the middle of the night the machine needs to be rebooted for whatever reason, the next Web request that is serviced by IIS will restart the COM server automatically. The key to having this happen is impersonation. Through the DCOMCNFG utility, a COM server can be told to start up as though it had been started by a particular user. So even though the server is not logged in, the COM server will run in the context of the specified user and assume all rights of that user. To set this up, do the following:

1. Click on Start | Run | DCOMCNFG | OK.

2. Select TODO.TODOSERVER from the list of applications.

3. Click on the Properties button.

4. Click on the Identity tab.

5. Click on the "This User" radio button.

6. Supply a username and password with the rights necessary to run the COM server.

7. Click OK twice to save.

When the Web site is hit with the first request, the COM server will start up but there will not be any visible server window. It runs in the background with no GUI. This is fine, because while it is running in the server, there will not be anyone around to watch it anyway! The only way to confirm that it is running is to start up the Task Manager and look for the listing in the Processes tab.

Overcoming the "Access Denied" error when running as a COM server

A very common problem when first running servers in COM mode is getting the "Access Denied" error. This is due to incorrect permission settings. The request that attempted to launch the COM server did actually launch the COM server. If Task Manager is used to view the list of running processes, the EXE file will be listed there. However, it is not being managed by the WC.DLL file and cannot be unloaded using the Web Connection administration page. The only way to unload it is to select the process in Task Manager and then click on "End Process." This will terminate the EXE. To make sure there are sufficient rights to launch the COM servers, make sure Step 9 in the prior section is performed correctly. The Access and Launch permissions page should look like **Figure 18**.

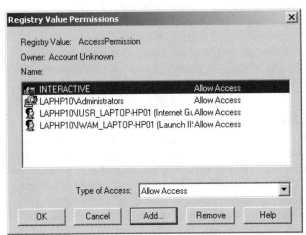

Figure 18. Accounts needed on Access and Launch Permissions.

The computer name "LAPHP10" would be replaced by the name of the local machine. Once these permissions are set and the site is hit again, the COM server will start properly.

Additional TODO features

The TODO application as shown in this chapter provides the forms for maintaining the TODO table. However, there should be Web pages to maintain the USERS and STATUS tables as well. This should be done through a maintenance page that only administration users have access to. The TODOADMIN.HTM page discussed earlier in this chapter could be used to gain access to the USERS and STATUS maintenance pages. The technique for doing these pages is exactly the same as for the TODO table. The complete version of this application with all necessary forms can be found at **www.webconnectiontraining.com**.

Conclusion

As you can see, there are a considerable number of new steps and technologies required to get a Web application running. Probably one of the most common problems is not having your custom application's INI file and the WC.INI file referring to the same TEMP paths when operating in file-based mode.

While the Visual FoxPro side of the equation remains pretty much the same, there are the new technologies of HTML pages, JavaScript, and IIS that need to be mastered. But, as we have seen here, these are variations in syntax (VFP Form DOM vs. Web Pages DOM) or implementation (File Type associations in Windows vs. script mapping in IIS). Study these examples in this book, and the process of building Web sites will become much easier.

Don't forget the RADWizard!

Appendix D of this book, the WebRad Project Wizard, is only available as an electronic download from the Hentzenwerke site. This project wizard is a greatly enhanced version of the project wizard that ships with Web Connection. The WebRad Project Wizard configures everything automatically for your new site and provides you with the same framework described in this chapter. Please download the PDF version of Appendix D and the WebRad Project Wizard source code!

Chapter resources

- **www.webconnectiontraining.com**: Author-run site with online demonstration of TODO application as well as all chapter videos, book resources, software, and updates.

- **www.faqs.org/rfcs/rfc1918.html**: Address allocation for private Internets: Document describes the use of the IP address blocks intended for private use.

- **www.stevedingle.com**: PJXSearch utility.

Chapter 13
Identifying Users and
Managing Session Data

Only the most basic Web sites can avoid the issues of tracking and identifying users. Before long you will have one or both of these needs. This chapter describes the concepts involved, the choices available, and how to implement your decision using Web Connection.

As discussed in previous chapters, Web applications are stateless. What does this mean for your applications? Simply that you are responsible for providing the glue that allows each individual user to navigate through your site and have a consistent, cohesive experience.

As an example, consider a graphics-intensive application that offers the user a choice between large, small, and no graphic images as a preference to assist users with low-speed connections. Once the user selects his or her preference, perhaps via a menu option on your home page, you will want to continue to honor that preference on all subsequent hits. As a novice Web developer, your first reaction might be to define either a property or variable to record this request. The problem is that your application is not serving that single user, but all users at once. Once you process one user's request, it is very likely that the next request will come from a different user, who doesn't have the same preferences. What to do?

The answer is to use one of several methods to establish the passing of identifying tokens between browser and Web server, such that you can maintain the context of each user's session independently. In this chapter, I will present four different such methods and show how to use each of these in a Web Connection application. I will then discuss how to manage state information during a user session by using the wwSession framework class. Finally, I will present some advanced topics in this area.

The basics

First, let me define a few terms I will be using.

What is user tracking?

By *user tracking*, I am referring to the need to follow each user as they navigate through your Web site, and store the various information about their actions that are required to provide the proper actions and responses on subsequent pages. The best-known usage of user tracking is in shopping cart functions, where the users' choices are saved while they continue to shop for additional items (or perform other actions) on your site.

When you employ user tracking, you may or may not know who the user is, but you definitely need to distinguish each user from all of the others who are visiting your site at the same time.

What is user identification?

On the other hand, by *user identification* I refer specifically to determining the identity of a given visitor to your site. The method by which the user identity is verified may vary widely— from a "guest book" application where users fill out a form about themselves and you accept them at their word, to applications that have user login forms, where you verify their entries against a known user table in your database.

Some applications require aspects of both user tracking and user identification.

The four basic methods

Whether or not your situation requires user identification and a login process, if your application requires any user tracking, you will have to choose a method whereby the browser and Web server exchange information that you will use to distinguish among users. There are four methods available to achieve this passing of tokens between browser and Web server:

- **Authentication** is a method by which you are able to use actual system user accounts in Web applications. These can be either local accounts on the Web server or domain accounts. (Note: If you need to log users in, but your user list is maintained in a database, you cannot use authentication. Instead, use one of the remaining three methods combined with a login form.)

- **Temporary cookies** provide a mechanism by which the server assigns an identifying token (or cookie) to the browser and requests that the browser send that cookie back with each subsequent request during that browser session.

- **Persistent cookies** are similar to temporary cookies, except they have an expiration date in the future. As such, they are recorded on the user's disk subsystem and continue to be sent back to your site in future browser sessions until the expiration date is reached.

- **License plates** are URL-based identifiers that are strictly created and maintained by your application. You assign a unique identifier to each new user to arrive at your site, and propagate this identifier into each dynamic hyperlink and form action that comprise your application. Although they represent the most difficult of the four methods from a developer perspective, in some circumstances license plates can avoid most of the disadvantages of the other three methods.

Each of these methods is presented in detail in the sections that follow. Depending on your environment and your design requirements, the decision of which method to use is usually straightforward. These methods are not mutually exclusive; however, you will typically employ only one for any single Web application. As an advanced topic at the end of this chapter, I discuss situations where you might combine more than one of these methods.

Authentication

Authentication is a method whereby the user agent (browser) and Web server communicate to verify the user's credentials. There are three techniques whereby you can force this authentication to occur.

First, you can set the security setting for your virtual directory or entire Web site not to allow anonymous access. While this will completely protect your site from anonymous users in one broad scope, and requires no code to implement, this technique applies only to (typically intranet) situations where your application has no public pages, including welcome information.

Second, if your file system type is NTFS, you can use the file system to protect specific files from use by anonymous Web users. You could even protect the WC.DLL file itself, thus removing all anonymous access to your dynamic pages. While again requiring no code to implement, this technique is too broad for most situations. It is also somewhat more difficult to audit and maintain.

Finally, you can build code right into the Process object of your Web Connection application. This can be as simple as:

```
LOCAL lcAuthUser
lcAuthUser = THIS.oRequest.GetAuthenticatedUser()
IF EMPTY( m.lcAuthUser )
  * Not yet logged in - abort here and authenticate:
  THIS.oResponse.Authenticate( THIS.oRequest.GetServerName())
  RETURN
ENDIF
```

This code uses the Request object to check who the current authenticated user is. If empty, the user has not been authenticated, and the response process is aborted with an authentication request.

Authentication and the end-user experience

Using any of the three approaches listed in the previous section, the Web server will return a "401 Not Authorized" HTTP result code, together with any realm name (either your entire site or a specific virtual directory) and an HTML response to be displayed if the authentication fails. Browsers receiving such a result will intervene and prompt the user for a user name and password. The style used for this prompt is browser- and platform-dependent, and is outside of your control as a developer. **Figure 1** shows the result using Microsoft Internet Explorer on a Windows 2000 platform.

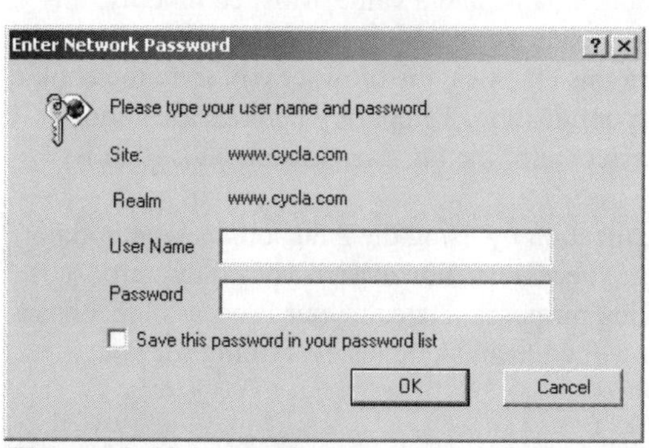

Figure 1. Using authentication, the client browser presents the user with a login dialog of its own format.

Pros and cons of authentication

Before deciding on using authentication, there are many factors to consider:

- If your users already have Windows accounts (such as on an intranet), authentication offers a method of identifying and tracking users that is automatic and requires no additional administrative effort.

- You must use basic (or "clear text") authentication if you want to be able to determine the user ID of the current user. If your Web server is configured to use Challenge Response Authentication (named Windows Authentication under Windows 2000), you will not be able to determine the identity of Microsoft Internet Explorer users, because this information is not made available as part of the ISAPI request. Thus, if you do not have control over this security policy decision, you will be unable to use authentication as an identifying strategy. It can still be used for security, however.

- To use authentication, there must be a Windows user account established for each user. This could present both administrative and licensing issues, depending on your situation. At minimum, involve your network administrator in any such decision.

- The Web Connection framework class for managing session state, wwSession, is designed for use with nine-character, randomly assigned session identifiers. Windows user IDs can be longer than nine characters. Thus, at minimum, you would need to subclass wwSession and override several methods to accommodate a longer identifier field. Alternatively, you might want to design your own session management class.

- There is no way to force a user logout once he or she has been logged in, unless the user closes the browser. You cannot control this at the server end. Depending on your security requirements, this may preclude the use of authentication.

Temporary cookies

Cookies are mechanisms by which a Web server sends the equivalent of a character-valued variable back to the browser. The cookie has both a name and a value. Most commonly, this would be an identifier to be used to track the user as he or she navigates through your site. If the user "accepts the cookie" (discussed later in this chapter), the browser will send the cookie back as part of each subsequent request to your application. Temporary cookies are almost always stored only in memory, and remain in effect until the browser session ends (that is, until the user closes the browser window).

You can add cookies manually in your application by using the AddCookie() method of the wwHttpHeader class. This manual step is not necessary, however, if your only purpose is to use the cookie as an identifier for user tracking purposes. Instead, your Process object has a single method that can be invoked with one line of code and handles everything for you:

```
THIS.InitSession()
```

By placing this method call in the Process method of your application, you can establish a single cookie that is used to control your user tracking across the entire application. For example:

```
FUNCTION Process
THIS.InitSession()
= DODEFAULT()
ENDFUNC  && Process
```

As long as you create your response using one of the standard Web Connection approaches, the framework does all of the work to create and send the cookie for you. (See the next section, "Ensuring your cookie gets delivered".) From this point on, you are free anywhere in your Process object methods to store and retrieve session state variables by making calls to Session.GetSessionVar() and Session.SetSessionVar(). The Session object is described further under "Managing session state" later in this chapter.

Also note that the Web Connection framework establishes the private variable Session, in addition to private variables Request, Response, and Server. These variables are created in the Process method of the parent wwProcess class, which gets called via DODEFAULT() in the preceding code. These variables can then be referenced in your individual page methods. This is merely a convenience, so that you do not need to always type references such as "THIS.oSession" (or, in scripts and templates, "Process.oSession").

For your initial attempt at using cookies, you can simply call InitSession as you saw earlier and reasonable defaults are established for you. There are, however, three optional parameters about which you should be aware:

1. The default name for the cookie that gets passed to the user is "wwSessionId". To use a different name, pass a string as the first parameter.

2. The default session timeout is 30 minutes (1800 seconds). If the user does not hit your site for that period of time, the session times out and any session variables are lost. If the same user then hits your site again, a new cookie will be generated and a new session opened. To change this timeout value, pass the desired value (in seconds) as a numeric second parameter.

3. InitSession creates a temporary cookie by default. A persistent cookie can be created by passing a logical True value as the third parameter. Persistent cookies are covered as a separate topic later in this chapter.

Thus, in the following command you are using your own cookie name and changing the session timeout to four hours.

```
THIS.InitSession( "MySessionId", 4 * 60 * 60 )
```

Ensuring your cookie gets delivered

When you use the InitSession() method of the Process object, a check is made of whether the user already has received the cookie. If not, properties in the Response object are set that are intended to write a cookie in the appropriate location of the response header. This automatic mechanism is very convenient, saving the developer several steps, but its success depends on your issuing your response in one of the following ways:

- by including a call to either Response.HTMLHeader() or Response.ContentTypeHeader() in your code;

- by sending basic response pages using either THIS.StandardPage() or THIS.ErrorMsg();

- by sending an expanded script or template using Response.ExpandScript() or Response.ExpandTemplate(); or

- by manually creating and using a header object using class wwHttpHeader and passing the Response object reference as a parameter to the Init() method.

This list covers virtually all of the standard response-generation techniques; therefore it is relatively simple to ensure your cookie is delivered. There are two common mistakes that developers make, however, that circumvent the cookie delivery process:

1. If you use HTTP redirection, via the Response.Redirect() method, you are replacing the standard HTTP header, which includes your cookie, with a special redirection header. If you do this, your cookie is never sent. Thus it is essential to avoid trying to redirect and send a cookie in the same response. This is a very common problem that arises on the West Wind support forums. (Note that if you construct the <head> section of your response manually, you can achieve a similar effect as redirection, while still preserving cookies, by including a <meta> tag with the http-equiv attribute setting of "refresh." Refer to an HTML reference for more information on this subject.)

2. If you create an HTTP header manually, or you instantiate an object from the wwHttpHeader class, but do not pass an object reference to the Response object, a cookie cannot be automatically created for you. It is still possible for you to add the cookie syntax yourself, but there is little reason to follow this manual path, when Web Connection provides a robust mechanism that handles everything for you.

Temporary cookies and the end-user experience

What the user will experience if you employ a temporary cookie strategy is outside of your control, except on tightly controlled intranets. Because of significant misinformation about cookies, many users fear cookies can compromise their privacy, and will not accept them.

Recent versions of both Netscape Navigator and Microsoft Internet Explorer allow users to set preferences to be employed when cookies are sent from a Web site. If users elect to accept all cookies, then response pages are displayed with no specific indication that a cookie has been sent. If, on the other hand, they choose to reject all cookies, any identifier you assign is never sent back by the browser.

Finally, most browsers now offer an option to be prompted when a new cookie arrives. In this case, users will see a dialog asking whether they wish to accept the cookie. **Figure 2** shows such a dialog with Netscape Navigator.

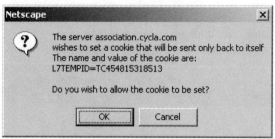

Figure 2. When your application sends cookies, your users may get warnings like this from their browser.

Pros and cons of temporary cookies

There are several pros and cons of using temporary cookies that are important to consider when choosing your strategy:

- Some older browsers do not support cookies at all. Today the percentage of browsers in this sad state is thankfully negligible.

- Some users may have set their browser options to reject cookies, or may reject your specific cookie when prompted. For corporate or government users, internal policies may dictate how browsers are configured. Fortunately, most users do accept cookies. But if your application must work in an environment where cookies are not accepted, you may be forced to choose an alternative strategy. *It is essential to know about your target audience at the beginning of your design phase.*

- Temporary cookies are very easy to implement in a Web Connection application. You have the entire mechanism at your fingertips simply by inserting a single line of code to call the InitSession() method of your Process object.

- Temporary cookies may be accepted in some situations where persistent cookies are not. As they are never stored permanently to the user's disk, they may be perceived as less of a privacy risk.

- By their very nature, there is no way to use temporary cookies by themselves to maintain state information from one user session to the next. If you have such a requirement, you will need to maintain a separate table of users, and design a login form in your Web application. You then store the user ID, once the user has logged in, to a session variable, and then use the cookie on subsequent hits to provide a crosswalk from the temporary session to the permanent user information. This is a very common design approach in Web applications. See "Managing session state" later in this chapter for an example that implements this strategy.

- Because temporary cookies expire as soon as the browser session ends, a user's session becomes effectively disconnected as soon as the user closes the browser, even if the session has not yet timed out on the server. This can enhance application security in environments where multiple users have physical access to the same computer.

Persistent cookies

Persistent cookies operate very similarly to temporary cookies, except that browsers store persistent cookies on disk, and then send them again unprompted in subsequent communications with your site. This can be a handy mechanism for applications with repeat visitors, since your site can "know who the user is" when he or she first arrives. This allows for adaptive behavior, such as inserting a customized "Welcome Back" message at the top of your page on the first hit.

Unless you provide some mechanism wherein users tell you who they are (such as by logging in), persistent cookies provide the only method for tracking users across multiple sessions.

Implementing persistent cookies in a Web Connection application could be very straightforward. The following line of code sets up the entire mechanism for you:

```
THIS.InitSession( , , .T.)
```

Note the optional third parameter, which directs that the cookie be persistent. From an implementation standpoint, this is the only difference from using temporary cookies. The problem with this approach is it gives you no real benefit over using temporary cookies, because all of the user's settings are dropped as soon as the session times out. Instead, you will want to choose from one of two basic approaches.

If you have an existing table of users, you can add a field to the table to store their persistent cookie values. When you process each hit, you will first check for the cookie, and if found, locate the current user in the table. If not, add a new record, assign a cookie value and send that cookie to the user. Here is a conceptual example:

```
LOCAL lcCookie
lcCookie = THIS.oRequest.GetCookie( "UserCookie" )
IF EMPTY( m.lcCookie )  && no cookie yet
   lcCookie = "C" + SYS(3)  && assign new random value
   INSERT INTO wwUser (UserCookie) VALUES (m.lcCookie)
   * Add cookie to response object:
   WITH THIS.oResponse
     .cAutoSessionCookieName = "UserCookie"
     .cAutoSessionCookie = m.lcCookie
     .lAutoSessionCookiePersist = .T.
   ENDWITH
ELSE
   SELECT wwUser  && assumes you've opened it elsewhere
   LOCATE FOR UserCookie = m.lcCookie
   IF NOT FOUND()  && bogus cookie
     * Possible hack attempt! Take action as appropriate!
   ENDIF
ENDIF
```

You can now store and retrieve user preference and state information from the user table, or you can instantiate a separate Session object to manage session data, while storing permanent user settings in the user table. The specific choice you make is dependent on your application requirements.

There is one other point to notice where the preceding code detects an invalid cookie. There are several possible explanations as to how this could occur, and the action you take depends on how you weigh these possibilities and the security requirements of your application. The situation could be caused by a problem at your end—for example, from the session table becoming corrupt or being improperly maintained. A second possibility is that another application, perhaps an Active Server Page, has set a cookie with the same name to a value unknown to you. Nevertheless, this situation could also indicate a hacker attempting to do something untoward on your site, by generating a false cookie and trying to see whether they can gain access. This is one reason why cookie values should be long random strings, rather than, say, integer primary key values. See Chapter 18, "Advanced Troubleshooting and Maintenance," for a discussion of handling hacker detection situations.

A second approach is available if you do not plan to maintain a separate user table. You can force the wwSession table to maintain persistent user information by employing an optional parameter in the NewSession() method of the session class that lets you force the session ID. This is again a manual approach, rather than using the automatic InitSession() method:

```
FUNCTION Process

LOCAL lcCookie
PRIVATE Session
THIS.oSession = CREATEOBJECT( [WWC_SESSION] )
Session = THIS.oSession
lcCookie = THIS.oRequest.GetCookie( "wwSessionId")
IF EMPTY( m.lcCookie )   && none yet assigned to this user
  lcCookie = Session.NewSession()
  WITH THIS.oResponse
    .cAutoSessionCookieName = "wwSessionId" && cookie name sent to client
    .cAutoSessionCookie = m.lcCookie  && assign value to cookie
    .lAutoSessionCookiePersist = .T.   && persistent (vs. temporary)
  ENDWITH
ELSE
  IF NOT Session.IsValidSession( m.lcCookie )
    Session.NewSession( , m.lcCookie )  && force the value
  ENDIF
ENDIF
* Call Web Connection default processing:
DODEFAULT()

ENDFUNC  && Process
```

Although the preceding code manages to employ the wwSession table to manage your permanent users, this approach requires some cautions. First, the user's "session" variables will persist from one session to the next. This may or may not be what you want. Depending on the situation, you may want to add code that detects the first hit of a session and resets some or all of the session variables. Second, you must avoid performing the built-in Web Connection maintenance functions on the session table, since they will delete and pack all records for which the user's session has timed out! Finally, be aware that you are committing to maintaining one record for every visitor who ever comes to your site. This could result in a huge table that affects performance. Be certain that the persistence of this information has sufficient value to your site to justify its costs.

Persistent cookies and the end-user experience

For typical users, there is no difference between what they see with persistent vs. temporary cookies. If their browser is set to accept all cookies, they are not even aware that a cookie has been sent. If instead their browser is set to prompt them when cookies arrive, they will see more information with persistent cookies.

Figure 3 show an example Microsoft Internet Explorer dialog after expanding the More Info option. Note the Expires field showing that the cookie expires far into the future.

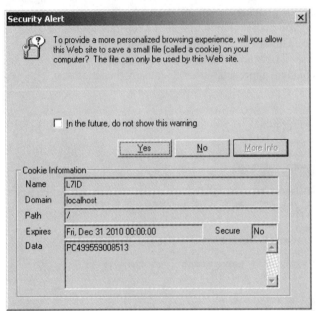

Figure 3. *Microsoft Internet Explorer shows extensive information about the cookie when you expand the dialog by pressing the More Info button.*

Figure 4 shows the same situation with Netscape Navigator. Notice the additional sentence that has been inserted advising the user of the cookie's persistence. Some users may be concerned about privacy and reject the cookie.

Figure 4. *Netscape shows additional persistence information for persistent cookies. Compare with Figure 2.*

License plates

The last alternative method for passing tokens between client and server is to use "license plates." This approach is the most difficult to implement for the Web Connection developer. Nevertheless, it offers the advantage of avoiding most of the shortcomings of the alternative methods.

A license plate is an identifier assigned to the user when he or she hits the first dynamic page on your site, and it is persisted in all subsequent URLs that a user encounters in navigating though your application. For example, if you assigned a random identifier of "L23891766" when the user arrived, you would attach "&lp= L23891766" to all of your dynamically generated URLs. On each incoming request, you simply check for the license plate via:

```
THIS.cLicensePlate = Request.QueryString( "lp" )
```

This code, of course, assumes you have added a property *cLicensePlate* to your process class. If there is no license plate (indicating the first hit for the current user), or if the value is not "current" (indicating a session timeout), you simply generate a new one. In fact, the wwSession class can be used to facilitate a license plate strategy, as shown later in this section.

Pros and cons of license plates

License plates are the most interesting and challenging of the methods presented. There are some vital issues to understand before committing to their use:

- The main advantage to license plates is that you avoid all of the issue of privacy concerns, security policies, and browser compatibility that hamper the other three methods. The license plate exists only in the query strings of URLs and on your server. If a user or entire organization prohibits the use of cookies, a license plate strategy still works. If a server administrator changes a site to use Windows Authentication, license plates are not affected.

- There are two major disadvantages to license plates. The first is that they involve a lot of work on the part of the Web Connection developer. You must ensure that the license plate value is persisted across every dynamic link that your application generates. This includes both hyperlinks and form actions. The first time the user trips on a single link without the license plate, the session thread is lost! If you are working on a shopping cart application, for example, this is a very bad outcome! Unless you develop a foolproof method for managing the URLs in your application, a license plate strategy is probably not one with which you will succeed.

- If your site includes static Web pages that your application must link to, be aware that the license plate becomes lost when the user navigates to such a page. Depending on the nature of your application, this could doom the use of license plates. (Note that neither cookies nor authentication are affected by this issue.) Although there are some advanced techniques to avoid this problem that are beyond the scope of this book, I recommend against using license plates if you must coexist with static pages.

It is crucial to understand the pros and cons discussed here before implementing a license plate strategy. In the next section, I will show how to implement the basics of such a strategy should you decide to select this approach.

Implementing a license plate strategy

There are plenty of challenges in implementing a license plate strategy. You have to be diligent in ensuring that the license plate gets "attached" to every single URL that your application generates. These include both form actions and standard hyperlinks (anchor tags). Given all of this effort, you should try to simplify the manual efforts as much as possible.

The simple approach shown here involves first adding a few properties and methods to your process class:

```
DEFINE CLASS myProcess AS WWC_PROCESS
* Add some properties:
cLicensePlate = ""
cUrlSuffix = ""
```

Next you add a new method that performs the equivalent functions as InitSession(), but for license plates:

```
FUNCTION InitLicensePlateSession
LPARAMETERS lcLPName, lnTimeout
LOCAL lcLPId

IF EMPTY(lcLPName)
  lcLPName =  "LP"
ENDIF

lcLPId = THIS.oRequest.QueryString( m.lcLPName )
THIS.oSession = CREATEOBJECT( [WWC_SESSION] )

IF NOT EMPTY( m.lnTimeout )
  THIS.oSession.nSessionTimeout = m.lnTimeout
ENDIF

IF NOT THIS.oSession.IsValidSession( m.lcLPId )
  * Pass a Request object reference, so other
  * items, such as IP address can be stored in the session.
  THIS.oSession.oRequest = THIS.oRequest

  lcLPId = THIS.oSession.NewSession()
ENDIF
* Now set license plate properties:
THIS.cLicensePlate = m.lcLPId
* This must be attached to every URL:
THIS.cUrlSuffix = "&" + m.lcLPName + "=" + m.lcLPId
RETURN lcLPId
ENDFUNC  && InitLicensePlateSession
```

You put this code to work in the same manner as temporary cookies. The easiest place is to override the Process method as follows:

```
FUNCTION Process
THIS.InitLicensePlateSession()
DODEFAULT()
ENDFUNC  && Process
```

Now you have a license plate mechanism in place that you can use in all of your pages. Now the hard part starts! It isn't hard technically, just very tedious. You need to ensure that you attach the license plate to all of your URLs. For example, if your code would otherwise read:

```
Response.Write( [<a href="wc.dll?myApp~myPage" title="Go to my page.">] + ;
  "[Link to My Page...]" + [</a>] + CR )
```

You would now want to use:

```
Response.Write( [<a href="wc.dll?myApp~myPage~] + THIS.cUrlSuffix +;
  [" title="Go to my page.">] + ;
  "[Link to My Page...]" + [</a>] + CR )
```

Similar considerations must be made for the *action* attributes on <form> tags in cases where the form is not simply submitted back to the same page. While this may look like a simple change, you can quickly become overwhelmed by the number of dynamic hyperlinks in your application. Remember that missing just one of these can cause your users' sessions to be lost!

Finally, if you deploy license plates in several applications, you might want to create a generic subclass of wwProcess that includes this approach and then derive your application classes from there. Subclassing of Web Connection framework classes is discussed in Chapter 16, "Extending the Framework."

Managing session state

Once you have selected the method you will use for passing tokens between client and server, you are ready to take advantage of your decision by adding the ability to manage the state of your user's session. By this, I am referring to the ability to store important actions, values, and preferences during the response to one request, such that this information can be retrieved and used in responding to subsequent requests from the same user.

This may sound like an obscure or difficult concept, but it is actually central to the design of robust Web Connection applications. As discussed at the beginning of this chapter, the need for managing state in this way arises from the stateless nature of Web applications. Once you start working with the concepts of state management, you will find it to be quite simple. Further, you will find seemingly limitless opportunities to manage state information in your applications. Here are just a few examples of state management in Web applications:

- For applications requiring user *logins*, you maintain session variables indicating both the user ID and whether they have successfully logged in. I show specific code to accomplish this task later in this section.

- Whenever the user takes any action indicating a *preference*, you save that information. Then, on any subsequent request for which that preference could apply, you retrieve the stored value and use it accordingly. Typical preference information might include use of frames, use of graphics, choice of colors, choice of language, and font size (for accessibility considerations).

- When a user selects from among a choice of categories or partitions of your data, you will often want to store this value and then use it in context later.

- When a user fills in selection criteria that you use to perform a query, you may encounter situations where you want to retrieve the user's most recent criteria, such as to redisplay a list.

Now that you have some ideas of typical state information, I will show you how to use the handy wwSession class from the Web Connection framework to make this effort a breeze.

Deploying the Session object

Although you could certainly design your own session management approach, Web Connection ships with a very useful class that can handle the needs of most applications for you. The wwSession class works automatically with temporary cookies and is easy to deploy with a license plate strategy as well. Once instantiated, your individual pages will only use two simple methods for all state management.

First you must instantiate the Session object. In general, you will want this object available across all pages in your application. As such you should insert your instantiation code in the Process method. By doing so, you need only include this code in one place. If you are using temporary cookies, here is the code you want to include:

```
= THIS.InitSession()
DODEFAULT()   && call framework wwProcess::Process code
```

Note that the default code in the Process method of the framework wwProcess class then takes care of creating a private variable *Session* that can be referenced in your individual page methods. This is both convenient and makes your code more consistent with ASP syntax, just as you do when you use *Request* and *Response*.

This step of deploying the Session object from the Process object creates an entire mechanism, whereby all of the hard work is accomplished for you. Specifically:

1. The Process object queries the Request object to determine whether a cookie value has been received.

2. The Process object instantiates the Session object, stores the object reference as the oSession property of the Process object, and optionally sets the session timeout value, if a non-default value was passed as the second parameter to InitSession.

3. The Process object then scripts the Session object to check whether the cookie value, if any, identifies a current valid session (one that has not timed out). If so, everything is established and the procedure ends.

4. If there is not a current valid session, the Process object directs the Session object to establish one.

5. The Session object takes care of assigning a new random session identifier, adds a new record to the session table if needed, and returns the session identifier to the Process object.

6. Finally, when a new session is created, the Process object sets property values in the Response object that control the automatic generation of a cookie in the HTTP header that accompanies the response.

By simply including a single call to the InitSession() method of the Process object, the Web Connection framework accomplishes all of the preceding steps for you, which consists of an orchestration of four separate objects. This should be strong incentive to use this valuable framework feature, rather than designing your own session management mechanism.

Putting the Session object to work

Now that you have deployed the Session object, it is ready and available for your use on every page of your application. All that is required is to use the SetSessionVar() method to save settings and the GetSessionVar() method to retrieve them. That's all there is to it!

Here is a simple example. Suppose you have a lot of users with very slow dial-up access and you want to offer the option of pages without graphics. First, you insert into your primary page a link by which the users can indicate their preference:

```
Response.Write( [<a href="wc.dll?myapp~mypage?graphics=no">] + ;
  "[Exclude Graphics]" + [</a>] + [ ] + ;
  [<a href="wc.dll?myapp~mypage?graphics=yes">] + ;
  "[Include Graphics]" + [</a>] )
```

This produces the links by which the users can indicate their preference. Note that you are not using the Session object here—you are simply providing the user interface.

Next, you include code in the method that processes these links if the user clicks on them:

```
LOCAL lcGraphicsPref
lcGraphicsPref = Request.QueryString( "graphics" )
IF NOT EMPTY( m.lcGraphicsPref )
  * they chose something
  Session.SetSessionVar( "graphics", m.lcGraphicsPref )
ENDIF
```

Now you have the user's preference stored for the remainder of the session. Whenever you need it, you just use code such as:

```
LOCAL lcGraphicsPref
lcGraphicsPref = Session.GetSessionVar( "graphics" )
IF NOT m.lcGraphicsPref == "no" && they don't mind graphics
  Response.WriteLn( [<img src="images/bigLogo.gif">] ) && let em have it
ENDIF
```

That is all there is to it! There is one point of interest in the last code segment. Note that I don't just check for the graphics setting being "yes" before sending the graphic. Instead, I take into account the possibility that no preference has yet been recorded. (In this case,

GetSessionVar() returns an empty string.) This is very frequently the case with session variables, and your application code often needs to have some default action in case no user setting yet exists. In this case, the application sends graphics unless the user has specifically requested otherwise.

Implementing user logins

If your application demands that users login, you will need to maintain user names and (unless using authentication) passwords in a database table. You will use a state management approach, such as via the Session object, to persist the login status from one hit to the next. This section provides an example that implements users logins.

For this example, I will assume you are using the standard Web Connection session approach with temporary cookies. I will also assume you have a table called User with at least two fields: *UserId* and *Password*. Further, in this basic example, I assume that all pages to your application require a login.

```
IF NOT THIS.IsLoggedIn()
   * user not yet logged in
   = THIS.LoginForm()
   RETURN .T.
ENDIF
...* remainder of Process method
```

All that happens here is we check to see whether the user is already logged in. If not, we display a login form and terminate further processing. That way we ensure that users never see anything to which they are not entitled. By including this code in the central Process method, all pages are protected. Here is the code that checks whether the user has already logged in successfully:

```
FUNCTION IsLoggedIn
LOCAL lcUser, lcFormUser, lcFormPass, Session, Request
Session = THIS.oSession
Request = THIS.oRequest
lcUser = Session.GetSessionVar( "UserId" )
IF EMPTY( m.lcUser )
   * they hadn't logged in before, let's see
   * if they just did
   lcFormUser = Request.Form( "txtUserId" )
   lcFormPass = Request.Form( "txtPassword" )
   IF NOT EMPTY( m.lcFormUser )
      SELECT User   && assume you opened it already
      LOCATE FOR UserId = PADR( m.lcFormUser, LEN( UserId)) AND ;
        Password = PADR( m.lcFormPass, LEN( Password))
      IF FOUND()
        lcUser = m.lcFormUser
        Session.SetSessionVar( "UserId", m.lcUser )
      ENDIF
   ENDIF
ENDIF
* Optional idea: THIS.cUserId = m.lcUser
RETURN NOT EMPTY( m.lcUser )
ENDFUNC
```

And finally, here is code to produce an example login form that appears if the user has not yet logged in:

```
FUNCTION LoginForm
WITH THIS.oResponse
  .WriteLn( [<H3>Please Log In</H3>] )
  .WriteLn( [<FORM METHOD=POST>] )
  .WriteLn( [User ID: ] + ;
    [<INPUT NAME="txtUserId" TYPE=TEXT SIZE=14><BR>] )
  .WriteLn( [Password: ] + ;
    [<INPUT NAME="txtPassword" TYPE=PASSWORD SIZE=20><BR>] )
  .WriteLn( [<INPUT TYPE=SUBMIT VALUE="Submit">] )
  .WriteLn( [</FORM>] )
ENDWITH
ENDFUNC
```

Forcing user logouts

When you design network applications, user logouts are fairly straightforward. Typically, the user logs out by exiting your application, or by selecting a menu option that logs that user out and presents a dialog for another user to log in.

A Web application is not as simple as this, because the end-user application is simply the browser. As an example, there is nothing to stop users from suddenly navigating to a completely different Web site just when, from the perspective of your application, they were about to do something important. Similarly, when they close their browser session, because of the disconnected nature of HTTP, your application is not informed. This difficult state of affairs leads to two additional requirements for the developer.

First, you should never write code that assumes the user will continue to hit your site. Each transaction needs to be atomic. For example, you cannot suddenly interject a modal dialog, such as a MESSAGEBOX. While you can send a response page that asks a question, you must assume *when you ask the question* that getting no response is one alternative. What this also means is that you cannot write cleanup code that counts on the users telling you when they are finished with their session.

Second, if you are using user logins, you may require some mechanism to allow a user to log out of your application. The most common need for this occurs when a machine is physically accessible to other people. When the user is done, you need to ensure that the browser is not left in a state where other people can access the site while still logged in as the previous user. An example scenario is a kiosk in an airport where a user logs into an online banking Web site.

The approach for achieving a user logout depends on the choice of method you select for maintaining state.

Using authentication by itself, there is no simple way to force a logout at the server end. You must hope the user closes the browser session, which does log the user out. While you can inform the user of this need, and even include JavaScript that might attempt a *window.close();* statement, the user can always defeat you. (In the JavaScript case, the browser warns the user that the Web page is trying to close the browser, and the user can elect not to do so.) You need to consider this when choosing authentication.

Using cookies or license plates in conjunction with a login scheme, such as the one presented in the previous section, you have much more control. First, the session itself has a timeout period. The default is 30 minutes. If no hit arrives from the same user in that time period, the session times out, and any user would have to log in again. If your security restrictions are tight, you can reduce this timeout value. I have noticed 15-minute timeouts on some financial Web sites. Second, you can include a "logout" hyperlink on all of the pages of your application. When the user clicks on this, you preempt the normal session timeout process and clear the setting of the current user ID. The following code shows an example of this:

```
FUNCTION Logout
Session.SetSessionVar( "UserId", "")  && clears the setting
THIS.StandardPage( "Logout Successful", ;
  "<P ALIGN=CENTER>Thanks for visiting our web site!</P>" )
RETURN
ENDFUNC  && Logout
```

When things go wrong

Depending on your choice of methodology, different problems can occur. Here are some of the more common problems to be aware of:

- Using authentication, if your administrator enables Windows (vs. plain text) authentication, your application will suddenly break for all Microsoft Internet Explorer users. The most common outcome is they will keep getting an authentication dialog, even after supplying a valid user ID and password. This is because your Web Connection application can no longer determine the authenticated user name. Your only solution is to convince the administrator to turn Windows authentication back off.

- Using either temporary or persistent cookies, you may encounter situations where the cookie mechanism does not appear to be working. If this affects just a single user or specific users, the most likely explanation is that those users are rejecting the cookies, either individually or via a global browser preference. If instead your application appears not to be sending cookies, you should verify that you are not using HTTP redirection with the same response with which you are trying to attach a cookie. These are mutually incompatible. Refer to the section "Ensuring your cookie gets delivered" earlier in this chapter.

- Using any session management option with the wwSession class and Visual FoxPro tables, the table can become very large rather quickly, depending on the volume of traffic on your Web site. It is important that expired session records be deleted and this table packed on a periodic basis. Code to accomplish these tasks is included in the Reindex() method of the wwSession class.

- New versions of Web Connection have sometimes altered the structure of the session table. When this occurs, you generally need to delete your old session table (usually called wwSession.DBF and found in the same directory as your EXE file), and allow Web Connection to create a new one automatically. If you do not do this, you will get a Visual FoxPro error, such as "variable <new_field> not found."

Beyond these possibilities, if things go wrong, you need to be adept at troubleshooting Web Connection applications in general. Throughout this book, we present ideas for handling things that go wrong. Also, refer to Chapter 18 for more ideas.

Advanced topics

This section covers a few advanced topics in the areas of user tracking and user identification. The topics covered here are definitely not for beginners.

Using Microsoft SQL Server to store session data

As of version 3.5, the Web Connection framework now includes a class wwSessionSql, which is a subclass of wwSession that allows you to deploy your session data on Microsoft SQL Server. The detailed instructions for implementing this approach are provided in the Web Connection documentation and are not repeated here. Here is an overview of this technology:

- You are responsible for manually creating the session table on the SQL Server machine. The Web Connection class does not do this for you.

- A new switch in the WCONNECT.H file, WWC_USE_SQL_SYSTEMFILES, is used to establish whether SQL Server, rather than Visual FoxPro data is being used for logging and session management.

- You specify the connection string to be used in your application's INI file using the SQLConnectString= line. This is loaded into the property Server.oConfig.cSQLConnectString.

- The InitSession() method in wwProcess takes care of instantiating the correct session class and all other details are handled for you.

Combining methods in a single application

In this chapter I presented four methods that can be used to pass information between browser and Web server for distinguishing among users and maintaining state information: authentication, temporary cookies, persistent cookies, and license plates. As I indicated previously, you generally select just one of these methods for any single application. Nevertheless, there may be circumstances where you want to combine two of these methods. This is certainly possible, as the methods are not mutually exclusive. In this section, I will discuss a few such combinations and the reasons you might want to choose them. No code is presented here, because of the number of different possible combinations and other considerations that are too specific to each individual application.

In many Web applications, you may choose to add one or more pages that contain links for performing database maintenance activities, such as packing and reindexing Visual FoxPro tables. By doing so, you can provide for remote maintenance from any location where you have a Web browser and Internet access. It is likely that you will want greater security associated with these methods than the remainder of your application. You can achieve this by combining authentication with any of the other methods, but only checking authentication on the relevant pages. Web Connection ships with a demo application that includes separate maintenance pages in file wwMaint.PRG. I recommend studying the simple authentication code used there, which involves specifying valid administrator account names in the WC.INI file.

There may also be situations where you want to combine persistent cookies with temporary cookies (or even with license plates). You may choose one of the latter for your application as the primary method, perhaps because you are concerned that some users will reject persistent cookies. But you may want to offer the option for some users to be "remembered" by your application in order to enhance their future sessions. This is an "opt in" situation where your user consents to the cookie. You can achieve this by adding a hyperlink to your application menu (or elsewhere) that the user can select in order to accept this offer. In your code that processes this request, you just send the user a persistent cookie that replaces the temporary one.

The potential combinations you can choose are numerous, as are the possible reasons for choosing them. I am not recommending any specific combination, as much as encouraging you to stretch your thought process and be aware of the options available to you in different situations.

Chapter 14
COM vs. File-Based Messaging

You probably feel that you have plenty to learn without getting into anything that might be considered optional. This chapter helps you understand why there is an alternative mechanism available to you—COM—and when this alternative might be worth your while to investigate.

Out of the box, a Web Connection application uses file-based messaging as the means of communicating between WC.DLL and your Visual FoxPro application. Nevertheless, Web Connection offers an alternative approach using COM messaging. There are potential advantages to COM—namely improved maintenance and performance—that prove compelling once you look toward longer-term issues facing your Web application.

Overview of COM and file-based messaging

The topics of COM and file-based messaging have already been introduced in this book. In Chapter 10, "Getting in Tune: Overcoming Conceptual Hurdles," you learned how file-based messaging works, and explored a few of the fundamental differences between file-based messaging and COM. In Chapter 12, "A Web Connection Application from Start to Finish," you learned the steps to convert a specific application from file-based messaging to COM. Now it is time to explore these concepts in more detail.

First, I want to review the basic differences. When using file-based messaging, the Web Connection DLL and your Visual FoxPro application function in a completely disconnected state. They use a pre-arranged temporary directory as a "drop zone" of sorts. First, the DLL will drop a file there describing an incoming Web hit. Your Visual FoxPro application discovers this file by continually checking the temporary directory for new files of this type. When your application has processed the hit and formulated a response, it too drops the information as a file back into the same directory, where the DLL is waiting for it in order to return the response to the client. As you can see, this is a very disconnected, trusting arrangement. The DLL has no control or even knowledge of what application, if any, will process the hits, and your Visual FoxPro application similarly has no control or knowledge of the origin of the temporary file.

COM operation is a different animal. When hits come in, the DLL knows (from INI file entries) both the name of the COM server class that will process the hits and the number of simultaneous instances to launch. After launching instances of your COM server, the DLL maintains object references in memory. Then, as each Web hit arrives, the DLL checks its pool for an instance that is not busy and, if one is available, calls the ProcessHit() method in that COM server instance, passing the same information as a string that under file-based messaging is "passed" in a temporary file.

Why move to COM?

So the big question, of course, is: Why move to COM? You have your application operating just fine using file-based messaging. It "ain't broke," so why fix it?

There are several reasons, and they all address more long-term issues:

- COM applications offer better performance. Instead of creating files on disk, communication occurs via strings passed and returned across a COM connection. Further, there is no latency due to the file-based timer approach of checking for new hits. The amount of performance improvement can vary significantly depending on both your server and your application. In some cases the improvement can be sufficient to defer making other scaling investments as your usage grows.

- COM applications are easier to maintain, particularly if off-site maintainability is important. Because COM instances are loaded and unloaded by the Web Connection DLL, that DLL is also able to respond to maintenance requests via the Web. This allows for server loading and unloading, killing hung server instances, and even updating to a newer EXE build, all via a remote browser. None of this is available in file-based operation.

- Under COM your servers are started automatically (on demand) after a server reboot, instead of your being required to ensure your executable is already running when a hit is received. More significantly, if your Visual FoxPro application crashes, COM operation allows the process to be killed, and a new one started, under control of WC.DLL.

- COM applications are easier to update. By setting up an update folder, it is easy to upload a new version of your executable to the production server (via FTP, pcAnywhere, or otherwise), after which a direct maintenance link on the admin.asp can be used to cause Web Connection to update the executable in a live setting. This is very convenient, and probably alone represents enough justification for many developers to make the switch to COM. (See Chapter 11, "Managing Your Configuration," for details of the WC.INI settings required to perform online updates of your executable.)

Against these are some counterpoints:

- COM is more difficult to get working in the first place, as many technologies are involved. Some of the required knowledge, such as security and networking, might also be beyond the expertise at your disposal.

- Some Web Connection developers have tried and failed to achieve successful COM operation, sometimes after investing significant energy in the attempt. In some further cases, running on Microsoft Windows 2000 servers, COM operation appears to have interfered with proper operation of the IIS management console, resulting in the occasional need to run the IISRestart utility program. This experience has led some developers to abandon the quest for COM operation. Although these situations have been reported on the West Wind support forums, the authors of this book have not encountered problems that precluded successful COM operation. Refer to this page

on the West Wind "wiki" for an up-to-date report on this subject:
www.west-wind.com/wiki/kb.wiki?wc~MMCLockingUpInCOMMode

- Bugs in your application can be more difficult to troubleshoot using COM.

- Some network security structures may preclude the use of COM. This can be true if your Web server operates in a "demilitarized zone" (DMZ) with a firewall between the Web server and your data.

The weighting of each of the preceding points varies from one situation to the next. In general, I consider COM a much better approach if you can get it to work for your situation. I recommend a strategy of getting your application tested and debugged using file-based messaging, and then attempting the switch to COM on either the development machine or a staging server.

COM principles

Before getting into a presentation of the steps involved in converting an application to COM, you need to have a solid understanding of some core principles. I present these for the purposes of relieving your anxiety and to give you an advanced understanding of the issues.

- The source code in your Visual FoxPro application requires no modification whatsoever to operate as a COM server. Thus, if your application operates properly in file-based mode, you are ready to attempt the move to COM.

- This does not mean your work in VFP is done. You must ensure that your project is built as an EXE, and that Server Instancing has been set to "Single Use" (the default is "Multi Use"). Because you cannot set Server Instancing until you have built the project into an EXE at least once, this means you must build the project at least one extra time to affect this change. The Server Instancing setting is available from the Servers tab of the Project Information dialog, as shown in **Figure 1**. (Note that this setting has no impact on your application when it is run in file-based mode, only when it is instanced under COM. Therefore, you can change the setting to "Single Use" and then never worry about it again.)

- Using COM, even when running multiple instances, you do not build your project into a DLL. You continue to use an EXE. Web Connection uses its own pool management scheme to manage instances of your application. Thus the same EXE is used whether your application is set to use COM or file-based messaging.

- In file-based mode, your application uses a timer to look continually for temporary files that indicate new requests to process. In COM mode, WC.DLL talks directly to your application when new requests arrive.

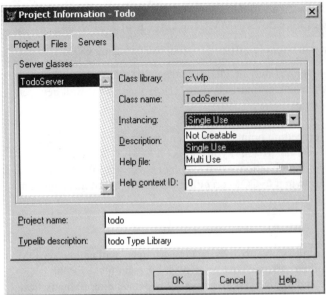

Figure 1. Server Instancing must be changed to "Single Use."

- In file-based operation, you must start your EXE manually, or arrange for the application to be started after server boot-up, such as by using the FileStartInstances setting in WC.INI or by specifying an auto-login account and including your EXE in the startup group for that account. In COM operation, you specifically do not start your EXE. Instead WC.DLL instantiates copies of your executable in response to Web activity, by using COM/DCOM information stored in the Registry.

- If your Visual FoxPro application crashes in COM mode, the process is eventually released and a new instance started as needed. In file-based mode, the process is left hanging, and no new process is started, thus requiring manual intervention at the server console.

- Most necessary Registry information required for COM is written by VFP when you build your EXE; however, that only helps when running on the development machine. You must take action to register your server on any production machine when you move your EXE to that machine.

- If using Visual FoxPro version 6, you must copy the type library (TLB) file along with the corresponding EXE file in order to register the server. Visual FoxPro version 7 removes this requirement by building sufficient information directly into the EXE file itself.

- In both cases (development and production), you must make further Registry settings, via DCOMCNFG, to establish identity and security settings before you can run in COM mode.

- The initial code in the main program (in other words, all code that appears before the first DEFINE CLASS statement) is *never executed* in COM mode. (This is true of any Visual FoxPro application when run as a COM server.) If you have included important code in this section, you should migrate it into either the SetServerEnvironment() or SetServerProperties() method of the server class (in the same PRG file). If your Visual FoxPro application does not appear to behave correctly in COM mode, this is a good factor to check.

- In COM mode, when using Microsoft Internet Information Server, you must be certain that the application protection setting for the virtual directory is set to "Low (IIS Process)" in order to avoid numerous pitfalls during server operation.

- If things don't work, suspect either permission issues or incorrect INI file settings.

- If an application was working properly, but suddenly stops working, suspect Registry corruption or permission changes.

Converting to COM: Step-by-step

In the following sections, I will present the steps that are involved in converting an application to run under COM. There are two types of conversions. First you will convert your development system (where your Visual FoxPro source code is). After confirming successful operation in development, you will convert servers that typically do not have Visual FoxPro installed, but only the run time.

A staging server

In some situations, there is only the development machine and the production server. This presents a challenge in that you have no ability to test the process of migrating from development without possibly impacting your production environment if this migration fails.

For those companies with adequate resources, a third machine is used that is often referred to as a "staging server." This staging server should be set up identically to the production server. This enables you to test an application deployment, using the exact steps you will use when you move to production.

Testing on the development system

This assumes your application has been tested and is running in file-based mode without error.

1. Ensure your EXE file has been built with Server Instancing set to "Single Use" as shown in the previous section.

2. Ensure that your EXE file has been built with DEBUGMODE set to false (.F.). If it was previously set to true (.T.), be certain to select "Recompile all" when building.

3. Start DCOMCNFG from the Windows Run box from the Start Menu. A dialog should appear with a list of applications, some with names and some with GUIDs, similar to that shown in **Figure 2**. If everything is well, you should be able to find

your own server in the list. Your server has an entry based on your EXE file name and the class name from your main program.

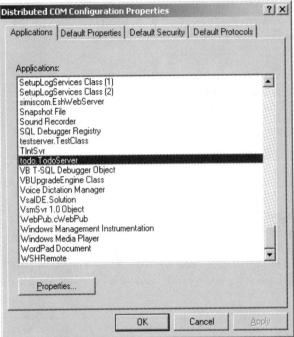

Figure 2. *Your COM server listed among the DCOMCNFG applications.*

4. Highlight your application in the list and either double-click the name or select the Properties button.

5. From the resultant Properties dialog for your application, select the Security tab as shown in **Figure 3**. From the first option group, select "Use custom access permissions." This will enable the associated Edit button.

6. Select the Edit button for access permissions. A further dialog will be provided, allowing access permissions to be set, as shown in **Figure 4**.

7. From the Permissions dialog, ensure that the IUSR_your_machine_name and IWAM_your_machine_name accounts have access. Furthermore, if you are using Windows Authentication (see Chapter 13, "Identifying Users and Managing Session Data"), you should ensure that other users/groups are included for access. At minimum, be certain to include both administrators and application developers (assuming they are not already administrators). The users and groups that will already be listed in this dialog are determined from the DCOM *default* settings (see the note that follows this procedure).

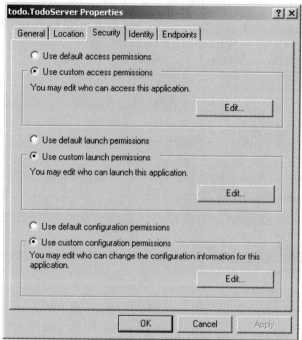

Figure 3. *The Security tab allows you to set access and launch permissions for your application.*

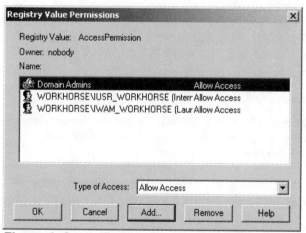

Figure 4. *Controlling access permissions to your application.*

8.   To add a user or group to this list, select the Add button. You will see the dialog shown in **Figure 5**. If your server is part of a domain, the List Names From dropdown will include choices for both your domain and your local machine. Select your local machine from this list. Select the Show Users button in order to include

individual users, rather than only groups, in the list. Find each user or group you wish to add, and click the Add button for each one. The users and/or groups you add will display in the Add Names edit box in the bottom half of the dialog. When you have finished, select OK to close this dialog. You will return to the Registry Value Permissions dialog (Figure 4), and the accounts you just selected should now appear in the list.

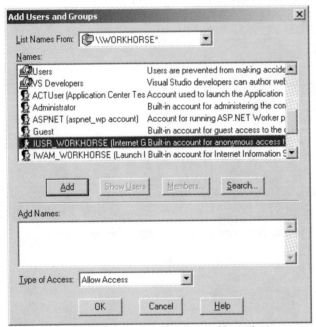

Figure 5. Adding users and groups. Note that you must click the Show Users button to see individual user accounts in the list.

9. Close the Registry Value Permissions dialog.

10. Back at the Security tab of the dialog for your application, select "Use custom launch permissions" from the second option group. Follow the same steps as for custom access permissions, selecting the same users and groups.

> *Launch permissions control the ability to launch (instantiate) your COM server, while access permissions control the ability to gain access to a COM server that has already been launched. Both of these must be set for COM operation to work.*

11. Now select the Identity tab for your application as shown in **Figure 6**. Select "The Interactive User" and click Apply. (Do this even if it already appears to be selected. Some versions of DCOMCNFG have a bug, requiring this to be done.) Setting this to the interactive user allows the server form to be displayed as long as someone is

logged in at the server console. This is easiest while debugging, but may not be desirable as a long-term production choice. The choices are as follows:

- Selecting "The interactive user" means that the security context for your COM application will be whomever happens to be logged in at the server console when the COM application is launched. If nobody is logged in, the application will fail to start. This setting is fine either during debugging, or if you know that this context will always be adequate given your security policies. A further advantage to this setting is that, when someone is logged in at the server console, you can see visual server forms while your Web Connection application is running.

- Selecting "The launching user" means that the context of the application that launched the COM application will be used. For Web Connection, this translates to the context provided by the Web server (IIS), which for many applications could be the anonymous user (IUSR_ account). This user probably does not have access to your data files, and therefore your application would fail if you selected this option. *Therefore, this choice is not recommended.*

- Selecting "This user" and then providing a specific user ID and password allows you to create a consistent security context that will be employed no matter who is logged in at the console or what user hits your Web site. A common strategy is to create a special User ID just for this purpose, which allows you to fine-tune access specifically for your application. Although you *could* also specify an existing user's account here, if that user happens to change his or her password, your application will stop functioning unless you also remember to change the password entry via DCOMCNFG. Selecting "This user" has strong appeal for production applications that have been debugged, as you can carefully control what network resources your application can access. One disadvantage to this selection is that you cannot see visual server forms while your Web Connection application is running.

NOTE *So, what's the difference between the Identity and Security tabs? This distinction is very important. The security settings control who has access to your application from the Web. The identity setting establishes the security context of your application as it goes about servicing Web hits. In other words, while processing hits, your application will take on the "identity" of the user you specify in the Identity tag.*

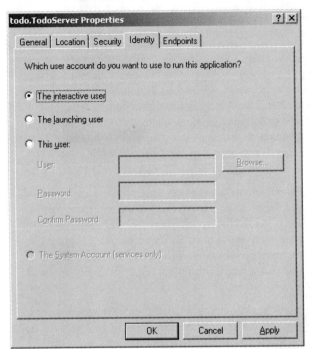

***Figure 6**. Selecting the DOCMCNFG identity setting.*

12. Close DCOMCNFG by clicking OK twice.

13. Next, you need to change the Mechanism setting in WC.INI to indicate COM operation (Mechanism=Automation). However, you should not make this change manually, unless you first want to stop the IIS Web service. Instead, ask WC.DLL to do this for you, either from the admin.asp page (by clicking on the "Switch to Automation Messaging" link) or via the URL wc.dll?_maintain~SetAutoMechanism. In either case, you will get a response page in your browser indicating "Message Mechanism Changed."

14. Ensure the Application Protection setting for the IIS virtual directory is set to "Low (IIS Process)." Refer to Chapter 12 for instructions on setting up the virtual directory for your application.

Your application can now be tested in COM mode. The remaining steps cover this testing.

15. Be sure to shut down any running file-based sessions or interactive Visual FoxPro sessions, so there is no confusion as to what process is handling your hits.

16. Go into your browser and request one of the pages from your application. (You may also just be able to refresh the current page.)

17. If everything has proceeded properly, you should see a new process launch with a Web Connection server window as a top-level form. You should also see the expected result returned to your browser.

This procedure covered the DCOM security settings for a single COM server class. DCOM also has "default access and launch permissions" that can be set from the Default Security tab of the main DCOMCNFG dialog. These settings control the permissions for any DCOM application for which the "use default" choices are selected on the Security tab of the server's properties. If you have total control over the use of the server, and you know it will only be used for Web Connection applications, you can elect to set the default permissions instead, using the same technique that was described earlier. The advantage in doing so is that it gives you the option of administering several separate Web Connection applications with one set of security values. You should do this only if you have a solid understanding of DCOM security.

If the COM mechanism fails to operate properly, check all of the preceding steps to make sure none were missed. Also refer to the section "Troubleshooting COM" later in this chapter.

Deploying COM on the production server

Once your application is operating under COM in a development environment, it is time to move it to production. All of the concepts are the same. The main difference is that you most likely will not have an interactive copy of Visual FoxPro installed on the production server, so you will simply be working with the EXE and run-time libraries.

 If you also have a staging server, first perform the procedure from this section on the staging server, prior to attempting the deployment to production.

Assuming you have already installed your application in production and have it running using file-based messaging, here are the steps to convert to COM:

1. Ensure that your COM server class is properly registered. This can be done by running your executable from a command prompt or the Run dialog with the /regserver switch (for example: D:\wcapps\todo\TODO /regserver). Note that this step was not required on your development machine, because the Visual FoxPro project manager takes care of registering any classes declared as OLEPUBLIC when you build the project.

   Caution! *Be certain that you always build your executable from the same Visual FoxPro project, and that you **do not** select the Project Manager option to "regenerate component IDs" when you do so. Otherwise, your COM Class ID will change, resulting in incorrect Registry settings in your production (and staging) server. If this happens, you must track down and remove previous Registry keys, and then register the new executable, and repeat any DCOM setup steps. This is a painful and error-prone exercise, to be avoided if possible.*

2. Follow the same step-by-step approach used for the development machine to create the proper permissions via DCOMCNFG, and to test your system by converting the Mechanism setting to Automation in the WC.INI file.

3. Again, ensure that the Application Protection setting for the IIS virtual directory is set to "Low (IIS Process)."

4. Test your system: a) from a browser on the server; b) from other browsers on your network; and c) from browsers on the Internet (for public Web sites). Use the admin.asp page to load and unload servers as you perform some of these tests (thus confirming launch and access settings). If Windows authentication is being used, be certain to test your application with users from different groups. (Often you get things working for anonymous users, and then find that they don't work for users in your domain!)

Troubleshooting COM

Despite your best efforts, COM problems can still occur. There are several guidelines to follow depending on the nature of your problem:

- Bugs in your Visual FoxPro code are harder to detect using COM, since you cannot use the Visual FoxPro debugger interactively when your application is running from a COM server. There are two approaches when this occurs. If the problem is straightforward, you might be able to use some of the advanced troubleshooting techniques described in Chapter 18, "Advanced Troubleshooting and Maintenance." Beyond this, you can often save time by reverting to file-based mode, preferably in a development environment, where you have more debugging tools available.

- Problems getting the COM servers themselves to launch can be more difficult to diagnose. If this occurs, review both the "COM principles" section and the step-by-step procedure for converting to COM earlier in this chapter. Several of the most-common mistakes are presented in Chapter 17, "The Mistakes We All Make," in the category "COM and file-based operational problems." Also refer to the Web Connection Help topic "Manual COM Server Configuration" for more troubleshooting ideas.

- Another helpful troubleshooting aide is to test whether your COM server can be instantiated from the Visual FoxPro IDE. What you do is attempt to use Visual FoxPro as a host for your COM server. This can be done via simple commands, such as:

```
loCom = CREATEOBJECT( "ToDo.ToDoServer")
loCom.Visible=.T.
```

If your server launches, this indicates your EXE is registered properly, and any problems are likely based on permission issues. (If you need to test this on a production machine that does not have Visual FoxPro, you may be able to use a simple Command Window replacement executable, such as that shown in Chapter 8, "Configuring Server Software," or use a different COM client, such as the Windows Script Host.)

- There have been some documented cases where developers followed all the proper steps and still the COM servers did not launch or respond properly. In more than one of these instances, the problem was caused by corrupt or altered IIS user accounts (IUSR_ and/or IWAM_). Fixing this problem is beyond the scope of this book, but could involve reinstallation of IIS and/or re-creation of these accounts, followed by resetting of the DCOMCNFG permissions.

- One troublesome problem can occur if you try to test in COM mode before getting your DCOMCNFG permissions set properly. This can result in an orphaned process that appears to prevent your fixing the problem (short of a server reboot). A solution is presented in the next section.

"Access Denied" errors under COM

If you do not set up your permissions correctly, you can get an "Access Denied" message when trying to launch a COM server for the first time. This can occur either in response to selecting Load Servers from the admin.asp page or when trying to access your application in the browser.

When this happens, it is possible that, even though the COM server did not fully launch, it is still loaded in memory, but not within the control of Web Connection. Therefore, attempting to shut down the COM server from Web Connection does not release this process. To see if this is the issue, perform the following steps:

1. Open the Windows Task Manager. Select the Processes tab, and check whether your COM server is listed. If so, select it and then click "End Process."

2. Go into DCOMCNFG, select the COM server, click on Properties, and verify that the application has proper access and launch permissions as discussed earlier.

3. Go back to the Web Connection admin page, and the COM server should now launch properly.

The challenge here is not realizing the COM server is loaded. You can click the Unload Servers link, and think you have released everything. But if this hidden process is not killed, even changing the DCOMCNFG settings to the correct permissions will not clear up the problem. The rogue process must be killed!

Trouble releasing COM servers

When using file-based messaging, shutting down an instance of your application is straightforward: You simply click the Exit button on the server form. This quits your application in a similar manner as a Visual FoxPro desktop application.

Using COM, this is not the case. Now your application has been instantiated as a COM object by WC.DLL. To shut down this instance, you must request WC.DLL to release its object reference. From the admin.asp page, it is easy to do this by simply selecting the Unload Servers link, which calls URL wc.dll?_maintain~release. If you are at the server console, you might still prefer to be able to click the Exit button on the server form, instead of using the browser interface.

Web Connection offers an indirect approach to allow this. When you click the Exit button in COM mode, your application actually initiates a separate HTTP request to trigger the same release URL mentioned earlier. In other words, clicking the Exit button causes your application to ask the WC.DLL to release it.

This is a handy provision, but in order for it to work, your application needs to know what URL to request. You specify this setting in your application INI file, using the COMReleaseURL setting. This URL needs to have the proper virtual directory to match your application. For example, if your application is in a virtual directory named "todo," the URL setting might be:

```
http://localhost/todo/wc.dll?_maintain~release
```

If instead you have hidden your DLL file and are using only script mapped URLs, you should also set this setting to use a script mapped extension. For example:

```
http://localhost/todo/wc.tsk?_maintain~release
```

Once this is set correctly, you should be able to click the Exit button on the Visual FoxPro form, and your browser should attempt to release your application. (Depending on the AdminUser setting in WC.INI, you may be prompted to enter your user ID and password.) If this does not work, double check that you have specified the URL setting correctly.

See Chapter 11 for details on adjusting all INI file settings.

The wcErrors.TXT file

Sometimes errors occur that are outside the scope of your Visual FoxPro application. Most of these involve COM problems that either prevent your application from running or keep hits from being processed. Most problems you will encounter involve incorrect permission settings.

The Web Connection DLL records any such errors in a text file named wcErrors.TXT located in the application temporary file path. It is helpful to examine this file both periodically and when problems occur. The interpretation and use of this error file is covered in Chapter 18.

Switching from COM back to file-based messaging

You may encounter situations where you want to switch an application from COM back to file-based messaging. For example, you will almost always want applications on your development machine running in file-based mode, where debugging is much easier.

To switch back to file-based messaging, perform the following steps:

1. From your browser, request the Web Connection DLL to switch itself to file-based messaging by activating one of the following URLs:

    - the Switch to File-Based Messaging link on admin.asp

    - the File Mode link on the DLL's own status page (wc.dll?_maintain~ShowStatus)

    - the immediate URL wc.dll?_maintain~SetFileMechanism

! **Caution!** *Do not attempt to edit the WC.INI file directly. Any manual changes to this file will not be recognized until the Web server has been stopped and restarted. Refer to Chapter 11 for a complete discussion of managing these settings.*

2. Start up a copy of your (file-based) executable. (Or, from a Visual FoxPro Command Window, DO your main program.)

3. That's all it takes. If you access your application from a browser, you should now see the hits being processed in the server window.

4. To switch back *again* to COM, you only need to request the Web Connection DLL to make the switch, using one of the links that triggers the wc.dll?_maintain ~SetAutoMechanism URL.

Note that, when switching back and forth between COM and file-based messaging, it is not strictly necessary to shut down any file-based instances of your application that are running. They will simply cease to process requests while you are testing in COM mode.

Sticking with file-based messaging

In some circumstances you might decide to stick with file-based messaging. Perhaps the potential advantages of COM are not important in your situation. Or maybe your security policy precludes the use of COM.

Improving file-based performance

Depending on your server hardware and software, there are several approaches you can take to improve the performance of your applications using file-based messaging. Some of these are good practices, while others are potential areas to test:

*   Do not specify your temp file path to be the same as the Windows temp directory setting. This directory gets cluttered with other files, thus slowing search time. (Other problems can also occur if you use the Windows temp directory, such as inadvertent "cleanup" by unknowledgeable system administrators.) If you have more than one logical drive, select a drive other than the system drive to protect against temporary file buildup filling the system drive such that critical maintenance cannot be performed.

*   When running more than one Web Connection application, specify separate temp file paths for each. This improves performance, because applications do not have to sort through each other's temporary files. Further, there will be a separate wcErrors.TXT file for each application, avoiding ambiguity over which application is causing errors.

*   On machines with independent physical drives, consider placing your temp path on a separate drive from your WC application. If you have three separate drives, consider placing your application on one, data on a second, and temp on the third. These moves can allow for higher performance, particularly when more than one file-based

instance is running, because data access can occur on one drive while temporary input and output files are being written to another.

- Consider not placing your temp files on certain RAID arrays, if this choice exists. (On a RAID-5 configuration, these short-lived files must be written to three or more drives at once, only to be deleted milliseconds later.) If you have three drives with two of them mirrored, place the temp files on the third drive. If you have the luxury of six drives, one interesting scenario, which I have seen recommended for SQL Server, is to have two drives mirrored for the operating system and applications, three drives in a RAID-5 array for data, and the final drive stand-alone for temp files, swap files, and so on. (Further, in these latter situations, if your security environment permits it, you could possibly look into making the temp drive Fat32 instead of NTFS for added performance.) Whether any of these ideas is right for you requires careful planning and testing. These are only offered as examples to promote further thinking, and may not be best in your specific situation.

- Turn off virus scanning of your Web Connection temp folder(s)! This can improve performance considerably. Alternatively, ensure that TMP and RET files are not scanned. (Be certain any choices you make here are compliant with your security policies!)

- Experiment/test to confirm the optimal number of file-based instances to run. This number varies based on several hardware factors (number of processors among the most significant), application factors, and what else your server is used for (other services, such as FTP, email, and other Web apps).

- Experiment with different timer interval values (the TimerInterval setting in the app INI file). The WC default value is 200 ms. The optimal value of this setting will vary based on several factors (including hardware, number of file-based instances, and median hit processing time). You may have to try varying both instance count and timer interval to find your best setting. If you change hardware in the future, repeat these tests.

- Remember that you can scale file-based messaging to the network. Other servers, or even workstations, can participate in processing hits by scanning for the temporary files and processing hits. To accomplish this, these other machines must have access to all necessary resources (data, temp files, and so forth) and path settings must be established using UNC naming (or perhaps some consistent drive mapping scheme).

Beyond these issues, there are some further ideas that apply whether you are using file-based messaging or COM:

- Don't run any services you don't need. For example, if you are not using FTP, set the startup setting for that service to either manual or disabled.

- If you can afford a new box, migrating something like Microsoft Exchange to a separate box can take a huge burden off your Web server.

- Marginal server hardware dollars usually have higher paybacks for added RAM and drive performance than for higher processor speeds.

- Don't leave gratuitous apps running under your workstation service. If you leave apps like a CHM (Help file) plus one or two MSIE windows open on the server desktop, these can quickly chew up resources (easily from 20-50MB of RAM or more).

- Also, carefully consider where your Web server (IIS) log files are being written. It may be an advantage to write those to a drive that is not involved in the processing of Web hits.

- If you run SQL Server on a separate box, and that box is less burdened than your Web server, experiment with moving your Web Connection session and logging files there. This can be accomplished by creating a SQL Server database and setting the WWC_USE_SQL_SYSTEMFILES flag in WCONNECT.H as discussed in the step-by-step Web Connection Help topic "Create SQL Server Tables."

Scaling with COM and file-based messaging

Scalability is a term that is often used in conjunction with Web sites. In simple terms, a system is scalable if you can meet increasing usage levels via a linear increase in resources. If a system either cannot meet a large usage level or requires an exponential increase in resources to do so, it is not scalable.

There are several factors beyond just your application that affect system scalability, including networking and telecommunications, which are beyond the scope of this book. Nevertheless, there are several factors that directly apply to your application. There are two areas involved in increasing the throughput of your system. First is to improve application performance so that the maximum number of hits can be processed by a single Visual FoxPro instance. Second is to increase the number of instances that simultaneously process hits.

The first of these areas requires monitoring, tuning, and testing throughout the lifetime of your system. The second area, adding instances, can be accomplished using one or more of several techniques, some of which depend on whether you are using COM or file-based messaging. These techniques include:

- Adding instances on the Web server

- Sharing the load with additional network machines

- Moving data to a different back end

- Scaling to a Web farm

- Additional physical separation of tiers

The next sections look at each of these in more detail.

Adding instances on the Web server

The first and easiest improvement can come from simply running additional instances of your Visual FoxPro application on the Web server, so that more than one Web hit can be processed in parallel. This is particularly effective on a multi-processor machine, but can be helpful in two situations. First, if some hits take longer than others to process, running multiple instances can appear to offer better performance to some users, since they may get a quick response without having to wait for a long-running response to complete. Second, if your data is on a different back-end server, your applications may experience significant waiting time as queries are processed, thus even allowing multiple instances to be helpful on a single processor machine.

Adding instances is possible with either COM or file-based messaging. Using COM, you simply add one line to the WC.INI file for each additional instance to be run. Refer to Chapter 11 for details on managing INI file settings. Using file-based messaging, you simply start additional instances of your Visual FoxPro executable. An approximate rule-of-thumb is to run two instances per processor; however, the optimum number can only be determined for any given system by rigorous stress testing. This determination should be reassessed whenever major system changes are made (such as adding processors, memory, or drives).

Also, remember that COM itself offers better performance than file-based messaging. Sometimes the simple task of switching your messaging mechanism to COM can result in a significant improvement to the throughput of your system.

Sharing the load with additional network machines

Once you have maximized the amount of processing that can be handled on your Web server, you can delegate other machines on your network to share the load. Although this is possible using either COM or file-based messaging, setup and administration issues greatly favor file-based messaging as the choice for this scalability model.

Sharing the load using file-based messaging requires little more than starting up copies of your application on one or more additional network machines. These can be either other servers or workstations. All machines look for new hits by checking one common temporary directory on the Web server. So that all participating machines know to use the same directory, either use a UNC setting in your INI file or employ a common network drive mapping strategy (for example, always mapping drive W: to the Web server, and then pointing to the temporary folder on the W: drive). You also need to make sure data paths are set to values that are accessible from all participating machines, and that permissions are set so that each machine has access to all resources needed to run your application.

Sharing the load in this manner using COM requires complex setup and administration, and is not recommended except for advanced developers with a solid Windows networking background. This topic is covered in the Web Connection Help topic "Scaling Web Connection Servers Across the Network."

Moving data to a different back end

If you move your data to a different back end (for example, Microsoft SQL Server) on a separate machine, you can remove a lot of the processing load from the Web server machine. This action alone can increase system throughput in some cases; however, you are likely to make best use of this move by also increasing the number of instances of your application that run on the Web server. This increase is possible because of the reduced level of activity for each instance, due to the data processing activity being offloaded to a different back end.

Scaling to a Web farm

Microsoft Windows 2000 Advanced Server includes a Network Load Balancing (NLB) service. Using this service, you can implement a Web farm to achieve even higher scalability levels. To use this strategy requires two or more Web server machines, each using Windows 2000 Advanced Server. Further, all of your data (including session and log files) must reside on a separate back-end machine. The following white paper on the West Wind Technologies Web site describes this strategy in detail: **www.west-wind.com/presentations/ LoadBalancing/LoadBalancing.htm**

Additional physical separation of tiers

Beyond the possibilities introduced so far, there is always a possibility of improving scalability through further separation of your system into more physical tiers. One such strategy is to create a separate data access tier that can be run as COM+ packages on separate servers. Another idea is to break out special, resource-intensive processes into components that can operate on other machines. Examples include credit card verification, email services, and maintenance and accounting tasks.

A final word: Know your enemy

Before embarking on any scalability strategy, make sure you have adequate knowledge of your overall system and what "problem" you are trying to solve. If your system throughput is insufficient, be certain that you know your Visual FoxPro application is actually the culprit before spending time and money on alterations. You could easily end up finding that your efforts are fruitless, because the problem was really elsewhere, such as a networking or telecommunications bottleneck.

Resources

- Web Connection Help topic "Manual COM Server Configuration"

- Web Connection Help topic "Create SQL Server Tables"

- White paper on load balancing: **www.west-wind.com/presentations/ LoadBalancing/LoadBalancing.htm**

Chapter 15
Data Entry on the Web

Creating applications that exist only on the Web means that all of your data entry must take place via Web-based forms. Whereas using the Visual FoxPro form designer is an obvious choice for Windows application, the best approach for designing Web-based forms is not so obvious. For developers accustomed to Windows-based graphical layout tools, some choices may feel like a return to the dark ages.

In this chapter, I discuss some of the solutions available to Web Connection developers for data entry on the Web. In order to get full value from this chapter, you should already have read:

- Chapter 9, "How a Web Page Works," which provides the anatomy of a Web page and shows how forms are structured;

- Chapter 10, "Getting in Tune: Overcoming Conceptual Hurdles," Concepts #8 and #9, which present some issues with Web forms; and

- Chapter 12, "A Web Connection Application from Start to Finish," in which a complete application, including data entry, is presented.

The majority of this chapter focuses on the many choices of approach that are possible for form design and deployment using Web Connection. Next comes an examination of the topic of binding Web forms to data. And finally, there is a section that outlines some common hacking techniques to be aware of.

Motivation

To understand why data entry is so much more difficult than other aspects of Web application design, consider the approach needed to update a single field in a Windows application compared to a hand-coded Web application.

In a Windows application you would use the form or class designer, drop a textbox control onto the form, and then bind the control to a data source (a view or a business object property). When the user enters a value into the text box, Visual FoxPro stores that value to the applicable control source with little more required by the developer.

In a hand-coded Web Connection scenario, things are not so automatic. Later in this chapter, I will discuss binding to data sources in general; however, even assuming you have a framework available (using either local/remote views, SQL pass-through, or business objects) to manage data access, consider the remaining chores involved with Web-based forms:

1. You must create an HTML form element name for each control.

2. You must render the form element as HTML to the browser, and ensure that the current data value is displayed.

3.   Separately, you must include code that reads the submitted value from the post buffer when the user submits the form.

4.   Because all HTML is string-based, you must convert all submitted values back to the native data type, including dealing with invalid values (that is, you do not have the strong typing that is automatic with Visual FoxPro controls).

5.   If the submittal is valid, you must store the submitted value back to the proper control source.

6.   If the submittal is not valid, you must have some strategy, such as displaying an error message and/or re-rendering the form for correction.

What does this all mean? Here is a crude example that assumes you are editing a single text field, and that you have already opened a view with the desired record as current. On the rendering side you have:

```
LOCAL lcStr
lcStr = [<tr><th>Customer Name:</th>] + CRLF
lcStr = m.lcStr + [<td><input name="txtCustomer_Name" type="text" value="] + ;
  TRIM( V_Customer.Customer_Name) + [" size=50>] + [</td></tr>] + CRLF
Response.Write( m.lcStr)
```

Then, on the form-processing end, which may be in the same or a different Web Connection method, depending on your design, you would have:

```
LOCAL lcCustomer_Name
lcCustomer_Name = Request.Form( "txtCustomer_Name")
IF (some validation check)
  REPLACE V_Customer.Customer_Name WITH m.lcCustomer_Name
ELSE
  THIS.ErrorMsg( "Invalid reponse.")
ENDIF
```

This may not appear so bad to you, but consider that the string "Customer_Name" appears *seven* times in the preceding code. Also consider that you are looking at the code for one field on one form with no validation. Just imagine what the code for this form would look like with 25 fields. Then consider an application with 40 data entry forms. You have a maintenance nightmare!

If you are not yet convinced, consider a few more factors:

•   The nature of Web forms exposes you to significant extra risk of errors going undetected. For example, if you accidentally omitted the underscore in "txtCustomer_Name" in the parameter passed to Request.Form() earlier, you would receive no error whatsoever! All that would happen is that the user's changes for this field would never be saved. This error would be noticed quickly enough in a one-field form, but what if it were buried in a 25-field form?

•   Imagine a form with 20 data entry fields, where some of those fields should not be visible for certain records, and others should be disabled (or omitted) from the form based on the user's security level. To implement these common requirements, you would have to add logic to the rendering portion of the code, and then repeat the same logic in the form-processing portion. The potential for making mistakes, either initially or during code maintenance, and the burden of keeping the logic in sync in both places, is enormous.

All of this, and the subjects of visual layout tools, consistent look-and-feel, and code reuse have not even been explored. Also important for many applications is the subject of accessibility, which involves making your applications available to all users, including those using assistive technology. Clearly if your applications will include a lot of data entry forms, more help is needed.

Design alternatives

There are several solutions that can provide this help. These solutions include everything from hand-coding, to using tools that come with Web Connection, to employing third-party products.

The solutions discussed in the subsequent sections of this chapter include:

- Hand-code all forms. This is the approach shown earlier.

- Hand-code the form processing, but use Web Connection scripts for visual layout.

- Use the wwShowCursor class, which has a TableEditor() method that can meet some basic needs.

- Use the wwForm and wwCtls classes to render Visual FoxPro forms in Web pages using DHTML (dynamic HTML).

- Use a third-party tool, such as the Voodoo Web Controls from EPS Software.

- Create your own class library.

- Attempt to combine a class library (third-party or your own) with visual form layout tools (such as Microsoft FrontPage).

Design attributes

Before exploring the different alternatives, it is useful to consider the attributes that determine the value of any particular solution. These include:

- **Maintainability:** How efficient and error-prone is the process of maintaining forms once the forms have been created?

- **Flexibility:** How flexible is the solution in implementing specific needs of individual forms, such as altering the layout, and selectively disabling and removing individual form elements?

- **Complex forms:** Does the solution readily support the creation of complex forms, such as those with page frames and grid-like controls?

- **Browser compatibility:** Does the solution readily produce output that can be accessed by the major browsers?

- **Visual layout capability:** Does the solution allow the use of a visual tool (such as Macromedia Dreamweaver, Adobe GoLive, or Microsoft FrontPage) to facilitate form layout?

- **Control of look-and-feel:** How effective is the solution in allowing the developer to create and maintain a consistent look-and-feel across an application with numerous data entry forms? Does the solution allow for usage of application-wide Cascading Style Sheets (CSS)?

- **Accessibility options:** How adaptable is the solution to coping with the needs of certain users, as outlined in the W3C accessibility guidelines? Requirements include: (1) associating labels with their controls (using the <label for=id> construct); (2) avoiding use of fixed font sizes so that users can scale their display; (3) avoiding reliance on absolute positioning or other features that prevent a page from being read without style sheets; and (4) avoiding the use of color schemes that are inaccessible to color-blind users (or allowing such users to alter the scheme).

- **Validation (client-side):** Does the solution support the inclusion of client-side JavaScript to support off-loading of some validation from the server and to improve the user experience?

- **Validation (server-side):** How well does the solution support server-side validation of form submittals?

- **Data binding:** How effective is the solution for supporting the binding of form controls to data elements? Does the approach support any preferred developer approach, including local/remote views, SQL pass-through, and business objects? (A separate discussion of data binding also appears later in the chapter, following the summary of these approaches to form design.)

- **Developer efficiency:** How quickly can the developer create new data entry forms?

- **Performance:** How does a Web application perform using the particular approach? (Also, refer to the section "Combo box issues" later in this chapter.)

- **Cost:** Does the solution require extra expenditures, beyond the cost of Web Connection?

- **Availability of solution:** Is the technology available to implement the solution?

Exploring the alternatives

Now I will evaluate each of the alternatives listed previously by examining each alternative in light of the attributes listed earlier. At the conclusion of this analysis is a table that summarizes the results.

Hand-coded forms

There is always the option to hand-code all of your forms. You have seen some of the drawbacks to this approach mentioned in the "Motivation" section earlier in this chapter. The primary concerns are in the areas of quality and maintainability. Nevertheless, there are many benefits to hand-coded forms, the most significant of which is the flexibility you gain.

Consider the case where you get a request to remove two fields from a certain form for all regular users, but to leave those fields on the form for managers and administrators. If you have hand-coded that form, a simple insertion of a few IF/ENDIF statements will suffice. But what if you were using a class library that did not support conditional removal of form controls? If you had no ability to alter the classes, or if the library was not amenable to a quick fix, you would be in some trouble. Possibly you would have to resort to creating and maintaining two separate forms, only slightly different from one another. This would be highly undesirable.

The conclusion to draw is that, if the maintenance cost of hand-coded forms is too high, be certain you choose an alternative that is sufficiently flexible to meet your needs.

Hand-coding plus scripts

Before abandoning the world of hand-coded forms entirely, there is a middle ground wherein you implement all of the form layout in Web Connection scripts[1] using a visual HTML editing tool, but perform all of the form processing in code. The TODO application presented in Chapter 12 uses this strategy.

Moving to a visual HTML editing tool can mitigate several of the shortcomings of the hand-coded approach, particularly if the tool of choice offers strong support for CSS and the ability to manage styles consistently across a collection of pages. Nevertheless, many of the maintenance headaches of the hand-coded approach remain. Additionally, you now have to coordinate changes between code and script files, which sometimes requires more than one person to make simultaneous coordinated changes, and for these changes to be deployed synchronously to the production server.

Use the wwShowCursor class

Web Connection includes a utility class, wwShowCursor, whose primary purpose is to facilitate rendering query results into HTML tables for display. Starting with version 3.65, this class has also included an EditTable() method, which provides a rapid technique for producing HTML data entry forms and binding to local Visual FoxPro data, with almost no code.

Although this can be a big time-saver in specific circumstances, it is really only designed for administrative functions, such as updating system tables. Presentation is limited to one field per row. No opportunity for field validation is available, and use with either buffered views or business objects is not possible. While fine for the purposes for which it was designed, this tool is not viable as a general-purpose form design alternative.

---

[1] Web Connection templates can also be used in some cases, but for more complex form requirements, scripts are essential.

Render Visual FoxPro forms via DHTML

Also included with Web Connection is a much more powerful alternative that allows you to render certain Visual FoxPro forms on the Web using DHTML. This approach uses a form class (in wwForm.PRG) and individual control classes (in wwCtls.PRG).

The secret to the operation of these classes is that Web Connection actually runs your form on the server, and then iterates the controls on that form and renders HTML counterparts. When the form is submitted, the form is run again on the server, in some cases allowing validation and other code to be run. This approach has tremendous appeal, particularly in cases where users are accustomed to the look of forms from an existing network application, which is to be deployed on the Web.

Regrettably this approach also has both limitations and drawbacks. Although this approach does let you leverage some Visual FoxPro SCX forms, performance can be poor, because a proxy form must be instantiated and run on the server for each Web hit. A further limitation is that the DHTML produced by these classes is compatible with Microsoft Internet Explorer only. (As browser support for CSS standards improves, this limitation may be reduced in the future.) Also, not all controls will render to DHTML.

In general, the less the code in the SCX, the more readily it can be adapted for DHTML use with Web Connection. Firing of method code for control-level events, such as GotFocus() and InteractiveChange(), is not supported at all, because these events occur on the client browser (that is, when navigating the HTML form), during which time your application is completely removed from the picture. There are a variety of ways to use and implement DHTML forms. You can bind directly to data or to data object properties. You can handle events either internally or externally to the form. In general, the best strategy appears to be handling as much as possible externally to the form, and to use the form primarily for rendering.

One remaining issue is that some developers have attempted to add features to the individual control classes in wwCtls.PRG and found the coding style not particularly amenable to subclassing.

If you can accept these limitations, particularly the browser restriction and slower performance, this approach is worthy of your consideration as a form design strategy. Carefully examine the DHTML examples in the Web Connection demo application to see whether this approach meets your needs. If the approach appears to suit you, try implementing it with a few of your forms. You will find out quickly whether they can be made operational.

Use the Voodoo Web Controls

The Voodoo Web Controls (or simply Voodoo) is a class library available from EPS Software (**www.eps-software.com/voodoo**). Voodoo is designed to be used in conjunction with ISAPI connector technology. Although Voodoo can be used with Active Server Pages (ASP) and potentially some other products, the platform of choice is Web Connection.

Voodoo is marketed with a "base package" and optional additional packages, the latter of which are available from both EPS and other developers. The base package license for one developer costs US $299. The base package is required to run any additional packages. The base package includes all of the controls for most data entry needs. Using Voodoo requires Visual FoxPro version 7 or later. Voodoo comes with Visual FoxPro source code, and is designed to allow subclassing as needed.

Voodoo's design was created with data binding in mind. In addition to binding to either views or business objects, Voodoo forms can bind directly to XML, which could be attractive in certain n-tier designs. The most straightforward data binding strategy, and one recommended in the Voodoo white paper, is to use data buffering with local data or remote views.

Implementing data binding by this strategy involves placing code in both the OnLoad() and Render() methods of the form object. The OnLoad() method is responsible for opening the view, for example:

```
FUNCTION OnLoad
  DODEFAULT()   && implement base class behavior
  SELECT 0
  USE (_SAMPLES + "Tastrade\Data\Customer")
  LOCATE FOR Customer_ID = Request.QueryString("ID")
  SET MULTILOCKS ON
  CURSORSETPROP("Buffering",5)
  THIS.AddObject("txtContact_Name","WebTextbox")
  WITH THIS.txtContact_Name
    .ControlSource = "Customer.Contact_Name"
    .Label = "Contact"
    .Width = 200
  ENWITH
  * ... load more individual controls here
ENDFUNC  && OnLoad
```

As you can see, each individual control has a ControlSource property, which you set in the same way as you would in a Visual FoxPro form. Now, when the form is submitted, the following code takes care of saving the data in the buffered view:

```
FUNCTION Render
  LOCAL lcOutput
  lcOutput = DODEFAULT()
  * The above causes all contained objects to be rendered.
  IF NOT THIS.lUpdate
    * lUpdate flag is set only when form is posted and no control
    * has rejected the submittal during validation
    TABLEUPDATE(.T.)   && save
  ELSE
    TABEREVERT(.T.)   && abort save
  ENDIF
  USE
  RETURN m.lcOutput
ENDFUNC   && Render
```

As you can see from this example code, working with Voodoo has more of a Visual FoxPro look than an HTML look, which may be a big comfort, depending on your background!

Voodoo also shines in the area of validation and browser-server coordination by providing straightforward properties and methods to control what is often a challenging aspect of Web form design. You can easily integrate JavaScript, specify your own event code, and designate which events on the browser cause a round-trip to the server. There is even a timer control that can be used to force a form to be submitted or aborted within a specified time frame, which can be a handy technique for implementing security requirements.

In reviewing version 1.1 of Voodoo, one shortcoming I noted was a lack of flexibility for meeting accessibility guidelines. The requirements presented in the "Design attributes" section earlier in this chapter cannot be easily met by subclassing Voodoo's base controls, because much of the relevant HTML is rendered in monolithic RenderTop() methods that do not lend themselves to easy subclassing. If you have the need to alter an entire form for specific users, the only approach that occurred to me was to write your own "visitor" code that would iterate each control of the form and alter each as needed (such as size and color scheme) just before rendering. I would like to see a property added to Voodoo to allow the optional specification of a CSS class for each control (possibly in external CSS files), in which case a class attribute would be rendered in place of the current style attribute[2]. If your applications must meet strict accessibility standards, such as on government Web sites, be certain to verify that Voodoo meets your needs. I reviewed an early version of the product, and it is certainly possible that future versions of Voodoo will add flexibility in this area.

Notwithstanding this issue, Voodoo is an impressive product, which responds to a significant need for Web Connection application development. Its compatibility with ASP could be a selling point for some organizations. Finally, because EPS uses Voodoo for its own development work, the chances are enhanced that the product will continue to be improved. To learn more about this product, I recommend reading the white paper available on the EPS Web site.

For those developers who desire a visual design tool, be forewarned that version 1.1 of Voodoo requires form design to be accomplished in code (that is, with no visual interface). Nevertheless, as this book went into print, developer Pertti Karjalainen had just announced a free, open source tool (covered under GNU license) named the "Visual Voodoo Designer" (VVD), which is intended to allow you to use the Visual FoxPro form designer to lay out forms that are then translated into their Voodoo counterparts. This tool, which is discussed in the "Voodoo Web Controls" forum of the West Wind message board, may be worthy of your consideration if you require a visual front end for designing Web forms.

Build your own class library

If a class library approach appeals to you, but licensing a third-party product such as Voodoo Web Controls is not your choice, your other option is to "roll your own" by designing a library of form and control classes.

Building a complete class library is well beyond the scope of this book. Nevertheless, it may be helpful to examine what such a library might include. At minimum, it would contain:

- A set of control classes, possibly derived from a single "base" class, that handle binding to data, rendering HTML, and processing submitted form values. They would also contain empty methods to support validation code within subclasses, as well as allowing interaction with business objects, which would perform their own separate validation.

---

[2] Using *class* instead of *style* allows swapping of CSS files for specific users to meet special user requirements, including font sizes and color schemes.

- A form class that serves as a container for the individual controls. This class could be designed to either interact directly with the Web Connection framework, or (more likely) to be scripted via methods in your application process subclasses.

- The ability to extend the class library with application-specific subclasses and additional controls.

- Optionally, you might also include some type of container classes to allow groups of controls to be nested in ways that could support pageframes, grids, and more complex form layout options.

A basic textbox class

To get you started, I will build the beginnings of a class to encapsulate the Web equivalent of a textbox control. First, the control must have basic rendering capability, as shown in **Listing 1**.

Listing 1. The beginnings of a textbox class. This one can at least render HTML.

```
* webradTextbox.PRG
DEFINE CLASS webradTextbox_1 AS CUSTOM
  cValue = ""
  FUNCTION Render
    RETURN [<input type="textbox" value="] + THIS.cValue + [">]
  ENDFUNC   && Render
ENDDEFINE
```

This simple class is already usable in a Web page. You can easily test this class. First, you would add the following line to the SetServerEnvironment() method of the server class (in your main program):

```
SET PROCEDURE TO webradTextbox ADDITIVE
```

Now you can "script" a text box from within any method in one of your Web Connection process classes:

```
LOCAL loTxt
loTxt = CREATEOBJECT( "webradTextbox_1")   && SET PROCEDURE first!
Response.Write( loTxt.Render())
```

The result should be a text box rendered to the browser. Alternatively, you can test the control from the Command Window:

```
DO wconnect   && load Web Connection utility classes
loTxt = NEWOBJECT( "webradTextbox_1", "webradTextbox.PRG")
ShowHTML( loTxt.Render())   && launches the browser
```

Pretty easy, right? After all, the class definition is only six lines of code. Well before going down this path, be forewarned that there are still many requirements remaining to be implemented, including style options, reading the posted results, binding to data, and accessibility considerations. And that is only to complete the textbox class, which is one of many necessary controls. On the other hand, your application code is suddenly absolved from the need to write out HTML tags with all the messy delimiters one encounters when embedding HTML strings in Visual FoxPro code. At this point, you should conclude that there is a lot of work remaining, but that the benefits may still be worth it.

So, the next step is to implement a few additional requirements. The next iteration is shown in **Listing 2** and includes:

- a text label;

- an HTML name, which is required when we later try to read what the user entered;

- an optional size attribute; and

- the beginnings of data binding.

Listing 2. We have added many additional capabilities to the basic textbox class.

```
DEFINE CLASS webradTextbox_2 AS CUSTOM
  cValue = ""
  lValueLoaded = .F.
  cControlSource = ""
  cHtmlName = ""
  cLabel = ""
  nSize = 0

  FUNCTION Render
    * "Template method" pattern—calls 2 other methods.
    RETURN THIS.RenderLabel() + THIS.RenderControl()
  ENDFUNC   &&Render

  FUNCTION RenderLabel
    RETURN IIF( EMPTY( THIS.cLabel), [], ;
      [<label for="] + THIS.cHtmlName + ["">] + ;
      THIS.cLabel + [:</label>]) + [ ]
  ENDFUNC   && RenderLabel

  FUNCTION RenderControl
    * This renders the actual textbox on the Web page.
    RETURN [<input] + ;
      [ type="textbox"] + ;
      [ name="] + THIS.cHtmlName + ["] + ;
      [ id="] + THIS.cHtmlName + ["] + ;
      [ value="] + THIS.cValue + ["] + ;
      IIF( THIS.nSize <= 0, [], ;
        [ size="] + TRANS( THIS.nSize) + ["]) + ;
      [>]
  ENDFUNC   && RenderControl

  FUNCTION cHtmlName_ACCESS
    * (See discussion in text below.)
    RETURN IIF( EMPTY(THIS.cHtmlName), THIS.Name, THIS.cHtmlName)
  ENDFUNC   && cHtmlName_ACCESS

  FUNCTION cValue_ACCESS
    * (See discussion in text below.)
```

```
   IF NOT EMPTY(THIS.cControlSource) AND NOT THIS.lValueLoaded
      THIS.LoadValue()
   ENDIF
   RETURN THIS.cValue
ENDFUNC

FUNCTION LoadValue
   * Seeds the textbox with the current database value
   * (vs providing an empty textbox).
   IF NOT EMPTY(THIS.cControlSource)
      THIS.cValue = TRANSFORM( EVAL( THIS.cControlSource))
      THIS.lValueLoaded = .T.
   ENDIF
ENDFUNC   && LoadValue
ENDDEFINE
```

Before discussing the additions, you might want to see some of the new features in action. Enter the following code in the Command Window:

```
DO wconnect  && load Web Connection utility classes
loTxt = NEWOBJECT( "webradTextbox_2", "webradTextbox.PRG")
loTxt.cLabel = "Version"
loTxt.cControlSource = "VERSION()"
loTxt.nSize = 60
ShowHTML( loTxt.Render())  && launches the browser
```

The result is shown in **Figure 1**. I used the expression "VERSION()" as the control source for ease of demonstration, so that no specific data source was required.

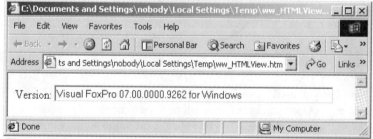

Figure 1. *The revised class sports a label and a control source.*

Quite a lot has been added to the class. What once was six lines has quickly grown to more than 40 lines. And this is only the beginning. On the positive side, the application code required to deploy the class remains very straightforward, and continues to require no HTML. If you examine the code for WebradTextbox_2, you will notice these features:

- Properties have been added to support the new features.

- In adding the label feature, the Render() method has been refactored to become a template method, which in turn calls two new hook methods, RenderLabel() and RenderControl(). This approach greatly increases flexibility by allowing either the hook method or the entire template method to be subclassed independently.

- An accessibility requirement has been met by wrapping the text label with an HTML <label> tag. This allows certain assistive technologies to help users by knowing how to associate the text of the label with the control to which it applies. By implementing this requirement in a generic textbox class, you have ensured that all text boxes in all forms meet this requirement with no further developer effort.

  Imagine the position you would be in if this requirement were added late in a development project. If each text box were based on a single parent class, the effort to implement this change would be minimal. If instead each text box in the application were hand-coded, you would have to alter every one individually!

- The revised class makes use of two "access" methods, each of which serves the purpose of simplifying the developer's job. For example, the access method for the cHtmlName property allows the developer the option of not assigning that property, in which case the HTML name defaults to the value of the Visual FoxPro control's Name property.

This class is only beginning to become remotely useful. To give you a further head start, a few more requirements will be implemented:

- Support for reading submitted values

- Saving back to the control source

- Basic CSS support

Support for reading the submitted values is straightforward:

```
FUNCTION ReadValue
  THIS.cValue = Request.Form( THIS.cHtmlName)
ENDFUNC  && ReadValue
```

There are several approaches you could take for saving values back to the control source. For this example, a new property, cControlSourceType, will be used to control this action, adding support for views as well as data objects. The code to save the value appears in a new method:

```
FUNCTION SaveValue
  DO CASE
  CASE THIS.cControlSourceType = "field"
    IF "." $ THIS.cControlSource
      LOCAL lcAlias
      lcAlias = LEFT( THIS.cControlSource, AT(".", THIS.cControlSource) - 1)
      REPLACE (THIS.cControlSource) WITH (THIS.cValue) IN (m.lcAlias)
    ELSE
      REPLACE (THIS.cControlSource) WITH (THIS.cValue)
    ENDIF
  CASE THIS.cControlSourceType = "property"
    STORE (THIS.cValue) TO (THIS.cControlSource)
  ENDCASE
ENDFUNC  && SaveValue
```

Finally, to add basic CSS support, four new properties will be added to allow control over possible CSS class and style attributes for the label and the control:

```
cLabelClass = "FormLabel"
cLabelStyle = ""
cControlClass = "FormControl"
cControlStyle = ""
```

These properties are used in the appropriate rendering methods. For example, the label is now rendered as follows:

```
FUNCTION RenderLabel
  RETURN IIF( EMPTY( THIS.cLabel), [], ;
    [<span] + ;
    IIF( EMPTY(THIS.cLabelClass), [], ;
      [ class="] + THIS.cLabelClass + ["]) + ;
    IIF( EMPTY(THIS.cLabelStyle), [], ;
      [ style="] + THIS.cLabelStyle + ["]) + ;
    [>] + ;
    [<label for="] + THIS.cHtmlName + [">] + ;
    THIS.cLabel + [:</label>]) + [ ] + [</span>]
ENDFUNC  && RenderLabel
```

Similar code is added to the RenderControl() method. By using this design, you can create style sheets that apply to all controls and include them in an application-wide CSS file. The entire application appearance can then be altered uniformly by modifying or replacing that file, without any change to your Visual FoxPro code. Similarly, specific user needs can be met by substituting a different CSS file reference, which you would implement by altering the file name in a single <link> tag in the <head> section of your response documents. This is a powerful and flexible approach to form design.

 The final WebradTextbox class, which implements the previous additions, is included in the downloadable source code for this chapter in WebradTextbox.PRG.

A basic form container class

You would not expect to manipulate text boxes and other controls independently in your application. Instead, you would group controls together into a data entry form. In order for you to have a starting place, **Listing 3** shows the beginning of what a form container class might look like.

Listing 3. A form class has the primary function of serving as a container for controls.

```
DEFINE CLASS webradForm AS CONTAINER
  cAction = ""
  cTableClass = "FormTable"
  cTitle = ""
  cBackColor = "#cccccc" && grey
  lResetButton = .T.
  cSubmitCaption = "Save"

FUNCTION Render
  LOCAL lcStr, loControl
```

```
* Open a <form>:
lcStr = [<form method="post"] + ;
  IIF( EMPTY(THIS.cAction), [], ;
    [ action="] + THIS.cAction + ["]) + ;
  [>]
* Wrap in a table:
lcStr = m.lcStr + [<table align=center] + ;
  IIF( EMPTY(THIS.cTableClass), [], ;
    [ class="] + THIS.cTableClass + ["]) + ;
  IIF( EMPTY(THIS.cBackColor), [], ;
    [ bgcolor="] + THIS.cBackColor + ["]) + ;
  [>]
* Optional title:
IF NOT EMPTY( THIS.cTitle)
  lcStr = m.lcStr + [<tr><th colspan=2>] + ;
    THIS.cTitle + [</th></tr>]
ENDIF
* Iterate the controls collection:
FOR EACH loControl IN THIS.Controls
  lcStr = m.lcStr + [<tr><th align="right">] + ;
    loControl.RenderLabel() + [</th><td>] + ;
    loControl.RenderControl() + [</td></tr>]
ENDFOR
* Submit and Reset buttons at the bottom:
lcStr = m.lcStr + [<tr><th colspan=2>] + ;
  [<input type="submit" value="] + ;
    THIS.cSubmitCaption + [">]
IF THIS.lResetButton
  lcStr = m.lcStr + [  ] + ;
    [<input type="reset" value="Reset">]
ENDIF
lcStr = m.lcStr + [</th></tr>]
lcStr = m.lcStr + [</table></form>]
RETURN m.lcStr
ENDFUNC  && Render

FUNCTION AddTextboxes( lcFields)
  * Not a real production method! Used for *demo*
  * purposes to load a form with fields.
  LOCAL aa[1], ii, llListPassed, lcField, ;
    loObj, lvVal
  IF EMPTY( m.lcFields)
    AFIELDS( aa)
  ELSE
    ALINES( aa, m.lcFields, .T., ",")
    llListPassed = .T.
  ENDIF
  FOR ii = 1 TO ALEN( aa, 1)
    IF m.llListPassed OR aa[ m.ii, 2] = "C"
      lcField = aa[ m.ii, 1]
      THIS.AddObject( m.lcField, "WebradTextbox")
      loObj = EVALUATE( "THIS." + m.lcField)
      loObj.cControlSource = ALIAS() + "." + m.lcField
      loObj.cLabel = PROPER( CHRTRAN( m.lcField, "_", " "))
      lvVal = EVALUATE( m.lcField)
      IF VARTYPE( m.lvVal) = "C"
        loObj.nSize = MIN( 60, LEN( m.lvVal))
      ENDIF
```

```
      ENDIF
    ENDFOR
ENDFUNC

FUNCTION Read
    LOCAL loControl
    FOR EACH loControl IN THIS.Controls
      loControl.ReadValue()
    ENDFOR
ENDFUNC   && Read

FUNCTION Save
    LOCAL loControl
    FOR EACH loControl IN THIS.Controls
      loControl.SaveValue()
    ENDFOR
ENDFUNC   && Read

ENDDEFINE   && webradForm
```

In addition to encapsulating the rendering of the <form> and </form> tags, this class is a basic container for the other controls. Note that there are three methods in the class where the container simply iterates its collection of members, passing the same message to each. The benefits of polymorphism are obvious, and you would extend these benefits by using the same method names in all other control designs. In fact, you might consider first creating an abstract class (for example, "AbstractWebControl") from which all other classes would be derived (subclassed).

In order to easily show the form class in action, it has an extra method named AddTextboxes(), which is intended for demonstration purposes only. You can take advantage of this by executing the following from the Command Window:

```
DO wconnect   && load Web Connection utility classes
OPEN DATABASE (_SAMPLES + [tastrade\data\tastrade])
USE Customer
loForm = NEWOBJECT( "webradForm", "webradTextbox.PRG")
loForm.cTitle = ALIAS() + " Form"
loForm.AddTextboxes()
ShowHTML( loForm.Render())   && launch the browser
```

That's all it takes to render the form. The results are shown in **Figure 2**.

There is little more required to render the same form within a Web Connection application. **Listing 4** shows a possible example.

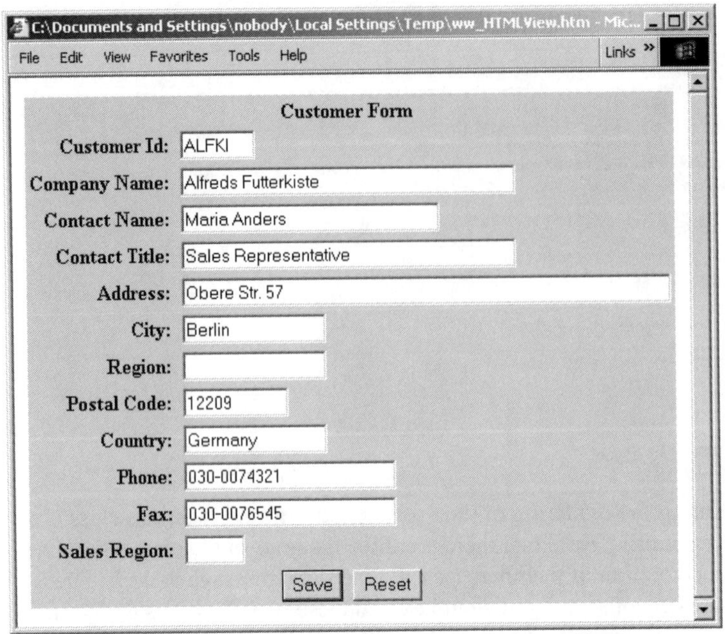

Figure 2. A simple form class rendered within a Web page.

Listing 4. The same form, now rendered from a Web Connection application.

```
FUNCTION CustForm
   OPEN DATABASE (_SAMPLES + [tastrade\data\tastrade])
   SLELECT 0
   USE Customer
   loForm = NEWOBJECT( "webradForm", "webradTextbox.PRG")
   loForm.cTitle = ALIAS() + " Form"
   loForm.AddTextboxes()
   Response.HTMLHeader()
   Response.Write( loForm.Render())
   Response.HTMLFooter()
   USE IN Customer
ENDFUNC   && CustForm
```

Of course, this is a simplified example. For one thing, it always will render the first record in the table. Refer to Chapter 12 for a more complete example of a functioning Web Connection application.

Before you conclude that these classes have given you a big head start, consider how much remains to be developed:

- Only a textbox control has been developed. At minimum, you still need controls for textareas (similar to Visual FoxPro edit regions), check boxes, radio buttons, drop-down lists, and hidden form controls. Each of these has its own intricacies, requiring careful attention to detail in the design process.

- You may also need to support multi-select lists and file upload components, as well as designing Web replacements for the grid control, pageframe, or other containers that have no HTML counterpart. These are much more complex tasks than designing a textbox control, and could be beyond either your capability or your budget.

- Even the textbox control that you have supports only character fields. Extending the control to include date and numeric entry involves extra work, as HTML text boxes have no concept of data types.

- The textbox control also does not yet support other features required for flexible form design, such as the ability to disable controls or conditionally remove them (for security or context reasons).

- Each of the controls needs further options such as Help text, on-screen instructions, and so forth.

- The form class is very basic and offers no alternative form layout strategies, besides rendering one field per row.

- Depending on your middle-tier design, you may also need validation hooks in the form and control classes.

Be forewarned that attempting to design your own class library is not a minor undertaking. For example, my company's library of form and control classes currently totals close to 4,000 lines of code, and there are still many desired features yet to be implemented.

The ultimate solution: What is still missing?

You should now recognize that either using the Voodoo Web Controls or designing your own class library would give you plenty of benefits via extensibility and code reuse. Nevertheless, neither of those approaches yields an obvious technique of combining a visual form-editing tool to maximum advantage. How one might combine two such technologies is far from obvious.

One approach is to combine the use of the class library with Web Connection scripts (edited using a visual tool). In this scenario, you would most likely forego use of a majority of the rendering code in the class library, in favor of simply accepting the visual layout in the script. For example, you might reference only the control objects' values, leaving it to the script layout to include the labels and other formatting. Depending on the flexibility of the editing tool you use, and how you divide the content creation between the scripts and the classes, you may or may not be able to achieve your desired results. Certainly some of the benefits gained through code reuse via the inheritance available in a pure code-based design could be lost when trying to combine the use of scripts. On the other hand, if your project team includes skilled Web page designers, your optimum choice could well be one that leverages these skills using a visual tool.

If you should attempt to combine two such technologies, be certain to consider the maintenance aspects. Envision typical changes to forms over time. If most of these changes will require alterations to both the Web page (script) and the Visual FoxPro code, the maintenance costs will remain sufficiently high that you may not end up with the gains you expected by pursuing the path of using a class library for form design.

Table 1 presents a summary and comparison of approaches.

Table 1. Summary of approaches.

Attribute	Hand-code	Hand-code + scripts	EditTable() in ShowCursor	DHTML with VFP forms	Voodoo Web Controls	Build class library	Ultimate (class lib + visual tool)
Maintainability	Poor	Fair	Good	Good	Good	Good	Good
Flexibility	Excellent	Medium	Poor	Good	Good	Good	Good
Complex forms?	Yes	Yes	No	Yes	Yes	Yes	Yes
Browser compatibility?	Yes	Yes	Yes	No (MSIE browser only)	Yes	Yes	Yes
Visual layouts?	No	Yes	No	Yes	No[3]	No	Yes
Control of look-and-feel	Excellent, but difficult to maintain	Good	Poor	Good	Good	Good	Good
Accessibility options	Good	Good	Fair	Poor	Poor	Fair-Good	Good
Validation (client-side)	Difficult	Difficult	None	Difficult	Good	Fair-Good	Fair-Good
Validation (server-side)	Hand-code	Hand-code	None	Good	Good	Good	Good
Data binding	None (manual process)	None (manual process)	Good[4]	Good	Good	Good	Good
Developer efficiency	Poor[5]	Poor	Excellent	Good	Good	Good	Good
Performance[6]	Best	Best	Best	Worst	Medium	Medium	Medium
Cost	N/A	HTML editing tool required	Included with Web Connection	Included with Web Connection	$299 for base package[7]	Development cost	Unknown
Available?	Yes	Yes	Yes	Yes	Yes (requires VFP 7)	No (developer must write)	No

---

[3] EPS Software has acknowledged the desirability of coupling a visual tool with Voodoo. Future revisions may include some alternative to do so. As stated in the text, the free Visual Voodoo Designer does provide one option in this area (using the Visual FoxPro form designer as opposed to an HTML editor).

[4] Assumes local table or similar (REPLACE statements used). A subclass would be needed to work with views. Not compatible with data objects.

[5] Can be improved with IntelliSense scripts and other productivity tools.

[6] Combo boxes on forms present their own performance issues, which are discussed separately in the next section of this chapter.

[7] Base package available from EPS Software. Additional controls may be available in the future, but will require that the base package be installed.

Combo box issues

In exploring various approaches to data entry on the Web, I found that combo boxes (or "select" lists) present challenges that none of the reviewed approaches attempt to address.

Specifically, the default technique for rendering a combo box is simply to embed all of the choices directly into the rendered Web form. The HTML source for one of these controls might look like this:

```
<select name="frmCust_cboState">
  <option value="AK"> Alaska </option>
  <option value="AL"> Alabama </option>
  <option value="AR"> Arkansas </option>
  ...etc.
</select>
```

Although this technique may be adequate for selecting one value from a list on a single form, consider these issues:

- If a form includes a grid of child records, where the combo box appears repeatedly as a column of the grid, the entire list of options would be repeated for each child record. Thus even the short state list, if repeated 10 times, could bloat the response size by approximately 20KB. This quantity obviously gets worse with more choices, longer text strings, or more child records.

- Even without a grid, if a lengthy list is encountered over and over from page to page, the server is both generating the list and embedding it in the response each time. This can impact both the performance of your site and your scalability options.

- Finally, if a single list is long enough, even though it might be encountered infrequently, the overhead associated with producing it dynamically for each Web hit might be too great[8].

These issues can be addressed via the use of JavaScript arrays. Essentially all modern browsers support JavaScript. By producing two arrays—one for the combo box values and another for the displayed text—the <select> tags could be rendered empty, and a JavaScript command could be issued after the page is loaded instructing the list to be populated from the arrays.

For the first issue, where lists are repeated for each item in a grid, the JavaScript approach would solve the problem, because the same array would be used to populate the list for each child record. In other words, the list would appear only once in the response. This would have the effect of reducing response size and improving server performance, with the minor cost of adding some processing burden to the client browser.

Without the repetition required for combo boxes in a grid, you might think the array approach would offer no benefit, because the list would only need to appear once. This is true if the lists are dynamic; however, many lists used in combo boxes are relatively (or completely) static in nature, such as the list of states. In this case, you adopt a caching

---

[8] These issues are somewhat like issues with combo boxes in a fat client Visual FoxPro application. You have to be really careful how you use combos no matter what!

architecture wherein you "publish" your lists as JavaScript arrays that exist in separate .JS files on the Web server. Using this architecture, you would then refer to these files using the src attribute of the <script> tag. Client browsers would then download these files separately, and the lists would not be included in the HTML response. Of equal importance, most client browsers would cache these files, in the same way they cache images that appear on many of your pages, thus avoiding the time and bandwidth involved in downloading the file each time it is referenced on a page.

Although I found no tool to facilitate this type of architecture, I would expect that, with increased usage of tools like Voodoo, some enterprising developer will soon develop a combo class for the Web that implements these ideas.

Data binding

In this chapter, I have examined several strategies for rendering and processing data entry forms on the Web. One attribute that I consider important is flexibility in the approach to data binding. For you, the developer, what is more important than flexibility is that the approach be compatible with your own data access tools and skills.

For example, if your organization uses a Visual FoxPro framework, such as Visual FoxExpress or Mere Mortals, for developing networked desktop applications, you should select a Web form approach that is compatible with the business class design employed by the framework that you use. If you fail to do this, you may find yourself unable to reuse your business objects in your Web applications, which can put your data and your reputation in jeopardy.

Review of data access strategies

If you already have a framework of choice, your job is to select a compatible approach to Web forms. If you are not using a framework, you should choose a flexible approach. First, consider some common data access approaches used in Visual FoxPro applications:

- Local data: You simply USE your tables, LOCATE your data, and update with REPLACE statements.

- Buffered local data or local views: Similar to the preceding approach, but the ability to issue a TABLEREVERT() command provides greater flexibility—essentially allowing the buffered table to act as a temporary work area while you validate form submittals to decide whether the input should be saved.

- Remote views: Provides an easy upsizing path, where data resides on a database server—typically Microsoft SQL Server or Oracle—while you can continue to use Xbase commands.

- SQL pass-through: In this case, again you have remote data, but you process updates by building actual SQL statements to be sent to the database server for processing. This approach provides greater flexibility than remote views, but requires more skill (or good tools) to implement. The wwBusiness class that comes with Web Connection encapsulates the process of updating remote SQL data in this manner.

- Business objects: Pure business objects hide the entire choice of data access methods by providing a standard interface to the data, usually via properties and methods, by which data is read and written. With a well-designed set of business classes, it would be possible for the entire data access layer to be changed without requiring a single change to the front-end (user interface) component.

Business object and data access object design is well beyond the scope of this book; however, I listed the approaches here as a reminder of the different interfaces with data that you might encounter. If searching for a flexible approach to Web forms, at minimum I would want an approach that worked well with both table buffering and business objects.

For example, earlier in this chapter, I showed an example of using Voodoo with table buffering. But Voodoo can also be easily used in a business object context. By specifying a control's ControlSource as a property of an object, instead of a field in a table, Voodoo will update that property, instead of replacing the field contents. Instead of issuing a TABLEUPDATE command to save the changes, you would call an appropriate method of whatever business object you are using—for example, Save(). One could even imagine a flag in your form subclass that could switch a form between buffered tables and business objects. The setting of this form flag could come from an application-level setting, thus allowing the entire application to be easily transformed.

A practical approach to data access

How can you employ these same principles to achieve a flexible design if you are not using a third-party product? One tool that can help is the wwBusiness class that comes with version 4 of Web Connection. This class, in supporting both local and remote data, allows you to design your front-end application with little worry about the possible need to upsize in the future.

If instead you want to design a flexible approach on your own, consider an approach where you use a simple data access object, even though you have no existing business class framework. Let me present this idea in the context of how the logic for a basic Web Connection data entry page might be constructed. In this example, imagine a design where the URL contains the primary key value of the record to be edited as a query string parameter "ID". **Listing 5** shows the pseudo-logic one would use.

Listing 5. Pseudo-code for form processing in Web Connection.

```
FUNCTION CustForm
  LOCAL lnId
  lnId = VAL(Request.QueryString("ID")) && convert string to integer
  <locate the data>
  IF <form was submitted>
    <read and validate form>
    IF <submittal valid>
      <save the data>
      <send the user somewhere else>
    ELSE
      <construct error message>
    ENDIF
  ENDIF
  <render the form>
ENDFUNC
```

Looking at this pseudo-logic, you can see that it would be desirable if only the locating and saving of data varied depending on the data access approach. But you might ask how that could be possible if you're working with local tables now, but hope to develop a middle-tier business object layer whenever you get the time. The first answer might be to use bracketed code. For example, your locate code might look like this:

```
LOCAL llBizObjs
IF llBizObjs
   ** Possible future code:
   ** LOCAL loCust
   ** loCust = CREATE("Customer")
   ** loCust.Load(m.lnId) && find their data
ELSE   && today's solution
   USE Customer
   LOCATE FOR CustID = m.lnId
ENDIF
```

Here you are coding for today while at least envisioning a better day tomorrow. But do a little more with your form, and you will run into some trouble. For example, your code to render a text box might look like this today:

```
Response.Write([<input name="txtName" type="text" value="] + ;
   Customer.CustName + [" size="20">])
```

You see the problem: This code is unique to today's approach in that it references a field name in a table. To move to a business object approach, you would have to bracket this code also (or at least use IIF() expressions). In fact, you would end up needing to put conditional code all over the place, including the "saving" code where you are writing back to the data source, because you would no longer be using REPLACE statements:

```
IF m.llBizObjs
   ** loCust.oData.CustName = Request.Form( "txtName")
   ** ... more properties
ELSE   && today's solution
   REPLACE CustName WITH Request.Form( "txtName") ;
      ... more fields
ENDIF
```

All of this bracketed code and repetition of names should not appear desirable. A better solution is to adopt a data object strategy today that provides a higher level of compatibility with a full middle-tier strategy in the future.

Suppose you anticipate a typical business class design where the business object includes a member data object, perhaps named "oData," that contains the values of the fields for the entity of interest. This data object will either be created from a view via SCATTER NAME or, in a distributed architecture, by reconstituting an XML string into an identical data object. If this is to be your interface to the data in the future, why not use the same interface today? If you could pull this off, there might be much less work in the future to adopt a new middle tier. Consider this minor alteration to the preceding code:

```
LOCAL llBizObjs, loData
IF llBizObjs
  ** Possible future code:
  ** LOCAL loCust
  ** loCust = CREATE("Customer")
  ** loCust.Load(m.lnId)   && find their data
  ** loData = loCust.oData   && member object!
ELSE   && today's solution
  USE Customer
  LOCATE FOR CustID = m.lnId
  SCATTER MEMO NAME loData
ENDIF
```

This may look similar, but the difference is profound! Now, in both cases, your code has produced an object named loData that has a property corresponding to each field in the record. This means that almost all of the need to bracket subsequent code disappears. For example, when rendering and reading the customer name text box, you can simply refer to loData.CustName. The only further bracketing you need to do is when you decide to save the record:

```
IF m.llBizObjs
  ** IF loCust.Validate()
  **    loCust.Save()   && bus obj knows what to do
  ** ENDIF
ELSE   && today's solution
  * manual validation checks, leading to:
  GATHER MEMO NAME loData
ENDIF
```

A complete example

With this entire strategy in hand, **Listing 6** shows a complete example of a Web Connection method that: (1) determines the record to be edited from a URL parameter; (2) retrieves the data using an approach that should be adaptable to a future, middle-tier design; (3) presents a Web-based form; and (4) saves the submitted data. This is a very simple example, in that only a single text box is edited, and there is no check to confirm that the primary key in the URL is valid, but you should easily be able to see how this would be extended.

Listing 6. A complete Web Connection example.

```
FUNCTION CustForm
  LOCAL llBizObjs, loData, lnId
  lnId = VAL(Request.QueryString("id"))
  IF m.llBizObjs   && set flag to .T. in the future
    ** LOCAL loCust
    ** loCust = CREATE("Customer")
    ** loCust.Load(m.lnId)
    ** loData = loCust.oData
  ELSE
    SELECT 0
    USE Customer
    LOCATE FOR CustID = m.lnId
    SCATTER MEMO NAME loData
```

```
  ENDIF
  IF Request.Form("FormName") == "CustForm"
    * form is being submitted, read the input:
    loData.CustName = Request.Form("txtCustName")
    * could do some validation here
    IF m.llBizObjs
      loCust.Save()
    ELSE
      GATHER MEMO NAME loData
    ENDIF
    THIS.StandardPage( "Data was saved!")
    RETURN
  ENDIF
  Response.HTMLHeader()
  Response.Write( [<form method="post">] + ;
    [<input type="hidden" name="FormName" value="CustForm">] + ;
    [ Customer Name: <input name="txtCustName" value="] + ;
      TRIM(loData.CustName) + [" size="30" type="text"><br>] + ;
    [<input type="Submit" name="btnSave" value="Save"><br>] + ;
    [</form>] )
  Response.HTMLFooter()
ENDFUNC  && CustForm
```

Although there are many approaches to data access, I hope this example has given you some ideas of how to design your front end in order to insulate you from the effects of future changes.

Fighting against form hackers

Once you shift gears from simply making your data accessible on the Web to allowing data entry via the Web, your security concerns immediately rise. Although not all specific to either Web Connection or Visual FoxPro, it is important to be aware of each of these threats.

URL manipulation

In this scheme, hackers edit the URL in their browsers in an attempt to access data that they are not supposed to see. For example, suppose you have a method named CustomerForm(), and the customer to be edited is ascertained from a URL parameter. An example URL might look like this: http://www.yourdomain.com/app/CustomerForm.wcs?id=2345.

A hacker looking at that URL might be curious to see what information he might see if he simply edits the final number in the URL. If this is all that is needed for hackers to access data to which they have no rights, your application is in big trouble! I will discuss the solution to this form of hacking in a moment, but first I will show hacking techniques that involve the form itself.

Form-variable hacking

Next are two different input form hacking techniques. The first involves hidden form variables, wherein the hacker actually modifies hidden values in your form prior to submitting data. Many Web designers use hidden form variables (using the <input type="hidden"> tag) to store variable information that is critical when processing the submitted form. Be aware that these variables are not truly hidden! Anyone can simply select the "View Source" option in his or her browser, and your dirty laundry is exposed.

You might think that this is not a problem as long as the hidden data isn't sensitive, because at least there is no visible form element, and thus the data cannot be altered by the user. Not so! It is trivial for a hacker to save the HTML source to a file on disk, and then edit the file locally, load that modified file in the browser, and submit the altered form back to your site. Is your application designed to cope with this possibility?

The final technique goes beyond hidden form variables and involves exposing inadequate validation in your application by hacking other form variables, such as pop-up lists. Using the same technique of saving and modifying the HTML source, a user can alter the choices in lists and radio buttons to include choices you never presented to them in the first place!

Round-Trip Principle

So, how do you respond to the threats of hacking illustrated in these examples? What I suggest is that you focus on an important concept that I call the "Round-Trip Principle." What this principle states is that security checks must be made and business rules employed on both sides of the round-trip involved in any transaction. In other words, when rendering a form, you check that the current user has rights to see the content on that form, and then when the form is submitted, you validate both the user's rights and the specific values submitted.

Some specific tips flow out of this principle:

- Just because a user hits a specific URL, do not assume he has any business accessing the information requested. Check the user's rights both when rendering hyperlinks that would lead him to a given page, and when he actually arrives at that page.

- After reading values in hidden form variables, validate that the current user has rights to whatever data is suggested by the form variable values, and that the values are indeed still valid.

- When processing submitted form values, you must validate all form elements, including values submitted from lists and radio buttons. Do not simply save the submitted values back to the database. Hackers can easily add invalid choices to these form objects.

Conclusion

The primary focus of this chapter was on the alternative choices available for designing data entry forms for the Web. There is no one conclusion that is right for all development situations. Each organization must make this decision for itself. Nevertheless, some generalizations can help in the decision process.

Hand-coding is certainly a viable approach for a modest development environment where a manageable number of forms is involved. This approach can be further leveraged via both some productivity tools and by combining hand-coded form processing with the use of scripts for the form layout work. As the number of forms increases, the maintainability costs, however, should lead you to explore other solutions.

The technique of using wwShowCursor::EditTable(), while fine for maintaining lookup tables and meta data, does not have sufficient flexibility (either in rendering or data binding) to be considered as a general development alternative.

The leveraging that you can gain from the option of rendering Visual FoxPro forms using DHTML can work in specific circumstances. Nevertheless, you must be willing to accept both the browser limitation (to Microsoft Internet Explorer) and the performance penalty.

Certainly if you are going to be developing many Web Connection applications that include data entry requirements, and cross-browser compatibility is a requirement, you should seriously consider one of the two class library approaches. If you have an existing framework and feel comfortable designing your own classes, you should consider creating a library of classes to encapsulate the rendering, processing, and data binding of Web forms. If you are not comfortable embarking on this approach, I recommend you consider using Voodoo.

You should be aware, however, that neither pure class library approach includes the visual layout potential that is available with either the use Web Connection templates or the approach of rendering Visual FoxPro forms via DHTML. So, keep an eye on the ultimate solution of combining a class library approach with a visual layout tool. This combination does not yet exist today. Perhaps you can be the first to create it!

Even if you are certain you will not choose the hand-coded approach, you should develop and test at least a few sample forms using this technique. Without this background, you will not be able to appreciate the challenges and analyze the relative merits of the other alternatives.

Finally, on a separate note, you create significant exposure to hacking when you allow data entry via the Web. No matter what tools you employ, you must be aware of the risks and take appropriate measures to safeguard your data.

Chapter 16
Extending the Framework

Once you have become comfortable with the basics, it is time again for new challenges. Extending the Web Connection framework classes and creating some of your own classes can significantly improve both your productivity and the quality of your applications.

Most of the important classes in the Web Connection framework can be easily subclassed when needed. In this chapter I will present the proper method for creating and installing such subclasses. I will also show several examples of useful extensions to the Web Connection framework. But first, I want to make sure that all readers are comfortable with the mechanics of subclassing in general in Visual FoxPro. The next section presents a primer on this subject. Developers who are already comfortable with these concepts can skip over this material.

A subclassing primer

To be successful as a developer of Web Connection applications, it is essential to become comfortable with object-oriented programming (OOP) in Visual FoxPro. As a developer, if you are new to both the Web and OOP, you will face a steep learning curve. After mastering the basics with Web Connection, you will encounter needs to create subclasses of your own. In this section I will show the basics of defining a subclass in code. With Visual FoxPro, you have the choice of creating your classes and subclasses with either the Class Designer, which is a visual tool, or with code alone. I am only going to discuss creating classes in code, because the Web Connection classes that you will be interested in subclassing are defined in code.

When you create a class, you start with a suitable Visual FoxPro base class, and then define all of its additional properties and methods from scratch. Properties are like variables that allow an object to have attributes assigned to it (such as height, width, color, and so forth). Methods are functions or procedures that are contained (or encapsulated) within an object. When you create a subclass, you are instead taking some existing class as a starting point and extending its properties and methods. The class from which you start is known as the parent class, or super class, if you are familiar with that terminology from another language. You extend and alter the parent class definition in the subclass. Any property or method in the parent that you do not specifically alter in the subclass is "inherited" by the subclass. You can make any combination of five types of alterations in a subclass:

- Add new properties.

- Override the initial values of parent properties.

- Add new methods.

- Completely override parent methods.

- Augment parent methods, while also calling the parent method code.

To see these five types of changes in action, you must start with a parent class—the class from which your subclass will be derived. Here is an example of a parent class named CoWorker that defines two properties and two methods:

```
DEFINE CLASS CoWorker AS CUSTOM
* Properties:
WorkerName = "Joe"
Efficiency = 1.0
* Methods:
FUNCTION SayHello
  MESSAGEBOX( "Hello, my name is " + THIS.WorkerName + "!" )
ENDFUNC
*
FUNCTION ListProperties
  ? "Name: " + THIS.WorkerName
  ? "Efficiency: " + TRANS( THIS.Efficiency)
ENDFUNC
ENDDEFINE && CLASS CoWorker
```

Class definition code is placed in PRG files just like other Visual FoxPro code. You can include one or more classes in a single PRG file. In this example class with two custom properties and two custom methods, you might create a file with the same name as the class (that is, CoWorker.PRG). You can easily deploy and test this class from the Visual FoxPro Command Window (see **Figure 1**).

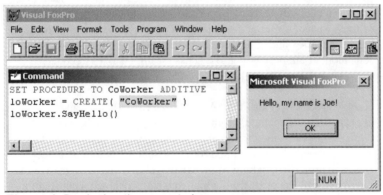

Figure 1. Deploying the parent class.

Now that you have created a working parent class, it is time to look at an example of creating a subclass that includes all five of the types of changes listed previously. Here is such an example, which you could package in the same PRG file with the parent, or in its own separate file:

```
DEFINE CLASS LazyCoWorker AS CoWorker
* (1) Add a new property:
LazinessQuotient = 10
* (2) Override a parent property:
Efficiency = 0.5
```

```
* (3) Add new method:
FUNCTION TakeCoffeeBreak( lnSeconds )
  DECLARE Sleep IN WIN32API INTEGER
  Sleep( 1000 * m.lnSeconds )
  MESSAGEBOX( "I'm awake now and raring to go." )
ENDFUNC

* (4) Completely override a parent method:
FUNCTION SayHello
  MESSAGEBOX( "Yawn... My name is " + THIS.WorkerName + ;
    ", and I sure am lazy." )
ENDFUNC

* (5) Augment a parent method:
FUNCTION ListProperties
  DODEFAULT() && call parent method
  ? "Laziness Quotient: " + TRANS( THIS.LazinessQuotient )
ENDFUNC
ENDDEFINE && CLASS LazyCoWorker
```

This is a complete working subclass that includes five modifications to the parent class. Notice how little source code a class can require. There are important factors to understand about each of the five types of changes in the subclass:

1. The first change was to add a new property called *LazinessQuotient*. When doing so, only the subclass and its descendents can reference this property. Thus, if you instantiate an object based on the parent class CoWorker, you could not refer to its *LazinessQuotient* property. When you discover that a parent class really requires a property that only exists in a subclass (for example, you discover that all co-workers can be lazy on occasions), you can simply add the property back to the parent class definition.

2. The second change was to override the value of a property that was defined in the parent—to change *Efficiency* from 1.0 to 0.5. This is a very frequent type of change to make in a subclass.

3. The third change was to add a brand-new method called TakeCoffeeBreak(). This is very similar to adding a new property—only objects derived from the subclass can utilize this method.

4. The fourth change was to completely override the SayHello() method from the parent. In this case, the interface to any object derived from the subclass remains the same as for those derived from the parent class; it is the implementation that changes. You still can call to loWorker.SayHello(), for example, and if you had passed parameters to the parent SayHello() method, you would pass the same parameters to the SayHello() method of the subclass, provided you included the same PARAMETERS or LPARAMETERS statement at the top of both the parent and subclass.

5. The fifth and final change is to augment a parent method, in this case the ListProperties() method. You do this when you want to retain some of the parent class behavior, while adding some additional code. The technique for implementing this is to call the DODEFAULT() function in the subclass. You have the flexibility of

calling this anywhere in the method code, although most commonly this will be either the first or last line of code.

Subclassing Web Connection framework classes

Web Connection provides significant functionality in its framework classes. When starting out, you will find this functionality almost overwhelming, such that subclassing is the last action you would consider. Nevertheless, after working with the framework for some time, you may encounter situations, such as tasks that are repetitive in nature, where you think framework extensions are in order. You may also discover behavior that you would like to create and fine-tune in one place and have it apply to your entire application, or to all Web Connection applications in your domain. In this section I will discuss several of the Web Connection framework classes and which of those are particularly amenable to subclassing.

In fact, if you have explored the sample code or created a project of your own, you can see that you are already working with subclasses of two of the framework classes. First, the main program for your project consists primarily of a subclass of the server class (wwServer). Second, each process program consists of a subclass of the process class (wwProcess). These two examples are cases of "implementation" subclassing, meaning that they represent a specific usage in a single application. Every Web Connection developer performs this type of subclassing. A more interesting form of subclassing involves actually extending the Web Connection framework for reuse. When you do this, you create functionality from which each of your implementation subclasses can benefit. This chapter focuses more on this latter concept of extending the framework itself.

An example extension to the response class

In each case where you identify a need to extend the Web Connection framework, there are at least four steps for you to perform:

- Define the need.

- Identify the correct framework class to be extended, if any.

- Implement the design.

- Integrate the design into your application.

Because I want to focus on the mechanics of successfully implementing a framework extension, I will start with a very simple example. In Chapter 18, "Advanced Troubleshooting and Maintenance," I discuss the advantage of using comments in your code, but with an unusual twist—by inserting the comments into your HTML output stream, you get the "double impact" of seeing the same comment in both your Visual FoxPro source code and in the HTML source for the page. This can be very convenient when debugging HTML layout and formatting problems.

To embed a comment into your HTML response, you could issue a command similar to the first line here:

```
Response.Write( [<!-- Beginning of TABLE for query results. -->] + CR )
Response.Write( [<table border=1 bgcolor="gray" cellpadding=2>] + CR )
```

Now suppose that you start embedding comments like this liberally in your code. If you are like me, you will find it repetitive to type that syntax for HTML comments each time. Further, you may not even remember the syntax and have to look it up in your trusty, dog-eared HTML reference. You realize that efficiency would be gained if you had a simple method for inserting comments into the HTML output. You have thus completed the first step of defining the need.

The next step is to identify the correct framework class to be extended. Sometimes, this will be obvious. Other times, you will not be certain, and will have to analyze the situation more closely. Sometimes there will not even be a good answer, which might suggest the need for designing a new class from scratch. The more you study and understand the Web Connection messaging model, the easier it is to identify the proper class to be extended.

Fortunately, this example fits into the first category. You see from the preceding code that it is the Response object that you wish to have the extended behavior of providing a simple interface for adding comments. The requirement is to have a method that is more specific than the Write method to the needs of inserting comments into the HTML output. WriteComment() might be a good choice of name for this method.

Now that you have identified the object whose behavior you want to enhance, you must discover the correct class name from which to derive your subclass. By examining the Web Connection documentation, you will discover that the Response object is defined in the wwResponse class. Thus you implement your design change by extending that class in a subclass called MyResponse, which you create in a new file named MyResponse.PRG as follows:

```
#INCLUDE WCONNECT.H
DEFINE CLASS MyResponse AS wwResponse
FUNCTION WriteComment( lcText )
  THIS.Write( [<!-- ] + m.lcText + [ -->] + CR )
ENDFUNC   && WriteComment
ENDDEFINE   && CLASS MyResponse
```

That's all it takes! You now have a class that allows easy insertion of HTML comments without your having to remember and type that syntax. And due to inheritance, your new class still has the Write method and all of the other methods in the base wwResponse class. Using the new WriteComment() method in your application code is simple:

```
Response.WriteComment( "Beginning of table for query results.")
```

You are probably thinking that it cannot be quite that easy, and you are correct. You still have to get this change installed into your application so that your class is recognized and used. If you did nothing more, your application would continue to implement the framework wwResponse class, rather than your new MyResponse class, which would mean the Response object would not have a WriteComment() method at all. There are two steps required to get your class recognized and used.

First, you must add the class to the active set of defined classes at run time. Because this class is defined in program code, the required statement is SET PROCEDURE..ADDITIVE. Thus you insert the following line near the top of your application's main program file, right after the line DO WCONNECT:

```
SET PROCEDURE TO MyResponse ADDITIVE
```

This step serves only to make your class available for use. How do you tell Web Connection to use it in place of its own wwResponse class? The answer lies in the use of compiler constants in the sometimes mysterious WCONNECT.H file. This file contains numerous constants for a variety of uses. Some are available for developer modification and some should never be touched! One set of constants that is definitely meant for developer modification is the one that is specifically included to facilitate subclassing. These constants all start with the prefix WWC_ , and in this case the one you are interested in is WWC_RESPONSE. If you examine the WCONNECT.H file, you will find this setting:

```
#DEFINE WWC_RESPONSE              wwResponse
```

This setting is used by the Web Connection framework to know the correct parent class to use when implementing framework-specific objects. Thus all you need to do in order to have your class used is to change the definition to:

```
#DEFINE WWC_RESPONSE              MyResponse
```

For the purpose of testing this simple example, you can make this change directly to the WCONNECT.H file. In the section that follows, I will present the preferred way of changing these constants, which minimizes maintenance problems when new revisions of Web Connection are issued.

You'll also notice that I included a #INCLUDE WCONNECT.H line at the top of MyResponse.PRG. This is because I'm using the constant CR in my code instead of having to type out CHR(13)+CHR(10). Any #INCLUDE compiler directive applies only to the current PRG file, so it is necessary to repeat this line in each PRG where you intend to use these constants.

One last detail to point out is that our WriteComment() method does not alter the output stream directly, but rather uses the existing Write() method and simply supplies the specifics that format a comment for HTML. Because the Write() method already encapsulates the proper mechanism for sending strings to the output stream, you leverage this code rather than trying to duplicate it. This is more important than it might sound. The Web Connection framework actually deploys further subclasses, wwResponseFile or wwResponseString, based on whether file-based messaging or COM messaging is in use. Each of these subclasses has different code to implement the Write method. By simply calling this method, you allow these differences to be handled for you automatically, rather than writing messaging-specific code yourself. In fact, you do not even need to be aware that two different mechanisms exist.

Managing changes to #DEFINE constants in WCONNECT.H

In the previous example, you had to change a #DEFINE constant in WCONNECT.H in order to implement a subclass of a Web Connection framework class. In this section I will explain why this is necessary. I will then present a more maintainable approach for altering these constants.

The important concept is why you need these constants at all. In other words, if you are subclassing the wwResponse class, why isn't:

```
DEFINE CLASS MyResponse AS wwResponse
```

sufficient in and of itself? Why do we need to change WCONNECT.H at all? The answer lies in the internal workings of the Web Connection framework. In many cases, including that of the Response object, another framework object is responsible for instantiating and manipulating that object. In this case, it is the Process object that instantiates the Response object. The problem is that other Web Connection framework objects have no knowledge of the details or even the existence of your subclass. Therefore, how could they know to instantiate your subclass instead of the framework class?

The answer, as you can probably guess, comes from the compiler constants. Each relevant framework class has an associated constant that defines the class name to be used. In the case of the wwResponse class, the constant is WWC_RESPONSE and its default definition is:

```
#DEFINE WWC_RESPONSE     wwResponse
```

Now for the trick! Rather than ever instantiating the wwResponse class directly, the constant is always used instead. Thus the code might look like:

```
THIS.oResponse = CREATEOBJECT( [WWC_RESPONSE] )
```

This technique of providing an indirect way of referring to the class name provides all of the flexibility you need to implement your subclassing. All you need to do is revise the value of the constant, and the framework will now use your subclass in all places where wwResponse was previously used. This is very elegant and powerful.

The second important concept is maintainability. Obviously WCONNECT.H is a file provided with the Web Connection framework. As such, it is subject to change from one revision to the next. In fact, it always changes with each revision, because one of the constants in WCONNECT.H defines the Web Connection revision number. If you also make several changes to this file, how will you ensure that these changes are not lost when you install a new revision of Web Connection? Further, suppose you have two or more separate Web Connection applications, and these applications do not use the same subclasses as one another. How would you manage the constants in that scenario?

The answer to both situations is *not* to make the changes in the WCONNECT.H file itself, but instead in a separate header file of your own for each application. This file will contain all of the values to override from the framework defaults. The secret is to ensure that your revised constants be used. After all, the framework classes will not know about your new header file. The trick to making this work is to insert these lines at the *very bottom* of WCONNECT.H that reference your own header file:

```
#IF FILE( "WCONNECT_OVERRIDE.H")
  #INCLUDE WCONNECT_OVERRIDE.H
#ENDIF
```

Starting with version 4 of Web Connection, the preceding lines are included by default. If you are working with prior versions, simply add the lines manually. Now, you can create your header file WCONNECT_OVERRIDE.H, which will need two lines for each class that you want to subclass. For the example I presented in the previous section, your header file would look like:

```
* WCONNECT_OVERRIDE.H
*   Application-specific overrides to WC framework constants.
*
* Subclass the Response class:
#UNDEF WWC_RESPONSE
#DEFINE WWC_RESPONSE     MyResponse
*
* more subclassing as required..
```

Note the use of the #UNDEF compiler directive. This causes the previous definition of this constant to be dropped, prior to substituting your own definition. Failure to include this line will produce a compile-time warning "Constant is already created with #DEFINE."

If you are managing multiple applications, this approach will still work. If you need different subclass definitions in each application, simply move the individual WCONNECT_OVERRIDE.H files into application-specific paths.

There is one potential problem you must be aware of when working with multiple Web Connection applications, if you also subclass framework classes. You must be very careful when testing these applications from the Command Window by simply running your main program file. If you do this after switching from one application to another, the framework classes may have been last compiled using the overrides from a different application, possibly leading to problems that could be very difficult to diagnose and debug. This is not an issue when running your compiled EXE files. This problem can be avoided, allowing you to test successfully from Visual FoxPro, by first recompiling all of your classes when switching to a different application.

Framework classes suitable for subclassing

Now that you have seen an example of how to implement a subclass, and you know how to manage the header files that control the compilation process properly, it is time to examine when you would want to create these subclasses.

Web Connection provides many framework classes. Some of these are well suited to subclassing, while others should probably never be considered. In this section, I will examine each of the major Web Connection classes plus a few of the supporting classes and discuss their suitability for subclassing.

Subclassing the wwServer class

The wwServer class is the basis for the primary Server object that runs your application. You always create a new subclass of this class in the main program of each Web Connection application. As such, it is trivial to add functionality to this object for a specific application, simply by adding the code to the class implementation in the main program. Beyond this basic extension, you can also create a subclass of wwServer from which each of your applications derives its server class. This would be appropriate if you identified additional Server object functionality that you wanted to apply to more than one of your applications.

From a completeness standpoint there is little reason to extend the wwServer class. This class already performs all of the functions needed to respond to requests from WC.DLL and to call the process classes that you design. Little could be added to this mechanism. Nevertheless, there is one tempting reason to add functionality here, and that involves persistence. Whereas the Request, Response, Process, and Session objects are instantiated and destroyed on every hit, the Server object persists until your EXE terminates. Because of this, the server becomes a tempting target for performing various tasks, even though they may be unrelated to Web Connection messaging. Tasks such as opening files and setting up the environment can be performed here.

Beyond that level, you are probably better off designing separate worker classes and instantiating them from the Server object, thus providing the persistence, but not adding to the complexity of the server class itself. The best place for adding such code is the SetServerProperties() method, which is always called from the Web Connection framework before the first hit is processed.

Subclassing the wwRequest class

The wwRequest class is used to encapsulate the incoming request for each Web hit. Although it is suitable for subclassing, for most situations there is no reason to do so, because it already contains the basic functionality required to read information about the incoming request. Some examples of reasons to subclass this class include:

- If you install a third-party ISAPI filter that alters the information received by WC.DLL, you might need one or more methods to facilitate parsing out this additional information.

- If your developers are all trained in Active Server Page (ASP) technology, you might want to revise the Form method in Web Connection so that it can handle multiple-selection popups in the same manner as ASP (via repeated calls to the Form method, rather than using the Web Connection GetFormMultiple() method).

- If your application includes any forms that include file upload controls, the wwRequest class is missing two methods that are needed to allow more flexibility in those forms. If you have multiple-selection popups on the same form, Web Connection does not include a method for reading the popup values. There is also not a method for verifying a form variable's existence. Neither the GetFormMultiple() nor the IsFormVar() method works with "multi-part" forms, which are the type used when uploading files. Following is a subclass that includes the needed methods. The methods GetMultipartFormMultiple() and IsMultipartFormVar() can be used for multi-part forms in exactly the same way that their counterparts work for basic forms.

```
DEFINE CLASS WebRadRequest AS wwRequest
* Sub-class of Web Connection wwRequest.
* ----------------------------------------------------------- *
FUNCTION GetMultipartFormMultiple(taVars,tcVarName)
* Adapted by Randy Pearson from other methods in wwRequest class.
*
* This method retrieves multipart, multiselect HTML form variables
* from the request buffer into an array.
*
* Multipart form variables are submitted on the client side by
* specifiying an encoding type of "multipart/form-data":
```

```
* <form METHOD="POST" ENCTYPE="multipart/form-data">

* Parameters:
* @taVars
*  An array that will receive the form variables. Pass by reference!!
* tcVarname
*  The name of the form variable to retrieve.

* Returns:
*  Numeric - count variables retrieved into the array.

* Example:
* DIMENSION laVars[1]
* lnVars=Request.GetMultipartFormMultiple(@laVars,"LastName")
* ------------------------------------------------------ *
LOCAL xx, lcValue, lnAt, lcFind, lcPointer
xx=0
lcPointer = THIS.cFormVars
lcFind = [NAME="] + m.tcVarName + ["]
lnAt = ATC(m.lcFind, m.lcPointer)
IF m.lnAt = 0
   RETURN 0
ENDIF

* Following is required as of WC 3.20, which adds new handling of
* multi-part borders:
IF EMPTY(THIS.cMultiPartBorder)
   THIS.GetMultiPartBorder()
ENDIF

DO WHILE m.lnAt > 0
  lcValue = Extract( @lcPointer, ;
    tcVarName + ["] + CHR(13) + CHR(10) + CHR(13) + CHR(10), ;
    CHR(13) + CHR(10) + "--" + THIS.cMultipartBorder)
  * Before WC 3.20, was: **  CHR(13)+CHR(10)+"---------"
  xx = m.xx + 1
  DIMENSION taVars[ m.xx]
  taVars[ m.xx] = m.lcValue
  lcPointer = SUBSTR( m.lcPointer, m.lnAt + LEN( m.lcFind))
  lnAt = ATC( m.lcFind, m.lcPointer)
ENDDO

RETURN m.xx
ENDFUNC  && GetMultipartFormMultiple

* ------------------------------------------------------ *
FUNCTION IsMultipartFormvar()
* Created by Harold Chattaway.
* Determines whether a form variable name was part of
* the current request submittal.
LPARAMETER lckey
LOCAL lcMultiPart, lnLoc
lcMultiPart = THIS.cFormVars
lnLoc = ATC([NAME='] + m.lckey + ['], m.lcMultiPart)
IF m.lnLoc=0
  RETURN .F.
ELSE
  RETURN .T.
```

```
ENDIF
ENDFUNC   && IsMultipartFormvar
* ------------------------------------------------------------ *
ENDDEFINE   && WebRadRequest
```

Subclassing the wwResponse class

In the example already presented in this chapter, you have seen the mechanism for subclassing the wwResponse class to enhance the methods available for simplifying the creation of HTML output. This class is very suitable for subclassing, and many Web Connection developers do so. You should weigh these situations carefully. This is a lightweight class with good performance. If you were to burden the class with properties and methods to automate every aspect of HTML, this performance would suffer. On the other hand, additional methods can improve your development productivity.

You need to find a good balance here. I suggest using the default Web Connection class for your first few projects, and moving to subclassing only after becoming convinced of the need to improve your productivity. Another alternative is to create helper classes that are instantiated only when the need arises. The wwShowCursor and wwDbfPopup classes, which are provided with Web Connection, are examples of such classes.

Subclassing the wwProcess class

The wwProcess class is at the heart of your application. If you develop more than one application, you are bound to identify ways that you want to extend this class to suit your own style and requirements. I have found almost limitless possibilities in this area. Just a few of these ideas are presented in the section "Extending the wwProcess class" later in this chapter.

Subclassing the wwSession class

The wwSession class provides a convenient tool for managing state in Web Connection applications. Chapter 13, "Identifying Users and Managing Session Data," presents this class in detail. Although the class can be subclassed, doing so is not simple, particularly if you want to support moving the session data to SQL Server using the wwSessionSQL class. Furthermore, the potential reasons for doing so are relatively minor.

The most frequent reason I have identified is when you have a session variable that you need to reference in most if not all of your process methods. Session variable names and values are stored in XML format in the Vars memo field of wwSession.DBF, which must be parsed to read the value. You could improve the performance of the Session object in this case by adding a field to the data structure that is specific to this session variable, thus allowing its value to be read directly, rather than by parsing through the Vars field. However, in order to use this technique, you must still create a method for storing data to and reading data from that field. It does not happen automatically. Nevertheless, one look through the source code for these classes will probably convince you not to implement such a change. There are several monolithic methods that embed the entire data structure in such a way that you would be forced to copy and paste the entire methods into your subclass for the purpose of addressing the one or two additional fields that you want to add. This would put you in a precarious position each time a new version of Web Connection is released.

Subclassing the wwHtmlHeader class

The wwHtmlHeader class in an optional class that provides an easy way to encapsulate the otherwise manual process of creating the detailed <head> section of an HTML response. This class already contains convenient methods for adding JavaScript, cascading style sheets (CSS) links, and some other frequent needs. It does not, however, encapsulate everything you might want to include in this section. Although you can address any further needs via the built-in AddMetaTag() method, or by addressing the *cHeadSection* property directly, these require that you know the often arcane syntax of the items that can be placed in this section of an HTML document. In addition, the AddMetaTag() method covers only the use of the *name* attribute in <meta> tags, while there are also needs to use the *http-equiv* attribute in some cases (such as adding content rating information). As you might be guessing, I find this a ripe area for subclassing.

Here is a simple subclass that adds some further functionality to this class:

```
#INCLUDE WCONNECT.H
DEFINE CLASS MyHtmlHeader AS wwHtmlHeader

* ------------------------------------------------------------ *
FUNCTION AddMetaEquivTag
* Adds a META tag to the header.
LPARAMETERS lcEquiv, lcValue
THIS.cHeadSection = THIS.cHeadSection + ;
  [<meta http-equiv="] + m.lcEquiv + [" content="] + ;
  m.lcValue + ["">] + CRLF
ENDFUNC   && AddMetaEquivTag

* ------------------------------------------------------------ *
FUNCTION AddKeywords
* Adds keywords to the header for indexing information.
LPARAMETERS lcKey
THIS.AddMetaTag( "keywords", m.lcKey )
ENDFUNC   && AddKeywords

* ------------------------------------------------------------ *
ENDDEFINE   && Class MyHtmlHeader
```

Your new class can easily be tested from the Command Window. The following shows some of the new functionality combined with some of the built-in framework functionality:

```
SET PROCEDURE TO MyHtmlHeader ADDITIVE
SET PROCEDURE TO wwHttpHeader ADDITIVE   && includes wwHtmlHeader
loHead = CREATE( "MyHtmlHeader" )
loHead.AddTitle( "My Special Web Page" )
loHead.AddStyleSheet( "styles/myAppStyle.css" )
loHead.AddKeywords( "widgets, cheap, best" )
? loHead.GetOutput()
```

The output produced is as follows:

```
<html>
<head>
<title>My Special Web Page</title>
<link rel="stylesheet" type="text/css" href="styles/myAppStyle.css">
```

```
<meta name="keywords" content="widgets, cheap, best">
</head>
<body>
```

Finally, I should note that you do not need to invoke the familiar technique of altering a define constant in order to implement this subclass. This is because the wwHtmlHeader class is an optional class for your own use and is never invoked directly by the Web Connection framework. Thus all you need to do is make certain that you instantiate your subclass rather than the framework class.

Subclassing the wwShowCursor class

The wwShowCursor class is a RAD tool that can be used to quickly convert a Visual FoxPro cursor to an HTML table with one row for each record in your cursor. This is a very handy tool for producing content with almost no code during the early stages of development in your applications. However, in many cases developers end up wanting more control over final appearance than the wwShowCursor class allows. There have been several questions posted on the West Wind support forums about the possibility of creating a subclass in order to gain this control.

Unfortunately, attempting to create such a subclass is not practical in most cases. An examination of the source code for wwShowCursor reveals a few monolithic methods that produce the bulk of the work for this class with very little use of customizable properties or hooks for added functionality. The only way to add control over the formatting would be to completely override the huge ShowCursor() method, and probably the BuildFieldListHeader() and ShowRecord() methods as well. Before undertaking this task, you should carefully evaluate either creating your own class from scratch, or hand-coding SCAN loops to generate your tables. This latter approach is more labor-intensive, but provides you with total control over the appearance of your application, which can be essential when those change requests are made.

The zero-maintenance subclass

You have now seen both the approach for creating subclasses and some of the candidate classes that can be altered to suit your needs. One point to remember is that there is some maintenance involved in using your own framework extensions. Always consider that there may be one other option: If your need is sufficiently generic that other Web Connection developers would also benefit from its inclusion, consider making a suggestion to West Wind Technologies that the framework itself be modified. Over the years I have recommended dozens of improvements to the Web Connection framework, many of which have been adopted. The best subclass is no subclass at all.

Extending the wwProcess class

As I discussed earlier, the wwProcess class is a great candidate for subclassing. Why is this? The Process object is at the heart of your application. It is a point of orchestration (or mediation) between the incoming request and the outgoing response. It is where you perform between 70 and 90 percent of your work (depending, for example, on whether you have separate business classes). There should be little surprise then that many opportunities to extend the framework are created at this point.

In this section I will present two extensions that could be used in any Web Connection application. The first is a Web-based assertion mechanism that can be very convenient for streamlining your development process. The second is a Web-based substitute for the ubiquitous MESSAGEBOX() function in Visual FoxPro. In each of these examples, the overriding design requirement is to simplify the coding for the Web Connection developer who uses these methods. In other words, these are ideal framework methods.

A Web-based assertion mechanism

The wwProcess class has a very convenient method to handle aborting out of one of your methods if a problem is identified. This method is called ErrorMsg(). It provides two services:

1. It aborts the current page, discards any content that has been generated up to that point, and ensures that no further output is sent to the user.

2. In place of the expected response, it displays a Web page back to the user with a description of the error or other condition that occurred. When deployed by the developer, this message can contain customized content explaining the situation.

A typical hypothetical example of how you might deploy this method would be:

```
IF NOT User.IsAdmin()
   THIS.ErrorMsg( "System Message", ;
     "Only administrators can perform this function." )
   RETURN .T.
ENDIF
.. remainder of processing code
```

As this example suggests, you might use this function frequently for security checks, to handle error conditions, and so forth. In fact, the Error() method of wwProcess calls the ErrorMsg() method to display a page to the user if an unhandled error occurs in your application.

What more could you ask than this? Well, first of all, you have already written four lines of code, and all you have accomplished is to advise the user of the error condition. It is very likely that, in this type of example, triggering this message is indicative of either a logic failure (this user should never have had a link to this page in the first place) or perhaps a hack attempt on your Web site. In either case, you definitely want to take other action. At minimum, you would want to log the event, but more likely you would want to alert a system administrator immediately, probably via email. Fortunately, there is the SendErrorEmail() method available to handle this situation. Thus you can alter your code as follows:

```
IF NOT User.IsAdmin()
   THIS.SendErrorEmail( "Invalid Access", ;
     "A non-administrator attempted to gain access to this page!" )[1]
   THIS.ErrorMsg( "System Message", ;
     "Only administrators can perform this function." )
```

---

[1] This code assumes you are already connected to your mail server. If your development machine requires a dial-up connection and you are not already connected, you'll need a command like wwipstuff.rasdial to establish a connection before this command.

```
   RETURN .T.
ENDIF
.. remainder of processing code
```

This is fine, but now you have a reasonable chunk of code to handle just one, possibly unlikely, scenario that you need to check. Web development presents countless needs to perform checks like this, given the stateless nature of the Web, sophisticated hacker tools, and so forth. The more code you have to write to check for conditions that may seem unlikely or impossible, the less likely you are to implement the checks. If you get lazy about performing such checks, you will be sorry in the long run. What is needed is a more convenient way for the developer to perform checks like the one shown previously.

When I tackled this need, I decided to create the programmatic interface that would do the best job and then develop the implementation to make that interface work. The solution is patterned after the Visual FoxPro assertion technique, wherein you can simply insert a single line in your code, such as:

```
ASSERT <condition>, <message>
```

What you do here is assert that a condition is true, and if not, display the message. If the condition is true, processing continues with the next line of code. If not, the program aborts with the message shown. This is not precisely what you want in your Web applications, but it is very close. It is not acceptable to be providing failure messages on the server or to quit the application, but you do want to stop further processing of the current page, and you do want to display a message back to the user. Thus, I decided that in the simplest form the developer should be able to enter a line of code like this:

```
THIS.Assert( <condition>, <message> )
```

In this simple form, if the condition is not true, a simple Web page should be returned to the user displaying the message, *and further processing of the page should be aborted*. The second factor is very important, because once you have identified an invalid condition of this nature, you want to ensure that this user does not perform the indicated task.

First, I will show a method that can be added to the wwProcess class to support this basic interface. After introducing that class, I will add some optional parameters to handle some interesting variations. Here is the first revision of the new method:

```
DEFINE CLASS MyProcess AS wwProcess
FUNCTION Assert( llCondition, lcMessage )
IF VARTYPE( m.llCondition) <> "L" OR NOT m.llCondition
   * assertion failed!
   THIS.ErrorMsg( "Assertion Failure", m.lcMessage )
   RETURN TO Process
ENDIF
ENDFUNC && Assert
ENDDEFINE   && CLASS MyProcess
```

This is all it takes to add the basic mechanism. Note the RETURN TO line, which aborts any possible further processing of your own method and returns to the point from which your method was called.

To test this, you need to install this subclass as described at the beginning of the chapter. This includes adding the following line to your main program right after the line "DO Wconnect":

```
SET PROCEDURE TO MyProcess ADDITIVE
```

Next, you need to make sure your class is recognized and used. Either choose a method in one of your current Web Connection applications (such as the "Hello World" method in the example application). At the top of the program file that includes this method, add these lines:

```
#UNDEF  WWC_PROCESS
#DEFINE WWC_PROCESS      MyProcess
```

Now you are able to test this basic mechanism. Open one of your Process methods and insert a line of code such as the second line of code here:

```
FUNCTION HelloWorld
THIS.Assert( CDOW(DATE()) = "Friday", "Page can only be shown on Fridays!")
*...remainder of method
```

Now fire up your browser and navigate to the page in question. For this example, I used the basic "Hello World" example that is provided with Web Connection. The result is shown in **Figure 2**.

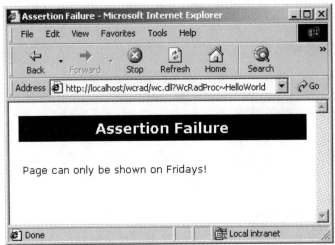

Figure 2. Users get a blunt message when they don't belong here.

You can probably see the advantage in using this function: Because it aborts from your method when the assertion fails, you need only enter a single line of code to check a critical condition and keep the user out if that condition is not met. I will often have five or more calls to the Assert() method near the beginning of most of my methods. Would I be so meticulous if each of these checks required several lines of code? Probably not!

I will now finish up the presentation of the assertion mechanism by adding three more features to enhance its power and flexibility:

- Notice that the result page in Figure 2 does not provide the user with any place to go. The method needs an optional URL parameter that, if provided, causes a hyperlink to display after the message.

- There needs to be a flag to control whether the assertion failure is sufficiently serious to require the generation of an email notice to the system administrator.

- There needs to be the ability for additional information to be provided to the system administrator that would not be appropriate to display to the user (typically for security reasons).

Here is the final Assert method, shown within the class definition:

```
DEFINE CLASS MyProcess AS wwProcess
FUNCTION Assert
LPARAMETERS llCondition, lcMessage, lcUrl, llEmail, lcExtraInfo
IF VARTYPE( m.llCondition) <> "L" OR ;
  NOT m.llCondition  && assertion failed!
  *
  IF m.llEmail  && send alert message to admin
    THIS.SendErrorEmail( "Assertion Failure", ;
      "Message Presented: " + m.lcMessage + ;
      IIF( EMPTY( m.lcExtraInfo), "", CHR(13) + CHR(10) + ;
      "Additional Info: " + m.lcExtraInfo ))
  ENDIF
  THIS.ErrorMsg( "Assertion Failure", m.lcMessage + ;
    IIF( EMPTY( m.lcUrl), "", [<BR><H3 ALIGN=CENTER><A HREF="] + ;
    m.lcUrl + [">OK</A></H3>] ))
  RETURN TO Process
ENDIF
ENDFUNC && Assert
ENDDEFINE  && CLASS MyProcess
```

There are plenty of ways to enhance this function and improve the displayed appearance. Then again, the messages should be displayed only when something goes wrong, so it does not need to be the flashiest part of your Web site! I am certain you can make extensive use of this method in your applications.

A Web-based MESSAGEBOX function

One area that every desktop application developer finds to be missing when they first start developing Web applications is the easy ability to interact with the user in a granular fashion by using functions such as the ubiquitous MESSAGEBOX() in Visual FoxPro. Although you can use the JavaScript alert and confirm functions to produce modal dialogs on the client system, these are seldom adequate substitutes for server-side needs. In addition, some browsers do not support JavaScript, while others allow the user to disable script languages for security reasons.

Consider a simple example where the user can click a "Delete" hyperlink in order to delete a customer record from the database. Suppose that you are not willing to delete a record this important without receiving confirmation. As a seasoned desktop developer, you might be tempted to include this code in your Process method:

```
lnConfirm = MESSAGEBOX("Delete this customer?", MB_YESNO, "Confirm")
```

The result of this would be a modal dialog appearing *on the server* waiting for a non-existent user to answer the question. This is equivalent to crashing your application, probably not your intention. What you need is a technique for posing this question to the client and processing the answer that the client provides back on the server. First, I will show how to ask a question in a specific case, and then I will generalize the approach for use in the framework.

For this example, suppose you are creating a DeleteCustomer() method wherein the ID of the customer to be deleted is passed as a URL parameter. In order to determine whether the user has confirmed his or her intention to delete the record, an additional URL parameter will be used. The technique will be to examine the URL and see whether there is evidence that the question has been answered. If so, the record will be deleted or not, depending on the answer. If there is not an answer, it means the question has not yet been asked, so you stop and ask the question, and defer any decision until the next hit from the current user.

The code presented here uses the named constants that are typically used with the MESSAGEBOX() function. Before implementing the actual code, you need to ensure that these constants are defined. The following definitions are best placed in your WCONNECT_OVERRIDE.H file, or equivalent; however, for this example it will suffice to place them at the top of the current process program file.

```
*-- MessageBox parameters
#DEFINE MB_OK                    0        && OK button only
#DEFINE MB_OKCANCEL              1        && OK and Cancel buttons
#DEFINE MB_ABORTRETRYIGNORE      2        && Abort, Retry, and Ignore buttons
#DEFINE MB_YESNOCANCEL           3        && Yes, No, and Cancel buttons
#DEFINE MB_YESNO                 4        && Yes and No buttons
#DEFINE MB_RETRYCANCEL           5        && Retry and Cancel buttons

#DEFINE MB_ICONSTOP              16       && Critical message
#DEFINE MB_ICONQUESTION          32       && Warning query
#DEFINE MB_ICONEXCLAMATION       48       && Warning message
#DEFINE MB_ICONINFORMATION       64       && Information message

*-- MsgBox return values
#DEFINE IDOK          1        && OK button pressed
#DEFINE IDCANCEL      2        && Cancel button pressed
#DEFINE IDABORT       3        && Abort button pressed
#DEFINE IDRETRY       4        && Retry button pressed
#DEFINE IDIGNORE      5        && Ignore button pressed
#DEFINE IDYES         6        && Yes button pressed
#DEFINE IDNO          7        && No button pressed
```

Now insert the following DeleteCustomer() method in your process program (for example, MyDemoProcess.PRG):

```
FUNCTION DeleteCustomer
LOCAL lnCust, lnAnswer, lcUrl
lnCust = INT( VAL( Request.QueryString( 'CustId')))
IF m.lnCust <= 0
```

```
    THIS.ErrorMsg( "No customer specified!" )
    RETURN
ENDIF
* [Code to confirm valid customer ID would go here.]
lnAnswer = INT( VAL( Request.QueryString( 'MsgBox')))
lcUrl = Request.GetCurrentUrl()
DO CASE
CASE m.lnAnswer = IDYES  && user said yes
   * [Actual code to delete the customer would go here.]
   THIS.StandardPage( "You have deleted customer #" + ;
     TRANSFORM( m.lnCust))
CASE m.lnAnswer = IDNO    && user said no
   THIS.StandardPage( "You elected <b>not</b> to delete customer #" + ;
     TRANSFORM( m.lnCust))
OTHERWISE
   THIS.StandardPage( "Confirm Customer Deletion", ;
     "Do you really want to delete customer #" + ;
     TRANSFORM( m.lnCust) + "?<P><P ALIGN=CENTER>" + ;
     [<A HREF="] + m.lcUrl + [&MsgBox=] + TRANSFORM( IDYES) + [">] + ;
     '<B><LARGE>[Yes]</LARGE></B></A>' + [  ] + ;
     [<A HREF="] + m.lcUrl + [&MsgBox=] + TRANSFORM( IDNO) + [">] + ;
     '<B><LARGE>[No]</LARGE></B></A>' + [</P>] )
ENDCASE
ENDFUNC  && DeleteCustomer
```

To see this code in action, navigate your browser to access the DeleteCustomer() method. You can do this by first navigating to the HelloWorld method and then manually changing the URL. In my case, the virtual directory is /wcrad and the class name is WcRadProc, so the complete local URL is:

```
http://localhost/wcrad/wc.dll?WcRadProc~DeleteCustomer
```

If you enter that URL by itself, you will trigger the "no customer specified" error message. Bypass that validation check by appending a hypothetical customer ID to the URL:

```
http://localhost/wcrad/wc.dll?WcRadProc~DeleteCustomer~&custid=2
```

Your code now verifies that a customer has been specified, but that no answer has yet been provided to a confirmation question. Therefore, as depicted in **Figure 3**, the user is asked to confirm the deletion.

If the user clicks the Yes hyperlink, pay careful attention to what transpires. The URL that corresponds to this hyperlink is identical to the previous one, except for the addition of &MsgBox=6 at the end. In other words, the hit will again be processed by the same DeleteCustomer() method, but in this case one more variable—the answer to the confirmation question—will be included in the query string. If you follow the code for this case, you should not be surprised that the result of the client clicking Yes is the confirming result page shown in **Figure 4**. In a real application, of course, you would also include the code that performs the customer deletion.

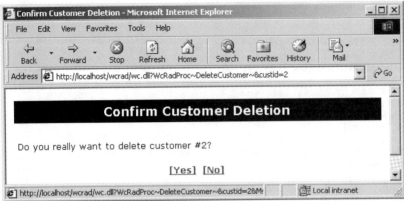

***Figure 3.** A confirming question is presented before performing a critical action.*

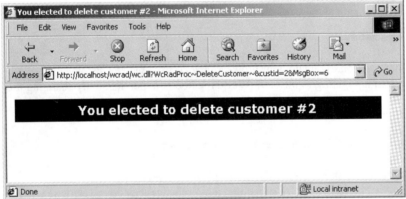

***Figure 4.** A confirming message provides feedback that the task was completed.*

One other important aspect of the DeleteCustomer() method is the manner in which the URLs for the Yes and No hyperlinks were constructed. Rather than building the URLs manually, the GetCurrentUrl() method of the Request object was used, and we simply appended a parameter to the query string. Because of this, our code does not explicitly reference the current class or method name, and is therefore much more suitable for reuse.

Although the approach shown previously is fairly simple, there are some shortcomings. First, although the additional code to produce the confirmation question is brief, it is still not nearly as simple as a call to MESSAGEBOX. Second, the style and layout of the HTML confirmation page is embedded in the code. If your application included a large number of these confirmations, you would need to manually ensure the consistency of each one, which can be an onerous task if a global change to the appearance is requested. A more generic solution is needed.

As with the assertion mechanism presented earlier, I will start with the interface. The goal is to produce a method that is as similar as possible to the desktop usage of MESSAGEBOX. A typical use of the method might look like:

```
IF THIS.MessageBox( <question>, MB_YESNO) = IDYES
 * do Yes stuff
ELSE
  * do No stuff
ENDIF
```

Notice that the only difference would be to use THIS.MessageBox() in place of MESSAGEBOX(). Achieving this result would greatly simplify application coding, and would be a particular benefit to developers used to coding for desktop applications. The trick is to make it happen. After studying the code in the DeleteCustomer() method shown earlier, you may have concluded that this goal is not possible in a Web application. After all, the preceding snippet does not appear to cover the case where the question has not been asked yet. In other words, it appears to presume that either a Yes or a No answer is forthcoming. As you will see, you can indeed achieve the desired result.

The secret is in using the same mechanism that the framework ErrorMsg method (and our new Assert method) uses, which is the ability to abort page processing, if needed. In this case, if no answer is available in the URL, the page processing will be aborted and the question will be presented in place of the result page. When the user then clicks on one of the allowed answers, your same method will be triggered again, except that this time there will be an answer ready to use in your decision tree. Following is the first working version of a subclass of wwProcess that can support this approach:

```
DEFINE CLASS MyProcess AS wwProcess
* ---------------------------------------------------------- *
FUNCTION MessageBox( lcMessage, lnType, lcTitle)
*
* Web approximation to MESSAGEBOX() function.
LOCAL lcAnswer, lnAnswer, lnDialog, lnIcon
lcAnswer = Request.QueryString( "MBAnswer")
IF NOT EMPTY( m.lcAnswer)
   * Pop and restore any previous form vars.
   Request.cFormVars = Session.GetSessionVar( "PreviousFormVars")
ENDIF
lnAnswer = INT( VAL( m.lcAnswer))
lnDialog = BITAND( m.lnType, 15)
lnIcon = m.lnType - m.lnDialog
DO CASE
CASE m.lnAnswer <= 0
   * No answer yet.
CASE m.lnDialog = MB_YESNO AND INLIST( m.lnAnswer, IDYES, IDNO)
   * Valid answer to YES-NO question.
   RETURN m.lnAnswer
CASE m.lnDialog = MB_OK AND INLIST( m.lnAnswer, IDOK)
   * Valid answer to OK dialog.
   RETURN m.lnAnswer
* [Additional CASE's removed for brevity.]
ENDCASE

* Save any form vars while we ask the question:
Session.SetSessionVar("PreviousFormVars", Request.cFormVars)

LOCAL lcMsg, lcBtn, lcUrl
lcUrl = Request.GetCurrentUrl() + "&MBAnswer="
IF VARTYPE( m.lcMessage) = "C"
```

```
   lcMsg = m.lcMessage
ELSE
   lcMsg = ""
ENDIF
lcBtn = ""
IF INLIST( m.lnDialog, MB_OK, MB_OKCANCEL)
   lcBtn = m.lcBtn + [ ] + [<A HREF="] + m.lcUrl + ;
     TRANSFORM( IDOK) + [">OK</A>]
ENDIF
IF INLIST( m.lnDialog, MB_YESNOCANCEL, MB_YESNO )
   lcBtn = m.lcBtn + [ ] + [<A HREF="] + m.lcUrl + ;
     TRANSFORM( IDYES) + [">Yes</A>]
ENDIF
IF INLIST( m.lnDialog, MB_YESNOCANCEL, MB_YESNO )
   lcBtn = m.lcBtn + [ ] + [<A HREF="] + m.lcUrl + ;
     TRANSFORM( IDNO) + [">No</A>]
ENDIF
IF EMPTY( m.lcTitle)
   lcTitle = "System Message"
ENDIF
THIS.StandardPage( m.lcTitle, ;
   m.lcMsg + [<P ALIGN=CENTER><B><FONT SIZE=3>] + m.lcBtn + ;
   [</FONT></B>] )
RETURN TO Process
ENDFUNC   && MessageBox
* ------------------------------------------------------- *
ENDDEFINE   && CLASS MyProcess
```

This class achieves our basic result, but there is still some work to do. First, I have included only a few of the standard dialog types. The complete version should include support for all types, including Abort-Retry-Ignore, and so forth. These are trivial extensions of the previous code and are omitted here to save space. The source code for this chapter, available at **www.hentzenwerke.com**, contains the full version.

This method also addresses one serious problem that I have not yet discussed. It considers the possibility of an HTML form submission. If we abort processing the page to ask a question, any form variables that were posted with the original request would be lost. This is clearly not acceptable. One solution would be to limit the use of our new MessageBox() method to only GET requests, and exclude POST requests. This would be too severe a restriction, because confirmation dialogs are often needed in response to form submissions. Instead, the solution is to employ the Session object to save the previous form variables while the question is being answered, and to restore the form variables afterward. This requires that you make sure you've added This.InitSession() to your Process method, or the Session variable won't be initialized.

Partitioning large applications

The first thing you will discover when you develop a Web Connection application is that the process program file can become very large. Even with some of the editor enhancements incorporated into version 7 of Visual FoxPro, this can become unwieldy.

What I always recommend is to create an application-level subclass of wwProcess (or your own framework extension) and then create subclasses of that in separate implementation PRG files. You can place common methods in the application-level class. These common methods might include Process(), Login(), standard look-and-feel items, and so forth. Each of the other PRGs will have its class definition based on this common subclass rather than on WWC_PROCESS.

Be forewarned that if you use script mapping in your Web Connection applications, and you divide your application into two or more process PRG files, you will need to define a separate script map extension for each, because that is the discriminator used in the main program to decide which program to call for each method.

You may also consider adding *properties* to the application-level classes. As an example, if some methods require the user to be logged in and others do not, you could add an lLoginRequired property and then split your methods between PRGs based on this division. I don't use that particular division technique, instead preferring to divide my methods into PRGs based on common functionality or modules. In either case, this is a highly recommended approach. While it is particularly important for projects with multiple developers, it is even useful for large applications when only a single developer is involved.

As an example, consider an application where you can divide all of the Process methods into one of two "modules." When you adopt this approach, your code might be structured as follows:

```
 * MainProc.PRG - This is the application-level subclass.
DEFINE CLASS MainProc AS WWC_PROCESS
cNewProp1 = ''
cNewProp2 = ''
FUNCTION Process
...your code here...
= DODEFAULT()
ENDFUNC
FUNCTION Login
...
ENDFUNC
ENDDEFINE && MainProc

* ModuleA.PRG
* Generic WC code that instantiates class:
LPARAMETER loServer
LOCAL loProcess
loProcess = CREATEOBJECT( "ModuleA")
loProcess.Process()
RETURN
********************************
* Actual class definition:
DEFINE CLASS ModuleA AS MainProc   && inheritance
FUNCTION PageA1
ENDFUNC
FUNCTION PageA2
ENDFUNC
ENDEFINE

* ModuleB.PRG
etc...
```

To implement this approach, you first need to ensure that your MainProc class is available by including an appropriate SET PROCEDURE TO..ADDITIVE statement in the main program. Next you add one CASE for each module in the Process method of your main program. For example:

```
CASE lcParameter == "MODULEA"
  DO ModuleA WITH THIS

CASE lcParameter == "MODULEB"
  DO ModuleB WITH THIS
* etc.
```

This is but one possible strategy for splitting up larger applications. Others have been discussed on the West Wind message board. You should consider your situation and your development environment carefully when choosing any such strategy.

Creating your own framework classes and tools

This chapter has endeavored to show you where and how the Web Connection framework can be extended. Sometimes you will need something additional, but none of the framework classes appear to be the right home for the required functionality. In this case, you may decide to purchase a third-party product, or to develop your own classes. In most instances it is easy to integrate new components with Web Connection.

If you design your own components, make sure you can test them as easily as possible. It is very inefficient to debug components that can run only within a complete, running Visual FoxPro application, and this is even more so for Web applications. My initial goal when designing any new class is *to be able to test it from the Command Window*. This may sound ambitious or even impossible, but it doesn't have to be that way. If you think outside the box a little bit and use a little creativity, you can usually meet this goal.

Web Connection also gives you some handy tools that allow you to test your designs more easily, such as from the Command Window. Browsing through the wwUtils.PRG file will often reveal something you had not used before. My favorite time saver is the ShowHtml() function, which is great for testing any component that generates either HTML or XML. All you do is pass any HTML as a string and this function calls up your default user agent (browser) and displays the result. If Microsoft Internet Explorer is your browser of choice, this works particularly well, because this browser is very flexible in what it will render. For example, because Microsoft Internet Explorer does not even require a <body> tag, or even an <html> tag, you can just pass little snippets of HTML and see how a browser would render it. You can see this function in action from the Visual FoxPro Command Window:

```
SET PROCEDURE TO wwUtils ADDITIVE  && pre-requisite
ShowHtml( [Two different browsers are often like <ul>]+;
  [<li>apples and<li>oranges.</ul>] )
```

I don't think you could ask for anything much easier than that!

The second important issue is how to install your classes so they are accessible when needed in your application. Typically, all that is required is one of these commands, depending on whether you use the code editor or the visual tools:

```
SET PROCEDURE TO <PRG_File_Name> ADDITIVE
SET CLASSLIB TO <VCX_File_Name> ADDITIVE
```

In almost all cases the best place to insert this code is in the main program, immediately after the line "DO Wconnect".

Leveraging existing code

When developing Web applications with Web Connection, you may encounter situations where there is an existing desktop application with its own large code base. Even though Web applications work quite differently, there may be strong incentives to reuse as much of the existing code base as possible.

Although there are countless possible variations to this situation, there are a few general areas worth covering:

- Making use of your application object class

- Integrating business objects

- Using FPD/FPW legacy code and data

Where does my application object go?

Many Visual FoxPro developers use either third-party frameworks or their own code that makes use of a master application object. This object is assigned to a public variable (or private variable created in the main program) with a name such as goApp. This object offers various services and performs actions that hold the entire application together. Further, many other modules in the application refer to the application object using the global variable name. When developing a Web application, developers often ask where their application object fits in.

First, you should be aware that you are not required to have an application object at all. Web applications work very differently from desktop applications. Each hit to your Web application is likely to come from a different user from the previous hit, so your application cannot simply log one user in and assume nothing changes until a subsequent logout. You are also not creating an application menu, toolbar, forms manager, or any of several other items that are unique to the desktop and not applicable to a Web application.

Second, your application must avoid all user interface (UI) code, such as message boxes and other dialogs that might pop up in the Visual FoxPro application. Your code must run unattended on the Web server. Thus, you must hunt down and eliminate any such code, possibly replacing it in a subclass with a Web-friendly approach. The less monolithic the application, the easier this task should be. Classic n-tier application components often can fit in quite easily. One technique for trapping any UI code is to insert a SYS(2335,0) statement in the SetServerEnvironment() method in your main Web Connection program. This causes any statements that would otherwise generate UI to instead trigger an error. You can use this technique only if you do not want to display the Web Connection server status form.

Those considerations aside, you may still want to use an application object. If you have an application class that is sufficiently flexible to exist in the stateless world of a Web application, and it provides services that would be helpful to your application, by all means use it. Most likely you will need to re-architect it for Web use, or design a Web-specific subclass. The question becomes where to instantiate it within the Web Connection framework.

In order to avoid having the application object be instantiated and destroyed on every hit, which could be very bad for performance, you need to create it from the Server object. Here I will consider a hypothetical class that includes a special method called BeforeProcess() that you have designed for Web use that adjusts the object to the changing user identity. What you could do is add a property oApplication to the server class in your main program. Then, in the SetServerProperties() method, add this line:

```
THIS.oApplication = CREATEOBJECT( "MyApplicationClass")
```

You now have an object that can be referenced by Server.oApplication, but when you are processing each hit you might prefer to refer to this object by the familiar goApp variable name. This may even be a requirement if you are calling other functions or classes that already refer to this variable. Further, you need to ensure that your clever new method has been called before the hit is processed. To accomplish this, you could add something like the following code to the Process method of your process class:

```
PRIVATE goApp
goApp = Server.oApplication
goApp.BeforeProcess()
DODEFAULT()
```

This is deliberately vague and is based on a hypothetical application class. You must analyze your own situation to determine whether you have this need, and whether your application class is sufficiently flexible for Web use. The purpose of the preceding discussion is to point you in the right direction when you are trying to determine how to plug such an object into your Web Connection application.

Integrating business objects into Web Connection applications

Business objects are very suitable for Web Connection applications. The Process object in the Web Connection framework is where incoming requests are analyzed and responses are generated. This is also the point at which you would deploy business objects.

A design goal should be to avoid any direct data manipulation in your Process object. Instead, you should deploy business objects to accomplish the same results. The design and use of business objects is beyond the scope of this book, but an example of how they might be deployed in a Web Connection Process method could be useful. Consider first this fragment of code, which uses direct data manipulation:

```
FUNCTION SaveOrder()
*
IF !USED('Orders')
  USE Orders IN 0
ENDIF
SELECT Orders
SET ORDER TO cOrderID
LOCAL lcOrderID
lcOrderID = Request.Form("OrderID")
IF NOT SEEK(lcOrderID)
  THIS.StandardPage ( 'Order not found!')
  RETURN
```

```
ENDIF
IF Request.Form('Amount') > Customer.MaxOrder
  THIS.StandardPage( 'Exceeded limit.')
  RETURN
ENDIF
IF RLOCK()
  REPLACE …
* etc.
```

Notice the problems inherent in this approach. First, it performs all of its data access using Xbase code (USE, SET ORDER, SEEK, and so forth), which is fine if you use local Visual FoxPro tables, but leaves you with a nightmare if you decide to migrate the application data to Oracle or SQL Server. Also, the data manipulation code is mixed in with user interface code, thus preventing future scaling to an n-tier architecture. Finally, the business rules are intertwined with specifics of the Web application. If you also needed a desktop version of this application, you would need to repeat all of the business rules there, creating a maintenance nightmare.

Consider now the following code fragment, in which a hypothetical business object is included:

```
FUNCTION SaveOrder()
*
LOCAL loOrder, lcOrderID
loOrder = CREATEOBJECT( "BizOrder")
lcOrderID = Request.Form("OrderID")
IF NOT loOrder.FindRecord(m.lcOrderID)
  THIS.StandardPage ( 'Order not found!')
  RETURN
ENDIF
loOrder.Amount = Request.Form('Amount')
IF NOT loOrder.Validate()
  THIS.StandardPage( loOrder.cErrorMessage )
  RETURN
ENDIF
loOrder.SaveRecord()
* etc.
```

In this code, a lot of the work has been delegated to the BizOrder business object. There is no assumption that the data resides in any particular format. Business rules are assumed to be implemented in the business object. This process code is simply orchestrating the business object with the Request and Response objects to create the Web version of this functionality. There are two big advantages to this. First, if the data was migrated to Oracle or SQL Server, no changes would be required in your Web Connection application code. Any changes would be made in either the business object classes or in other classes that the business objects utilize (such as separate data access classes). Second, you could create a desktop application that uses the same business objects and be assured that all of the business rules would be consistent between the two applications.

Alternatives to designing your own business classes

Rather than designing your own business classes, there are two interesting alternatives. The first alternative is to use a commercial third-party Visual FoxPro framework in conjunction with Web Connection. If you already are familiar with one of these frameworks, you might want to investigate the suitability of its business class approach, if any, for use with Web Connection.

A second alternative, available starting with version 4 of Web Connection, is to use the wwBusiness class, which is provided with Web Connection as an optional utility class. wwBusiness is a light-weight class, which is more of a data access class than a true business class. In other words, its built-in methods are more oriented to the mechanics of reading and writing data from their sources, rather than providing a robust mechanism for enforcing business rules. Nevertheless, if you are looking for an easy object-oriented approach to data access that also allows easy migration from a Visual FoxPro to a SQL Server back end, this class could be worth investigating. Refer to the Web Connection Help documentation for detailed information on the use of this class.

West Wind also sells an add-on application that implements a Web-based store using Web Connection. This add-on uses the wwBusiness class for all of its data access. If you purchase this add-on, the source code can be very useful for learning one approach to integrating business objects.

When things go wrong

Although it is difficult to anticipate the specific problems that might occur, there are a few common difficulties that can arise.

Symptom: You get a Visual FoxPro "class definition not found" error.

Diagnosis: This can be one of two problems. The first is that you created a subclass but did not take the proper action to ensure that the class is available at run time. The simplest way to correct this is to insert a SET PROCEDURE TO <your class> ADDITIVE statement in your main program. This command can appear just after the DO WConnect line, which sets up the Web Connection framework classes. The second possibility is that you issued a SET PROCEDURE statement somewhere and failed to include the ADDITIVE clause. This causes all previously declared procedure files to be dropped.

Symptom: Your subclasses no longer work after upgrading to a new version of Web Connection.

Diagnosis: You have overwritten the previous copy of WCONNECT.H with the one from the new version, but failed to edit that file to contain the same #INCLUDE statement as before. See the previous section in this chapter, "Managing changes to #DEFINE constants in WCONNECT.H," for specific information on this topic.

Symptom: You created a subclass, but its methods are not being invoked.

Diagnosis: If the object is instantiated by your own code, check to be certain that you are instantiating your subclass rather than the default framework class. If the object is instantiated automatically by the framework, either you have not provided the proper override to the constant in WCONNECT.H, or you have not recompiled the framework classes since doing so. This problem is more common when testing from the Command Window (DO MainProg). Correct the problem by compiling all framework classes:

```
COMPILE CLASS \wconnect\classes\*.vcx
COMPILE \wconnect\classes\*.prg
```

There may also be other problems if, for example, the Web Connection console application is running (Console.EXE). This causes compile copies of classes to be loaded into memory, which may prevent new copies from loading. The following commands help clear the Visual FoxPro environment:

```
CLEAR ALL
CLOSE ALL
CLEAR PROG
SET CLASSLIB TO
```

If this still doesn't fix the problem, sometimes the only solution is to quit Visual FoxPro and start back up. Also, remember to test correctly from your browser. Often you may have to back up a few pages and refresh the content, or perhaps even start a fresh browser session, in order to have a clean scenario for testing your modifications.

Once you take the plunge and follow the path of extending the Web Connection framework, you also become more responsible for diagnosing problems that occur. Good troubleshooting skills are a must. See Chapter 18 for a general discussion of troubleshooting Web Connection applications. Also, remember that the West Wind support forums provide an opportunity to get help from other developers.

Chapter 17
The Mistakes We All Make

The world of Web applications is a complex one. There is plenty to learn, no matter what development tools you choose. Some mistakes are so common, they seem to be made by almost every Web Connection developer.

This chapter attempts to coalesce the most common problems and mistakes that the Web Connection developer will encounter. The criteria for an item being listed in this chapter are that it seems to surface over and over again for many developers, and that it is not specific to a bug or specific version of Web Connection.

The items have been divided into seven categories:

- Installation and setup

- Visual FoxPro development

- Problems specific to scripts and templates

- Operational issues

- COM and file-based messaging issues

- Debugging

- Email and client-side tools

Each item has three components: symptom, cause, and solution. For more complex items, you are often referred back to the chapter in this book in which the concepts are presented in detail.

Symptom: After installing a new version of Web Connection, my previous framework subclasses are no longer recognized.

Cause: You made changes to WCONNECT.H that have been overwritten by installing a new version.

Solution: This was a common issue prior to version 4 of Web Connection. Refer to Chapter 20, "Updating to New Web Connection Versions," and use the technique of placing all override information in a WCONNECT_OVERRIDE.H file.

Installation and setup problems

Getting started, either for the first time or after installing an update, can be a frustrating time. Chapters 1-4 cover the area of first-time installation. Chapter 20 addresses version updates. Following are some of the most frequent problems we have noticed.

Symptom: You still get the "shareware" message after purchasing and installing the full licensed copy of Web Connection.

Cause: Files unique to the shareware version still remain on disk.

Solution: The Web Connection installation package does not delete files unique to the shareware version. In this case, you must delete the WConnect.APP file. This is because of a line of code in your main program, DO wconnect. In the full version, this line should call the WConnect.PRG file; however, if the WConnect.APP file, which is unique to the shareware version, still exists, Visual FoxPro's priority rules will cause that to be executed instead.

Symptom: After installing a new version, previous changes you made to Web Connection default behavior are no longer recognized.

Cause: You had previously changed the Web Connection framework files directly, and now you have overwritten those changes.

Solution: Do not directly change the Web Connection framework. Instead, create subclasses, using the technique described in Chapter 16, "Extending the Framework."

Symptom: After installing a new version of Web Connection, your previous framework subclasses are no longer recognized.

Cause: You made changes to WCONNECT.H that have been overwritten by installing a new version.

Solution: This was a common issue prior to version 4 of Web Connection. Refer to Chapter 20, "Updating to New Web Connection Versions," and use the technique of placing all override information in a WCONNECT_OVERRIDE.H file.

Symptom: After installing a new version of Web Connection, your application no longer responds to Web requests.

Cause: You ran the Setup program after unzipping the new version, and selected a different value for at least one setting from what you had selected previously.

Solution: Determine which setting you changed and restore the correct value. A likely choice is the setting for the temporary file path. If you set this originally to something other than the Web Connection default, the Setup program does not realize that, and again proposes the default location. Refer to Chapter 20 for a complete discussion of updating to new versions of Web Connection.

Symptom: Your browser displays "Access denied" errors when trying to run the basic Web Connection sample application (or another application) for the first time.

Cause: Anonymous user does not have full access to the temporary directory.

Solution: Grant the anonymous user (iusr_<machinename>) full access to the application's temporary directory, as described in Chapter 3, "Installing, Configuring, and Testing Web Connection."

Visual FoxPro application problems

Problems in this category are those that occur within your code or when working to develop and test your application within the Visual FoxPro integrated development environment. Problems specifically related to use of scripts and templates, however, appear in a separate category.

Symptom: You encounter errors when trying to build a project using the shareware version of Web Connection.

Cause: Executables cannot be created using the shareware version.

Solution: Upgrade to the full version. Until this is possible, run your application from the Command Window (DO <mainprogram>).

Symptom: Some form variables are truncated, incorrect, or dropped.

Cause: Your form is using the GET method instead of the POST method of HTTP.

Solution: The GET method puts all the variables into the URL itself, and this is limited by specification. The proper technique for allowing large numbers of form variables is to use the POST method, which is attained via <form method="post">. Note that this change requires that you use the Form() method instead of the QueryString() method to read the posted variables.

Symptom: One user seems to get another user's results or to inherit another user's permissions or session settings.

Cause: You have used either public or application-wide private variables to record information specific to a single user's session.

Solution: It is important to understand the stateless nature of Web applications. Immediately after serving one user's request, your application must be immediately prepared for the next hit to come from a different user. Therefore, maintaining user information in application-wide variables is not viable. This is a dangerous practice, but it does not get exposed until you start testing an application with multiple simultaneous users. Refer to Chapter 10, "Getting in Tune: Overcoming Conceptual Hurdles," for an explanation of the stateless concept.

Symptom: You create a new project using the Web Connection Management Console, but cannot find your MyProcess.PRG file in the project after the wizard completes.

Cause: Due to file contentions, some files are not added by the wizard.

Solution: Close the Management Console and re-build the project from the VFP Project Manager. Your MyProcess.PRG file (and a few others, like CodeBlockClass.PRG) will be added.

Symptom: Your application works correctly on your development machine when you build and execute an EXE file, but it does not work correctly when you DO <main> from the Command Window.

Cause: The main program is located in a different folder than your project and EXE file.

Solution: Move the main program to the same folder as the project, even if all other source code is located elsewhere. The nature of how the Web Connection framework operates causes the startup path to be stored in the Registry. When running the main program as a PRG, the path of that file will be used, which will cause your application not to find the INI file, and numerous problems will occur that can be a nightmare to troubleshoot.

Script and template problems

These are problems unique to using Web Connection script and template technology.

Symptom: You put a Response.Write() statement in your template, but the result appears at the beginning of your output, rather than in its intended location.

Cause: Response.Write() is not supported in templates, only scripts.

Solution: To force output from a Visual FoxPro code block into the current response location, you must RETURN a string at the end of the code block. See Chapter 10 for information about the difference between scripts and templates.

Symptom: Expressions in scripts/templates don't appear to get evaluated.

Cause: You have SET EXACT ON somewhere in your application.

Solution: Not only script/template processing, but many framework classes will not work with this setting. I recommend never setting EXACT to ON. There are other techniques in almost all circumstances. If absolutely necessary, turn it OFF immediately following the line of code for which it is needed to be ON!

Symptom: When using templates or scripts, your custom HTTP header is ignored.

Cause: The ExpandScript() and ExpandTemplate() methods create their own headers, unless you explicitly pass one as a parameter.

Solution: Pass your header object as the second parameter to either method. If you are using the Web Connection default template handling technique, where you do not call ExpandTemplate() yourself, you may be able to include a Response.Clear() command within the template itself, followed by writing your own header, but this approach to Web Connection development is not recommended.

Symptom: You encounter variable not found and similar errors.

Cause: Variables are LOCAL instead of PRIVATE or are not declared early enough in the code.

Solution: Due to the interpreted, recursive nature of CodeBlock processing, variables need to be PRIVATE so they can be seen when recursive processing is performed for Visual FoxPro control structures (IF, SCAN, and so forth). Ensure that variables in code blocks are declared as PRIVATE (not LOCAL) and that the declaration appears prior to the beginning of control structures.

Operational problems

Operational problems include those associated with operating your Web Connection application on a Web server. This category excludes COM and file-based issues, which appear in their own category, later in this chapter.

Symptom: You are seeing the HTTP header appear in the browser (for example, text beginning with HTTP 1.1 200 OK).

Cause: You have sent two HTTP headers with your response.

Solution: Various framework header methods insert a complete header. These include Response.ContentTypeHeader(), Response.HTMLHeader(), Response.ExpandTemplate(), and Response.ExpandScript(). If you call another of these methods, or the same one a second time, the section that normally would not show becomes part of the displayed page.

Symptom: When using Windows 95 or Windows 98, your script maps do not work properly.

Cause: PWS does not have very good support of script maps. It often has problems when you have multiple mappings. Additionally, you need to reboot after adding the mappings.

Solution: Try removing any script maps you do not need and moving the ones you have created to the top of the list. Be certain you reboot the machine after making any script map changes in these operating systems. For this and other reasons, these operating systems do not tend to be good choices for Web application development.

Symptom: Cookies disappear or a new cookie is written on every hit.

Cause: There are two common causes for this: (1) Your code uses AddCookie() without regard to whether a cookie already exists on the client. (2) The client does not accept cookies.

Solution: For (1), review and correct your code. Consider using the InitSession() method instead of "rolling your own" cookie code. For (2), if you cannot convince the user to accept cookies for your site (most browsers allow this to be a site-by-site decision), you must either face the exclusion of a small fraction of the user base, or you could consider implementing a "license plate" approach. See Chapter 13, "Identifying Users and Managing Session Data," for a full discussion of user identification and state management.

Symptom: Cookies are not being received by users, leading to issues such as repetitive login forms and empty session variables.

Cause #1: You have attempted to combine HTTP redirection with the sending of cookies.

Solution: If you use HTTP redirection, via the Response.Redirect() method, you are replacing the standard HTTP header, which includes your cookie, with a special redirection header. If you do this, your cookie is never sent. Thus it is essential to avoid trying to redirect and send a cookie in the same response. This is a very common problem that arises on the West Wind support forums. (Note that if you construct the <head> section of your response manually, you can achieve an effect similar to redirection, while still preserving cookies, by including a <meta> tag with the http-equiv attribute setting of "refresh." Refer to an HTML reference for more information on this subject.)

Cause #2: Some users may have their browser set not to accept cookies. This is a possible cause only if the symptom is occurring for some users, but not others.

Solution: See the previous item for a discussion of users who do not accept cookies.

Symptom: Your clients keep getting a login form even after they have correctly entered their username and password.

Cause: The user's authentication is not being stored correctly or is expiring too early. Also, the client may have cookies turned off (even if you are using sessions, the client needs to accept the session ID cookie).

Solution: See the previous item.

Symptom: In response to hits, the client receives a "file download" dialog prompting them to download WC.DLL.

Cause: Execute Permissions have not been set correctly in IIS for the virtual directory.

Solution: Set Execute Permissions to either "scripts only" (if using script maps exclusively) or "scripts and executables" (if supporting URLs that include "wc.dll"). Note: This is a Web server setting, not a file system permission setting!

Symptom: Your application crashes intermittently with C0000005 errors.

Cause: Corrupt index or memo field.

Solution: Try to isolate the problem, either by examining log files to determine which table is the likely culprit, or by other methods. Fix the source of corruption. If all else fails, restore from a previous backup.

Symptom: After installing a certificate and switching your URLs to require HTTPS, your application does not receive hits.

Cause: IIS has not been set to listen on port 443 for HTTPS traffic.

Solution: HTTPS, using secure socket layers (SSL), typically operates on port 443, and this must be specified in the "Web Site" tab of the IIS properties for your site.

Symptom: No hits are processed. Browsers display a timeout message (such as "Cannot reach server" or the misleading "DNS Error") after a lengthy delay.

Cause: Temporary file path or template settings are mismatched between WC.INI and the application INI file.

Solution: Both Path and Template settings must match in order for file-based messaging to operate. See Chapter 11, "Managing Your Configuration," for complete details on proper configuration settings.

Symptom: Your browser is unable to connect to your application on a development machine, even though you have a local Web server installed.

Cause #1: TCP/IP is not loaded.

Solution: On development machines without network cards (such as notebook machines out of their docking stations), TCP/IP will not be loaded. The workaround, when adding a NIC bound with TCP/IP is not an option, is to attempt a dial-up (an actual connection is not even necessary) on a modem where TCP/IP is bound. This will load the TCP/IP stack.

Cause #2: You are running a version of Microsoft Internet Explorer that has a bug.

Solution: The original version of Internet Explorer 5.0 had a bug that would cause it to offer the choices of "Work offline" or "Try again" when going to Localhost if you did not have a connection to the Internet. Although selecting the unintuitive option of "Try again" works, this dialog is annoying. The problem can be avoided altogether by patching or upgrading Internet Explorer.

Symptom: The AdminUser setting is not honored after altering the setting in WC.INI.

Cause: WC.DLL will only allow users specified by in the AdminUser setting to make administrative changes. If you try to add yourself, you create a Catch-22 situation, which requires that you stop and restart IIS for the setting to be honored.

Solution: Modify the WC.INI file manually. Then stop and restart IIS, which causes WC.DLL to be unloaded from memory, and then reloaded, thus causing it to reread the WC.INI settings.

Symptom: The user gets a blank screen when a PDF file is returned.

Cause: Microsoft Internet Explorer compatibility issue.

Solution: Rather than returning the physical PDF directly, you can write the file to disk, and then return an HTML response with a link to the file. Alternatively, check whether current browsers still have this problem and, if not, recommend that users upgrade.

Symptom: Users are repeatedly prompted with an authentication dialog, and even after supplying a valid network user ID and password, cannot gain access to your application.

Cause: You have not enabled basic (or "plain text") authentication.

Solution: In order for your application to be able to ascertain the Windows user ID, using Request.GetAuthenticatedUser(), basic authentication must be enabled, at least for your virtual directory. See "Pros and cons of authentication" in Chapter 13, "Identifying Users and Managing Session Data," for more detail.

Symptom: Internet Information Server Management Console (MMC) locks up when trying to manage IIS settings with Web Connection COM servers running.

Cause: An undiagnosed bug, presumed to be attributable to either the IIS Admin interface or Visual FoxPro COM servers. Occurs only on Windows 2000 (not Windows NT).

Solution: Running the IIS Restart program (IISReset.EXE) resolves the problem. Refer to **www.west-wind.com/wiki/kb.wiki?wc~MMCLockingUpInCOMMode** for up-to-date information about this problem.

COM and file-based operational problems

The subject of COM vs. file-based operation is discussed at length in Chapter 14, "COM vs. File-Based Messaging." The following are some of the most frequently reported issues in this area.

Symptom: You receive COM invocation error messages in the browser while running in file-based mode.

Cause: Accidentally or otherwise, the setting in WC.INI has been changed to Mechanism=Automation.

Solution: Change the setting back to Mechanism=File. (See Chapter 11, "Managing Your Configuration," for the proper technique for making this change.) Also, if you are unaware of how this switch occurred, it is possible that you have not set your AdminUser setting in WC.INI to restrict access to administrative functions in WC.DLL.

Symptom: You encounter numerous Web server problems when running in COM mode, including error messages such as "The parameter is incorrect," "Access denied," and "COM object invocation error." Other problems include the inability to unload COM servers after they have been loaded.

Cause: A virtual directory is not set to "low" isolation mode.

Solution: Using IIS, set the application isolation level for each Web Connection virtual directory to "low." Chapter 8, "Configuring Server Software," discusses server software configuration in general. (Note: In IIS 4, instead you must ensure that "Run in a separate memory space" is not checked.)

Symptom: When running more than one instance of the server, problems are encountered and each instance has the same Windows process ID (as listed in the Task Manager or on the Web Connection status page).

Cause: The Visual FoxPro project was built with server instancing set to "Multi Use."

Solution: The executable must be built as "Single Use," which is not the Visual FoxPro default. In the project manager, change this setting on the Servers tab of the Project Information dialog. Then rebuild the executable, and try again.

Symptom: After switching to COM operation, your application behaves slightly differently, and seems to ignore environmental settings (such as SET commands) or other code that were respected in file-based mode.

Cause: You have placed important code at the beginning of your main program, in the initial code that precedes the first DEFINE CLASS statement.

Solution: In Visual FoxPro COM servers, "main procedure" code never executes. Instead, the "entry point" to your application is via the creation of an OLEPUBLIC object. To ensure that this code is executed, move it to the SetServerEnvironment() method of the server class in your main program. This code is executed only once, and before any Web hit is processed.

Symptom: Access denied problems are encountered when running in COM mode.

Cause: DCOM security and/or identity settings are not correct.

Solution: See Chapter 14, "COM vs. File-Based Messaging," for details on how to establish proper COM settings.

Symptom: You experience difficulty with COM operation after deploying a new version of your application that also incorporates a new version of Web Connection.

Cause: Mixed files from two different Web Connection versions.

Solution: Make certain that the latest version of WC.DLL was also deployed to your Web server. Trying to run a new application with an old version of WC.DLL can cause problems that are almost impossible to isolate. Refer to Chapter 20, "Updating to New Web Connection Versions," for a complete discussion of the proper procedures for deploying new versions of Web Connection.

Symptom: A "No such interface supported" error is returned when trying to launch the COM server.

Cause: You have set the Visual FoxPro COM server to run in unattended mode, and then attempted to display a user interface element, such as by setting ShowServerForm to On in the application INI file.

Solution: Attempting to force unattended mode via the Visual FoxPro SYS(2335,0) command is not recommended for Web Connection servers. If you must do so, try to localize the duration of unattended mode to process class implementation.

Debugging problems

The following are a few of the more common debugging problems. See Chapter 18, "Advanced Troubleshooting and Maintenance," for general debugging guidance.

Symptom: When you try to trace through code, you get "source not available" in many places. Mostly this happens when trying to trace through the Web Connection framework classes.

Cause: The source file and the compiled file of the library you are tracing through are not in synch.

Solution: Erase all .FXP files and recompile your app. If you use VCX classes, you may also need to recompile these. Further, you may need to issue the CLEAR PROGRAM and CLEAR ALL commands. See Chapter 12, "A Web Connection Application from Start to Finish," for details of installing a macro to perform these and other commands to reset the Visual FoxPro environment.

Symptom: After fixing a bug in your code, when you test the change, the old code seems to be used.

Cause: The function or class is still loaded into Visual FoxPro's memory.

Solution: Again, you need to reset the Visual FoxPro environment. See the previous item.

Symptom: After erasing all .FXP files, restoring the Visual FoxPro environment, and recompiling, you still cannot trace through certain libraries.

Cause: If you are launching VFP via the WC shortcut, certain files are loaded at startup via WCStart.PRG. One of them is Console.EXE, which contains several of the standard Web Connection class libraries. These libraries will stay in memory and will be used by your application.

Solution: Remove all old copies of Console.EXE and recompile the Console.PJX project.

Email and other IP tools problems

These problems are mostly associated with the use of the wwIpStuff classes, which are mostly used for client-side applications, but are also used for sending email from a server and for some server-to-server communications.

Symptom: HTML content in email messages is not rendered as HTML on the client.

Cause: Two common causes are: (1) not specifying the proper content-type for the message; or (2) the recipient's email client software does not support HTML content.

Solution: If (1), set the content type property (cContentType) of the wwIpStuff object to "text/html" prior to sending. If (2), encourage specific clients to upgrade their mail software, or else modify your application to allow a preference for plain text messages.

Symptom: Email messages are truncated.

Cause: The maximum length of email message line has been exceeded.

Solution: Many mail servers do not permit long lines of text in email messages. It is best, even when sending HTML content, for which it would not seem to matter, to convert paragraphs in email messages to individual lines not exceeding 70 characters per line. If email is central to your application, write your own function or class to handle formatting.

Symptom: Email messages are received by some recipients, but not others.

Cause: Recipient lists are too long.

Solution: Ensure that neither to "to" nor the "cc" field of any email message exceeds 1024 characters.

Symptom: Attempts to send email using wwIpStuff fail with one of various 500-series errors, including 553 (unauthorized host) and 572 (relay not allowed).

Cause: The mail server you are contacting does not accept anonymous posting from your host machine.

Solution: In an attempt to limit unsolicited commercial email (UCE, or "spam"), many email administrators block the use of the server for mail relay purposes. In some cases, they require authentication, which is not part of basic SMTP, and is not supported by wwIpStuff. Most mail servers, however, allow specific hosts to be accepted, so your best bet is to convince the mail administrator to add the IP address of your Web server to the list of accepted hosts. Another alternative is to run the local SMTP service that comes with IIS, and simply post messages to the local machine.

Symptom: Inexplicable bugs are encountered when using wwIpStuff, particularly after installing a new version.

Cause: You are using an old version of wwIpStuff.DLL that is not compatible with the latest Visual FoxPro code in wwIpStuff.VCX.

Solution: Deploy the latest copy of wwIpStuff.DLL to your application folder.

Chapter 18
Advanced Troubleshooting and Maintenance

Web applications can be more difficult to troubleshoot than desktop applications, because of the need to understand the role of the browser, Web server, and network, in addition to just your Visual FoxPro application. Although the Web Connection framework offers some assistance, as your applications progress, so will your need for better troubleshooting techniques.

Your entire application consists of not just a Visual FoxPro executable, but also the Web Connection DLL, the Web server, and other supporting components, such as scripts and images. As such, troubleshooting goes beyond the scope of basic Visual FoxPro error handling and debugging. Although these are both still important, other techniques are needed as well. This chapter looks as several areas where problems arise and presents approaches that have proven helpful for other developers.

Eliminating common mistakes

This chapter explores some advanced techniques for troubleshooting Web Connection applications. Many mistakes, however, are common ones that developers seem to make over and over again. The most frequent ones have been gathered and categorized in Chapter 17, "The Mistakes We All Make." You should review this chapter regularly.

Where to look when problems arise

When problems occur with your application, there are many places to look for evidence of the source of the problems.

If your application does not respond at all, or indicates an error, you have to consider several possibilities:

- The Web server itself may not be running. Confirm this by navigating to a static HTML page and verifying that it displays. As this page may be in the browser cache, be sure to refresh the page to be certain you are getting a current response from the Web server.

- The Web Connection DLL file may be missing or improperly configured. Rather than hitting your application, you can ask the DLL directly for its status using a URL such as http://yourdomain/wconnect/wc.dll?_maintain~ShowStatus. If properly set up, the DLL responds quickly with a formatted status page. (You may also examine the settings shown on this page for further hints of what else may be wrong.)

- If the DLL is responding, make certain your application is running. Remember that when using file-based messaging, your application does not start by itself. Be certain either that your EXE is running, or that you have started the main program from the Command Window.

- If the DLL is responding and your application is running, but your application does not see any action, you are likely to have a mismatch between the temporary file path and template settings in the two relevant INI files. (See Chapter 13, "Identifying Users and Managing Session Data," for details.) One way to check this is to open Windows Explorer and navigate to the temporary file folder for your application. Now make a request to your application from a browser and note whether files are created in the temporary folder.

- If the Web Connection DLL has difficulty communicating with your application, it will record brief text entries of each difficulty in the file wcErrors.TXT, which is located in the temporary folder. These messages become more important if you switch to COM messaging, but can be helpful for some file-based messaging problems as well. If this file becomes large, you can periodically delete or rename it. (A new file will be created when the next error occurs.)

- If requests are making it through to your application, but errors in your code are trapped by Visual FoxPro while processing the requests, then information about the errors is recorded in the request log in your application's main directory (default name: wwRequestLog.DBF). Check for records where the logical field Error is set to true (.T.).

- Finally, by setting the appropriate INI file properties, you can arrange for email notifications of errors to be sent to an administrator. The settings for doing so are discussed in detail in Chapter 13.

DEBUGMODE

When you are first creating a new application, the Web Connection framework provides a great mechanism for debugging—the DEBUGMODE compiler directive. By setting this value to .T. (in WCONNECT.H or WCONNECT_OVERRIDE.H, as applicable) and recompiling everything, you establish a state wherein all Web Connection framework error handling is removed.

With no error handling, Visual FoxPro traps your errors in the familiar way in which the offending source code is opened in an editor window. You are now able to stop your application, fix the error, and try again.

Web Connection accomplishes this feat by a clever trick of wrapping the Error() method of its classes with compiler directives:

```
#IF DEBUGMODE = .F.
  FUNCTION Error( nError, cMethod, nLine)
  ... error handling code here
  ENDFUNC
#ENDIF
```

Note that the compiler directive is not inside the method, but outside. What this means is that when DEBUGMODE is .T., there simply is no Error() method! In this state, errors occurring in a class are referred to the global error handler defined by ON ERROR, or by Visual FoxPro itself. Because the same trick is used for the global error handler, Visual FoxPro handles all errors.

Beyond DEBUGMODE

Although the DEBUGMODE switch is powerful during early application development, it becomes burdensome when most of your application is working and you are dealing with isolated bugs. The issue is that DEBUGMODE applies to your entire application and the Web Connection framework as a whole. Whenever you make the switch, you are required to recompile everything, or the debugging mechanism will not work properly. This can be more trouble than it is worth for tracking down minor problems.

Clearly, your arsenal will require some additional strategies. In Chapter 12, "A Web Connection Application from Start to Finish," you have already seen the powerful and highly useful DebugProcess class, which can be invoked from an INI file switch and provides extensive debugging information back to the browser with each request that is processed. Although shown in use with the "To Do" application, that debugging class can be easily incorporated into any Web Connection application. In the next sections, I will present some further ideas for adding debugging capabilities to your applications.

Debug this!

I often find that my debugging session is isolated to a problem with a single class. When this occurs, there is a simple technique that can assist in debugging, while not interfering with the DEBUGMODE mechanism (whether on or off). Insert a compiler constant that is limited to only the class in question:

```
DEFINE CLASS MyClass AS CUSTOM
#DEFINE DEBUG_THIS .T.
… rest of class
#UNDEF DEBUG_THIS
ENDDEFINE  && MyClass
```

Now you have a simple flag that you can use anywhere in the class. For example, if you are debugging a standard Web Connection process subclass, you can insert extra information in the response object, such as in the following example:

```
#IF DEBUG_THIS
  Response.Write( [<p>Debug Info, query string: ] + ;
    Request.QueryString() + [</p>])
#ENDIF
```

When you are done debugging, just clear the flag:

```
#DEFINE DEBUG_THIS .F.
```

You don't even need to remove all the bracketed code until you are certain you have solved the current problem.

Debugging object creation and memory leaks

One problem that is easy to create in your Visual FoxPro applications is memory leaks due to failure to fully release the memory used by objects that your application creates. Although Visual FoxPro offers excellent garbage collection that absolves you from most of the requirements to clean up after your objects, there are programming errors that prevent the garbage collection mechanism from occurring. A common cause of this problem is creating Object B from Object A and storing object references to each in the other. In this case, you cannot destroy the first object without first clearing the reference in the second object.

This type of error could go unnoticed in a desktop application, but that is unlikely in a server application such as one using Web Connection. The problem is that the leaks will continue to mount as more and more users hit your application, until performance slows to a crawl. It is critical to identify and fix these problems.

If you suspect problems like this in your application, because you have created dependencies like this between classes, using the DEBUGOUT window to view object creation and removal can provide valuable insights. A simple approach is to modify each affected class to include this line:

```
#DEFINE DEBUG_OBJECTS .T.
```

Next, in each class, add code to the INIT() and DESTROY() methods to send output when objects are created and destroyed. For example:

```
FUNCTION INIT
   ... existing code
   #IF DEBUG_OBJECTS
     DEBUGOUT THIS.Name + " (" + THIS.Class + ")" + " created."
   #ENDIF
ENDFUNC   && INIT

FUNCTION DESTROY
   ... existing code, if any
   #IF DEBUG_OBJECTS
     DEBUGOUT THIS.Name + " (" + THIS.Class + ")" + " destroyed."
   #ENDIF
ENDFUNC   && INIT
```

Now run your code and watch the Debug Output window as you hit your application. The results should be enlightening. If objects are created and destroyed in the proper order, you are probably in good shape. If not, you have work to do.

Further background information on problems related to garbage collection in Visual FoxPro applications, and effective solutions, can be found at **http://fox.wikis.com/ wc.dll?Wiki~ManualGarbageCollection**.

Error handling and error messages

A substantial majority of your Web Connection code will exist in implementation subclasses of the core wwProcess class. Therefore, it is reasonable to expect that most errors you make will also occur in these classes. Because of this, the technique used for handling errors that occur in these classes is particularly important.

Fortunately, Web Connection shines in this area. There are two very important techniques for handling errors that occur in Process objects of production Web Connection applications. First is to display error information back to the user as a Web response. Second is (optionally) to send error information to a designated administrator in an email message. Each of these serves an important purpose.

When an error occurs while processing a Web request, it is generally not possible to complete the request. Nevertheless, failing to send any response would be particularly bad form: The browser would time out and the user would have no idea why. Instead, the wwProcess class has an Error() method that traps the error and returns an indication of the error to the user. To demonstrate this, I will insert the following line in the ListTasks() method of the Class_Tsk process class of the "TODO" application described in Chapter 12:

```
= A + B  && force an error!
```

Figure 1 shows what the user sees when he or she next navigates to this page. Note that in the run-time environment, the current line of code would not be shown.

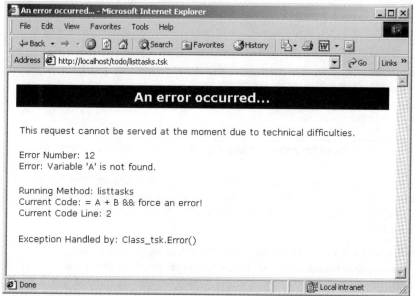

Figure 1. When an error occurs, at least the user is informed.

Although informing the user is nice, fixing the error is more important. You cannot fix what you do not know about, and the preceding message is being delivered only to the user of your application. Fortunately, Web Connection offers a nice solution, assuming a mail server is available: An email message can be sent to a designated administrator whenever an error occurs. This is accomplished by coordinating three settings in your application's INI file. The AdminSendErrorEmail switch, when set, indicates that email messages should be sent when errors occur. Messages are sent to the person identified by AdminEmail using the mail server identified by AdminMailServer. **Figure 2** shows the email message generated by the same error as earlier. Note that more information is provided, including some information that may not be appropriate to show regular users, such as physical file locations and login names.

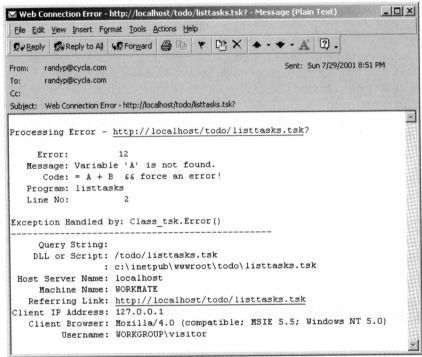

Figure 2. The error email includes more information than was shown to the user.

When an error occurs, the Error() method of the wwProcess class checks your INI settings and, if indicated, calls the SendErrorEmail() method, passing the content shown in Figure 2. This mechanism should suggest a few additional ideas to enhance your troubleshooting repertoire:

1. The SendErrorEmail() method can be called elsewhere by your own code whenever a situation occurs where you want to advise the administrator of a problem. By "problem," I do not mean errors, which are already trapped, but perhaps other anomalies, including security events. Here are some cases when I issue these messages:

    *   Multiple login failures from a single IP address over a short time period.

    *   Requests for data with primary keys that do not exist (possible hacker).

    *   Logic error found in an unanticipated OTHERWISE catch-all statement.

2. The Error() method could be overridden in a subclass if you found standard information you always want to send in the error emails. For example, if the request

is a POST request, and an error occurs, I always send the post buffer (Request.cFormVars) with the error email messages.

Getting more from your error messages

As shown earlier, the Web Connection framework provides a convenient combination for responding to errors: A simple message is shown to the user, while somewhat more information is sent to the administrator in an email message. Although this is an excellent mechanism, you might find the information included in the emails to be insufficient for your debugging purposes. I will examine how you can get more information in these messages.

The framework method that handles the errors that occur while your code is executing is wwProcess::Error. If you examine that method, you will find the code that produces the error result pages and sends the email messages. Unfortunately, your examination will find that this method is not really suitable for easy subclassing. For example, the method could benefit from a hook to send additional information. Nevertheless, if this subject is sufficiently important to you, one possibility is to override the SendErrorEmail() method. The code that follows is an example that inserts the program stack into the automatic error messages that are sent.

```
FUNCTION SendErrorEmail( lcErrorHeader, lcMessage, ;
  lcRecipient, lcSender, llForce )
  *-- Insert program stack as well into error messages.
  * Program Stack:
  LOCAL lcProgStack, lnPointer, lnLevel
    lcProgStack = TRANS( m.lcMessage)   && start with any string passed in
  lnLevel = PROGRAM(-1)
    lcProgStack = m.lcProgStack + "Program Stack:" + CRLF + CRLF
  FOR lnPointer = m.lnLevel TO 1 STEP -1
    lcProgStack = m.lcProgStack + ;
      TRANS( m.lnPointer) + [. ] + PROGRAM( m.lnPointer) + CRLF
  ENDFOR
  * Now call the default framework method in wwProcess:
  DODEFAULT( m.lcErrorHeader, m.lcProgStack, ;
    m.lcRecipient, m.lcSender, m.llForce )
ENDFUNC  && SendErrorEmail
```

I tested this code by inserting it into the DebugProcess class presented in Chapter 12; however, you could also insert this code into your own subclass of wwProcess (see Chapter 16, "Extending the Framework," for a discussion of how to subclass Web Connection framework classes), or directly into the top-level process class in your application. **Figure 3** shows an example email message with this expanded error information.

If you are using Visual FoxPro version 7 or later, the new ASTACKINFO() function can be used to provide even more detail of the program stack, including the line number from each module in the stack. The function L7ShowProgramStack(), included with the source code for this book in L7ShowData.PRG, provides an easy mechanism for inserting this information into either an HTML page or a text string.

There is one important caveat to this technique. When you alter any error handling code, you must be certain that your code does not have errors of its own! Introducing new errors when processing other errors can have disastrous effects, including preventing you from discovering that the original error even occurred. Make certain that any code that undertakes this task is carefully debugged!

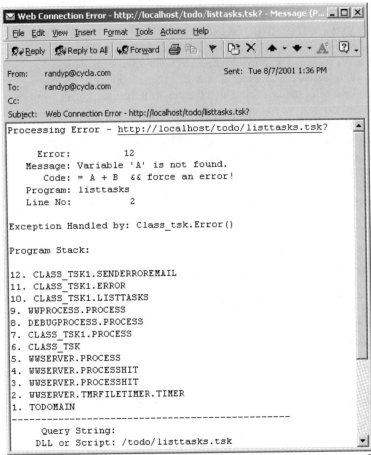

Figure 3. Error messages delivered via email can be more useful with more information inserted. Here we have added the full Visual FoxPro program stack.

Getting information on object state

The most common mode of testing your application will be navigating the application yourself using a Web browser. Therefore, some of the most useful debugging techniques involve providing information back to the browser. For example, instead of using the standard Visual FoxPro troubleshooting techniques of embedding WAIT WINDOW or MESSAGEBOX statements in the code (which display at the server console, if anywhere), you should instead embed information in the Response stream that is returned to the client browser.

Returning information to the browser can involve interrupting the response creation with a message, such as:

```
THIS.StandardPage( "Code worked up to here!")
RETURN .T.
```

This would simply return a single message to the browser. More often, you will want to produce the complete response, but also embed some additional debugging information. Single pieces are easily handled using Response.Write, for example:

```
Response.Write( "<P><B>Request was:</B> " + Request.QueryString())
```

That approach is handy enough for inserting simple values, but if you are performing some serious troubleshooting, you will usually need more information. Two of the most common pieces of information I require are object property values and data field values. I have developed two simple functions, L7ShowObject() and L7ShowRecord(), which create quick-and-dirty HTML tables showing the state of either an object or a record. These functions, shown in the following code, are also included in L7ShowData.PRG in the source code for this chapter. First is the code to show an object's properties:

```
FUNCTION L7ShowObject
* RAD Debugging Tool - shows all object property values in an HTML table.
LPARAMETERS loObject, lcTitle
IF VARTYPE( m.loObject) <> 'O'
  RETURN "<P><B>No object passed [L7ShowObject].</B>"
ENDIF
* Pass a .T. for no title, a string for a specific title,
* and no parameter or .F. for self-generated title.
IF VARTYPE( lcTitle) = "L"
  IF m.lcTitle
    lcTitle = ""
  ELSE
    LOCAL lcObjName
    lcObjName = SYS(1272, m.loObject)
    lcTitle = IIF( m.lcObjName = "empty", "Data Object Properties", ;
      "Object " + m.lcObjName + " Properties" )
  ENDIF
ENDIF
LOCAL lcText, lcFieldText, lnProps, ii, lcType
LOCAL ARRAY laProps[1]
lnProps = AMEMBERS( laProps, m.loObject )
lcText = []
lcText = m.lcText + [<table align=center class="ContentTable">] + ;
  CHR(13) + CHR(10)
IF NOT EMPTY( m.lcTitle)
  lcText = m.lcText + ;
    [<tr><td colspan=2 align=center class="ContentTitle">] + ;
    m.lcTitle + [</td></tr>] + CHR(13) + CHR(10)
ENDIF
FOR ii = 1 TO m.lnProps
  lcType = TYPE( 'loObject.' + laProps[ m.ii] )
  DO CASE
  CASE lcType = "O"
    lcFieldText = [(object)]
  CASE lcType = "U"
    lcFieldText = [(not defined)]
  OTHERWISE
    lcFieldText = TRANSFORM( EVAL( 'loObject.' + laProps[ m.ii] ))
```

```
    ENDCASE
    lcFieldText = [<tr valign=top><td align=right class="ContentLabel">] + ;
      PROPER( STRTRAN( laProps[ m.ii], "_", " ")) + [:</TD>] + ;
      [<TD CLASS="ContentValue">] + ;
      m.lcFieldText + [</td></tr>]

    lcText = m.lcText + m.lcFieldText + CHR(13) + CHR(10)
ENDFOR
lcText = m.lcText + [</table>] + CHR(13) + CHR(10)
RETURN m.lcText
ENDFUNC  && L7ShowObject
```

Note that this function returns the HTML as a string. Thus to insert the table into a page you are constructing, you would use Response.Write in conjunction with this function. For example, the following code inserts all information from the Request object into the result page:

```
Response.Write( L7ShowObject( Request ))
```

Here is the equivalent function for showing all field values for the current record of the selected alias:

```
FUNCTION L7ShowRecord
* RAD Debugging Tool - shows all field values in an HTML table.
LPARAMETERS lcTitle
* Pass a .T. for no title, a string for a specific title,
* and no parameter or .F. for self-generated title.
IF VARTYPE( lcTitle) = "L"
  IF m.lcTitle
    lcTitle = ""
  ELSE
    lcTitle = ALIAS() + " Record " + TRANSFORM( RECNO()) + ;
      " of " + TRANSFORM( RECCOUNT())
  ENDIF
ENDIF
LOCAL lcText, lcFieldText, lnFields, ii
lnFields = FCOUNT()
IF m.lnFields = 0
  RETURN "<P><B>No data table selected [L7ShowRecord].</B>"
ENDIF
lcText = []
lcText = m.lcText + [<table align=center class="ContentTable">] + ;
  CHR(13) + CHR(10)
IF NOT EMPTY( m.lcTitle)
  lcText = m.lcText + ;
    [<tr><td colspan=2 align=center class="ContentTitle">] + ;
    m.lcTitle + [</td></tr>] + CHR(13) + CHR(10)
ENDIF
FOR ii = 1 TO m.lnFields
  lcFieldText = [<tr valign=top><td align=right class="ContentLabel">] + ;
    PROPER( STRTRAN( FIELD( m.ii), "_", " ")) + [:</td>] + ;
    [<td class="ContentValue">] + ;
    TRANSFORM( EVAL( FIELD( m.ii))) + [</td></tr>]
  lcText = m.lcText + m.lcFieldText  + CHR(13) + CHR(10)
ENDFOR
```

```
lcText = m.lcText + [</table>] + CHR(13) + CHR(10)
RETURN m.lcText
ENDFUNC   && L7ShowRecord
```

More information in error messages

In addition to the functions described in the preceding section, the source code for this chapter also includes functions L7ShowWorkAreas() and L7ShowMemory(). The former shows all work areas open in all data sessions; and the latter provides a wrapper around Visual FoxPro's DISPLAY MEMORY command, to make the output suitable for inclusion in an HTML page. Both of these functions can prove useful in some debugging situations. They are also both included in L7ShowData.PRG.

Combining several of the functions that have been discussed, you can create error messages, particularly those delivered to the administrator by email, that provide sufficient information to help debug most errors in your application. My current preferences for information to include in administrator email messages are:

- Request object properties, using L7ShowObject(Request)

- Program stack, using L7ShowProgramStack()

- Work areas in all data sessions, using L7ShowWorkAreas()

- (Optional) SHOW MEMORY output, using L7ShowMemory()

Because some of these functions provide for more visually appealing HTML output options, you should consider using these options and sending the error email messages using the "text/html" content type. To do so, you would need to completely override the default behavior of the SendErrorEmail() method, as the default has no provision for changing the content type.

Errors in business objects and other tiers

When errors occur in other objects, such as business objects in the same tier, they do not necessarily trigger the error reporting mechanism described earlier. Whether or not this occurs depends on whether the class from which the object was instantiated has its own Error() method. If it does not have an Error() method, the preceding mechanism will be utilized and you should become aware of any errors in your application, provided that you have enabled email error notifications.

A bigger problem occurs when your business object classes have their own Error() methods. This might seem like smart design, but that is not always the case. Because a business object is non-visual, it has no user interface for displaying error messages. Thus, a typical approach is to set internal properties to indicate the occurrence of errors, and then for host objects to check these properties to see whether any errors occurred. My experience is that this design approach works poorly, because you never check completely for these error conditions. My preference is to exclude Error() methods from business classes, so that any resulting error passes control back to a UI-enabled class that can handle the situation in a reasonable way.

This problem is similar when you add physical tiers to your system architecture; you definitely cannot attempt to present UI elements, such as dialogs and message boxes, to the user. In this instance there are two approaches you can use. One is to have no error handling in your component at all, in which case any errors are trapped by Visual FoxPro and returned via the COM subsystem to the calling object in your front-end application. A second approach can be used when you communicate with middle-tier components via XML. In this case, you can define an <Error> element in your XML return schema wherein you can advise of any errors that occurred. With this approach, you can use Error() methods in these components. The Error() methods are responsible for recording error information such that it is included in the XML that is returned. As long as your front end *always* checks the XML return string for error information, this can be a reliable approach for error handling in middle tiers. Further, this approach isolates you from using the COM subsystem for communicating errors, which makes your middle-tier components more readily capable of being migrated to Web services. (In a Web service, you return error information as part of the overall XML return string.)

Debugging Web Connection scripts

Web Connection Scripts (WCS) are files that consist of both HTML and Visual FoxPro code. Each script file is processed either at run time, using CodeBlock, or by pre-compiling the scripts as described in the Web Connection documentation. There are a few tricks that can be used to help debug problems that occur in the middle of a script.

If the script runs to completion (that is, with no Visual FoxPro errors), but the results are not what you expected, you can simply edit the script file and insert either a SUSPEND or a SET STEP ON command. When you then test your application interactively in Visual FoxPro, the usual debug window will open and you can proceed from there.

The efficacy of this approach may vary, however. If your application is set to execute scripts at run time using CodeBlock (ScriptMode=3 in your application INI file), when you suspend code execution, you will be debugging the actual CodeBlock execution itself, which can be both confusing and time-consuming.

A better approach is to pre-compile your scripts, which results in Visual FoxPro code, which is much easier to understand and debug. Scripts can be compiled using the WCSCompile function that is part of wwUtils.PRG. For example:

```
SET PROCEDURE TO wwUtils
WCSCompile( "c:\inetpub\wwwroot\myApp\myScript.WCS")
```

There is also a Web interface on the admin.asp page that comes with Web Connection that accomplishes the same task. An extra benefit to pre-compiling scripts occurs when debugging Visual FoxPro errors in your application with DEBUGMODE set on (.T.). Now when an error occurs even in your script page, the standard Visual FoxPro debug window will open.

One thing to remember when debugging scripts this way is that you need to make any corrections in the original script file and re-compile it in order to test your corrections. Refer to Chapter 12 for further discussion about pre-compiling scripts.

Debugging slow processes

Often, once your application is in testing or production, you will find some of the processes to be running slower than you would prefer. It is possible that you already know the reason (for example, a slow query that requires further optimization). But sometimes you are not certain which parts of your process are responsible for the performance problem.

I have created a simple class, L7PerformanceInfo, that can help pinpoint these problems. All the class does is encapsulate an array that tracks the amount of time your process has been running at different key milestones. You establish the milestones by inserting calls in your process code to the AddItem() method of this class. At the end of your process, you can choose various options for using the results. The easiest option is simply to display the results in the browser.

The class code is as follows:

```
* L7PerformanceInfo.PRG
#INCLUDE WCONNECT.H
*** ====================================================== ***
DEFINE CLASS L7PerformanceInfo AS RELATION
*** ====================================================== ***
PROTECTED nItems
DIMENSION aItems[ 1, 2]
nItems = 0
nStart = 0
nLast = 0
* ---------------------------------------------------------- *
FUNCTION INIT
THIS.Reset()   && allow object reuse!
ENDFUNC
* ---------------------------------------------------------- *
FUNCTION Reset
THIS.nStart = SECONDS()
THIS.nLast = THIS.nStart
THIS.nItems = 1
DIMENSION THIS.aItems[ 1, 2]
THIS.aItems[ 1, 1] = "Performance Object Initiated"
THIS.aItems[ 1, 2] = 0
ENDFUNC
* ---------------------------------------------------------- *
FUNCTION AddItem( lcText)
LOCAL lnSeconds, lnDiff
lnSeconds = SECONDS()
lnDiff = MOD( m.lnSeconds - THIS.nLast, 86400 )
THIS.nLast = m.lnSeconds
THIS.nItems = THIS.nItems + 1
DIMENSION THIS.aItems[ THIS.nItems, 2]
THIS.aItems[ THIS.nItems, 1] = m.lcText
THIS.aItems[ THIS.nItems, 2] = m.lnDiff
* ---------------------------------------------------------- *
FUNCTION GetOutput( lcLang)
lcLang = "HTML"
LOCAL ii, lcStr, lnCum, lnAmt, lnTot
lcStr = CRLF + ;
  [<TABLE STYLE="background-color: white; font-size: x-small;"] + ;
  [ BORDER=1 ALIGN=CENTER>] + CRLF + ;
  [<CAPTION ALIGN=TOP>Performance Information</CAPTION>] + CRLF + ;
  [<THEAD><TR VALIGN=BOTTOM>] + CRLF + ;
```

```
[<TH>Process Milestone</TH><TH>Incremental<BR>Time</TH>] + ;
[<TH>Cumulative<BR>Time</TH><TH>Graph</TH>] + ;
[</TR>] + CRLF + [</THEAD><TBODY>] + CRLF
lnCum = 0
lnTot = MOD( SECONDS() - THIS.nStart, 86400)
lnTot = MAX( 0.01, m.lnTot)  && avoid divide by 0
FOR ii = 1 TO THIS.nItems
  lnAmt = THIS.aItems[ m.ii, 2]
  lnCum = m.lnCum + m.lnAmt
  lcStr = m.lcStr + [<TR><TD>] + THIS.aItems[ m.ii, 1] + ;
    [</TD><TD ALIGN=RIGHT>] + ;
    IIF( m.lnAmt >= 0.05, [<B>], []) + TRANS( m.lnAmt, "999.99") + ;
    [</TD><TD ALIGN=RIGHT>] + TRANS( m.lnCum, "999.99" ) + ;
    [</TD><TD>] + REPL( "x", INT( 50 * ( m.lnAmt / m.lnTot ))) + ;
    [ </TD></TR>] + CRLF
ENDFOR
RETURN m.lcStr + [</TBODY></TABLE>] + CRLF
ENDFUNC  && GetOutput
*** ===================================================== ***
ENDDEFINE && CLASS L7PerformanceInfo
```

This class has no formal ties to the Web Connection framework, and thus can be deployed in any manner that suits your own situation and style. I will show a straightforward approach using the "TODO" application from Chapter 12. I start by ensuring that the class is available for use, by adding the *second* line here to the main program (ToDoMain.PRG):

```
DO WCONNECT
SET PROCEDURE TO L7PerformanceInfo ADDITIVE
```

Next, I add a setting to the application configuration class, to enable performance debugging to be turned on and off via an INI file setting, by inserting the second line here into the class definition near the bottom of ToDoMain.PRG:

```
DEFINE CLASS todoprocConfig AS wwConfig

  lDebugPerformance = .F.
```

Simply adding the preceding property would establish the performance debugging flag, but it would default to being disabled. To enable performance debugging, create (or alter if already created) the physical INI setting, as shown in bold here:

```
[TodoProc]
DebugPerformance=On
```

Next I add code to check the INI file setting, and instantiate the debugging object in the Process() method of the main program. I also create two PRIVATE variables that can be used from anywhere in my further processing as follows:

```
PROTECTED FUNCTION PROCESS
    * Check if performance debugging is ON:
    PRIVATE plDebugPerformance, poPerformanceInfo
    plDebugPerformance = THIS.oConfig.oToDoProc.lDebugPerformance
    IF m.plDebugPerformance
```

```
    poPerformanceInfo = CREATEOBJECT( "L7PerformanceInfo" )
ENDIF
```

Now I choose key places in the code of the "troubled method" and insert calls to the AddItem() method of our debugging class. As a hypothetical example, if I suspected a SQL statement of being a major culprit in the slow performance, I might make two calls as follows:

```
IF m.plDebugPerformance
  poPerformanceInfo.AddItem( "Just before inventory query.")
ENDIF
SELECT * FROM Parts JOIN ...  && the suspect query
IF m.plDebugPerformance
  poPerformanceInfo.AddItem( "Just after inventory query.")
ENDIF
```

Finally, at the bottom of my suspect method, I can insert code to display the results as an HTML table right in the page returned to the browser:

```
IF m.plDebugPerformance
  Response.Write( poPerformanceInfo.GetOutput() )
ENDIF
```

To see an example of the output, I inserted several milestone events into the ListTasks page of the "TODO" application. **Figure 4** shows the performance information in the browser.

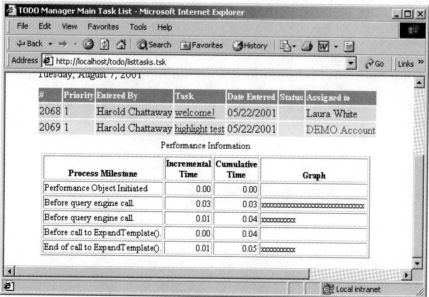

Figure 4. A performance information table can help pinpoint the potential slow points in your application.

Remember to turn the setting On in your application INI file when you want to test the application, and back Off when you are done!

One result I have found when running tests like these is that the performance problems are not always where you first suspect. For example, if you build large HTML result pages, the basic string concatenation in building those pages can often take more processing time than performing the SQL query to support the result. Information such as that displayed by the class presented earlier can steer you in the right direction when trying to tune your application.

Isolating the cause of Visual FoxPro crashes

Sometimes, despite your best efforts, your Visual FoxPro application will simply appear to be crashing. You know something is wrong, but you do not know how to isolate it. Usually, you can reproduce the problem by examining hit logs, observing what users were doing, and making educated guesses about what the next action might have been that caused the crash.

Nevertheless, there are times when your application simply crashes and you cannot reproduce the sequence during testing. In these cases you cannot use the Web Connection hit log to find the source of the crash, because Web Connection does not log a hit until after processing has been completed. Thus if a crash occurs, there is no trace in the log. Often these crashes are the result of corrupted index or memo files, so knowing what the incoming request was can be a big step in finding the problem.

One solution is to rig your application to employ a simple class that uses both pre- and post-logging. Prior to processing each hit, most of the usual information is written to the log, with the exception that the Error field is set to .T. and the Duration field is set to -1. If the hit is processed without incident, the record is then altered to clear the Error field and save the actual Duration. If instead your Visual FoxPro application crashes, you can examine the hit log for records where Error = .T. AND Duration = -1 to find the sources of the crashes. (Other trapped errors may also be recorded in the log, but in these cases Duration will be 0.)

 The class that implements this logging is called WcRADDebugServer. The full source code including comments is included with the source code for this book. An abbreviated version is shown here. One attractive feature of this approach is that the entire mechanism can be turned off via a single constant, WCRAD_DEBUG_SERVER, thus allowing it to be easily switched on only when needed should crashes start to occur.

```
* WcRADDebugServer.PRG
#INCLUDE WCONNECT.H
* Developed by J. Randy Pearson, Cycla Corporation
* during the writing of "WC RAD" for Hentzenwerke.
* --------------------------------------------------------------- *
DEFINE CLASS wcRadDebugServer AS WWC_SERVER

* IMPORTANT NOTES:
* 1. Even if you use SQL Server for logging, you will return to
*    local .DBF logging when you use this class.
* 2. This class lowers application performance. Revert to
*    the regular approach after you're done debugging.

* New Property:
nLogRecordNo = 0
```

```
* ---------------------------------------------------------------- *
FUNCTION ProcessHit(lcRequestBuffer,llFile)
* Override the ProcessHit() method with our own.
* The idea here is to pre-log each hit, but to mark the log record
* in anticipation of an error. If the app crashes, you can find the records
* where Error = .T. AND Duration = -1.
* If the hit processes OK, the record is "adjusted" at the end.

LOCAL lnSeconds, lvResult
lnSeconds = SECONDS()

* Make sure default method doesn't also log the result:
THIS.lLogToFile = .F.

THIS.PreLogRequest()
lvResult = DODEFAULT( m.lcRequestBuffer, m.llFile)

THIS.PostLogRequest( MOD( SECONDS()- m.lnSeconds, 24 * 60 * 60) )
RETURN m.lvResult

ENDFUNC && ProcessHit
* ---------------------------------------------------------------- *
FUNCTION PreLogRequest

IF !USED("CGILOG")
  THIS.SetLogging(.T.)
ENDIF
SELECT CGILOG
APPEND BLANK
IF RLOCK()
  THIS.nLogRecordNo = RECNO()
  REPLACE ;
    TIME WITH DATETIME(), ;
    QueryStr WITH THIS.oRequest.QueryString(), ;
    REMOTEADDR WITH THIS.oRequest.GetIPAddress(), ;
    Duration WITH -1, ;
    Error WITH .T., ;
    Script WITH JUSTFNAME( THIS.oRequest.ServerVariables("Executable Path")), ;
    MemUsed WITH SYS(1016)
  UNLOCK
ELSE
  THIS.nLogRecordNo = -1  && indicate failure
ENDIF

ENDFUNC && PreLogRequest

* ---------------------------------------------------------------- *
FUNCTION PostLogRequest( lnSeconds)
IF THIS.nLogRecordNo >= 1
  IF !USED("CGILOG")
    THIS.SetLogging(.T.)
  ENDIF
  SELECT CGILOG
  GOTO THIS.nLogRecordNo
  IF RLOCK()
    REPLACE Duration WITH m.lnSeconds, ;
    Error WITH .F., ;
    MemUsed WITH SYS(1016)
  ENDIF
ENDIF
```

```
ENDFUNC && PostLogRequest
* ------------------------------------------------------------------ *


ENDDEFINE  && CLASS wcRadDebugServer
* ------------------------------------------------------------------ *
```

It is easy to implement this new class in any Web Connection application that is based on version 3.6 or greater of the Web Connection framework. First, in your application main program, just *after* the line that says #INCLUDE WCONNECT.H, add the following lines:

```
#DEFINE WCRAD_DEBUG_SERVER .T.
#IF WCRAD_DEBUG_SERVER  && debugging ON
  #UNDEF WWC_USE_SQL_SYSTEMFILES
  #DEFINE WWC_USE_SQL_SYSTEMFILES .F.  && turn off SQL Server logging
#ENDIF
```

Next, right after the line DO WConnect, add:

```
SET PROCEDURE TO WcRadDebugServer ADDITIVE
```

Then, in your main class definition (DEFINE CLASS), instead of something like:

```
DEFINE CLASS TodoServer AS WWC_SERVER OLEPUBLIC
```

change this to read (make sure to use your own class name!):

```
#IF WCRAD_DEBUG_SERVER
  DEFINE CLASS TodoServer AS wcRadDebugServer
#ELSE
  DEFINE CLASS TodoServer AS WWC_SERVER OLEPUBLIC
#ENDIF
```

You are ready to rebuild and run your app in server debugging mode! You can either just wait for your crash to occur, or try forcing a crash to make sure your new class is working. The latter can be simulated, by using the special administrative URL wc.dll?wwMaint~ CrashGPF. Note that if you are testing this with the "TODO" application from Chapter 12 and have located WC.DLL in the suggested "scripts" subfolder, you will need to insert that path into the URL, which then might be:

```
http://localhost/todo/scripts/wc.dll?wwMaint~CrashGpf
```

After your app crashes, look at the records where WwRequestLog.Error = .T.. The items where Duration = 0 are trapped errors. The items where Duration = -1 are new entries that this class has helped to isolate. This should give a clue of what method is causing your crashes, hopefully. After that, it is up to you to isolate the cause further!

Note that using the WcRadDebugServer class imposes a performance penalty on your application by having two logging operations per hit (the first one adds a record, and the second one updates the record). Further, if you had been logging to SQL Server, this is suspended during use of this class. Therefore, you should deactivate this mechanism whenever it is not needed. You do this by setting the debugging constant WCRAD_DEBUG_SERVER to .F. in your main program and rebuilding your application:

```
#DEFINE WCRAD_DEBUG_SERVER .F.
```

Once this feature is deactivated, there is no cost in leaving your application rigged to use this debugging aid in the future.

Detecting hackers

If your application is available to the public on the Internet, sooner or later you will be subject to hacking attempts. Most types of hacking, such as "denial of service" attacks, never involve your application directly, and therefore are outside the scope of this book, but there are some areas where your application can take an active role.

Failed login attempts

If your application uses user logins, you can record the IP address and user ID of any invalid attempts. You can then take various actions, such as locking out accounts or sending email warnings to system administrators when these attempts are identified.

Invalid cookies and license plates

A similar problem to watch for is when a request supplies an invalid cookie or license plate value. (See Chapter 13 for a full discussion of cookies and license plates.) Receiving an invalid value could well be an attempt by a hacker to hijack another valid user's session, possibly gaining access to privileged information. Again, recording these incidents and advising system administrators can help to identify and deal with such situations.

Invalid primary or surrogate keys in URLs

Much like the invalid cookie scenario, you should be suspicious of requests that specify invalid primary or surrogate keys in the query string of the URL. This could indicate hackers attempting to "guess" the identification of data that they have no business seeing. Once they discover these keys, even if your application denies them access to view the data, they may decide it is then worth trying to hack further into your system by accessing another user's account.

Be on the lookout for situations where you detect cases like this that do not make sense. Record and analyze all invalid attempts to access your data. But before making accusations, remember there can be several legitimate reasons for situations like this:

- Someone can bookmark a URL linking to a record that is subsequently deleted.

- A URL can be mistyped, thus resulting in an invalid ID. (This is why you would tend to ignore single incidents, but might look instead just for trends.)

Invalid form values

Input forms can be hacked very easily. Anyone can do it simply by saving the HTML source of the page locally, editing the HTML of the form itself, and then opening the edited version of the form and submitting the modified version to your application.

This type of hacking poses a serious threat unless you validate all submissions and enforce all security rules during both rendering and post processing. One area ripe for hacking is the use of radio buttons or drop-down lists. Perhaps you populate these from values in a database when you render forms. But do you also confirm the submitted values are from these valid lists? If not, a hacker can add his or her own extra values and submit these, which could wreak havoc on your application.

Locking out specific IP addresses

If you identify a potential hack attempt coming from a specific IP address or network, you should take action immediately. At the lowest level, you can block specific IP addresses from being served by your application in any of several ways:

- You could create an IPLockout table in your application to record problem IP addresses, and then check Request.GetIPAddress() on each hit and refuse to process the hit if the address is in the table.

- You can configure most Web servers, including IIS, to deny any requests from a specific IP address or range of IP addresses. The benefit of this is that all resources on your Web site are protected, rather than just your application.

- If you have access to your router or firewall, you may be able to block the malicious user from even entering your network.

Depending on the nature of the attempt, you might decide that someone is attempting something that may even be a crime. One possible approach is to contact the FBI. A preliminary step is to determine whose network the hacker is using to originate their attempts. Be aware that some hackers can spoof their IP address, so this determination may not always be reliable. By running the Windows NSLookup utility and entering the hacker's IP address, you can find the originating domain name. (To do this, simply type NSLookup followed by the IP address from a Windows command prompt.) It may be possible to contact the system administrator for that domain and advise them of the problem. Sometimes I have found that what appeared to be a hacker was actually a Web crawler or other indexing tool not performing correctly.

Frequent Visual FoxPro coding mistakes

By watching the messages on the Web Connection support forums for several years, I have seen some recurring problems that cause big debugging headaches.

- The most-frequent mistake I have noticed is when developers SET EXACT ON in their code, and fail to turn it back off. Many methods in the Web Connection framework simply will not work when this occurs. There are actually almost no legitimate instances in the powerful Visual FoxPro language where you need to use this setting. If you have any such situations, be certain to restore the setting to OFF immediately thereafter. Problems with this setting have been very difficult to debug.

- Problems with delimiters (quotes and brackets) are particularly frequent and troublesome to detect when developing Web applications. The primary reason is that you are often using one language (Visual FoxPro) to create "source code" in other languages (HTML, JavaScript, and so forth). As such, you encounter situations where you must nest delimiters, and frequently will use all three types that Visual FoxPro supports (quotes, apostrophes, and brackets). Further, although the Visual FoxPro compiler usually catches these mistakes when developing desktop applications, that is not always the case in Web applications. For example, you may create valid Visual FoxPro syntax that writes improper HTML code. Mistakes such as a missing closing quotation mark in an HTML page can be maddening to discover, particularly because different browsers have different behaviors in how they render such pages.

Other common development problems

In addition to Visual FoxPro coding mistakes, several other common problems occur in the Visual FoxPro development environment:

- Developers often encounter the inability to trace their code. This occurs whenever your FXP files are out of synch with the corresponding PRG files. This can also occur when classes still exist in memory, perhaps to an application not terminating cleanly back to the Command Window. The following code, also recommended in Chapter 12, should help to restore your development environment:

```
SET DEVELOPMENT ON
CLEAR ALL
RELEASE ALL
CLEAR PROGRAM
SET PROCEDURE TO
SET CLASSLIB TO
CLEAR
```

- A closely related problem occurs when you are tracing your code, but cannot trace through Web Connection framework classes and functions. If you are currently running the Web Connection Management Console (Console.EXE), some of the Web Connection framework that is built into that executable will continue to reside in memory, even if your application terminates properly. The only solution to this problem, if you need to trace through the framework code, is to start Visual FoxPro without using the console program.

- Be careful what commands you place in your CONFIG.FPW file. In particular, be careful about what folders comprise your PATH statement. You can easily create paths to duplicate or out-of-date versions of files (perhaps a backup of your database), which can cause the wrong copy of one or more files to be utilized, which can be very difficult to detect during troubleshooting.

- When updating your production application to a new version of Web Connection, a frequent mistake is forgetting to deploy new versions of the DLL files onto the server. In addition to copying in the latest version of WC.DLL, which requires stopping and re-starting the Web service, you must also copy the latest version of wwIpStuff.DLL into the application directory (where your Visual FoxPro executable resides).

Understanding the wcErrors.TXT File

Having read this far, you might think that all sources of potential problems have been covered. Not so! Web Connection applications have another source of errors, which are logged in a simple text file named wcErrors.TXT. The entries in this file are not written by your Visual FoxPro application, but rather by WC.DLL itself. I will examine the purpose and contents of this important file.

The first important piece of information is where the file is located. If your WC.INI file has a proper entry for the temporary file Path setting, then the wcErrors.TXT file will be located there. If this entry points to either an invalid directory or one for which there is no write access, this file will instead be created in a location such as the \WinNT\System32 subdirectory. (Note that there is no wcErrors.TXT file until the first time an entry is written.)

The next step is to understand the nature of entries that are written to this file. These include the following:

- Normal, everyday events

- Problems with your application's availability or responsiveness

- Problems limited to COM operation

The first thing to notice is that not all entries are unexpected. For example, when using COM messaging without the KeepAlive option, it is normal for instances of your application to be released and reloaded following periods of inactivity. Nevertheless, you will see an entry in the error log each time that occurs. This entry might look like this:

```
RPC Server Unavailable due to thread timeout: Attempt to Reload Server...
```

Entries such as this one are not indicative of problems and can be ignored.

Many entries can be indicative of problems with your application. For example, if your application does not respond quickly enough to a new request, you will see an entry such as "Web Connection request timed out." This can also occur if you fail to start your file-based application prior to the receipt of Web requests, which is a common occurrence during development and testing.

If you switch to COM messaging, the wcErrors.TXT file becomes much more important in diagnosing system problems. The format and number of distinct messages that can appear in this file is constantly evolving with each new release of Web Connection. To see a technical description of the important possible messages, refer to the latest Web Connection Help document in the topic named "Web Connection ISAPI Error log (wcErrors.txt)."

Trouble with your HTML

In addition to problems with your Visual FoxPro code, you will often have problems with the appearance of the HTML pages that you return. There are some standard practices and troubleshooting techniques that you can use to help in these situations:

1. Embed comments in your HTML output. This helps you determine what your HTML is attempting to accomplish, and is particularly important when you start nesting <table> elements. If your HTML is generated from Visual FoxPro code, these comments can actually serve double duty—helping both when you review your code and when viewing the generated HTML source. Chapter 13 presents a subclass of wwResponse that adds a WriteComment method for facilitating this practice.

2. Indent your HTML when practical to show nesting of structural elements. This has the same benefit as indenting your Visual FoxPro code, and is helpful when diagnosing problems, particularly when nesting <table> elements.

3. If your problem involves page structure, it can be a slow process to try fixing this in your Visual FoxPro code, and testing each incremental change. Another idea is to use the "Save As" function of your browser to save the page source as a local file. You can then use a text or HTML editor to experiment with fixes to the structure of your page. Navigate to the physical file in your browser to view the results. Once you determine the proper adjustments, you can apply the change to your Visual FoxPro application.

4. Also useful are Web sites and tools to validate your HTML. Examples can be found at **www.w3.org/** (in particular: **http://validator.w3.org/** and **www.w3.org/People/ Raggett/tidy/**). Another option is to use an HTMLTidy-endowed text editor like UltraEdit32.

5. If your browser renders a page in a way that looks completely wrong, always check the HTML source for both missing closing tags and missing closing delimiters. For example, failure to supply a closing quotation mark in the attribute value of a tag can cause the entire document to look completely wrong.

6. Browser issues can be the most frustrating problems of all. If you are supporting clients with different browser makes and versions, it is critical to be able to view your application from these different browsers *during the development process.* Browser issues are much easier to correct when identified early. The most common problems include:

a. One browser is more forgiving of HTML errors than another. If you test your application using the more forgiving browser, you will have trouble when your users later claim the application is not working. Historically, I have found Microsoft Internet Explorer to be more forgiving than Netscape Navigator. For example, if you do not close a <table> with a matching </table>, Microsoft Internet Explorer will make an assumption of where your table ends, while Netscape Navigator might not render the page at all.

b. Not all browsers support the same features, or may support them differently. Cascading Style Sheet (CSS) features are a particular source of inconsistent browser treatment, particularly prior to version 6.2 of Netscape Navigator.

c. New browsers may come to the market of which you are unaware.

d. Some browsers have bugs. I have found most versions of Netscape Navigator prior to 6.2 to have bugs and idiosyncrasies that you become aware of only by viewing your application using that browser.

7. Consider adding the "View Partial Source" feature to your Microsoft Internet Explorer installation, as described in the next section.

View Partial Source

If a Web page doesn't look right, the first step many developers take is to use the "View Source" tool from the browser. This displays the original HTML in a simple editor window. For any but the simplest pages, finding the problem in this window can be extremely time-consuming. (It is generally harder in Microsoft Internet Explorer than Netscape Navigator, but neither makes it easy.)

Fortunately, Microsoft provides a great free add-on to Microsoft Internet Explorer at its Web site, called "View Partial Source." This option allows you to select a portion of a Web page (using click-and-drag), and then view only the portion of the HTML that is responsible for the selected portion.

You can download and install this option by navigating to **www.microsoft.com/ Windows/IE/WebAccess/**.

Download and install the "Microsoft Web Developer Accessories" (as opposed to "Web Accessories from Microsoft" available on the same site) and you will have "View Partial Source" available from your right-click menu when you highlight a portion of a Web page. Using this feature is demonstrated in **Figures 5** and **6**.

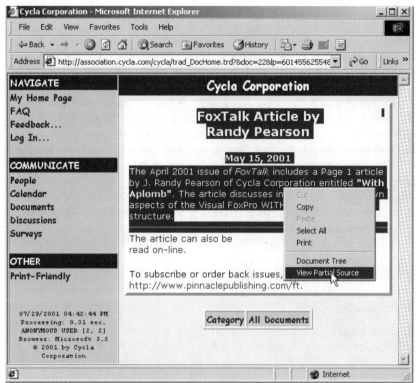

***Figure 5**. You can focus on the portion of the page you are interested in.*

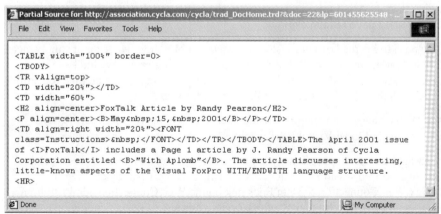

***Figure 6**. You see only the relevant HTML, rather than the source for the entire page.*

Maintenance requirements of Web Connection applications

There are several routine maintenance tasks that need to be performed on a production Web Connection application in order to ensure that it continues to operate with acceptable performance:

Ensure that the temporary file folder is periodically purged of extraneous files with either TMP or RET extensions. In the course of normal operations, Web Connection deletes these files for you. Nevertheless, in the case of certain error conditions or server crashes, this does not occur. You can either purge these files manually or create an automated routine to do this for you. One such mechanism is presented in Chapter 19, "Asynchronous and Scheduled Operations."

You should periodically examine and delete (or rename) the wcErrors.TXT file that the Web Connection DLL file creates. This file gives you clues about communication problems in your application. An approach I like is to have this file sent to the administrator daily via email, after which it is deleted. An automatic mechanism for doing this is presented in Chapter 19.

If you log individual Web hits, the request log can become large, thus hurting system performance, because a new record is appended on each hit. There are several options available to you in this situation:

- Turn off request logging in the application INI file if you do not need each hit logged. Note that Web Connection will still record errors when they occur.

- Frequently purge the request log. Web Connection comes with a maintenance routine that allows you to trigger this action remotely via the Web (wwMaint::ClearLog). Exclusive use is required, so if you are running more than one server instance via COM, you need to first stop all but one instance and hold other requests while purging the log. All of this can be accomplished from the Web Connection administration page (admin.asp).

- If you need to keep all of your historical request information, you cannot simply clear the request log. One approach I use is to create a new log each day, and have a scheduled process append all of these logs together into an off-line archive for further analysis. Chapter 19 shows an example of this approach.

- As of Web Connection version 3.60 and later, you can log your requests to SQL Server instead of local Visual FoxPro tables.

- If your application uses sessions, you have a periodic need to pack the session table to remove expired session records. This is easily accomplished by clicking the Reindex Web Connection System Files link on the Web Connection administration page (admin.asp). The frequency of performing this task is dependent on the usage level of your application. For a busy Web site with thousands of users, tasks like this should be performed at least once per day.

You may periodically need to PACK or REINDEX your own production database. In this situation, exclusive use will be needed, so the same considerations apply as discussed earlier for clearing the request log. I recommend creating a Web-based interface for performing these tasks. This allows you to run specific maintenance tasks remotely over HTTP, which can be handy when you are off-site.

There may be periodic, perhaps daily, tape backups performed on your data. Although some backup systems are supposedly capable of performing reliable backups of Visual FoxPro tables even when the files are open, I do not trust these scenarios and prefer to try to close all tables during the time that the backup is performed. (If your data is on SQL Server or Oracle, this is not an issue.)

One approach I have employed is to specify a maintenance interval, either in code or as INI file settings, and to refuse to operate on data tables during this time. There are numerous ways of accomplishing this. One way might be to place the following code at the beginning of the Process() method in your main program:

```
LOCAL lcStartMaint, lcEndMaint
lcStartMaint = "02:45"   && or read a value from INI
lcEndMaint = "03:15"
IF BETWEEN( TIME(), m.lcStartMaint, m.lcEndMaint)
   CLOSE DATA ALL
   LOCAL Response
   Response = CREATE( "wwResponseString")
   Response.StandardPage( "Maintenance Advisory", "Sorry, but we are " + ;
      "performing maintenance right now. Check back after " + ;
      m.lcEndMaint + " (eastern time). Thank you for your patience.")
   IF THIS.lCOMObject
      THIS.cOutput=Response.GetOutput()
   ELSE
      File2Var(THIS.oRequest.GetOutputFile(),Response.GetOutput())
   ENDIF
   RETURN   && avoid any further processing!
ENDIF
```

Note that this approach may not always work, since it counts on receiving a hit after entering the maintenance interval, but before the backup device starts. One solution would be to perform your backup in a batch file, in which an HTTP request is sent to your application before the backup command is issued, thus causing your tables to be closed. Still, this is a crude and imperfect solution. For robust backups, either ensure your application is not running during the backup, or migrate your data to a back-end database, such as SQL Server or Oracle.

If you are using Visual FoxPro data and a maintenance window is not an option (that is, your application must run 24x7), another option is to make a live copy of your data, using the Visual FoxPro COPY TO command. You could then arrange for the copies, which would not need to be open, to be backed up onto tape. This approach is discussed further at **http://fox.wikis.com/wc.dll?Wiki~BackupOpenFiles.**

Online maintenance approach using COM

If you are using COM instead of file-based messaging (see Chapter 14, "COM vs. File-Based Messaging"), you have more flexibility when it comes to performing maintenance tasks. In COM mode, there is a special link available from admin.asp that lets you "unload all servers but one and hold requests." When you do this, only one request can be serviced at a time, and only those from administrators are accepted (as determined by the AdminUser setting in

WC.INI). This means you have the ability to perform actions like PACK and REINDEX, which require exclusive use. Once finished, you release the "hold" and now other users can once again reach your application. In the interim they see a (customizable) message advising them that maintenance is being performed.

To implement this strategy, you would create Web Connection Process() methods to perform your maintenance, thus allowing you to call the methods from a Web page. For example, a method to pack a table could be as simple as:

```
FUNCTION PackCustomer
  CLOSE DATABASES
  IF OpenExclusive( "Customer")
    PACK
    USE
    THIS.StandardPage( "Customer table was packed.")
  ELSE
    THIS.ErrorMsg( "Could not get exclusive use of Customer table.")
  ENDIF
ENDFUNC  && PackCustomer
```

Obviously, you would probably do something more elaborate, such as creating a PackTable() method instead, where the name of the table was passed as a URL parameter, but you get the idea. Now your server operator would perform this, perhaps weekly, function by following a procedure similar to the following:

1. Put the server into maintenance mode by selecting the "unload all servers but one and hold requests" link from admin.asp (the equivalent query string is "_maintain~maintholdrequests").

2. Perform one or more maintenance functions, such as the pack operation shown earlier. Ideally you would create a page that served as a menu of administrator functions. You could then add a link to your maintenance menu from the admin.asp page, and vice versa, thus enabling easy navigation among all maintenance tasks.

3. After performing all tasks, release the hold either by selecting the "load all servers from INI" link from admin.asp (the equivalent query string is "_maintain~load") or by clicking the "switch" toggle link on the Web Connection status page (the equivalent query string is "_maintain~HoldRequests").

Finally, be aware that some maintenance tasks take longer that the standard Web browser timeout. These tasks should not be performed synchronously from a Web-based maintenance page. Chapter 19 presents other techniques for dealing with this type of maintenance activity, including the use of the wwAsyncWebRequest framework tool.

Online maintenance of lookup tables and metadata

If you have lookups and/or metadata that you would prefer to maintain online, normally the only option would be to develop your own Web-based data entry forms and Process() methods.

Starting with Web Connection version 3.65, there is an alternative. The wwShowCursor class now has an EditTable() method that provides for quick and easy table editing, which is handy for maintenance functions. Refer to the example method TableEditor() in wwDemo.PRG to see an example of this new method in use. You can also run this example from the demo application that installs with Web Connection.

Conclusion

Developing Web Connection applications can be challenging, because of the numerous technologies that are involved. When things don't go quite right, you need to be ready to diagnose the source of the trouble. This chapter presented various ideas and techniques for approaching some of the more frequent issues you will face.

Chapter 19
Asynchronous and
Scheduled Operations

The needs of a Web application quickly grow beyond simple responses to Web requests. Some periodic activities need to occur in the background. And some requests require processing that takes longer than most simple requests. In this chapter I explore those needs and present some solutions.

As your applications mature and grow in complexity and database size, additional needs arise that cannot be met by simply adding more features to your basic Web Connection application. These needs fall into two categories:

Asynchronous operations are required when some of the incoming requests take too long to process and return results in a timely fashion. One example is a long-running query, perhaps one that performs either a text search or many table joins on a large database. An absolute need is reached when the processing time exceeds either the browser or Web server timeout values. But a practical limit occurs much sooner, because users are not provided any feedback while long requests are running, thus causing them to take undesirable actions including (1) re-submitting the request (which requires your application to run the burdensome request a second time), and (2) leaving your site. Therefore, any request that is likely to take more than a few seconds to complete should be considered for migration to an asynchronous operation.

Scheduled operations are different in that they are not responses to incoming requests at all. Rather, they represent recurring needs that must be performed on a regular basis. Examples of these include:

- Sending queued messages to a mail server.

- Making a live backup copy of your database.

- Emailing the error log to the administrator.

- Deleting temporary files.

Your Web Connection application cannot perform these operations by itself, because it only responds to incoming Web hits, whereas these represent ongoing needs that are not specific to any given request. While you could create a page full of URLs that request these operations, you would also have to ensure that an employee always remembered to trigger each operation in a timely fashion. This is both a costly and an error-prone approach.

In the remainder of this chapter, I will look at both asynchronous and scheduled operations in more detail.

The asynchronous and scheduled task code shown in this chapter is not presented as "industrial strength" designs, but rather is intended to provide examples of the general approach one might take in meeting the needs discussed herein. I have grafted these examples onto the TODO application presented in Chapter 12, "A Web Connection Application from Start to Finish," for ease of demonstration, even though that application was never designed with these additions in mind.

Asynchronous operations

Some Web requests take longer to process than others. If a request takes too long, one of several things can occur:

- The client browser times out, giving the user a generic message over which you have no control. The user has no idea whether the server got the request, the site is down, they made a mistake, and so on.

- The Web server or Web Connection DLL gives up and times out, sending the user an error page indicating that no output was generated. Under file-based messaging, your application will finish processing, but the response goes nowhere. Under COM messaging, your application can eventually be terminated after a timeout of sufficient length occurs.

- The user, accustomed to the other snappy pages on your site, assumes he or she did something wrong and submits the request a second time. This is a particularly bad result, because now the first process is abandoned following completion, and the same request is repeated. Your response takes even longer to get to the user, and your site's resources are tied up doing twice as much work.

- The user assumes your site isn't responding and gives up, possibly navigating to a competitor's site. Obviously, this is the worst outcome of all.

- Even if the user "hangs in there" and gets a response within the timeout period, the user received no feedback during that time indicating there would be a wait. If nothing more, this may leave the user with a bad impression of the quality of your site.

Asynchronous operations are required when some of incoming requests take too long to process and return results in a timely fashion. As a practical guideline, any request that is likely to take more than 5-10 seconds to complete should be considered for migration to an asynchronous operation. For many sites, this threshold will be even lower.

Why asynchronous?

The most difficult concept to assimilate is why an asynchronous operation is needed in the first place. After all, can't your application send a "please wait" message back to the client, and then run the request to completion?

The answer, as you might have guessed, is "no."

Once you provide an interim response, no further interaction with the client browser is possible without that client initiating further contact. Thus, even if you could arrange to run the entire request following delivery of the message, that effort would fall on deaf ears. You should also be aware that Web Connection is not designed to perform further processing of a request after a response has been returned.

How does an asynchronous request operate?

The solution to this is to break the request processing into two parts, in which you return a message quickly that indicates the request is being processed, and at the same time arrange for that processing to occur via a separate application using some type of messaging mechanism. The design of this approach would include these steps:

1. A typical Web Connection method receives the incoming request and analyzes the requirements (form variables, URL parameters, and so forth).

2. Instead of processing the full request, the Web Connection method simply logs the request into a queue for a back-end application to handle. This queue can be as simple as a single DBF file created as a free table.

3. Depending on the architecture you choose, the Web Connection method could also launch the back-end application that will do the actual processing, by using the Visual FoxPro RUN command, or the ShellExecute API. You might choose this approach if you have very infrequent needs of this type. Alternatively, you could create a back-end application that runs in the background and continuously polls for new entries in the queue. This gains efficiency, because you are not launching a new instance of Visual FoxPro upon each request. On the other hand, you must take the proper steps to ensure that the back-end application is always running and available when needed. One approach for doing this is including the back-end application in the Windows startup group, assuming your server always boots to a logged-in condition. Other approaches are also possible depending on your system configuration and security policies.

4. The Web Connection method immediately returns a response that indicates the request is being processed. This response also includes an HTML refresh instruction (using a META tag) that causes the browser to poll your Web Connection application every few seconds to see whether the process is completed. An example is shown later in this chapter.

5. Your back-end application updates the status of the request in the queue as the processing occurs, and inserts the final response there when the processing has been completed. (The amount of in-process updating depends on what your specific process does. For example, you could not update the status in the middle of running a long SQL SELECT statement.)

6. During this time, your Web Connection application receives repeated polling requests from the client browser, because of the META refresh tag you include in each response. Upon each request, your method checks the status of the item in the queue,

and either returns a status update page (with a further refresh instruction) or returns the final result when completed.

7.   Additional coding can be included to handle timeouts, user cancellation, and so on.

It is entirely possible, given this strategy, to write your own code to handle all of these steps; however, as described in the next section, Web Connection includes a handy class that helps to automate this process.

The wwAsyncWebRequest class

As of version 3.65, Web Connection includes a new class that facilitates the handling of asynchronous requests.

The wwAsyncWebRequest class is a utility class that is invoked by both the Web Connection application and a back-end application to communicate progress via a messaging table. The Web Connection application both writes new requests to the table and checks the table for status messages as new polling requests are received. The back-end application checks the table for new requests to be processed and updates the table with the status of requests as it processes them. The wwAsyncWebRequest class simply abstracts this communication into a class that is easy to deploy.

Asynchronous processing example

In this section, I will present a simple example of how to deploy this strategy. The example is derived from the TODO application that was developed in Chapter 12.

The Class_Tsk class of the TODO application includes a method named ListTasks, which lists all open tasks. Imagine a time in the future when there are so many open tasks that this request could not be completed in a timely manner. I will simulate that condition by inserting a delay into the process, thus allowing an example of an asynchronous process to be created without having to generate large quantities of sample data. **Listing 1** shows a new method in the same class titled SlowListTasks to use for this example. This code can be inserted as a new method in Class_Tsk.PRG.

Listing 1. A Web Connection method wrapping an asynchronous process.

```
*****************************************
FUNCTION SlowListTasks
*****************************************
SET PROCEDURE TO wwAsyncWebRequest ADDITIVE  && not set in WCONNECT.PRG
LOCAL loAsync, lcAction, lcJobId, lnRefreshPeriod, ;
   lnRetries, lnTry, lcMessage
loAsync = CREATEOBJECT( "wwAsyncWebRequest")
* See if this is a new request or polling for a current request:
lcAction = Request.QueryString( 'Action')
lcAction = IIF( EMPTY( m.lcAction), 'New', PROPER( m.lcAction))
IF m.lcAction == 'New'
   lcJobId = loAsync.SubmitEvent( , "Slow Task List")
   * Optionally, fire up the process here. (Note: You
   * can also run a continuous background process that
   * polls for new requests.)
   LOCAL lcRunCmd
   lcRunCmd = [RUN /n4 TODOAsyncHandler.EXE ] + m.lcJobId
```

```
   &lcRunCmd
ELSE   && not new
   lcJobId = Request.QueryString( 'JobId')
ENDIF

* Set refresk periond (in seconds):
lnRefreshPeriod = 1
* How many polls before we give up:
lnRetries = 50
* Which retry are we on:
lnTry = 0

DO CASE
CASE m.lcAction == 'Check'
   LOCAL lnStatus
   lnStatus = loAsync.CheckForCompletion( m.lcJobId)
   * 0 means still running, negative numbers are error conditions
   DO CASE
   CASE m.lnStatus = -2   && bad ID
     THIS.ErrorMsg( "Invalid Request", ;
       "Sorry, your request was either invalid or has been lost." + ;
       " Please try again." )
     RETURN
   CASE m.lnStatus = -1   && cancel
     THIS.ErrorMsg( "Request Cancelled", ;
       "Your request has been cancelled." )
     RETURN
   CASE m.lnStatus = 1   && completed
     LOCAL lcResult, loReturnXML
     lcResult = loAsync.oEvent.ReturnData

     #IF .F.   && return XML
     Response.ContentTypeHeader( "text/xml")
     Response.Write( m.lcResult )
     #ELSE   && return HTML page
     loReturnXML = CREATEOBJECT( "wwXML")
     loReturnXML.XMLToCursor( m.lcResult, "TaskList")
     Response.ExpandScript( Process.cHTMLPAGEPATH + ;
       "tasklist.wcs", 3, THIS.Header)
     USE IN TaskList
     #ENDIF

     RETURN
   ENDCASE
CASE m.lcAction == "Cancel"
   loAsync.CancelEvent( m.lcJobId)
   THIS.StandardPage( "Your request has been cancelled.")
   RETURN
ENDCASE

* If we get this far, we want to return a status update page:
lnTry = loAsync.oEvent.ChkCounter
IF m.lnTry > m.lnRetries
   THIS.StandardPage( "Request Timeout", ;
     "Sorry, but your request could not be completed in a " + ;
     "timely fashion." + ;
     " Please try again later.")
   RETURN
ENDIF
```

```
lcMessage = 'Please wait. Your request is being processed. <br>' + ;
   [<table cellpadding=0 cellspacing=0 ] + ;
   [style="border: medium solid orange;" width=] + ;
   TRANSFORM( 5 * m.lnRetries) + [>] + ;
   [<tr><td style="background-color: blue;"] + ;
   [ width=] + TRANSFORM( 5 * m.lnTry) + ;
   [> </td><td> </td></tr></table>] + ;
   [<BR>] + loAsync.oEvent.Status

THIS.StandardPage( "Asynchronous Task List", m.lcMessage, , ;
   m.lnRefreshPeriod, ;
   'SlowListTasks.tsk?action=Check&JobId=' + m.lcJobId )

ENDFUNC   && SlowListTasks
```

That takes care of the various steps that are performed in the Web application itself. **Listing 2** shows the code that makes up the back-end application.

Listing 2. The back-end application code produces the actual result.

```
* ToDoAsyncMain.PRG
#INCLUDE WCONNECT.H
PARAMETERS lcJobId

IF EMPTY( m.lcJobId)
   RETURN
ENDIF
SET EXCLUSIVE OFF
SET TALK OFF
SET SAFETY OFF

DO wconnect
SET PROCEDURE TO wwasyncwebrequest ADDITIVE
SET PROCEDURE TO ToDoConfig ADDITIVE
SET PROCEDURE TO queryengine ADDITIVE

ON ERROR DO AsyncError IN ToDoAsyncMain WITH ;
   ERROR(), MESSAGE(), MESSAGE(1), SYS(16), LINENO()

DO PATH WITH '.\Data'

* Need some dummy objects to "simulate" the Server
* and Process objects in the TODO environment:
PRIVATE goWCServer, Process
goWCServer = CREATEOBJECT( "DummyServer")    && see below
Process    = CREATEOBJECT( "DummyProcess")   && see below

LOCAL loAsync, lcTitle
loAsync = CREATEOBJECT( "wwAsyncWebRequest")

IF NOT loAsync.LoadEvent( m.lcJobId)
   ON ERROR
   RETURN
ENDIF
```

```
loAsync.oEvent.Started = DATETIME()
loAsync.SaveEvent()

lcTitle = TRIM( loAsync.oEvent.Title)
DO CASE
CASE lcTitle == "Slow Task List"
  = DelayEvent( loAsync, m.lcJobId, 20)
  LOCAL loQuery, loXML, lcResult
  loQuery = CREATEOBJECT("QueryEngine")
  loQuery.Execute( "TASKLISTALL")
  loXML = CREATEOBJECT( "wwXML")
  loXML.nCreateDataStructure = 2 && include DTD
  lcResult = loXML.CursorToXML()
  loAsync.CompleteEvent( m.lcJobId, m.lcResult)
ENDCASE


ON ERROR
RETURN


* -------------------------------------------------------- *
FUNCTION AsyncError( lnErr, lcMess, lcCode, lcMethod, lnLine)
ON ERROR
WAIT WINDOW TIMEOUT 2 m.lcMess + [ (error ] + TRANS( m.lnErr) + [)]
IF NOT FILE( FULLPATH( ".\AsyncError.DBF"))
  SELECT 0
  CREATE TABLE AsyncError FREE ;
    ( Error I, Message C(80), Code M, Method C(50), Line I, MoreInfo M)
  USE
ENDIF
LOCAL lcLogString, lnLevel, lnPtr

lnLevel = PROGRAM(-1)
lcLogString = ""
lcLogString = m.lcLogString + "Program Stack" + CRLF + CRLF
FOR lnPtr = lnLevel TO 1 STEP -1
  lcLogString = m.lcLogString + ;
    TRANS( m.lnPtr) + [. ] + PROGRAM( m.lnPtr) + CRLF
ENDFOR
INSERT INTO AsyncError ;
    ( Error, Message, Code, Method, Line, MoreInfo) ;
    VALUES ;
    ( lnErr, lcMess, lcCode, lcMethod, lnLine, lcLogString )
ENDFUNC   && AsyncError


* -------------------------------------------------------- *
FUNCTION DelayEvent( loAsync, lcId, lnSecs)

DECLARE Sleep IN WIN32API INTEGER
LOCAL ii
FOR ii = 1 TO m.lnSecs
  Sleep( 1000)
  IF NOT loAsync.LoadEvent( m.lcID)
    LOOP
  ENDIF
  IF loAsync.oEvent.Cancelled
    RETURN
  ENDIF
  loAsync.oEvent.Status = TRANS( m.lnSecs - m.ii) + " seconds remaining."
  loAsync.SaveEvent()
ENDFOR
```

```
ENDFUNC   && DelayEvent
* ------------------------------------------------------ *
DEFINE CLASS DummyServer AS Custom
  oConfig = NULL
  cIniFile = "ToDo.INI"
  FUNCTION INIT
      THIS.SetEnvironment()
  ENDFUNC
  * ---------------------------------------------------- *
  FUNCTION SetEnvironment
      THIS.cIniFile = ADDBS( GetAppStartPath()) + THIS.cIniFile
      LOCAL lcStr

      THIS.oConfig = CREATE( "ToDoServerConfig")
      THIS.oConfig.cFileName = THIS.cIniFile
      THIS.oConfig.Load()
  ENDFUNC
ENDDEFINE
* ------------------------------------------------------ *
DEFINE CLASS DummyProcess AS Custom
  cTempPath = ""
  cShowPlanResults = ""
  * ---------------------------------------------------- *
  FUNCTION INIT
      THIS.cTempPath = goWcServer.oConfig.oTodo.cTempPath
  ENDFUNC
ENDDEFINE
```

Before you can test the new asynchronous operation, you must build the back-end executable. Create a new project named ToDoAsyncHandler, and add the preceding program as the main program. This project can be created in the same folder as your main TODO application. Build the project into an executable ToDoAsyncHandler.EXE.

You are now ready to test the system. Start your TODO application. Next go to your browser and enter a URL of http://localhost/todo/SlowListTasks.tsk.

If all is well, you should see responses such as shown in **Figure 1** during the delay period while the request is running. This response is constructed by checking a counter and a status line value from the wwAsync object. Notice that after each page refresh, more dots are replicated giving the impression of a stream of progress. You could obviously enhance this display with graphics and/or color in a production application.

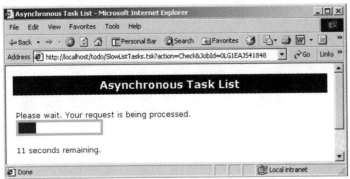

Figure 1. The user gets some comforting feedback while a long request is running.

Once the request has been completed, the expected response is then displayed.

Another feature of the wwAsyncWebRequest class is support for canceling a long request before completion. This can be easily accomplished by adding an extra link to the status result page shown in Figure 1. Simply change the code for building the message in the SlowListTasks method by adding:

```
lcMessage = m.lcMessage + ;
  [<p align=center>] + ;
  Response.Href( 'SlowListTasks.tsk?action=Cancel&JobId=' + m.lcJobId, ;
    "Cancel", .T.)
```

That's all it takes! Now while the processing is running, the status result will appear as in **Figure 2**. The cancel action works because of the CASE statement in the SlowListTasks() method that calls the CancelEvent() method of the wwAsyncWebRequest class.

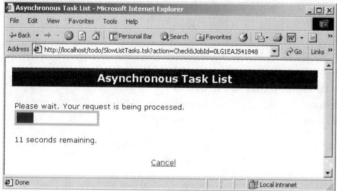

Figure 2. *The addition of a Cancel link gives your users more control.*

Pressing the Cancel link yields the result in **Figure 3**. (Note that in a production application, you would want to provide further guidance, and one or more links to allow navigation to a reasonable point in your application from which the user session should continue.)

Figure 3. *The user can cancel a request that is taking too long.*

Back-end deployment alternatives

In the previous example, a separate Visual FoxPro executable was launched in response to each request that requires asynchronous processing. If these requests are infrequent, the overhead of starting and stopping a Visual FoxPro instance might be acceptable.

Another alternative is to create an application that runs continuously and polls for new asynchronous requests. Once found, the request is processed. By deploying a back-end application in this fashion, the overhead of starting Visual FoxPro on each hit is eliminated. This is a more suitable choice if your Web Connection application must service frequent asynchronous processes. Further, you could design the back-end application to be scalable such that other servers (or workstations) could share the processing load. In the second half of this chapter, I present an application whose purpose is to process other scheduled tasks. In that presentation I also demonstrate how asynchronous processing could be incorporated.

SQL Server version

For developers who prefer to maintain all of their data in Microsoft SQL Server, there is a subclass of wwAsyncWebRequest class, called wwSQLAsyncWebRequest, that performs the same functions but with the asynchronous queue maintained in a SQL Server database. Refer to the Web Connection documentation for instructions on using that class.

When are asynchronous operations needed?

Now that you have seen how to build an asynchronous operation, you might be wondering what situations lead to this need. The most common situations are:

- Potentially long-running queries, such as those that require several joins, or perhaps contain full text searches or non-optimizable query conditions.

- Methods that interact with other components, possibly on other servers, such as building dynamic PDF files.

- Maintenance requests, such as reindexing or packing a database.

- Interacting with other services, such as a credit card processing service.

Scheduled operations

While asynchronous operations are important in dealing with lengthy processes in response to user requests, scheduled operations represent an entirely different need of handling tasks that need to be performed on a regular basis. Because these requirements are not driven by specific incoming Web hits, something else must trigger them.

In several of my systems, I run a separate Visual FoxPro application that I refer to as my Scheduled Task Server (STS). This is a simple application that scans through a Visual FoxPro job table for tasks to be run. Various fields allow the tasks to be customized as to their frequency and other important attributes.

Here are some of the examples of tasks that I perform using these applications:

- Sending queued messages to a mail server. I never send email messages directly from Web applications. There is too much of a risk of those messages being lost, for example if the mail server has crashed. Instead I always use a store-and-forward strategy for email messages. The STS then sends the messages only if it can confirm a connection to the mail server.

- Making a live backup copy of your database. In addition to tape backup strategies, I like to make a periodic live backup of certain databases (using basic COPY TO commands). This gives me extra protection in case of certain kinds of failures.

- Emailing the error log to the administrator. Web Connection records certain difficult communication problems outside of your Visual FoxPro application in a file named wcErrors.TXT. These errors can often go unnoticed by a system administrator. Therefore, I like to email this message file to the administrator on a daily basis.

- Deleting temporary files. In general, Web Connection cleans up its temporary files. Nevertheless, during periods of testing and problem solving, temporary files can build up, causing decreased system performance. I like to have a scheduled task delete any remaining temporary files on a daily basis.

- Maintaining the request log. The Web Connection request log can grow large fairly quickly on a busy site. Nevertheless, there are applications for which you will want to analyze site usage over an extended time period. If, however, you start adding indexes to the request log, performance of your Web Connection applications will suffer greatly. The approach I take is to create a new request log every day with no indexes. The date is encoded as part of the log file name, and the server knows to create a new log file, and release the handle to the previous file, when the date changes. I then create a separate archive that is used for long-term analysis. The archive has numerous indexes. Each night, a scheduled task appends the log from the previous day into the archive and then deletes any old log files.

- Running application-specific tasks. Each application has its own needs of this type. For example, the TODO application tracks actions that are due. In addition to providing a Web interface from which a person can review their open items, it might be nice if the application sent out email messages as items approached their due date. Another example is a Web store, where customers are notified of any delays or when their orders actually ship. Yet another example is the servicing of "subscription" choices, where users are notified via email when new information is posted to the database.

The one feature that all of these examples have in common is that you would like the action to occur automatically, and independently of any activity in the Web application. In the next section, I will present a simple application that can handle some basic Web Connection application tasks, and can be easily extended to add tasks of your own.

A Scheduled Task Server

The Scheduled Task Server (STS) applications that I use are simple engines that scan a job table looking for tasks that are within their schedule window. The application has built-in support for email and shares the configuration settings in your application INI file, for ease of maintenance.

In the following sections I will describe the general steps you would follow to build an STS application. While describing these steps I will also present an actual example to accompany the TODO application from Chapter 12. The source code for this STS application is included with the download for this chapter.

The example application has the following features:

- The main program instantiates a server class that controls individual task classes by running them when the schedule dictates.

- Each task has its own schedule parameters (maintained in a DBF file) to control frequency of execution.

- An optional status form shows tasks being performed and allows the server to be stopped.

- Individual tasks can be deactivated, placed on hold, or run additional (that is, unscheduled) times.

- Scalability is built-in so that additional machines can share the load. A task record must be locked before the task can be run, thus preventing two instances from running the same task simultaneously.

- The STS application shares use of the same configuration INI as the base Web Connection application, thus streamlining maintenance and ensuring consistent usage of shared settings.

The first iteration of the application will cover only generic tasks that apply to any Web Connection application. In subsequent iterations I will show how to add tasks that are specific to a given application, in this case the TODO application. All of these files are included in the source code for this book. I will address some of the features here. The files to be used with the STS application include:

- TodoSTSMain.PRG—The main program for the STS application.

- TodoConfig.PRG—Configuration classes discussed earlier.

- TodoSTSTask.PRG—Task definition classes for each individual task.

- TodoSTSProc.PRG—Procedure file containing special functions.

Step 1: Place the config classes in a separate file

The first step I suggest you need to take is to remove the various configuration classes from the main program of your application and place the code in a separate file. (This is the code in your main program that starts with a line like DEFINE CLASS ToDoConfig AS wwServerConfig and proceeds to the end of the main program.) In this example, the new file for the configuration classes is called ToDoConfig.PRG.

The reason to do this is that you are going to reuse these configuration classes in the STS application, in order to share the configuration settings in the application INI file. If you attempt to do this by simply using a SET PROCEDURE TO ToDoMain ADDITIVE statement, this would cause the Project Manager both to build the entire Web Connection framework into your supplemental applications, and to create additional, unwanted COM entries in the Registry. If instead you move the classes to a separate program file, you avoid these problems, because the main program with the OLEPUBLIC class will not be included in the STS project. Just be sure to adjust your main program so that it includes the statement:

```
SET PROCEDURE TO ToDoConfig ADDITIVE
```

As a warning, there is one downside to migrating to a separate configuration program file. You will no longer be able to use the New Process Wizard for this application, because that wizard tries to find the configuration class code in the main program. If you cannot deal with this limitation, you can still share use of the same INI file, but you will have to read any settings manually, using the wwAPI::GetProfileString method.

As you migrate the code to this new file, you will also be adding an additional object to represent a new [Schedule] section in the INI file. **Listing 3** shows an example of the completed program.

Listing 3. *The configuration class definitions migrated to their own PRG file.*

```
* ToDoCONFIG.PRG
**********************************************************************
DEFINE CLASS TodoServerConfig AS wwServerConfig
   oTodo = .NULL.
   oqeconfig = .NULL.
   odebug = .NULL.
   oSchedule = NULL

   FUNCTION INIT
      THIS.oTodo = CREATEOBJECT("todoConfig")
      THIS.oqeconfig = CREATEOBJECT("QEConfig")
      THIS.odebug = CREATEOBJECT("debugconfig")
      THIS.oSchedule = CREATEOBJECT("ScheduleConfig")
   ENDFUNC
ENDDEFINE

DEFINE CLASS todoConfig AS wwConfig
   cHTMLPagePath = ""
   cDatapath = ""
   cTempPath = ""
   cAdminPagePath=""
   lDebugPerformance = .F.
ENDDEFINE

DEFINE CLASS QEConfig AS wwConfig
   cEntityTable = "e:\webradsource\todosource\todo\data\querydefs"
   cDataSource="VFP"
ENDDEFINE

DEFINE CLASS debugconfig AS wwconfig
   cSHOWDEBUGINFO="NO"
   cDEBUGIP=""
   cSHOWMEMORY="NO"
   cSHOWSTATUS="NO"
   cDebugAdminPath="e:\webradsource\todosource\wwwroot\todo\admin\"
```

```
ENDDEFINE
*** Configuration class for Schedule Task Server:
DEFINE CLASS ScheduleConfig AS wwConfig
  cExecutable = "ToDoSTS.EXE"
  cFullURL    = "http://www.yourdomain.com/todo/" && supports URL creation
cTitle       = "TODO Scheduler"
  nLoopSleep  = 10   && pause between loops (seconds)
  nTaskSleep  = 1    && pause between tasks within a loop (seconds)
  lTesting    = .T. && if TRUE, email all sent to "cTestingEmail"
  cTestingEmail = "your_email@your_domain.com"
  nTestingEmailPercent = 10 && percent of messages to send when testing
  lRunOnce    = .F. && if TRUE, only loop through tasks once, then exit
  lStatusForm = .T. && if TRUE, show top-level status form
ENDDEFINE  && ScheduleConfig
```

Step 2: Create a main controlling program

Next you will create the main program for the STS. In the example, this is entitled
ToDoSTSMain.PRG. This program includes the startup code, the controlling server class
code, error handling, and code for an (optional) status form. As with main programs for Web
Connection applications, you must place this main program in the main project folder (with
your project and EXE), even if you place all other source code in a subfolder.

You will also use a few auxiliary files.

Step 3: Create abstract class for individual tasks

Your primary server class will have the responsibility of launching the individual tasks when
they are scheduled to be executed. By creating an abstract class with a standard interface,
subclasses for each concrete class can be created that will be compatible with the server.

To understand this point, first examine the code in the server that calls each task:

```
loTask = CREATEOBJECT( TRIM( THIS.oJob.Class), THIS )
THIS.NewStatusLine( TRANS( DATETIME()) + [ "] + loTask.cTitle + [" ])
* Run the task:
= loTask.Execute()
IF loTask.lError
  * stamp record with error indication
ELSE
  * stamp record with time run and success info
ENDIF
```

What happens here is that the server finds the class name for the task in the Class field of
the task table, and instantiates that class when the task is to be performed. The server then calls
the Execute() method of that class. Thus, at the simplest level, your class need only have an
Execute() method and a few specified properties to have an interface that is compatible with
the server. Rather than creating these for each class, however, you can create an abstract class
that provides this interface, such as that shown in **Listing 4**, and then subclass each concrete
task from there. In the examples for this chapter, both the abstract and concrete tasks are found
in TodoSTSTask.PRG. I will discuss some of the code here.

Listing 4. *Abstract class for executing scheduled tasks.*

```
* ======================================================= *
DEFINE CLASS StsTask AS SESSION
* ======================================================= *
* Abstract class for individual tasks. All task
* definitions are subclassed from this task.
cTitle = ""

lDisabled = .F.       && Flag to temporarily disable task.
oServer = NULL        && Reference back to calling server.

lError = .F.          && Flag indicating an error has occurred.
cErrorMessage = ""    && Property for error handler.
cErrorInfo = ""       && Property for error handler.

* Optional-use properties for counting individual results:
nSuccesses = 0
nFailures = 0
nSkips = 0

* ------------------------------------------------------- *
FUNCTION cTitle_ACCESS
  RETURN IIF( EMPTY( THIS.cTitle), THIS.Name, THIS.cTitle)
ENDFUNC
* ------------------------------------------------------- *
FUNCTION ERROR( nError, cMethod, nLine)
  * Error handling mechanism. Sets flag and stored error
  * info for server to use in communicating problems to admin.
  THIS.lError = .T.
  THIS.cErrorMessage = MESSAGE()
  THIS.cErrorInfo = ErrorToXml( THIS.Class, nError, cMethod, nLine)
  DO StsError WITH nError, cMethod, nLine, ;
    THIS.Class, THIS.cErrorInfo
  IF UPPER( m.cMethod) == "EXECUTEIMPLEMENTATION"
    RETURN TO Execute
  ENDIF
ENDFUNC && ERROR
* ------------------------------------------------------- *
FUNCTION RELEASE
  THIS.oServer = NULL
  CLOSE DATA ALL   && We're in a private datasession.
ENDFUNC
* ------------------------------------------------------- *
FUNCTION DESTROY
  THIS.RELEASE()
ENDFUNC
* ------------------------------------------------------- *
FUNCTION INIT( loServer)
  * Repeat this, since it's a new private datasession:
  DO StandardVfpSettings
  THIS.oServer = m.loServer
  = THIS.Setup()
ENDFUNC  && INIT
* ------------------------------------------------------- *
FUNCTION Setup
ENDFUNC  && Setup
* ------------------------------------------------------- *
FUNCTION Reset
```

```
      THIS.nSuccesses = 0
      THIS.nFailures = 0
      THIS.nSkips = 0
      THIS.lError = .F.
      THIS.cErrorMessage = ""
      THIS.cErrorInfo = ""
   ENDFUNC   && Reset
   * ------------------------------------------------------ *
   FUNCTION Execute
      = THIS.PreExecute()
      IF NOT THIS.lError
         * Call the actual implementation code in the
         * individual task's class definition:
         = THIS.ExecuteImplementation()
      ENDIF
      CLOSE DATA ALL
      RETURN NOT THIS.lError
   ENDFUNC   && Execute
   * ------------------------------------------------------ *
   FUNCTION PreExecute
      = THIS.Reset()
   ENDFUNC   && PreExecute
   * ------------------------------------------------------ *
   FUNCTION ExecuteImplementation
      * Must be overridden in specific class code!
      THIS.lError = .T.
      THIS.cErrorMessage = "No class code for ExecuteImplementation()!"
      RETURN .F.
   ENDFUNC   && ExecuteImplementation
   * ====================================================== *
   ENDDEFINE   && StsTask
   * ====================================================== *
```

The abstract class is designed for easy subclassing. Your only absolute requirement is to implement the ExecuteImplementation() method. Thus a (not very useful) task could be as simple as:

```
DEFINE CLASS TestTask AS StsTask
FUNCTION ExecuteImplementation
   WAIT WINDOW TIMEOUT 1.0 "Hello. I was executed."
ENDFUNC
ENDDEFINE
```

That is rather straightforward. Although this class doesn't really do anything, in further examples, you will notice that the code is often almost as simple. Before examining some concrete examples, there are some interesting features of the abstract class to understand.

- Although I indicated that the server calls an Execute() method, the preceding example shows that you must implement a method called ExecuteImplementation(). That is because the abstract class has an Execute() method that sets up the environment and calls your ExecuteImplementation() method in a controlled manner. This is a simple example of the "template" design pattern.

- A hook is provided for a method named Setup(). This can be convenient if creating a class hierarchy for a group of related tasks, and you want some common code implemented prior to execution, such as opening a database.

- The class is based on the Visual FoxPro Session base class. Because the Session base class sets up a private data session, this allows you to create very simple implementations without worrying about opening and closing files and other Visual FoxPro environmental issues.

- The Error() method checks to see whether the error occurred in your ExecuteImplementation() code, and if so attempts to RETURN TO Execute. This approach allows clean recovery from lots of problems and reduces to some degree the sensitivity of the system to errors in your concrete class code.

The intent behind this design is to allow new tasks to be added as easily as possible. To see this in use, **Listing 5** shows one of the tasks in the sample application, which deletes any temporary Web Connection files that may have accumulated.

Listing 5. *A concrete task derived from the abstract class.*

```
DEFINE CLASS DeleteTempAppFilesTask AS StsTask
* Delete old files in TEMP folder.
* ---------------------------------------------------- *
FUNCTION ExecuteImplementation
  LOCAL lcPath, lnFiles, lnSkips, lnFails
  lcPath = ADDBS( THIS.oServer.oConfig.cTempFilePath )
  STORE 0 TO lnFiles, lnSkips, lnFails

  * Delete temp files more than 1 hour old:
  lnFiles = m.lnFiles + StsDeleteFiles( m.lcPath + "*.RET", ;
    60 * 60, @lnSkips, @lnFails )
  lnFiles = m.lnFiles + StsDeleteFiles( m.lcPath + "*.TMP", ;
    60 * 60, @lnSkips, @lnFails )
  * Optional code that updates server status display window:
  THIS.nSuccesses = m.lnFiles
  THIS.nSkips = m.lnSkips
  THIS.nFailures = m.lnFails
ENDFUNC   && ExecuteImplementation
ENDDEFINE   && DeleteTempAppFilesTask
```

As you can see, this code is very simple and is dedicated to the task at hand. In fact, about half of the code is optional and is used only to update the status shown in the server status form. This class calls a simple utility function named STSDeleteFiles() that is included in TodoSTSProcs.PRG.

Step 4: Test with just the basic tasks

Before adding any custom tasks of your own, make sure that the basic server application is operating correctly. If you want to try this with the TODO application using the sample files included with the source code for this chapter, you can test the application from the Command Window as follows:

```
DO TodoSTSMain
```

As with all Web Connection applications, be certain the main program is located in the current directory, or the server class will not behave properly when tested from the Visual FoxPro IDE. If all is well, you should see a Visual FoxPro application running in a top-level form such as in **Figure 4**.

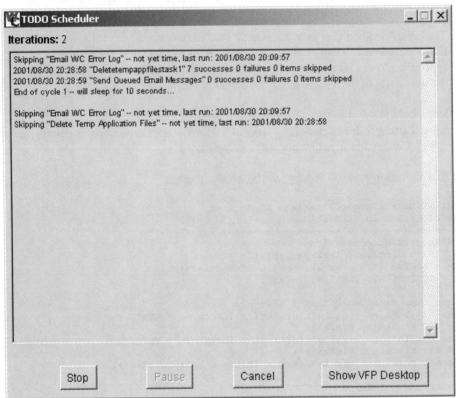

Figure 4. *The Schedule Task Server in operation.*

If all is working and there are some Web Connection error entries in the wcErrors.TXT file, you should receive an email message such as that shown in **Figure 5**.

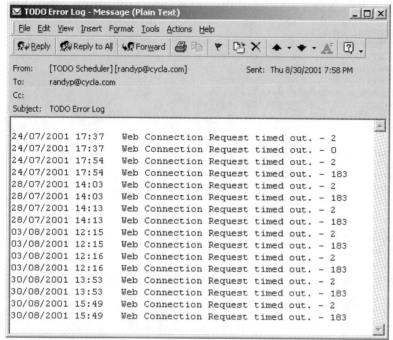

Figure 5. *The Web Connection error log arrives via a daily email message.*

Step 5: Add your own additional tasks

The real payoff to the STS application comes when you can add your own custom tasks that are specific to your Web Connection application.

As an example, suppose in the TODO application you would like to send daily messages reminding people of incomplete action items that are assigned to them and are either overdue or due on that day. To add a task of your own, there are two steps.

 First, you create the new class. An example is shown in **Listing 6**. (Note that the class is already included in the source code, but it will not be triggered until a record is added to the job table as described later.)

Listing 6. *A further concrete class to send email reminders.*

```
DEFINE CLASS TaskDueEmailTodoTask AS TodoTask
* -------------------------------------------------- *
FUNCTION ExecuteImplementation

SELECT iTaskIdPK, cTask, mNotes, mSolution, dEntered, ;
    dEstFinish, iUserIdPK, cEmail ;
  FROM Todo ;
    JOIN Users ON iAsgnIdFK = iUserIdPK ;
  WHERE EMPTY( dCompleted) AND ;
    EMPTY( dEstFinish) OR dEstFinish <= DATE() ;
  INTO CURSOR Items_Due_
```

```
LOCAL lcSubject
SCAN
  IF IsValidEmail( TRIM( cEmail))
    lcMessage = [<HTML><BODY>] + ;
      [<H2 ALIGN=CENTER>Action Due Notice</H2>] + ;
      [<P>The following action is assigned to you and ] + ;
      IIF( EMPTY( dEstFinish), ;
        " does not have a schedule date", ;
        " has a due date of " + TRANS( dEstFinish)) + ;
      [.<P>] + TRIM( cTask) + [<P>] + mNotes + ;
      [</BODY></HTML>]

    THIS.oServer.SendMessage( ;
      TRIM( cEmail), ;
      "TODO Action Due Notice", ;
      m.lcMessage, ;
      .F., .F., .F., .F., "text/html" )
  ENDIF
ENDSCAN
ENDFUNC  && ExecuteImplementation
ENDDEFINE  && TaskDueEmailTodoTask
```

Second, manually add a record to the StsJob table with the class and schedule attributes. You want to run this task once every day, so your entry would look like that shown in **Figure 6**.

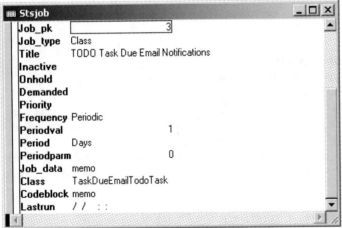

Figure 6. A record must be added to the Job table to control the task.

Now run the application again, and if there are any items due in the TODO database, a set of email messages should be sent. An example of a test message is shown in **Figure 7**.

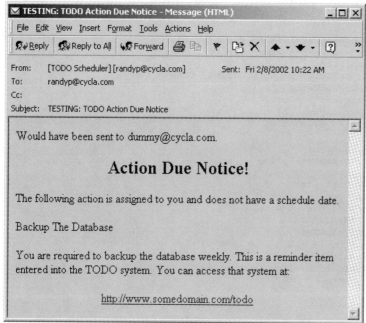

Figure 7. Example email message sent in test mode.

Notice that both the subject and the text of the message appear slightly different from what you might expect by examining the Visual FoxPro code for the task. This is because the STS application is designed with a "testing" mode, configurable via an INI file setting. When Testing=On, all email messages are routed to the address indicated by the "TestingEmail" setting. This lets you confirm that your system operates properly without sending actual messages to real users, who might be confused about the purpose of the message if your system is only in a test mode.

Also notice that in this example, the email has been formatted with a content type of "text/html" so that it can contain rich content. If your users have email clients that do not support rich content, you will need to revise your approach to send your content as "text/plain" (the default) and without the HTML markup.

Serving asynchronous requests

As you recall, the first half of this chapter was devoted to deploying asynchronous operations to handle lengthy Web requests. One of the requirements was to have another application perform the actual request. In the example given, an entire EXE was launched for each such request.

If your application involves frequent long-running requests, launching a copy of Visual FoxPro for each request will not be an efficient use of resources. As you have just seen, the STS application runs continuously looking for tasks to perform. Thus it is a perfect match for the requirement of running these back-end requests. All you need to do is add a task that performs the same operation shown in the asynchronous example. **Listing 7**, which can be found in TodoSTSTask.PRG, does just that.

Listing 7*. Processing asynchronous requests from a scheduled task server.*

```
DEFINE CLASS ProcessAsyncRequestsTask AS StsTask
* ------------------------------------------------------ *
FUNCTION ExecuteImplementation
LOCAL loAsync, lcJobId, lcTitle, loQuery, loXML, lcResult
loAsync = CREATE( "wwAsyncWebRequest")
DO WHILE loAsync.GetNextEvent() = .T.
  lcJobId = TRIM( loAsync.oEvent.ID)
  IF NOT loAsync.LoadEvent( m.lcJobId)
    LOOP
  ENDIF
  lcTitle = TRIM( loAsync.oEvent.Title)
  DO CASE
  CASE lcTitle == "Slow Task List"
    THIS.DelayEvent( loAsync, m.lcJobId, 20)
    loQuery = CREATEOBJECT("QueryEngine")
    loQuery.Execute( "TASKLISTALL")
    loXML = CREATEOBJECT( "wwXML")
    loXML.nCreateDataStructure = 2 && include DTD
    lcResult = loXML.CursorToXML()
    loAsync.CompleteEvent( m.lcJobId, m.lcResult)
  ENDCASE

  THIS.oServer.ShowProgress()
ENDDO
ENDFUNC  && ExecuteImplementation
* ------------------------------------------------------ *
FUNCTION DelayEvent( loAsync, lcId, lnSecs)

DECLARE Sleep IN WIN32API INTEGER
LOCAL ii
FOR ii = 1 TO m.lnSecs
  Sleep( 1000)
  IF NOT loAsync.LoadEvent( m.lcID)
    LOOP
  ENDIF
  IF loAsync.oEvent.Cancelled
    RETURN
  ENDIF
  loAsync.oEvent.Status = TRANS( m.lnSecs - m.ii) + " seconds remaining."
  loAsync.SaveEvent()
ENDFOR
ENDFUNC  && DelayEvent
* ================================================== *
ENDDEFINE  && ProcessAsyncRequestsTask
```

Once again, you need to add a corresponding record to the StsJob table. This one, shown in **Figure 8**, has a much smaller time period, because you want to check frequently for new asynchronous requests.

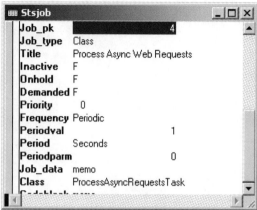

Figure 8. *Checking for new asynchronous requests every second.*

With this in place, you should return to the code for the SlowListTasks() method, and remove the code that launched the separate EXE on each request. In other words, you would *delete or comment out* these lines that were used before:

```
LOCAL lcRunCmd
lcRunCmd = [RUN /n4 TODOAsyncHandler.EXE ] + m.lcJobId
&lcRunCmd
```

As long as your STS is running, this approach is no longer needed. If you do handle these requests in this manner, you may want to adjust the sleep intervals in the [Schedule] section of the TODO.INI file, in order to improve the responsiveness of the application to new asynchronous requests.

 If you want to test the implementation of the STS servicing the asynchronous requests, you need to compile the STS into a separate EXE file and run the EXE as a separate process. You can do this by building the TodoSTS.PJX project that is included with the source code for this chapter. Start the executable and also start your TODO Web application. You should be able to return to the SlowListTasks page and observe your new mechanism in action.

Conclusion

This chapter has presented the concepts for both asynchronous and scheduled operations to accompany a Web Connection application. These can become important supporting components for mature Web applications.

Resources

The wwAsyncWebRequest class and ideas for its usage is described in the following article:
www.west-wind.com/presentations/wwAsyncWebRequest/wwAsyncWebRequest.htm

Chapter 20
Updating to New Web
Connection Versions

Working with a third-party product adds extra variables to your application life cycle. One of these variables occurs when a new version of the third-party product is released. This chapter discusses strategies to consider when deciding if and when to update your applications when new versions of Web Connection are released.

Web Connection is frequently updated. Because the primary medium for sale and distribution is the Internet, posting frequent updates is very efficient. Whenever an update is posted, licensed users are advised via an email message. This email message describes the changes that are included in the update. Changes include both enhancements and bug fixes.

Should you update?
Each time a new version of Web Connection is released, you certainly are not required to update. Whether or not to update should be based on three factors:

- Pricing and licensing

- Enhancements and bug fixes

- The cost of your time

These factors are discussed in the following sections.

Pricing and licensing
In the past, an upgrade price has been incurred only when a major version was released. All incremental version updates with the same major version number have been free. In addition, there is typically a grace period wherein you receive the upgrade for free if you purchased your license recently (say, a few months or less) before a new major version was released.

Therefore, pricing is a factor in your decision only when you are facing a major version release (for instance, 2.x to 3.0, or 3.x to 4.0).

Enhancements and bug fixes
Each new version incorporates either enhancements to the product or bug fixes. Most versions include some of both. Therefore, a major determinant in whether to update should be your assessment of whether you will use any new enhancements or whether you are currently affected by any bugs that have been fixed.

Unless you notice changes of interest, you probably will not want to update with each minor release. Nevertheless, it is useful to remain reasonably current. For example, conversations on the West Wind Message Board typically focus on the latest product release.

If you are far behind the curve, you may not be able to benefit from the latest approaches being discussed. Further, if you encounter a problem that has already been fixed by a subsequent release, you may need to update in a hurry, sometimes at an inconvenient time.

The cost of your time

The final factor to consider is the cost of your time in performing the update. The degree of this cost depends on the developer. Expert Web Connection developers can probably download an update, rebuild their applications, and install the changes on a production server in 15-30 minutes. Inexperienced developers probably cannot come close to this mark. The amount of time it will take any individual is difficult to predict; however, if you read this book and follow the guidance in this chapter, you should find updating to be a fairly straightforward exercise. Further, help is always available via the West Wind Message Board.

Toward a successful update

In order to enhance your chances of performing a successful update in a minimum amount of time, you should be aware of what needs to be accomplished. Specifically:

- The previous Web Connection framework source code is replaced with that from the new version.

- A new version of WC.DLL is provided. You will need to replace the previous version, copies of which may reside in several folders (one for each Web Connection application on your system).

- You will receive a new version of header file WCONNECT.H. You need to ensure that any changes you made to this file previously are migrated to the new version. This approach has often made updating more difficult than necessary. Starting with version 4.0, this has been improved. See the next section, "WCONNECT.H file considerations," for more details.

- You must rebuild your entire executable, using the RECOMPILE option of the BUILD command (or the Recompile All Files check box of the Build dialog). This step is required to ensure that the latest compiler directives are reflected in all source code modules. Also, see the caution below concerning generation of component IDs.

> ❗ *Caution! If you use COM messaging, be certain that you always build your executable from the same Visual FoxPro project, and that you **do not** select the Project Manager option to "regenerate component IDs" when you do so. Otherwise, your COM Class ID will change, resulting in incorrect Registry settings in your production (and staging) server. Refer to Chapter 14, "COM vs. File-Based Messaging," for details about COM messaging.*

- To test your application within VFP by running your main program from the Command Window, you will also need to recompile individual source code modules.

- You will receive an updated copy of wwIpStuff.DLL. When you migrate your re-compiled executable to the production server, you must copy the latest copy of the wwIpStuff.DLL file to the server as well.

WCONNECT.H file considerations

In early versions of Web Connection, the most problematic aspect of updating was often figuring out how to deal with the WCONNECT.H file.

Why is a small text file such a problem? The answer is that it contains numerous framework constants, some of which developers are free to alter, but others that should never be touched. Additionally, new versions of Web Connection often add new constants and change the values of other constants. (The WWVERSION and WWVERSIONDATE date constants, for example, change with every new version.)

This created a dilemma with each version update. If you retained your old version of this file, you would be excluding new (required) constants, and using some outdated values for others. Conversely, if you used the new version of the file, you would be overwriting any constants that you had previously changed from their defaults. Choosing either of these courses could result in broken applications, or at least unexpected behavior.

The solution that many developers used was to compare the two file versions line-by-line, and merge the two into a version that included all of the right values. This was an error-prone and somewhat tedious process.

When version 3 of Web Connection was released, a somewhat better technique was suggested by Web Connection developer Michael Dyer. What you would do is add a single final line to the bottom of WCONNECT.H to #INCLUDE a further file in which you would make any changes to the framework constants by using the #UNDEF directive, prior to redefining each constant. To illustrate, suppose you wanted to change the DEBUGMODE setting to true, and to subclass the wwProcess class with your own class. You would create a new file called, for example, MY_WCONNECT.H, that might look like this:

```
* MY_WCONNECT.H
#UNDEF DEBUGMODE
#DEFINE DEBUGMODE  .T.

#UNDEF WWC_PROCESS
#DEFINE WWC_PROCESS myWwProcess
```

Then, to cause these definitions to be used, you would add the following line to the end of WCONNECT.H:

```
#INCLUDE MY_WCONNECT.H
```

Now, when a new version of Web Connection was released, you could freely copy the new WCONNECT.H file over the previous one, and all you needed to remember was to add the #INCLUDE directive to the end.

This was indeed an improvement, but it still required you to remember this one additional step. A final improvement to this process has now been recommended, and its use will become standard with Web Connection version 4. First, all developers will now standardize on the name of the file used for overriding the constants. This file name will be WCONNECT_OVERRIDE.H. Second, to ensure that this file is always honored, while not causing problems when there is no such file, the following lines will appear at the end of WCONNECT.H:

```
#IF FILE( "WCONNECT_OVERRIDE.H")
  #INCLUDE WCONNECT_OVERRIDE.H
#ENDIF
```

This approach now solves all of the original update problems.

Even if you are not yet planning to update to version 4 of Web Connection, you can still prepare for the eventual update by using this naming convention for your #INCLUDE file (assuming you have such a file). If instead you have been changing constants directly in the WCONNECT.H file, I suggest you immediately stop this practice and start using the technique described here.

Update procedures

The process for updating is straightforward. First you install the update on your development machine and get your application working with the new version. Then you move the requisite files onto the production server.

Updating your development machine

The procedure for updating to a new version of Web Connection on your development machine is:

1. Back up your current files, including your installation of Web Connection and your application source code files.

2. Before doing anything else, read any instructions provided with the update. These are generally provided via an email message that announces the update.

3. Download the new version, which is packaged as a single, password-protected, self-extracting executable file. The file name depends on the version number. For example, the file name for version 3.65 was wc_365.EXE. As of version 4 this naming convention appears to have changed slightly, such that the file name for version 4.01 was wwwc_401.EXE. The email announcements for each new version always include the specific file name.

4. Delete all files from the .\classes and .\tools subfolders of your Web Connection installation directory. This step ensures that outdated framework files are not retained. Note, however, that you should not simply delete the entire \wconnect folder, because you might remove important files that you have created or altered, such as WCONNECT_OVERRIDE.H.

5. Also delete all FXP files from your own application source code. This ensures that any new compiler constants are utilized, and that testing from the Command Window can be performed without accidentally using any outdated code modules. If your main

PRG is in the application's root directory, but all others are in a separate directory (for example, .\Progs), make sure you delete FXP files from both locations.

6. Start the unzipping process by opening the downloaded file. For most situations, it is recommended that you use the Unzip button, rather than the Run WinZip button. Use the Run WinZip button for situations where you only need to unzip selected files.

7. When prompted, supply the password that was provided in the email message. Passwords are case-sensitive. The password changes with each minor version in a predictable manner based on version number. With each major version, which requires an upgrade fee, the root of the password scheme changes so that those not paying the upgrade fee cannot "guess" the new password scheme.

8. When prompted for a directory to unzip the files, choose the same directory where you previously installed Web Connection (for example, c:\wconnect\).

9. If there is a check box labeled "When done unzipping open: setup.exe," be certain it is *not* checked! Leaving this checked causes steps to be performed that are appropriate only for first-time installations—not updates.

10. Start Visual FoxPro using the same method you normally use to access Web Connection (via a shortcut or the Start menu option, for instance).

11. Review the earlier section titled "WCONNECT.H h file considerations" to determine whether any actions are necessary. Once you have migrated to the new approach of using a WCONNECT_OVERRIDE.H file, this entire step will become a thing of the past.

12. Stop your Web Service, so that the previous WC.DLL file is released from memory and can be overwritten. If your Web Service is Microsoft Internet Information Server (IIS), you can stop the service from the "services" applet, available from the Control Panel in Windows NT, or from the "Services and Applications" item under Computer Management in Windows 2000. The specific service is labeled, "World Wide Web Publishing Service."

13. Copy the new WC.DLL file over the previous version in each applicable virtual directory. (The new file is found in the .\scripts subfolder of your Web Connection installation directory.)

14. Start the Web Service that was stopped in step 12.

15. In general you can also copy the latest admin.asp file (found in the .\html subdirectory) into each virtual directory to replace the previous version. Nevertheless, you need to be aware of whether you had previously altered this file for your own purposes. If so, you should retain the old version. You can then review the new version to see whether any new options have been added, and merge any HTML as you deem appropriate. Note that, in general, old versions of this file tend to operate correctly with new versions of Web Connection.

16. Now open the Visual FoxPro project manager, and rebuild your EXE. Be certain to select the choice to Recompile All Files. (If during this process the project manager

complains of files missing, choose Remove—you have probably encountered file names that have been removed or renamed in the framework.)

17. Test your application on the development machine to verify that operation has not been affected by the new version of Web Connection.

Updating a staging or production server

Once you have confirmed that your application operates properly with the new Web Connection version on your development system, it is time to move the application into production.

1. Re-read the instructions that accompanied the update to determine whether anything discussed will affect your production environment.

2. Stop the Web Service on the applicable server. (If using IIS, the Service is named "World Wide Web Publishing Service." See step 12 in the previous procedure for more details.)

3. If you are using file-based messaging, also close any running instances by selecting the Exit button on the Web Connection server window.

4. Copy the new WC.DLL file into proper folder for the application virtual directory. (For example, c:\inetpub\wwwroot\yourApp\.)

5. Copy the new version of your EXE file from the development machine to the proper location on the server. (Note: If you have used the "online code update" feature of Web Connection, that process does not apply when updating Web Connection versions. You want to copy the EXE directly over the previous production copy on the server.)

6. Copy the new version of wwIpStuff.DLL to the same folder as your EXE file.

7. If you found it necessary to copy the new admin.asp into your development directories, don't forget to do this on the server as well.

> *Web Connection documentation also recommends that you install the wwIpStuff.DLL file in the Windows System32 folder. I have not found this to be necessary. Nevertheless, if the production server already has a copy of this file in the Windows System32 folder, there is no reason not to copy the newest version there as well.*

8. If using file-based messaging, start your application EXE.

9. Start the Web Service that was stopped in step 2.

10. Test to confirm proper operation.

Updating more than one application

If you have more than one Web Connection application, the process to follow is highly dependent on the specific approach and directory structures you have used. If, for example, you have a separate copy of the Web Connection framework for each application, you will obviously have to update each application separately. Note, however, that many different Web Connection revisions can coexist on the same machine, so you are never required to update all applications at the same time.

If instead you have used a common copy of the Web Connection framework for all of your applications, such as in some of the example applications presented in this book, you have one of two choices available. The first option is to simply update the Web Connection installation using the procedure presented in this chapter. Adopting this option constrains you to updating all of your applications to the new version. That does not mean, however, that you are obliged to deploy revisions of all applications to production servers immediately.

The second option is to create a second installation of the Web Connection framework in a separate directory structure. For example, if the previous version is in the c:\wconnect folder, you could install version 4 in c:\wc4. Now you can make your update decisions one application at a time by changing paths and/or migrating application-specific files. The exact process is too dependent on the specific choices you have made to allow for a generalized procedure to be presented in this book.

Migrating from a Web Connection 2.x application

If you still have applications based on version 2 of Web Connection, there is more work to be done. Numerous changes were made in version 3 that broke backward compatibility. Although most of these were simple name changes, some required more effort.

Fortunately, Web Connection developer Paul Mrozowski and I have written a migration tool. To accompany this tool, a detailed procedure was also written that describes two different potential strategies for migrating from version 2. Refer to the Help topic "Migration to Web Connection 3.x" for this procedure and details on using the migration tool.

> ❗ *Caution!* The Help topics for migrating from version 2 have been removed as of Web Connection version 4. If you are attempting to migrate directly from version 2 to version 4, and do not have a copy of the version 3 Help file, you may need to request specific assistance. The migration tool and procedure will work for this migration.

Mistakes to avoid while updating

Following the instructions that accompany the update while using the procedures presented here should see you through to a successful update. Nevertheless, there are some common mistakes to be avoided:

- Do *not* copy the new WC.INI file over your current copies. This file contains several settings that are specific to your environment. Copying this file will overwrite these settings and cause your applications to fail. Do not worry about the new version—

new settings are seldom added to this file. In the event one is, the update instructions will be clear in advising you how to add the new setting to your existing WC.INI file.

- When unzipping the new Web Connection version, do not check the box to run Setup.EXE after unzipping. This is only appropriate for first-time installations, and could cause you to overwrite some of your existing work if you run the executable and make the wrong choices.

- If you have made alterations to any Web Connection framework code, you have special issues to face. As discussed in Chapter 16, "Extending the Framework," altering the framework is a bad practice. Instead, there are techniques for extending the framework via subclasses that remove this burden when updating to new versions. What should you do in the meantime? I recommend comparing the new source code module to the prior version line-by-line using a tool such as Beyond Compare. While doing so, note the changes that are needed. Now is the time to convert to a subclassing approach using the guidance from Chapter 16.

- You cannot use the "Update Code Online" option when updating to a new version of Web Connection. There are simply more tasks to perform than this process could ever offer. Most notably, you will be replacing the WC.DLL file itself, which precludes the possibility of having this file control the update process. Additionally, you will be updating to a new wwIpStuff.DLL file, which is not offered by the "Update Code Online" process.

- Although not specifically an "updating" issue, there is a frequent problem encountered when *upgrading* from the shareware version to the licensed version of Web Connection. When doing so, if you do nothing more than unzip the full version into the same directory as the shareware version, you will continue to see "shareware" messages. You must also delete the WCONNECT.APP file to resolve this issue. If, however, you also run Setup.EXE after unzipping, this action is performed for you.

Resources

- Web Connection Help topic titled, "Updating to a New Web Connection Version."

Chapter 21
Marketing Your Web Site

Marketing is one of those areas in which many developers lack significant working knowledge. If you are an independent consultant, knowing something about marketing is fundamental to your survival. If you are working in a larger company where there is a separate marketing department, you may never get any exposure to this area. Even in this environment, it can be important to know what is going on in marketing so you can determine your company's prospects—the fact is, without marketing, your company will not survive. This chapter will introduce the concepts of marketing your Web site so your hard work does not go to waste.

Marketing is the process of driving qualified leads to your company. Ideally your sales force, whether that consists of you or a 20-person sales team, should not have to make cold calls. The marketing presence that is out in the community should be able to inform prospective clients that you have a product or service that will solve some problem they are having. If this is not happening, either customers will never know you exist or your sales team will be spending valuable resources making cold calls. Cold calling is a highly inefficient way to generate sales. Too much time has to be spent explaining your product or service to people who may not even be interested. Ideally, a sales team should be in place to close the sales that come in as the result of marketing material that your company produces.

Marketing is just another one of the skills a successful developer must know in order to survive. It is just like having to know some of the other new skills that have been discussed in this book. It may not be as technical as knowing how to configure IIS, but it is just as vital.

Great technology in and of itself does not generate sales. As everyone in the Visual FoxPro community knows, Visual FoxPro is a great database development environment, but people outside the community had no idea what it does. That is now changing. Some of the things the FoxPro team is now doing will be discussed here.

Some marketing successes

See if you can think of some really successful marketing campaigns. One that may come to mind is Beanie Babies. These stuffed toys are really no different from the hundreds of other stuffed toys that are on the market. One of the things that made Beanie Babies stand out was the notion of "limited supply." Each line of Beanie Babies had a limited run and was then retired. This created a tremendous perceived need in the minds of consumers to by them now before they ran out. It worked! People would by each line of the stuffed toys before they ran out. When the final consumer is a child, that child exerts a tremendous influence on the parent to buy the product before it is "gone forever."

Microsoft is a marketing-driven company. Some of its products are not the market leaders in innovation, but with its marketing department, Microsoft is able to generate the perceived need for its products. Being picked by IBM to provide the DOS operating system helped Microsoft and gave it the chance to be first in the PC market. When you are first, the market gives you a lot more latitude. This gave Microsoft the clout to control the operating system that PC manufacturers installed on their machines. This served as a way to market the rest of its software applications as well. Everyone already had Windows, so it was much easier to sell other Microsoft software to the same people.

Some other marketing success stories are:

- eBay: It was the first online auction house. Being first is what helped make it a success. This is one of the few dot-com businesses that has had real staying power. It is profitable and is here to stay. The eBay site is very simple to use, lightweight, and has attracted so much traffic that it is possible to find almost anything there.

- McDonalds: Wherever you go, if you see the Golden Arches, you know exactly what you will be getting. McDonalds is the same everywhere you go. McDonalds has built such a strong brand that its restaurants can be recognized a mile away. You can be sure there will be no other hamburger restaurant with a trademark resembling the arches any time soon!

- George Foreman Grill: These grills have sold tremendously well. The technique of using endorsement marketing has been very successful. George's commercials are enjoyable to watch, he is a household name, and the products work well.

Marketing failures

There have been some big marketing failures in the business world. Many of them were based on bad business models from the outset, while others were great ideas foiled by poor marketing. Here are some examples:

- New Coke: What was wrong with the old Coke? When there is an established hold on the market, there is no need in the mind of the consumer to replace it.

- IBM PC: IBM is the leader in "big iron" computing, but not in the PC market. This was a case of over-extension. It was believed that IBM could sell a computer no matter what form it took. In the consumer's mind, however, PCs were not what IBM was about.

- Numerous online retailers: Sites such as pets.com failed due to poor market research. Their products might have been marginally cheaper, but then shipping had to be added to the price. In the world of e-commerce there is no loyalty. Another site is simply a click away. Consumers felt more comfortable going to stores and picking up their pet supplies for the same price. You need to figure out whether your pricing model both solves a perceived consumer problem and is sufficient to keep you in business!

- USDatacenters, Inc: This company spent $17 million in 18 months to build an Internet data center. Now, the timing was bad, but they also *never* did any marketing. The potential customer base never knew they existed. Consequently, in two years the company went bankrupt and all its assets were sold for $400,000.

So why market your site?

Great technology in and of itself means almost nothing. The very best ideas and products need to find their way into the consumer's mind. Marketing takes care of this necessary step. When a Web site is first made live on the Internet, it is only the beginning. This simply is the publishing step. Think of a book. If a book is written and printed, but is never put in a book store or listed on a site like Amazon, the author should not wonder why there are no sales! With conventional tangible products, the retail outlet helps a great deal in the marketing. It is able to put the product in front of the consumer. A Web site is a different story, however. Publishing to a Web server that has a domain attached to it does not mean the site will be found. You have to take an active role in driving traffic to it. This chapter will examine the techniques that work and the ones that don't.

What doesn't work

From firsthand experience, I can say that the one thing that does *not* build customer goodwill is using *spam*. People hate getting unsolicited email. There are utilities available that can be used to scour newsgroups for email addresses. They will de-dupe the list for you. The idea here is that you can download email addresses from newsgroups that are targeted to the product or service you are offering. Even when an effort is made to target your audience like this, the recipient still hates it! Usually the first question is, " Why does everyone hate spam? Just delete it!" Well, with the explosive growth of the Internet and Internet scams, an increasingly large portion of the traffic is spam. This puts a huge burden on the recipient to read and delete all this email. Many spam emails contain links to allow removal from the list. However, a great many of these links are invalid, and most emails do not contain them to begin with. This trick also serves to validate that the email address is active. This makes it far more valuable to spammers. You will see a reference in a great many emails that it "complies with Bill XXX on Unsolicited email." Currently there are no federal laws on spamming, so this proposal can be referenced but there's no teeth in it. Some other reasons why recipients hate spam:

- The recipient pays for the bulk of the email, not the sender. Virtually all Internet traffic is metered. The ISPs are metering all traffic they send to their customers, and the upstream providers for the ISPs are metering them on their traffic. Also, if a person is accessing an account through a dial-up connection, that user might be paying for the connect time. All of this spam counts as metered traffic, so a lot of people get stuck paying for it!

- Spam consumes a lot of resources. Spam accounts for a significant amount of disk space on mail servers. Sometimes spam causes outright theft as well. Spammers will sign up for trial accounts, send thousands of emails, and then bail on the account, leaving the ISP to clean up the mess.

- Most of the offers from spam email are fraudulent—get-rich-quick schemes, weight loss formulas, and the like.

If enough people complain to your ISP about the spam email, your ISP can and will have your account terminated. If it does not, it runs the risk of having its email server blacklisted on the Internet. If this happens, any email, even legitimate, will be blocked by other mail servers and no mail will be delivered. Your ISP will *not* let this happen!

Another technique that does not have great returns is direct mail. Direct mail takes a lot of work to prepare, print, and mail, and the return on it is very low. You can expect less than a 5% return on direct mail. Now, this might be okay depending on the pricing of your product or service. If you have a very low-priced service, you would have to get a return on direct mail pieces way above the usual rate. However, if your product or service is priced high, then you could live with the business generated by only a 2% increase in sales. It is very important when doing direct mail that the list you are using be very clean and up-to-date. You do not want to pay for names that are undeliverable! You also have to factor in the time to track your responses. When undeliverables get returned, you need to update the address database.

Banner ads also have some of the same problems as direct mail. Banner advertising can be *very* expensive. On Google.com, for example, its premier advertising package requires spending $10,000 over 3 months! Another option with Google is to use its "AdWords." Current rates are $15, $12, and $10 (per thousand ads shown) for positions 1, 2, and 3, respectively, and $8 per thousand for positions 4-8. These are the ads that appear on the right-hand margin when doing a keyword search. You pay for certain keywords, so your ad only appears when those keywords are used. Your position is also based on how many people click on your link. The more clicks, the better the positioning. Banner advertising that is not targeted like this is a total waste of money. It is the same with any type of advertising. If you are selling lawn mowers, don't advertise in *Glamour* magazine!

It is important to know the cost per click-through. For example, prices are usually quoted in "CPM," a holdover from print ad days that means "cost per thousand." For example, if the CPM for a particular campaign is $20, then it would cost $2,000 for 100,000 impressions. On a per-click-through basis, if you have been getting an average click-through ratio of 0.5%, then your cost per click would be $4.00 ($20 divided by five click-throughs). The math has to be done to determine whether this is an acceptable cost for the sale opportunity. Remember, this gets prospective customers to the site, but they are not yet sold. If they were able to click on your banner ad after doing a search on a specific keyword that you had bought, at least they are in the market for your product. Now it is up to you to make your site compelling enough for them to choose to spend their money with you.

What does work

For finding sites on the Web, the de facto standard is search engines. If you are already online, you are not going to get a magazine out to find what you are looking for. You will simply go to one of the major search engines and type in your keywords of interest. Since the primary goal of marketing is to pre-qualify your customers, getting and keeping a good position in a search engine is vital to a Web site's success. One of the huge benefits of a search engine listing over an email campaign is its staying power. An email campaign or a physical mailing is very fleeting. Most times the email is deleted or the mail piece is thrown out before it is even read. But having a good position in a search engine for your keywords is like having a 24x7 marketing manager on your staff. Search engines are always open for business, and by their nature will attract very qualified leads to your site. The only way people will find your link is if they are looking for what you sell!

There are basically three types of search registries:

- Search engines: Google, AltaVista, HotBot, MSN, and Lycos are search engines. These sites will go out and index a Web site. They need to be told to do this. Search engine submission will be covered next.

- Pay-per-click: Some sites like goto.com (now overture.com) charge for the positioning in the engine. It is run like an auction. For the keywords you are interested in, there will be a listing showing what each spot is paying to be listed there. So if you want to be listed in the #1 spot, you need to outbid the person who is paying for that spot. This fee is for every click-through, so be careful what you pay for! Overture.com's listings also appear in other search engines listings. So if you are able to get into the top three positions on Overture, when users of Yahoo!, America Online, Lycos, and AltaVista do a search for your keywords, they will see the listing you entered in Overture. On Overture, you can go to **www.overture.com/d/search/ tools/bidtool/** and type in your keywords. It will show a listing of the sites using those keywords and what they are paying to be listed in each position. You have to decide where you want to be listed and then bid for that position. It is set up so you can specify a monthly budget that is not to be exceeded. Or you can have an open-ended account that will remain open so there is no interruption of service. All account information can be checked online. Since these paid listings now come before the once-free listings, it is important to consider using this technique for search engine placement!

- Directories: Yahoo! is a directory-type search engine. With directories such as Yahoo!, they do not go and index sites automatically. Companies wanting to be listed in Yahoo! need to submit their link to the proper category with the Yahoo! directory. Then there are people who manually go and check out the site to see whether it fits into the category selected. All commercial sites on Yahoo! now have to pay a $200 fee to be included in the index. This does not even really guarantee a listing, it just means that Yahoo! will consider the site for listing.

When you pay for a new domain name at any of the registration companies, usually they offer the service of submitting your site to the various search engines for some fee. At **www.register.com**, for example, you can have your site submitted once a month for a year for $29.95. This includes sending it to 400 search engines. Be aware that there are only a few engines you need to be concerned with:

- Yahoo!

- Google

- MSN

- AOL

- AltaVista

- Go Network

- Lycos

- Excite

These represent 88.86% of the total search engine queries per day, or approximately 283 out of 319 million.

This leaves 11.14% left for *all* other engines/directories/pay-per-bid engines, or approximately 36 out of 319 million. There is a lot more to search engine submissions than just routinely submitting them on a monthly basis. It takes some time to analyze where you are in the rankings and examine what can be done to increase that ranking.

Most search engine services work in a similar fashion. You will get more for your money if you do the search engine analysis yourself. An excellent tool that automates all of the steps in getting and keeping your site listed is WebPositionGold. It is a very easy-to-use tool, and chances are most services that do search engine placement for you are using this tool or one very similar.

One directory service that is very important to be in is the "open directory" located at **www.dmoz.org**. This site is hosted by Netscape and is run by volunteer editors. This is a completely free directory service that other search engines tap into to determine placement of query results. AOL Search, HotBot, Lycos, and Netscape all use the directory for query results on their pages. DMOZ stands for "directory Mozilla" and is a link to the Mozilla open-source browser project that Netscape manages. Netscape administers the DMOZ directory as a non-commercial entity and does not really care how other search engines use its data. When a query is done at DMOZ, the results are listed in alphabetical order—no ranking criterion other than the alphabet is used. They are like the yellow pages in this regard; they are simply a directory of Web sites.

To get listed, type in the keywords under which your site would be listed. The result page shows a listing of categories under which your keywords were found, as well as specific sites that match your keywords sorted alphabetically. Select the category listed that best matches your site. On the category page, click on "Add URL" at the top of the page. The form that appears just asks for the site URL, a title, a brief description, and an email contact. That is it. The site is then reviewed by a human reviewer; it is not indexed automatically. It may take four to eight weeks for the site to be listed.

Keywords

Before diving into submitting your site to search engines, you need to think about what keywords you want to use to identify your site. Keywords are the words or phrases that potential customers will type into their search engines to locate your site, or so you hope. The KEYWORD meta tag that can appear in the header section of your Web pages is not the only place the keywords need to appear. Many search engines now do not even read the KEYWORD meta tag. The search engines go through an involved process of analyzing the content of the Web page for the appearance of keywords. It is important that keywords appear often but not too often. The engines are smart enough now to realize that a page with a keyword repeated 300 times is an attempt to spam the search engine. Physical placement on the page is important also. The closer to the top of the page they are, the more relevance the keywords are deemed to have. Placing the keywords in the TITLE tag can also be very important. For example, if your site name is Exodus, and your main business is Web hosting, it would be a good idea for your TITLE tag to be "Web hosting at Exodus.com."

It is important to keep in mind that in order for your site content to be indexed, it has to be in HTML. If you place the text of your pages in GIF or JPG files, the search engines can't index them. Some do look for the ALT tag on images. Use this to describe what the image is saying.

Search engines also have different rules about what constitutes good ratios between the total number of words on a page and how often your keywords appear. One of the power features of WebPositionGold is that it has a knowledge base of the rules for the top engines and will critique your pages and tell you how to improve them.

A great way to start off developing a list of keywords is to go to **www.wordtracker.com**. This site maintains a database of the keywords that are searched for on a daily basis. You supply the keywords you are thinking of using and it will tell you how many searches have been done with those keywords. It will also tell you related keywords. Maybe including these related words in your page could help greatly in positioning.

Using WebPositionGold, you can also run a report for your keywords and see what other sites (competition) are using the same words. Taking a look at the sites that appear in the top 10 spots could give you a great idea as to how to construct your pages. Let's take a look at how to use WebPositionGold to create a ranking report for your keywords.

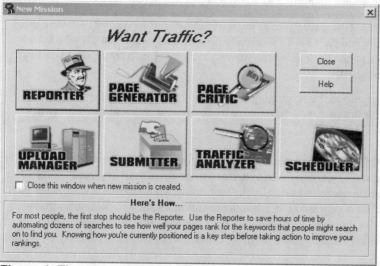

Figure 1. The main screen for WebPositionGold.

Figure 1 shows the main WebPositionGold page. The first button, "Reporter," will generate a report for your keywords across the top search engines showing how your site ranks among your competitors. When you click on the button, you will be asked for your domain name, keywords, and search engines to report on. When completed, you will have several reports to choose from. The "Concise" report shows rankings for each search engine: In this example, the domain used was **www.universalthread.com** and the keywords used were "Visual FoxPro" and "VFP." The chosen search engines were AltaVista, HotBot, Google, and

MSN. For each search engine, it shows where universalthread.com ranks for each keyword. If you are not in the first 10-15 rows, it becomes much tougher for people to find your site. Most people do not scroll through pages and pages of listings to view all results. The "Detail" report shows the sites that rank above and below yours. You could create these reports yourself. But this product does the job of distilling all the information into one easy-to-read report. The other buttons are:

- Page Generator: This will create pages for you via a template that you fill in. You will be asked for the keywords, page description, and what search engine to optimize the page for.

- Page Critic: This will critique your page against the knowledge base of a particular search engine to see what can be improved. It can also compare your pages against a competitor's to see whether there is anything they are doing differently that could help your page.

- Upload Manager: This can manage the files that you want to have indexed. If particular pages other than the home page are going to be indexed, this will make sure they exist.

- Submitter: This will submit your site to the major search engines. It can also check to make sure you are not submitting to them too often.

- Traffic Analyzer: This is a service to track traffic patterns to your site—where users are coming from and the like. This is really not necessary. You can get all of this information out of the IIS logs on the server your site is hosted on. How to do this will be covered shortly.

- Scheduler: This allows the submitting functionality to be scheduled automatically. Each month, for instance, you could have it submit your pages so the engines are kept updated.

After getting a feel for your keywords using the **www.wordtracker.com** site and running the report shown in **Figure 2**, you can make better decisions about your keyword choices. For example, if you do Web development using Web Connection, your keywords should not be "Web development." This is way too broad, and the resulting listing will contain so many listings you will be lost in the noise. However, if your keywords are "Web Connection development," the resulting listing will be far more concise and your site will really stand out.

AltaVista

June 23rd, 2001: AltaVista is currently alternating their rankings at times. Therefore, you may rank in a certain position on the first search, and then a subsequent identical search a few minutes later may show somewhat different rankings. We assume this is temporary and will eventually be corrected by AltaVista.

Keyword	Position	Page	Last Position	Change	URL
Visual FoxPro	12	2	NA	NA	http://www.universalthread.com/
Visual FoxPro	13	2	NA	NA	http://www.universalthread.com/Forum5.asp
VFP	Not in first 30.	Not in first 3.	NA	NA	No pages found.

HotBot

Keyword	Position	Page	Last Position	Change	URL
Visual FoxPro	NM	NM	NA	NA	No pages found.
VFP	Not in first 30.	Not in first 3.	NA	NA	No pages found.

Google

Keyword	Position	Page	Last Position	Change	URL
Visual FoxPro	2	1	NA	NA	www.universalthread.com/
Visual FoxPro	12	2	NA	NA	www.universalthread.com/Forum5.asp
VFP	Not in first 30.	Not in first 3.	NA	NA	No pages found.

MSN

Keyword	Position	Page	Last Position	Change	URL
Visual FoxPro	Not in first 30.	Not in first 2.	NA	NA	No pages found.
VFP	Not in first 30.	Not in first 2.	NA	NA	No pages found.

Figure 2. Concise WebPositionGold report.

Doorway Pages

Doorway pages use a technique for optimizing the page for a particular keyword. Your home page cannot be optimized for each keyword at the same time. Doorway pages are pages that contain content relevant to the keyword. They contain links that point to your main home page. These individual doorway pages can be submitted to search engines in addition to the home page. WebPositionGold provides a tool to create these doorway pages. The idea here is to give them the same look and feel as your home page, but to tailor the page content to each keyword. There could be a link on the page that states, "For more on <keyword> please click here." This link would then direct users to the home page.

Foreign language translations

It is important to keep in mind that, while English is likely the most widely used language on the Web, people like to be able to search in their native language too. It would be a good idea to have foreign language versions of your home page and doorway pages. These foreign language version pages can also be submitted separately to search engines for indexing. Instead of using an automated translation service like **www.babblefish.com**, it would be better to have it translated by a human. You want to make sure the translation is proper! One site that does human translations is **www.worldlingo.com**. You can upload your document via the Web and a human translator will translate the document. Translating a Web site's home page runs around $100. For the increased business this could bring in, it could be an excellent investment.

Cross-promotion

Cross-promotion involves getting your site listed on other related sites. For example, if you have a new service or product related to Visual FoxPro, it would be a good idea to get it mentioned on the Universal Thread home page. This site gets a lot of traffic, and being listed in the news section would generate a lot of click-throughs.

Also, if your product is targeted to a particular market, find out whether there are industry Web sites that can possibly do a review of your Web site. Many industry association Web sites have pages that link to sites of interest to that community. Being listed there can also be a tremendous help. These are all highly targeted leads, since they are already looking for your type of service that is meant for their industry. And similar to a search engine, these links stay around for a while. Virtually all forms of marketing other than search engines and cross-promotional marketing as discussed here are temporary. They exist for the person reading it, and when that person deletes the email or throws away the direct mail piece, it is gone. Search engine placement stays around. Consider sources of cross-promotion a form of search engine.

PR: Trade shows, articles

Trade shows can be an important way of getting your site noticed in the industry you are targeting. Virtually every industry has a trade show and professional organization. Having a booth at a trade show for your Web site can put you in front of your target audience. However, trade shows can be very expensive. Booth rental fees, professional-looking literature, and the cost of having a professional-looking display can run into the thousands of dollars. You also need to factor in the follow-up costs for any prospects. For staying power, trade shows can have the same problems as email and direct mail.

Many local and regional newspapers and business journals have sections geared toward small business and the entrepreneur community. Many are eager to hear stories of successful Web sites and are willing to help them become successful. Check with the business editors of publications to see whether they are interested in hearing your story.

Opt-in mailings

There are a number of opt-in emailing services that can be used to send out bulk email that is *not* spam. Opt-in email lists are those for which people voluntarily sign up. They want to receive information on a particular topic. Many services such as **www.bulletmail.com** and **www.listbazaar.com** will rent out their lists to your demographic. They typically do not sell you the list outright. You provide them with the copy that you want to appear in the email, and they do the actual mailing. They can have hundreds of categories to choose from. This type of email marketing is much more successful because the target audience is looking for information on the categories they signed up for.

Testimonials

Testimonials or "endorsement marketing" is a very powerful technique to persuade customers to use your company. People feel a lot more comfortable when they know someone else has already tried your product and has found it to be a good deal. Endorsement marketing is used quite often for television commercials. Just about everyone has seen the George Foreman Grill commercials on TV. He is a well-known person and has a likeable personality, so this makes it much easier for the manufacturer to sell those grills. Most people figure that George Foreman would not risk his reputation by endorsing a bad product. This same psychology can be used to endorse your product or service as well. Most readers would not have the budget to hire a nationally known personality, but what is very effective and free is to solicit testimonials from your customer base. Most customers are very willing to help you out. While these people may not be household names, they are still very valuable as users of your product/service.

There should be a page devoted to testimonials on your Web site. Before using testimonials, however, make sure you get permission first! Since at some level these people are risking their reputations endorsing your product, you need to make sure they feel totally comfortable giving you a public endorsement! It is a good idea when soliciting comments to ask for different viewpoints. For example, ask some people to comment on your customer support and others on product quality. This way, new customers who read the testimonials can get a much better overview of your business.

Here is an example letter you can use to solicit testimonials:

Mr. Joe Smith
Product Supervisor
XYZ Corporation
Anyplace, USA

Dear Joe:
I have a favor to ask of you.
I'm in the process of putting together a booklet of testimonials—a collection of comments about my services, from satisfied clients like yourself.
Would you please take a few minutes to give me your opinion of my consulting services?
There's no need to dictate a letter—just jot your comments on the back of this letter, sign below, and return to me in the enclosed envelope. (The second copy is for your files.)
I look forward to learning what you like about my service... but I also welcome any suggestions or criticisms, too.
Many thanks, Joe:
Regards, Bob Bly

YOU HAVE MY PERMISSION TO QUOTE FROM MY COMMENTS, AND USE THESE QUOTATIONS IN ADS, BROCHURES, MAIL, AND OTHER PROMOTIONS USED TO MARKET YOUR SERVICES.
Signed_____ Date_____

Notice that you should be getting a release from this person to use his comments not only on your Web site but also for any marketing material you may be doing in the future. You should be able to use it in brochures, direct mail pieces, and opt-in email campaigns.

Logging your traffic

Before the various marketing techniques discussed earlier are put into place, you need to make sure that your Web site is set up to record the traffic that will be coming to the site. It is vital that logging is turned on for your Web site! To do this, do the following:

1. In Windows 2000 Server, go to Start | Programs | Administrative Tools | Internet Services Manager.

2. In the tree view on the left side of the IIS Manager, select your Web site.

3. Right-click and choose "Properties."

4. On the Web Site tab of the dialog shown in **Figure 3**, make sure the Enable Logging check box is checked.

5. Click on the Properties button.

6. Click on the Extended Properties tab.

7. Make sure the following items are checked:

    a. Client IP address

    b. Method

    c. URI Stem

    d. URI Query

    e. Bytes Sent (for bandwidth calculations)

    f. Bytes Received

    g. Time Taken

    h. Host

    i. User Agent (Browser)

    j. Referrer (Where did they come from?)

8. Click on General Properties.

9. In the Log File Directory box, specify a location for the files. If there are multiple sites on the server, segment out the log files in a directory for just that site. If there are multiple physical drives on the server, specify a different physical drive from the virtual directory's drive. This helps spread the load over different spindles. Logging is very write-intensive. Everything that your server sends out over the wire is logged into the log files. This includes GIFs, JPGs, stylesheets, and so forth.

10. Click OK.

11. Click OK again to save the site settings.

This will create log files that can now be analyzed and reported on. Knowing where your prospects are coming from is one of the most important pieces of data for judging the effectiveness of your marketing campaigns.

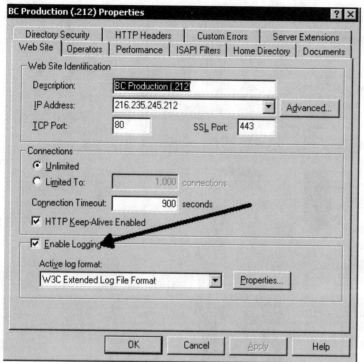

Figure 3. The Web Site tab of the Properties dialog.

Analyzing your log files

It is a good idea to analyze your log files every week to see where the traffic is coming from. There are many log-file reporting tools. WebTrends is a very popular one, but it is also very expensive. A very nice *free* tool is Analog, available at **http://analog.sourceforge.net**. It produces the same reports that WebTrends does. It is not as polished as WebTrends, but it is free! Analog is a single EXE file that does not need to be registered. Simply drop it in a directory and it can be run by simply double-clicking on it. It is configured through an INI file. All you need to tell it is where the log files are located and what date ranges you are interested in reporting on, and it will translate the raw log files into meaningful reports. The output produced by Analog is presented in table format with simple graphs. To produce professional reports, there is another free add-on tool called Report Magic, available at **www.reportmagic.com**. This is meant to work with Analog. It too is driven by a single INI file and is easy to set up. With Report Magic, you can produce reports like the one in **Figure 4** from the raw log file data.

```
216.235.245.212 80 GET /images/clicktolearn.gif - 200 1104 257
216.235.245.212 80 GET /subheads/sub-2weektrial.gif - 200 1135
216.235.245.212 80 GET /subheads/sub-memberlogin.gif - 200 100
216.235.245.212 80 GET /banner/banner.jpg - 200 40525 251 672
216.235.245.212 80 GET /subheads/sub-emailsupport.gif - 200 13
216.235.245.212 80 GET /images/bluebullet.gif - 200 271 255 26
216.235.245.212 80 GET /login.htm - 200 5861 342 78 www.bugcen
216.235.245.212 80 GET /subheads/sub-login.gif - 200 1926 265
- 216.235.245.212 80 HEAD /default.wp - 200 6178 67 31 - Ipswi
216.235.245.212 443 POST /entry.wp - 200 18839 505 703 www.bug
216.235.245.212 443 GET /stylesheets/bugstyle.css - 200 5596 2
216.235.245.212 443 GET /mainmenu/menustyle.css - 200 2377 296
216.235.245.212 443 GET /mainmenu/scrollspy-091.js - 200 6254
216.235.245.212 443 GET /mainmenu/menufunctions.js - 200 4238
216.235.245.212 443 GET /images/fill_square.gif - 200 278 296
216.235.245.212 443 GET /banner/banner.jpg - 200 40525 291 422
```

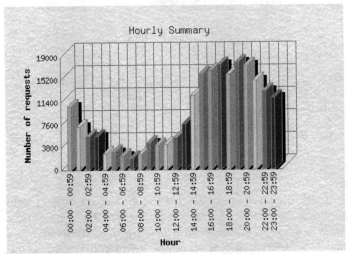

Figure 4. From raw log files to polished reports.

Log reports can show exactly how visitors got to your site. If they came from a search engine, it will show the link they clicked on in the search engine, which will contain even the keywords they used in that particular search engine. These reports can be used to determine what search engines people are using to find you and what keywords they used. Log reports can also report on what browsers your user base is using. This data is vital in understanding your community. Are you testing the site enough in the browsers that people are using?

The first section of a log report is a summary showing the bandwidth being used by your site. This is important if you are being billed for bandwidth. You want to have an independent means of checking bandwidth from the way the data center calculates it.

With Analog, the date range of the report has to be changed manually in the INI file before running the report, but that is reasonable for a free tool. You can also specify where the report is sent. If you specify a subdirectory off of your site's root, you can view the results from any browser.

Most log analyzers will report on the most active directories also. For instance, if you created a direct mail piece or placed an ad in a magazine, you should specify a URL such as http://www.mydomain.com/ad1. Then, when you're looking over the log reports, you can see whether anyone actually visited that link. If they did, it was due strictly to that ad. Each ad would have its own unique directory. The page the users are brought to may be a copy of your regular home page, or it could be a custom page with some special offer for people who read the ad.

If you've placed banner ads on other sites or had cross-promotion agreements with other sites, you have control over the link that is placed on those pages. In this case you can supply a link such as http://www.mydomain.com?referral=sitex. There are functions you'll see in the next section that will allow you to query the URL for the "referral" parameter and store that in a table and/or store that with the customer record if that person signs up at your site.

Tracking users in Visual FoxPro

As discussed in Chapter 12, "A Web Connection Application from Start to Finish," the home page to your Web site can be a dynamic page that your Web Connection application can process. As mentioned earlier, it is always a good idea to know where your site traffic is coming from. Even though the links mentioned earlier would be stored in the IIS logs, you would not be able to associate them with where a particular customer came from. If, however, your home page is dynamic, you can store the "referral" parameter and the user's previous URL in a customer record if there is a registration process. This way, each customer gets stamped with where he or she came from. This makes it possible to credit the other site with the sale if you have such an arrangement.

So let's assume you have set your default home page to be "listtasks.tsk," as the sample TODO application does. Let's also assume there is a scriptmap set up that directs any "TSK" page extension to be routed to your site's copy of WC.DLL. When someone hits your site, the listtasks method is processed in the class_tsk library. In this method, you could have the following lines of code:

```
cReferral = request.querystring("referral")
cPreviousURL = request.getpreviousurl()

if !empty(creferral)
   loheader.addcookie("referral",creferral)
endif

*--- where did they just come from?
If !empty(cpreviousurl)
   Loheader.addcookie("previousurl",cpreviousurl)
Endif
```

If a user found your site by searching on Google, his previousurl link might look like this:

```
http://www.google.com/search?q=bug+tracking+software&hl=de&lr=
```

With these two items set as cookies, they could then be stored with the customer's record during a registration process as a permanent record of how that customer came to your site.

Conclusion

Marketing your Web site is yet another skill that is needed to make your site successful. It may not be as technical as other pieces of the puzzle, but it is just as important. Whether you do this part yourself or hire a marketing consultant, be aware that marketing can make or break your project. If you work in a larger company that has a marketing department, that certainly helps. But if you are a one-man shop, knowing the basic aspects of marketing is as important as knowing how to code a SQL SELECT statement. Your best leverage is to get into the search engines and maintain a good position. The tools described here will help greatly in getting you there and reporting on site statistics going forward. Also, read the information at **www.searchenginewatch.com** listed in the "Chapter resources." This site is a great resource for the latest information on how search engines work and the criteria they use to rank sites.

Chapter resources

Anti-spamming sites:

- **http://spam.abuse.net/spam/**

- Why is spam bad? **http://spam.abuse.net/spam/spambad.html**

- Anti-spamming laws: **http://law.spamcon.org/us-laws/us/index.shtml**

- Proposed U.S. anti-spamming law: **www.spamlaws.com/federal/hr95.html**

- State anti-spamming laws: **www.spamlaws.com/state/index.html**

Search engine submission:

- Search engine submission tool: **www.webpositiongold.com**

- Back issues of the Web position newsletters. Excellent articles on how to position yourself in the engines: **www.webposition.com/newsletters.htm**

- Pay-per-click listing on **www.overture.com** (formerly **www.goto.com**): **www.overture.com/d/search/tools/bidtool/**

- Keep up with the latest search engine news: **www.searchenginewatch.com/**

- Picking keywords: **www.wordtracker.com**

Log analysis:

- Log File Analyzer: **http://analog.sourceforge.net**

- Log Reporting Add On: **www.reportmagic.com**

Miscellaneous:

- Translation service: **www.worldlingo.com/products_services/document_translations.html**

Index

Note that you can download the PDF file for this book from **www.hentzenwerke.com** (see the section "How to download files" at the beginning of this book). The PDF is completely searchable and will provide additional keyword lookup capabilities not practical in an index.